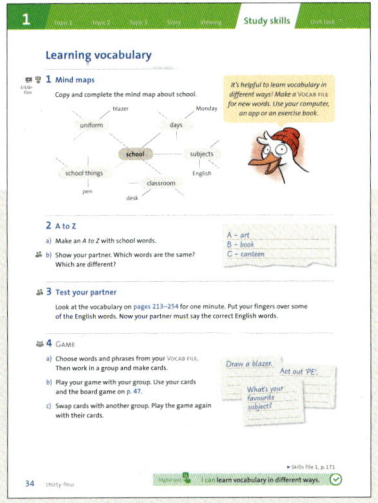

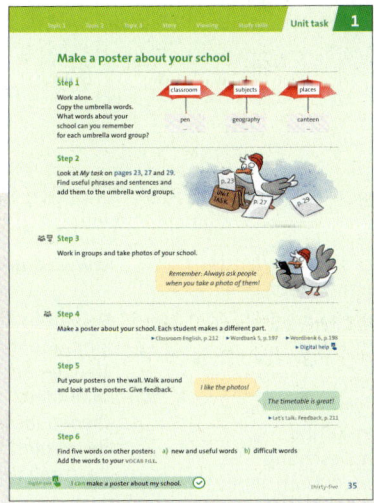

Lern- und Arbeitstechniken

Auf der *Study skills*-Seite übst du wichtige Lern- und Arbeitstechniken, z. B. wie du neue Wörter am besten lernst.

Eine Aufgabe am Unit-Ende

In der *Unit task* erstellst du ein größeres Produkt, z. B. eine Präsentation. Dabei wendest du das Gelernte aus der Unit an.

Im *Checkpoint* wiederholst du

Hier überprüfst du, wie gut du die Lernziele der Unit schon erreicht hast.

Im Anschluss findest du ein *Text file* mit interessanten Texten zum Thema der Unit.

Diese Verweise führen dich in die *Diff bank* am Ende der Unit

▶ More help	▶ Parallel exercise	▶ More practice	▶ Challenge
Hilfen zu den Aufgaben	einfachere Variante einer Übung	weitere Übungen	weitere Übungen mit höherem Schwierigkeitsgrad

Diese Lernangebote findest du im hinteren Teil des Buches

▶ Skills file	▶ Language file	▶ Wordbank
eine Übersicht über die Lern- und Arbeitstechniken	die wichtigsten Sprachregeln	zusätzliche Wörter zu bestimmten Themen

Let's talk	Vocabulary	Dictionary
Redewendungen nach wichtigen Themen und Situationen geordnet	eine Liste der neuen Vokabeln einer Unit mit hilfreichen Tipps	alphabetische Wörterlisten zum Nachschlagen (Englisch – Deutsch, Deutsch – Englisch)

lighthouse 1

Lehrkräftefassung Plus

Die **Unterrichtsvorschläge** und **Kopiervorlagen** der *Lehrkräftefassung Plus* wurden erarbeitet von Anke Barth, Plauen und Denise Heckmann, Hannover
sowie Martin Bastkowski, Schellerten *(Vorwort)*

in Zusammenarbeit mit der Englischredaktion
Klaus Unger (Projektleitung), Jenny Dames (verantwortliche Redakteurin), Lisa Ahmadi, Josephine Bienert-Köhler, Sandhya Gupta, Chelsea Ledvinka-Heß, Anja Zieschang
sowie Anke Kellerhoff, Wilnsdorf *(Unit 2, Unit 3)*, Nadja Prinz, Köln *(Unit 5)*, Georg Raspe, Düsseldorf *(Lehrkräftefassung und Lösungen)* und Katrin Gütermann, Berlin *(Glossar)*

Schulbuch (978-3-06-036252-3)

Im Auftrag des Verlages herausgegeben von
Martin Bastkowski, Schellerten;
Sonja Mahne, Basel; Ulrike Rath, Aachen;
Berit Schaarschmidt, Aschaffenburg

Erarbeitet von
Rebecca Robb Benne, Kopenhagen;
Zoe Thorne, Royston
sowie Jennifer O'Hagan, Bristol *(Checkpoints)*
und Ulrike Rath, Aachen *(Skills file)*

Vocabulary, Dictionary E–G
Ingrid Raspe, Düsseldorf

Beratende Mitwirkung
Anke Barth, Plauen; Peer Brändel, Gütersloh;
Claudia Görner, Maxdorf; Silvana Green, Potsdam;
Denise Heckmann, Hannover; Lara Jano, Rottweil;
Nathalie Schlosser, Berlin; Steffen Schmidt, Weimar;
Christoph Ullrich, Lemgo sowie
Vertr.-Prof. Dr. Christian Ludwig, Berlin;
Prof. Dr. Bernd Rüschoff, Essen;
Prof. Dr. Michaela Sambanis, Berlin

Illustrationen
Harald Ardeias, Schelklingen; Irina Zinner, Hamburg

Fotos
Anja Poehlmann, Brighton
Für die freundliche Unterstützung danken wir
der *Varndean School, Brighton*

Umschlaggestaltung
Rosendahl, Berlin

Layoutkonzept
Klein & Halm, Berlin

Layout und technische Umsetzung
Straive *(Schulbuch)*;
Klein & Halm Grafikdesign, Berlin *(Lehrkräftefassung Plus)*;
MatMil & Kollegen, Berlin *(Kopiervorlagen)*

www.cornelsen.de

Soweit in diesem Lehrwerk Personen fotografisch abgebildet sind und ihnen von der Redaktion fiktive Namen, Berufe, Dialoge und Ähnliches zugeordnet
oder diese Personen in bestimmte Kontexte gesetzt werden, dienen diese Zuordnungen und Darstellungen ausschließlich der Veranschaulichung und dem
besseren Verständnis des Buchinhaltes.

Dieses Werk berücksichtigt die Regeln der reformierten Rechtschreibung und Zeichensetzung.

Die Webseiten Dritter, deren Internetadressen in diesem Lehrwerk angegeben sind, wurden vor Drucklegung sorgfältig geprüft. Der Verlag übernimmt keine Gewähr für die Aktualität und den Inhalt dieser Seiten oder solcher, die mit ihnen verlinkt sind.

1. Auflage, 2. Druck 2023

Alle Drucke dieser Auflage sind inhaltlich unverändert und können im Unterricht nebeneinander verwendet werden.

Die *Cornelsen Lernen App* ist eine fakultative Ergänzung zu *Lighthouse*, die die inhaltliche Arbeit begleitet und unterstützt. Als solche unterliegt sie nicht der Genehmigungspflicht.

© 2022 Cornelsen Verlag GmbH, Berlin

ISBN 9783060345427

Druck: AZ Druck und Datentechnik GmbH, Kempten

PEFC-zertifiziert
Dieses Produkt stammt aus nachhaltig bewirtschafteten Wäldern und kontrollierten Quellen
PEFC/04-31-2260 www.pefc.de

lighthouse 1

Cornelsen

Inhalt

Symbole und Markierungen in der Lehrkräftefassung Plus

busy	Lernwortschatz (produktiv zu lernen)
*pair	situativer Wortschatz (nicht produktiv zu lernen)
+blazer	Wort, dessen Bedeutung sich erschließen lässt
she's tired	neue grammatische Strukturen
1 Lily • 2 Willow	Lösungen zu geschlossenen Aufgabenformaten
4 Lösungsbsp. S. 286	Verweis auf Lösungsbeispiele (s. S. 286–299)
► Box: Voc., p. 214	Verweis auf Merkboxen im *Vocabulary*
Sunita [səˈniːtə]	Auf den Abbildungen sind jeweils die Namen (mit Aussprachehinweisen) der wichtigen Personen angegeben.
Campbell[1] 1 [ˈkæmbəl]	Aussprachehinweis bei Eigennamen und schwierigen Wörtern
🔊 1.10	CD- und Tracknummern aller für das SB aufgenommenen Hörtexte/Buchtexte
graue Schrift	fakultative Angebote

Schwerpunkte des sprachlichen Skills-Training

🦻 Listening 　 💬 Speaking 　 📖 Reading 　 ✏️ Writing 　 ⇥ Mediation 　 🔁 Medienkompetenz inkl. Viewing

Verweise

► Bus stop	Verweis auf Einträge im methodisch-didaktischen Glossar (S. 300–322)
► KV 0.1	Verweis auf eine Kopiervorlage im Anhang der *Lehrkräftefassung Plus* (S. 323–360)
► Wordbank 6, S. 198	Verweis auf eine unterstützende *Wordbank* mit Seitenangabe
► Good to know, S. 20	Verweis auf eine *Good to know*-Box mit Seitenangabe
► Tippbox, S. 118	Verweis auf eine Tippbox mit Seitenangabe
► LF1, S. 182	Verweis auf das *Language file* im Anhang des SB (S. 182–191)
► SF1, S. 171	Verweis auf das *Skills file* im Anhang des SB (S. 170–181)

Abkürzungen

AA	Arbeitsanweisung	KV	Kopiervorlage(n) (s. Anhang S. 323–360)
App	Cornelsen Lernen App	L	Lehrkraft
Ausw.	Auswertung	MH	More help
Ch	Challenge	MP	More practice
DIFF	Extra Differenzierung	PA	Partnerarbeit
EA	Einzelarbeit	S	Schüler/in(nen)
Ex	Exercise	SB	Schulbuch
GA	Gruppenarbeit	Sich.	Sicherung
GSE	Grundschulenglisch	TA	Tafelanschrieb
HA	Hausaufgabe	UMA	Unterrichtsmanager Plus
INKL	Lern- und Arbeitsheft für Lernende mit erhöhtem Förderbedarf	WB	Workbook

So funktioniert die *Lehrkräftefassung Plus*

Unit-Übersicht:
- enthält Informationen zur **Storyline**, zu den neuen **Strukturen** sowie zum **Viewing** jeder Unit und nennt die **Unit task**

2

Unit-Übersicht

Storyline: Die S erfahren mehr über Sunita und Lily, ihre Familien und Haustiere. Die vier Lehrwerkskinder beschreiben, wo sie wohnen. Es gibt eine Videotour durch Sunitas Haus und auch Lily stellt ihre Wohnung vor. Sunita beschreibt ihr Zimmer. In der *Story* beschweren sich Sunita und Nish über Bens Gesang. Die Familie versucht, das Problem konstruktiv zu lösen.
Strukturen: Fragen und Kurzantworten mit *to be* (S. 51) • *There's / There are* (S. 54)
Viewing: Tour durch Sunitas Haus (S. 55) • zwei neue Mutproben für Daisy und Emir, in denen die S Informationen über die Familie von Emir und von Mrs Collins erhalten (S. 63)
Unit task: ein Traumzimmer präsentieren

Handreichungen

Kommentierungen:
- methodisch-didaktische Hinweise zu jeder Aufgabe
- übersichtlich und schnell erschließbar in der Randspalte neben der jeweiligen Schulbuchseite

Differenzierungsangebote und Zusätze:
- Differenzierungsvorschläge für lernstärkere (⊠) oder lernschwächere (⊡) S bzw. *Early finisher* in grauer Schrift (optional)
- Alternativvorschläge und Zusätze ebenfalls in grauer Schrift

Glossar und Kopiervorlagen:
- gut sichtbare Verweise auf das umfangreiche methodisch-didaktische Glossar und eine Vielzahl an Kopiervorlagen

---

Unit 2 Einstieg:
- (SB zu) ► Five-finger brainstorming: S sammeln je fünf bekannte *family words* und nennen sie dann im Plenum.
- L notiert die Wörter (TA Stammbaum, ► Vokabelarbeit).
- S tauschen sich im ► Milling around über die Namen ihrer fünf Familienmitglieder aus. L: *Talk about one member of your family for each finger.*
- ⊠ Lernstärkere S nennen auch Alter, Hobbys etc.
- TA: Vokabeln für Ex 1 im *Vocab file* sichern.

Ex 1 Einstieg:
- (SB auf) Bildbeschreibung als *Pre-listening*: L: *What or who can you see in the pictures?*
- ⊠ Lernstärkere S stellen Vermutungen an, wer die unbekannten Personen sein könnten: *Maybe the boy is …*

Erarbeitung:
- S lesen die Satzanfänge A–J. Kurze Wdh.: Bedeutung von *'s*.
- S lesen die Wörter im Reservoir und erfragen die ihnen unbekannten (► Semantisierung).
- Ggf. im TA (s. Unit-Einstieg) neue Wörter ergänzen.
- S notieren die Buchstaben A–J und rechts daneben die *family words* aus dem Reservoir untereinander im Heft.
- **1. Hören:** S verbinden die Buchstaben und *family words*.
- **2. Hören:** S überprüfen ihre Lösungen.
- ► Partner check
- **Ausw.:** ► Five-minute teacher

Unit 2
My family and home

🔊 **1** WORDS **Sunita's family**

🔊 1.30
Listen to Sunita and Lily and look at the photos. Complete the sentences with the words in the box.

A is Meera, Sunita's …   F is Rahi, Sunita's …
B is Nish, Sunita's …   G and H are Jay and
C is Ben, Meera's …   Anika, Sunita's …
D is Willow, Ben's …   I is Sunita's …
E is Priya, Sunita's …   J is Sunita's …

aunt • brother • cousins • daughter • grandpa • grandma • mum • partner • uncle

► More practice 1, p. 75

> **1** A mother • B brother • C partner • D daughter •
> E aunt • F uncle • G and H cousins • I grandpa • J grandma

48   forty-eight

48

III

2

Lead-in Inhalt

Lernschwerpunkt: Familienverhältnisse verstehen (Sunita und Lily betrachten Familienfotos und einen *circle of important people*)

Kompetenzen: Listening Dialogen Informationen über Familienverhältnisse entnehmen • Speaking sich über Familie, Freunde und Nachbarn austauschen

Redemittel: Wortfeld *family words*

Vorbereitung

Material: Ex 1 UMA/CD • Ex 2 UMA/CD, von L vorbereiteter *circle of important people*, ▶ KV 2.1: My circle of important people (Klassensatz), ggf. Handpuppe Scout

Zeitbedarf: ca. 2 Std.

Begleitmedien: WB (S. 26), App (Digital quiz), INKL (S. 48–49), DIFF (2.1)

Nach dieser Unit kann ich ... ✓

○ über meine Familie und unsere Haustiere sprechen
○ mein Zuhause und mein Zimmer beschreiben
○ Wörter buchstabieren

Unit task ✓

○ mein Traumzimmer präsentieren

Nach dieser Unit ...
- L bespricht mit S die Lernziele der Unit (s. links) und kündigt die *Unit task* an.
- Am Ende der Unit überprüfen die S das Erreichen der Ziele mithilfe des *Checkpoint* (S. 66–69) bzw. gemeinsam im Plenum.

Ex 2 Einstieg:
- (SB zu) L präsentiert vorbereiteten *circle* als TA (eigene oder Scouts imaginäre Familie/ Freunde).
  L (ggf. als Scout): *This is my circle of important people. Let me tell you about them.*
- L führt dabei auch die neue Vokabel *neighbour* ein.

Erarbeitung:
a) (SB auf) *Pre-listening*: Vermutungen anstellen.
L: *Look at the picture. What are Lily and Sunita talking about? Who are the people in this circle?*
- S schreiben die Namen (1–9) ins Heft.
- **1. Hören:** S notieren die Lösungen im Heft.
- **2. Hören:** S prüfen.
- **Ausw.:** im Plenum

b) ▶ Partner talk
- S nutzen ▶ KV 2.1.
- ▶ Double circle: S tauschen sich mit mind. fünf anderen S aus.
- **Ausw.:** Ein/e S stellt den *circle* eines/einer Mit-S im Plenum vor.
- S heften ihren *circle* in ihr ▶ Dossier.
- **Zusatz:** S ergänzen ggf. als HA Fotos oder Zeichnungen der Personen im *circle*.

Lehrkräftefassung

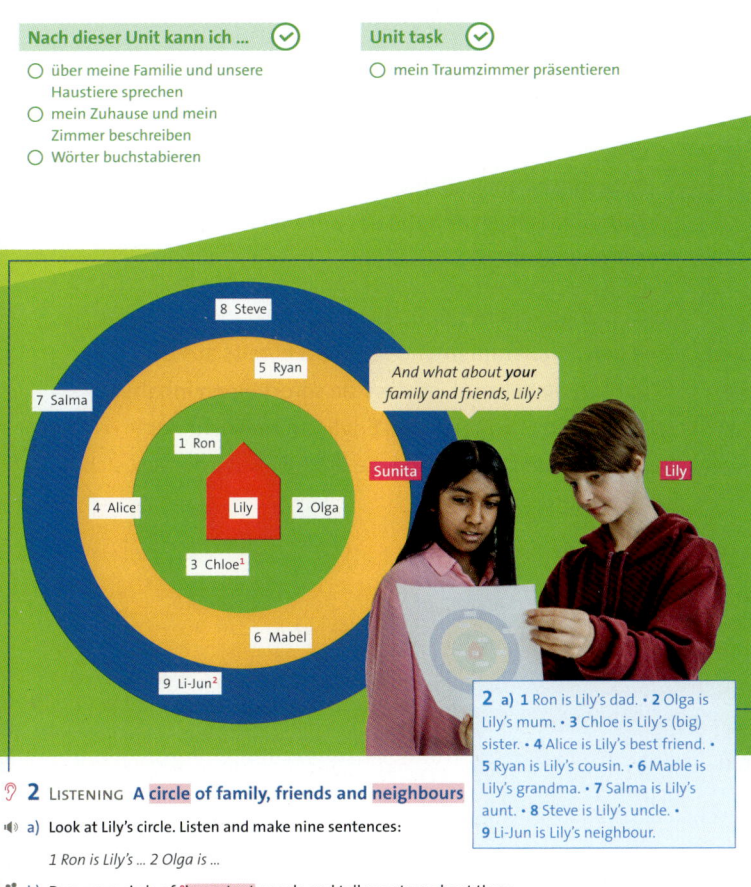

8 Steve
5 Ryan
7 Salma
1 Ron
*And what about **your** family and friends, Lily?*
Sunita
Lily
4 Alice
Lily
2 Olga
3 Chloe¹
6 Mabel
9 Li-Jun²

2 a) 1 Ron is Lily's dad. • 2 Olga is Lily's mum. • 3 Chloe is Lily's (big) sister. • 4 Alice is Lily's best friend. • 5 Ryan is Lily's cousin. • 6 Mable is Lily's grandma. • 7 Salma is Lily's aunt. • 8 Steve is Lily's uncle. • 9 Li-Jun is Lily's neighbour.

🧩 **2** LISTENING **A** circle of family, friends and neighbours

◀)) a) Look at Lily's circle. Listen and make nine sentences:
1 Ron is Lily's ... 2 Olga is ...

b) Draw your circle of °important people and tell a partner about them:
Gabriela is my stepmum. ▶ Box: Voc., p. 228

Put your circle of important people in your DOSSIER.

▶ Wordbank 7, p. 199

2 b) individuelle Lösungen

▶ Workbook, p. 26

Digital quiz 🟢 I can **talk about my family.** ✓ 1 ['kləʊi:] 2 [li: 'dʒu:n]

forty-nine **49**

49

IV

1 Grundschul-Übergang

Mit dem neuen Lighthouse wird ein differenziertes
Lernen und lebendiges Unterrichten durch lebensnahe
Themen und multimediales Üben ermöglicht. Dabei liegt
ein umfassendes Differenzierungskonzept für Lernende
an differenzierenden Schulformen und Orientierungsstu-
fen ab Klasse 5 vor. Speziell mit der Lehrkräftefassung
Plus möchten wir Ihnen als Lehrkräften zudem eine
effektive Entlastung bei der Unterrichtsvorbereitung
und -durchführung an die Hand geben.
Im folgenden Vorwort finden Sie zu den Grundsätzen und
zentralen Charakteristika des neuen Lighthouse konkrete
Beispiele und Erklärungen.

Rolle von *Hello! Nice to meet you*

Ein wichtiges Ziel des neuen *Lighthouse* ist es, die
Schülerinnen und Schüler mit ihren unterschiedlichen
Vorkenntnissen in punkto Grundschulenglisch auf ihrem
Leistungsstand gezielt abzuholen und mit niedrigschwel-
ligen Aktivitäten von Anfang an für den Englischunter-
richt der Sekundarstufe I zu begeistern.

Hello! Nice to meet you dient in diesem Sinne als soge-
nannte *pick-up unit*, d.h. als eine Übergangsunterrichts-
einheit, in der Elemente des Englischunterrichts an
Grundschulen Anwendung finden: typische Aktivitäten
und Übungen (s.u. Übergangsaktivitäten), Medien (z.B.
Bilder, Lieder), thematische Bezüge (eigene Vorstellung,
Ferien, Freizeit etc.) sowie bereits erlernte kommunikative
Fertigkeiten (s.u. Skills-Schwerpunkte). Somit bietet *Hello!
Nice to meet you* neben der motivatorischen Funktion
eine diagnostische Grundlage über den Ist-Stand der
Schülerinnen und Schüler.

Skills-Schwerpunkte

Der Englischunterricht an Grundschulen legt einen klaren
Fokus auf die kommunikativen Fertigkeiten des Hör-/
Sehverstehens und des Sprechens. Demgegenüber sind
Schreiben und Sprachmittlung als nachrangig zu betrachten.

Um den Grundschul-Übergang für die Lernenden zu
vereinfachen, sind die ersten Seiten in *Lighthouse* daher
den o.g. Fertigkeiten gewidmet, wie die verschiedenen
Aktivitäten auf den abgebildeten Buchseiten zeigen.

Die Zielsetzung für die weiteren Units ist eine sukzessive
Anbahnung der produktiven Fertigkeiten des Schreibens
und der Sprachmittlung sowie eine Vertiefung der
rezeptiven Fertigkeiten des Hör-Sehverstehens und des
Lesens.

Übergangsaktivitäten

Die ersten Seiten von *Lighthouse* bieten eine ganze
Palette an fachdidaktischen Mitteln für den Grundschul-
übergang an, um die Begeisterung für die englische
Sprache auch in der Sekundarstufe I aufrechtzuerhalten.
Dazu gehören:

- ein hoher Grad an visuellen Inputs (s. die Bilder auf
  der Doppelseite)

- abwechslungsreiche Aufgabenstellungen (z.B. *listen,
  find, point, act, sing, walk* etc.)

- die gezielte Einbindung von Bewegungselementen
  (z.B. Aufgabe Nr. 3 mit *Walk around*)

- ein großes Repertoire an *Scaffolding* (*sentence starters*,
  Sprachvorgaben)

- niedrigschwellige kommunikative Aktivitäten (z.B.
  kurzer dialogischer Austausch über die eigene Person)

- spielerische Aspekte (*Look at the picture for 30 seconds.
  Close your books. What can you remember?*)

- die Adressierung verschiedener Lernkanäle (z.B.
  musikalisch anhand des Liedes, visuell anhand der
  Bilder, sprachlich anhand der *phrases*, interpersonell
  anhand des *Walk around* etc.).

Alle oben genannten Aufgabenformate und Aktivitäten
sind den Schülerinnen und Schülern bereits aus der
Grundschule bekannt, so dass sie sofort einen inhaltlich-
sprachlichen Einstieg in den Englischunterricht der
Sekundarstufe I finden und die Möglichkeit erhalten, sich
aktiv zu beteiligen.

Goodbye, holidays!

1 In the picture

a) Look at the picture. Listen, find and point.

b) Find, point and say.
► Wordbanks 1–2, p. 194 ► Language file 1, p. 182

Scout the seagull • Leo's mum • Ben's dad • two numbers •
three animals • four colours • three drinks •
two things to eat • three other things

*Here's Scout.
And here's Leo's mum.
I can see a dog / …*

c) Look at the picture for 30 seconds again. Close your books.
What can you remember?

I remember Scout and a dog.

I remember Scout.

I remember Scout and a dog and a …

2 SONG Scout's song

a) Listen and act out the song. Then listen again, act and sing.

*Hi, hello, nice to meet you today!
How are you? I'm fine, I'm OK.
I live here in Brighton, right by the sea.
It's a nice day to meet
And to find something to eat.
Oh, what's that?
(Look out! It's Scout!)
Wheeeeeeee!*

*I'm a seagull, I'm Scout the seagull.
Just look how high
In the sky I can fly.
That's where I like to be.
I'm a seagull, I'm Scout the seagull.
Just look how high in the sky I can fly
Over the sea.*

b) Ask and answer.

A: *Ali, how are you?*   B: ☺ *I'm fine/OK. Mia, how are you?*   C: ☹ *I'm not so good. Ole, how …*
► Workbook, p. 8

Digital quiz I can **talk about a picture.** ✓

Lighthouse (General Edition) Band 1 (9783060362523), S. 12–13

3 Hello, class

WALK AROUND Find out about other students.

1 *Hello! I'm … What's your name?*

2 *Hi! I'm … I'm … (years old). How old are you?*

3 *I'm … (years old). I'm from … Where are you from?*

4 *I'm from … (too). I like … What about you?*

5 *I like … Nice to meet you!*

6 *Nice to meet you too. Bye!*

Digital quiz I can **say hello.** ✓

Lighthouse (General Edition) Band 1 (9783060362523), S. 11

VI

2 Kommunikatives Handeln

Zielsetzung des Englischunterrichts

Das neue *Lighthouse* leistet einen essenziellen Beitrag, um die zentrale Zielsetzung des Englischunterrichts zu erfüllen, nämlich die Schülerinnen und Schüler zu befähigen, inhaltlich-sprachlich sowie kulturell adäquat in Realsituationen zu handeln.

Dazu werden im Verlaufe der Schuljahre konsekutiv die drei Handlungsebenen der Rezeption, Produktion sowie Interaktion geschult und anhand zahlreicher Aufgaben und Übungen trainiert.

Um dies erfolgreich umzusetzen, benötigen die Lernenden zum einen kommunikative Fertigkeiten, also Sprechen, Schreiben und Sprachmittlung als produktive Fertigkeiten sowie Hör-/Seh- und Leseverstehen als rezeptive Fertigkeiten. Zum anderen benötigen sie sprachliche Mittel wie Grammatik, Wortschatz, Ausspra-che etc., die als Vehikel zur Umsetzung der kommunikati-ven Fertigkeiten dienen.

Desweiteren müssen auch interkulturelle Kompetenzen (z. B. kulturelle Aspekte) sowie Methodenkompetenzen (Lernstrategien, Mediennutzung etc.) vorhanden sein, um die Zielsetzung zu erfüllen.

Die zahlreichen kommunikativen Aufgaben in *Lighthouse* leisten hierfür einen wichtigen Schritt.

Kommunikative Ausrichtung der Aufgaben

Die Übungen und Aufgaben in *Lighthouse* basieren auf modernen fachdidaktischen Modellen und aktuellen Leitprinzipien. Das sind z. B. das Prinzip des Übens (d.h. die Integration inhalts- und sprachbezogener Übungssi-tuationen) und das Prinzip der Authentizität (d.h. die Einbindung alltagsnaher Themen und Kommunikations-szenarien). Hinzu kommen die Merkmale guten Englisch-unterrichts, die konsequent im Schulbuch eingebettet sind:
- hoher Grad an Scaffolding
- effektive Mediennutzung
- Fokus auf die Lernenden
- thematische Behandlung von bedeutungsvollen Inhalten
- die Umsetzung kommunikativer Szenarien.

Das Beispiel rechts von Aufgabe 4 *A conversation with Ryan* zeigt, wie viele Merkmale guten Englischunterrichts in einer Aufgabe platziert werden können.

Mit *I can talk about my free time* liegt ein für die Schüler und Schülerinnen authentisches, bedeutungsvolles und realitätsnahes Thema vor. Daneben ist die Aufgabe kommunikativ in eine Konversation eingebettet und wird durch zahlreiche *Scaffolding*-Elemente (in diesem Falle *Phrases*) unterstützt. Weiterhin fungiert Lilys Kalender mit mehreren Aktivitäten als zielführender Medieninput, um das kommunikative Szenario erfolgreich umzusetzen. Mit dieser Aufgabe werden die Lernenden so befähigt, sich kommunikativ über ein Thema auszutauschen. Darüber hinaus erfahren sie anhand der sprachlichen Mittel auch eine echte Sprachprogression.

Die kommunikative Ausrichtung der Aufgaben gilt nicht nur für die produktiven Fertigkeiten (Sprechen, Schrei-ben), sondern auch für rezeptive Fertigkeiten (Hör- und Leseverstehen).

Anhand der *profiles* bauen die Lernenden in der Aufgabe *FindAPet* sukzessive ihre Lesefertigkeit auf. Dabei nutzt *Lighthouse* das fachdidaktische Modell der *pre-/while-/post*-Phasen.

Zunächst beschreiben die Lernenden in Nr. 7a) anhand mehrerer Bilder und sprachlicher Hilfestellungen (vgl. oben effektive Mediennutzung und *Scaffolding*) drei verschiedene Haustiere. Das ist die *pre*-Phase, in der für das gesamte Unterrichtsszenario zunächst ein kontextu-eller Rahmen geschaffen wird.

Mit Hilfe klarer Leseaufgaben in Nr. 7b), bei der den jeweiligen Haustierprofilen Adjektive zugeordnet werden müssen, wird niedrigschwellig das Leseverstehen in der *while*-Phase aufgebaut.

Die *post*-Phase in Nr. 7c) animiert die Lernenden, eine eigene Meinung zu bilden, sowie eine persönliche Präferenz zu äußern (Nr. 7d)).

Mit diesem Modell erfährt der Englischunterricht eine klare und logisch aufgebaute Schrittigkeit mit einem im Mittelpunkt stehenden *Skills*-Fokus (hier: Leseverstehen).

7 READING *FindAPet*

Lily wants a new pet.

a) BEFORE YOU READ Look at the photos of the three pets. Guess what they're like. Use the words in the box.

> active • big • cute • fast • friendly • hungry • interesting • loud • mean • old • quiet • slow • small • special

I think Rex is … He isn't …

b) Now read the profiles from *FindAPet* and match the words from a) to the three pets.
Rex: big, …
Axel: …
Maude: …

c) Read about Lily's dream pet. Which pet from *FindAPet* is right for Lily?

I think … is right for Lily (because …)

> My dream pet is different and interesting. It isn't too big or loud and it's nice.

d) Which of the three pets is your favourite and why?

My favourite pet is … because he's/she's … and he/she isn't …

Rex is big, but he isn't mean. He's a very friendly and active dog. But he's always hungry and he's very loud!

Axel is a special pet – he's a small, green lizard. He's very quiet, but he's interesting. And he isn't slow!

Maude is quite old, but still very fast. She's cute, but be careful – she isn't friendly!

---

4 SPEAKING A conversation with Ryan

I can talk about my free time.

Ryan asks Lily about her free time. Look at Lily's calendar and say her answers.

> Are you in a school club, Lily? Tell me what other activities you do and how often.

Phrases
- (Yes,) I'm in the … club.
- I also like/do/play/go to/…
- I (sometimes/often/always) play/walk/do …

Monday	Tuesday	Wednesday	Thursday	Friday	Saturday	Sunday
5.30 p.m.: table tennis		4.30 p.m.: parkour	After school: art club		10 a.m.: parkour	11 a.m.: walk with Dad

Check

ninety-nine **99**

Lighthouse (General Edition) Band 1 (9783060362523), S. 53 u. 99

VIII

3 Grammatik-Vermittlung

Engage – Discover – Activate: kommunikative Vermittlung grammatischer Phänomene

Die Vermittlungsform grammatischer Phänomene ist seit Jahrzehnten ein kontrovers diskutiertes Feld. Mittlerweile liegen zahlreiche Modelle mit unterschiedlich komplexen Phasierungen und Fokussierungen vor. Mit dem neuen *Lighthouse* offerieren wir mit *Engage-Discover-Activate* eine neue Grammatikkonzeption, die praktikabel, flexibel und kleinschrittig angewendet werden kann. Dabei steht vor allem eine kommunikativ-kontextuelle Einbettung des grammatischen Phänomens im Mittelpunkt.

In der *Engage*-Phase erfolgt zunächst eine inhaltliche Hinführung zum Thema. Anhand eines Inputs (z. B. Lied, Lesetext, Bild etc.) wird eine Kontextualisierung hergestellt und eine inhaltliche Beschäftigung mit dem Input initiiert. Das grammatische Phänomen ist dabei bereits in den Input eingebettet, so dass die Schülerinnen und Schüler es bereits unbewusst kennenlernen.

In dem Beispiel rechts (Nr. 4 *Before and after school*) besteht die thematische Kontextualisierung in Zanes Tagesablauf. Das grammatische Phänomen des *Simple present* ist in den Zeitungsartikel *Best Kids Competition* eingebettet. Dabei arbeiten die Schülerinnen und Schüler zunächst inhaltlich (*focus on meaning*) mit dem Text, wie in Aufgabe 4b)) umgesetzt.

Mit Blick auf den Erwerb einer neuen grammatischen Struktur sollen die Lernenden die *target structure* auch bereits reproduktiv umsetzen (*reproducing chunks*). Dazu werden die einzelnen Tagesabläufe von Zane (s. Aufgabe 4c)) in die richtige Reihenfolge gebracht, wobei das *Simple present* in dieser Phase unbewusst angewendet wird. Damit ist die gesamte *Engage*-Phase primär inhaltlich ausgerichtet, beinhaltet aber bereits die angestrebte grammatische Struktur.

In der Folgephase *Discover* erfolgt ein klarer Fokus auf die *target structure* (in unserem Beispiel das *Simple present*) und die Aspekte *form, function* und *use*. Diese werden von den Lernenden (selbst-)gelenkt entdeckt oder von der Lehrkraft präsentiert. Dazu eignen sich u.a. auch Erklärfilme (wie hier in Aufgabe 5 angeboten) und sprachbewusste Aufgaben, wo die Lernenden Unterschiede in den Verbformen beim *Simple present* erkennen (s. 5a) und 5b)). Um die Sprachbewusstheit der Lernenden zusätzlich zu steigern, können in dieser Phase auch weitere Schritte zum Einsatz kommen, z. B. die Umsetzung von *timelines*, *grammar posters* oder *grammar cards*.

Mit **Activate** erfolgt nun die dritte Phase der Grammatikvermittlung. Diese teilt sich in rezeptiv-kommunikative und produktiv-kommunikative Aktivitäten ein. Die Ursache liegt darin, dass nach dem sprachlichen Fokus in der *Discover*-Phase kein zu schneller Übergang in die kommunikative Umsetzung erfolgen sollte. Daher stärken die Lernenden zunächst rezeptiv ihre Sprachbewusstheit durch das Finden der richtigen Verbform (s. Nr. 6) sowie musikalisch anhand eines Liedes (Nr. 8).

Im Anschluss erfolgt eine produktive Aktivität im Rahmen der *My task*, wo das *Simple present* als *target structure* kontextualisiert und mit einem klaren *Outcome* (*Write a post about your day*, s. Nr. 9) angewendet wird. Dazu erhalten die Lernenden einen hohen Grad an *Scaffolding* (s. *Digital help, More help, Wordbank*) als Unterstützung, um die Aufgaben inhaltlich und sprachlich erfolgreich zu bewältigen.

4 READING **Before and after school**

My son is the best ever!

Today's letter for our 'Best Kids Competition' is from Louise Adebayo. It's about her son Zane (11). Remember: you choose the winner, readers!

5 I have a bad illness and I use a wheelchair. My husband Eno has a cafe and he works long days. On weekdays, my son Zane helps me.

Zane gets up at 7 o'clock, has a shower
10 and gets dressed. His little sister Holly gets up at 7.30. Eno makes breakfast for us and we all eat breakfast. Zane takes Holly to her school at 8.15 and then he goes to his school. Then I work – I write
15 books with special software.

Zane meets Holly at her school at 3.20 and they walk home. Zane makes a snack

for us and tidies the kitchen. Then he does his homework. It takes an hour. On
20 some days Zane helps me with dinner. Or he talks with his friends or watches TV. On Friday he goes to swimming training. He goes to bed at 9 o'clock.

Zane, you help me a lot. You're the best
25 son ever!

c) Read the full article. Put Zane's day in the correct order: *1f, 2 …*

a He does his homework.
b He eats
c Zane tak
d He make

e Zane goes to bed at 9 o'clock.

---

5 LOOKING AT LANGUAGE **Simple present**

Erklär-film

a) Complete the sentences from the article.

1 You … the winner, readers! (line 4)
2 I … a wheelchair. (lines 5–6)
3 We all … breakfast. (line 12)
4 They … home. (line 17)
5 Zane, you … me a lot. (line 24)

6 He … long days. (line 7)
7 Zane … me. (line 8)
8 She … up. (lines 10–11)
9 It … an hour. (line 19)
10 He … with his friends. (line 21)

b) Look at the verbs in **a)**. What's different? Answer the question in the box below.

Bei regelmäßigen Tätigkeiten und Aktionen verwendest du das *simple present*.
Wann endet das Verb auf *-s*? Bei:
– I / you / we / they?
– he / she / it?

Be careful with these verbs:
have – has
do – does
go – goes
watch – watches
tidy – tidies

► Language file 10, p. 187   ► More practice 5, p. 106

My task

9 My school day

WRITING **Read Zane's post. Write a post about your day. You can use the words in the box. Put your post in your DOSSIER.**

in the morning • after school • in the afternoon •
in the evening • get up • have a shower •
get dressed • walk / go by … • go to school •
school starts • have lunch • school ends • go to bed

Hi, Zane
My name is … and I live in … This is my day:
In the morning I get up at …

Hello, everybody
My class has a project about the school day in other countries. Please tell us about your school day. Thanks.

► Digital help   ► More help, p. 108   ► Wordbank 10, p. 201

► Workbook, p. 43

Digital quiz   I can **describe my daily routine.**

Lighthouse (General Edition) Band 1 (9783060362523), S. 83–85

X

4 Bewegtes Lernen

Skills-Förderung durch Bewegungselemente – Verknüpfung von Bewegung und Sprache

Die zielführende Einbindung bewegungsreicher Aktivitäten offeriert ein enormes Potential zur Förderung verschiedener kommunikativer Fertigkeiten (Hör- und Leseverstehen, Sprechen, Schreiben etc.).

Zum einen steigert Bewegung die Lern-, Leistungs- und Konzentrationsfähigkeit der Lernenden und ermöglicht in diesem Zuge günstige Bedingungen für den Spracherwerb, z. B. durch die Reduzierung des Stress- und Angstgefühls. Zum anderen verbessern Bewegungselemente die Unterrichtsatmosphäre für alle Beteiligten, da Bewegung Spaß, Freude und das Lernen mit allen Sinnen befördert.

Generell kann zwischen zwei Formen der Lernbewegung unterschieden werden: lernbegleitend und lernerschließend. Lernbegleitende Aktivitäten umfassen z. B. Bewegungspausen (Dehnungs- und Lockerungsübungen) oder eine direkte Einbindung von Bewegung in der Lernorganisation, z. B. bei einer szenischen Darstellung, beim Stationenlernen oder einem Expertenpuzzle. Lernerschließende Aktivitäten beinhalten ein Lernen mit Bewegung. Das bekannteste Beispiel dafür ist die Erschließung unbekannter *lexical items* anhand von Gestik und Mimik.

Zielführende Bewegungsaktivitäten

Das neue *Lighthouse* bindet bewusst die o. g. positiven Aspekte des bewegten Lernens anhand zahlreicher bewegungsreicher Aktivitäten direkt in den Englischunterricht mit ein. Die Aufgaben 9 und 10 aus der Unit *My new school* zum Thema *school subjects* umfassen gleich zwei verschiedene Bewegungselemente: *Get-up song* (bei *The timetable song*) sowie das *Speed dating* (bei *Favourite subjects*).

Beim *Get-up song* (Nr. 9) stehen die Schülerinnen und Schüler sofort auf, wenn sie ein Schulfach im Lied hören. Diese Aufgabe ermöglicht eine motivierende und bewegungsreich gestaltete rezeptive Wahrnehmung des Wortschatzes anhand des musikalischen Inputs durch das Lied.

Das sich anschließende *Speed dating* (Nr. 10), wo sich zwei gegenüberstehende Reihen über ihre Lieblingsfächer unterhalten, schafft für die Lernenden den Rahmen, sich produktiv in einem angstfreien Raum mit wechselnden Partnerinnen und Partnern beim *Speed dating* über das Thema auszutauschen, und zeichnet sich durch eine hohe Sprechaktivierung aus.

Mit der Aufgabe *Where is it?* (Nr. 3) in der Unit 2 zu *My family and home* erhalten die Lernenden die Möglichkeit, ihre eigene Meinung körperbetont anhand einer Meinungslinie darzustellen. Kontextuell eingebettet in die Fragestellung *Is your room messy or tidy?* stellen sich alle Schülerinnen und Schüler dabei je nach persönlicher Haltung im Klassenraum auf. Damit erfährt der Englischunterricht eine deutliche dynamisch-räumliche Umsetzung der Aufgabe.

Eine enorm hohe sprachliche Aktivierung wird durch die Bewegungsaktivität *Quiz-quiz-swap* initiiert, hier eingebettet in der Unit 4 *Where I live*. Die Schülerinnen und Schüler notieren sich eine Frage auf einer Fragekarte und lassen sich diese im *Walk around* von einem Mitschüler bzw. einer Mitschülerin beantworten. Anschließend werden die Fragekarten getauscht, so dass mit einer nun neuen Frage ein neuer kurzer Austausch stattfinden kann. Die Umsetzung dieser Aufgabe bietet zahlreiche Vorteile, u. a. eine entspannte Lernatmosphäre durch die persönliche Interaktion in Partnerarbeit, einen dynamischen kommunikativen Austausch durch wechselnde Fragekarten sowie auch eine gezielt kontextuelle Anwendung grammatischer Phänomene (z. B. Fragebildung).

🔊 **9** SONG **The timetable song**

▣ a) Listen. Stand up when you hear a school subject.

b) Listen again. Write the correct subject (a–f) for 1–6.

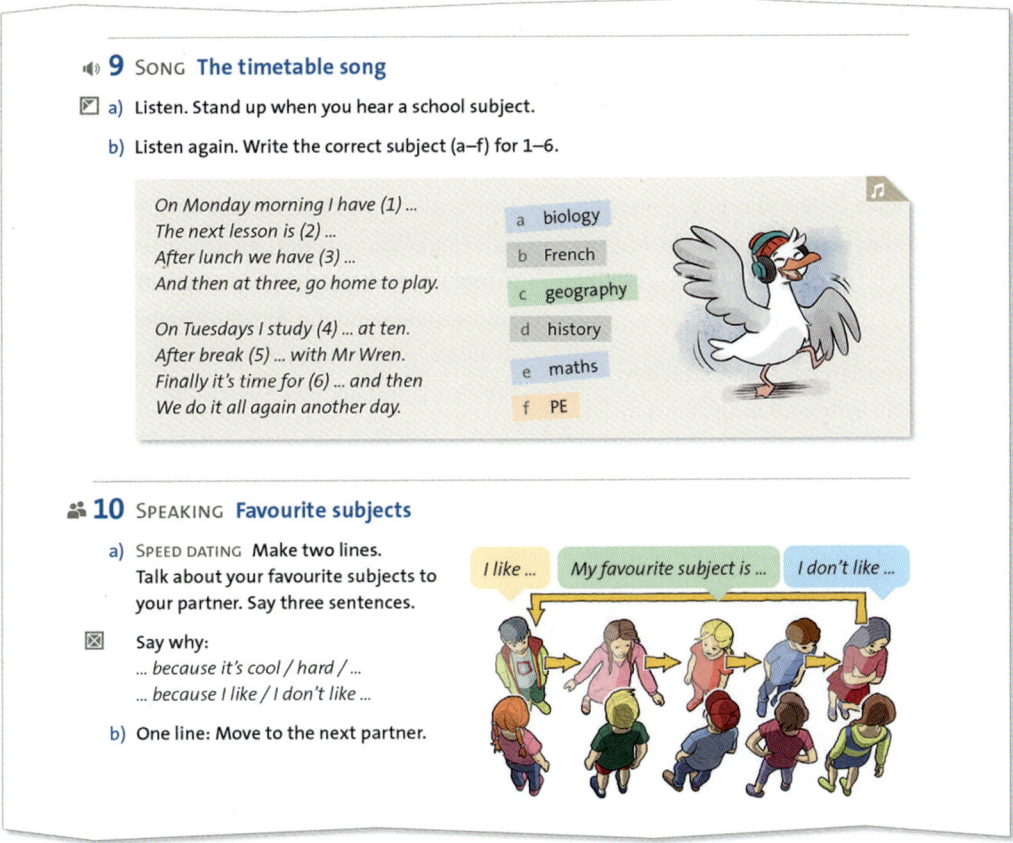

On Monday morning I have (1) ...
The next lesson is (2) ...
After lunch we have (3) ...
And then at three, go home to play.

On Tuesdays I study (4) ... at ten.
After break (5) ... with Mr Wren.
Finally it's time for (6) ... and then
We do it all again another day.

a biology
b French
c geography
d history
e maths
f PE

👥 **10** SPEAKING **Favourite subjects**

a) SPEED DATING Make two lines.
Talk about your favourite subjects to
your partner. Say three sentences.

▣ Say why:
... because it's cool / hard / ...
... because I like / I don't like ...

b) One line: Move to the next partner.

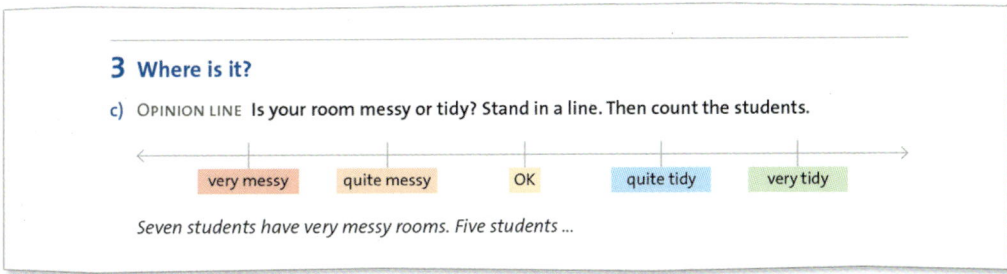

I like ...   My favourite subject is ...   I don't like ...

3 Where is it?

c) OPINION LINE Is your room messy or tidy? Stand in a line. Then count the students.

very messy   quite messy   OK   quite tidy   very tidy

Seven students have very messy rooms. Five students ...

My task

5 Quiz-quiz-swap

a) Write one question about your town or village and the weather on a card.
Use the notes in the table to help you.

What do you do
when it's snowy?

What ... do Where ... go How ... travel	when it's	sunny / rainy / snowy / cloudy / windy / hot / cold / warm?

👥 b) WALK AROUND
Find a partner and ask your question.
Answer your partner's question about your town.

When it's hot, I go swimming.

▶ Digital help 🔗   ▶ More help, p. 139

c) Swap cards and walk around again. Find a new partner and ask your new question.

▶ Workbook, pp. 62–63

Digital quiz 🔗   I can **talk about sights in Brighton and the weather.** ✅   one hundred and twenty-one **121**

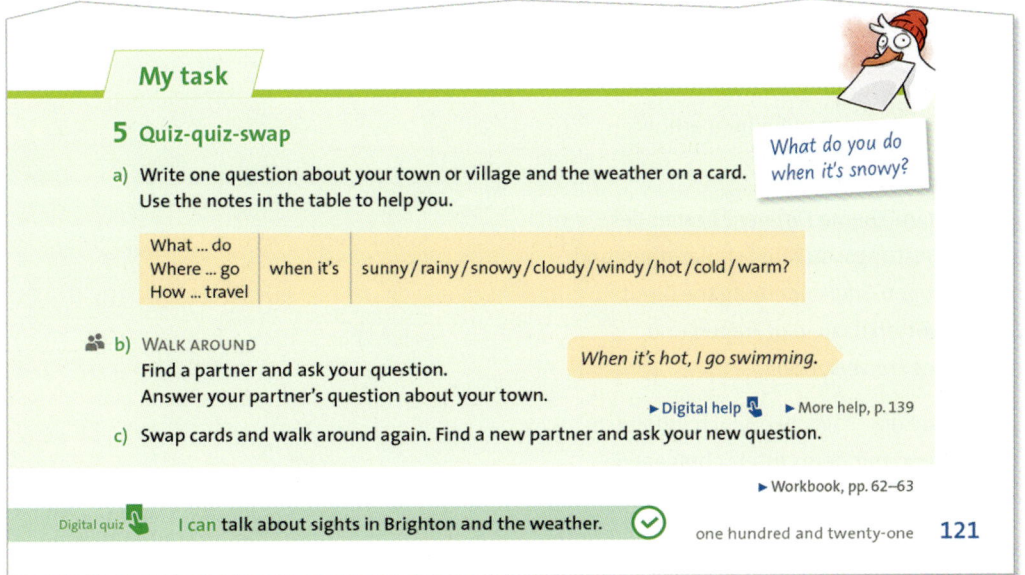

Lighthouse (General Edition) Band 1 (9783060362523), S. 27, 57 und 121

5 Differenzierung / Diff bank

More help / More practice / Challenge / Parallel-Aufgaben

Das vielseitige und fundierte Differenzierungskonzept stellt eines der Säulen des neuen *Lighthouse* dar. Insgesamt liegen vier unterschiedliche Differenzierungsformen vor:

1. *More help*: Diese Differenzierungsform bietet den Lernenden eine zusätzliche Unterstützung und Hilfe zu den Aufgaben an.

Im Falle von *My pet or dream pet* (siehe Beispiel rechts) erhalten die Lernenden zur erfolgreichen Umsetzung der *My task* zum Beispiel *sentence starters* und Beschreibungskategorien (*colour, size* etc.) sowie Adjektive, die sie verwenden können. Damit erhalten insbesondere Lernschwächere ein hilfreiches *Scaffolding*.

2. *More practice*: Mit dieser zweiten Differenzierungsform wird es den Lernenden ermöglicht, weitere (teils vertiefende) Aufgaben zum Thema zu bearbeiten. Damit erfüllt sich ein Grundpfeiler des Englischunterrichts – das Prinzip des Übens. Innerhalb des *Topic* 2 haben sich die Schülerinnen und Schüler mit dem Thema *A special house* beschäftigt und das Haus von Zanes Freund beschrieben.

Mit *More practice* 3 können die Lernenden ihr inhaltlich-sprachliches Wissen zur Beschreibung eines Hauses in einer weiteren Übung anwenden, indem sie eines der sechs vorgegebenen Bilder wählen und einem Partner / einer Partnerin beschreiben und erraten lassen, um welches Bild es sich handelt.

3. *Challenge*: Das Differenzierungskonzept fördert nicht nur Leistungsschwächere (s. *More help*), sondern fordert auch Leistungsstärkere. Dafür fungieren die *Challenge*-Aufgaben, also weitere Übungen mit einem erhöhten Schwierigkeitsgrad.

Weiterhin eingebettet im Thema *Different homes* des *Topic* 2 befassen sich leistungsstärkere Schülerinnen und Schüler in der zugehörigen *Challenge*-Aufgabe 1 mit einem Dialog, beantworten dazu in *a)* Fragen und komplettieren in *b)* eine *conversation*.

Damit bietet *Lighthouse* die Möglichkeit, sich inhaltlich und sprachlich vertiefend mit dem Unterrichtsgegenstand auseinanderzusetzen.

4. Parallel-Aufgaben: Mit den Parallel-Aufgaben als vierte Differenzierungsform wird den Schülerinnen und

Schülern die einfachere Variante einer Übung angeboten. Dies ist insbesondere sinnvoll, wenn zum Beispiel der identische Input (wie bei einem Hörtext) genutzt wird. Die Parallel-Aufgabe ist inhaltlich gleich, umfasst aber eine deutliche Reduzierung im Anspruch. Im Beispiel von *Is that your pet?* ist die Ursprungsaufgabe eine offene Hörverstehensübung. Bei der Parallelaufgabe sind die Antworten bereits geschlossen vorgegeben und müssen nur richtig mit der Frage verbunden werden (*Matching*).

More help, More practice, Challenge und die Parallel-Aufgaben sind übersichtlich auf den *Diff bank*-Seiten platziert, die sich jeweils direkt im Anschluss an die Unit befinden und somit eine einschlägige thematische Einheit bilden.

Zuweisung von Aufgabenformaten (einfach / schwierig / Wahl)

Neben den vier Differenzierungsformen können die Aufgaben auch selbst ein unterschiedliches Anspruchsformat aufweisen: einfach ▱ (z. B. erhöhter Grad an *Scaffolding* oder Reduzierung der Teilaufgaben), schwierig ▨ (z. B. offene oder sprachlich vertiefende Aufgaben) und eine Wahlaufgabe ⅄ (z. B. Wahl, welches Lernprodukt umgesetzt werden soll). So erkennen die Lernenden und Lehrkräfte sofort, auf welchem Niveau sie gerade arbeiten bzw. welche Aufgaben gezielt bestimmten Lernenden zugewiesen werden können.

► Page 53

More help **8** MY TASK **My pet or dream pet**

a) Copy the table and make notes about your pet or dream pet.

Animal	I have a … / My dream pet is a …
Colour	He's / She's brown / …
Characteristics	He's / She's / He isn't / She isn't friendly / …
Size	He's / She's very small / …

active • big • cute • fast •
friendly • happy • hungry •
loud • old • mean • quiet •
slow • small

► Page 54

More practice 3 **Different houses**

a) **Partner A:** Choose a picture – don't tell your partner! Talk about the home.
Partner B: Guess the picture: *I think it's picture 1 / 2 / …*

	a bi…
	a lo…
In this picture there's	a bi…
There are	a re…
	a ga…

b) **Partner B:** Choose a different …
Partner A: Guess the picture.

Challenge 1 **New homes**

a) Zane asks his friend Alfie about his family's new house. Read their conversation.
Copy the list on the right and write *yes* or *no*.

Zane	Are there kids at the neighbour's house?
Alfie	No, there aren't. But there are a lot of kids in our street.
Zane	Is there a garden?
Alfie	There is. There isn't a really big garden, but it's nice.
Zane	Is there a trampoline in the garden?
Alfie	No, there isn't. But there's a swimming pool!
Zane	Wow!

1 kids at the neighbour's house
2 a lot of kids in the street
3 a garden
4 a really big garden
5 a trampoline
6 a swimming pool

b) Lily's friend Kinza has a new home. Complete their conversation.

Lily	(1) … a lot of floors in the building?
Kinza	Yes, (2) … There are twelve floors.
Lily	(3) … a lot of rooms in your flat?
Kinza	No, (4) … There are three rooms.
Lily	(5) … one room for you and your sister?

🏆🏆 **Step 2**

YOU CHOOSE **Do task A or B.**

Task A	Task B
Draw a comic of your activities from step 1. Write your sentences from step 1 under your comic pictures. ☒ You can add speech bubbles too.	Make a video: Record your sentences from step 1 on your phone. You can show things, for example headphones for music.

Check that the light is good for your video. Speak clearly.

Lighthouse (General Edition) Band 1 (9783060362523), S. 76–77, S. 97

6 Individualisierung

Arbeit mit dem Checkpoint

Mit den *Checkpoints* wird allen Schülerinnen und Schülern die Möglichkeit gegeben, sich einerseits selbst zu überprüfen und sich andererseits gezielt auf Tests oder Klassenarbeiten vorzubereiten.

Die strukturelle Grundlage für die Arbeit mit den *Checkpoints* stellen die *I-can-statements* dar, die den Lernenden einen roten Faden bieten. Die *I-can-statements* werden während der Unit behandelt und bilden bei den *Checkpoints* hilfreiche inhaltliche Eckpfeiler, zu denen verschiedene Aufgaben und Übungen bearbeitet werden müssen, z. B. *I can talk about my family* oder *I can describe my home or dream home*.

Die *Checkpoints* bieten den Lernenden eine ganze Palette an Aufgabenformaten zu verschiedenen sprachlichen Mitteln (*Words, Language*) oder kommunikativen Fertigkeiten (*Writing, Speaking, Listening*) an. Damit werden bereits behandelte Themen und Aufgabenformate der Unit noch einmal zielführend umgewälzt und trainiert.

Aus methodischer Sicht hat die Lehrkraft verschiedene Möglichkeiten, die *Checkpoints* in den Englischunterricht einzubinden.

So können diese vier Seiten zum einen individuell in autonomen Arbeitsprozessen von den Lernenden bearbeitet werden. Eine beliebte Möglichkeit ist dabei die *Bus stop*-Methode, bei der die Lösungen der *Checkpoint*-Aufgaben an verschiedenen *Bus stops* zur selbstständigen Überprüfung ausgelegt werden. Die Lösungen finden Sie als KVs im Anhang dieses Buchs (ab S. 322).

Zum anderen können die Übungen auch in dynamischer Form anhand von Partner- oder Gruppenarbeitsprozessen bearbeitet werden.

Das neue *Lighthouse* bietet zudem die Möglichkeit, alle Übungen des *Checkpoints* auch in digitaler Form zu bearbeiten. Der *Digital checkpoint* stellt hierbei eine digitale Alternative zum Schulbuch dar. Die Lernenden bearbeiten die Aufgaben in der Cornelsen Lernen App und erhalten dort ein sofortiges Feedback zu ihrer Leistung.

Auch wenn die Schülerinnen und Schüler die Aufgaben nicht digital, sondern in ihrem Heft bearbeiten, können sie die Cornelsen Lernen App nutzen, um sich die Lösungen zu den Aufgaben anzuschauen, so dass sie die Ergebnisse selbstständig überprüfen und ggf. korrigieren können.

Damit wird dem hybriden Gedanken des neuen *Lighthouse* Rechnung getragen.

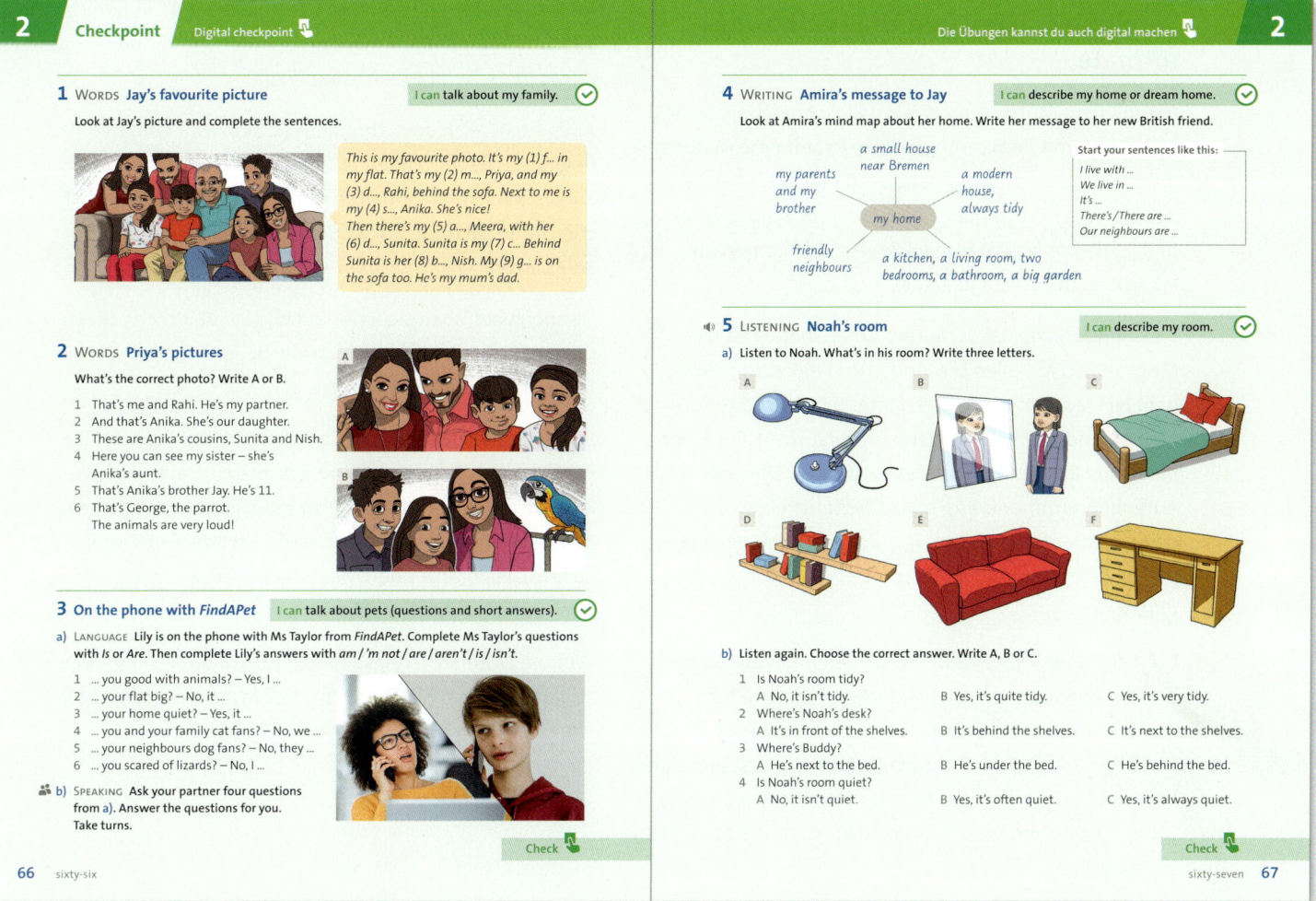

1 WORDS **Jay's favourite picture** | I can **talk about my family.** ✓

Look at Jay's picture and complete the sentences.

*This is my favourite photo. It's my (1) f... in my flat. That's my (2) m..., Priya, and my (3) d..., Rahi, behind the sofa. Next to me is my (4) s..., Anika. She's nice!
Then there's my (5) a..., Meera, with her (6) d..., Sunita. Sunita is my (7) c... Behind Sunita is her (8) b..., Nish. My (9) g... is on the sofa too. He's my mum's dad.*

2 WORDS **Priya's pictures**

What's the correct photo? Write A or B.

1 That's me and Rahi. He's my partner.
2 And that's Anika. She's our daughter.
3 These are Anika's cousins, Sunita and Nish.
4 Here you can see my sister – she's Anika's aunt.
5 That's Anika's brother Jay. He's 11.
6 That's George, the parrot. The animals are very loud!

3 **On the phone with** *FindAPet* | I can **talk about pets (questions and short answers).** ✓

a) LANGUAGE Lily is on the phone with Ms Taylor from *FindAPet*. Complete Ms Taylor's questions with *Is* or *Are*. Then complete Lily's answers with *am / 'm not / are / aren't / is / isn't*.

1 ... you good with animals? – Yes, I ...
2 ... your flat big? – No, it ...
3 ... your home quiet? – Yes, it ...
4 ... you and your family cat fans? – No, we ...
5 ... your neighbours dog fans? – No, they ...
6 ... you scared of lizards? – No, I ...

b) SPEAKING **Ask your partner four questions from a). Answer the questions for you. Take turns.**

Check ⬇

4 WRITING **Amira's message to Jay** | I can **describe my home or dream home.** ✓

Look at Amira's mind map about her home. Write her message to her new British friend.

my parents and my brother
a small house near Bremen
a modern house, always tidy
my home
friendly neighbours
a kitchen, a living room, two bedrooms, a bathroom, a big garden

Start your sentences like this:
I live with ...
We live in ...
It's ...
There's / There are ...
Our neighbours are ...

🔊 **5** LISTENING **Noah's room** | I can **describe my room.** ✓

a) Listen to Noah. What's in his room? Write three letters.

A   B   C

D   E   F

b) Listen again. Choose the correct answer. Write A, B or C.

1 Is Noah's room tidy?
A No, it isn't tidy.   B Yes, it's quite tidy.   C Yes, it's very tidy.
2 Where's Noah's desk?
A It's in front of the shelves.   B It's behind the shelves.   C It's next to the shelves.
3 Where's Buddy?
A He's next to the bed.   B He's under the bed.   C He's behind the bed.
4 Is Noah's room quiet?
A No, it isn't quiet.   B Yes, it's often quiet.   C Yes, it's always quiet.

Check ⬇

Lighthouse (General Edition) Band 1 (9783060362523), S. 66–67

XVI

7 Lern- und Arbeitsheft

Vereinfachungen und Unterstützungsformate

Gemäß dem Motto „Gemeinsam Ziele erreichen" bietet *Lighthouse* mit dem Lern- und Arbeitsheft eine Materialgrundlage speziell für Lernende mit erhöhtem Förderbedarf an. Das Heft ist dabei besonders für Schülerinnen und Schüler mit dem Förderschwerpunkt Lernen im inklusiven Unterricht geeignet.

Ein Grundprinzip des Lern- und Arbeitsheftes ist die Möglichkeit, mit allen Lernenden im Englischunterricht parallel – auch im inklusiven Unterricht – arbeiten zu können und sie bestmöglich zu unterstützen. Für einen parallelen Einsatz sind daher Layout, die Seitenzahl und Aufgabennummerierung sowie die Lernziele und *I can*-statements gleich zum Schulbuch. Damit ist eine leichte Orientierung für alle Lernende und Lehrkräfte garantiert.

Das Lern- und Arbeitsheft enthält vereinfachte Aufgaben und Übungen, die gleich direkt im Heft bearbeitet werden können. Am Beispiel von *Four students at Varndean School* wird exemplarisch der Unterschied zum Lern- und Arbeitsheft deutlich. Im Schulbuch sollen die Schülerinnen und Schüler anhand eines Hörtextes Sätze komplettieren.

Im Lern- und Arbeitsheft erhalten die Lernenden bereits alle Satzfragmente in reduzierter Form und können diese direkt im Heft zuordnen (*Matching*).

Auch im Bereich des Schreibens (s. 1c) *Write about you*) beginnen die Lernenden mit Förderbedarf zunächst mit kurzen Sätzen und erhalten *sentence starters* als zusätzliche Unterstützung. Im Schulbuch sollen hingegen komplexere Satzstrukturen gebildet werden.

Dennoch befinden sich alle Lernenden inhaltlich auf der gleichen Ebene, wodurch sich alle bei der Vorstellung der Ergebnisse beteiligen können.

Lighthouse bietet über die Cornelsen Lernen App zusätzlich auch den Zugriff auf vereinfachte Hörtexte an, um den Anspruch der Aufgaben zu reduzieren und Erfolgserlebnisse für die Lernenden mit Förderbedarf zu ermöglichen. Die ergänzenden Medien auf der App umfassen auch zum Beispiel Erklärfilme.

Weitere Unterstützungselemente beinhalten Aufgabenstellungen auch auf Deutsch, klare Symbole und sprachliche Hilfen sowie zahlreiche konkrete Beispiele.

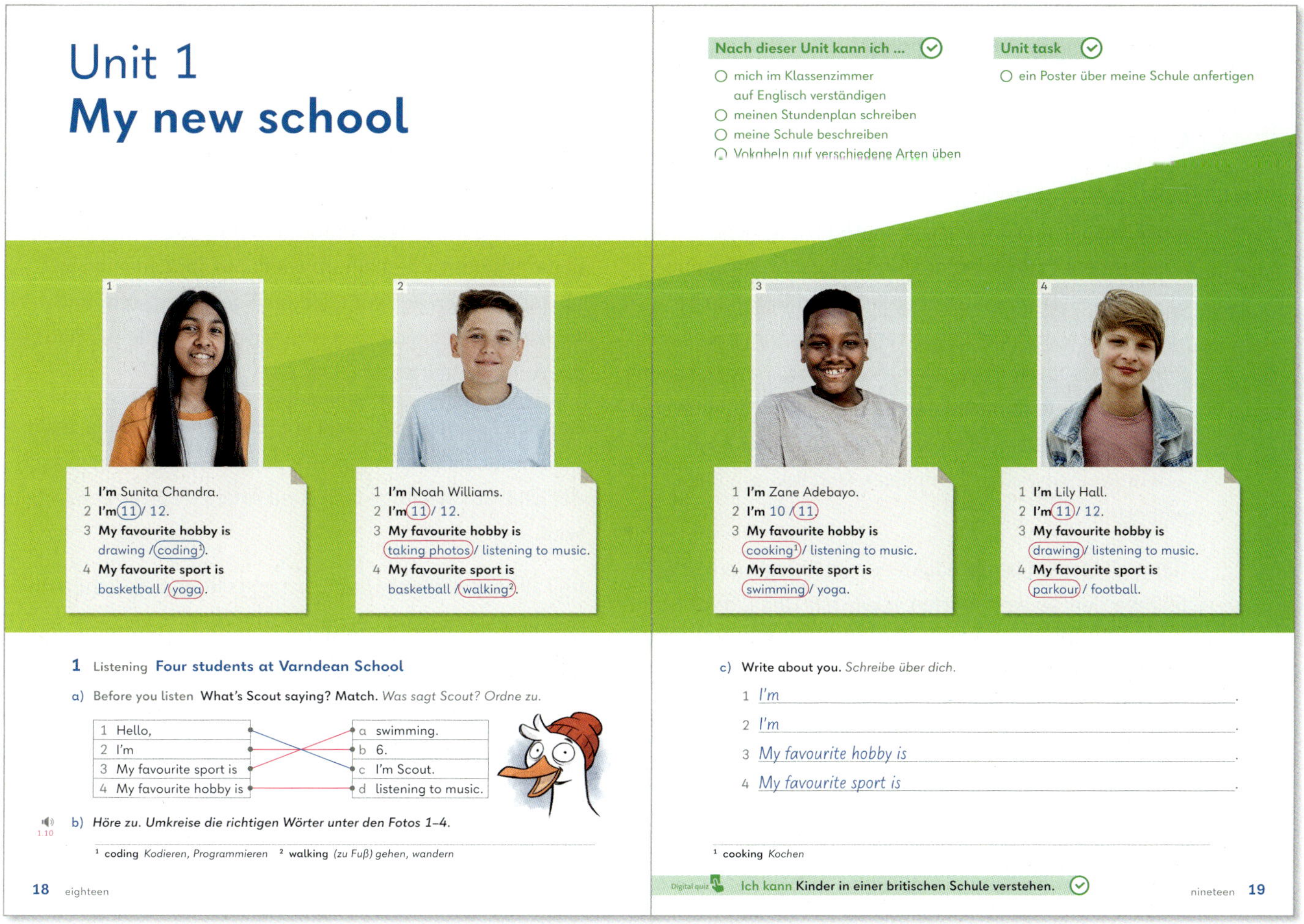

Unit 1
My new school

Nach dieser Unit kann ich ... ✓
- ○ mich im Klassenzimmer auf Englisch verständigen
- ○ meinen Stundenplan schreiben
- ○ meine Schule beschreiben
- ○ Vokabeln auf verschiedene Arten üben

Unit task ✓
- ○ ein Poster über meine Schule anfertigen

1
1 I'm Sunita Chandra.
2 I'm (11) / 12.
3 My favourite hobby is drawing / (coding²).
4 My favourite sport is basketball / (yoga).

2
1 I'm Noah Williams.
2 I'm (11) / 12.
3 My favourite hobby is (taking photos) / listening to music.
4 My favourite sport is basketball / (walking²).

3
1 I'm Zane Adebayo.
2 I'm 10 (11)
3 My favourite hobby is (cooking¹) / listening to music.
4 My favourite sport is (swimming) / yoga.

4
1 I'm Lily Hall.
2 I'm (11) / 12.
3 My favourite hobby is (drawing) / listening to music.
4 My favourite sport is (parkour) / football.

1 Listening **Four students at Varndean School**

a) Before you listen **What's Scout saying? Match.** *Was sagt Scout? Ordne zu.*

1 Hello,	a swimming.
2 I'm	b 6.
3 My favourite sport is	c I'm Scout.
4 My favourite hobby is	d listening to music.

b) *Höre zu. Umkreise die richtigen Wörter unter den Fotos 1–4.*
1.10

¹ **coding** *Kodieren, Programmieren* ² **walking** *(zu Fuß) gehen, wandern*

c) **Write about you.** *Schreibe über dich.*
1 *I'm* _____ .
2 *I'm* _____ .
3 *My favourite hobby is* _____
4 *My favourite sport is* _____

¹ **cooking** *Kochen*

Digital quiz **Ich kann Kinder in einer britischen Schule verstehen.** ✓

18 eighteen

nineteen 19

Lighthouse Lern- und Arbeitsheft für Lernende mit erhöhtem Förderbedarf Band 1, Lehrkräftefassung (9783060345465), S. 18–19

Zum Vergleich: die gleiche Seite im Schulbuch der Lighthouse General Edition

Lighthouse (General Edition) Band 1 (9783060362523), S. 18–19

8 My task / Unit task

Outcome-Orientierung

Das finale Lernprodukt (*Outcome*) spielt in einem modern-kommunikativ ausgerichteten Englischunterricht eine zentrale Rolle. Hierbei zeigt sich, ob die Lernenden das Erlernte (aus inhaltlicher oder sprachlicher Sicht) auch situativ und kontextuell anwenden können. *Lighthouse* schafft bewusst mehrere Szenarien, in denen die Schülerinnen und Schüler kommunikativ agieren und ein Lernprodukt erstellen, anhand der *My task* nach jedem Topic sowie der komplexen *Unit task* am Ende einer Unit.

Generell können Lernprodukte in vier Kategorien einge-teilt werden: *spoken, written, multi-skill* und *digital outcomes*. Die *Unit tasks* greifen diese vier Kategorien verteilt über alle Units des Schulbuches auf, um mög-lichst viele Lern-Typen einzubinden und eine hohe Variation an Aufgabenformaten zu offerieren. Die Lernenden zeigen als summative Leistung bei der *Unit task* auf, was sie bisher in dieser Unit gelernt haben.

Das hier abgebildete Beispiel der *Unit task* zu *Present your top three places for kids* zeigt die typische kleinschrittige Struktur auf.

In einzelnen *Steps* erarbeiten die Lernenden Schritt für Schritt die einzelnen Aufgaben, um am Ende das Lernpro-dukt einer visuell unterstützten Präsentation zu geben. Aufgrund eines klaren kommunikativen Ergebnisses, der inhaltlich-sprachlichen Umsetzung, der interaktiven Gestaltung sowie des Einsatzes zielführender Medien beinhalten die *Unit tasks* unübersehbare Elemente von TSLT (*Task-Supported Language Teaching*).

Die insgesamt fünf *Steps* der Beispiel-Aufgabe rechts führen sukzessive zu einem finalen *Outcome*. Auf dem Weg dorthin erarbeiten sich die Lernenden (hier in Gruppenarbeit) inhaltliche und sprachliche Aspekte, erstellen eine *Slide show* und üben ihre Präsentation, bevor diese im Plenum vorgestellt wird und sie ein Feedback erhalten. Alle *Steps* werden durch *Scaffolding*-Elemente flankiert, z. B. *Digital help*, Wortschatzgrundla-gen auf Basis der *Wordbanks*, *Study skills* sowie sprachli-che Mittel zum Erteilen von Feedback.

Vorbereitende Lern- und Arbeitstechniken (Study skills)

Um ein produktives Lernprodukt erfolgreich umzusetzen, bedarf es neben den inhaltlichen und sprachlichen Vorkenntnissen aus der Unit auch gezielten Lern- und Arbeitstechniken, die den Lernenden bei der Bewältigung der Aufgabe helfen.

Das neue *Lighthouse* bietet vor jeder *Unit task* eine *Study skills*-Seite an, auf der eine für das *Outcome* (Lernprodukt) der *Unit task* wichtige Lern- und Arbeitstechnik behandelt wird.

Im Falle der Beispiel-*Unit task* rechts lernen die Schülerin-nen und Schüler auf der vorgeschalteten *Study skills*-Seite, wie medial gestützte Präsentationen erarbeitet, geübt und umgesetzt werden. Damit wird eine zentrale Grundlage geschaffen, den kommunikativen Anforderun-gen der *Unit task* gerecht zu werden. Die *Study skills*-Seite mit dem Fokus auf Präsentationen schult die Lernenden, wie sie inhaltlich strukturiert vorgehen (Nr. 1), wie eine *Slide show* aufgebaut werden kann (Nr. 2) sowie welche sprachlichen Mittel beim Präsentieren zum Einsatz kommen (Nr. 3). Abschließend erhalten die Lernenden die Möglichkeit, eine exemplarische Präsentation zu geben und dazu Feedback zu erhalten (Nr. 4).

Mit dieser Vorbereitung sind die Lernenden nun gut gewappnet, erfolgreich die *Unit task* zu bewältigen.

Give a presentation

1 Plan your presentation

Put topics A–E in the correct order for Scout's presentation about her favourite places.

Help me plan a presentation, please!

A Talk about other good places in Brighton
B Explain why it's my favourite place
C Say hello and what the presentation is about
D Ask for questions and say thank you
E Say my favourite place

2 Make a slide show

Scout's notes are too long on this slide.
Help her choose five words or phrases.

My favourite place
My favourite place in Brighton is the beach because a lot of people come here and they often eat fish and chips or sandwiches. And I love fish and chips too!

Me on the beach!

Make the title big.
Use short notes.
Use some colour.
Choose big pictures.

3 Find useful phrases

Copy the table. Put the phrases in the correct place.

In this photo you can see • I'd like to talk about • In the end • Next • Do you have any questions? • Let's look at this picture of • My presentation is about • Thank you for listening.

Start the presentation	Continue the presentation	Talk about pictures	End the presentation
I'd like to talk about	...	...	...

4 Practise your presentation

a) Give your presentation on Scout's favourite places to your partner or film yourself.

b) Give your partner or yourself feedback. Draw one, two or three ☺ or ☹.

Speak loudly: ...   Speak clearly: ...   Look at your partner / group: ...

▶ Skills file 5, p. 179

Digital quiz **I can plan and practise a presentation.** ✓

Present your top three places for kids

Step 1

Use a placemat in a group. First write ideas about your top places for kids. Then compare your ideas. Write the best ideas in the middle of your placemat.

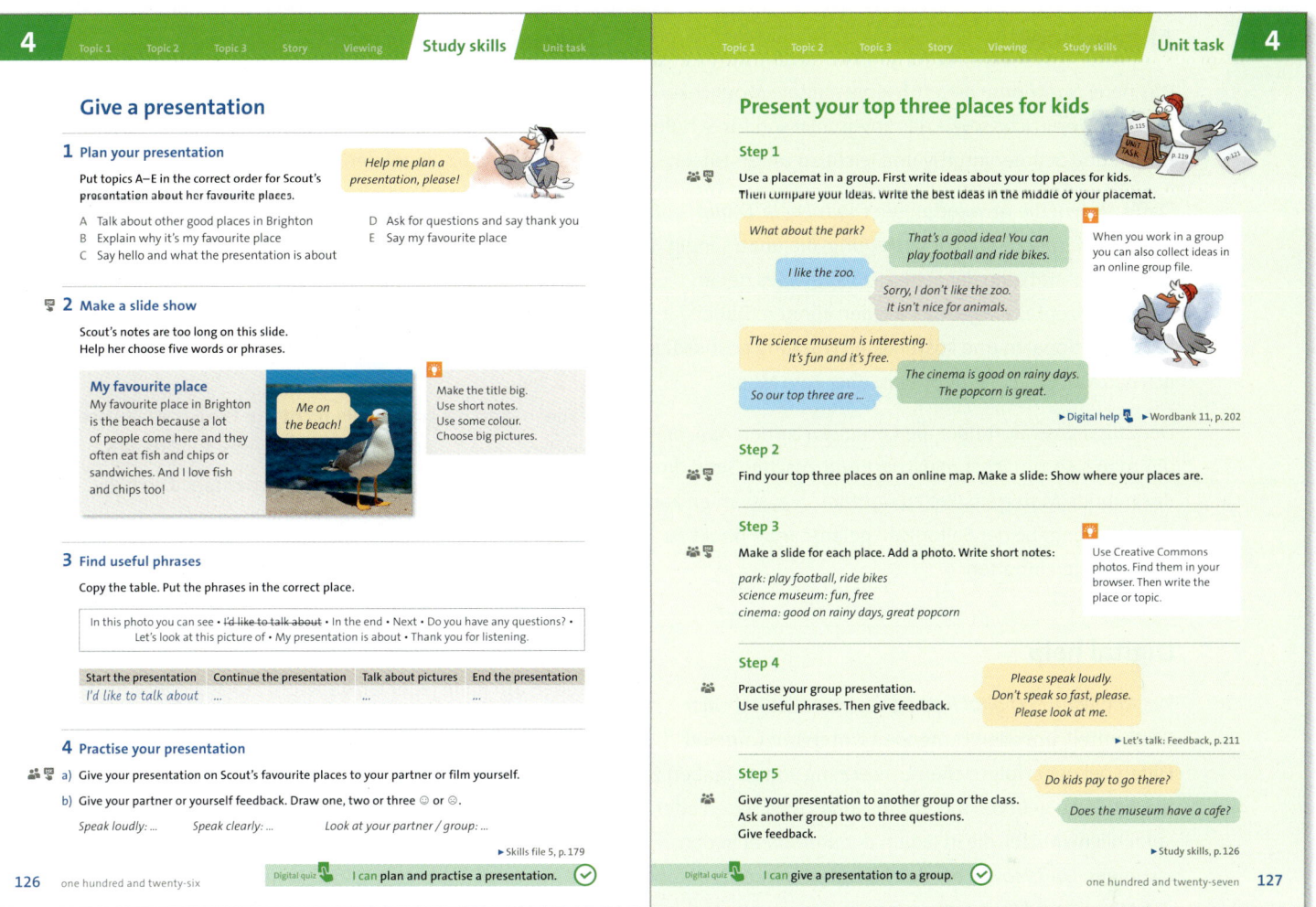

What about the park?
That's a good idea! You can play football and ride bikes.
I like the zoo.
Sorry, I don't like the zoo. It isn't nice for animals.
The science museum is interesting. It's fun and it's free.
The cinema is good on rainy days. The popcorn is great.
So our top three are …

When you work in a group you can also collect ideas in an online group file.

▶ Digital help   ▶ Wordbank 11, p. 202

Step 2

Find your top three places on an online map. Make a slide: Show where your places are.

Step 3

Make a slide for each place. Add a photo. Write short notes:

park: play football, ride bikes
science museum: fun, free
cinema: good on rainy days, great popcorn

Use Creative Commons photos. Find them in your browser. Then write the place or topic.

Step 4

Practise your group presentation. Use useful phrases. Then give feedback.

Please speak loudly. Don't speak so fast, please. Please look at me.

▶ Let's talk: Feedback, p. 211

Step 5

Give your presentation to another group or the class. Ask another group two to three questions. Give feedback.

Do kids pay to go there?
Does the museum have a cafe?

▶ Study skills, p. 126

Digital quiz **I can give a presentation to a group.** ✓

Lighthouse (General Edition) Band 1 (9783060362523), S. 126–127

XX

9 Hybrides Arbeiten

Allgemeines

Das neue *Lighthouse* bietet flexible digitale Möglichkeiten, den Unterricht sowie das Englischlernen für Schülerinnen und Schüler intuitiv und leicht zu unterstützen.

Dafür stehen die Anwendungen *Digital help*, *Digital quiz* und *Digital checkpoint* zur Verfügung, die unabhängig von der Ausstattung der Schule im Sinne des neuen Hybridkonzeptes eingesetzt werden können. Dabei gilt bei der optionalen und kostenlosen Nutzung grundsätzlich das Motto: „Ein großes Plus, aber kein Muss".

Der Zugang verläuft über die Cornelsen Lernen App, bei der man sich zunächst registriert und anschließend direkt das hybride Materialpaket zu *Lighthouse* auswählen kann. Über die Eingabe der Seitenzahl gelangt man direkt zu den digitalen Inhalten.

Digital help

Die Applikation *Digital help* ist ein zentraler hybrider Bestandteil, um allen Lernenden Unterstützung und Hilfen bei der erfolgreichen Umsetzung von Aufgaben zu bieten. Dazu gehören z. B. ergänzende Tipps, Ideen oder sprachliche Mittel, die in jedem der drei *Topics* in den einzelnen *Units* sowie bei den komplexeren Lernaufgaben der *My task* und *Unit task* zu finden sind.

Beim rechten Beispiel, eingebettet in die Aufgabe *My home*, sollen die Lernenden über ihr eigenes Zuhause bzw. Traumzuhause an einen Freund / eine Freundin schreiben. Dies steht im Einklang mit den klar strukturierten *I-can statements*, in diesem Falle *I can describe my home or dream home*. Somit fungiert *Digital help* immer als feste Unterstützungskomponente für das Erreichen der *I-can statements*. Beim rechten Beispiel haben die Lernenden bei eventuellen Schwierigkeiten nun die Möglichkeit, digitale Unterstützung zu erhalten. Dafür können sie eine Audioerklärung der Aufgabe erhalten, sprachlich-inhaltliche Starthilfen nutzen oder eine Erinnerung in Form einer Checkliste (ob sie an alle Punkte gedacht haben) verwenden. Damit kann jeder in seinem Tempo lernen. *Digital help* beinhaltet somit eine vielseitige mediale Ergänzung und Unterstützung (Audios, Videos, Erklärfilme) für den Englischunterricht.

Digital quiz

Die Vielfalt des Englischunterrichts beinhaltet auch, eine hohe Abwechslung für die Lernenden zu ermöglichen. Das *Digital quiz* als spielerische Applikation leistet hierfür einen zentralen Beitrag. Innerhalb der einzelnen *Topics*, *Stories*, *Study skills* und *Unit tasks* erhalten die Schülerinnen und Schüler immer wieder die Möglichkeit, das Gelernte in Form motivierender digitaler Quizaufgaben anzuwenden. Dazu dienen Aufgabenformate wie z. B. *Put the words in the right order* oder *Memory*.

Dabei haben die Lernenden nicht nur Erfolgserlebnisse, sondern sehen gleichzeitig ihren Lernfortschritt. Ein Feedbacksystem (z. B. positive Kommentare durch die Leitfigur) schafft zusätzliche Motivation.

Digital checkpoint

Im Sinne der hybriden Ausrichtung des neuen *Lighthouse* stehen am Ende jeder Unit sowohl ein analoger *Checkpoint* im Schulbuch als auch ein digitaler *Checkpoint* in der Cornelsen Lernen App zur Verfügung. Für beide Versionen gilt, dass bisher erworbene Kompetenzen und sprachliche Mittel in Form eines *self-assessment* direkt angewendet werden können. Beim *Digital checkpoint* erhalten die Lernenden nach der Bearbeitung sofort eine Rückmeldung, wie viele Aufgaben richtig beantwortet wurden, und somit eine transparente Übersicht über den aktuellen Lernstand.

13:26

← Materialpaket zum Schulbuch   ooo

‹ **59** ›

Unit 2 | My family and home

Topic 3 | In my room
8a) My room

💡 **Ich brauche eine Erklärung der Aufgabe.**
ⓘ Digital help | Audio

💡 **Ich brauche Starthilfen.**
ⓘ Digital help | Text / HTML

💡 **Ich möchte mir einen Erklärfilm ansehen: Das Verb be - Fragen und Kurzantworten**
ⓘ Digital help | Video

Digital quiz | I can describe my room.

👆 **I can describe my room.**
ⓘ Digital quiz

13:25

✕   I can describe my daily routine.   **1/6**

🔊 **Look at the picture of Karim and make a sentence. Put the words in the correct order.**

| Karim | at | 7.30. | gets up |

Überspringen   **Auswerten**

©

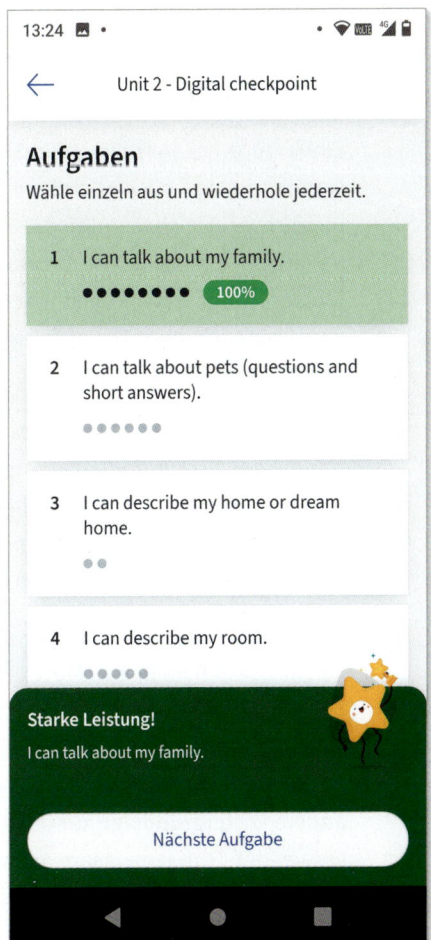

13:24

←   Unit 2 - Digital checkpoint

Aufgaben
Wähle einzeln aus und wiederhole jederzeit.

1   I can talk about my family.
●●●●●●●● **100%**

2   I can talk about pets (questions and short answers).
● ● ● ● ● ●

3   I can describe my home or dream home.
● ●

4   I can describe my room.
● ● ● ● ●

Starke Leistung!
I can talk about my family.

Nächste Aufgabe

Lighthouse (General Edition) Band 1 Hybrides Material Paket Cornelsen Lernen App (220058915)

10 Medien- und Aufgabenvielfalt

Unterschiedliche Zugänge für die Vielzahl an Lernenden

Englischunterricht bedeutet Vielfalt und vor allem die Einbindung der vielseitigen und interessanten Typen von Lernenden. Um so viele Schülerinnen und Schüler wie möglich zu erreichen, sollte der Englischunterricht im Verlaufe der einzelnen Units bezüglich des Einsatzes von Medien, Aufgaben und Methoden balanciert und variantenreich gestaltet sein. Das neue *Lighthouse* bietet dafür die richtige Grundlage.

Von Bildimpulsen und Videoclips über *chat messages* und *mind maps* zu *questionnaires* und Liedern – die Buchseiten von *Lighthouse* offerieren eine ganze Palette an verschiedenen Medieninputs und Aufgabenformaten, um eine spannende Variation in den Englischunterricht zu bringen.

So befasst sich im Beispiel rechts die Aufgabe *A missing pet* (Nr. 6) mit der Komplettierung eines unvollständigen Posters. Die fehlenden Wörter müssen jedoch vom Partner / von der Partnerin ergänzt werden, der/die eine andere Postergrundlage auf den *Diff bank*-Seiten verwendet. Nur gemeinsam anhand der beiden unterschiedlichen Poster kann die Aufgabe erfolgreich gelöst werden. Dieses Aufgabenformat zeigt die Verknüpfung von Sprachprogression, Spaß und dem zielführenden Einsatz eines Medieninputs.

Insgesamt berücksichtigt das neue *Lighthouse* die Vielzahl an Lernenden-Typen durch eine Methoden-, Aufgaben- und Themenvielfalt:

- intrapersonelle Angebote für individuelles Arbeiten

- interpersonelle Angebote für die Zusammenarbeit mit anderen Lernenden

- musikalische Angebote mit kreativen und bewegungsreichen Aufgaben mit einem Liedinput (vgl. das Beispiel rechts, Aufgabe 1 *Ben's song*)

- visuelle Angebote, z. B. durch die Beschreibung von Bildern oder das Anschauen von Videos wie im Beispiel rechts in Aufgabe 2 *Time for a new dare*

- logisch-mathematische Angebote, indem z. B. Informationen im Sinne einer *Info-gap activity* herausgefunden werden müssen, siehe z. B. *A missing pet*

Weiterhin werden die Lernenden anhand variantenreicher Aufgabenstellungen befähigt, sich inhaltlich und sprachlich mit dem Unterrichtsgegenstand auseinanderzusetzen. Beispiele dafür sind *Listen and repeat, short interviews, read the profiles, watch the tour, make word webs, do the role-plays, stand in a line, compare the photo, write questions in the correct order* etc.

In diesem Zuge offeriert *Lighthouse* auch eine Wahldifferenzierung bei möglichen *outcomes* (Lernprodukten). Wie das Beispiel von Step 2 rechts zeigt, können die Schülerinnen und Schüler zwischen zwei verschiedenen Lernprodukten wählen (entweder *draw a comic* oder *make a video*) und somit ihren persönlichen Präferenzen und Interessen Ausdruck geben.

6 SPEAKING A missing pet

a) Noah and Zane see some *Missing Pet* posters, but they have rain on them.

Partner B: Look at p. 74.
Partner A: Copy the poster.
Read the first three sentences to partner B.
Your partner completes the missing words in his/her poster.
Then listen to your partner and complete your missing words.

b) Read the completed poster.
Which pet is missing? Tell your partner.

I think the missing pet is …

MISSING

Our friendly parrot is missing. He's blue and orange and he's ten years old. He likes talking and flying, and he's very nice. But we think he ▨ happy because we have a lot of ▨ in our ▨. It's very ▨.

▨ call **07700 900426** if you find him.

At home with Sunita

My little flat

a And the living room is always very messy
b There are two small bedrooms, there aren't three
c And it isn't new or modern at all
d There aren't expensive pictures on the wall
e But my little flat is perfect for me
f People ask, 'Is your flat big?' No, it's small
g There's my family, that's enough
h My little flat is perfect for me
i Because there's music, there's love

1 SONG Ben's song

a) Listen to the song about Ben and Willow's flat. Put the lines in the correct order: *1f, 2c, 3 …*

b) Listen again and check on p. 74.

c) Describe the flat in one sentence.

It's …

---

2 VIEWING Time for a new dare

Watch the video. Choose the correct picture (A or B) for each dare.

Daisy's dare for Emir is to …

wear underpants[1] on his head.

wear pink hair.

Emir's dare for Daisy is to …

make a street drawing.

play street music.

⚥ Step 2

YOU CHOOSE Do task A or B.

Task A	Task B
Draw a comic of your activities from step 1. Write your sentences from step 1 under your comic pictures. ⊠ You can add speech bubbles too.	Make a video: Record your sentences from step 1 on your phone. You can show things, for example headphones for music.

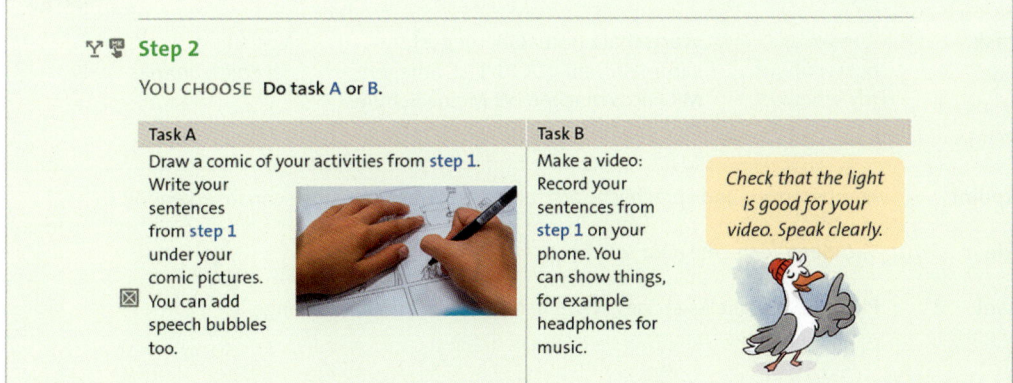

Check that the light is good for your video. Speak clearly.

Lighthouse (General Edition) Band 1 (9783060362523), S. 52; 60; 95; 97

Inhalt

Inhalt

Anhang

Die Angebote des Schulbuchs sind nicht obligatorisch abzuarbeiten.
Die Auswahl der Übungen und Übungsteile richtet sich nach den
Schwerpunkten des schulinternen Curriculums.

Unit-Übersicht

Storyline: Das Maskottchen Scout stellt sich und ihre Lieblingsdinge, -farben, -tiere und Hobbys vor. Dabei wird Grund-schulvokabular wiederholt.

Hello! Einstieg:

- (SB zu) L stellt sich mithilfe der Handpuppe von Scout verschiedenen S vor:
  L (verstellte Stimme): *Hello. I'm Scout. What's your name?*
  Die S antworten.
- ▶ TA als Hilfe: *Hi, I'm …*
- ☒ L stellt den S zusätzlich die Fragen von S.11, Bild 4, z. B. *How old are you?* (max. eine zusätzliche Frage pro S).

- **Alternative:** L nutzt ein alternatives Maskottchen, das den S evtl. schon bekannt ist (z. B. Klassenmaskottchen) – es kann bei Einstiegen u. Ä. eingesetzt werden.

Ex 1 Erarbeitung:

- (SB auf) gemäß AA
- **Sich.:** L liest die Sätze vor. S antworten jeweils.

- ☒ **Zusatz:** (SB zu) L zeigt die Bilder von S.10–11 (UMA). L: *What can you see in the pictures?* S: *I can see …*
- TA: L sammelt die Begriffe.

Ex 2 Erarbeitung:

a) (SB auf) gemäß AA (▶ Mitlese-verfahren)
- **Sich.:** S lesen den Dialog vor.

b) AA klären: In PA ersetzen die S die blauen Wörter im Dialog durch Infos über sich selbst und üben den Dialog gemeinsam.
- S können L nach unbekannten Wörtern fragen. Wichtige Wörter werden an der ▶ Vokabeltafel gesammelt.
- **Sich.:** Freiwillige S tragen den Dialog in PA vor.

Hello!
Nice to meet you

📖 **1 Hello, Scout**

1	1 right	3 right	5 wrong
	2 wrong	4 wrong	6 right

°Look at °pages 10–11. Right °or wrong?

Right!

1 Scout is a seagull. 3 Scout is hungry. 5 Scout is from Hove.
2 Scout is white and green. 4 Scout is 7 years old. 6 Scout is clever.
▶ Box: Voc., p. 215

Wrong!

👂💬 **2 What about you?**

🔊 a) Look at Scout and Leo on p. 11. °Listen and °repeat. 👥 b) °Now °ask and °answer °about you.
1.1
▶ Numbers, p. 277 ▶ Wordbank 1, p. 194

10 ten

Lead-in Inhalt

Lernschwerpunkt: sich selbst vorstellen

Kompetenzen: Reading *right/wrong*-Fragen zu einer Bildergeschichte beantworten • Listening Gehörtes nachsprechen • Speaking sich vorstellen und Alter, Wohnort und Hobby nennen

Redemittel: sich vorstellen (Wdh. von GSE)

Vorbereitung

Material: Einstieg Handpuppe Scout (od. Klassenmaskottchen) • Ex 1 UMA • Ex 2 UMA/CD • Ex 3 ▶ KV 0.1: Hello, class (Klassensatz), weißes Papier (A4, Klassensatz)

Zeitbedarf: 1–2 Std.

Minimalversion: Ex 2 auslassen

Begleitmedien: App (Digital quiz), INKL (S. 10–11), DIFF (0.1)

Ex 3 Erarbeitung:

- (SB auf) AA klären: *Walk around* ist ein sog. ▶ Milling around.
- L führt mit S mind. einen Beispieldialog vor.
- Mindestzahl an zu befragenden S festlegen.
- ☑ S nehmen ihr SB od. ▶ KV 0.1 (Ex 1a) mit und lesen den Dialog ab.
- **Sich.:** S notieren sich die Ergebnisse ihrer Interviews, z. B. auf ▶ KV 0.1 (Ex 1b).
- ▶ Early finisher: S nutzen ▶ KV 0.1 (Ex 1c).
- ☒ L stellt weiterführende Fragen im Plenum, z. B.: *Who is from …?* *Who is … years old?* *Who is this?* (L zeigt auf S.) *What does … like?*
- S antworten mithilfe ihrer Notizen auf der KV.

- **Zusatz:** ▶ KV 0.1 (Ex 2–3): S ergänzen erst die gesuchten Informationen zu Scout (Ex 2). Als Hilfe dienen die Bilder von S. 11.
- In Ex 3 gestalten die S ein Poster über sich selbst auf einem Extrablatt.
- S können (freiwillig) z. B. Fotos od. Zeichnungen auf den Postern ergänzen (als HA).
- Die fertigen Poster werden im Klassenraum präsentiert, z. B. mit einem ▶ Gallery walk.
- individuelle Ablage im ▶ Dossier

3 Hello, class

°WALK AROUND °Find out about other students.

1 Hello! I'm … What's your name?

2 Hi! I'm … I'm … (years old). How old are you?

3 I'm … (years old). I'm from … Where are you from?

4 I'm from … (too). I like … What about you?

5 I like … Nice to meet you!

6 Nice to meet you too. Bye!

Digital quiz 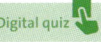 I °can °say hello.

Goodbye, holidays! | Inhalt

Lernschwerpunkt: über ein Wimmelbild sprechen
Kompetenzen: Listening Geräusche und kurze Dialoge Ereignissen auf einem Wimmelbild zuordnen • ein Lied anhören und zum Text passende Bewegungen ausführen • Speaking Dinge auf einem Wimmelbild benennen
Strukturen: *s*-Genitiv und *of*-Fügung (lexikalisch)
Redemittel: Wortfelder *food and drink, colours, animals, numbers*

Ex 1 Einstieg:
- (SB zu) L bahnt an:
  L: *This is my favourite place in Brighton. What is it?*
  (L zeichnet einen Strand mit Wellen usw., bis S das Wort *beach* erraten.)
- ☒ ▶ Five-finger-brainstorming:
  L: *What can you see at the beach?*

Erarbeitung:
a) (SB auf) **1./2. Hören** gemäß AA. L zeigt das Bild von S. 12–13 (UMA).

b) AA im Plenum klären: L lässt S z.B. *Scout* und *two numbers* auf der SB-Seite (UMA) suchen, ggf. weitere Beispiele.
L: *Point at two numbers, please. Can you say the two numbers?*
S: *Here's …*
- In PA: S1 sucht einen Begriff aus dem Reservoir auf dem Bild, zeigt darauf und sagt, was zu sehen ist. Dann übernimmt S2.
- ▶ Early finisher: S-Paare suchen und benennen weitere Dinge auf dem Bild.
- **Sich.:** Vergleich im Plenum (mit dem UMA).
- S zeigen auf das SB-Bild und sagen, was sie sehen.
- TA/UMA: L sammelt Begriffe und sichert den Lernwortschatz (▶ Semantisierung).
- L leitet ▶ Vokabelarbeit an, die S notieren die neuen Wörter im *Vocab file* (s.a. ▶ SF 1, S. 173).
- bei Bedarf ▶ LF 1, S. 182

c) gemäß AA (s.a. ▶ Kimspiel)
- **Sich.:** in einer ▶ Meldekette
  ▶ Chain game

Hello!

Goodbye, holidays!

1 a) 4

1 b) two numbers

NUMBER 1

1 a) 3

1 a) 6

🎧💬 **1 In the picture**   **1** im Bild u. Lösungsbsp. S. 286

🔊 1.2 a) °**Look at** the picture. °**Listen**, °**find** and °**point**.

👥 b) Find, point and °**say**.   ▶ Wordbanks 1–2, p. 194   ▶ Language file 1, p. 182

> Scout the seagull • Leo's mum • Ben's dad • two numbers •
> three animals • four colours • three drinks •
> two things to eat • three other things

Here's Scout.
And here's Leo's mum.
I can see a dog / …

👥 c) Look at the picture °**for** 30 °**seconds** °**again**. °**Close** your °**books**.
What can you remember?

I remember Scout and a dog.

I remember Scout.

I remember Scout and a dog and a …

12   twelve

Goodbye, holidays! **Vorbereitung**

Material: Ex 1 UMA/CD • Ex 2 UMA/CD, Handpuppe Scout (od. vorhandenes Klassenmaskottchen)
Zeitbedarf: ca. 2 Std.
Minimalversion: Ex 2 auslassen
Begleitmedien: WB (S. 8), App (Digital quiz), INKL (S. 12–13)

Hello!

- **1 b)** two numbers
- **1 b)** Scout the seagull — Leo
- **1 b)** Leo's mum
- **1 b)** Ben's dad
- **1 a)** 1
- **1 a)** 2
- **1 a)** 5

2 SONG **Scout's +song**

a) Listen and °act out the song. Then listen again, act and sing.
1.3

> Hi, hello, nice to meet you °today!
> How are you? I'm fine, I'm OK.
> I °live here in Brighton, °right by the sea.
> It's a nice °day to meet
> And to °find °something to eat.
> Oh, what's °that?
> (°Look out! It's Scout!)
> Wheeeeeeee!

> I'm a seagull, I'm Scout the seagull.
> °Just look how °high
> In the °sky I can °fly.
> °That's where °I like to °be.
> I'm a seagull, I'm Scout the seagull.
> Just look how high in the sky I can fly
> °Over the sea.

b) °Ask and °answer.

A: Ali, *how are you?*   B: ☺ *I'm fine/+OK.* Mia, how are you?   C: ☹ *I'm not so good.* Ole, how …

► Workbook, p. 8

 Digital quiz   I can **talk about a picture.** ✓

Ex 2 Einstieg:

- (SB zu) L mit Handpuppe:
Scout: *Hello, how are you? Do you like my beach? I like music. Do you like music? Let's sing a song!*
- S antworten spontan.

- **Alternative:** Anderes Maskottchen od. L selbst moderiert den **Einstieg** (s. o.).

Erarbeitung:

a) (SB zu) **1. Hören:** L spielt mit Scout die Bewegungen auf den kl. Bildern vor. Die S ahmen sie nach (► TPR).
L (als Scout): *Now listen and act! Look at me!*
Bild 1: winken
Bild 2: Wellenbewegungen
Bild 3: essen
Bild 4: Ausschau halten
Bild 5: Flügelbewegungen
Bild 6: Daumen/Flügel hoch
Bild 7: s. Bild 2
- (SB auf) **2. Hören:** S singen mit und machen die Bewegungen nach.

b) L mit Scout-Handpuppe (fragt erst sich selbst)
Scout: *Hello, who are you?*
L: *I'm Mr/Ms/Mrs …*
Scout: *Hello, Mr/Ms/Mrs … nice to meet you. How are you today?*
L: *I am not so good. And how are you?*
Scout: *I am fine. Thank you.*
- L fragt einzelne S, dann ► Meldekette.

- **Alternative:** L führt den Dialog zunächst mit freiwilligen S od. alternativem Maskottchen vor.

About me | Inhalt

Lernschwerpunkt: Lieblingstiere nennen, über Hobbys und Lieblingsdinge sprechen

Kompetenzen: Reading Tierbilder ihren korrekten Bezeichnungen zuordnen • Sätze den passenden Gegenständen auf einem Bild zuordnen • Listening Tiere an ihren typischen Lauten erkennen • Gegenstände beim Hören erkennen und auf sie zeigen • Speaking Tiere nachahmen, zeichnen oder benennen • sich mit anderen über Lieblingssportarten und Hobbys austauschen

Redemittel: Wortfelder *animals, colours, hobbies*

Ex 1 Erarbeitung:

a) (SB auf) gemäß AA
- **Sich.:** L/S schreibt das jeweilige Tier mit der korrekten Zahl an die Tafel.

b) gemäß AA
- **Sich.:** Vergleich im Plenum: S: *Number one is a …*
- L sichert die Aussprache durch chorisches Sprechen (▸Lautschulung).

c) AA im Plenum klären
- S arbeiten in PA: S1 zeichnet oder ahmt ein Tier nach oder macht seine typischen Geräusche. S2 errät das Tier.
- Dann wird gewechselt.

- **Alternative:** (SB zu) Einsatz ▸KV 0.2 A+B: Die Aufgabe wird als Kartenspiel durchgeführt (in PA od. GA).
- S1 zieht eine Tier- und eine Aktionskarte und führt die beschriebene Aktion aus. S2 bzw. die Gruppe errät das Tier.

- **Sich.:** S schreiben den neuen Lernwortschatz ins *Vocab file* (s. a. ▸SF 1, S.173, ▸Vokabelarbeit).
- ▸Early finisher: S können die passenden Tiere zu den Wörtern malen.

d) (SB zu) eine Variation des ▸Fruit salad-Spiels:
- Zur Vorbereitung merken sich die S ihr jeweiliges *favourite animal* (▸Wordbank 3, S.195) und nennen es im Plenum.
- L sichert ggf. die Aussprache für neue Tiervokabeln im Plenum durch chorisches Sprechen (▸Lautschulung).

Hello!

About me

📖 **1 My favourite animal**

💬 a) What animals can you see? °Match the °words to the pictures.

> 1 a) **1** a horse • **2** a dog • **3** a parrot • **4** a monkey • **5** a lion • **6** a cat • **7** a snake • **8** an elephant

In picture 1 I can see …   In picture 2 there's …

a cat • a dog • an elephant • a horse • a lion • a monkey • a parrot • a snake

▸ Box: Voc., p. 216

🎧 1.4 b) °Listen. °Write six animals from a).

> 1 b) **1** a monkey • **2** a parrot • **3** an elephant • **4** a horse • **5** a lion • **6** a snake

💬 c) °Mime, °draw or °make an animal °noise. Your °partner °says the animal.   *It's a dog!*

👥 d) GAME °Stand in a °circle. One student says °his/her favourite animal. Students °with °the same favourite animal °change °places.   ▸ Wordbank 3, p. 195

My favourite animal is a fish.

▸ Workbook, p. 9

14   fourteen

About me Vorbereitung

Material: Ex 1 UMA/CD, ▶ KV 0.2A + B: GAME Activity cards / Animal cards (vorbereitete Spielkarten, ein Satz pro S-Gruppe) • Ex 2 UMA, ▶ KV 0.3: My favourite hobbies (Klassensatz), ▶ KV Extra: Bus stop (eine Kopie pro *Bus stop* in der Klasse) • Ex 3 UMA/CD

Zeitbedarf: ca. 2 Std.

Minimalversion: Ex 1c) und d) auslassen

Begleitmedien: WB (S. 9–10), INKL (S. 14–15), DIFF (0.2, 0.3)

---

2 My favourite hobbies

🖊 a) Look at the °code.
°Write Scout's hobbies and sports.

a	e	i	o	u
∞	m	Ж	□	◆

I like …

Scout

f□□tb∞ll ▶ Box: Voc., p. 216

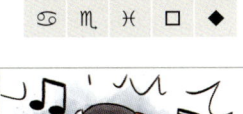

lЖstm_nЖng t□ m◆sЖc

dr∞wЖng

d∞ncЖng

swЖmmЖng

t∞kЖng ph□t□s

👥 b) DOUBLE CIRCLE °Think about your °free time. °Talk to a partner.
💬 One °circle °moves to °find a new partner.

> 🙂 *I like/love … too.*

> *My favourite hobby/sport is …*
> *What about you?*

> ☹️ *I don't like …*
> *My favourite hobby/sport is …*

2 a) 1 football • **2** listening to music • **3** drawing • **4** dancing • **5** swimming • **6** taking photos

▶ Wordbank 4, p. 196

3 My favourite things

🔊 🔊 a) Listen and point.
1.5

b) Look at the picture °again. Read 1–8 and °say what it is.

a guitar   a bike   a cap   a chain   a ⁺rucksack
a book   a phone   a scooter

1 My favourite thing is small, new and black.
2 It's big and blue.
3 This thing is small and gold.
4 I love it – it's big and silver.
5 I can ⁺play music with it.
6 It's ⁺cool and white.
7 This thing is small and old. I read it.
8 It's red and I put things in it.

3 b) 1 a phone • **2** a scooter • **3** a chain • **4** a bike • **5** a guitar • **6** a cap • **7** a book • **8** a rucksack

▶ Workbook, pp. 9–10

fifteen **15**

Ex 2 Erarbeitung:

a) (SB auf) gemäß AA
• S notieren ihre Lösungen für die gesuchten Hobbys.
• ▶ Early finisher: S ergänzen eigene/weitere Hobbys in Code auf der ▶ KV 0.3 (Ex 1) (▶ Wordbank 4, S. 196).
• S lösen die Begriffe in PA od. S finden Partner/in am ▶ Bus stop (Einsatz: ▶ KV Extra).
• **Sich.:** gemeinsames Überprüfen der Lösungen im Plenum: L zeigt die sechs Bilder mit dem UMA und notiert die richtigen Lösungen darunter.
• ▶ Lautschulung durch chorisches Sprechen.

b) S nutzen die ▶ KV 0.3 (Ex 2a–b) zur Vorbereitung auf den ▶ Double circle.
• 🖳 Lernschwächere S nutzen ▶ KV 0.3 (Ex 2a–b) als *prompts* im ▶ Double circle.
• L präsentiert die Sprechblasen aus 2b) als TA oder mit dem UMA.
• **Sich.:** S stellen im Plenum eine/n Mit-S aus dem ▶ Double circle vor.

Ex 3 Erarbeitung:

a) (SB auf) gemäß AA
• **Sich.:** L zeigt auf einen Gegenstand (SB/UMA):
L: *What is this?*
S: *This is a …*
• L berichtigt ggf. die Aussprache (▶ Lautschulung).

b) S lesen jeweils den Satz laut vor und sagen: *It's a …*
• L achtet weiterhin auf die Aussprache (▶ Lautschulung).

Lernschwerpunkt: über Lieblingsdinge reden (Forts. von S. 15)

Kompetenzen: Listening ein Lied über Lieblingsdinge anhören • Speaking ein Lied singen • Writing ein Gedicht/Lied über die eigenen Lieblingsdinge schreiben (mit Hilfen) • sechs Lieblingsdinge aufschreiben

Redemittel: Wortfelder *animals, colours, numbers, things, hobbies*

Material: Ex 4 UMA/CD, weißes Papier (A4, Klassensatz)

Zeitbedarf: ca. 1 Std.

Minimalversion: Ex 4 kann ausgelassen werden, wenn S sicher im GSE sind

Begleitmedien: WB (S. 10), App (Digital quiz), INKL (S. 16)

Ex 4 Einstieg:
- (SB zu) L notiert als TA:
  Partner A: *What is your favourite colour/sport/...*
  Partner B: *My favourite colour/thing/ ... is ...*
- L präsentiert 1–2 Beispieldialoge mit freiwilligen S, dann arbeiten S in PA.

Erarbeitung:

a) (SB auf) gemäß AA

b) S sammeln Beispiele zu jeder Kategorie. L sichert durch TA:
L: *Which animals/colours/ ... do you know?*
- S können ▶ Wordbanks 1–4, S. 194–196 und ▶ Wordbanks 8–9, S. 200 nutzen.
- S gestalten individuell ein Gedicht auf einem A4-Blatt.
- **Ausw.:** ▶ Gallery walk
- ggf. Ablage im ▶ Dossier

Ex 5 Erarbeitung:
- (SB auf) gemäß AA
- Vorbereitung auf Ex 6
- **Sich.:** ▶ Five-minute teacher

Ex 6 Einstieg:
- (SB zu) L stimmt S ein:
  L: *My top six are ... What are your top six?*

Erarbeitung:

a) (SB auf) gemäß AA
- S erstellen ihre *top six* mithilfe der Vorlage aus Ex 5.

b) ▶ Milling around gemäß AA
- S nutzen Notizen aus a).

c) S gestalten ihre *top six* (individuell) auf einem Blatt für das ▶ Dossier (z. B. als HA).

Hello!

4 SONG **My favourites**

🔊 1.6 a) Listen. Then listen again and sing.

b) Make a new song or °poem with your favourite **animals**, **colours**, **numbers**, **things** and **hobbies**.

▶ Wordbanks 1–4, pp. 194–196

▶ Wordbanks 8–9, p. 200

4 Lösungsbsp. S. 286

> 🎵
> *What's your favourite animal?*
> *My favourite animal is a °kangaroo.*
> *What's your favourite colour?*
> *My favourite colour is blue. What about you?*
>
> *I like silver and I don't like gold.*
> *Ten is my favourite number °'cause I'm ten years old.*
> *I like my bike and I love my football,*
> *But my scooter is my favourite thing of all.*
>
> *What's your favourite hobby?*
> *Dancing is my favourite thing to do.*
> *What's your favourite sport?*
> *I like swimming too. What about you?*

'cause *weil*

5 Scout's ⁺**top six**

Write the °**correct** words.

animal • colour • ⁺film • hobby • sport • thing

My favourite ... is a fish.
My favourite ... is orange.
My favourite ... is singing.
My favourite ... is my hat.
My favourite ... is *Finding Nemo*.
My favourite ... is swimming.

5 1 animal • **2** colour • **3** hobby • **4** thing • **5** film • **6** sport

6 My top six

a) Write your top six.

b) WALK AROUND Ask and answer six questions. Who has the same favourite things?

What's your favourite film / ...?

My favourite film / ... is ...

I like that too.

Sorry, I don't like that. My favourite film / ... is ...

💡 Im DOSSIER kannst du deine wichtigen und schönen Arbeiten sammeln.

c) Put your top six in your DOSSIER.

▶ Workbook, p. 10

 Digital quiz **I can talk about what I like.** ✓

Ready for school — Inhalt | Vorbereitung

Lernschwerpunkt: Ansagen von Lehrkräften verstehen
Kompetenzen: Listening Anweisungen einer Lehrkraft hören und dazu passende Bewegungen ausführen • ein Lied hören und den Text vervollständigen • Reading *Book rally* (Bilder von Scout finden und dabei die unterschiedlichen Teile des Buches kennenlernen)
Redemittel: *classroom English*

Material: Ex 1 UMA/CD, Handpuppe Scout • Ex 2 UMA/CD, Handpuppe Scout • Ex 3 UMA/CD, ► KV 0.4: My book (Klassensatz)
Zeitbedarf: ca. 1 Std.
Minimalversion: Ex 2 auslassen
Begleitmedien: WB (S. 6–7, S. 11), App (Digital quiz), INKL (S. 17), DIFF (0.4)

Hello!

Ready for school

1 b) 1 G · 2 A · 3 F · 4 D · 5 H · 6 E · 7 B · 8 C

1 a) und **c)** Lösung S. 286

1 Listen, please!

a) Listen. Point to the correct pictures. *(1.7)*

b) °Match the °speech bubbles and the pictures.

1 *Quiet, please.* 2 *Listen.* 3 *Open your books.*
4 *Sit down.* 5 *Look at the board.* 6 *Stand up.*
7 *Put your hand up.* 8 *Close your books.*

c) Listen. °Do the °actions. *(1.8)*

d) °Now you're the °teacher: Read a speech bubble, and the students do the actions.

2 SONG The school song

a) Listen. °Then listen °again and sing. *(1.9)*

b) °Complete the song.

Ready, steady, 1, 2, 3
(1) … and °repeat after me
°First (2) … down and °then stand up
Don't °forget, (3) … your hand up
(4) … your book °at page four
(5) … at me, look at the °board
(6) …, please, don't °make a °sound
(7) … the °question, °write it down
°Quick, put °all your (8) … °away
°Now it's °break, it's °time to (9) …

2 b) Ready, steady, 1, 2, 3 (1) *Listen* and repeat after me / First (2) *sit* down and then stand up / Don't forget, (3) *put* your hand up / (4) *Open* your book at page four / (5) *Look* at me, look at the board / (6) *Quiet*, please, don't make a sound / (7) *Read* the question, write it down / Quick, put all your (8) *things* away / Now it's break, it's time to (9) *play*.

3 Lösung S. 286

3 Where's Scout?

°Find °these pictures of Scout. What °part of the book is °she in?

A   B   C   D   E   F   G

► Workbook, pp. 6–7, p. 11

 Digital quiz   I can understand classroom English. ✓

seventeen **17**

Ex 1 Einstieg:
• (SB zu) Einsatz Maskottchen:
L: *Hi Scout! How are you?*
Scout: *I'm sad!* (Scout weint.)
L: *What? Why?*
Scout: *I don't understand my teacher!*
L: *Hey class. Let's help Scout!*

Erarbeitung:
a) (SB auf) gemäß AA

b) gemäß AA
• Sich. im Plenum

c) + d) gemäß AA (► TPR)

Ex 2 Einstieg: (SB zu)
L: *Well, Scout, do you understand your teacher now?*
Scout: *Yes, I do. But I forget the words.*
L: *Maybe this song can help you! Listen, please.*

Erarbeitung:
a) (SB zu) 1. Hören
• (SB auf) S lesen und singen beim 2. Hören mit (► Mitleseverfahren).

b) gemäß AA
• Sich.: ► Five-minute teacher.

Ex 3 Einstieg:
• (SB auf) L zeigt Bilder von Scout (UMA):
L: *Scout likes hats. Which hat is the best?*
• S nennen den Buchstaben ihres Lieblingshuts.

Erarbeitung:
• S suchen die Bilder im Buch und tragen die Lösungen z.B. in ► KV 0.4 ein.
• Sich.: ► Meldekette

Unit-Übersicht

Storyline: Die vier Lehrwerkskinder Sunita, Noah, Zane und Lily werden vorgestellt. Die S lernen die Varndean School kennen. Es gibt Informationen über die Schuluniform, den Fächerkanon und den Alltag an einer britischen Schule. In der Story erleben Lily und Sunita, wie Noah von Kindern einer anderen Schule gemobbt wird und helfen ihm. Scout hat einen großen Auftritt.
Strukturen: s-Genitiv und *of*-Fügung (S. 19) • unbestimmter Artikel *a/an* (S. 21) • Plural der Nomen (S. 22) • Personalpronomen (S. 24) • Verb *to be* (Kurzform u. Langform (S. 24), Verneinung (S. 29))
Viewing: Emir und Daisy, die auch auf die Varndean School gehen, stellen einander lustige Mutproben, sog. *dares* (S. 33)
Unit task: Gestaltung eines Posters über die eigene Schule

Unit 1 Einstieg:
- (SB zu) L führt einen Dialog mit Handpuppe Scout:
  L: *Hello Scout. Today we are in a school.*
  Scout: *What's the name of the school?*
  L: *It's Varndean School.*
  (L schreibt Namen an die Tafel.) *And here are four students.*
  Scout: *That's great.*
- UMA mit Bildern von S. 18/19
  L: *Look, here they are: this is ...*
  (L zeigt aufs Bild und nennt den jeweiligen Namen.)

Ex 1 Erarbeitung:
a) (SB auf) S vervollständigen Sätze von Scout in PA oder im Plenum (S nutzen ihr Vorwissen von S. 10–11).
- S-Paare vervollständigen die Sätze mit ihren eigenen Angaben und tauschen sich im ▶ Partner talk aus.
- **Ausw.:** Einzelne S-Paare berichten im Plenum über sich.

b) AA gemeinsam klären
- S lesen die Informationen über die Lehrwerkskinder.
- Vorentlastung des neuen Wortschatzes (▶ Semantisierung, ▶ Lautschulung)
- **1. Hören:** S notieren die Buchstaben in EA im Heft.
- **Sich.:** ggf. **2. Hören** und Vergleich im Plenum
- L/S markiert Lösung an der Tafel/UMA.
- ☑ **Alternative:** Einsatz von ▶ KV 1.1: S bilden Dreiergruppen.
- S teilen die Höraufträge in der Gruppe auf, s. Ex 1a): **1. Hören**.
- **Ausw.** in GA, s. Ex 1b) schriftl. auf der KV
- Forts. Ex 1, s. S. 19

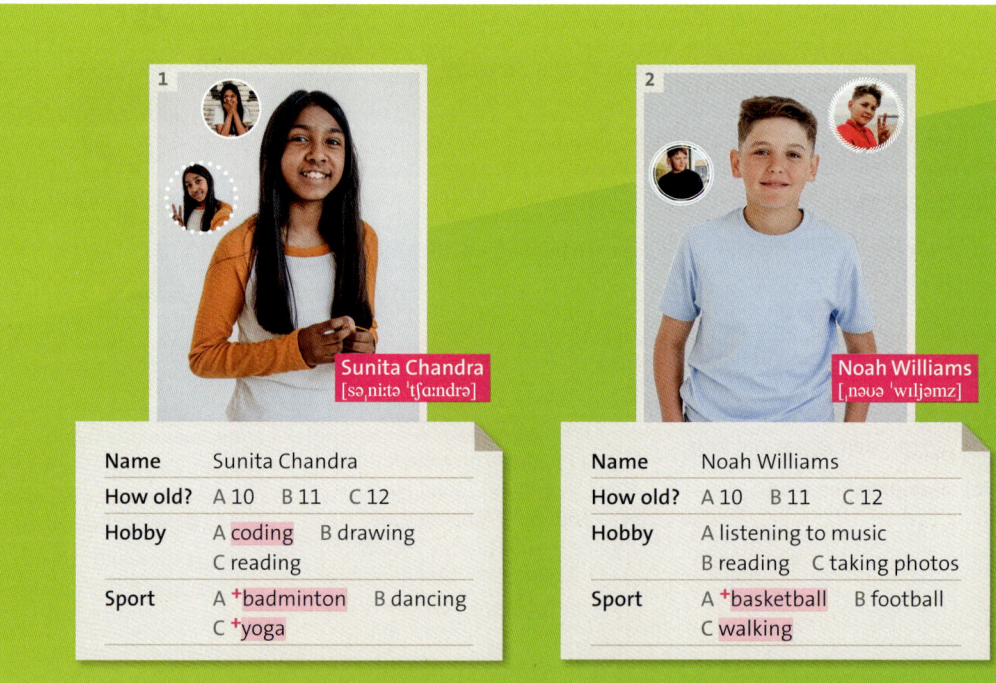

Unit 1
My new school

Name	Sunita Chandra		Name	Noah Williams	
How old?	A 10	B 11 C 12	How old?	A 10	B 11 C 12
Hobby	A coding	B drawing C reading	Hobby	A listening to music B reading C taking photos	
Sport	A +badminton	B dancing C +yoga	Sport	A +basketball B football C walking	

Sunita Chandra [səˌniːtə ˈtʃɑːndrə]

Noah Williams [ˌnəʊə ˈwɪljəmz]

🎧 **1** LISTENING **Four students at Varndean¹ School**

💬👥 a) BEFORE YOU LISTEN Complete Scout's sentences. Then tell a partner about you.

1 a) Lösungsbsp. S. 287

Hello, I'm ...   I'm ... years old.   I like ...   My favourite hobby is ...   My favourite sport is ...   What about you?

🔊 1.10 b) Look at the pictures of four students from Brighton and read about them. Then listen. Write A, B or C for the answers.

1 b) Sunita: B • A • C   **Noah:** B • C • C   **Zane:** B • B • C   **Lily:** B • A • B

18 eighteen

¹ [vɑːnˈdiːn]

Lead-in Inhalt

Lernschwerpunkt: Kennenlernen der Lehrwerkspersonen
Kompetenzen: Listening Informationen über Personen verstehen • Speaking über sich und andere Personen sprechen
Redemittel: sich vorstellen • Lieblingshobby/-sport nennen und erfragen
Strukturen: *s*-Genitiv und *of*-Fügung (lexikalisch)

Vorbereitung

Material: Ex 1 UMA/CD, Handpuppe Scout / alternatives Maskottchen, ▸ KV 1.1: Four students (Klassensatz)
Zeitbedarf: ca. 2 Std.
Begleitmedien: WB (S. 12), App (Digital quiz), INKL (S. 18–19), DIFF (1.1)

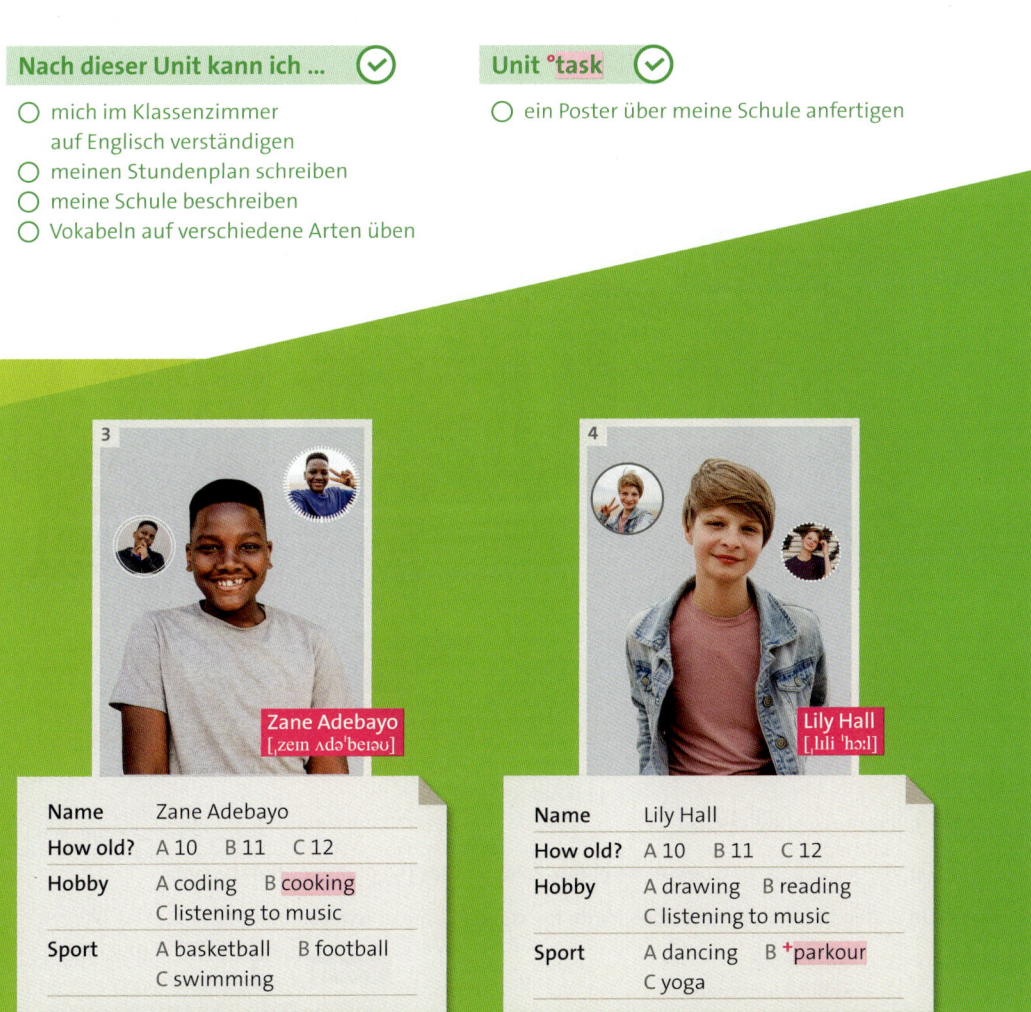

Nach dieser Unit kann ich ... ✓

○ mich im Klassenzimmer auf Englisch verständigen
○ meinen Stundenplan schreiben
○ meine Schule beschreiben
○ Vokabeln auf verschiedene Arten üben

Unit °task ✓

○ ein Poster über meine Schule anfertigen

3

Zane Adebayo
[ˌzeɪn ʌdəˈbeɪəʊ]

Name	Zane Adebayo
How old?	A 10 B 11 C 12
Hobby	A coding B cooking C listening to music
Sport	A basketball B football C swimming

4

Lily Hall
[ˌlɪli ˈhɔːl]

Name	Lily Hall
How old?	A 10 B 11 C 12
Hobby	A drawing B reading C listening to music
Sport	A dancing B ⁺parkour C yoga

💬👥 **c)** Choose Sunita, Noah, Zane or Lily. What's the same or what's °different for you?

Sunita is ... years old. I'm ... too. / But I'm ...
I like ... too. / I don't like ...
Sunita's favourite hobby is ...   My favourite hobby is ...
Sunita's favourite sport is ...   My ...

1 c) Lösungsbsp. S. 287

▸ Language file 1, p. 182

▸ Workbook, p. 12

Digital quiz **I can understand students at a British school.** ✓

nineteen **19**

Nach dieser Unit ...
• L bespricht mit S die Lernziele der Unit (s. links) und kündigt die *Unit task* an.
• Am Ende der Unit überprüfen die S das Erreichen der Ziele mithilfe des *Checkpoint* (S. 36–39) bzw. gemeinsam im Plenum.

Ex 1 Erarbeitung (Forts.)
c) L oder freiwillige/r S demonstriert ggf. ein Beispiel (*Sunita*) im Plenum.
• Durchführung im ▸ Partner talk
• **Ausw.:** S tragen die Ergebnisse im Plenum vor.
• s. a. ▸ LF 1, S. 182
• 🖵 **Alternative:** Einsatz von ▸ KV 1.1 (Ex 2a): S arbeiten schriftlich in EA.
• S lesen sich im Anschluss die Ergebnisse in PA vor ▸ KV 1.1 (Ex 2b) (▸ Partner check).
• **Ausw.:** individuelle Überprüfung durch L (KV einsammeln) od. S tragen ihre Ergebnisse im Plenum vor.

Topic 1 Inhalt

Lernschwerpunkt: der erste Schultag • Dinge, die man in der Schule benötigt • sich positionieren zur Schuluniform
Kompetenzen: Listening Schulhofgesprächen Informationen entnehmen • Vokabeln aus dem Wortfeld *school things*
verstehen • Speaking sich über Schuluniformen äußern • Gegenstände auf einem Bild benennen • Study skills sprachliche
Regelmäßigkeiten entdecken
Redemittel: *adjectives to describe feelings/emotions* • *parts of school uniforms* • Wortfeld *school things*
Strukturen: unbestimmter Artikel *a/an*

Ex 1 Einstieg:

- (SB zu) L zeigt das vergrößerte Foto von **Ex 1** (UMA):
  L: *It's time for school. Look at the picture. What can you see?*
  S: *I can see …*
- ▶ Semantisierung des neuen Wortschatzes

Erarbeitung:

a) (SB auf / UMA), gemäß AA
  S: *This is …*

b) gemeinsames ▶ Klären der AA
- S notieren während des **1. Hörens** die Namen im Heft.
- ⊠ S schreiben Sätze vor dem **1. Hören** ab und ergänzen dann die Namen.
- **Ausw.:** S lesen Ergebnisse vor (▶ Meldekette).
- **Sich.:** ggf. **2. Hören**
- ▶ Good to know, S. 20

Ex 2 Einstieg:

- (SB auf) L zeigt auf vergrößertes Foto von **Ex 1** (UMA):
  L: *What can you say about the uniform?*
  S: *The uniform is blue and black. The uniform is nice / isn't nice …*

Erarbeitung:

- In PA, anschließend tragen S ihre Ergebnisse im Plenum vor.

- **Zusatz:**
- L plant einen ▶ Uniform day mit der Klasse.

| 1 | °Topic 1 | Topic 2 | Topic 3 | Story | °Viewing | Study skills | Unit task |

Time for school

🦻 **1** LISTENING **At school**

⊠ **a)** BEFORE YOU LISTEN **Look at the photo. Point and say the names of the students.**

> **1 a)** (The students are labelled.)

🔊 **b)** Listen to two °conversations. Write the correct name or names.
1.11

1 … are friends.
2 … is busy and tired.
3 … is +happy about the school tie.
4 … is scared of the school.
5 … like the uniform.
6 … are in the same class.

> **Good to know**
> British schools have a school uniform, often with a +blazer and a tie.

> **1 b) 1** Lily and Zane • **2** Zane • **3** Lily • **4** Noah •
> **5** Sunita and Noah • **6** Sunita and Noah (in class 7C)

💬 ⊠ **2** SPEAKING **School uniform**

> **2** Lösungsbsp. S. 287

Say your opinion of the school uniform.

> *I like / I don't like the uniform.*
> *The uniform is nice / cool / great / horrible.*
> *I like / I don't like the colour.*

▶ Workbook, p. 13

20 twenty

Topic 1 Vorbereitung

Material: Ex 1 vergrößertes Foto von Ex 1, UMA/CD, Handpuppe Scout kann immer anstelle von L im Einstieg eingesetzt werden • **Ex 2** vergrößertes Foto von Ex 1, ggf. UMA • **Ex 3** Federmäppchen mit entsprechenden Realien, UMA/CD • **Ex 4** Federmäppchen mit Realien (wie in Ex 3) • **Ex 5** UMA

Zeitbedarf: ca. 2 Std.

Minimalversion: Ex 5 auslassen

Begleitmedien: WB (S. 13–14), **INKL** (S. 20–21)

---

3 WORDS **School things**

3 a) pencil case • ruler • rubber • pencil • pen • pen • glue stick • pencil sharpener • exercise book • English book

a) Sunita's school things are on her desk. Look at the picture, listen and point.
1.12

an English book

a glue stick

an exercise book

English

a pencil

a pencil case

a pen

an apple

an orange

a rubber

a pencil sharpener

a ruler

a desk

3 b) a desk • a pencil case • an apple • a ruler • a rubber • a pencil • a pen • an orange • a glue stick • pencil sharpener • an exercise book • an English book

b) Listen to the words and repeat.
1.13

4 LOOKING AT °LANGUAGE *a/an*

4 a rubber • a glue stick • an exercise book • a pencil sharpener • an English book • a ruler
Rule: *an* vor Vokalen

Complete the °list of Sunita's things with *a* or *an*. Find the °rule.

► More practice 1, p. 42
► Language file 2, p. 183

... rubber
... glue stick
... exercise book

... pencil sharpener
... English book
... ruler

5 a desk • a blue pencil case • a pink pen • a brown pencil • a white rubber • a red pencil sharpener • a yellow glue stick • a grey exercise book • an orange / a brown ruler • a green English book • an apple • an orange

5 I can remember

Close your books.
What things from 3a) can you remember?

I can remember a pink ...

I can remember an orange ...

► Workbook, pp. 13–14

Ex 3 Einstig:
• ✉ (SB zu) ► Semantisierung:
L zeigt ein Federmäppchen mit den Realien von **Ex 3a**).
L: *Look, it's my pencil case.*
• L hält die Gegenstände hoch:
L: *What is this?*
S/L: *It's a/an …*

Erarbeitung:
a) (SB auf / UMA) **1. Hören**
• **Ausw.:** S/L zeigen beim **2. Hören** auf die korrekten Gegenstände.

b) gemäß AA (► Lautschulung)
• **Sich.:** S übertragen den neuen Lernwortschatz ins *Vocab file* (► SF 1, S. 171ff.).

Ex 4 Erarbeitung:
• (SB auf) S arbeiten schriftl.
• **Ausw.:** im Plenum mit TA:

a	an
...	...

• gemeinsame Regelfindung (s. Vorwort, S. IX) im Plenum mithilfe der Lösungen im TA
• **Sich.:** ► LF 2, S. 183
• S übertragen die Regel in den Merkteil des ► English folder.

Ex 5 Erarbeitung:
• (SB auf) L zeigt vergrößertes Bild von **Ex 3a**) (UMA):
L: *Look at the picture for one minute.* (evtl. Zeit stoppen)
• L entfernt das Bild. / S schließen SB.
• ► Partner Talk gemäß AA

• **Zusatz:** S1 beschreibt S2 den Inhalt des eigenen Federmäppchens aus dem Gedächtnis (in PA).

Topic 1 Inhalt

Lernschwerpunkt: Erarbeitung von *classroom phrases*

Kompetenzen: Reading einen Dialog lesen und mit verteilten Rollen spielen • Listening ein Gespräch hören und Informationen zuordnen • Speaking Informationen zu Schulsachen austauschen • Fragen und Antworten zum Thema *classroom English* • Writing eigene *classroom phrases* schreiben und gestalten

Redemittel: Wortfelder *school things, classroom phrases*

Strukturen: Pluralbildung (lexikalisch)

Ex 6 Einstieg:
- (SB zu) L legt Realien entspr. den Bildern von S. 21/42 auf den L-Tisch (Wortschatz von Ex 3, S. 21, reaktivieren)
L: *Look here, what can you see?* (L hält Realien hoch.)
S: *I can see a blue pen / two green books / ...*

Erarbeitung:
- (SB auf) ▶ Info-gap activity gemäß AA; *Partner A* arbeitet mit dem Bild von Ex 3a), S. 21, *Partner B* auf S. 42.
- **Ausw.:** S-Paare präsentieren ihre Ergebnisse im Plenum.
- ▶ LF 3, S. 183
- ☑ ▶ Scaffolding als TA:
In my picture (A) I can see ...,
In my picture (B) I can see ...
- ▶ Early finisher: ▶ MP 2, S. 42

Ex 7 Einstieg:
- (SB zu) L zeigt vergrößertes Foto von S. 22 (UMA):
L: *What can you see in the picture? Where are they?*
S: *I can see ... They are in the classroom.*
- ▶ Semantisierung des Lernwortschatzes im Plenum
- ▶ Vokabelarbeit, ▶ Vokabeltafel

Erarbeitung:
a) (SB auf) lesen gemäß AA (▶ Mitleseverfahren)
- **Ausw.:** S präsentieren die Lösung in der ▶ Meldekette.
- ▶ Good to know, S. 22

b) S in Kleingruppen à fünf S (▶ Gruppenbildung): S lesen den Text in verteilten Rollen (▶ Role-play).
- **Ausw.:** Freiwillige S-Gruppen spielen/tragen den Text im Plenum vor.

| **1** | **Topic 1** | Topic 2 | Topic 3 | Story | Viewing | Study skills | Unit task |

💬 👥 **6** SPEAKING **Different desks**

6 Lösung S. 287

Partner A: Look at Sunita's desk on p. 21.
Partner B: Look at Noah's desk on p. 42.
Find six different things.

a/one pencil   two pencils

In my picture I can see one brown pencil.

In my picture I can see two brown pencils.

▶ More practice 2, p. 42
▶ Language file 3, p. 183

🔲 **7** READING **Hello, class 7C!**

7 a) 1 Emma • **2** Ravi • **3** Layla • **4** Mel

🔊 1.14 **a)** Read and find the students in the picture.

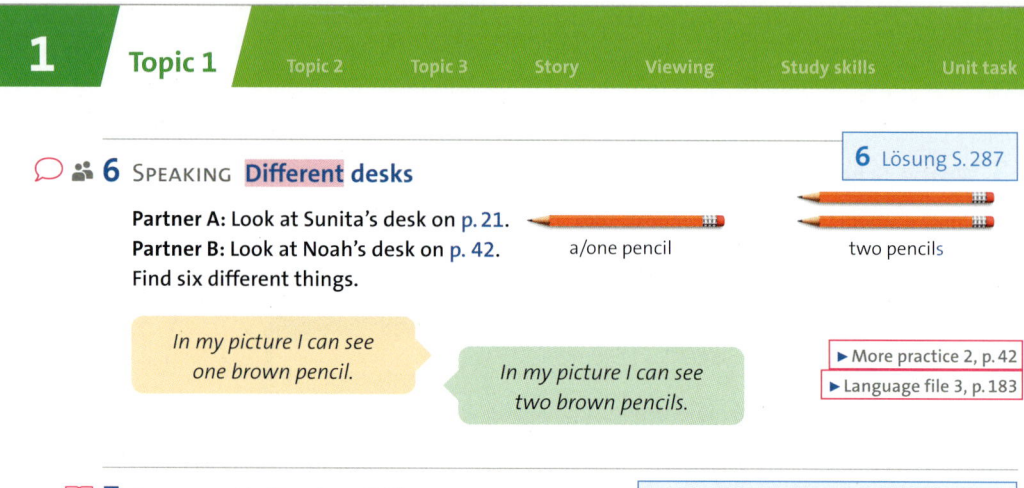

Mr Lee	Hello, class 7C! I'm Mr Lee, your class teacher and English teacher.	**Layla**	Can I go to the toilet?
		Mr Lee	Yes, you can. Now, please take your pencil case and your exercise book.
Emma	Sorry I'm late, Mr Lee.		
Mr Lee	OK, please sit down. Don't be late again.	**Mel**	Can you say that again, Mr Lee?
		Mr Lee	Yes. Please take your pencil case and your exercise book. Don't talk! Now, let's start!
Ravi	Can I open the window, please?		
Mr Lee	Yes, you can.		

💬 👥 **b)** ROLE-PLAY **Act out the conversation in a).**

Good to know

In England the first year of secondary school is year 7.

▶ More practice 3, p. 43 ▶ Challenge, p. 43

▶ Workbook, p. 14

Topic 1 Vorbereitung

Material: Ex 6 Realien wie auf den Bildern von S. 21/42, Ex 7 vergrößertes Foto von S. 22 (UMA), UMA/CD • Ex 8 UMA/CD, Ex 9 weißes Papier (Klassensatz)

Zeitbedarf: ca. 2 Std.

Minimalversion: Ex 9a) auch als HA moglich, Ex 9 auslassen

Begleitmedien: WB (S. 14, S. 15), App (Digital quiz), INKL (S. 22–23), DIFF (1.2, 1.3, 1.4)

1

🗣💬 **8** SPEAKING In class

🔊 a) Listen. Match what Noah and Sunita say.
1.15

1 What page is it?
2 I don't understand exercise 1.
3 Can you help me with question 2?
4 What's the answer to question 3?
5 Can I use your book?
6 Thanks.

a Yes, here you are.
b The answer is b.
c It's page 9.
d You're welcome.
e Let's ask Mr Lee.
f Yes, I can.

1 a) 1 c • **2** e • **3** f • **4** b • **5** a • **6** d

🔊 b) Listen to the questions in a). Say the answers.
.16

▶ Box: Voc., p. 222

👥 c) WALK AROUND Practise the questions and answers in a) with different partners.

1 b) It's page 9. • Let's ask Mr Lee. • Yes, I can. • The answer is b. • Yes, here you are. • You're welcome.

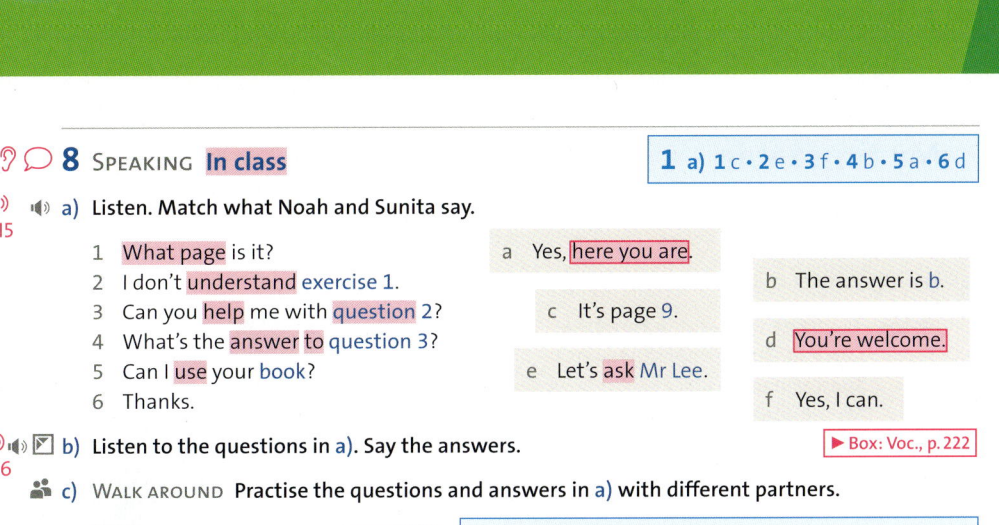

My task

✏️💬 **9** My classroom questions and answers

9 a) Lösungsbsp. S. 287

👥 a) Write new questions and answers: Change the parts in blue in 8a). Practise with your partner.

👥 b) Present your questions and answers to °another °pair.

▶ Workbook, p. 15

 Digital quiz I can understand and use classroom English. ✓

Ex 8 Einstieg:
- (SB zu) L gibt Anweisungen:
  L: *Open a window, please. Take a blue pen. Open your book. Close your book.* (S führen aus.)
  L: *Do you know more classroom phrases?*
  S geben mögliche Beispiele.
- ☒ S können als Hilfe die bekannten *phrases* von **Ex 7a)**, S. 22 und **Ex 1**, S. 17 nutzen.

Erarbeitung:

a) (SB auf) S lesen alle Fragen und Antworten still in EA und notieren die Zahlen 1–6 in ihr Heft.
- Beim **1. Hören** schreiben S den Buchstaben der passenden Antwort ins Heft.
- **Ausw.:** ▶ Meldekette

b) gemäß AA

c) Klären der AA
- L demonstriert Bsp. (s. a. ▶ Market-place activity / ▶ Milling around)
- ☒ Lernstärkere S führen die Aufgabe ohne Hilfen durch.

My task Ex 9 Einstieg:
- (SB auf)
  L: *Let's find some more classroom questions and answers.*

Erarbeitung:

a) gemäß AA
- **Ausw.:** im Plenum

- **Zusatz:** S gestalten ein Poster mit *classroom phrases*. Fragen und Antworten in Sprechblasen und Gestaltung mit Bildern od. Zeichnungen (▶ English corner).

Topic 2 Inhalt

Lernschwerpunkt: den eigenen Stundenplan auf Englisch schreiben können

Kompetenzen: Reading einen Dialog lesen und verstehen • Information zuordnen • Speaking Personen oder Gegenstände auf Bildern benennen • Listening Aussprache der Wochentage • ein Lied zu den Wochentagen anhören • Writing über Personen in der eigenen Klasse schreiben

Strukturen: Personalpronomen • Verb *to be* (Kurz- und Langformen)

Redemittel: Personen beschreiben • Hobbys • Wochentage • Wortfeld *in the classroom*

Ex 1 Einstieg:
• (SB zu) ▶ Semantisierung des Lernwortschatzes im Plenum

Erarbeitung:
a) (SB auf) **1. Lesen/Hören:** im
  ▶ Mitleseverfahren
• ☒ L u. zwei gute S lesen vor.
• **2. Lesen:** S lesen in verteilten Rollen laut vor.

b) S schreiben die vier Sätze in ihren ▶ English folder.
• Ein Bsp. wird im Plenum bearbeitet.
• **Ausw.:** S lesen Sätze und Antworten laut vor.

Ex 2 Einstieg:
• (SB zu) L zeigt die vergrößerten Bilder von b) (Tafel/UMA).
• L zeichnet eine leere Tabelle darunter (eine Spalte pro Bild).

Erarbeitung:
a) (SB auf) gemäß AA
• L ergänzt die 1. Zeile der Tabelle (TA).

b) gemäß AA
• L/S ergänzen die 2. Zeile der Tabelle (TA) mit dem Personalpronomen (▶ LF 4, S. 184).

Ex 3 Einstieg:
• (SB zu) Wdh. der Personalpronomen, z. B. mit ▶ Flashcards

Erarbeitung:
• (SB auf) S lesen den Text von Ex 1a) in verteilten Rollen, anschl. gemäß AA.
• S finden die Lösungen mithilfe des Textes von Ex 1a)
• **Sich.:** als TA im Plenum
• S übertragen die Tabelle in den Merkteil (▶ English folder).
• s. a. ▶ LF 6, S. 185, Erklärfilm (UMA/App)

My timetable

1 The English lessons

🔊 **a)** Read the conversation.
1.17

Mr Lee	7C, please look at your timetable. Can you see the English lessons? They're in room 2.
Lily	Mr Lee, look at Tim. He's asleep. I think he's tired.
Mr Lee	You're right, Lily. And Emma – she's tired too. Emma and Tim, I know you're tired, you're at a new school. We're all tired! But it's time for break soon. It's in five minutes.
Tim	I'm sorry, Mr Lee.

✏ **b)** Write the things or students.

1 They're in room 2.
2 He's asleep.
3 She's tired.   ▶ Box: Voc., p. 222
4 It's in five minutes.

> **1 b)** **1** the English lessons • **2** Tim • **3** Emma • **4** break

💬 **2 People and things in class**

a) Who or what can you see in the pictures?   *I can see …*

b) °Match the people and things to the correct words in the °box.

> **2 a)** **1** Mr Lee • **2** the timetable • **3** Sunita and Noah • **4** chairs • **5** Lily

`he • she • it • they (2 x)`

Mr Lee   Sunita and Noah   Lily

> **2 b)** **1** he • **2** it • **3** they • **4** they • **5** she

▶ More practice 4, p. 43   ▶ Language file 4, p. 184

✏ 🖥 **3 LOOKING AT LANGUAGE** *to be*

Erklär-film

Read the conversation in **1** again. °Copy and complete the °table.

> **3** Lösung S. 287

°long form	°short form	long form	short form
I am	…	we are	…
you are	…	you are	…
he is	…		
she is	…	they are	…
it is	…		

▶ Language file 6, p. 185
▶ Workbook, pp. 15–16

24   twenty-four

Topic 2 Vorbereitung

Material: Ex 1 UMA/CD • Ex 2 UMA • Ex 3 vorbereitete Flashcards (Personalpronomen), UMA/App (Erklärfim) • Ex 5 Handpuppe Scout, ▶ KV Extra: Bus stop • Ex 6 Handpuppe Scout, UMA/CD
Zeitbedarf: ca. 2 Std.
Minimalversion: Ex 4b) als HA vorbereiten lassen, Ex 6b), c) bei Zeitmangel auslassen
Begleitmedien: WB (S. 15–16), App (Erklärfilm), INKL (S. 24–25)

4 Varndean students and teachers

a) Write the correct name(s) or word.

> Emma and Tim • Lily • Mr Lee • Sunita and Noah • break • Zane

1 "I'm an English teacher."
2 He's a good swimmer.
3 "We're tired."
4 It's after lessons 1 and 2.
5 She's in a parkour class.
6 They're a girl and a boy in 7C.

> **4 a) 1** Mr Lee • **2** Zane • **3** Emma and Tim • **4** break • **5** Lily • **6** Sunita and Noah

Zane   Noah   Sunita

b) Say sentences about people in your class. The class °guesses the person.   ▶ More help, p. 44

He's ...   She's ...   They're ...

> **4 b)** individuelle Lösungen

5 Messages   ▶ Parallel exercise, p. 44

Complete the messages from Noah and his mum. Use short forms.

Noah

Hi, Mum! I like the classroom. (1) ... big.
I like Mr Lee, my teacher, too. (2) ... cool.
And I like my new friends. (3) ... nice. ☺ ✓

👍 Great! (4) ... lucky, Noah! Varndean School
is big, but (5) ... a good school. Sorry, (6) ...
busy now. *See you!* ☺ ✓

> **5 1** It's • **2** He's • **3** They're • **4** You're • **5** it's • **6** I'm

▶ More practice 5, p. 44
▶ More practice 6, p. 45

6 Song Days of the week

a) Words Look at the days. Listen to the song and put them in the correct °order.

> Thursday   Tuesday   Sunday   Friday
> Monday   Wednesday   Saturday

1 Monday   2 ...

> **6 a) 1** Monday • **2** Tuesday • **3** Wednesday • **4** Thursday • **5** Friday • **6** Saturday • **7** Sunday

▶ Box: Voc., p. 223

b) Now sing the song.

c) Complete the sentence: *My favourite day of the week is ...*

▶ Workbook, p. 16

Ex 4 Erarbeitung:
a) (SB auf) schrift. gemäß AA

b) gemäß AA
• L gibt Bsp.: *He's in a football team. / She is from ...*
• S notieren eigene Sätze.
• 🖪 ▶ More help, S. 44 bietet ▶ Scaffolding.
• **Ausw.:** ▶ Meldekette

Ex 5 Einstieg:
• (SB zu) L/Scout: *Noah is new at school. Is he happy?*
• L holt Stimmungsbild ein (▶ Thumbs up).

Erarbeitung:
• (SB auf) gemäß AA (s. a. S. 44)
• 🖪 ▶ Parallel ex, S. 44 auf leichterem Niveau
• L kann S individuell zuweisen.
• **Ausw.:** ▶ Partner check bzw. am ▶ Bus stop (Einsatz ▶ KV Extra)

Ex 6 Einstieg:
• (SB zu) ▶ Semantisierung des Lernwortschatzes, z. B.:
Scout: *What day is today?*
S: *Today is ...*
Scout: *What are the days of the week?*
S: *Monday ...,*

Erarbeitung:
a) gemäß AA
• **Sich.:** S schreiben die Wochen-tage als TA.

b) gemäß AA
• 🖪 UMA/TA mit den Wochen-tagen als Hilfe (s. **Ex 6a)**)

c) gemäß AA
• **Ausw.** ▶ Meldekette:
L: *What is your favourite day, Scout?*
Scout: *My favourite day is ....*
(Scout fragt S1, S2 etc.)

Topic 2 **Inhalt**

Lernschwerpunkt: Unterrichtsfächer kennenlernen und Stundenpläne lesen und erstellen
Kompetenzen: Listening Unterrichtsfächer verstehen und zuordnen • einen Dialog verstehen und Aussagen ergänzen •
ein Lied hören • Speaking sagen, welche Unterrichtsfächer man mag oder nicht mag (mit Begründung für Lernstärkere) •
Writing den eigenen Stundenplan schreiben
Redemittel: Wortfelder *school subjects*, *days of the week*

Ex 7 Erarbeitung:

a) (SB auf) L zeigt den vergrößerten Stundenplan von S. 26 (Tafel/UMA).
• gemeinsame ▶ Semantisierung gemäß AA
• **Sich.:** TA der *subjects* und dt. Entsprechungen (▶ Vokabeltafel)
• gemeinsame ▶ Lautschulung, ▶ Vokabelarbeit

b) In EA notieren S die Nrn. und ergänzen das *subject*.
• **1. Hören**, dann ▶ Partner check
• **Ausw.:** ▶ Meldekette:
  S1: *Number 1 is ...*
  S2: *Number 2 is ... etc.*

Ex 8 Einstieg:

• (SB zu) L verweist auf den Stundenplan im Raum oder HA-Heft:
  L: *Look at your timetable. What are your lessons today?*
  (S antworten in ▶ Meldekette):
  S1: *Lesson 1 is ....*
  S2: *Lesson 2 is ...*
  L: *Let's find out about Lily's timetable on Fridays.*

Erarbeitung:

• (SB auf) gemäß AA, schriftl. in EA
• **Ausw.:** L schreibt *lessons 1–6* untereinander an die Tafel:
  L: *What's lesson 1?*
• S schreiben die Lösung an.
• ▶ Early finisher: Schnellere S können ▶ MP 7, S. 45 direkt im Anschluss an **Ex 8** bearbeiten.
• **Zusatz:** ▶ Info-gap activity zum Üben der *subjects*:
• Einsatz von ▶ KV 1.2 A + B: je ein Stundenplan pro S
• gemeinsames ▶ Klären der AA
• **Ausw.:** im Plenum (TA)

---

1 | Topic 1 | **Topic 2** | Topic 3 | Story | Viewing | Study skills | Unit task

---

🎧 ☑ **7** WORDS **School subjects**

📖 **a)** Look at the timetable for 7C. Which words can you understand?
(German and other languages can help you.)

Lesson	Monday	Tuesday	Wednesday	Thursday	Friday
°registration and assembly					
1	English	art	French	computing	🔵
2	English	maths	French	computing	🔵
break					
3	history	English	science	geography	🔵
4	geography[1]	music	science	history	🔵
lunch					
5	maths	science	design and technology[2]	PE	🔵
6	maths	science	computing	PE	🔵

🔊 1.19 🔊 **b)** Match the pictures to the subjects in the timetable. Then listen and check.

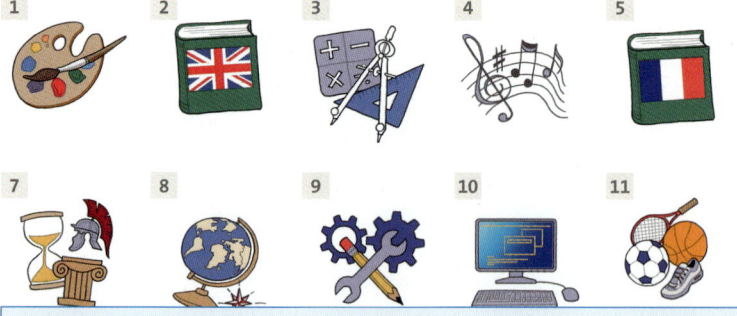

> **7 b) 1** art • **2** English • **3** maths • **4** music • **5** French • **6** science • **7** history • **8** geography •
> **9** design and technology • **10** computing • **11** PE

🎧 🔊 **8** LISTENING **7C's timetable**

🔊 1.20 Listen to Lily and Zane. Complete 7C's timetable for Friday in your exercise book.

Lesson 1: ...   *Lesson 2: ...*   *...*   ▶ More practice 7, p. 45

> **8** Lesson 1: music • Lesson 2: maths • Lesson 3: English •
> Lesson 4: French • Lesson 5: art • Lesson 6: design and technology

▶ Workbook, p. 17

26 twenty-six   **1** [dʒiˈɒgrəfi]   **2** [tekˈnɒlədʒi]

Topic 2 **Vorbereitung**

Material: Ex 7 vergrößerter Stundenplan von S. 26 (UMA), UMA/CD • Ex 8 UMA/CD, Stundenplan der Klasse, ▶ KV 1.2 A + B: My timetable (1/2 KV pro S) • Ex 9 vergrößerte Bilder von Ex 7b), UMA/CD, geeignete Aufnahmegeräte • Ex 10 Handpuppe Scout, akustisches Signal (z. B. Gong) • Ex 11 vorbereiteter englischer Stundenplan der Klasse mit Lücken (als TA), weißes Papier (A4, Klassensatz)

Zeitbedarf: ca. 3 Std.

Minimalversion: Ex 8 oder Ex 9a) auslassen, Ex 11 als HA möglich

Begleitmedien: WB (S. 17–18), App (Digital help, Digital quiz), INKL (S. 26–27), DIFF (1.5)

1

9 SONG **The timetable song**

a) Listen. Stand up when you °hear a school subject.

1.22

b) Listen again. Write the correct subject (a–f) for 1–6.

> **9 b) 1** history • **2** geography • **3** biology • **4** French • **5** PE • **6** maths

On Monday morning I have (1) ...
The next lesson is (2) ...
After lunch we have (3) ...
And then °at three, go home to play.

On Tuesdays I °study (4) ... at ten.
After break (5) ... with Mr Wren[1].
°Finally it's time for (6) ... and then
We do it all again another day.

a biology
b French
c geography
d history
e maths
f PE

Scout

---

10 SPEAKING **Favourite subjects**

> **10 a)** Lösungsbsp. S. 287

a) SPEED DATING **Make two °lines.** Talk about your favourite subjects to your partner. Say three sentences.

Say why:
... because it's cool / hard / ...
... because I like / I don't like ...

I like ... *My favourite subject is ...* *I don't like ...*

b) One line: Move to the next partner.

My task

11 **My timetable**

Write your timetable in English for an English friend. Put your timetable in your DOSSIER.

Write about your timetable:

English is on ... and on ...
German lessons are in lesson ... on ... and in ... on ...

> **11** individuelle Lösungen

▶ Wordbank 5, p. 197
▶ Digital help
▶ Workbook, pp. 17–18

Digital quiz • I can **write my timetable in English.** ✓ 1 [ren]

Ex 9 **Einstieg:**
• (SB zu) Als Wdh. zeigt L die vergrößerten Bilder von Ex 7b), S. 26 (UMA):
L: *What subject is it?*
S: *It's ...*

Erarbeitung:
a) (SB zu) **1. Hören** gemäß AA
b) (SB auf) **2. Hören** gemäß AA
• **Zusatz:** Lied gemeinsam an den eigenen Stundenplan anpassen und ggf. aufnehmen.

Ex 10 **Erarbeitung:**
a) (SB auf) Vorbereitung aufs ▶ Speed dating gemäß AA
• Satzanfänge als TA, L führt mit S Bsp. vor.
• Lernstärkere S begründen ihre Aussagen (▶ Scaffolding).
b) gemäß AA
• **Ausw.:** L/Scout fragt freiwillige S:
L: *What about you?*

My task Ex 11 **Einstieg:**
• (SB zu) engl. Stundenplan der Klasse mit Lücken als TA
L: *Look, I have a problem with our timetable. Can you help me?*
S: *Lesson 1 on Monday is ...*

Erarbeitung:
• (SB auf) gemäß AA, S schreiben und gestalten ihren Stundenplan auf Englisch (A4-Blatt)
• gemäß AA
• **Ausw.:** ▶ Gallery walk oder Präsentation, z. B. in der ▶ English corner
• **Sich.:** Ablage im ▶ Dossier

Topic 3 Inhalt

Lernschwerpunkt: Vorstellung von Schulräumen • einen Brief über die Schule lesen und schreiben
Kompetenzen: Reading ein Gespräch zwischen Zane, Lily, Sunita und Noah über das Schulgebäude lesen und die Schul-
räume erkennen • Listening/Speaking Aussprache von Wörtern (*places at school*) üben • Writing einen Brief über die
eigene Schule schreiben
Strukturen: Verb *to be* (Verneinung)
Redemittel: Wortfeld *places at school* • Adjektive

Ex 1 Einstieg:
- (SB zu) L zeigt die vergrößerten
  Bilder von S. 28 (UMA/Tafel).
  L: *What places can you see in
  the pictures? Guess the names.*
  S: *I can see the …*
  (L notiert die Vorschläge, TA)

Erarbeitung:
a) (SB auf) gemeinsames Klären
  der AA
- S lesen/hören mit (▶ Mitleseverfahren) und notieren die
  korrekten Wörter im Heft.
- **Ausw.:** ▶ Partner check, dann
  im Plenum: Korrigieren des
  TA, s. **Einstieg.**

b) gemäß AA, S sprechen im
  Chor nach (▶ Lautschulung),
  ▶ Vokabelarbeit
- S lesen den Text in verteilten
  Rollen.

Ex 2 Erarbeitung:
- (SB auf) gemeinsames Klären
  der AA
- Lösung der Sätze 1 und 2 im
  Plenum (TA)
- S notieren die übrigen Sätze
  mit richtiger Verbform in ihr
  Heft.
- **Ausw.:** ▶ Five-minute teacher

| **1** | Topic 1 | Topic 2 | **Topic 3** | Story | Viewing | Study skills | Unit task |

It's a big school!

1 WORDS **Places at school**

a) Look at the pictures. Read the conversation and complete the rooms with *a, e, i, o, u*.
1.23

the c■rr■d■r `corridor`   the c■nt■■n `canteen`   the c■mp■t■r r■■m   `computer room`

the sp■rts h■ll `sports hall`

the ■rt r■■m `art room`

Zane	Hi, Lily! I'm not alone in 7B. Our friends are in my class.
Lily	Hi, Zane. That's great! This is Sunita and Noah from 7C.
Sunita	Nice to meet you, Zane.
Noah	I'm hungry. My sandwich isn't in my bag. Where's the canteen?
Sunita	I don't know. Let's look in this corridor … No, this room isn't the canteen, it's the art room.
Zane	This is the computer room. And the toilets are here.
Lily	Look at this map! We're in building 1. The canteen and the sports hall aren't in this building. They're in building 2. It's a big school!
Noah	Yes, and we aren't near the canteen. I'm really hungry.
Lily	Oh, Noah isn't happy!
Sunita	You're lucky, Noah, I'm not hungry. Maybe I have two sandwiches. You can have one.
Noah	You aren't hungry, Sunita … I'm always hungry! Thanks!
Sunita	You're welcome.

b) Listen and repeat the places.   ▶ More practice 8, p. 45
1.24

2 What's right?

2 **1** I'm not • **2** I'm • **3** is • **4** isn't • **5** are • **6** We aren't • **7** You're • **8** You aren't

Choose the correct words.

1 Zane: I'm / I'm not alone in 7B.
2 Noah: I'm / I'm not hungry.
3 The computer room is / isn't in building 1.
4 The canteen is / isn't in building 1.
5 The students are / aren't in building 1.
6 Noah: We're / We aren't near the canteen.
7 Sunita: You're / You aren't lucky, Noah.
8 Noah: You're / You aren't hungry, Sunita.

▶ Workbook, p. 18

28 twenty-eight

Material: Ex 1 UMA/CD • Ex 3 UMA/CD, UMA/App (Erklärfilm) • Ex 5 Brief im Umschlag, UMA
Zeitbedarf: ca. 2 Std.
Minimalversion: Ex 4 bei sicherem Umgang mit den Kurzformen auslassen, Ex 5b) als HA vorbereiten lassen
Begleitmedien: WB (S. 18–19), App (Erklärfilm, Digital help, Digital quiz), INKL (S. 28–29), DIFF (1.6)

1

3 LOOKING AT LANGUAGE **to be (negative)**

Erklär-film

Look at exercises **1** and **2** on **p. 28**. Copy and complete the table.

I'm *not*	we …
you …	you *aren't*
he … she *isn't* it …	they …

Your sandwich isn't in your bag. It's in here.

▶ Language file 7, p. 185

3 Lösung S. 288

---

4 **The new school**

Choose the correct picture (a or b) for the sentence.

1 The school isn't small.　　2 We aren't scared!　　3 The teacher is nice.

4 The food isn't bad.　　5 I'm happy at my school.　　6 My new school is cool!

▶ More practice 9, p. 46

4 1 a • 2 a • 3 b • 4 a • 5 b • 6 a

My task

5 **My school**

a) Read what Lily writes to her °grandparents about her school. What two things are wrong?

b) Write about your school. Write two wrong things.

c) Read your text to your partner. Your partner must say the wrong things.

The school isn't …, it's …

> Hi, Grandma and ⁺Grandpa!
> The name of my school is Varndean School.
> It's an old school and it's very big.
> I'm in class 7B. My class teacher is Mr Lee.
> My favourite place at school is the art room.
> My favourite day is Monday because lesson 1
> is music and lesson 5 is art. My school is great.
> See you
> Lily

▶ Digital help 　▶ Wordbank 6, p. 198

5 a) **1** Lily is in class 7C, not 7B. **2** Monday: lesson 1 is English and lesson 5 is maths.

▶ Workbook, p. 19

Digital quiz 　I can °describe my school. ✓

Ex 3 Einstieg:
• (SB auf), L zeigt Ex 3 (UMA).
• L leitet die Lösungsfindung an: L: *Let's find the forms in exercise 1 and 2.*

Erarbeitung:
• gemeinsam im Plenum
• S nennen Formen von *to be*, L ergänzt die Übersicht (TA).
• **Sich.:** S schreiben den TA in ihren Merkteil ab (▶ English folder).
• ▶ LF 7, S. 185 gemeinsam lesen u. Erklärfilm (UMA/App) anschauen.

Ex 4 Einstieg:
• (SB zu) vorab ▶ Semantisierung von *food, bad* (Satz 4)

Erarbeitung:
• (SB auf) gemäß AA
• mündliche oder schriftliche Bearbeitung durch S
• **Ausw.:** ▶ Five-minute teacher

My task Ex 5 Einstieg:
• (SB zu) L hält einen Brief in der Hand: *Look, here is a letter from Lily. It's for her grandparents. Let's read it.*

Erarbeitung
a) (SB auf) gemeinsames Klären der AA
• stilles Lesen gemäß AA
• **Ausw.:** im Plenum

b) Klären der AA im Plenum
• S arbeiten schriftl. mit ▶ Wordbank 6, S. 198 als Hilfe.
• Lilys Brief (Ex 5) dient als Wortgerüst (TA/UMA).

c) gemäß AA, ▶ Partner talk
• **Ausw.:** Einzelne S lesen ihre Briefe in der Klasse vor.

Story   Inhalt

Lernschwerpunkt: eine Bildgeschichte über einen Mobbing-Fall und solidarisches Verhalten verstehen
Kompetenzen: Speaking einen guten Freund beschreiben • Reading eine (bildgestützte) Geschichte lesen, dazu Fragen beantworten und Aussagen korrigieren
Redemittel: Adjektive zum Wortfeld *describe a friend*

Ex 1 Einstieg:
- (SB zu) ▶ Five-finger-brain-storming:
 L: *What can you say about your friend? Find a word for each finger.*
 S: *nice, cool, great, careful, sporty, ...*

Erarbeitung:
- (SB auf) gemäß AA
- ▶ Semantisierung; ▶ Vokabel-arbeit
- S schreiben Sätze auf.
- **Ausw.:** Satzanfänge als TA, L fordert S1 auf, ein Wort zu ergänzen, dann S2 etc. (▶ Meldekette)

Ex 2 Einstieg:
- (SB auf) L zeigt die Bilder der Story (UMA):
 L: *Look at the pictures. Who and what can you see?*
 S: *I can see ...*
- **Alternative:** L zeigt die Bilder von S. 30–31 einzeln als Präsentation (UMA).
 L: *What can you see in this picture?*
- S beschreiben Personen und Orte einzeln für jedes Bild.

Erarbeitung:
- gemeinsames Lesen der Fragen im Plenum
- S stellen Vermutungen an, z. B. mithilfe der Bilder.
- L/S notieren sie (TA).
- **1. Lesen/Hören** im ▶ Mitlese-verfahren
- ▶ Semantisierung des Lern-wortschatzes; ▶ Vokabelarbeit
- **Ausw.:** gemeinsames Über-prüfen des Globalverstehens durch Beantwortung der Fragen (z. B. ▶ Meldekette)

30

| **1** | Topic 1 | Topic 2 | Topic 3 | **⁺Story** | Viewing | Study skills | Unit task |

After school

💬 **1** BEFORE YOU READ **A good friend**

Describe a good friend.

A good friend is ...   A good friend isn't ...

> **1** A good friend is *brave • friendly • helpful • kind • nice.* A good friend isn't *horrible • mean.*

> brave • friendly • helpful • horrible • kind • mean • nice

📖 ▶ **2** READING **Characters in the story**

> **2 1** Zane • **2** Kyle, Jade / those bullies • **3** Noah • **4** the seagulls • **5** Lily • **6** Buddy / Noah's dog

Read the story. Answer the questions about the people in the story.

1 Who is busy?
2 Who is mean?
3 Who is sad?

4 Who is helpful?
5 Who is scared, then brave?
6 Who is friendly?

Zane   Lily   Sunita

Kyle, Jade
Noah

🔊 1.25

Lily	Hey, Zane! Are you free after school today? It's a nice day – let's go to the beach!
Zane	Sorry, I'm busy! It's time for ⁺band now and I'm the ⁺star! Bye!
Lily	Zane is always busy.
Sunita	He's so cool!

Kyle[1]	Move! You're too slow!
Jade[2]	He's so weird.
Noah	I'm not weird!
Lily	Who are they?
Sunita	They aren't from Varndean. They're bullies.

Lily   Sunita

Noah
Scout

Lily	That's Noah from our class. He's in trouble! Those bullies are really mean.
Sunita	Can we help him?
Lily	I don't know. I'm scared of them!

Noah	Hi, seagull. Those bullies aren't kind, but you're nice. You understand me. I'm sad. Some people are mean to me because they think I'm different. But I'm clever.

1 [kaɪl]   2 [dʒeɪd]

Story Vorbereitung

Material: Ex 2 UMA/CD
Zeitbedarf: ca. 1–2 Std.
Begleitmedien: INKL (S. 30–31)

1

🔊 1.26

Lily Oh no! Noah is so nice, but he's alone. We aren't good friends ...
Sunita Let's help him!

Jade Look! The weird boy is still here!
Kyle You're in trouble now ...
Sunita No! He's our friend. Go away!
Lily We aren't scared of you!

Here are my friends!

Noah That's my friend, the seagull! And her friends too – they're very helpful!
Kyle °Ugh! Let's go!
Jade Those seagulls are horrible!

Noah Thanks. You're good friends. And you're brave.
Lily You're welcome!
Sunita That seagull is very clever! You're good with animals, Noah.

Noah Hi, Dad. These are my friends Lily and Sunita.
Dad Hello! Nice to meet you. This is Noah's dog Buddy. He's very friendly.
Lily He's cool! ▶ Box: Voc., p. 226

📖 3 READING What's wrong?

✏️ Write the correct sentences. ▶ Parallel exercise, p. 46

1 Zane is free after school.
2 Kyle and Jade are nice to Noah.
3 Sunita and Lily aren't scared of the bullies at first.
4 Lily and Sunita aren't Noah's friends.
5 The seagulls are nice to Kyle and Jade.
6 Noah's dog is mean.

3 Lösung S. 288

thirty-one **31**

Ex 3 Erarbeitung:
- (SB auf) L klärt AA im Plenum
- 🖼 ▶ Parallel ex, S. 46: Lernschwächere S erhalten mehr Hilfen.
  L: *Read the senctences.*
- S lesen die Sätze laut vor.
  L: *What's wrong with sentence number 1? Can you tell me?*
  S: *Yes, I can. Zane isn't free after school.*
- L schreibt den ersten Satz als Beispiel an die Tafel.
- S bearbeiten die Aufgabe (Sätze 2–6) schriftlich.
- **Ausw.:** ▶ Five-minute teacher
- ▶ Early finisher: Schnelle S bilden entsprechend weitere „falsche" Sätze.
- **Ausw.:** gemeinsames Lösen im Plenum

Story Inhalt | Vorbereitung

Lernschwerpunkt: eine Geschichte nachspielen
Kompetenzen: Speaking eine Geschichte in verteilten Rollen aufführen • Personen beschreiben • Writing über den besten Freund schreiben
Redemittel: Adjektive • Wortfeld *my friend*

Material: Ex 4 vorbereitete Rollenkarten • Ex 5 vorbereitete Wortkarten (z. B. ▶ KV 1.3: Swap cards) • Ex 6 persönliches Foto von L, weiße Blätter (A4, Klassensatz)
Zeitbedarf: ca. 2 Std.
Minimalversion: Ex 6 kann als HA erteilt werden
Begleitmedien: WB (S. 20), App (Digital quiz), INKL (S. 32), DIFF (1.7)

Ex 4 Erarbeitung:
a) (SB auf) L verteilt vorbereitete Rollenkarten (s. a. ▶ Gruppen-bildung).
• S ziehen je eine Rolle.
• Die Sechsergruppen lesen/proben gemeinsam.

b) S spielen die Geschichte nach (▶ Scenic play), ggf. nutzen sie Schulhof, Aula o. Ä.
• **Ausw.:** Gruppen spielen vor der Klasse (▶ Feedback).

Ex 5 Einstieg:
• (SB zu) Wdh. der *adjectives* (s. Reservoir) mithilfe von ▶ Swap cards (z. B. ▶ KV 1.3) L: *Let's talk about the people in the story. Who are they?* (S/L notiert die sechs Namen (TA).)

Erarbeitung:
• (SB auf) freiwilliges S-Paar liest Bsp. aus dem SB vor, weitere Bearbeitung in PA.
• ⊠ gemäß AA
• **Ausw.:** S präsentieren ihre Meinungen im Plenum.

Ex 6 Einstieg:
• (SB zu) L zeigt ein persönliches Foto: *Look, here is a picture of my best friend.*
• L beschreibt die fiktive Person und nutzt dabei Noahs Text als ▶ Scaffolding.

Erarbeitung
a) (SB auf) S liest Beispiel vor.
• ▶ S nutzen Noahs Text als ▶ Scaffolding.
• S schreiben ihre Texte auf ein weißes Blatt und gestalten es.

b) gemäß AA
• **Ausw.:** ▶ Gallery walk für a) und b)

---

1 | Topic 1 | Topic 2 | Topic 3 | **Story** | Viewing | Study skills | Unit task

👥 **4** SHOWTIME **Action!**

💬 a) Make groups of six students:
Noah, Lily, Sunita, Kyle, Jade and Zane/Scout.
Read the scenes.

📖 b) Act out the °scenes for the class or another group.
Use actions and °feelings.

Scout

💬👥 **5** SPEAKING **What's your opinion?**

5 individuelle Lösungen

Talk about the people in the story: *I like … because …*

> *I like Noah because he's nice and clever and he's good with animals. What about you?*

brave • cool • clever • friendly • a good friend • good with people / animals • happy • helpful • kind • nice

⊠ Say more: *I don't like … because …*

> *I like Noah too. But I don't like Jade because she isn't kind to Noah.*

✏ **6** LIFE SKILLS **Your best friend**

a) Write about your best friend. Look at Noah's description.

Noah

Buddy

> *My best friend is my dog Buddy. He's clever and friendly. He's very helpful when I'm sad.*

⊠ b) Write more:

6 individuelle Lösungen

He/She's my best friend because …
He/She isn't …

▶ Workbook, p. 20

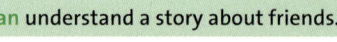 Digital quiz   **I can understand a story about friends.** ✓

32 thirty-two

Viewing Inhalt | Vorbereitung

Lernschwerpunkt: kleine Filmszenen über lustige Mutproben verstehen

Kompetenzen: Reading Bildunterschriften richtig zuordnen •
Viewing Filmszenen verstehen • Speaking die eigene
Meinung äußern

Redemittel: Adjektive zur Beschreibung von Personen und
Tätigkeiten

Material: Ex 1 Realien: z. B. lustige Krawatte • Ex 2 UMA/
DVD

Zeitbedarf: ca. 1 Std.

Begleitmedien: INKL (S. 33)

| Topic 1 | Topic 2 | Topic 3 | Story | **Viewing** | Study skills | Unit task | 1 |

The Brighton dares[1]: At school

📖 1 The two dares

BEFORE YOU WATCH **Daisy and Emir[1] do funny[2] dares.**
Match the dares to the pictures.

a   Wear a funny school tie.
b   Wear a beard[3].
c   Don't wear shoes.
d   Speak backwards[4].
e   Walk backwards.
f   Write words backwards.

> **1** a 2 • b 4 • c 5 • d 3 • e 6 • f 1

ruoy erad.
old years eleven am I

💻 2 VIEWING At school

> **2 a)** Daisy's dare for Emir: *Wear a beard.* • Emir's dare for
> Daisy: *Speak backwards and walk backwards.*

a) **Watch the video from 00:00 to 02:17. Write the correct dares from 1.**

Daisy's dare for Emir: ...   Emir's dare for Daisy: ... and ...

b) **Watch all the video. Choose the correct answer.**

1   Mr Campbell[2], the teacher, has a brown / black beard.
2   Mrs Collins has Emily's school bag / pencil case.
3   Emir / Mr Campbell looks for Emily.
4   Emily is in Room 12 / the school garden.
5   Mr Campbell is OK with / isn't happy about Emir's beard.
6   Mrs Collins really can't see well / can see fine.

> **Good to know**
>
> Dares are often funny.
> You do dares because other
> people ask you.
> Dares can show you are
> clever or brave.

> **2 b)** Lösung S. 288

c) **Compare your answers with a partner. Then watch the video again and check.**

✏️💬 3 My opinion

> **3** Lösungsbsp. S. 288

Copy and complete the sentences for you. Then tell a partner.

I think …
1   the beard dare is …
2   the backwards dare is …
3   Mr Campbell is …
4   Mrs Collins is …

> bad • clever • cool • friendly •
> funny • good • great •
> horrible • kind • mean • nice •
> OK • weird

¹ **dare** *Mutprobe*   ² **funny** *witzig*   ³ **beard** *Bart*   ⁴ **backwards** *rückwärts*

1 [eˈmɪə]   2 [ˈkæmbəl]

thirty-three   **33**

Ex 1 Einstieg:
• (SB zu) L trägt lustige Krawat-
  te, Hut o. Ä.
  L: *There is a school dare today.
  Look at me. What can you see?*
  S: *You have a funny tie/hat/ …*
• Begriffsklärung im Plenum

Erarbeitung:
• (SB auf) L stimmt die S ein:
  L: *Let's find out more about
  funny dares.*
• S arbeiten in EA od. PA und
  notieren die Lösungen.
• **Ausw.:** ▶ Meldekette

Ex 2 Einstieg:
• (SB auf)
  L: *Let's watch a video.*

Erarbeitung:
a) Klären der AA im Plenum
• **1. Sehen** (Teil 1), schriftl. in EA
• **Ausw.:** im Plenum

b) Klären der AA
• **2. Sehen** (ganzer Film),
  schriftl. in EA

c) ▶ Partner check gemäß AA
• **Ausw.:** ▶ Meldekette
• ▶ Good to know, S. 33

Ex 3 Einstieg:
• (SB zu) spontanes Feedback
  im Plenum (▶ Thumbs up):
  L: *What do you think about
  the beard dare / the backwards dare?*

Erarbeitung:
• (SB auf) S notieren Sätze in EA
• ▶ Partner talk gemäß AA
• **Ausw.:** im Plenum

• **Zusatz:** S bereiten eigene
  dares für die nächste Stunde
  vor.

Study skills Inhalt | Vorbereitung

Lernschwerpunkt: Techniken, um Wortschatz zu lernen
Kompetenzen: Reading Informationen zum Wörterlernen •
Speaking Fragen und Antworten in einem Spiel • Writing
eine Mindmap ergänzen • eine alphabetische Wortliste
erstellen • Study skills Vokabellerntechniken ausprobieren
Redemittel: Redewendungen für ein Spiel • Wortschatz der
Unit 1

Material: Ex 2 ggf. Poster (A3/A4, Klassensatz) •
Ex 3 UMA/App (Erklärfilm) • Ex 4 ▶ KV 1.4: GAME New words
(pro Gruppe eine Kopie)
Zeitbedarf: ca. 1 Std.
Minimalversion: Ex 3 auslassen, Ex 4a) als HA vorbereiten
lassen
Begleitmedien: App (Digital quiz, Erklärfilm), INKL (S. 34)

Ex 1 Erarbeitung:
- (SB zu) ▶ Brainstorming:
  L: *Can you tell me more words
  about school?* (*school* als TA)
- L erstellt die ▶ Mindmap aus
  dem SB als TA und ergänzt sie
  mit den Wörtern der S.
- (SB auf) S übertragen die
  fertige Mindmap ins Heft od.
  Vocab file (▶ Vokabelarbeit) und
  ergänzen ggf. eigene Wörter.
- **Ausw.:** L prüft die Ergebnisse
  z. B. durch Einsammeln.
- ▶ SF2, S. 174 lesen u. besprechen.

Ex 2 Einstieg:
- (SB auf)
  L: *Let's look at some more
  ways to learn words.*

Erarbeitung:
  a) + b) gemäß AA
- **Sich.:** S erstellen ein gemeinsames *A to Z* (TA bzw. als
  Poster in der ▶ English corner).

Ex 3
Erarbeitung:
- gemäß AA in PA
- **Ausw.:** L sammelt spontanes
  ▶ Feedback zum Test ein.
- ▶ SF1, S. 171 lesen und im
  Plenum besprechen: welche
  anderen Lernmöglichkeiten
  gibt es? (▶ Vokabelarbeit)
- Erklärfilm (UMA/App)

Ex 4 Erarbeitung:
a) (SB auf) gemeinsames Klären
  der AA
- S wählen passende *phrases/
  activities* u. gestalten die Spielkarten mithilfe von ▶ KV 1.4.

b) + c) gemäß AA (s. a. S. 47)

Erklär-
film

Learning vocabulary

1 Mind maps

Copy and complete the mind map about school.

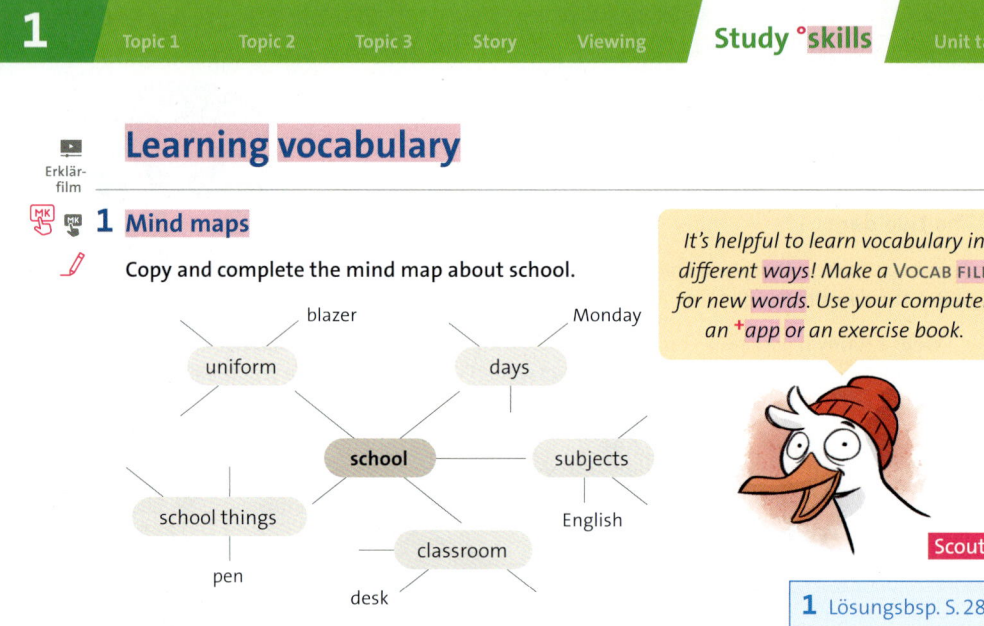

> It's helpful to learn vocabulary in
> different ways! Make a VOCAB FILE
> for new words. Use your computer,
> an ⁺app or an exercise book.

Scout

1 Lösungsbsp. S. 288

2 A to Z

a) Make an *A to Z* with school words.

b) °Show your partner. Which words are the same?
   Which are different?

A – art
B – book
C – canteen

2 a) Lösungsbsp. S. 288

3 ⁺Test your ⁺partner

Look at the Vocabulary on pages 223–224 for one minute. Put your °fingers over some
of the English words. Now your partner must say the correct English words.

4 GAME New words

a) Choose words and °phrases from your VOCAB FILE.
   Then work in a group and make °cards.

b) Play your game with your group. Use your cards
   and the board game on p. 47.

c) Swap cards with another group. Play the game again
   with their cards.

Draw a blazer.
Act out 'PE'.
What's your
favourite
subject?

▶ Skills file 1, p. 171
▶ Skills file 2, p. 174

Digital quiz 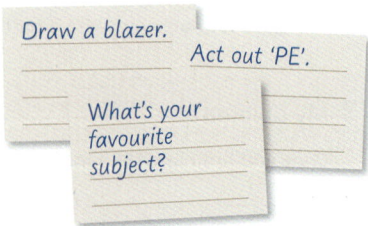 I can **learn vocabulary in different ways.**

Unit task · Inhalt | Vorbereitung

Lernschwerpunkt: ein Poster über die eigene Schule gestalten

Kompetenzen: Speaking ein Feedback geben • Study skills Vokabeln zu Wortfeldern sammeln • Media skills Fotos machen, ein Poster erstellen

Redemittel: Wortfelder *subjects, classes, places at school*

Material: evtl. Kameras, Papier für Poster (mögl. A3, pro Gruppe), UMA

Zeitbedarf: ca. 2 Std.

Begleitmedien: App (Digital help, Digital quiz), INKL (S. 35)

| Topic 1 | Topic 2 | Topic 3 | Story | Viewing | Study skills | **Unit task** | **1** |

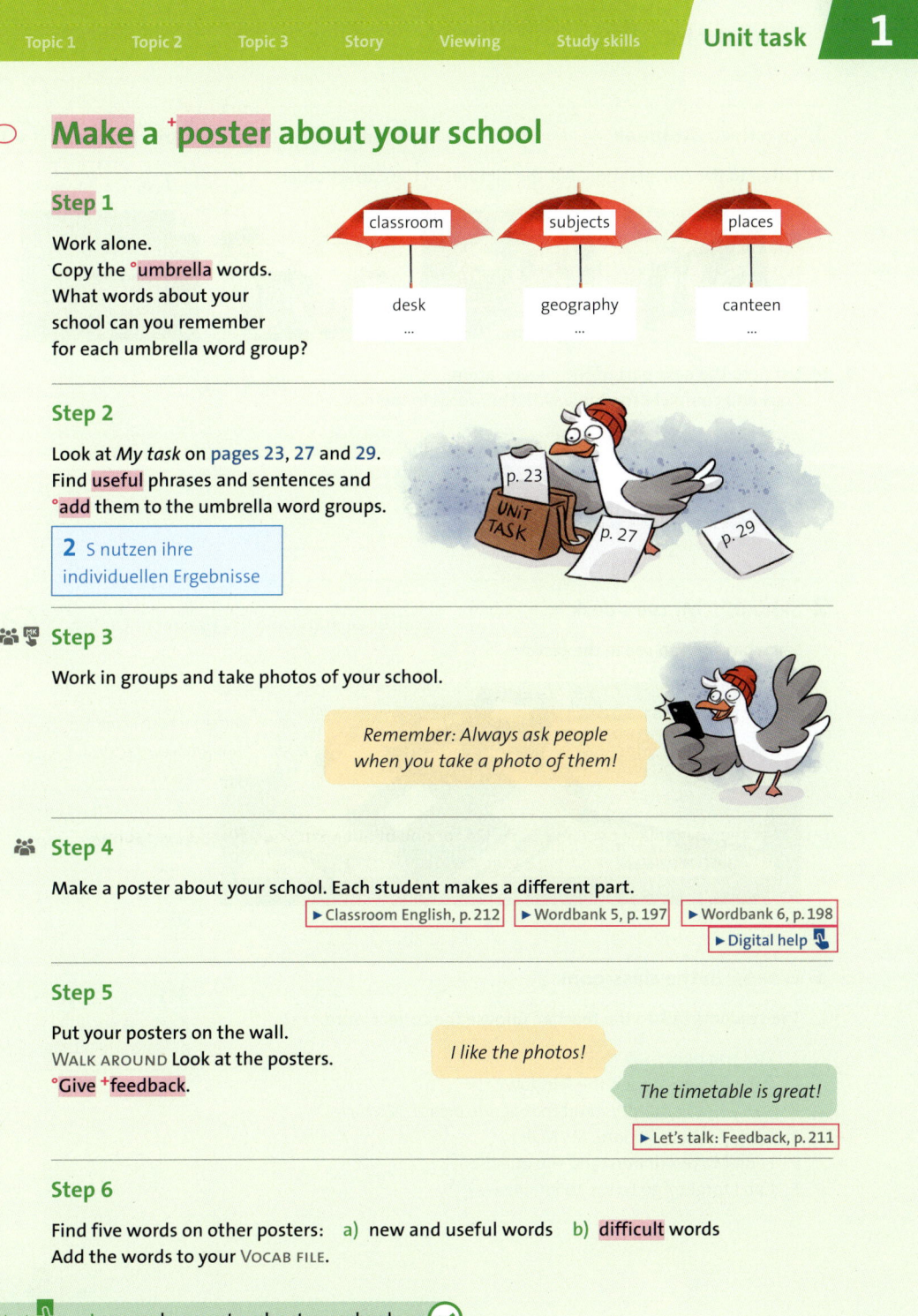

Make a ⁺poster about your school

Step 1

Work alone.
Copy the °umbrella words.
What words about your school can you remember for each umbrella word group?

classroom — desk ...

subjects — geography ...

places — canteen ...

Step 2

Look at *My task* on pages **23**, **27** and **29**.
Find useful phrases and sentences and °add them to the umbrella word groups.

2 S nutzen ihre individuellen Ergebnisse

p. 23
UNIT TASK
p. 27
p. 29

Step 3

Work in groups and take photos of your school.

Remember: Always ask people when you take a photo of them!

Step 4

Make a poster about your school. Each student makes a different part.

► Classroom English, p. 212   ► Wordbank 5, p. 197   ► Wordbank 6, p. 198
► Digital help

Step 5

Put your posters on the wall.
WALK AROUND Look at the posters.
°Give ⁺feedback.

I like the photos!

The timetable is great!

► Let's talk: Feedback, p. 211

Step 6

Find five words on other posters: a) new and useful words   b) difficult words
Add the words to your VOCAB FILE.

Digital quiz   I can make a poster about my school. ✓

thirty-five **35**

Step 1 Einstieg:
- (SB zu) L erklärt *Unit task*:
  L: *Each unit has a unit task – it can be a project. In Unit 1 you make a poster about our school.*

Erarbeitung:
- (SB auf) in EA gemäß AA
- ► Partner check

Step 2 Erarbeitung:
- (SB auf) gemäß AA,
- S ergänzen ihre *word groups* von **Step 1**.

Step 3 Erarbeitung:
- (SB auf) S arbeiten in Gruppen à 3–4 S (► Gruppenbildung).
- L erklärt AA
- Belehrung zum Datenschutz
- evtl. Bereitstellung von Kameras

Step 4 Erarbeitung:
- (SB auf) gemäß AA
- L stellt Papier zur Verfügung bzw. gibt die Größe des Posters an.
- In GA entwerfen die S ihre Schulposter, verteilen Arbeitsaufträge etc.

Step 5 Erarbeitung:
- (SB auf) gemäß AA
- **Ausw.:** ► Milling around bzw. ► Gallery walk
- ► Let's talk: Feedback, S. 211: L visualisiert Hilfen als TA (od. mit UMA)

Step 6 Erarbeitung:
- (SB auf) gemäß AA
- S notieren die Wörter im *Vocab file*.
- Poster werden in der ► English corner ausgehängt.

Checkpoint Inhalt

Lernschwerpunkt: Kompetenzen und sprachliche Mittel üben, Lernfortschritte erkennen
Kompetenzen: Listening einen Dialog hören • Bilder zuordnen • Detailinformationen erfassen • Speaking Schulsachen
und *classroom phrases* korrekt benennen • Writing einen Kommentar über Schule schreiben
Redemittel: Wortfelder *school, school things, classroom phrases*
Strukturen: Verb *to be* (Kurz- und Langformen, Verneinung)

Allgemeine Anmerkung:
Die Aufgaben auf den *Checkpoint*-Seiten dienen den S zum Überprüfen, ob sie die Lernziele (*I can ...*) erreicht haben (s. Vorwort S. XVf.).
S schätzen ihr Können vor der Bearbeitung und nach der Besprechung der Lösungen ein.
Bei Nutzung des *Digital checkpoint* (APP) arbeiten die S selbstständig. Die Lösungen werden im Programm überprüft.

Ex 1 Einstieg:
- (SB auf) S lesen das Lernziel zu diesem Abschnitt vor (*I can ...*).
- S schätzen ihr Können zum Lernziel ein, z. B. mit ▶ Thumbs up, und notieren das Ergebnis.

Erarbeitung:
a) 1. **Hören** gemäß AA
- 2. **Hören** zur Überprüfung (EA)

b) S notieren die Tabelle ins Heft u. ergänzen sie beim 1. **Hören**.
- **Ausw.:** ▶ Bus stop (▶ KV Extra): S vergleichen ihre Lösungen mithilfe von ▶ KV 1.5A.
- nach der Lösungskontrolle erneute Einschätzung des Könnens (wie im **Einstieg**)

Ex 2 + 3 Einstieg:
- s. Ex 1 (Selbsteinschätzung)
- ▣ (SB zu) ggf. Poster von **Ex 9, Zusatz**, S. 23 zur Aktivierung des Wortschatzes

Erarbeitung:
- gemäß AA
- **Ausw.:** ▶ Bus stop (▶ KV Extra): S vergleichen ihre Lösungen für Ex 2 + Ex 3 mithilfe von ▶ KV 1.5A.
- erneute Selbsteinschätzung

🎧 1 LISTENING At break

I can **understand students at a British school.** ✓

🔊 1.27 a) Listen to the conversation. Put the pictures in the correct order.

1 a) D • B • C • A

 A
 B
 C
 D

🔊 1.28 b) Listen to the next part of the conversation.
Copy and complete the table with the words in the box.

Name	Favourite lesson today	Why?
Zane	...	geography	The teacher is ...	nice
Sunita	...	computing	It's ...	cool
Lily	...	PE	It's ...	fun

computing • geography • PE • cool • fun • nice

💬 2 SPEAKING Mr Lee's desk

I can **understand and use classroom English.** ✓

Say what you can see in the picture.

In the picture I can see a white computer, ...

2 ... three (brown/orange) rulers, four green exercise books, five red glue sticks.

📖 3 WORDS In the classroom

The students talk to the teacher. Choose the correct word.

1 Can you help / say me?
2 Can I answer / open the window?
3 Can you say / understand that again, please, Ms Miller?
4 Sorry / Please I'm late, Ms Miller.
5 I don't take / understand the question.
6 Can I forget / go to the toilet, please?

3 1 help • 2 open • 3 say • 4 Sorry • 5 understand • 6 go

Check

Checkpoint Vorbereitung

Material: alle Aufgaben ▸ KV Extra: Bus stop, ▸ KV 1.5A: Checkpoint answers • Ex 1 UMA/CD • Ex 2/3 ggf. Poster mit *classroom phrases* (Ex 9, Zusatz, S. 23)

Zeitbedarf: ca. 2 Std.

Minimalversion: Auswahl der Aufgaben erfolgt aufgrund der zu überprüfenden Lernziele

Begleitmedien: App (Digital checkpoint), INKL (S. 36–37)

Die Übungen kannst du auch digital machen 👆   1

4 LANGUAGE Sunita's email

I can write my timetable in English *(to be).* ✅

Sunita and her friend Jasmine are at different schools.
Complete Sunita's message with *am / is / are.*

> Hi, Jasmine!
> How (1) … you? I (2) … now in class 7C at Varndean School. My timetable (3) … great! English lessons (4) … on Mondays, Tuesdays and Fridays. I have two music lessons. One (5) … in lesson 4 on Tuesdays and one (6) … in lesson 1 on Fridays. Science lessons (my favourite lessons) (7) … on Tuesdays and Wednesdays. And PE (8) … in lessons 5 and 6 on Thursdays. Is your timetable OK? What's your favourite day?
> See you
> Sunita

4 1 are • 2 'm/am • 3 is • 4 are • 5 is • 6 is • 7 are • 8 is

5 LANGUAGE Jasmine's school

I can describe my school *(to be – negative).* ✅

Jasmine talks about her school. Look at the picture and complete Jasmine's sentences with *is / isn't / are / aren't.*

5 1 aren't • 2 is • 3 is • 4 are • 5 isn't • 6 aren't • 7 isn't

> This is my school in Hove. The students (1) … in the building because it's break. The uniform is nice – the blazer (2) … red and the tie (3) … blue. There are two seagulls – they (4) … friendly. But they like our sandwiches! The canteen (5) … very big and the food there is great. But the classrooms are in building 1 – they (6) … near the canteen. The sports hall (7) … in building 1 – it's near the canteen.

6 WRITING Seb's school

Seb is Lily's friend from Bochum. Read his notes about his school. Write his message to Lily.

Hi, Lily! My school is Schiller School. It's …

- Schiller School
- in Bochum
- not big
- students: friendly
- class teacher: Ms Lang
- favourite place: sports hall

6 Lösungsbeispiel: *Hi Lily! My school is Schiller School. It's in Bochum. It isn't big. The students are friendly. My class teacher is Ms Lang. My favourite place is the sports hall. See you, Seb*

Check 👆

thirty-seven **37**

Ex 4 Einstieg:
- s. Ex 1 (Selbsteinschätzung)

Erarbeitung:
- gemäß AA.
- ▸ Early finisher: S notieren vollständige Sätze.
- **Ausw.:** ▸ Bus stop (▸ KV Extra): S vergleichen ihre Lösungen mithilfe von ▸ KV 1.5A.
- erneute Selbsteinschätzung

Ex 5 + 6 Einstieg:
- s. Ex 1 (Selbsteinschätzung)

Ex 5 Erarbeitung:
- gemäß AA
- ▸ Early finisher: S notieren vollständige Sätze.
- Ausw: ▸ Bus stop (▸ KV Extra): S vergleichen ihre Lösungen mithilfe der ▸ KV 1.5A.
- erneute Selbsteinschätzung

Ex 6 Erarbeitung:
- (SB auf) ggf. Klären der AA
- schriftl. Bearbeitung in EA
- ☑ ▸ Scaffolding (als TA)
- **Ausw.:** ▸ Bus stop: S vergleichen ihre Lösungen mithilfe von ▸ KV 1.5A.
- **Alternative:** ▸ Partner check
- erneute Selbsteinschätzung
- **Zusatz:** Auswertung, wie gut sich S bei den Aufgaben dieser Doppelseite selbst eingeschätzt haben (▸ Thumbs up): Stimmt die Einschätzung vor der Aufgabe mit der Einschätzung nach der Aufgabe überein?

Lernschwerpunkt: Kompetenzen und sprachliche Mittel üben, Lernfortschritte erkennen
Kompetenzen: Reading eine szenische Geschichte verstehen, detaillierte Informationen entnehmen • Informationen und
Bilder zuordnen • Study skills eine Mindmap erstellen
Redemittel: Wortfelder *school, hobbies, favourite things*

Ex 7 Einstieg:

- (SB auf) S lesen das Lernziel zu diesem Abschnitt vor (*I can ...*).
- S schätzen ihr Können zum Lernziel ein, z. B. mit ▶ Thumbs up, und notieren sich das Ergebnis.
- ⬚ (SB zu) L zeigt vergrößerte Bilder (UMA):
  L: *What can you see?*
- S beschreiben die Bilder.

Erarbeitung:

a) (SB auf) gemäß AA
- S lesen/hören still mit (▶ Mitleseverfahren).

b) + c) gemäß AA
- S notieren die Antworten im Heft.
- **Ausw.:** ▶ Bus stop (▶ KV Extra): S vergleichen ihre Lösungen mithilfe der ▶ KV 1.5B.
- **Alternative:** ▶ Meldekette
- erneute Selbsteinschätzung

- **Zusatz:** S können den Text mit verteilten Rollen lesen.
- Freiwillige Gruppen tragen ihren szenischen Text im Plenum vor (▶ Scenic play) oder nehmen sich mit geeignetem Aufnahmegerät/Smartphone auf.

---

1 Checkpoint   Digital checkpoint

📖 **7** READING **Zane's homework**   I can **understand a story about friends.**

🔊 **a)** Read the story.
1.29

Mr King °So, class 7B. This is your homework. Make a poster about your favourite band, with °facts and photos.

Zane Erm ... °Sir ... Can I ask a ...
Mr King Sorry Zane, I'm busy. Let's talk at break.

Sunita Why are you sad, Zane? You like music! And you're in a band!
Zane I want to make a great poster. But my computer is old and slow.
Sunita Where's your computer? I can help with that.

Zane Wow. You're good with computers. Thanks, Sunita.
Sunita You're welcome!

b) Complete the sentences with the words from the box.

1 Mr King is ...
2 Sunita is ... and ...
3 Zane is ... then ...

busy • clever • happy • helpful • sad

7 b) 1 busy • **2** helpful and clever • **3** sad then happy

c) Choose the correct answer.

1 Mr King is the A maths teacher B French teacher C music teacher.
2 Mr King can talk A now B at break C at lunch.
3 Zane likes A computers B music C posters.
4 Zane's computer isn't A old B new C big.
5 Sunita is good with A problems B music C computers.

7 c) 1 C • **2** B • **3** B • **4** B • **5** C

Check

Checkpoint Vorbereitung

Material: alle Aufgaben ▸ KV Extra: Bus stop, ▸ KV 1.5B: Checkpoint answers • Ex 7 UMA/CD, geeignete Aufnahmegeräte • Ex 8 UMA

Zeitbedarf: ca. 2 Std.

Minimalversion: Auswahl der Aufgaben erfolgt aufgrund der zu überprüfenden Lernziele

Begleitmedien: App (Digital checkpoint)

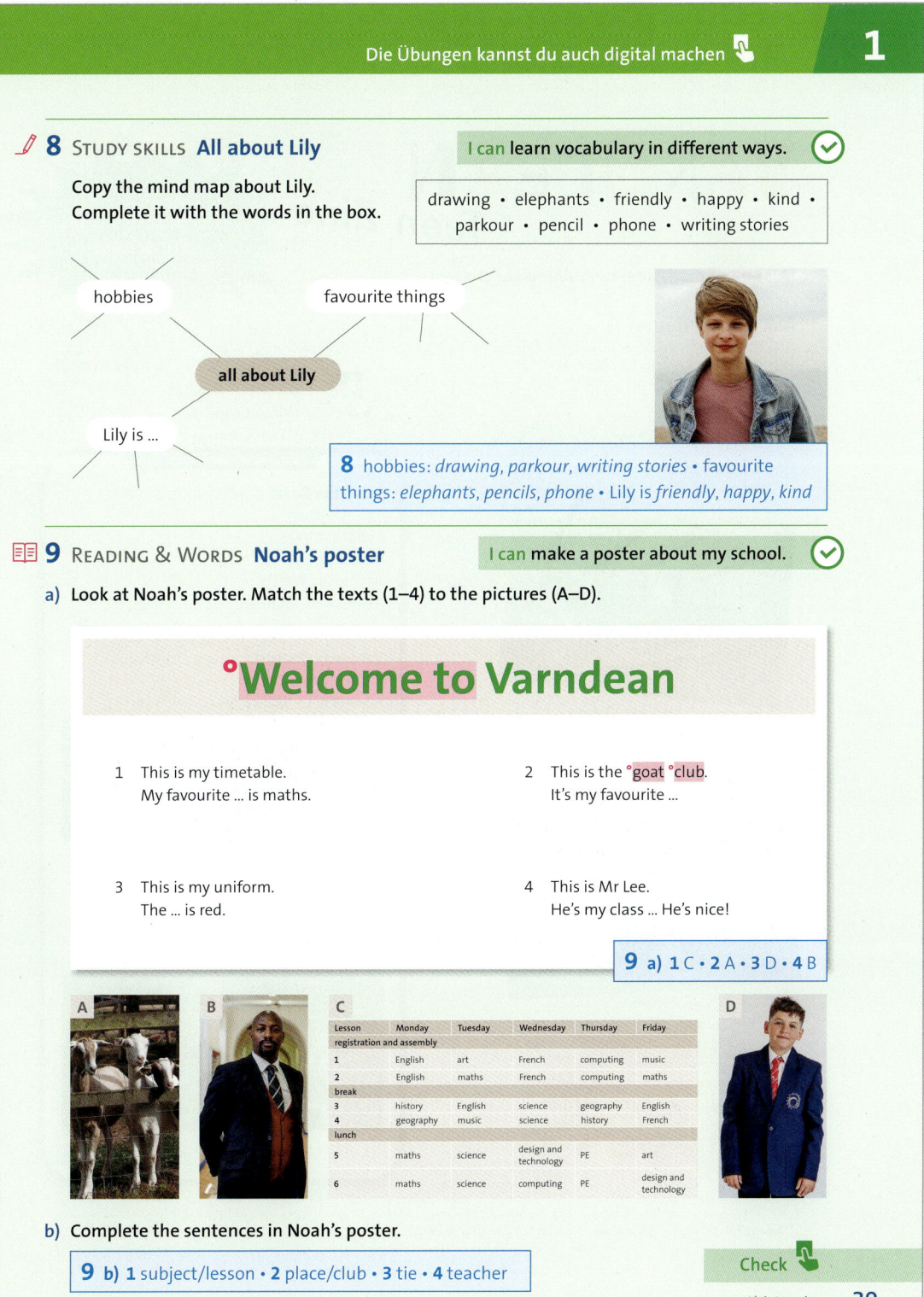

Die Übungen kannst du auch digital machen 👆 **1**

🖊 **8** STUDY SKILLS **All about Lily**

I can learn vocabulary in different ways. ✓

Copy the mind map about Lily.
Complete it with the words in the box.

drawing • elephants • friendly • happy • kind •
parkour • pencil • phone • writing stories

hobbies

favourite things

all about Lily

Lily is …

8 hobbies: *drawing, parkour, writing stories* • favourite
things: *elephants, pencils, phone* • Lily is *friendly, happy, kind*

📖 **9** READING & WORDS **Noah's poster**

I can make a poster about my school. ✓

a) Look at Noah's poster. Match the texts (1–4) to the pictures (A–D).

°Welcome to Varndean

1 This is my timetable.
   My favourite … is maths.

2 This is the °goat °club.
   It's my favourite …

3 This is my uniform.
   The … is red.

4 This is Mr Lee.
   He's my class … He's nice!

9 a) **1** C • **2** A • **3** D • **4** B

Lesson	Monday	Tuesday	Wednesday	Thursday	Friday
registration and assembly					
1	English	art	French	computing	music
2	English	maths	French	computing	maths
break					
3	history	English	science	geography	English
4	geography	music	science	history	French
lunch					
5	maths	science	design and technology	PE	art
6	maths	science	computing	PE	design and technology

b) Complete the sentences in Noah's poster.

9 b) **1** subject/lesson • **2** place/club • **3** tie • **4** teacher

Check 👆

thirty-nine **39**

Ex 8 Einstieg:
• s. Ex 7 (Selbsteinschätzung)
• ✉ ggf. ▸ Semantisierung des Wortschatzes

Erarbeitung:
• gemäß AA
• S übertragen die Mindmap in ihr Heft.
• **Ausw.:** ▸ Bus stop (▸ KV Extra): S vergleichen ihre Lösungen mithilfe der ▸ KV 1.5B.
• **Alternative:** S präsentieren Ergebnisse im Plenum über UMA/Tafel.
• erneute Selbsteinschätzung
• **Zusatz:** S gestalten eine Mindmap über sich selbst (z. B. als HA).

Ex 9 Einstieg:
• s. Ex 7 (Selbsteinschätzung)

Erarbeitung:
a) + b) Bearbeitung gemäß AA schriftl. in EA.
• **Ausw.:** ▸ Bus stop (▸ KV Extra): S vergleichen ihre Lösungen mithilfe von ▸ KV 1.5B.
• erneute Selbsteinschätzung
• **Zusatz:** Auswertung, wie gut sich S bei den Aufgaben dieser Doppelseite selbst eingeschätzt haben, mit ▸ Thumbs up: Stimmt die Einschätzung vor der Aufgabe mit der Einschätzung nach der Aufgabe überein?

Text file Inhalt

Lernschwerpunkt: ein *school magazine* lesen
Kompetenzen: Reading kurzen Texten entnehmen, welche Lieblingsorte es an der Varndean School gibt • kennenlernen der *Varndean goats* • ein Rätsel lösen • Viewing eine *video tour* über Varndean School anschauen
Redemittel: *places at school, colours*

Allgemeine Anmerkung:
Die Bearbeitung der *Text file*-Seiten ist optional. Die Seiten können zur Differenzierung und als Zusatzangebot genutzt werden, z. B. für ▶ Early finisher und lernstärkere S. Die Seiten dienen aber auch als Abwechslung für die gesamte Klasse. Die Aufgaben können wahlweise bearbeitet werden. S wählen selbst, an welchen Stellen sie sich produktiv einbringen können/wollen. Ggf. gibt L eine Minimalvorgabe für ein eingeführtes Portfolio (▶ Dossier).

Ask the students Einstieg:
• (SB zu) L schreibt *Teen Zine* an die Tafel (▶ stummer Impuls) u. sammelt spontane Reaktionen/Vermutungen der S.
• **Alternative:** u. U. Verweis auf eigene Schülerzeitung:
L: *The students at Varndean have a school magazine too, like at our school. Let's have a look and find out more.*

Erarbeitung:
• (SB auf) S lesen in PA (▶ Leseacht).
• S betrachten die *school video tour* in der App.
• Austausch im Plenum:
L: *What's your favourite place at Varndean School?*
• S antworten individuell.

• **Zusatz:** S berichten über ihre Lieblingsorte in der eigenen Schule:
S: *My favourite place is … because I love …* (kann auch als TA oder auf einem Poster festgehalten werden.)

VARNDEAN Teen Zine

This month's topic: our school

Our school magazine: by students for students

Ask the students

What's your favourite place at Varndean School?

Lin, 7B: *My favourite place is the theatre because I love acting!*

Kate, 8A: *Books, books, books … I love the library!*

Check out our school video tour in the app!

Say hello to the Varndean goats on social media!
@VarndeanGoats

Varndean Goats @varndeangoats · Dec 16
The sun is up
The sky is blue
It's beautiful[1]
And so are we![2]
#Varndean #Sunrise

Varndean Goats @varndeangoats · Jul 9
Band photo
#Goats with #Attitude

Varndean Goats @varndeangoats · Mar 11
And here's number 13 in the list of things goats can do that you can't …
#goatskills

---

[1] **beautiful** *schön* [2] **So are we.** *Wir auch. / Das sind wir auch. / Das gilt auch für uns.*

Text file · Vorbereitung

Material: Ask the students ggf. Schülerzeitung der eigenen Schule, App (für alle S od. per L-Zugang) • Puzzle time Realien: Krawatte, ggf. Poster (A3/A4, Klassensatz)

Zeitbedarf: ca. 1 Std.

Minimalversion: alle Texte sind optionale Zusatztexte

Begleitmedien: App (Film)

Puzzle time

Find[1] the small school and the tie colour for these five Varndean students.

Varndean is one big school with five small schools.
The small school names are famous[2] people and the ties are different colours: blue, blue-green, purple, red and silver.

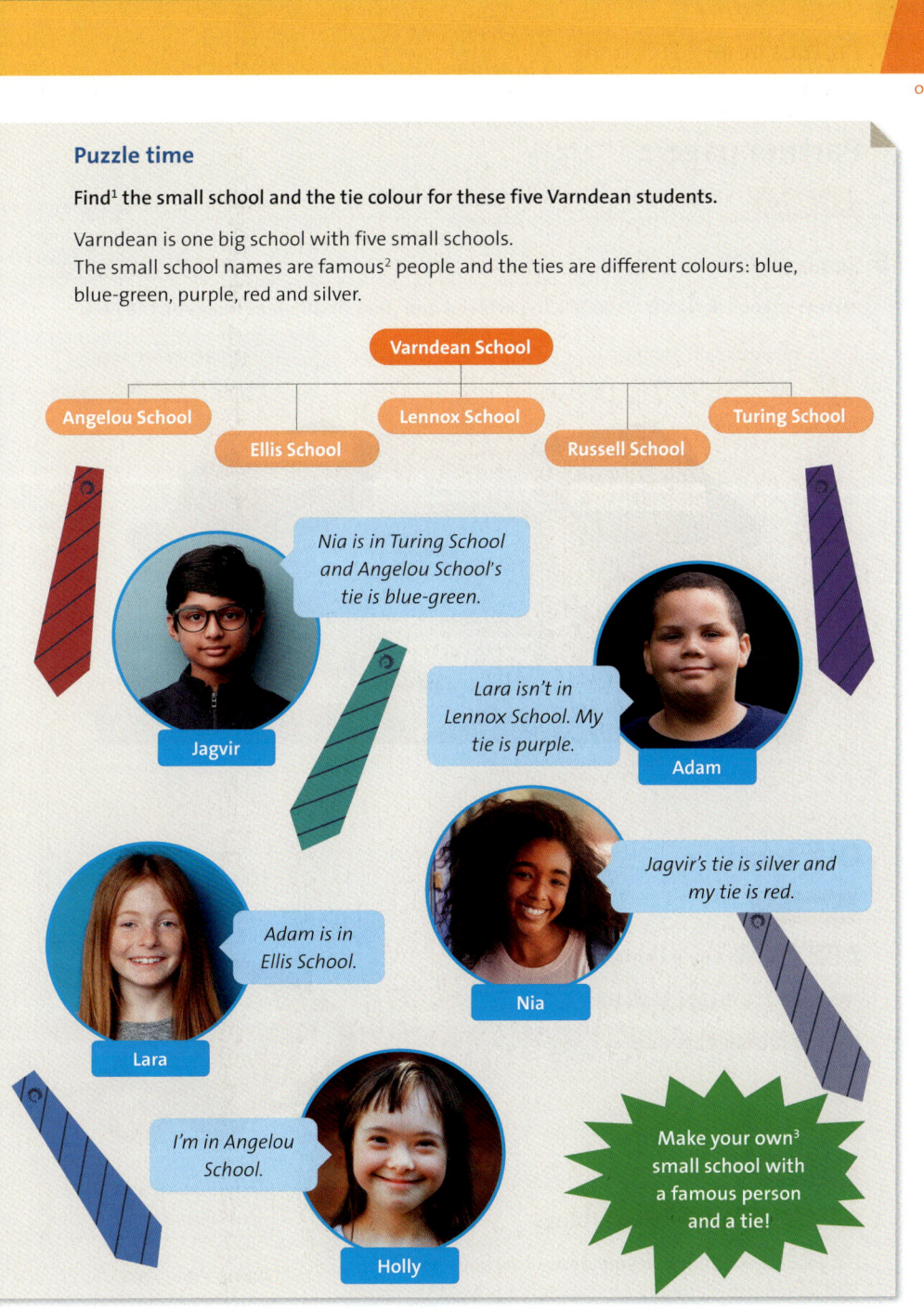

Varndean School

Angelou School · Ellis School · Lennox School · Russell School · Turing School

> Nia is in Turing School and Angelou School's tie is blue-green.

Jagvir

> Lara isn't in Lennox School. My tie is purple.

Adam

> Jagvir's tie is silver and my tie is red.

> Adam is in Ellis School.

Nia

Lara

> I'm in Angelou School.

Make your own[3] small school with a famous person and a tie!

Holly

[1] **find** finden [2] **famous** berühmt [3] **own** eigene, eigener, eigenes

Puzzle time Einstieg:
- (SB zu) ▶ Semantisierung: *puzzle time*
- Aktivierung: *tie* (z. B.: L zeigt/trägt echten *tie* als ▶ stummen Impuls)

Erarbeitung:
- (SB auf) Klären der AA im Plenum
- evtl. Vorgabe einer Tabelle als TA:

school	student	tie
...	...	...

- S bearbeiten die Aufgabe in EA/PA.
- **Ausw.:** S präsentieren Ergebnisse im Plenum.
- Projekt: S kreieren ihre eigene *small school* in EA/PA/GA.

- **Zusatz:** S recherchieren, wer die *famous people* sind, nach denen die fünf *small schools* benannt sind:
  - *Angelou School = Maya Angelou, poet and civil rights activist*
  - *Ellis School: Ethel Ellis, former headteacher*
  - *Lennox School: Annie Lennox, pop singer*
  - *Russell School: Bertrand Russell, philosopher*
  - *Turing School: Alan Turing: mathematician and cryptanalyst*
- **Ausw.:** Poster, Mini-Vorträge o. Ä., je nach vorhandenen Möglichkeiten

1

Partner page / Diff bank Inhalt

Lernschwerpunkt: zusätzliche Übungen, Differenzierungs- und Hilfsangebote
Kompetenzen: Speaking Austausch von Informationen • Schulsachen nennen und beschreiben • Writing den Inhalt eines
Rucksacks beschreiben • Regeln im Klassenraum schreiben
Redemittel: Wortfeld *school*
Strukturen: unbestimmer Artikel *a/an* • Pluralbildung • Personalpronomen

Allgemeine Anmerkung:
• *Partner page* enthält die
  Informationen für *Partner B*
  (▶ Info-gap activity). Die
  didaktischen Hinweise für
  diese Aufgaben befinden sich
  im vorderen Teil der Unit bei
  Partner A.
• *Diff bank*: s. Vorwort S. XIIIf.

Ex 6 Erarbeitung: s. S. 22
• gemäß AA

MP 1 Einstieg:
• ▶ (SB zu) L zeigt eine Tasche
  mit diversen *school things*:
  L: *What can you see?*
  S: *I can see ...*

Erarbeitung:
• (SB auf) Aussprache von
  rucksack wdh. (▶ Lautschulung,
  s. Nachsprechen im Chor)
• S arbeiten schriftl. gemäß AA.
• **Ausw.** ▶ Partner check, anschl.
  Vergleich im Plenum

MP 2 Erarbeitung:
• (SB auf) gemäß AA in PA
• **Ausw.:** ▶ Partner check
• L prüft individuell und
  korrigiert ggf. die Aussprache.

---

1 Partner page / Diff bank

Partner page
▶ Page 22

💬 **6 SPEAKING Different desks**   6 Lösung S. 288

Partner B: Look at Noah's desk. Talk to partner A and °find six different things on the desk.

In my picture I can see one brown pencil.   *In my picture I can see two brown pencils.*

an English book • a pencil sharpener • a pencil case • a rubber • a glue stick • an exercise book • a pen • a pencil • a ruler • a desk

Diff bank
▶ Page 21

🖊 **More practice 1 Lily's things**

°Write what's in Lily's rucksack.

In Lily's rucksack I can see ...

1 an orange pencil case • a blue cap • three books •
an exercise book / a pink exercise book • a ruler •
an elephant • two sandwiches

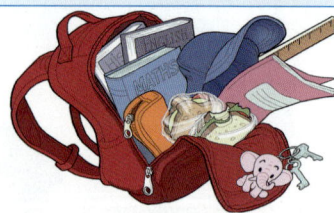

▶ Page 22

💬 **More practice 2 Your school things**   2 individuelle Lösungen

Put your school things on your desk. Close your °eyes.
°Tell your partner about your school things and the colours.

I have a / an / two ...

Diff bank Vorbereitung

Material: MP 1 Schultasche mit Realien • Challenge UMA • MP 4 UMA
Zeitbedarf: abhängig davon, welche Aufgaben bearbeitet werden
Minimalversion: *More practice-* und *Challenge*-Aufgaben sind stets Zusatzaufgaben

More practice 3 Class °rules

Complete the rules.
Use the words in the box.

be (2 x) • eat • listen • put • remember • stand up • talk

3 1 be • 2 Remember • 3 Stand up • 4 Listen • 5 talk • 6 Put • 7 Be • 8 eat

1 Don't … late.
2 … your school things.
3 … when the teacher comes °into the classroom.
4 … to the teacher.
5 Don't … when the teacher talks.
6 … your hand up to °speak.
7 … nice to other students.
8 Don't … in the classroom.

Challenge Open the window, please

Write the sentences in the speech bubbles.   1 *Open the window, please.*   2 *Don't …*

 open
 eat
 walk
 listen
 talk
 take

Ch 2 Don't eat in the classroom. • 3 Walk in the corridor, please. • 4 Listen to me, please. • 5 Don't talk. • 6 Don't take my sandwich.

▶Page 24

More practice 4 Scout's conversation

Complete Scout's sentences with the words in the box.

I • you • ~~he~~ • she • it • we • you • they

1 Zane is a busy boy. *He*'s always tired.
2 Noah and Sunita are good students. …'re clever.
3 Lily is nice. …'s always happy.
4 The °kids and I are from Brighton. …'re friends.
5 …'re new here, Blue °Bird. °Welcome to Brighton!
6 Brighton is a nice place. …'s °by the sea.
7 …'m hungry.
8 Blue Bird and Black Bird, I think …'re hungry too. Let's °find lunch!

4 2 They • 3 She • 4 They • 5 You • 6 It • 7 I • 8 you

MP 3 Einstieg:
• (SB zu) Verben der Aufgabe als TA vorgeben u. aktivieren (u. a. ▶ Lautschulung)

Erarbeitung:
• (SB auf) L u. S erarbeiten ein od. zwei Beispiele im Plenum.
• S notieren die Sätze ins Heft.
• **Ausw.:** ▶ Meldekette

Challenge
• Diese Aufgabe kann zur Differenzierung für lernstärkere oder schnelle S verwendet werden (s. Vorwort S. XIII).

Einstieg:
• (SB zu) L zeigt die vergrößerten Bilder von S. 43 (UMA): L: *What can you see in picture 1, 2, …?* S: *In picture 1 I can see …*

Erarbeitung:
• gemäß AA schriftl. in EA
• **Ausw.** ▶ Partner check, anschl. Vergleich im Plenum

MP 4 Einstieg:
• (SB zu) L visualisiert das Reservoir mit den Personalpronomen als TA (od. UMA).
• S lesen vor (▶ Lautschulung).

Erarbeitung:
• (SB auf) gemäß AA, schriftl. in EA
• Ausw: ▶ Partner check und abschließend im Plenum

Diff bank — Inhalt

Lernschwerpunkt: zusätzliche Übungen, Differenzierungs- und Hilfsangebote
Kompetenzen: Speaking Beschreibung von Personen • Writing über sich und den Tag schreiben • Listening einen Dialog hören • Detailinformationen erfassen
Redemittel: Wortfelder *describing people, school subjects*
Strukturen: Verb *to be* (Kurz- und Langform, Verneinung)

MH 4 s. S. 25
• Durch diese Hilfe erhalten S mehr Vorgaben zur Bildung von Sätzen (▶ Scaffolding).

Erarbeitung:
• (SB auf) gemäß AA, s. S. 25

Parallel ex 5 s. S. 25
• Lernschwächere S erhalten hier mehr Vorgaben.

Erarbeitung:
• (SB auf) gemäß AA
• **Ausw.:** s. S. 25

MP 5 **Einstieg:**
• (SB zu) L schreibt untereinander (TA): *Tim, my friends, I, the school*
L: *Let's make (short) sentences with am, is, are.*
• Im Plenum werden Sätze gebildet und als TA gesichert.

Erarbeitung:
a) (SB auf) gemäß AA, schriftl. in EA
• **Ausw.:** ▶ Partner check, dann Besprechung der Ergebnisse von a) im Plenum

b) ▶ Klären der AA
• Bearbeitung in EA
• S präsentieren ihre Texte im Plenum.

---

1 **Diff bank**

▶ Page 25

💬 **More help** **4** **Varndean students and teachers** | **4** individuelle Lösungen

b) Say sentences about people in your class. The class °guesses the °person.

She's in a football /… team.   *They're good friends.*
He's in a band.   *She's from …*
They like sandwiches / …   *He's … years old.*
She can sing / make music / play the guitar.   *They like the colour blue / red / …*
He can draw.

✎ **Parallel exercise** **5** **Messages**

🖉 Complete the messages from Noah and his mum. °Choose the correct short form.

Hi, Mum! I like the classroom. (1) *It's / They're* big.
I like Mr Lee, my teacher, too. (2) *She's / He's* cool.
And I like my new friends.
(3) *They're / We're* nice. ☺

👍 Great! (4) *It's / You're* lucky, Noah! Varndean
School is big, but (5) *she's / it's* a good school.
Sorry, (6) *you're / I'm* busy now.
See you! ☺

5 **1** It's • **2** He's • **3** They're • **4** You're • **5** it's • **6** I'm

📖 **More practice 5** **Zane's message**

a) Complete Zane's message to a friend in London. Use *am / is / are.*

Hi, Zara
How *are* you? Please °come to Brighton soon! Brighton (1) … great. The beach (2) … my favourite place. I (3) … at my new school now. My new school friends (4) … nice. Noah (5) … cool and Sunita (6) … friendly. Noah and Sunita (7) … in a different class. My friend Lily (8) … in °their class too. °I must go. I (9) … very busy!
°Write soon.
Zane ☺

5 **1** is • **2** is • **3** am/'m • **4** are • **5** is • **6** is • **7** are • **8** is • **9** am/'m

🖉 ⊠ **b)** Write a message to Zane. Use his message to help you.

Diff bank Vorbereitung

Material: MP 7 UMA/CD
Zeitbedarf: abhängig davon, welche Aufgaben bearbeitet werden
Minimalversion: *More practice*-Aufgaben sind stets Zusatzaufgaben

More practice 6 Scout's day

a) Write the correct short forms.

1 I... tired!
2 Remember my friend Black Bird? He... tired too.
3 And my new friend Blue Bird? She... tired too.
4 We... all tired!
5 Today is a nice day. But it... busy.
   What about you and your day?

b) Write about you and your day.

Me: ... tired / happy / hungry / ...
My day: ... nice / busy / horrible / ...

▶Page 26

6 a) 1 I'm • **2** He's • **3** She's • **4** We're • **5** it's

6 b) individuelle Lösungen

More practice 7 I like English

1.21

a) Copy the table. Then listen and write the subjects.

Name	❤	☺	☹
Sunita	science	design and technology	art
Lily	art	PE	French
Noah	maths	history	PE
Zane	PE	English	maths

b) Listen again and °check.

☒ °Make notes °why the students like °their favourite subjects.

▶Page 28

7 b) Sunita: Science is great. • Lily: Art is so cool. • Noah: The maths teacher is nice. • Zane: PE, because sport is great.

More practice 8 Places at school

a) Write the correct place.

1 You can use computers in this room.
2 You can draw pictures here.
3 You can go to different rooms here.
4 You can °do sport in this place.
5 You can eat lunch and °snacks here.
6 You have lessons in this room.

b) Complete the sentence.

My favourite place in school is ...

Yum! School lunch is good!

8 a) 1 the computer room • **2** the art room • **3** the corridor • **4** the sports hall • **5** the canteen • **6** the classroom

8 b) individuelle Lösungen

forty-five **45**

MP 6 Einstieg:
• (SB zu) Zur Aktivierung schreibt L die *long forms* von *to be* an die Tafel.
  L: *What are the short forms?*
• S ergänzen *short forms* an der Tafel.

Erarbeitung:
a) (SB auf)
• S schreiben die Sätze in ihr Heft und ergänzen die korrekten *short forms*.
• **Ausw.:** ▶ Five-minute teacher

b) gemäß AA
• S notieren die Sätze in ihr Heft.
• **Ausw.:** im Plenum

MP 7 Einstieg:
• (SB zu) Wdh. der *subjects* mithilfe der Bilder von Ex 7b) S. 26 (UMA)

Erarbeitung:
a) S ergänzen die Lücken in der Tabelle beim **1. Hören**.

b) S vergleichen ihre Ergebnisse beim **2. Hören** u. ergänzen/korrigieren ihre Lösungen.

• ☒ gemäß AA beim **3. Hören**
• **Ausw.:** ▶ Partner check, abschließend im Plenum

MP 8 Erarbeitung:
a) (SB auf) Klären der AA: L/S löst ein Bsp. mündl. im Plenum.
• S arbeiten in EA und notieren die Begriffe im Heft.
• **Ausw.:** ▶ Five-minute teacher

b) gemäß AA
• **Ausw.:** S präsentieren Ergebnisse im Plenum.

Diff bank Inhalt

Lernschwerpunkt: zusätzliche Übungen, Differenzierungs- und Hilfsangebote
Kompetenzen: Reading Informationen einer Geschichte korrigieren • Writing Personen, Tiere und Gegenstände beschreiben •
Speaking ein Brettspiel spielen
Redemittel: Adjektive • Wortschatz Unit 1

MP 9 Einstieg:
- (SB zu) L bringt einen Gegenstand mit, z. B. ein altes od. großes Buch und stimmt S ein:
L: *What can you see? Can you describe it?*
S: *I can see a book. It's old/ big/...*

Erarbeitung:
a) (SB auf) Klären der AA: L/S bearbeiten mind. ein Beispiel (positiver und negativer Satz) gemeinsam im Plenum.
- S schreiben die Sätze in ihr Heft.
- **Ausw.:** ▸ Five-minute teacher

b) gemäß AA
- **Ausw.:** Freiwillige S lesen ihre Sätze im Plenum vor.

Parallel ex 3 s. S. 31
- Für lernschwächere S sind die zu korrigierenden Formen im Satz schon gekennzeichnet.

Einstieg:
- (SB auf) gemeinsames Klären der AA im Plenum
- S bearbeiten die Aufgabe schriftlich. Die Sätze werden ins Heft geschrieben.
- **Ausw.:** ▸ Five-minute teacher (gemeinsam im Plenum, s. a. S. 31)

---

1 **Diff bank**

▸Page 29

☒ More practice 9 **Big or small?**

🖉 a) °Describe the students, things and animals.
Write two sentences for °each picture with the words °below.

> 9 a) **2** ... nice. They aren't horrible • **3** The book is old. It isn't new • **4** The sandwiches are good. They aren't bad • **5** The seagull is grey. It isn't black • **6** Zane is hungry. He isn't tired.

1 *The dog is big. It isn't small.*
2 *Lily and Noah are ...*

big/small   nice/horrible   old/new

 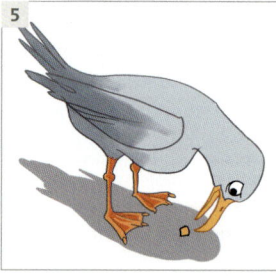 

good/bad   grey/black   hungry/tired

b) Write two sentences about students or things in your class.

▸Page 31

☑ Parallel exercise **3** READING **What's wrong?**

📖 Make the sentences correct. °Change the words in blue.

1 Zane is free after school.
2 Kyle and Jade are nice to Noah.
3 Sunita and Lily aren't scared of the bullies at first.
4 Lily and Sunita aren't Noah's friends.
5 The seagulls are nice to Kyle and Jade.
6 Noah's dog is mean.

> 3 **1** isn't • **2** aren't • **3** are • **4** are • **5** aren't • **6** isn't

Vorbereitung

Material: MP 9 passende Realien (z. B. altes Buch), Game UMA, vorbereitete Spielkarten s. Ex 4, S. 34 od. ► KV 1.4: GAME New words (mind. eine Kopie pro Gruppe)

Zeitbedarf: abhängig davon, welche Aufgaben bearbeitet werden

Minimalversion: *More practice*-Aufgaben sind stets Zusatzaufgaben

1

► Page 34

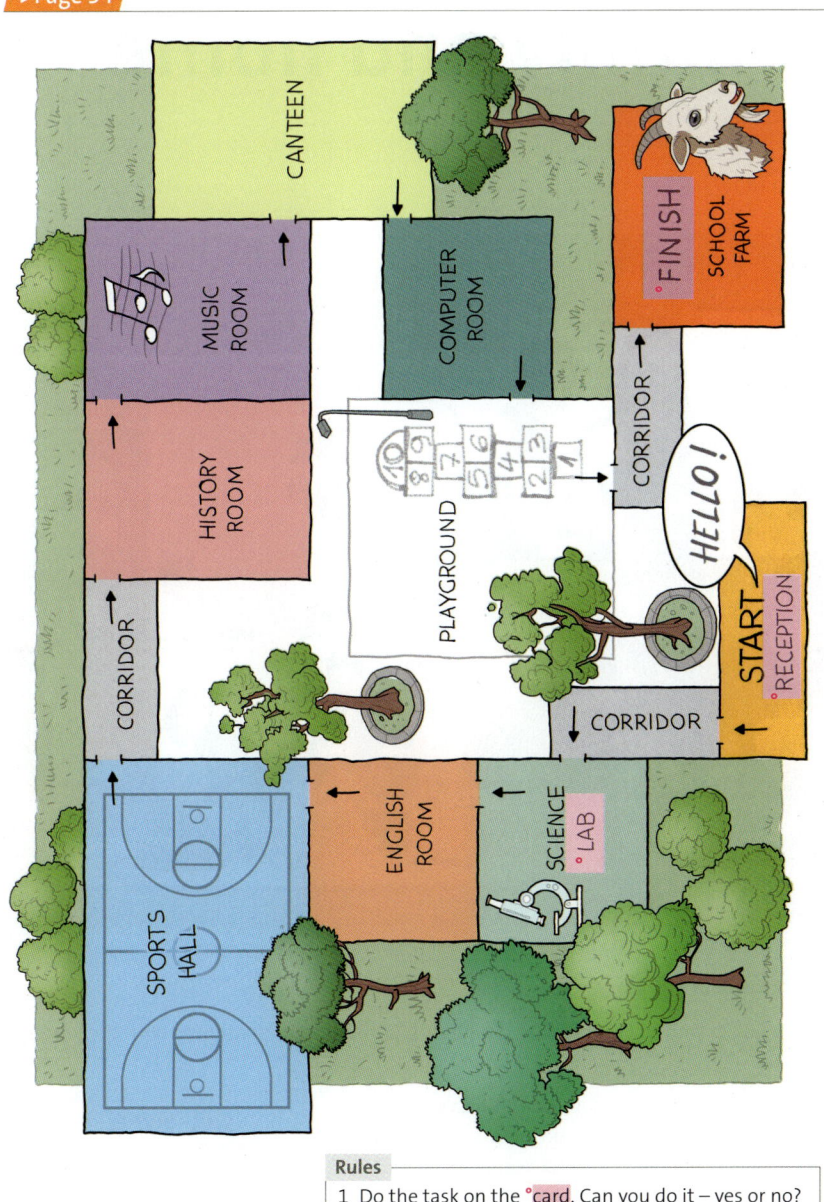

Rules
1 Do the task on the °card. Can you do it – yes or no?
  Yes: Move to the °next room.
  No: Don't move to the next room.
2 The next student takes a card.

Game
- (SB auf) Vorbereitung mithilfe von Ex 4a), S. 34: S gestalten in GA ihre Spielkarten (► KV 1.4).

Erarbeitung
- (SB auf) L visualisiert die vergrößerte Spielvorlage für alle (UMA). So können die Regel und der Ablauf gut erklärt werden.
  L: *Let's play the game. First let's read the rules.*
- S/L liest Regeln vor.
- L nutzt zwei oder drei Spielkarten der S, um den Ablauf beispielhaft zu präsentieren, anschließend spielen die Gruppen gemäß Ex 4b) u. 4c), S. 34.
- **Sich.:** Ggf. prüft L individuell Aussprache und Korrektheit.

Unit-Übersicht

Storyline: Die S erfahren mehr über Sunita und Lily, ihre Familien und Haustiere. Die vier Lehrwerkskinder beschreiben, wo sie wohnen. Es gibt eine Videotour durch Sunitas Haus und auch Lily stellt ihre Wohnung vor. Sunita beschreibt ihr Zimmer. In der *Story* beschweren sich Sunita und Nish über Bens Gesang. Die Familie versucht, das Problem konstruktiv zu lösen.
Strukturen: Fragen und Kurzantworten mit *to be* (S. 51) • *There's / There are* (S. 54)
Viewing: Tour durch Sunitas Haus (S. 55) • zwei neue Mutproben für Daisy und Emir, in denen die S Informationen über die Familie von Emir und von Mrs Collins erhalten (S. 63)
Unit task: ein Traumzimmer präsentieren

Unit 2 Einstieg:

- (SB zu) ▶ Five-finger brain-storming: S sammeln je fünf bekannte *family words* und nennen sie dann im Plenum.
- L notiert die Wörter (TA Stammbaum, ▶ Vokabelarbeit).
- S tauschen sich im ▶ Milling around über die Namen ihrer fünf Familienmitglieder aus.
  L: *Talk about one member of your family for each finger.*
- ☒ Lernstärkere S nennen auch Alter, Hobbys etc.
- TA: Vokabeln für Ex 1 im *Vocab file* sichern.

Ex 1 Einstieg:

- (SB auf) Bildbeschreibung als *Pre-listening*:
  L: *What or who can you see in the pictures?*
- ☒ Lernstärkere S stellen Vermutungen an, wer die unbekannten Personen sein könnten: *Maybe the boy is …*

Erarbeitung:

- S lesen die Satzanfänge A–J. Kurze Wdh.: Bedeutung von *'s*.
- S lesen die Wörter im Reservoir und erfragen die ihnen unbekannten (▶ Seman-tisierung).
- Ggf. im TA (s. Unit-Einstieg) neue Wörter ergänzen.
- S notieren die Buchstaben A–J und rechts daneben die *family words* aus dem Reservoir untereinander im Heft.
- **1. Hören:** S verbinden die Buchstaben und *family words*.
- **2. Hören:** S überprüfen ihre Lösungen.
- ▶ Partner check
- **Ausw.:** ▶ Five-minute teacher

Unit 2
My family and home

🎧 ◀) **1 WORDS Sunita's family**

◀)
1.30 Listen to Sunita and Lily and look at the photos. Complete the sentences with the words in the box.

A is Meera, Sunita's …   F is Rahi, Sunita's …
B is Nish, Sunita's …   G and H are Jay and
C is Ben, Meera's …   Anika, Sunita's …
D is Willow, Ben's …   I is Sunita's …
E is Priya, Sunita's …   J is Sunita's …

aunt • brother • cousins • daughter • grandpa • grandma • mum • partner • uncle

▶ More practice 1, p. 75

1 A mother • **B** brother • **C** partner • **D** daughter •
E aunt • **F** uncle • **G and H** cousins • **I** grandpa • **J** grandma

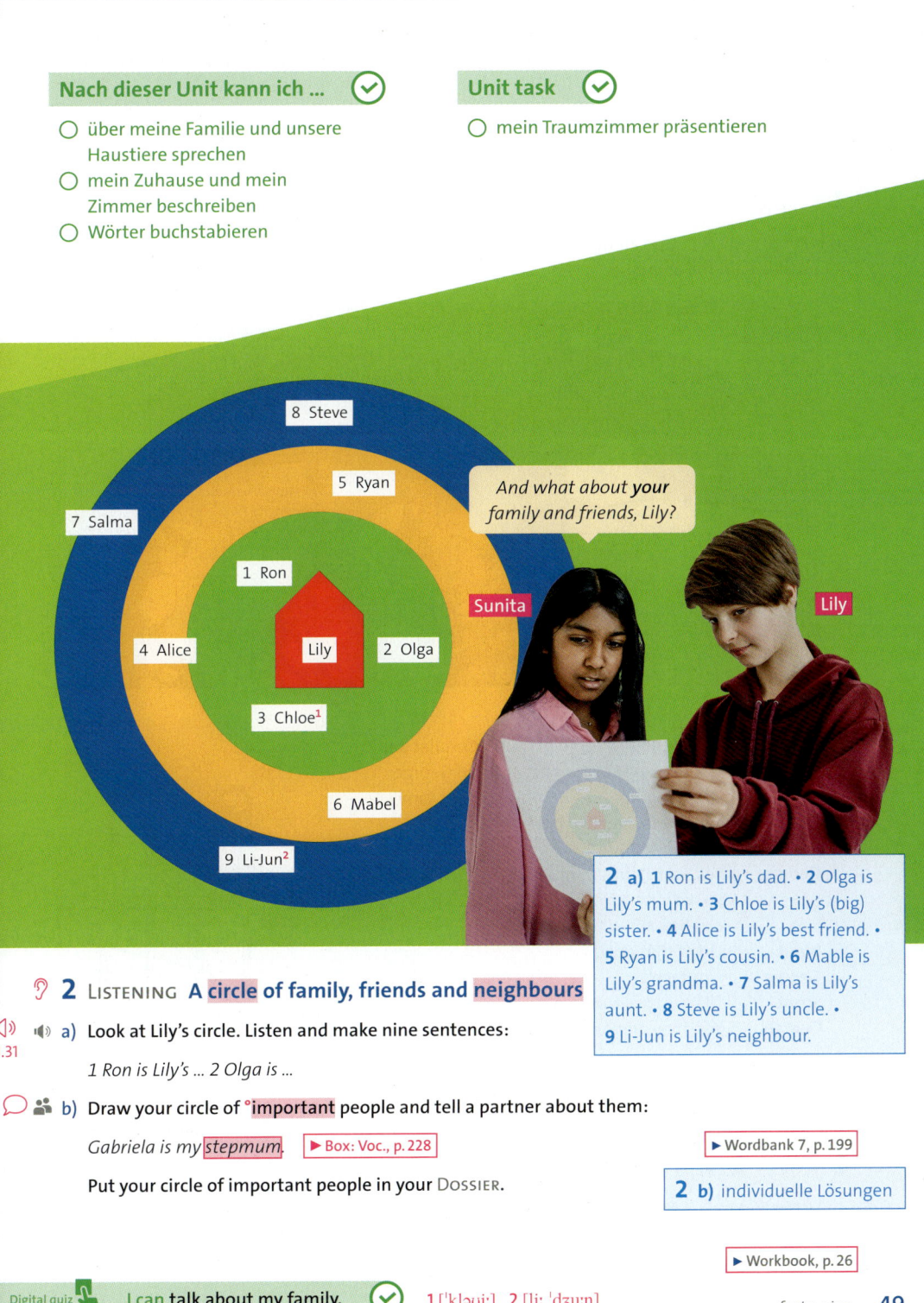

Lead-in Inhalt

Lernschwerpunkt: Familienverhältnisse verstehen (Sunita und Lily betrachten Familienfotos und einen *circle of important people*)
Kompetenzen: Listening Dialogen Informationen über Familienverhältnisse entnehmen • Speaking sich über Familie, Freunde und Nachbarn austauschen
Redemittel: Wortfeld *family words*

Vorbereitung

Material: Ex 1 UMA/CD • Ex 2 UMA/CD, von L vorbereiteter *circle of important people*, ▶ KV 2.1: My circle of important people (Klassensatz), ggf. Handpuppe Scout
Zeitbedarf: ca. 2 Std.
Begleitmedien: WB (S. 26), App (Digital quiz), INKL (S. 48–49), DIFF (2.1)

Nach dieser Unit kann ich ... ✓
○ über meine Familie und unsere Haustiere sprechen
○ mein Zuhause und mein Zimmer beschreiben
○ Wörter buchstabieren

Unit task ✓
○ mein Traumzimmer präsentieren

Nach dieser Unit ...
• L bespricht mit S die Lernziele der Unit (s. links) und kündigt die *Unit task* an.
• Am Ende der Unit überprüfen die S das Erreichen der Ziele mithilfe des *Checkpoint* (S. 66–69) bzw. gemeinsam im Plenum.

Ex 2 Einstieg:
• (SB zu) L präsentiert vorbereiteten *circle* als TA (eigene oder Scouts imaginäre Familie/Freunde).
L (ggf. als Scout): *This is my circle of important people. Let me tell you about them.*
• L führt dabei auch die neue Vokabel *neighbour* ein.

Erarbeitung:
a) (SB auf) *Pre-listening*: Vermutungen anstellen.
L: *Look at the picture. What are Lily and Sunita talking about? Who are the people in this circle?*
• S schreiben die Namen (1–9) ins Heft.
• **1. Hören:** S notieren die Lösungen im Heft.
• **2. Hören:** S prüfen.
• **Ausw.:** im Plenum

b) ▶ Partner talk
• S nutzen ▶ KV 2.1.
• ▶ Double circle: S tauschen sich mit mind. fünf anderen S aus.
• **Ausw.:** Ein/e S stellt den *circle* eines/einer Mit-S im Plenum vor.
• S heften ihren *circle* in ihr ▶ Dossier.
• **Zusatz:** S ergänzen ggf. als HA Fotos oder Zeichnungen der Personen im *circle*.

*And what about **your** family and friends, Lily?*

Sunita   Lily

8 Steve / 5 Ryan / 7 Salma / 1 Ron / 4 Alice / Lily / 2 Olga / 3 Chloe¹ / 6 Mabel / 9 Li-Jun²

2 a) 1 Ron is Lily's dad. • **2** Olga is Lily's mum. • **3** Chloe is Lily's (big) sister. • **4** Alice is Lily's best friend. • **5** Ryan is Lily's cousin. • **6** Mable is Lily's grandma. • **7** Salma is Lily's aunt. • **8** Steve is Lily's uncle. • **9** Li-Jun is Lily's neighbour.

2 LISTENING **A circle of family, friends and neighbours**

a) Look at Lily's circle. Listen and make nine sentences:
1 Ron is Lily's ... 2 Olga is ...

b) Draw your circle of °important people and tell a partner about them:
Gabriela is my stepmum. ▶ Box: Voc., p. 228
Put your circle of important people in your DOSSIER.

▶ Wordbank 7, p. 199
2 b) individuelle Lösungen
▶ Workbook, p. 26

Digital quiz **I can talk about my family.** ✓ 1 [ˈklɔʊiː] 2 [liː ˈdʒuːn]

Topic 1 Inhalt

Lernschwerpunkt: einen Text über Haustiere lesend verstehen • Fragen und Kurzantworten mit *to be*
Kompetenzen: Reading einen Dialog über Haustiere lesen • eine kurze Zusammenfassung des Textes lesen und vervollständigen • im Text Fragen finden und abschreiben • Speaking Lautschulung Tierwörter • Fragen mit *to be* stellen und mit Kurzantworten beantworten • Writing Fragen mit *to be* in die richtige Reihenfolge bringen • Study skills sprachliche Regelmäßigkeiten entdecken
Strukturen: Fragen und Kurzantworten mit *to be*
Redemittel: Wortfeld *pets*

Ex 1 Einstieg:
- (SB auf) TA: *In the picture I can see ...*
- S nennen die Tiere im großen Bild zuerst in PA, dann im Plenum.
- TA: L sammelt Tierwörter. S übersetzen sie (▶ Vokabelarbeit).

Erarbeitung:
a) AA gemeinsam lesen, Aufgabe im Plenum lösen.
- **Zusatz:** L: *Who or what can you see in the small picture on the right?* S beschreiben das kleine Bild.

b) Text leise lesen, unbekannte Wörter im Plenum klären (▶ Semantisierung)
- ☒ Wörter im *Vocabulary* (S. 228–229) nachschlagen lassen
- Sätze im ▶ Think-Pair-Share vervollständigen
- **Ausw.:** TA der Lösungen in der *Share*-Phase

Ex 2 Erarbeitung:
- (SB auf) gemäß AA
- **1. Hören:** L spielt im ▶ Mitleseverfahren die Wörter mit UMA/CD vor. S zeigen auf das Wort, das vorgelesen wird.
- **2. Hören:** S sprechen die Wörter nach (▶ Lautschulung).
- **Ausw.:** Freiwillige S sprechen die Wörter vor.
- **Zusatz:** S üben das Lesen des Textes mit verteilten Rollen (PA).
- **Alternative:** Den Dialog mit der Handpuppe Scout und einem Stofftier nachspielen.

My pets

📖 **1** READING **A lot of animals!**

▶ **a)** BEFORE YOU READ One animal in the box isn't in the picture. Find the animal.

> a cat • a fish • a horse • a parrot • a rabbit • a snake • two hamsters

> **1 a)** A *fish* isn't in the picture.

George

🔊 1.32	
Scout	Hello, I'm Scout. Are you lost?
George	No, I'm not. I'm here because it's quiet and I'm not happy! Nice to meet you, I'm George.
Scout	You're George. Oh, is Sunita in your family?
George	Yes, she is. Are you and Sunita friends?
Scout	Yes, we are. Are you angry?
George	Yes, I am. Sunita's mum is a vet. It's the weekend, so we have a lot of animals from Meera's work in our house.
Scout	Oh, is that good?
George	No, it isn't!
Scout	Oh, are they too loud?
George	Yes, they are! And the house is so messy!

George Scout

> **1 b)** George is *Sunita's* pet. He isn't *happy* because the animals in his house are too *loud*.

b) Read the conversation and complete the sentences.

George is ...'s pet. He isn't ... because the animals in his house are too ...

🎤💬 ─────────────────────

🔊 **2** WORDS **A cat, a fish ...**

🔊 1.33 Listen and repeat the words from the box in 1a).

▶ Workbook, p. 27

Topic 1 Vorbereitung

Material: Ex 2 UMA/CD, Handpuppe Scout und Stofftier/Papagei • Ex 3 UMA/App (Erklärfilm) • Ex 4 von L vorbereitete Karten mit Fragen (*swap cards*)
Zeitbedarf: ca. 2 Std.
Minimalversion: Ex 2 auslassen
Begleitmedien: WB (S. 27–28), App (Erklärfilm), INKL (S. 50–51)

2

Erklär-film

3 LOOKING AT LANGUAGE **Questions and short answers**

a) Read the conversation on p. 50 again. Find the matching questions. What's different?

1	You are lost.	→ Are you lost?
2	Sunita is in your family.	→ Is …?
3	You are angry.	→ …?
4	That is good.	→ …?
5	They are too loud.	→ …?

> **3 a) 1** *Are you* lost? • **2** *Is Sunita* in your family? • **3** *Are you* angry? • **4** *Is that* good? • **5** *Are they* too loud?

b) Match the questions to the answers.

1	Is George happy?	A	Yes, it is.
2	Are the animals too loud?	B	No, they aren't.
3	Is Sunita's house messy?	C	Yes, he is.
4	Is George Sunita's pet?	D	Yes, they are.
5	Are the hamsters quiet?	E	No, he isn't.

💡 It's not polite to answer only *Yes* or *No*. Use short answers:
Are you lost? – Yes, I am.
– No, I'm not.

▶ Language file 8, p. 186

> **3 b) 1** E • **2** D • **3** A • **4** C • **5** B

---

4 Scout's questions

> **4 a)** Lösung S. 289

🖊 **a)** Scout has some questions for you. Write the questions in the correct order.

1 you / good with animals / are / ?

2 your favourite animal / friendly / is / ?

3 in your house / loud / it / is / ?

4 your favourite animals / are / monkeys / ?

5 are / scared of snakes / you / ?

6 you and your family / cat ⁺fans / are / ?

💬👥 **b)** Ask your partner the questions in a). Answer your partner's questions with short answers.

> **4 b)** Lösung S. 289

Are you good with animals?

Yes, I am. / No, I'm not. What about you?

▶ More practice 2, p. 75

▶ Workbook, p. 28

fifty-one **51**

Ex 3 Einstieg:
• (SB auf) Falls neue Stunde: Text von S. 50 mit verteilten Rollen lesen/spielen.

Erarbeitung:

a) S suchen die Fragen im Text auf S. 50 und schreiben sie ins Heft.
• **Ausw.:** L sammelt Ergebnisse (TA) und unterstreicht jeweils Verb und Subjekt in verschiedenen Farben.
• S beschreiben den Unterschied zwischen Aussage und Frage. TA: Regel notieren.

b) ▶ Think-Pair-Share. S notieren die Lösung im Heft.
• **Ausw.:** ▶ Five-minute teacher
• S beschreiben, wie man Kurzantworten bildet.
• s. a. ▶ LF 8, S. 186, Erklärfilm (UMA/App)
• 🔲 Wdh. der Personalpronomen: ▶ LF 4, S. 184
• TA: Regel zu den Kurzantworten notieren.
• S übertragen die Regeln in den Merkteil (▶ English folder).

Ex 4 Einstieg:
• (SB zu) ▶ Swap cards: L verteilt dazu Karten mit Fragen wie in Ex 3b).
• Regel zu den Fragen und Kurzantworten wiederholen.

Erarbeitung:

a) (SB auf) gemäß AA
• **Ausw.:** ▶ Five-minute teacher
• ▶ Early finisher: Gedichte auf S. 70 lesen

b) S üben die Fragen und Antworten im ▶ Double circle.
• **Ausw.:** ▶ Meldekette mit Fragen und Antworten

Topic 1 Inhalt

Lernschwerpunkt: über Haustiere sprechen, Haustiere beschreiben und Informationen erfragen
Kompetenzen: Listening einen Dialog über Haustiere hören und Fragen dazu beantworten • Reading Tierbeschreibungen Informationen entnehmen und sich damit für das richtige Haustier für Lily entscheiden • Speaking in einer *Info-gap activity* eine Vermisstenanzeige vervollständigen • in PA Fragen zu einem Haustier stellen und beantworten • Writing sich Notizen zu einem Haustier machen
Redemittel: Wortfeld *pets* • Adjektive zum Beschreiben von Tieren

---

Ex 5 Einstieg:
• (SB zu) Zur Wiederholung der Tierwörter zeigt L Bilder von Tieren bzw. ▶ Flashcards.
  L: *Do you know which animal this is?*
• S antworten. L schreibt die Wörter nochmal an die Tafel.

Erarbeitung:
a) (SB auf) gemäß AA, im Plenum

b) 1. **Hören** gemäß AA
• **Ausw.:** im Plenum

c) S schreiben die Fragen ab und notieren die Antworten beim 2. **Hören.**
• ▣ ▶ Parallel ex, S. 75: S ordnen die richtigen Kurzantworten zu.
• **Ausw.:** ▶ Meldekette

Ex 6 Einstieg:
• (SB zu) Handpuppe Scout: *Help! My friend is missing! Can you help me find him?*
  S: *Yes!*
  Scout: *Thank you! I have a poster but some words are missing.*

Erarbeitung:
a) (SB auf) L erläutert AA
• S schreiben den Plakattext in ihr Heft ab (Plakat für *Partner B* s. S. 74).
• ▣ Langsamere S erhalten ▶ KV 2.2.
• ▶ Info-gap activity gemäß AA
• **Ausw.:** ▶ Five-minute teacher

b) S lesen sich das vervollständigte Poster still durch und beantworten die Frage in PA.
• **Ausw.:** im Plenum
  Scout: *Thank you for your help! Now we can find him!*

---

2 | **Topic 1** | Topic 2 | Topic 3 | Story | Viewing | Study skills | Unit task

👂 **5** LISTENING **Is that your pet?**

💬 🖻 a) BEFORE YOU LISTEN **What animals can you see?**

5 a) I can see ... **A** a dog • **B** a dog • **C** three hamsters • **D** two fish • **E** (no pets)

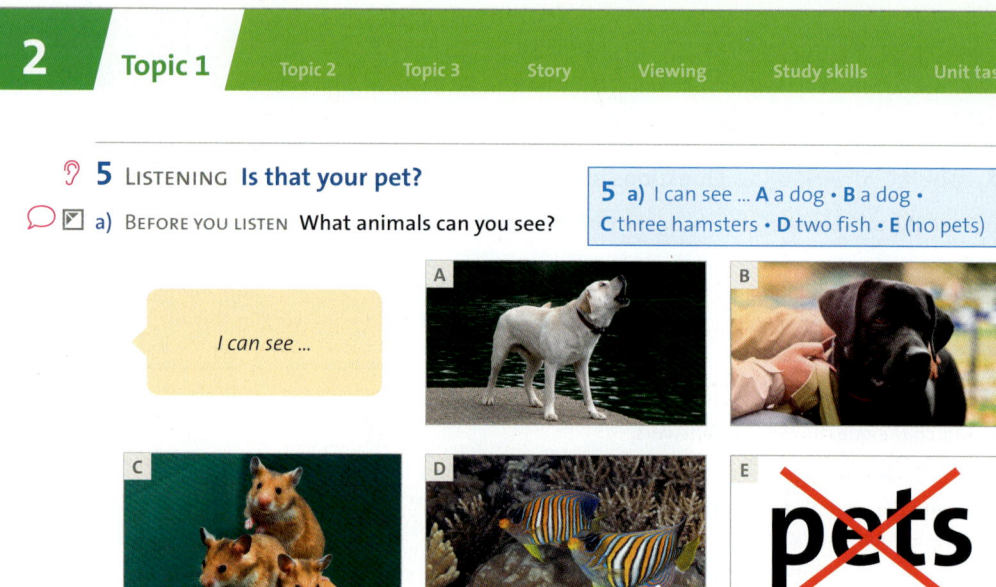

I can see ...

🔊 b) Listen to the conversation about pets. Which picture (A–E) is correct for:
1.34

1 Noah **B**   2 Zane **E**   3 Zane's aunt **A**   4 Lily? **D**

🔊 c) Listen again and write the answers.

1 Are you OK, Sunita? – *No, I'm not.*
2 Is it hard to do your homework? – ...
3 Is your dog Buddy loud? – ...
4 Are you too busy for pets? – ...
5 Are they your pets? – ...

5 c)
1 No, I'm not.
2 Yes, it is.
3 No, he isn't.
4 Yes, I am.
5 No, they aren't.

▶ Parallel exercise, p. 75

▶ Box: Voc., p. 229

💬 👥 **6** SPEAKING **A missing pet**

a) Noah and Zane see some *Missing Pet* posters, but they have °rain on them.

Partner B: Look at p. 74.
Partner A: Copy the poster.
Read the first three sentences to partner B.
Your partner completes the missing words in his/her poster.
Then listen to your partner and complete your missing words.

b) Read the completed poster.
Which pet is missing? Tell your partner.

I think the missing pet is ...

6 b) George! (Sunita's parrot)

MISSING

Our friendly parrot is missing. He's blue and orange and he's ten years old. He likes talking and flying, and he's very nice. But we think he ▯ happy because we have a lot of ▯ in our ▯ . It's very ▯ .

call 07700 900426 if you find him.

6 a) isn't • animals • home • loud • Please

Vorbereitung

Material: Ex 5 UMA/CD, von L recherchierte Bilder/Bildkarten mit Haustieren • Ex 6 Handpuppe Scout, ▸ KV 2.2: A missing pet (je nach Bedarf) • Ex 7 UMA, vergrößerte Tierfotos von S. 53 • Ex 8 ggf. Handpuppe Scout
Zeitbedarf: ca. 2–3 Std.
Minimalversion: Ex 6 auslassen, Ex 7d) für *Early finishers* oder ganz überspringen
Begleitmedien: WB (S. 29), App (Digital help, Digital quiz), INKL (S. 52–53), DIFF (2.2, 2.3)

2

📖 7 READING *FindAPet*

Lily wants a new pet.

a) BEFORE YOU READ **Look at the photos of the three pets. Guess what they're like. Use the words in the box.**

> active • big • cute • fast • friendly • hungry • interesting • loud • mean • old • quiet • slow • small • special

I think Rex is … He isn't …

b) Now read the °profiles from *FindAPet* and match the words from a) to the three pets.
Rex: big, …
Axel: …
Maude: …

c) Read about Lily's dream pet. Which pet from *FindAPet* is right for Lily?

I think … is right for Lily (because …)

My dream pet is different and interesting. It isn't too big or loud and it's nice.

d) Which of the three pets is your favourite and why?

My favourite pet is … because he's/she's … and he/she isn't …

7 a) individuelle Lösungen

Rex is big, but he isn't mean. He's a very friendly and active dog. But he's always hungry and he's very loud!

Axel is a special pet – he's a small, green lizard. He's very quiet, but he's interesting. And he isn't slow!

Maude is quite old, but still very fast. She's cute, but be careful – she isn't friendly!

7 b) Rex big, friendly, active, hungry, loud, not mean
Axel special, small, quiet, interesting, not slow
Maude old, fast, cute, not friendly

7 c) I think Axel is right for Lily because he's different, interesting, nice, and not too big.

7 d) individuelle Lösungen

My task

8 My pet or dream pet

8 individuelle Lösungen

 a) Make notes about your pet or dream pet: animal, colour, °size, other things.
▸ Digital help   ▸ More help, p. 76   ▸ Wordbank 8, p. 200

 b) °Interview your partner about his/her pet or dream pet.

I have a … / My dream pet is a …   *Is it cute / active / …?*   *Yes, it is. / No, it isn't.*

▸ Workbook, p. 29

Digital quiz   **I can talk about pets.** ✓

Ex 7 Einstieg:
• (SB zu) ▸ Semantisierung der Adjektive aus dem Reservoir
• ▸ Vokabelarbeit

Erarbeitung:
a) (SB auf) ▸ Klären der AA
• L zeigt die vergrößerten Tierfotos ohne Texte (UMA).
• S bilden Sätze.
• **Ausw.:** im Plenum

b) S bearbeiten die Aufgabe im Heft, stilles Lesen.
• **Ausw.:** ▸ Five-minute teacher

c) gemäß AA
• **Ausw.:** im Plenum

d) ▸ Appointments
• TA: L zeichnet Tabelle mit ▸ Scaffolding aus d) in drei Zeilen, mit Spalten für drei S.
• S nennen Mit-S ihr Lieblingstier und notieren Antworten der Mit-S in der Tabelle.
• **Ausw.:** S stellen Antworten ihrer Mit-S im Plenum vor.

My task Ex 8 Einstieg:
• (SB zu) Handpuppe Scout oder L erzählt bildgestützt von ihrem Wunschhaustier.

Erarbeitung:
a) (SB auf) S sammeln Adjektive und machen sich Notizen gemäß AA.
• ▸ More help, S. 76
• **Ausw.:** L sammelt Ideen als TA, S ergänzen.

b) L zeigt mit lernstärkeren S zwei oder drei Modelldialoge.
• TA: ▸ Scaffolding aus b)
• S üben die Dialoge im ▸ Milling around.
• **Ausw.:** im Plenum

Topic 2 Inhalt

Lernschwerpunkt: Beschreibungen von unterschiedlichen Wohnsituationen
Kompetenzen: Listening ein Gespräch über Wohnsituationen verstehen und Bilder den Aussagen zuordnen •
Speaking Bilder von Wohnsituationen beschreiben • Reading die Beschreibung eines Hauses lesen und das Haus zeichnen •
Viewing einer Videotour durch Sunitas Haus Informationen zu Personen, Räumen und Einrichtung entnehmen •
Writing eine kurze Nachricht über das eigene Zuhause verfassen
Strukturen: *There's / There are*
Redemittel: Wortfelder *rooms and things in a house, different homes*

Ex 1 Einstieg:
- (SB zu) ► Semantisierung:
  L zeigt die Fotos von S. 54
  (UMA) und stellt Fragen: *Who
  lives in a flat? / Who has a
  balcony? / …*
- ► Vokabelarbeit

Erarbeitung:
a) (SB auf) S beschreiben die
Bilder im ► Partner talk.
- **Ausw.:** im Plenum

b) S übertragen die Namen der
vier Kinder ins Heft.
- **1. Hören:** S notieren die
Lösungsbuchstaben.

c) **2. Hören:** S prüfen.
- **Ausw.:** ► Five-minute teacher

Ex 2 Einstieg:
- (SB zu) L gibt Beispiele (mit
TA): *In my garden, there are
many trees. But there's only
one apple tree.*
- S beschreiben die Regel zu
There's / There are (► LF 9, S. 186)
und übertragen sie in den
Merkteil (► English folder).

Erarbeitung:
- (SB auf) gemäß AA
- **Ausw.:** ► Meldekette

Ex 3 Einstieg:
- (SB zu) L sagt Sätze mit
There's / There are über das
Klassenzimmer. S stehen auf,
wenn der Satz falsch ist.

Erarbeitung:
a) (SB auf) gemäß AA
- **Ausw.:** ► Five-minute teacher

b) gemäß AA
- ► Early finisher: ► Challenge 1,
  S. 77
- **Ausw.:** S zeigen ihre Bilder,
  Vergleich mit Foto auf S. 74.

54

Different homes

◎ 1 LISTENING Four homes

1 a) Lösungsbsp. S. 289

○ a) BEFORE YOU LISTEN Talk about the homes in the photos.

*The home in photo A / B / …
is a house / flat.*

*The flat is on the ground /
top floor.*

It's old / new / big / small.

*It has a garden / a balcony /
a garage.* ► Box: Voc., p. 230

◁)) 1.35 ◁) b) Listen. What's the
correct photo for Zane,
Sunita, Lily and Noah?

◁) c) Listen again and check.

1 b), c) Zane **B** • Sunita **A** • Lily **C** • Noah **D**

✎ 2 About the homes

Complete the sentences about the four homes. Put the things and people in the correct list.

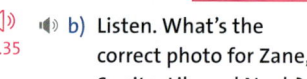

There's …	There are …
a balcony	friendly neighbours
a garage	a lot of flats
a nice garden	some trees

a balcony • friendly neighbours • a garage •
a lot of flats • a nice garden • some trees

► Language file 9, p. 186

🔖 3 A special house

a) Zane's friend has a special house. Choose the correct words for Zane's sentences.

1 There's / There are eleven floors. The building is white and red.
2 There's / There are one room on each floor.
3 There's / There are eleven rooms. The top two floors are red.
4 On the top floors there's / there are big balconies.
5 There's / There are a red lamp at the top of the building.
6 There's / There are no garden.

3 a)
1 There are
2 There's
3 There are
4 there are
5 There's
6 There's

👥 b) Draw the house with a partner. Then °compare with the photo on p. 74.

► More practice 3, p. 76 ► Challenge 1, p. 77

3 b) individuelle Lösungen

Topic 2 **Vorbereitung**

Material: Ex 1 UMA/CD, vergrößerte Bilder von S. 54 • Ex 4 + 5 UMA/DVD
Zeitbedarf: ca. 2–3 Std.
Minimalversion: Ex 3 bei sicherem Umgang mit *There's / There are* auslassen
Begleitmedien: WB (S. 30), App (Digital help, Digital quiz), INKI (S. 54–55), DIFF (2.4)

2

4 VIEWING **A tour of Sunita's home**

4 a) Lösungsbsp. S. 289

a) BEFORE YOU WATCH **What can you remember about Sunita's family, pet and home?
In your group, °collect °information and make notes. Then compare with another group.**

Meera is Sunita's mum. – Yes, and Meera's partner is …

b) **Watch the tour of Sunita's house. Write the people and animals that Sunita talks about.**

4 b) Ben • a cat • mum • George (the parrot) • Nish (big brother)

5 WORDS **Rooms**

a) **Look at the picture of Sunita's house.
Write the rooms:**

5 a) Lösung S. 289

1 Meera's bedroom   2 …

bathroom • dining room • hall • kitchen •
living room • Meera's bedroom •
Nish's bedroom • Sunita's bedroom

b) **Watch again and check your answers in a).**

c) **Watch the +video again. Write what's in these rooms: hall, kitchen, living room, Meera's bedroom.**

hall: shoes and …

5 c) Lösungsbsp. S. 289

My task

6 **My home**

a) **Read Lily's online chat message to a new friend. Say what's in her message:**

a the rooms in her home
b her family
c how big her home is
d how old her home is
e what floor her home is on
f other places (garden or balcony)

6 a) a • b • c • f

*I live with my mum and dad.
We live in a flat in Brighton.
It's a small flat and it's very nice.
There's a kitchen, a bathroom
and three other rooms: a living
room and two bedrooms.
There's a big balcony too.
Tell me about your home!*

b) **Write about your home or dream home for a new friend.
Change the words in blue. You can add other things.**

▶ Digital help   ▶ More help, p. 77
▶ Workbook, p. 30

6 b) individuelle Lösungen

 Digital quiz   **I can** describe my home or dream home. ✓

Ex 4 Einstieg:
• (SB zu) TA: Vorlage für eine
  ▶ Mindmap mit drei Kategorien
  (family, pet, home), Mitte:
  Sunita.

Erarbeitung:
a) (SB auf) ▶ Klären der AA
• S brainstormen in Dreier-/
  Vierergruppen und nutzen die
  Mindmap für Notizen.
• Je zwei Gruppen vergleichen
  ihre Lösungen.
• **Ausw.:** im Plenum

b) gemäß AA
• **Ausw.:** im Plenum

Ex 5 Einstieg:
• (SB zu) Wdh. von GSE:
  L: *What rooms are there in
  your house or flat?*
  S: *There's / There are …*
• TA an ▶ Vokabeltafel.

Erarbeitung:
a) (SB auf) gemäß AA

b) S prüfen ihre Lösungen.
• **Ausw.:** ▶ Five-minute teacher

c) gemäß AA, TA: Räume aus AA
• **Ausw.:** ▶ Meldekette, L sammelt
  Wörter an der Tafel.

My task Ex 6 Einstieg:
• TA von Gegensatzpaaren, z. B.:
  flat/house, small/big …
• S laufen zu dem zu ihrer Wohn-
  situation passenden Wort und
  bilden damit einen Satz.

Erarbeitung:
a) gemäß AA in PA
• **Ausw.:** Vergleich im Plenum

b) gemäß AA, S nutzen a) als
  Struktur.
• ▶ More help, S. 77
• **Ausw.:** im Plenum vorlesen.

55

2

Topic 3 | **Inhalt**

Lernschwerpunkt: ein Zimmer beschreiben
Kompetenzen: Speaking Sunitas Zimmer beschreiben • Lautschulung *things in a room* • Reading eine bildgestützte Zimmerbeschreibung verstehen
Redemittel: Wortfeld *things in a room* • Präpositionen zur Beschreibung des Ortes

---

Ex 1 Einstieg:
- (SB zu) ▶ Milling around: L teilt vergrößerte Wort- und Bildkarten der ▶ KV 2.3 aus.
- S suchen Partner/in.
- Wort-Bild-Paare an die Tafel heften, ▶ Vokabelarbeit und chorisches Sprechen
- ☒ In schwächeren Klassen den Wortschatz mit der ▶ KV 2.3 aktivieren

Erarbeitung:
a) (SB auf) gemäß AA
- **Ausw.:** im Plenum

b) S schreiben Lösungen ins Heft.
- **Ausw.:** ▶ Five-minute teacher

Ex 2 Einstieg:
- (SB zu) ▶ Milling around: L verteilt nur die Bilder der ▶ KV 2.3.
- S fragen: *Do you have a ...?* und suchen Partner/in mit demselben Bild.
- ▶ Early finisher: S erzählen sich, was sie in ihrem Zimmer haben.

Erarbeitung:
a) gemäß AA

b) L: *Which words did you hear?*
- TA: Wortschatz aus a)
- (SB auf) S übertragen die ▶ Mindmaps in ihr Heft und ergänzen Beispiele.
- **Ausw.:** ▶ Appointments: Austausch mit jeweils drei S
- L gibt für jedes *Appointment* eine Mindmap vor, über die sich die S austauschen.
- S stellen Partner/in ihre Mindmap vor. Partner/in ergänzt ggf. Ideen in der eigenen Mindmap.

56

| 2 | Topic 1 | Topic 2 | **Topic 3** | Story | Viewing | Study skills | Unit task |

In my room

💬 **1** SPEAKING **Sunita's room**

👥 **a)** Look at the picture. What can you see? Tell your partner. | **1 a)** Lösungsbsp. S. 289 |

> *I can see ...*

> *There's a ...*
> *There are two / three / some ...*

b) Right or wrong? **Correct** the wrong sentences. | **1 b)** Lösung S. 289 |

1 There are three red cushions on the bed.
2 There's a bag under the bed.
3 There's a big table with a yellow lamp.
4 There's a chair in front of the desk.
5 There are a computer and a book on the desk.
6 The computer is behind a robot.
7 There are a lot of books on the shelves.
8 There's a mirror next to the desk.

🔊💬 **2** WORDS **Things in my room** | **2 a)** bed • chair • clothes • computer • cushion • desk • lamp • mirror • shelves • shoes • sofa • table • wardrobe |

1.36
🔊☒ **a)** Listen and repeat the words.

✏️ **b)** Make mind maps for things in a room. | **2 b)** Lösungsbsp. S. 289 | ▶ Skills file 2, p. 174

```
  ...        ...      ...          ...        ...           ...

     things in and         things on, under        things on and
    on my wardrobe          and next to my bed      next to my desk

  ...        ...      ...          ...        ...           ...
```

▶ Workbook, p. 31

56 fifty-six

Topic 3 Vorbereitung

Material: Ex 1 vergrößerte Wort- und Bildkarten der ▶ KV 2.3: Things in a room, ggf. Magnete, ▶ KV 2.3 (Klassensatz) •
Ex 2 UMA/CD, vergrößerte Bildkarten der ▶ KV 2.3 • Ex 3 von L vorbereitete A4-Blätter mit der Aufschrift *very messy /
quite messy / …*
Zeitbedarf: ca. 2 Std.
Minimalversion: Ex 2 und Ex 3c) auslassen
Begleitmedien: WB (S. 31), INKL (S. 56–57)

2

3 Where is it?

a) Look at the picture of Sunita's room and answer the questions.

1 What's different to the room on p. 56? *The room in this picture is …*
2 Who is in the room? *I can see …*

> **3 a) 1** messy • **2** George (the parrot) and Scout (the seagull)

Scout

George

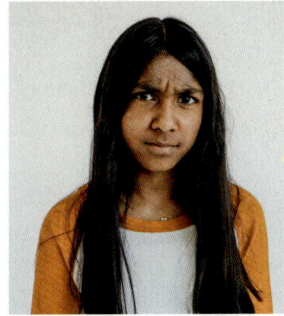

> Oh no! Look at my room! It's so messy!
> Who is in here? George, I can see you.
> And who is that under the bed? Is it Scout the seagull?
> Where's my lamp? Where are the cushions?
> What's on the floor?
> And where's Robbie the robot?
> Are you OK, Robbie?
> My chocolate isn't on my desk. I know where that is!
> Chocolate is Nish's favourite thing!
> Hey Nish, where's my chocolate?

b) Read what Sunita says. Look at her room and answer the questions.

1 Who is behind the door? – … is behind the door.
2 Who is under the bed? – … is under the bed.
3 Where's the lamp? – The lamp is …
4 Where are the cushions? – The cushions are …
5 What's on the floor next to the lamp? – … is on the floor next to the lamp.
6 Who is Robbie? – Robbie is Sunita's …
7 What's in Nish's room? – Sunita's … is in Nish's room.

> **3 b) 1** George (the parrot) • **2** Scout (the seagull) • **3, 4** on the floor / next to the bed • **5** a book • **6** robot • **7** chocolate

c) OPINION LINE Is your room messy or tidy? Stand in a line. Then °count the students.

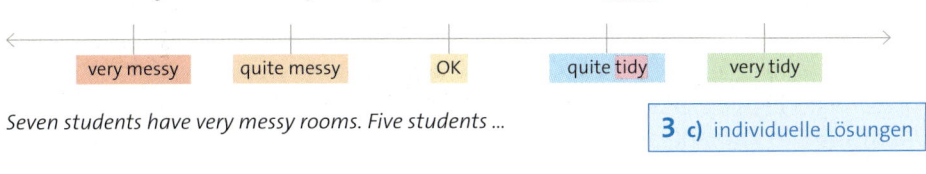

| very messy | quite messy | OK | quite tidy | very tidy |

Seven students have very messy rooms. Five students …

> **3 c)** individuelle Lösungen

Ex 3 Einstieg:

• (SB zu) ▶ Five-finger brainstorming: L: *Name five things Sunita has in her room.*

Erarbeitung:

a) (SB auf) gemäß AA
• **Ausw.:** S beantworten die Fragen im Plenum.

b) L: *Look at Sunita. Is she OK?* S: *No, she's angry.*
• **1. Lesen:** L liest laut vor. S zeigen auf die Dinge, die im Text erwähnt werden.
• **2. Lesen** in Stillarbeit
• S beantworten die Fragen im Heft.
• ▶ Partner check
• **Ausw.:** TA der Antworten
• Präpositionen unterstreichen.
• Bedeutungen der Präpositionen auf E und D an ▶ Vokabeltafel schreiben (▶ Vokabelarbeit).

c) gemäß AA
• **Alternative:** L legt Blätter mit den entsprechenden Wörtern auf den Fußboden und S ordnen sich zu. Anschließend wird die jeweilige S-Anzahl erfasst.

Topic 3 | Inhalt

Lernschwerpunkt: sagen/fragen, wo sich Dinge befinden und wie ein Zimmer aussieht
Kompetenzen: Speaking sagen/fragen, wo sich etwas befindet • Fragen mit *who, where, what* stellen und beantworten • das eigene Zimmer beschreiben • Study skills Notizen machen
Redemittel: Präpositionen zur Beschreibung des Ortes • Fragewörter *who, where, what* • Wortfeld *things in a room*

Ex 4 Einstieg:
- (SB zu) L setzt Scout (oder Stofftier) an verschiedene Orte. L: *Where is Scout?*
- ▣ Hilfe: TA Präpositionen

Erarbeitung:
a) (SB auf) gemäß AA
- **Ausw.:** ▶ Five-minute teacher

b) gemäß AA
- **Ausw.:** Einige S zeigen ihre Bilder im Plenum. Die Klasse sagt, wo Scout ist.
- **Zusatz:** L sammelt die Bilder ein und nutzt sie in den folgenden Stunden als ▶ Swap cards.

Ex 5 Einstieg:
- (SB auf) L: *What can you see in the picture?*

Erarbeitung:
a) gemäß AA, ▶ Partner talk
- **Ausw.:** im Plenum

b) gemäß AA
- **Ausw.:** im Plenum
- TA: Fragewörter auf E und D an ▶ Vokabeltafel

Ex 6 Einstieg:
- (SB zu) ▶ Five-finger brainstorming: S überlegen sich pro Finger eine Frage mit *who, where, what.*
- ▶ Milling around: S stellen sich die Fragen gegenseitig.

Erarbeitung:
a) (SB auf) gemäß AA. S notieren die Lösungen im Heft.
- **Ausw.:** ▶ Meldekette

b) gemäß AA, ▶ Partner talk
- S notieren die Antworten.
- **Ausw.:** Fragen und Antworten im Plenum vortragen.

---

2 | Topic 1 | Topic 2 | **Topic 3** | Story | Viewing | Study skills | Unit task

💬👥 **4 Where's Scout?**

a) Choose a picture. Tell your partner where Scout is. Use the words in the box. Your partner says the picture. Take turns.

Partner A: *Scout is ...*
Partner B: *That's picture 1/2/...*

behind • in • in front of • next to • on • under

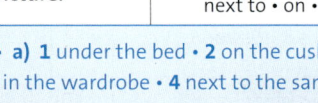
4 a) 1 under the bed • **2** on the cushion • **3** in the wardrobe • **4** next to the sandwich • **5** behind the lamp • **6** in front of the computer

b) Draw another picture with Scout.
WALK AROUND Show your picture to different partners. Your partner says where Scout is. You say where Scout is on your partner's picture.

4 b) individuelle Lösungen

▶ More practice 4, p. 78

📖 **5 Question words**

5 a) 1 George is a parrot. • **2** George is on a chair. • **3** George's favourite food is an apple.

a) Look at the picture and answer the questions.

WHO is George?
WHERE is George?
WHAT is George's favourite food?

b) What are the three question words in German?

5 b) 1 wer? • **2** wo? • **3** was?

📖 **6 Questions for you**

1 Who / Where is your home?
2 What / Who is your favourite person in your family?
3 Who / What is your favourite room in your home?
4 Where / Who is your room in your home?
5 Who / What is your favourite thing in your room?
6 Where / Who are your neighbours?

a) Your teacher has a °questionnaire for you. Choose the correct question word.

💬👥 b) Ask and answer the questions with a partner.

6 a) 1 where • **2** who • **3** what • **4** where • **5** what • **6** who

6 b) individuelle Lösungen

▶ Workbook, p. 32

Topic 3   Vorbereitung

Material: Ex 4 Handpuppe Scout oder ein Stofftier, A4/A5-Blätter zum Zeichnen • Ex 8 ggf. Handpuppe Scout,
▶ KV 2.4: My room (Klassensatz)

Zeitbedarf: ca. 2 Std.

Minimalversion: Ex 4b) überspringen, Ex 5 bei sicherem Umgang mit den Fragewörtern auslassen, Ex 8 Einsatz von
▶ KV 2.4 spart viel Zeit

Begleitmedien: WB (S. 32–33), App (Digital help, Digital quiz), INKL (S. 58–59), DIFF (2.5, 2.6)

📖 7 Where are my things?

| 7 a) 1 where • 2 who • 3 who • 4 where • 5 what • 6 where |

a) Sunita can't find her things. Complete Sunita's questions with the correct question word.

1 … are my sandwiches?
2 … has my blazer?
3 … has my 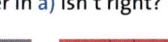sweets?
4 … is my black shoe?
5 … animals are in the house today?
6 … is the snake?

Nish: Ask George. He's a sandwich fan.
Mum: Not me! Maybe it's in the hall.
Nish: Not me! I like chocolate.
Nish: Maybe with the other black shoe!
Mum: A dog, a cat and a snake.
Mum: It's in its terrarium[1].   ▶ Box: Voc., p. 232

b) Look at the pictures. Which answer in a) isn't right?

| 7 b) Answer 6 isn't right. |

▶ More practice 5, p. 78   ▶ Challenge 2, p. 78

My task

💬👥 8 My room

| 8 individuelle Lösungen |

a) SPEAKING Ask your partner questions about his/her room. Make notes.

▶ Digital help 👆   ▶ More help, p. 79   ▶ Wordbank 9, p. 200

Is it your own room?
Or is it your sister's / brother's room too?
Is your room big or small?
Where's your room?
What's in your room?
Are there pets in your room?
What colour are the walls?
What's on the walls?
Is it loud or quiet in your room?

b) Use your notes. Draw your partner's room.

c) Swap pictures with your partner.
Is the picture of your room correct?

▶ Workbook, p. 33

Digital quiz 👆   I can describe my room. ✓   1 [teˈrearɪəm]

Ex 7 Einstieg:
• (SB zu) TA: *who, where, what.*
L: *What do these words mean in German?* (S antworten.)
L: *Who can make a question with one of these words?* (L sammelt Fragen an der Tafel.)

Erarbeitung:

a) (SB auf) gemäß AA, in EA
• S notieren die kompletten Fragen im Heft.
• ▶ Early finisher: S schreiben zwei bis drei Sätze über die Bilder in **b)**.
• ☒ ▶ Early finisher:
▶ Challenge 2, S. 78
• **Ausw.:** ▶ Five-minute teacher

b) gemäß AA
• **Ausw.:** im Plenum

My task Ex 8 Einstieg:
• (SB zu) L oder Handpuppe Scout: *Some people have cool rooms. What about your rooms?*
• L/Scout stellt die Fragen aus a) im Plenum. S antworten. L/Scout: *That sounds cool. I want to see your rooms!*

Erarbeitung:

a) (SB auf) gemäß AA, in PA
• 🔲 Hilfe: ▶ Wordbank 9, S. 200 und ▶ More help, S. 79

b) gemäß AA, in EA
• **Alternative:** ▶ KV 2.4: S schneiden die Gegenstände aus und ordnen sie im skizzierten Raum richtig an.

c) S zeigen sich in PA ihre Bilder und besprechen, ob alles richtig gezeichnet wurde.
• **Ausw.:** ▶ Gallery walk

Story **Inhalt**

Lernschwerpunkt: eine Geschichte über einen Konflikt in der Familie lesen
Kompetenzen: Listening ein Lied über Bens Wohnung verstehen • Speaking Gefühle beschreiben • Reading eine Geschichte über einen Konflikt zu Hause verstehen
Redemittel: Wortfeld *feelings* • Sätze/Ausdrücke, um über Probleme zu sprechen

Ex 1 Einstieg:
- (SB auf, S. 48) als Wdh:
  L: *Who is Ben? Who is Willow? Describe the photo.*

Erarbeitung:
a) (SB auf, S. 60) **1. Hören:**
S ordnen die Zeilen und notieren die Reihenfolge in ihr Heft (gemäß AA).
- ⊠ Lernschwächere S nutzen die ▶ KV 2.5 (Ex a–d).

b) 2. Hören: S prüfen.
- **Ausw.:** S vergleichen mit S. 74.

c) S ergänzen den Satz im Heft.
- **Ausw.:** im Plenum
- ▶ Early finisher: S bearbeiten in PA ▶ KV 2.5 (Ex e).

Ex 2 Einstieg:
- (SB zu) ▶ Five-finger brainstorming: *feelings* (mit TA)
  L: *How do you feel at home? Do you sometimes feel angry or sad? Why?/When?*
- S antworten im Plenum.

Erarbeitung:
a) L zeigt vergrößerte Bilder von S. 60–61 (UMA). S beschreiben die Gefühle gemäß AA.
- ⊠ ▶ More help, S. 79 für lernschwächere S

b) (SB auf) **1. Lesen, Teil 1:** Text absatzweise erarbeiten.
  L: *Read the chat. What's Sunita's problem? What does Lily tell her to do?*
- S beantworten die Fragen (globales Verstehen).
- ▶ Vokabelarbeit mit unbekannten Wörtern aus diesem Teil.

- **Zusatz:** S hören den Text absatzweise und lesen mit (▶ Mitleseverfahren).

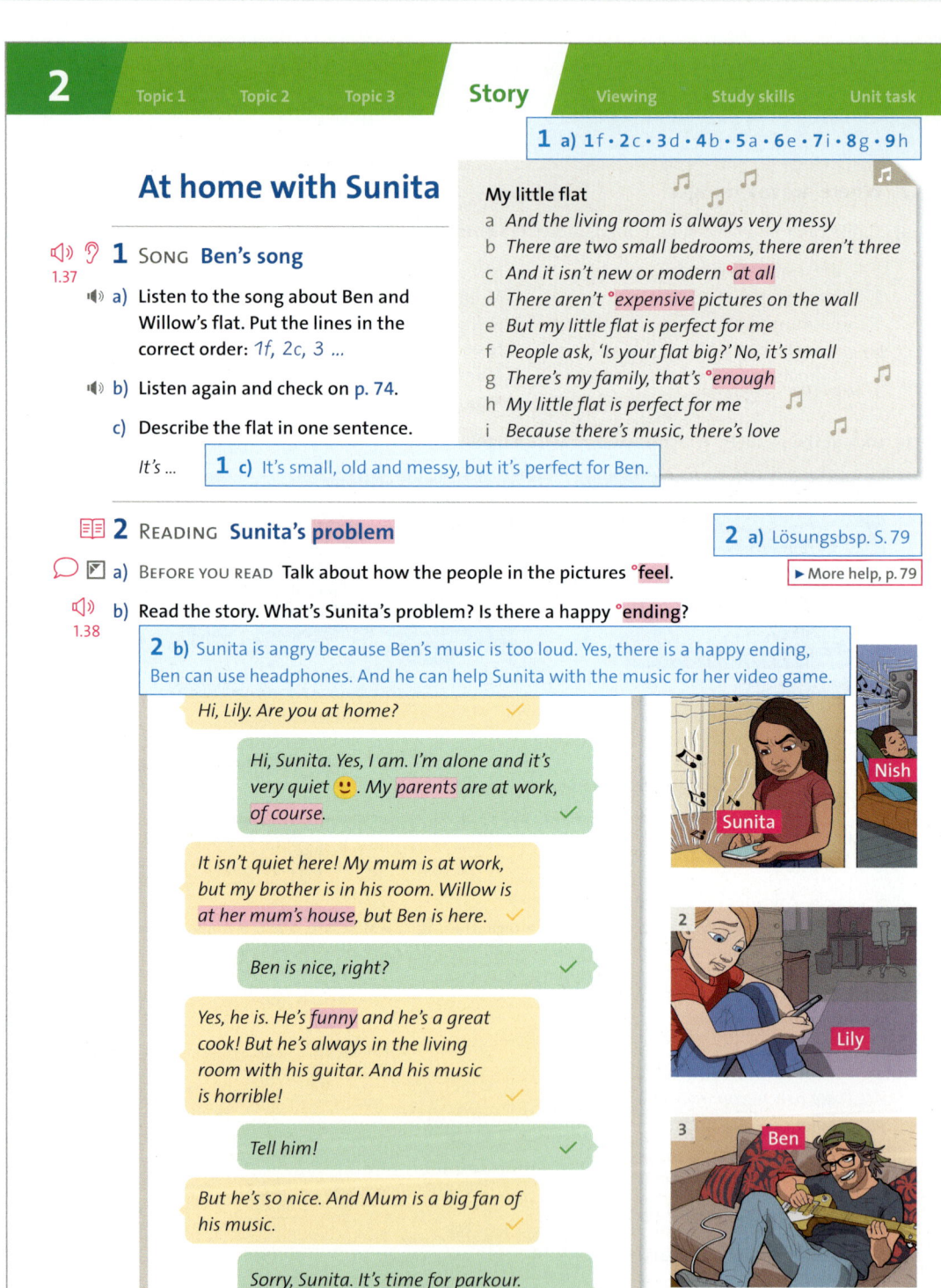

Story Vorbereitung

Material: Ex 1 UMA/CD, ▸ KV 2.5: Ben's song (je nach Bedarf) • Ex 2 UMA, vergrößerte Bilder von S. 60–61, UMA/CD
Zeitbedarf: ca. 1–2 Std.
Minimalversion: Ex 1 auslassen
Begleitmedien: INKL (S. 60–61)

1.39

Later in the dining room ...
Sunita Thanks for dinner, Ben. You're a really good cook!
Meera Yes, thanks, love.
Ben Let me play my new song.
Nish Erm, I have a lot of homework ...
Sunita Me too.
Meera Nish, Sunita ... don't be rude. You can listen.

Later in the living room ...
Ben ♫ ♫ ♫ My little flat is perfect for me ...
Nish Erm ... look, Ben, I like you, but I don't like your music. It's really bad! You can play your music in your flat. This isn't your house!
Sunita And your music is too loud, Ben. I can't do my homework or code.
Meera Nish and Sunita, this isn't Ben's home, but he's part of our family. We can talk about problems – but be polite!
Nish Erm ... sorry, Ben.
Ben That's OK. It's an electric guitar. I can use headphones.
Sunita Thanks, Ben. ... And Nish, you can use headphones too!
Ben Sunita, I can play different music. Maybe I can help you with the music for your video game?
Sunita Erm ... OK, thanks.

1.40

Hi, Sunita. I'm home.

Hi, Lily! Are you tired?

Yes, parkour is hard! Is there still a problem with Ben's music?

No, it's OK now. And not all Ben's music is bad. Listen to this ♫ – it's for my video game.

That's great! ... Oh, Mum is back at home now – time for dinner! 🙂 See you!

Bye, Lily. See you at school!

sixty-one **61**

Einstieg Teil 2:
• (SB auf) L: *Look at the pictures. What happens at dinner?* Mögliche S-Antworten: *Sunita and Nish talk to Ben. / They are angry. / ...*
• ▸ Semantisierung und ▸ Vokabelarbeit für Wortschatz von Teil 2

Erarbeitung:
• Stilles Lesen von Teil 2
• **Ausw.:** L: *Who wants to sing a song? Who isn't polite? What can Ben do so the music isn't too loud? What can Ben do to help Sunita?*
S: *Ben wants to sing. Nish isn't polite. Ben can use head-phones. Ben can play music for Sunita's video game.*

Einstieg Teil 3:
• (SB auf) L: *Look at the pictures. How does Sunita feel?*
• ▸ Semantisierung und ▸ Vokabelarbeit für Wortschatz von Teil 3

Erarbeitung:
• S lesen den letzten Teil der Geschichte.
• **Ausw.:** L: *Does Sunita still have a problem?*
S: *No. (She is happy now.)*
• S beschreiben die Bilder auf S. 62 oben.
L: *So is there a happy ending?*
S: *Yes, there is.*
• ☒ Lernstärkere S schreiben das Ende der Geschichte, indem sie drei bis fünf Sätze über die Bilder auf S. 62 bilden.
• Mögliches ▸ Scaffolding:
... plays the guitar.
... has headphones.
... is happy.
... sings the new song too.

Story Inhalt | Vorbereitung

Lernschwerpunkt: eine Geschichte über einen Konflikt in der Familie lesen
Kompetenzen: Reading einem Text detaillierte Informationen entnehmen • Speaking / Life skills über Probleme und mögliche Lösungen sprechen (*Role-play*)
Redemittel: Sätze/Ausdrücke, um über Probleme zu sprechen

Zeitbedarf: ca. 1 Std.
Minimalversion: Ex 5 auslassen
Begleitmedien: WB (S. 34), App (Digital quiz), INKL (S. 62), DIFF (2.7)

Ex 3 Einstieg:
- (SB auf) Falls neue Stunde:
  L: *Look at the pictures again. What do you remember about the story?*
- ▶ TA mit ▶Scaffolding: *problem, music, loud, Ben, Sunita, talk to/about, help*

Erarbeitung:
a) gemäß AA
- 2. Lesen in EA. S schreiben die Lösungen ins Heft.

b) Ausw.: ▶ Partner check
- Vergleich im Plenum
- ▶ Early finisher: *What do you learn about Lily and her home in the story?* S schreiben zwei bis drei Sätze.

Ex 4 Erarbeitung:
- (SB auf) gemäß AA
- **Ausw.:** ▶ Five-minute teacher
- ☒ ▶ Three truths, two lies: S schreiben Sätze über die Geschichte, lesen sie im Plenum vor. Klasse sagt, welche Sätze wahr und welche falsch sind.

Ex 5 Einstieg:
- (SB zu) TA: Gerüst des Dialoges wie in der Aufgabe: L: *Let's make up a dialogue between Sunita (A) and Ben (B).*
- Dialog erarbeiten:
  A:... *play loud music.*
  B:... *use headphones.*
- Zwei S spielen Dialog vor.

Erarbeitung:
- (SB auf) L: *Now it's your turn. Read the problems and the ideas. Then do the role-plays.*
- S üben die Dialoge in PA (▶ Role-play).
- **Ausw.:** Präsentation im Plenum

62

| 2 | Topic 1 | Topic 2 | Topic 3 | **Story** | Viewing | Study skills | Unit task |

📖 **3** READING **The story**

a) Read the story again. Are the sentences right or wrong?

1 Sunita is on her phone with Lily. She isn't happy about the noise at home.
2 Sunita, Nish, Meera and Ben eat dinner.
3 Nish is polite about Ben's new song.
4 Meera isn't happy with Nish and Sunita.
5 Nish isn't sorry.
6 Ben has an idea about the noise.
7 Ben has an idea to help Sunita.
8 Sunita and Lily think Ben's music for the video game is really bad.

> **3 a) 1** right • **2** right (+ Willow) • **3** wrong (Nish is rude about Ben's song) • **4** right • **5** wrong (Nish is sorry) • **6** right • **7** right • **8** wrong (they think Ben's music for the video game is great)

👥 **b)** Check with a partner.

📖 **4** **Who is it?**

Write the names.

> **4 1** Lily • **2** Lily • **3** Ben • **4** Sunita • **5** Meera • **6** Ben, Nish

1 ... is alone at home.
2 ... is tired after parkour.
3 ... is nice and a great cook.
4 ... can't code because it's loud.
5 For ... it's important to be polite.
6 ... and ... can use headphones.

💬👥 **5** ROLE-PLAY & LIFE SKILLS **Talk about problems**

> **5** Lösungsbsp. S. 289

SPEAKING Do the °role-plays.
Use the ideas in the table.
Take turns to be A and B.

A I have a problem when you ...
B I'm sorry. I can ...
A That's a good idea. Thanks.
B You're welcome.

A: problem		B: idea
play loud music	→	be quiet
be in the bathroom a long time	→	be fast
make the kitchen messy	→	be tidy
put shoes on the floor in the hall	→	put my shoes away

> ▶ Workbook, p. 34

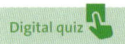 Digital quiz I can understand a problem and talk about it. ✓

62 sixty-two

Viewing | Inhalt | Vorbereitung

Lernschwerpunkt: Filmszenen über Mutproben verstehen
Kompetenzen: Viewing / Intercultural compentence
Filmszenen verstehen • Speaking Ergebnisse vergleichen •
eine Filmszene beschreiben
Redemittel: Wortschatz zum Vergleichen von Lösungen

Material: Ex 2 + 3 UMA/DVD
Zeitbedarf: ca. 1 Std.
Minimalversion: Ex 3 auslassen
Begleitmedien: INKL (S. 63)

| Topic 1 | Topic 2 | Topic 3 | Story | **Viewing** | Study skills | Unit task | 2 |

The Brighton dares: Family

Daisy   Emir

📖 1 What are the dares?

👥 BEFORE YOU WATCH **Look at the pictures and complete the sentences.**

1   hug   postbox

from   to

cards

string

> **1 1** ... to *hug* a *postbox* for *two* hours. • **2** ... to make a 3D family *tree* with *cards* and *string* in public.

1   One dare is to ... a ... for ... hours[1].
2   The other dare is to make a 3D family ... with ... and ... in public[2].

🖥 2 VIEWING **Two families**

> **2 a) 1** in front of • **2** ... to make a family tree.

a) **Watch the video from 00:00 to 01:30 and check your answers from 1.**
✉👥 **Complete the sentences. Then check with a partner.**

Daisy isn't happy about her dare because the postbox is ... Luke's house.
Mrs Arinze's homework for Daisy and Emir is ...

b) **Watch all the video. True (T) or false (F)?**   > **2 b) 1** T • **2** F (her cousin) • **3** T • **4** F (in the city) • **5** T

1   Mr Campbell and Mrs Collins have letters[3] for the postbox.
2   Mrs Collins wants to find her father.
3   Mrs Collins has tea and biscuits[4] for Daisy after her dare.
4   Emir and Gloria do his dare on the beach.
5   Mrs Collins and Robert Collins speak on the phone.

💬👥 **c)** **Compare your answers with a partner.**
Take turns. Then watch the video again and check.

> *Is sentence 1 true or false?*

> *I think it's true. / I think it's false.*

🖥 3 **Emir's family tree**

> **3** Lösungsbsp. S. 290

🖥 **Stop the video at 10:00. What do you think of Emir's tree?**

I think Emir's tree is ...

---

[1] **hour** *Stunde*   [2] **in public** *in der Öffentlichkeit*   [3] **letter** *Brief*   [4] **tea and biscuits** *Tee und Kekse*

Ex 1 Einstieg:
• (SB zu) TA: *Dare.* S erinnern sich, was *dare* heißt (vgl. S. 33).
L: *Let's take a look at different dares.*

Erarbeitung:
• (SB auf) S vervollständigen die Sätze schriftlich.
• **Ausw.:** s. Ex 2

Ex 2
a) Erarbeitung:
• (SB auf) **1. Sehen** (bis 01:30): S überprüfen ihre Lösungen aus Ex 1.
• ✉ S vervollständigen noch die zusätzlichen Sätze und vergleichen die Lösungen im ▶ Partner check.
• **Ausw.:** ▶ Five-minute teacher, L sichert die Ergebnisse im TA.

b) Gemeinsames Lesen der Sätze, ggf. Klären von Vokabeln
• **2. Sehen** (komplett): S notieren die Zahlen 1–5 und T oder F.

c) ▶ Partner check: S vergleichen ihre Ergebnisse und nutzen dabei die in den Sprechblasen vorgegebenen Sätze.
• Überprüfen beim **3. Sehen** (komplett).
• **Ausw.:** ▶ Meldekette

Ex 3 Erarbeitung:
• L stoppt das Video bei 10:00.
• S beantworten die Frage im ▶ Partner talk.
• **Ausw.:** ▶ Meldekette

Study skills Inhalt | Vorbereitung

Lernschwerpunkt: Wörter richtig buchstabieren
Kompetenzen: Listening das Alphabet kennenlernen •
Namen, Adressen und Telefonnummern verstehen •
Speaking/Writing Namen, Adressen und Telefonnummern
erfragen, buchstabieren und schreiben
Redemittel: *numbers 0–9 • the alphabet • name, address,
phone number*

Material: Ex 1 UMA/CD, Handpuppe Scout mit Formular •
Ex 2 UMA/CD • Ex 3 von L vorbereitete Karten mit Tierwör-
tern, Karteikarten oder A6-Blätter (3 pro S)
Zeitbedarf: ca. 1 Std.
Minimalversion: Ex 1b) und Ex 3 auslassen
Begleitmedien: App (Digital quiz), INKL (S. 64)

Ex 1 Einstieg:
• (SB zu) Handpuppe Scout mit
Formular: *Hello! Can you help
me? I need to spell my name.*

Erarbeitung:
a) (SB auf) **1. Hören:** S lesen leise
mit, ggf. ▶ Lautschulung.
• **2. Hören:** S singen mit.

b) S singen/lesen die Zeilen des
Liedes abwechselnd laut vor.
• ▶ Partner check
• **Ausw.:** im Teilchor

Ex 2 Einstieg:
• (SB zu) TA des leeren Formu-
lars, Klären der Kategorien.

Erarbeitung:
a) (SB auf) S schreiben das
Formular ins Heft ab.
• Lesen der ▶ Tippbox, S. 64
• **1. Hören:** S vervollständigen
das Formular im Heft.
• **2. Hören:** S prüfen.
• **Ausw.:** ▶ Meldekette, L hält
Lösungen an der Tafel fest.

b) Fragen in den Sprechblasen
und Buchstabieren der
Namen im Plenum üben,
dann Vorgehen gemäß AA.
• **Ausw.:** ▶ Partner check

Ex 3 Einstieg:
• (SB zu) L gibt S Karten mit
Tierwörtern. S buchstabieren,
die Klasse schreibt mit.

Erarbeitung:
a) (SB auf) gemäß AA, S schreiben je ein Wort auf eine leere
Karteikarte.

b) gemäß AA

• **Zusatz:** Karten aus a) in den
Folgestunden als ▶ Swap cards
nutzen

Spelling

🔊🎙 **1 SONG The alphabet**
1.41

🔊 a) Look at the alphabet song in the box
and listen. Then listen again and sing.

👥 b) Sing or say the alphabet °in pairs.

    Partner A: black °lines.
    Partner B: blue lines.

The alphabet
A B C D E
F G H I J
K L M N O
P Q R S T
U V W
X Y Z
That's the alphabet!

🎙 **2 Name, address and phone number**

🔊 🔊 a) Sunita is on the phone about a coding °course. Copy the °form.
1.42   Then listen and complete it.   ▶ Numbers: p. 277

⁺First name: *Sunita*
⁺Family name:
Address: Chandra
Phone number: 22 Palmeira Rd,
     Hove, BN3 2JN
     07700 900567

Say phone numbers in English
like this: 07700 900638

*oh–seven–seven–oh–oh
nine–oh–oh–six–three–eight*

▶ Box: Voc., p. 233

💬👥 b) **Partner A:** Copy the form in a) again. Ask partner B the yellow questions and complete the
form. Use the green questions to check.
Partner B: Answer the questions: *It's …*

     2 b) individuelle Lösungen

What's your family name?   *What's your address?*   *What's your phone number?*

Is that right?   *Can you say that again, please?*   *Can you spell that, please?*

💬👥 **3 Spell, write and say**
✏   **3 a)** Lösungsbsp. S. 290

a) Write three long words from this unit.
Don't °show your partner!   *bathroom, …*

     B-A-T-H-R-O-O-M

b) **Partner A:** Spell a word for partner B.
Partner B: Write the word.
Then say it and check
the spelling.   *B or P?*   *It's "bathroom". B-A- …*
°Take turns.

     Can you say that again, please?

         ▶ Skills file 3, p. 176

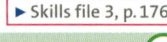

Digital quiz   **I can spell words correctly.** ✓

Unit task Inhalt | Vorbereitung

Lernschwerpunkt: das eigene Traumzimmer präsentieren
Kompetenzen: Writing ein Traumzimmer beschreiben •
Speaking eine kurze Präsentation halten • Media skills
Bilder aus dem Internet verwenden
Redemittel: Wortfelder *things in a room, colours, pets,
adjectives* • Feedback geben

Material: Step 4 von L vorbereitete Präsentation ihres
dream room, ggf. Handpuppe Scout
Zeitbedarf: ca. 1–2 Std.
Begleitmedien: App (Digital help, Digital quiz), INKL (S. 65)

| Topic 1 | Topic 2 | Topic 3 | Story | Viewing | Study skills | Unit task | **2** |

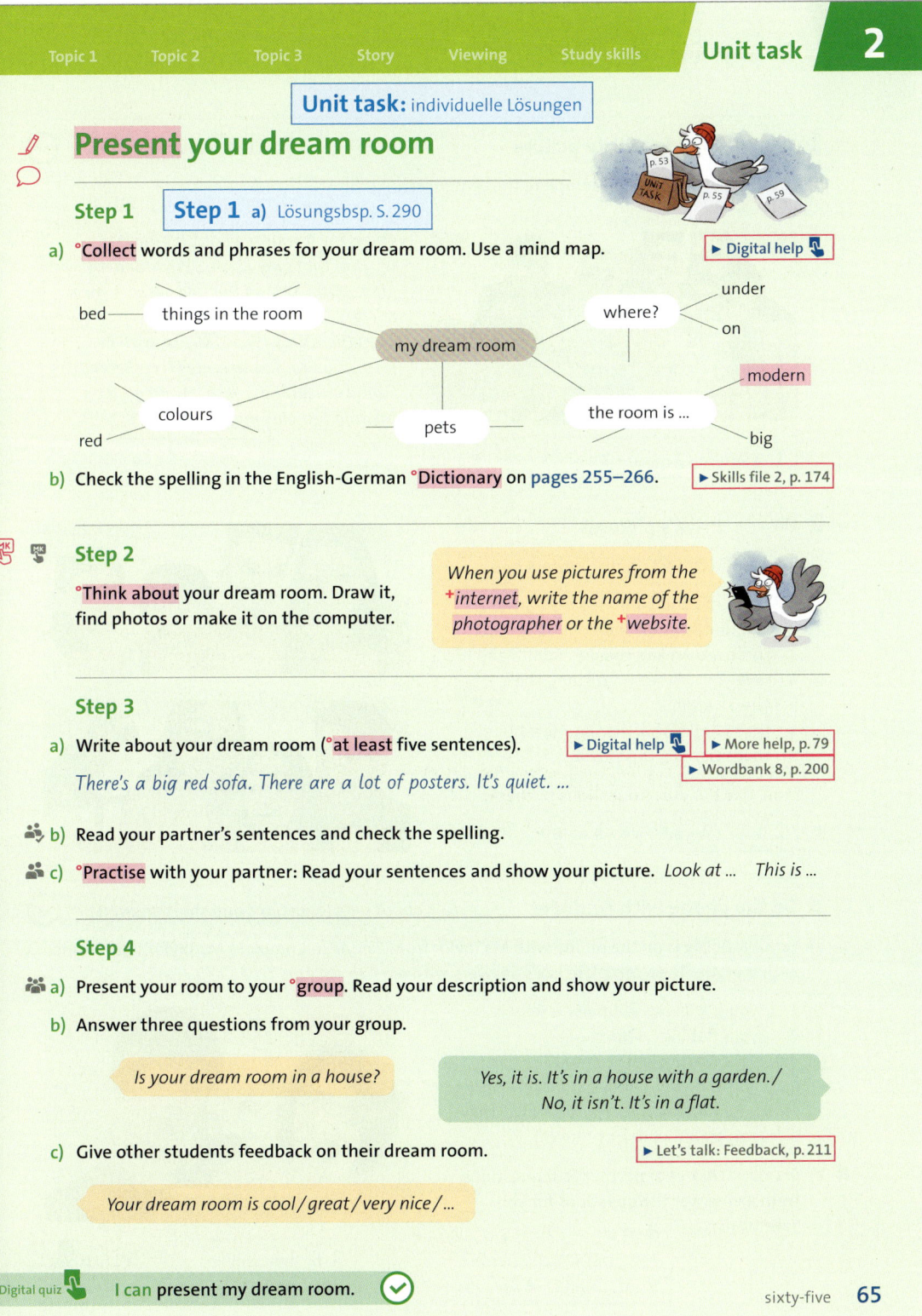

Unit task: individuelle Lösungen

✎ Present your dream room
💬

Step 1 **Step 1 a)** Lösungsbsp. S. 290

a) °Collect words and phrases for your dream room. Use a mind map. ▶ Digital help 🔖

bed — things in the room
my dream room
colours
red
pets
where?
under
on
the room is ...
modern
big

b) Check the spelling in the English-German °Dictionary on **pages 255–266**. ▶ Skills file 2, p. 174

Step 2

°Think about your dream room. Draw it, find photos or make it on the computer.

When you use pictures from the ⁺internet, write the name of the ⁺photographer or the ⁺website.

Step 3

a) Write about your dream room (°at least five sentences). ▶ Digital help 🔖 ▶ More help, p. 79 ▶ Wordbank 8, p. 200

There's a big red sofa. There are a lot of posters. It's quiet. ...

b) Read your partner's sentences and check the spelling.

c) °Practise with your partner: Read your sentences and show your picture. *Look at ...   This is ...*

Step 4

a) Present your room to your °group. Read your description and show your picture.

b) Answer three questions from your group.

Is your dream room in a house?   *Yes, it is. It's in a house with a garden. /
No, it isn't. It's in a flat.*

c) Give other students feedback on their dream room. ▶ Let's talk: Feedback, p. 211

Your dream room is cool / great / very nice / ...

Digital quiz 🔖 **I can present my dream room.** ✓

sixty-five **65**

Unit task Einstieg:
- (SB auf) L bespricht mit S Ziel der *Unit task* und die Schritte zum Erreichen des Ziels.
- Step 2 sollte als vorbereitende HA aufgegeben werden.

Step 1 Erarbeitung:
a) S schreiben die Mindmap in ihr Heft ab.
- S ergänzen ihre Mindmap und vergleichen sie im ▶ Think-Pair-Share.
- **Ausw.:** im Plenum, Sammeln von Wortschatz an der Tafel

b) gemäß AA

Step 2 Vorbereitende HA, s. o.

Step 3 Erarbeitung:
a) gemäß AA. L weist auf Hilfen hin (ggf. TA).

b) ▶ Peer correction der Sätze bezüglich Rechtschreibung

c) S üben die Präsentation in PA, ggf. ▶ Read-and-look-up.

Step 4 Einstieg:
- L oder Handpuppe Scout präsentiert ihren *dream room* und fordert S auf, Fragen zu stellen und Feedback zu geben.
- TA: Redemittel aus ▶ Let's talk: Feedback, S. 211, ggf. ▶ Semantisierung

Erarbeitung:
- S stellen sich ihre Räume in Kleingruppen vor und befolgen die Schritte a) bis c).
- **Ausw.:** Einige S präsentieren ihren Raum im Plenum.
- **Zusatz:** ▶ Gallery walk

Lernschwerpunkt: Kompetenzen und sprachliche Mittel üben, Lernfortschritte erkennen
Kompetenzen: Reading einen kurzen Text lesen und mit passenden Wörtern vervollständigen • Bilder einem Satz zuordnen • Speaking Fragen zum eigenen Zuhause und zu Haustieren stellen und beantworten • Writing mithilfe einer Mindmap einen Text über ein Zuhause verfassen • Listening Beschreibungen eines Zimmers Informationen entnehmen
Strukturen: Fragen und Kurzantworten mit *to be*
Redemittel: Wortfelder *family, pets, homes, rooms*

Allgemeine Anmerkung:
s. Unit 1, S. 36

Ex 1 + Ex 2 Einstieg:
- (SB auf) S lesen das Lernziel rechts oben auf der Seite vor (*I can …*).
- S schätzen ihr Können zum Lernziel ein, z. B. mit ▶ Thumbs up, und notieren sich das Ergebnis.

Erarbeitung:
- gemäß AA, möglichst in EA
- **Ausw.:** ▶ Bus stop (▶ KV Extra): S vergleichen ihre Lösungen mithilfe der ▶ KV 2.6A.
- Nach der Lösungskontrolle erneute Einschätzung des Könnens (gleiche Methode wie im Einstieg).

Ex 3 Einstieg:
- (SB auf) Selbsteinschätzung s. Ex 1 + 2

Erarbeitung:
a) S schreiben die vollständigen Fragen und Antworten ins Heft ab.
- **Ausw.:** ▶ Bus stop (▶ KV Extra): S vergleichen ihre Lösungen mithilfe der ▶ KV 2.6A.

b) ▶ Partner talk
- **Ausw.:** Lösungskontrolle im Plenum, dann erneute Selbsteinschätzung

---

2 | **Checkpoint** | Digital checkpoint 👆

1 WORDS **Jay's favourite picture** | I can **talk about my family.** ✓

Look at Jay's picture and complete the sentences.

This is my favourite photo. It's my (1) f… in my flat. That's my (2) m…, Priya, and my (3) d…, Rahi, behind the sofa. Next to me is my (4) s…, Anika. She's nice!
Then there's my (5) a…, Meera, with her (6) d…, Sunita. Sunita is my (7) c… Behind Sunita is her (8) b…, Nish. My (9) g… is on the sofa too. He's my mum's dad.

1 1 family • **2** mum • **3** dad • **4** sister • **5** aunt • **6** daughter • **7** cousin • **8** brother • **9** grandpa

2 WORDS **Priya's pictures**

What's the correct photo? Write A or B.

1 That's me and Rahi. He's my partner.
2 And that's Anika. She's our daughter.
3 These are Anika's cousins, Sunita and Nish.
4 Here you can see my sister – she's Anika's aunt.
5 That's Anika's brother Jay. He's 11.
6 That's George, the parrot. The animals are very loud!

2 1 A • **2** A • **3** B • **4** B • **5** A • **6** B

3 On the phone with *FindAPet* | I can **talk about pets (questions and short answers).** ✓

a) LANGUAGE Lily is on the phone with Ms Taylor from *FindAPet*. Complete Ms Taylor's questions with *Is* or *Are*. Then complete Lily's answers with *am / 'm not / are / aren't / is / isn't*.

1 … you good with animals? – Yes, I …
2 … your flat big? – No, it …
3 … your home quiet? – Yes, it …
4 … you and your family cat fans? – No, we …
5 … your neighbours dog fans? – No, they …
6 … you scared of lizards? – No, I …

b) SPEAKING Ask your partner four questions from a). Answer the questions for you. Take turns.

3 a) 1 Are … am. • **2** Is … isn't. • **3** Is … is. • **4** Are … aren't. • **5** Are … aren't. • **6** Are … 'm not.

3 b) individuelle Lösungen

Check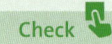

66 sixty-six

Checkpoint Vorbereitung

Material: alle Aufgaben ▶ KV Extra: Bus stop, ▶ KV 2.6A: Checkpoint answers • Ex 5 UMA/CD
Zeitbedarf: ca. 2 Std.
Minimalversion: Auswahl der Aufgaben erfolgt aufgrund der zu überprüfenden Lernziele
Begleitmedien: App (Digital checkpoint), INKL (S. 66–67)

Die Übungen kannst du auch digital machen 2

✎ **4** WRITING **Amira's message to Jay** | I can describe my home or dream home. ✓

Look at Amira's mind map about her home. Write her message to her new British friend.

a small house
near Bremen

my parents
and my
brother

a modern
house,
always tidy

my home

friendly
neighbours

a kitchen, a living room, two
bedrooms, a bathroom, a big garden

Start your sentences like this:

I live with …
We live in …
It's …
There's / There are …
Our neighbours are …

4 Lösungsbsp. S. 290

🎧 ▶) **5** LISTENING **Noah's room** | I can describe my room. ✓

◁)) a) **Listen to Noah. What's in his room? Write three letters.**
1.43

5 a) C · D · F

A

B

C

D

E

F

b) **Listen again. Choose the correct answer. Write A, B or C.**

5 b) 1 C · **2** A · **3** B · **4** C

1 Is Noah's room tidy?
   A No, it isn't tidy.   B Yes, it's quite tidy.   C Yes, it's very tidy.
2 Where's Noah's desk?
   A It's in front of the shelves. B It's behind the shelves.   C It's next to the shelves.
3 Where's Buddy?
   A He's next to the bed.   B He's under the bed.   C He's behind the bed.
4 Is Noah's room quiet?
   A No, it isn't quiet.   B Yes, it's often quiet.   C Yes, it's always quiet.

Check ⬇

Ex 4 Einstieg:
• (SB auf) Selbsteinschätzung zum Lernziel mit ▶ Thumbs up. S notieren sich das Ergebnis.

Erarbeitung:
• S schreiben die Nachricht in ihr Heft.
• **Ausw.:** ▶ Bus stop (▶ KV Extra): S vergleichen ihre Lösungen mithilfe der ▶ KV 2.6A.
• **Alternative:** Vergleich im Plenum mit ▶ Meldekette (mit TA)
• erneute Selbsteinschätzung

Ex 5 a + b Einstieg:
• (SB auf) Selbsteinschätzung zum Lernziel mit ▶ Thumbs up

Erarbeitung:
• gemäß AA, S notieren Lösungen im Heft.
• **Ausw.:** ▶ Bus stop (▶ KV Extra): S vergleichen ihre Lösungen mithilfe der ▶ KV 2.6A.
• erneute Selbsteinschätzung

• **Zusatz:** Auswertung, wie gut sich S bei den Aufgaben dieser Doppelseite selbst eingeschätzt haben, mit ▶ Thumbs up: Stimmt die Einschätzung vor der Aufgabe mit der Einschätzung nach der Aufgabe überein?

Checkpoint Inhalt

Lernschwerpunkt: Kompetenzen und sprachliche Mittel üben, Lernfortschritte erkennen
Kompetenzen: Reading einem Text Informationen entnehmen und Bilder passend zum Text ordnen • Writing buchstabierte Wörter richtig schreiben • Listening einem Gespräch Informationen entnehmen und damit Steckbriefe ausfüllen • Speaking ein Zimmer beschreiben
Strukturen: Aussagen mit *to be, There's / There are*
Redemittel: Wortfelder *family, homes, rooms, pets* • Präpositionen

---

Ex 6 Einstieg:
- (SB auf) S lesen das Lernziel vor.
- S schätzen ihr Können zum Lernziel ein, z. B. mit ▶ Thumbs up. Sie notieren sich das Ergebnis.

Erarbeitung:
a) S lesen die Nachrichten und schlagen unbekannte Wörter möglichst selbstständig im *Dictionary* (S. 255–266) nach.
- S ordnen die Bilder.

b) S notieren die richtige Antwort im Heft.
- **Ausw.:** ▶ Bus stop (▶ KV Extra): S vergleichen ihre Lösungen zu a) und b) mithilfe der ▶ KV 2.6B.
- nach der Korrektur erneute Selbsteinschätzung

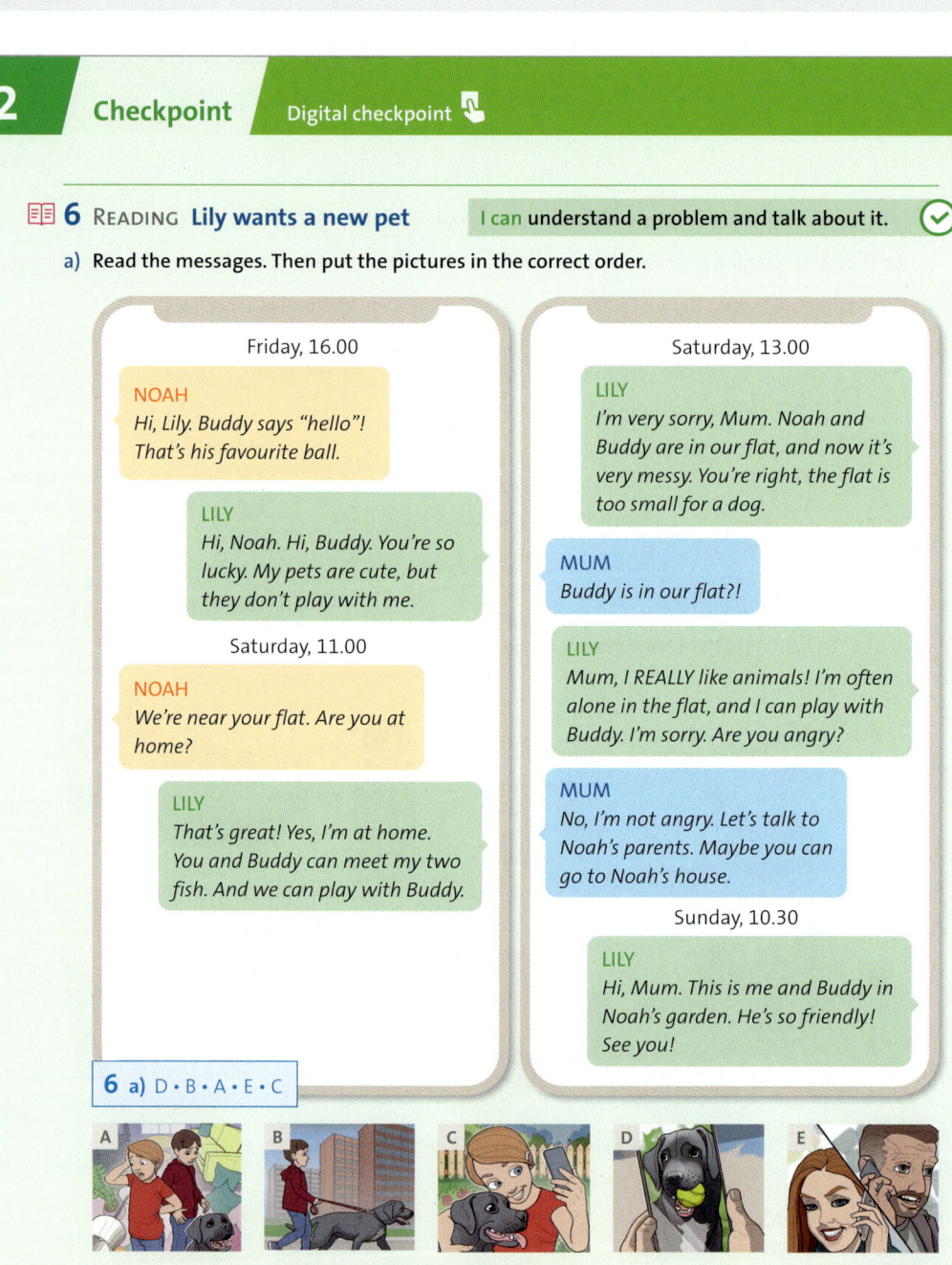

2 Checkpoint   Digital checkpoint

📖 6 READING **Lily wants a new pet**   I can **understand a problem and talk about it.** ✓

a) Read the messages. Then put the pictures in the correct order.

Friday, 16.00

NOAH
Hi, Lily. Buddy says "hello"! That's his favourite ball.

LILY
Hi, Noah. Hi, Buddy. You're so lucky. My pets are cute, but they don't play with me.

Saturday, 11.00

NOAH
We're near your flat. Are you at home?

LILY
That's great! Yes, I'm at home. You and Buddy can meet my two fish. And we can play with Buddy.

Saturday, 13.00

LILY
I'm very sorry, Mum. Noah and Buddy are in our flat, and now it's very messy. You're right, the flat is too small for a dog.

MUM
Buddy is in our flat?!

LILY
Mum, I REALLY like animals! I'm often alone in the flat, and I can play with Buddy. I'm sorry. Are you angry?

MUM
No, I'm not angry. Let's talk to Noah's parents. Maybe you can go to Noah's house.

Sunday, 10.30

LILY
Hi, Mum. This is me and Buddy in Noah's garden. He's so friendly! See you!

6 a) D • B • A • E • C

A · B · C · D · E

b) What's Lily's problem? Choose the correct sentence. Write A, B or C.   6 b) B

A Lily's mum is angry because Buddy is in the flat.
B Lily is often alone and wants to play with a pet.
C Lily can't go to Noah's house.

Check 📥

Checkpoint Vorbereitung

Material: alle Aufgaben ▶ KV Extra: Bus stop, ▶ KV 2.6B: Checkpoint answers • Ex 8 UMA/CD
Zeitbedarf: ca. 2 Std.
Minimalversion: Auswahl der Aufgaben erfolgt aufgrund der zu überprüfenden Lernziele
Begleitmedien: App (Digital checkpoint)

Die Übungen kannst du auch digital machen 📱 **2**

---

7 STUDY SKILLS **Sunita's messages**

| I can spell words correctly. ✓ |

One word is wrong in each message. Write the correct word.

1 Ben's music is too <u>lodu</u> – again! 🙂
2 Hi, Lily, the art <u>homwork</u> is hard – can you help me?
3 Coding isn't °<u>easy</u> to <u>lern</u>, but °<u>it's fun</u>!
4 Nish, 😊 thank you for the <u>chocolade</u>!
5 °<u>Have a nic weekend</u>, Anika. 🙂
6 Mum, what's for <u>dinnre</u>? I'm really hungry.
7 Hello, Zane. What's your <u>addres</u>, please?
8 Hi, Mum. I'm <u>bak</u> at home now. See you.

> **7 1** loud • **2** homework •
> **3** learn • **4** chocolate • **5** nice •
> **6** dinner • **7** address • **8** back

8 LISTENING **At the vet**

🎧 1.44

There are two new animals at the vet. Copy the forms. Listen and complete them.

1
Pet's name: ...
Animal: ...
Family name: ...
Phone number:

> Queenie
> hamster
> Fruin ['fruːn]
> 4960162

2
Pet's name: ...
Animal: ...
Family name: ...
Phone number: ...

> Hermes ['hɜːmiːz]
> parrot
> Lui [liː]
> 07700 900835

9 SPEAKING **Zane's dream room**

| I can present my dream room. ✓ |

Look at Zane's picture of his dream room. Say at least five sentences about it. You can use the words in the boxes.

> **9** Lösungsbsp. S. 290

| big • cool • great • messy • modern • nice • small • yellow |

| bag • bed • cat • computer • desk • football posters • guitar • sofa • walls |

> This is Zane's dream room.
> It's ... and ...
> The ... is / are ...
> There's / There are ...
> The ... is / are on the ...

Check 📥

Ex 7 Einstig:
- (SB auf) Selbsteinschätzung s. Ex 6

Erarbeitung:
- S schreiben die korrigierten Wörter in ihr Heft.
- **Ausw.:** ▶ Bus stop (▶ KV Extra): S vergleichen ihre Lösungen mithilfe der ▶ KV 2.6B.
- **Alternative:** Auswertung im Plenum. S buchstabieren das falsch geschriebene Wort. Der Rest der Klasse klopft auf den Tisch, wenn sie einen Fehler hören.
  L: *Knock on the table if you hear a mistake.*

Ex 8 Erarbeitung:
- (SB auf) S schreiben die Steckbriefe in ihr Heft ab.
- **1. Hören:** S ergänzen die Steckbriefe.
- **2. Hören:** S prüfen.
- **Ausw.:** ▶ Bus stop (▶ KV Extra): S vergleichen ihre Lösungen mithilfe der ▶ KV 2.6B.
- **Alternative**: TA der Steckbriefe, gemeinsam ausfüllen.
- erneute Selbsteinschätzung

Ex 9 Einstig:
- (SB auf) Selbsteinschätzung s. Ex 6

Erarbeitung:
- S sprechen über das Zimmer im ▶ Partner talk.
- **Ausw.:** ▶ Bus stop (▶ KV Extra): S vergleichen ihre Beschreibungen mithilfe der Musterlösung auf der ▶ KV 2.6B.
- **Alternative:** ▶ Partner check: Partner/in klopft, wenn er/sie einen Fehler hört.
- erneute Selbsteinschätzung

69

Text file Inhalt

Lernschwerpunkt: Texte zum Thema *pets, homes and families* lesen

Kompetenzen: Reading Gedichte über Haustiere lesen • einen informativen Text über ein Haustier lesen • Rätsel lösen • etwas nach einer Anleitung basteln

Redemittel: Wortfelder *pets, adjectives* • Präpositionen

Allgemeine Anmerkung:
s. Unit 1, S. 40

Lucy's poems **Erarbeitung:**
- (SB auf) Lesen der Gedichte in PA
- S können versuchen, ein eigenes Gedicht zu schreiben. Die Zeilen müssen sich nicht unbedingt reimen.
- Falls Reime erwünscht sind, sammelt die Klasse vorab sich reimende Wörter und Namen an der Tafel (z. B. *cat – hat, Jack – black*) oder L gibt ein ▶ Scaffolding vor.

My pet **Erarbeitung:**
- (SB auf) S lesen den *model text*.
- S können einen ähnlichen Text über ein Tier ihrer Wahl schreiben.
- Ggf. recherchieren sie Informationen im Internet.

---

2 **Text file**

OPTIONAL

VARNDEAN Teen Zine

This month's topics: pets, homes and families

Our school magazine: by students for students

Lucy's poems
I love writing poems! Here are three poems about pets.
You can write a pet poem too and send it to Teen Zine!

I have a mouse
In my room in our house
She has a little cap
And she's really good at rap!

I have a dog
She has a blog
She's always fine
When she's online!

I have a snake
His name is Jake
He's white and green
And very mean!

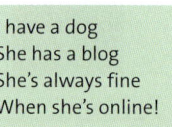

My pet by Max
I have a bearded dragon[1] or a 'beardie'. Here's a photo of him – isn't he cute? His name is Drago and he's grey and yellow.

Beardies can swim and run[2] fast. Beardies can live for 10–12 years. Drago is four. He's active in the day and he's very funny.

Drago has a big terrarium with a lamp. It's nice and warm under the lamp. Bearded dragons eat insects, fruit[3] and vegetables[4].

I think a bearded dragon is a fantastic pet!

Hello!

We think Max has a great pet! What about you?
Do you have a great pet? Write to us and send a photo!

---

[1] **bearded dragon** *Bartagame (Echsenart)* [2] **run** *rennen, laufen* [3] **fruit** *Obst* [4] **vegetable** *Gemüse*

Text file **Vorbereitung**

Material: Make a paper family ggf. weißes A4-Papier, Scheren
Zeitbedarf: abhängig davon, welche Texte bearbeitet werden; pro Text ca. 25 Minuten
Minimalversion: alle Texte sind optionale Zusatztexte
Begleitmedien: INKL (S. 68–71)

°Puzzle time

What am I?
Can you say the animals?

> I have four legs[1], but I'm not a dog
> I can run fast, but I'm not a lion
> I like carrots, but I'm not a rabbit
> You can ride me, but I'm not a camel
> What am I?

> I'm small, but I'm not a mouse
> I'm gold, brown or white, but not often black
> I'm very active, but not in the day
> You can play with me, but I like being alone
> What am I?

Where do they live?
Emma, Zendaya, Leon and Danny all live in the same street[2]. What are their house numbers?

1 Emma's house number isn't 2 or 6.
2 Zendaya's neighbours are Emma and Leon.
3 Leon's house is next to Danny's house.

Make a °paper family

You °need:
- a piece of paper (DIN A4)
- a pencil
- scissors[3]
- coloured pens

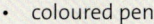

1	2	3

 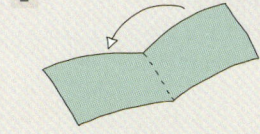 

Fold[4] an A4 piece of paper in half. Cut[5] it in two.

Take one piece. Fold it in half.

Fold it in half again.

4	5	6

Draw a person on one side of the folded paper.

Cut out the person.

Open the paper. Draw faces[6] and clothes on the people.

---

[1] **leg** *Bein* [2] **street** *Straße* [3] **scissors** *Schere* [4] **fold** *falten* [5] **cut** *schneiden* [6] **face** *Gesicht*

Puzzle time **Erarbeitung:**
- (SB auf) S lesen die Rätsel und notieren ihre Lösungen.
- **Ausw.:** ▶ Partner talk
- **Zusatz:** S verfassen eigene Rätsel gemäß den Beispielen im SB über ein (Haus-)Tier, einen Gegenstand im Haus oder ein Zimmer.

Make a paper family
Erarbeitung:
- (SB auf) Handlungsorientierte Umsetzung eines Lesetextes: S basteln anhand der Anleitung ihre eigene *paper family*.
- Die entstandenen Papierfamilien können weiter farbig gestaltet werden.
- Ggf. können die entstandenen Familien auch verwendet werden, um die eigene Familie darzustellen.
- **Ausw.:** Die Familien sollten im Klassenraum ausgehängt werden (▶ Gallery walk).

Lernschwerpunkt: Texte zum Thema *Festivals* (*Christmas, Chinese New Year*) lesen

Kompetenzen: Reading / Intercultural competence Texten Informationen über Weihnachten in Großbritannien und das chinesische Neujahrsfest entnehmen

Wortschatz: Wortfelder *Christmas, Chinese New Year*

Teen Zine special: Festivals

- Die hier vorgestellten *holidays* können auch im Plenum behandelt werden, z. B. vor Weihnachten.

Einstieg:

- (SB zu) L zeigt vergrößertes Bild von Lyle und Astra (UMA). L: *This is Lyle and his sister Astra.*
- L leitet über die Kleidung hin zum Thema *Christmas*: L: *When do you wear jumpers like this? What do you know about Christmas in the UK?*

Christmas Erarbeitung:

- (SB auf) Lesen des Textes. Im Plenum könnte eine Text-Bild-Zuordnung erfolgen. L: *What can you see in the photos?*
- Interkulturelles Lernen/ Mediation: Wiedergabe der wichtigsten Informationen zu Weihnachten in Großbritannien auf Deutsch im Plenum.
- **Ausw.:** S sagen, was sie Neues über Weihnachten in Großbritannien gelernt haben.

What holidays ... Erarbeitung:

- Im Anschluss schreiben/reden die S über die eigene Familientradition in der Weihnachtszeit.
- L bietet dazu ▶ Scaffolding an, z. B.: *We celebrate / make / eat / decorate / play / ...*
- S wählen weitere Feste oder Feiern aus (z. B. Ostern, Geburtstag) und schreiben/ reden darüber auf Englisch.

Teen Zine Special: Festivals

Christmas

I'm Lyle and this is my sister Astra. This is how we celebrate[1] Christmas in my family:

Before Christmas

★ We send e-Christmas cards to my grandparents. My parents send cards and messages on social media to friends.

★ We decorate a Christmas tree.

★ My friends and I go to the neighbours' houses and sing Christmas carols[2].

1.45

> We wish[3] you a merry Christmas
> We wish you a merry Christmas
> We wish you a merry Christmas
> and a happy New Year.

Christmas Eve[4] (24th December)

★ We hang up[5] our stockings.

★ We make Christmas cookies.

★ We put cookies and milk under the tree for Father Christmas, and a carrot for reindeer Rudolph.

Christmas Day (25th December)

★ We open our presents[6] in the morning. There are always some small presents in the stockings and some big presents under the tree.

★ My parents make the turkey for dinner.

★ My grandparents and my aunt and uncle and cousins come for Christmas dinner. We eat at about 2 o'clock[7] in the afternoon[8].

★ After dinner we play a game.

What holidays do you celebrate?

What are your family's Christmas traditions?

---

[1] **celebrate** *feiern* [2] **Christmas carol** *Weihnachtslied* [3] **wish** *wünschen* [4] **Christmas Eve** *Heiligabend*
[5] **hang sth. up** *etwas aufhängen* [6] **present** *Geschenk* [7] **2 o'clock** *14 Uhr* [8] **afternoon** *Nachmittag*

Text file Vorbereitung

Material: Christmas UMA, vergrößertes Foto von S. 72 oben • Chinese New Year UMA, vergrößerte Fotos von S. 73 oben
Zeitbedarf: abhängig davon, welche Texte bearbeitet werden; pro Text ca. 25 Minuten
Minimalversion: alle Texte sind optionale Zusatztexte

Chinese New Year

> I'm Vivian and my family is Chinese. There are about 400,000 Chinese people in the UK and Chinese New Year is a very important festival for us.
> It can be in January or February. Some British cities have big parties for the festival and Brighton is one of them!

There are 15 days of Chinese New Year celebrations[1] and we do something special each day.

Day 1 We visit[2] the oldest people in our family, eat sweets and drink tea.
Day 2 We give[3] food to dogs in the streets[4] because today is a special day for dogs.
Day 3 This is a quiet day: We respect the dead, stay[5] at home and go to bed early.
Day 4 We welcome the Kitchen God and make meals for the week.
Day 5 We clean[6] the house and welcome the God of Money[7].
Day 6 We throw away[8] old things.
Day 12 We get ready[9] for the Lantern[10] Festival.
Day 13 We eat simple vegetarian meals[11] to give our body a rest[12].

> Kung Hei Fat Choi!
> Happy New Year!

Tell us about you and your family's New Year's traditions: the food you eat, the things you do …

---

[1] **celebration** *Feier* [2] **visit** *besuchen* [3] **give** *geben* [4] **street** *Straße* [5] **stay** *bleiben* [6] **clean** *putzen*
[7] **God of Money** *Gott des Geldes* [8] **throw away** *wegwerfen* [9] **get ready** *sich vorbereiten* [10] **lantern** *Laterne*
[11] **meal** *Mahlzeit* [12] **rest** *Ruhe, Pause, Erholung*

Chinese New Year Einstieg:
• (SB zu) L zeigt vergrößerte Fotos der S. 73 (UMA).
  L: *Describe the photos. / This is the Chinese New Year.*

Erarbeitung:
• (SB auf) S lesen den Text.
• **Ausw.:** S sagen im ▶ Partner talk, welchen der beschriebenen 15 Feiertage sie am besten finden.
• ▶ Scaffolding: TA: *I like day __ best because …*
• **Alternative:** Der Text kann auch im Plenum erarbeitet werden.
• **Zusatz:** S schreiben ▶ Three truths, two lies über den Text und stellen sie in PA oder im Plenum vor, z. B.: *The Chinese New Year is on 1st January. (wrong) / There are 13 days of celebrations. (wrong) / Day 3 is a quiet day. (right) …*

Tell us about you … Erarbeitung:
• S berichten über eigene Neujahrstraditionen und bekommen ggf. Zeit, ihre Sätze schriftlich zu formulieren.

Lernschwerpunkt: zusätzliche Übungen, Differenzierungs- und Hilfsangebote
Kompetenzen: Writing Fragen mit *to be* schreiben • Listening passende Kurzantworten zu Fragen mit *to be* finden
Strukturen: Fragen und Kurzantworten mit *to be*
Redemittel: Wortfeld *family*

Ex 6 Erarbeitung: s. S. 52
- *Partner A* schreibt das Poster von S. 52 ab, *Partner B* das Poster von S. 74.
  - ▶ Langsamere S erhalten
    ▶ KV 2.2

Ex 3 Erarbeitung: s. S. 54
- ▢ Lernstarke S vergleichen das Haus, das sie gezeichnet haben, in einem ▶ Partner talk mit dem Foto.
- Mögliches ▶ Scaffolding:
  The house in our picture has a …
  The house in the photo has no …
  There's a …. in our picture / in the photo.
  There are … in our picture / in the photo.
  There's no … in our picture / in the photo.
  The house in our picture is …
  The house in the photo isn't …

Ex 1 Erarbeitung: s. S. 60
- S finden zum Überprüfen ihrer Lösung hier den Songtext in der richtigen Reihenfolge.

---

2   **Partner page**

Partner page

▶ Page 52

💬 **6** SPEAKING **A missing pet**

👥 **a)** Noah and Zane see some *Missing Pet* posters, but they have °rain on them.

Partner B: Copy the poster.
Listen to partner A and complete the missing words in the first three sentences. Then read the next sentences to your partner and he/she completes the missing words in his/her poster.

6 a) parrot • blue • ten • talking • nice

MISSING

Our friendly ____ is missing. He's ____ and orange and he's ____ years old. He likes ____ and flying, and he's very ____. But we think he isn't happy because we have a lot of animals in our home. It's very loud.

Please call **07700 900426** if you find him.

▶ Page 54

👥 **3** **A special house**

💬 °Compare your drawing with the photo.

▶ Page 60

1 SONG **Ben's song**

My little flat ♫ ♫ ♫
People ask, 'Is your flat big?' No, it's small
And it isn't new or modern °at all
There aren't °expensive pictures on the wall
There are two small bedrooms, there aren't three
And the living room is always very messy
But my little flat is perfect for me
Because there's music, there's love ♫
There's my family, that's °enough ♫
My little flat is perfect for me ♫

Diff bank Vorbereitung

Material: Ex 6 ▶ KV 2.2: A missing pet • Parallel ex 5 UMA/CD
Zeitbedarf: abhängig davon, welche Aufgaben bearbeitet werden
Minimalversion: *More practice*-Aufgaben sind stets Zusatzaufgaben

---

Diff bank

▶Page 48

🖊 **More practice 1** **Family words**

a) Copy and complete the table.
Use the words from the box.

> aunt • ~~brother~~ • cousin • dad • daughter • grandma • grandpa • mum • partner • sister • son • uncle

👤	👤	👤 or 👤
brother • dad • grandpa • son • uncle	aunt • daughter • grandma • mum • sister	cousin • partner

b) Read about Noah's family. Complete the sentences with the words from a).

1 Mark is Noah's dad. → Noah is Mark's …
2 Amy is Mark's sister. → Amy is Noah's …
3 Eliana is Amy's daughter. → Eliana is Noah's …
4 Albert is Mark's dad. → Albert is Noah's …
5 Gladys is Noah's grandma. → Gladys is Mark's …

> **1 b)**
> **1** son
> **2** aunt
> **3** cousin
> **4** grandpa
> **5** mother

▶Page 51

🖊 **More practice 2** **Scout's family and friends**

Read the sentences about Scout's family and friends. Make questions.

1 Sally is Scout's cousin.
  Is Sally Scout's cousin?
2 Scout's parents are from Brighton.
3 Scout's brothers are loud.
4 She is very friendly.
5 We are all Scout's friends.

> **2 1** Is Sally Scout's cousin? • **2** Are Scout's parents from Brighton? • **3** Are Scout's brothers loud? • **4** Is she very friendly? • **5** Are we all Scout's friends?

▶Page 52

 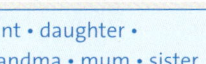 **Parallel exercise** **5** LISTENING **Is that your pet?**

 c) Listen again and match the answers to the questions.
1.34

1 Are you OK, Sunita? a No, they aren't.
2 Is it hard to do your homework? b Yes, I am.
3 Is your dog Buddy loud? c No, I'm not.
4 Are you too busy for pets? d No, he isn't.
5 Are they your pets? e Yes, it is.

> **5 c)** 1 c • 2 e • 3 d • 4 b • 5 a

MP 1 **Einstig:**
• (SB zu) L zeichnet die Tabelle an die Tafel und zeigt nacheinander auf die Symbole.
L: *Give me a family word for a boy / for a girl / a word that can be both boy or girl.*
• L trägt je ein Beispiel in die Tabelle ein.

Erarbeitung:
a) (SB auf) gemäß AA
• **Ausw.:** ▶ Five-minute teacher

b) S schreiben die Sätze ins Heft und ergänzen.
• 🔲 Hilfe: ▶ Wordbank 7, S. 199
• **Ausw.:** ▶ Five-minute teacher oder ▶ Meldekette

MP 2 **Einstig:**
• (SB zu) L stellt drei bis vier Fragen mit *to be*, z. B.: *Are you happy? Is my pencil case red?*
• Dann ▶ Meldekette mit Fragen.

Erarbeitung:
• (SB auf) gemäß AA. S schreiben die Fragen ins Heft.
• **Ausw.:** ▶ Five-minute teacher

Parallel ex 5 s. S. 52
• Diese Aufgabe eignet sich besonders für lernschwächere S und Hörbeeinträchtigte.

Erarbeitung:
• S schreiben die Sätze 1–5 in ihr Heft ab. Sie hören den Dialog und notieren zunächst nur den Buchstaben der richtigen Lösung. Dann ergänzen sie die jeweiligen Kurzantworten.
• **Ausw.:** s. S. 52

Diff bank Inhalt

Lernschwerpunkt: zusätzliche Übungen, Differenzierungs- und Hilfsangebote
Kompetenzen: Speaking verschiedene Häuser beschreiben • Reading einem Text Informationen über ein Zuhause entnehmen • Writing das eigene Zuhause beschreiben
Strukturen: *There's / There are*
Redemittel: Wortfelder *adjectives, rooms and houses*

MH 8 Erarbeitung: s. S.53
- Diese zusätzliche Hilfe bietet den Lernenden eine gute Struktur. In schwächeren Klassen sollte sie allen S zur Verfügung gestellt werden.
- Sie kann als ▶ Scaffolding beim Sprechen benutzt werden. So wird vermieden, dass S nur vorgeschriebene Sätze vorlesen.

MP 3 Einstieg:
- (SB auf) L wiederholt das Lernziel: „Ich kann mein Zuhause beschreiben." (s. S. 49 Nach dieser Unit kann ich …)
- S schätzen sich selbst ein mit ▶ Thumbs up.
  L: *Let's practice more!*

Erarbeitung:
a) + b) Zwei bis drei freiwillige S beschreiben als Beispiel eins der abgebildeten Häuser im Plenum. Dabei nutzen sie das unter den Bildern angebotene ▶ Scaffolding. Die Klasse rät.
- ▶ Partner talk: S wechseln sich gemäß AA ab mit Beschreiben und Raten.
- **Ausw.:** S schätzen sich erneut ein (wie im **Einstieg**).
- Unsichere S tragen ggf. ihre Beschreibung nochmal im Plenum vor.

---

2 **Diff bank**

▶Page 53

✏ More help **8** MY TASK **My pet or dream pet** | **8** individuelle Lösungen

a) **Copy the table and make notes about your pet or dream pet.**

Animal	I have a … / My dream pet is a …	
Colour	He's / She's brown / …	active • big • cute • fast • friendly • happy • hungry • loud • old • mean • quiet • slow • small
Characteristics	He's / She's / He isn't / She isn't friendly / …	
Size	He's / She's very small / …	

▶Page 54

💬 👥 More practice 3 **Different houses** | **3 a)** Lösungsbsp. S. 290

a) **Partner A: °Choose a picture – don't tell your partner! Talk about the home.**
  Partner B: °Guess the picture: *I think it's picture 1 / 2 / …*

In this picture there's There are	a big / small / old / modern house / building a lot of trees a big window / two windows a red / blue / … door a garden / a balcony	on the ground floor. on the top floor.

b) **Partner B: Choose a different picture and talk about it.**
  Partner A: Guess the picture.

Diff bank Vorbereitung

Material: Challenge 1 ▸ KV Extra: Bus stop, ggf. von L vorbereitete Lösungsblätter • MH 6 UMA
Zeitbedarf: abhängig davon, welche Aufgaben bearbeitet werden
Minimalversion: *More practice*- und *Challenge*-Aufgaben sind stets Zusatzaufgaben

---

2

Challenge 1 **New homes**

Ch 1 **a)** **1** no • **2** yes • **3** yes • **4** no • **5** no • **6** yes

a) Zane asks his friend Alfie about his family's new house. Read their °conversation.
Copy the list on the right and write *yes* or *no*.

Zane Are there °kids at the neighbour's house?
Alfie No, there aren't. But there are a lot of kids in our °street.
Zane Is there a garden?
Alfie There is. There isn't a really big garden, but it's nice.
Zane Is there a °trampoline in the garden?
Alfie No, there isn't. But there's a °swimming pool!
Zane Wow!

1 kids at the neighbour's house
2 a lot of kids in the street
3 a garden
4 a really big garden
5 a trampoline
6 a swimming pool

b) Lily's friend Kinza has a new home. Complete their conversation.

Lily (1) ... a lot of floors in the building?
Kinza Yes, (2) ... There are twelve floors.
Lily (3) ... a lot of rooms in your flat?
Kinza No, (4) ... There are three rooms.
Lily (5) ... one room for you and your sister?
Kinza Yes, (6) ... It's a nice big room.
Lily (7) ... a balcony?
Kinza No, (8) ... Our flat is on the ground floor.

▸Page 55

Ch 1 **b)** **1** Are there • **2** there are. • **3** Are there • **4** there aren't. • **5** Is there • **6** there is. • **7** Is there • **8** there isn't.

More help **6** MY TASK **My home**

b) Write about your home or dream home for a new friend.

I live with my	dad / mum / grandma / grandpa / .... little brother / sister. big brother / sister. two sisters and my brother.
We live in	a house / flat in ...
It's	old / new / big / small / nice / quiet / loud / ....
There's a kitchen and a bathroom and	a living room / a dining room / a TV room / a toilet / three bedrooms / ...
There's	a garden / a balcony.
Our neighbours are	nice / friendly / not very friendly / ...

6 b) individuelle Lösungen

Challenge 1

• Diese Aufgabe kann zur Differenzierung für lernstärkere oder schnelle S verwendet werden.

Erarbeitung:

a) (SB auf) S lesen AA und stellen ggf. Fragen.
• S schreiben die Liste ins Heft ab.
• S lesen den Text und notieren die Ergebnisse im Heft.
• **Ausw.:** ▸ Bus stop (▸ KV Extra): S treffen sich und vergleichen ihre Ergebnisse. Ggf. vorbereitete Lösungsblätter auslegen.

b) Anhand des Dialoges von a) und ggf. ▸ LF 9, S. 186 wiederholen S bei Bedarf die Regeln zu *There is / There are* (Fragen, bejahte und verneinte Aussagesätze, Kurzantworten).
• S lesen die AA und notieren die Lösungen im Heft.
• **Ausw.:** ▸ Bus stop (▸ KV Extra), ggf. Lösungen auslegen.

MH 6 Erarbeitung: s. S. 55

• Diese Hilfe kann benutzt werden, um lernschwächeren S die Struktur des Modelltextes auf S. 55 zu verdeutlichen und ihnen das Befolgen dieser Struktur zu erleichtern. Die rechte Spalte bietet Ideen bzw. Vokabelhilfen zum Vervollständigen der Sätze.

• **Alternative:** L schreibt für lernschwächere S die Satzanfänge und mögliche Ergänzungen an die Tafel oder präsentiert sie vergrößert mithilfe des UMA.

Diff bank Inhalt

Lernschwerpunkt: zusätzliche Übungen, Differenzierungs- und Hilfsangebote
Kompetenzen: Speaking beschreiben, wo Dinge in einem Zimmer sind • Writing Fragen mit *who, where, what* stellen und beantworten
Redemittel: Wortfelder *things in a room, feelings* • Präpositionen • Fragewörter *who, where, what*

MP 4 Einstieg:
- (SB zu) TA: Präpositionen von S. 58
- ▶ Words in the air: PA: *Partner A* schreibt eine Präposition in die Luft. *Partner B* legt Federmäppchen, wie die Präposition es beschreibt, und sagt einen Satz. Bsp.: A schreibt *under* in die Luft. B legt Federmappe unter den Stuhl und sagt: *My pencil case is under the chair.*

Erarbeitung:
- (SB auf) gemäß AA, ▶ Partner talk
- **Ausw.:** im Plenum, ▶ Melde-kette
- ☒ **Zusatz:** ▶ Three truths, two lies: Die Klasse hört zu und findet die falschen Aussagen.

MP 5 Einstieg:
- (SB zu) ▶ Five-finger brain-storming: *What do you know about Sunita?*

Erarbeitung:
a) (SB auf) gemäß AA, S notieren die Antworten im Heft.

b) gemäß AA, ▶ Partner check
- **Ausw.:** im Plenum

Challenge 2
- Diese Aufgabe kann zur Differenzierung für starke oder schnelle S verwendet werden.

Erarbeitung:
- (SB auf) gemäß AA, S notieren die Fragen in EA.
- **Ausw.:** im Plenum. S stellen eine Frage (andere Reihenfol-ge), andere S antworten.

---

2 | **Diff bank**

▶Page 58

👥 More practice 4 | **Where is it?**

4 Lösungsbsp. S. 290

💬 Say where the things or animals are. Your partner says the thing or animal. Take turns.

I see a brown animal under the desk. – It's a rabbit!

▶Page 59

More practice 5 | **Who? What? Where?**

✏️ a) Can you remember? Do the quiz. Write the answers.

1 Who is Meera? – She's ...
2 What room is next to the dining room in Sunita's house? – The ...
3 Where's Nish's bedroom? – It's ...
4 What colour are the walls in Sunita's bedroom? – They're ...
5 Who is Ben? – He's ...
6 Where's the snake? – It's ...

5 a) 1 She's Sunita's mum. • **2** The living room. • **3** It's upstairs / next to the bathroom and Meera's bedroom. • **4** They're brown. • **5** He's Meera's partner. • **6** It's under the bed.

💬👥 b) Now ask a partner the questions in a). Check your partner's answers. Take turns.

✏️ Challenge 2 | **Who is it?**

Write questions for the answers. Use *Who, Where* or *What*. Who is the student?

1 ... – The name of this student's school is Varndean.
2 ... – This student's home is in Hove.
3 ... – This student's mum is Meera.
4 ... – This person's favourite thing is chocolate.
5 ... – This student is ...

Ch 2 1 What is the name of this student's school?
2 Where is this student's home?
3 Who is this student's mum?
4 What is this person's favourite thing?
5 Who is this student?
Answer: This student is *Nish*.

78 seventy-eight

Diff bank Vorbereitung

Material: MH 2 ggf. UMA, Bilder von S. 60–61
Zeitbedarf: abhängig davon, welche Aufgaben bearbeitet werden
Minimalversion: *More practice-* und *Challenge-*Aufgaben sind stets Zusatzaufgaben

More help **8** MY TASK **My room**

a) SPEAKING **Answer your partner's questions.**

I have my own room. / I have a room with …
My room is big / small.
My room is next to …
There are / There aren't a lot of things in my room.
There's a bed and a wardrobe / desk / …
There are pets in my room: I have …
The walls are white / blue / …
On my walls there are posters / photos / …
My room is quiet / loud.

> **8** individuelle Lösungen

▶ Page 60

More help **2** READING **Sunita's problem**

a) BEFORE YOU READ **Talk about how the people in the pictures feel.**

angry • happy • not happy • sad • tired

In picture 1 I think Sunita is …
In picture 2 I think Lily is …

> **2 a)**
> **Picture 1** … Sunita is angry / not happy.
> **Picture 2** … Lily is sad / not happy.
> **Picture 3** … Ben is happy.
> **Picture 6** … Lily is happy and tired.
> **Picture 7** … Sunita is happy again.

▶ Page 65

More help UNIT TASK **Present your dream room**

Step 3 **Write about your dream room.**

> **Step 3** individuelle Lösungen

a)

There's	a big red sofa / a wardrobe for my clothes / … a dog on the bed / a parrot / … a guitar / a computer / a lamp / …
There are	purple / red / … walls. a lot of posters / photos / lamps / cushions / … two cats / hamsters / …
It's	big / small. quiet / loud. tidy / messy.

MH 8 Erarbeitung: s. S. 59
- Diese Hilfe ist vor allem für lernschwächere S geeignet.
- S lesen die Hilfe, bevor sie mit der PA auf S. 59 beginnen. In der PA können ganz schwache S die ganze Zeit auf die Hilfe zurückgreifen. Stärkere S können die Hilfe abdecken und nur gucken, wenn sie nicht weiterkommen.
- Um das Hin- und Herblättern zu vermeiden, öffnet *Partner A* während des Gesprächs S. 59 und *Partner B* S. 79.

MH 2 Erarbeitung: s. S. 60
- Diese Aufgabe bietet ▶ Scaffolding für leistungsschwächere S.
- Da die zu beschreibenden Bilder ebenfalls im SB sind, bietet es sich an, entweder die Bilder mit dem UMA zu zeigen oder das Scaffolding als TA vorzugeben, damit ständiges Blättern entfällt.

MH Unit task Erarbeitung: s. S. 65
- Leistungsschwächere S bekommen hier sprachliche Hilfen, mit deren Unterstützung sie ihr Traumzimmer beschreiben können.

Unit-Übersicht

Storyline: Die S erfahren, wie die Lehrwerkskinder zur Schule kommen, wie der britische Schulalltag aussieht und welche Aktivitäten an britischen Schulen angeboten werden. In der *Story* gewinnt Zane einen Wettbewerb, weil er besonders viel zu Hause hilft und seine kranke Mutter unterstützt.

Strukturen: *simple present* (bejahte Aussagesätze) (S. 84) • Adverbien der Häufigkeit (lexikalisch) (S. 87)

Viewing: Emir und Daisy stellen sich weitere herausfordernde Mutproben: Emir muss beim Fußballspielen eine Unterhose auf dem Kopf tragen und Daisy soll Straßenmusik machen, obwohl sie nicht musikalisch ist. (S. 95)

Unit task: in einem selbst gezeichneten Comic oder einem Video die Höhepunkte der eigenen Woche vorstellen

---

Unit 3 Einstig:

- (SB zu) L hängt ▶ Flashcards mit Bildern von Verkehrsmitteln (*go by bus / go by car / go by bike / go by train* und *walk*) verdeckt an die Tafel.
- Handpuppe Scout ggf. dem Wetter anpassen, zerzaust oder mit Schirm: *Sorry, I'm late. My journey to school was very hard today! It's raining / windy / … and I fly to school. It isn't nice! How do you go to school?*
- L antwortet: *I go to school by …* und deckt die entsprechende Karte auf.
- S antworten ebenfalls und erfragen ggf. die fehlenden Redemittel (*What is … in English?*).
- L deckt nach und nach alle Redemittel auf und spricht sie vor.
- ▶ Vokabeltafel

Ex 1 Einstig:

- (SB auf) L verteilt die Flashcards aus dem Unit-Einstieg im Raum. L (oder starke/r S) liest den Text in dem Smartphone-Rahmen auf S. 80 langsam vor, S laufen jeweils zu dem Bild mit dem vorgelesenen Transportmittel.

Erarbeitung:

a) gemäß AA in EA. S schreiben die Sätze ab und vervollständigen sie.
- **Ausw.:** ▶ Five-minute teacher

b) S lesen die Sätze und schreiben die Nummern 1–5 ins Heft.
- **1. Hören:** S notieren T/F.
- **2. Hören:** S prüfen.
- **Ausw.:** ▶ Five-minute teacher

Unit 3
My day

School journeys
Our students come from different places in Brighton and Hove. Some come to school by bus, by car and by train. A lot of students walk or go to school by bike. ♥
😊 #greenschooljourneys

> **1 a) 1** walk • **2** bus. • **3** to school by car. • **4** I go to school by bike. • **5** I go to school by train.

🎧 1 LISTENING **School journeys**

✏️ ✉️ **a)** BEFORE YOU LISTEN **Look at the photos. Write how the students go to school.**

  1 Zane: I … to school. 2 Sunita: I go to school by … 3 Noah: I go …
  4 Lily: … 5 Alice: …

🔊 **b)** **Listen to the students. °True or °false?**
2.1

  1 Zane's flat is near the school.
  2 Sunita's bus is electric.
  3 Noah's school journey is very short.

  4 Lily has a long journey to school.
  5 Alice is alone on her school journey.

> **1 b) 1** true • **2** false • **3** true, only 5 minutes • **4** true • **5** false, she goes to school with her big brother

Lead-in Inhalt

Lernschwerpunkt: über den Schulweg sprechen
Kompetenzen: Listening Sprachnachrichten Informationen über den Schulweg entnehmen • Speaking sich über den Schulweg austauschen • Umfrageergebnisse versprachlichen
Redemittel: Wortfeld *school journey*

Vorbereitung

Material: Unit-Einstieg von L vorbereitete Flashcards mit Verkehrsmitteln, Handpuppe Scout / alternatives Maskottchen • Ex 1 UMA/CD, Flashcards (s.o.) • Ex 2 Flashcards (s.o.)
Zeitbedarf: 1–2 Std.
Begleitmedien: WB (S. 40), App (Digital quiz), INKL (S. 80–81), DIFF (3.1)

Nach dieser Unit kann ich ... ✓

○ über meinen Schulweg sprechen
○ meinen Alltag beschreiben
○ mich verabreden
○ neue Wörter nachschlagen und lernen

Unit task ✓

○ die Höhepunkte meiner Woche vorstellen

Nach dieser Unit ...

• L bespricht mit S die Lernziele der Unit (s. links) und kündigt die *Unit task* an.
• Am Ende der Unit überprüfen die S das Erreichen der Ziele mithilfe des *Checkpoint* (S. 98–101) bzw. gemeinsam im Plenum.

Ex 2 Einstieg:
• (SB auf) TA: #greenschooljourneys
L: *Are we a green class? Why (not)?*

Erarbeitung:
a) L schreibt die fünf Transportmittel (s. Unit-Einstieg) untereinander an die Tafel.
L: *Talk to your classmates. Say how you go to school and find students with the same transport.*
• L spielt Beispiel mit zwei bis drei S vor.
• ▶ Milling around: S tauschen sich aus und bilden eine Gruppe mit den S, die dasselbe Transportmittel benutzen.
• ⊠ Lernstärkere S bilden gemäß AA ausführlichere Sätze.
• **Ausw.:** L legt wieder die Flashcards aus Ex 1 im Raum aus. L: *Let's check. How do you go to school? Please go to the right picture.* S gehen in ihren Gruppen zu den Flashcards.

b) Gemeinsames Zählen.
• Ergebnisse im TA festhalten.
• **Ausw.:** S sprechen im Plenum über die Ergebnisse mit dem ▶ Scaffolding aus b).

Noah

Lily

Alice [ˈælɪs]

💬 **2** SPEAKING **My school journey**

👥 a) WALK AROUND Tell different partners about your school journey. Make groups of students with the same °transport.

I go to school by bus. – Me too!

⊠ Say °more in your group: *I walk to school with my sister / dad / friend / ...*
It's a short / long journey.

▶ More practice 1, p. 105

b) Say how students go to school.

A lot of students in my class ...   Some ...

▶ Workbook, p. 40

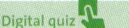 Digital quiz   I can **talk about my school journey.** ✓

Topic 1 Inhalt

Lernschwerpunkt: Zeitangaben und Tagesabläufe verstehen
Kompetenzen: Listening Hörtexten Zahlen und Uhrzeiten entnehmen • Speaking sagen, wie viel Uhr es ist •
Reading einem Lesetext Informationen über Zanes Tagesablauf entnehmen
Redemittel: Zahlen von 10 bis 60 • digitale Uhrzeiten • Wortfeld *daily routine*

Ex 1 Einstieg:
- (SB auf) L schreibt die Zahlenwörter aus a) in gemischter Reihenfolge an die Tafel und liest sie laut vor.
  L: *Match the numbers from your book with the right words.*
- S ordnen die Zahlen den Wörtern zu.

Erarbeitung:
a) + b) gemäß AA
- **Sich.:** Zahlenwörter ins *Vocab file* schreiben.

Ex 2 Einstieg:
- (SB zu) Spiel: S zählen durch (eine Zahl pro S). L nennt zwei Teiler (z. B. 3 und 5). Bei Zahlen, die durch 3 und 5 teilbar sind, klatschen S statt zu zählen. Bei einem Fehler startet das Zählen wieder bei Null.

Erarbeitung:
a) (SB auf) **1. Hören:** S klatschen den Rhythmus nach.
- **2. Hören:** S klatschen den Rhythmus und sprechen die Uhrzeiten nach.

b) gemäß AA, L erklärt die Bedeutung von *a.m.* und *p.m.*
  (▶ Good to know, S. 82).
- **Ausw.:** ▶ Five-minute teacher

c) S schreiben die Programmpunkte ins Heft.
- **1. Hören:** S notieren die Uhrzeiten.

d) S prüfen ihre Antworten im ▶ Partner check. Dann **2. Hören.**
- **Ausw.:** im Plenum (mit TA)

Ex 3 s. S. 104

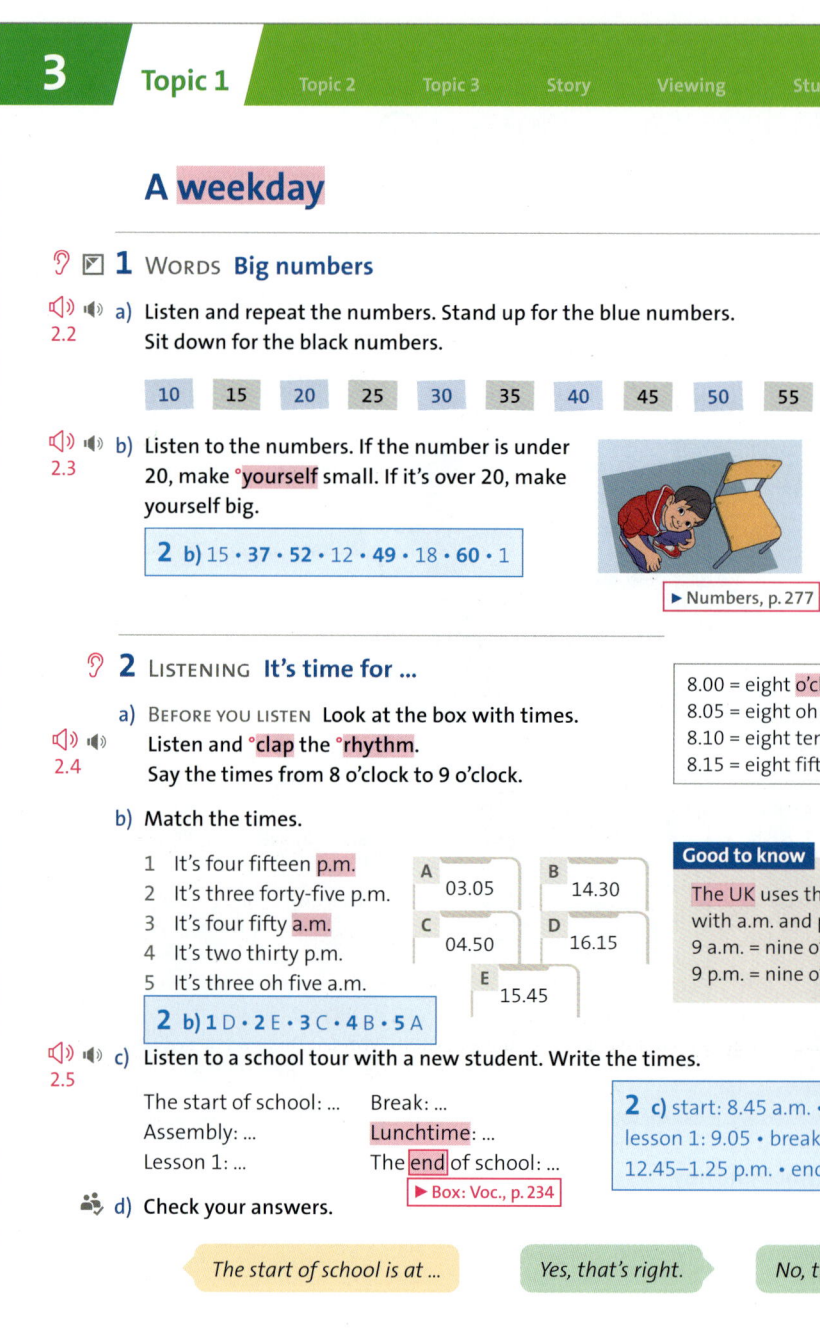

Topic 1 Vorbereitung

Material: Ex 1 UMA/CD • Ex 2 UMA/CD • Ex 4 UMA, vergrößertes Foto von S. 83
Zeitbedarf: ca. 2 Std.
Begleitmedien: WB (S. 41), INKL (S. 82–83), DIFF (3.2)

4 READING Before and after school ▶ Box: Voc., p. 234

a) BEFORE YOU READ **What's true about Zane? Talk to a partner. Then check in Units 1 and 2.**

His hobby is parkour: I think that's false. – Yes, you're right. / I think you're wrong. Let's check.

1 His hobby is parkour. (Unit 1, p. 19)
2 He's a swimmer. (Unit 1, p. 19)
3 He's always busy. (Unit 1, p. 30)
4 He has time for his friends after school. (Unit 1, p. 30)
5 He has a new computer. (Unit 1, p. 38)
6 His dream room is messy. (Unit 2, p. 69)

> **4 a) 1** false (that's Lily's sport) •
> **2** true • **3** true • **4** false • **5** false
> (it's old and slow) • **6** true

b) **Look at the picture, the °headline and the first two °paragraphs. Answer the questions.**

1 Why is Zane's family in the newspaper? *It's a letter from his … for a competition.*
2 Why is Zane always busy on weekdays? *He helps his … because she has a …* ▶ Box: Voc., p. 235

> **4 b) 1** mum • **2** mum, bad illness

🔊 2.7

My son is the best +ever!

Today's letter for our 'Best +Kids Competition' is from Louise Adebayo. It's about her son Zane (11). Remember: you choose the winner, readers!

5 I have a bad illness and I use a wheelchair. My husband Eno has a cafe and he +works long days. On weekdays, my son Zane helps me.

Zane gets up at 7 o'clock, has a shower
10 and gets dressed. His little sister Holly gets up at 7.30. Eno makes breakfast for us and we all eat breakfast. Zane takes Holly to her school at 8.15 and then he goes to his school. Then I work – I write
15 books with special +software.

Zane meets Holly at her school at 3.20 and they walk home. Zane makes a snack

for us and tidies the kitchen. Then he does his homework. It takes an hour. On
20 some days Zane helps me with dinner. Or he talks with his friends or watches +TV. On Friday he goes to swimming +training. He goes to bed at 9 o'clock.

Zane, you help me a lot. You're the best
25 son ever!

Zane's mum / Zane

▶ Box: Voc., p. 235

c) **Read the °full °article. Put Zane's day in the correct order:** *1f, 2 …*

a He does his homework.
b He eats breakfast with his family.
c Zane takes Holly to her school at 8.15.
d He makes a snack and tidies the kitchen.
e Zane goes to bed at 9 o'clock.
f Zane gets up at 7 o'clock, has a shower and gets dressed.
g He meets Holly at her school at 3.20.

> **4 c) 1** f • **2** b • **3** c • **4** g • **5** d • **6** a • **7** e

eighty-three **83**

Ex 4 Einstieg:
• (SB zu) L zeigt das vergrößerte Foto von S. 83 (UMA).
L: *Who is this? Who is the woman?*
• S raten die Antwort auf die zweite Frage.
L: *Let's see now what you know about Zane.*

Erarbeitung:
a) (SB auf) PA gemäß AA
• **Ausw.:** ▶ Five-minute teacher

b) L: *Zane is always busy. Let's find out why! Read the headline and the first two paragraphs of the article.*
• S lesen die Aufgabe und die ersten zwei Absätze des Textes.
• Sie ergänzen die Lücken in den Sätzen 1 und 2.
• **Ausw.:** im Plenum

c) **1. Lesen:** S lesen den Text / hören mit (▶ Mitleseverfahren). Sie erfragen unbekannten Wortschatz.
• ▶ Vokabelarbeit: L sammelt neuen Wortschatz an der ▶ Vokabeltafel.
• **2. Lesen:** S lesen die Sätze a–g und bringen sie in die richtige Reihenfolge.
• Sie überprüfen ihre Antworten durch erneutes Lesen.
• **Ausw.:** ▶ Meldekette

• ▶ Early finisher: S schreiben einige wahre und falsche Aussagen zum Text und stellen sie der Klasse vor. Die Klasse ordnet die Sätze als *true* bzw. *false* ein.

Topic 1 Inhalt

Lernschwerpunkt: den eigenen Tagesablauf beschreiben und über die Tagesabläufe anderer sprechen
Kompetenzen: Listening Song zum Tagesablauf verstehen • Speaking über den eigenen Tagesablauf sprechen • den Song zum Tagesablauf mitsingen • Writing Sätze mit dem *simple present* vervollständigen • einen Post zum eigenen Tageslauf schreiben
Strukturen: *simple present* (bejahte Aussagesätze)
Redemittel: Uhrzeiten, Wortfeld *daily routine*

Ex 5 Einstieg:
- (SB auf, S. 83) L: *What do you remember about Zane's day?*
- S nennen Informationen (vorbewusste Nutzung des *simple present*).

Erarbeitung:
a) (SB auf, S. 84) gemäß AA
- **Ausw.:** ▶ Five-minute teacher mit TA der jeweiligen Sätze

b) S lesen die linke Box. Sie untersuchen die Sätze aus a).
- **Ausw.:** Ergebnisse werden im Plenum verglichen.
- L erklärt die Grammatik u. lässt die ▶ Tippbox, S. 84 gemeinsam lesen.
- S übertragen Regeln mit Beispielen in den Merkteil (▶ English folder).
- s. a. ▶ LF 10, S. 187 und Erklärfilm (UMA/App)

Ex 6 Einstieg:
- (SB auf) L: *Describe the picture. What does Zane do on Saturday?*
- PA: S beschreiben das Bild. L: *Let's find out more.*

Erarbeitung:
- S wählen die richtige Verbform und schreiben sie ins Heft.
- **Ausw.:** ▶ Five-minute teacher
- ▶ Early finisher: ☒ ▶ KV 3.1
- ☒ ▶ Challenge 1, S. 107

Ex 7 Einstieg:
- (SB zu) L übt den Dialog beispielhaft mit einigen S.

Erarbeitung:
- (SB auf) S arbeiten gemäß AA in Kleingruppen.
- ☒ Stärkere S wiederholen die Aussagen von mehreren S.

---

3 | Topic 1 · Topic 2 · Topic 3 · Story · Viewing · Study skills · Unit task

5 LOOKING AT LANGUAGE °Simple present

Erklär-film

a) Complete the sentences from the article.

1 You ... the winner, readers! (line 4)
2 I ... a wheelchair. (lines 5–6)
3 We all ... breakfast. (line 12)
4 They ... home. (line 17)
5 Zane, you ... me a lot. (line 24)

6 He ... long days. (line 7)
7 Zane ... me. (line 8)
8 She ... up. (lines 10–11)
9 It ... an hour. (line 19)
10 He ... with his friends. (line 21)

5 a) 1 choose • **2** use • **3** eat • **4** walk • **5** help • **6** works • **7** helps • **8** gets • **9** takes • **10** talks

b) Look at the verbs in a). What's different? Answer the question in the box below.

> Bei regelmäßigen Tätigkeiten und Aktionen verwendest du das *simple present*. Wann endet das Verb auf -s? Bei:
> – I / you / we / they?
> – he / she / it?

Be careful with these verbs:
have – has
do – does
go – goes
watch – watches
tidy – tidies

5 b) Bei *he/she/it* endet das Verb auf -s.

▶ Language file 10, p. 187 ▶ More practice 5, p. 106

---

6 On Saturday

Zane's mum tells a friend about the family's weekend. Choose the correct verb.

On Saturday Zane and Holly (1) get up / gets up late. Eno (2) get up / gets up first and he (3) do / does the shopping. Then he (4) make / makes breakfast for us and we all (5) eat / eats. In the afternoon I (6) work / works. Eno and the kids (7) go / goes to the ⁺park or they (8) play / plays a game at home.

▶ Box: Voc., p. 236

Eno ['iːnəʊ]
Holly   Zane

▶ More practice 6, p. 106 ▶ More practice 7, p. 107 ▶ Challenge 1, p. 107

6 1 get up • **2** gets up • **3** does • **4** makes • **5** eat • **6** work • **7** go • **8** play

---

7 GAME Weekdays

Talk about your weekday like this:

Student 1	I get up at six thirty.
Student 2	He/She gets up at six thirty. I have a shower and get dressed.
Student 3	He/She has a shower and gets dressed. I eat breakfast.
Student 4	He/She ... I ...
Student 1	He/She ... I ...

7 individuelle Lösungen

▶ Workbook, pp. 41–43

84 eighty-four

Topic 1 Vorbereitung

Material: Ex 5 UMA/App (Erklärfilm) • Ex 6 ▶ KV 3.1: Scout's day (je nach Bedarf) • Ex 8 UMA/CD
Zeitbedarf: ca. 3 Std. (Die 3. Person Singular sollte gut geübt werden.)
Minimalversion: Ex 8 auslassen
Begleitmedien: WB (S. 41–43), App (Erklärfilm, Digital help, Digital quiz), INKL (S. 84–85), DIFF (3.3)

🎵 8 SONG **Good morning!**

8 a) 1 d • 2 c • 3 a • 4 e • 5 b

a) BEFORE YOU LISTEN **Match the times to the °activities.**

1	07.00	a	eat your breakfast
2	07.15	b	go to school
3	07.30	c	have a shower
4	07.45	d	get up
5	08.00	e	brush your teeth

🔊 2.9 b) **Listen to the song. Compare your answers in a) with the song.**

🔊 2.10 c) **Listen to °verse 6. It's not on this page. Say how the song ends. Then check your answer on p. 104.**

The girl says that it's …

d) ROLE-PLAY **Sing and °act out the song.**

> **8 c)** The girl says that it's Saturday. It's 8 o'clock, go back to bed.

The morning song 🎵

Get up, it's seven o'clock (It's too °early!)
Get up, it's seven o'clock
It's seven °already, it's time to °get ready
Get up, it's seven o'clock.

Have a shower, it's seven fifteen
(But I'm tired!)
Have a shower, it's seven fifteen
It's seven fifteen, now it's time to °get clean
Have a shower, it's seven fifteen.

It's seven thirty, eat your breakfast (I'm not hungry!)
It's seven thirty, eat your breakfast
I say it's °the most important °meal of the day
It's seven thirty, eat your breakfast.

It's seven forty-five, brush your teeth
(The bathroom's °cold!)
It's seven forty-five, brush your teeth
It's °almost eight, you don't want to be late
It's seven forty-five, brush your teeth.

It's eight o'clock, go to school (°Wait, Dad …)
It's eight o'clock, go to school (Dad!)
Don't °make a fuss, time to °catch the bus
It's eight o'clock, go to … (Dad!!!)

My task

9 My school day | **9** individuelle Lösungen |

WRITING **Read Zane's °post. Write a post about your day. You can use the words in the box. Put your post in your DOSSIER.**

> in the morning • after school • in the afternoon •
> in the evening • get up • have a shower •
> get dressed • walk/go by … • go to school •
> school starts • have lunch • school ends • go to bed

Hi, Zane
My name is … and I live in … This is my day:
In the morning I get up at …

Zane
Hello, everybody
My class has a project about the school day in other countries.
Please tell us about your school day.
Thanks.

▶ Digital help   ▶ More help, p. 108   ▶ Wordbank 10, p. 201

▶ Workbook, p. 43

 Digital quiz   **I can °describe my °daily °routine.** ✅

Ex 8 Einstieg:
- (SB zu) TA mit ▶ Scaffolding für Aktivitäten aus a) *I get up at … and I eat my breakfast at … When do you get up?*
- S sagen in PA, wann sie die Aktivitäten tun.
- ✉ S sprechen über den Tag ihres Partners / ihrer Partnerin.

Erarbeitung:
a) (SB auf) gemäß AA

b) **Ausw.** von a), gemäß AA

c) 1. Hören: ▶ Partner talk: S besprechen, was sie verstanden haben.
- **Ausw.:** 2. Hören: S lesen auf S. 104 mit.

d) S lesen Songtext und erfragen unbekannten Wortschatz.
- GA: S überlegen sich Bewegungen zum Song (▶ TPR).
- **Ausw.:** S singen mit und zeigen die Bewegungen.

My task Ex 9 Einstieg:
- (SB zu) L gibt Beispiele für Unterschiede zwischen deutschen und britischen Schulen (Unterrichtszeiten s. Ex 2c), S. 82).
- Ggf. S fragen, an welche Unterschiede sie sich noch erinnern.

Erarbeitung:
- (SB auf) S lesen Zanes Nachricht.
- S schreiben einen Text über ihren Schultag.
- ▶ More help, S. 108
- **Ausw.:** S lesen Texte in der Klasse vor.
- **Sich.:** Ablage im ▶ Dossier

3

Topic 2 Inhalt

Lernschwerpunkt: über Hobbys und sportliche Aktivitäten sowie deren Häufigkeit sprechen
Kompetenzen: Listening einem Hörtext Informationen über AGs und Hobbys entnehmen • Speaking sich äußern, welche Aktivitäten man regelmäßig, oft oder nie macht • Intercultural competence erfahren, welche *school clubs* es in Großbritannien gibt
Strukturen: Adverbien der Häufigkeit (lexikalisch)
Redemittel: Wortfeld *sports and hobbies*

Ex 1 Einstieg:
• (SB zu) L: *What's your favourite sport/hobby? Are you in a club?* S antworten.

Erarbeitung:
a) (SB auf) gemäß AA. S lesen Wörter vor und nennen Bedeutung. Evtl. vergrößerte Bilder von ▶ KV 3.2 als Flashcards zur visuellen Unterstützung einsetzen, anschließend ▶ Lautschulung und ▶ Vokabelarbeit.
• L verweist dann auf ▶ Good to know, S. 86, S/L liest vor, Beantworten der beiden Fragen im ▶ Think-Pair-Share.
• **Ausw.:** S: *There is/are ... at our school. / I/We want a ... club at our school.*

b) S notieren beim **1. Hören** die Buchstaben in der richtigen Reihenfolge.
• **Ausw.:** im Plenum

c) Gemeinsames ▶ Klären der AA, S notieren beim **2. Hören** die richtigen Namen.
• **Ausw.:** ▶ Partner check, anschließend im Plenum

d) (SB zu) L mit Handpuppe Scout: *I remember table tennis and cricket. What about you?*
• S fragen und antworten in PA.

e) (SB auf) S tauschen sich im ▶ Milling around aus.
• **Ausw.:** Einige S stellen ihre Dialoge im Plenum vor.
• ▶ Early finisher: ☑ ▶ KV 3.2
• ☒ ▶ Challenge 2, S. 108
• **Zusatz:** S spielen mit den ausgefüllten Dominokarten der ▶ KV 3.2 ▶ Menschen-Domino.

86

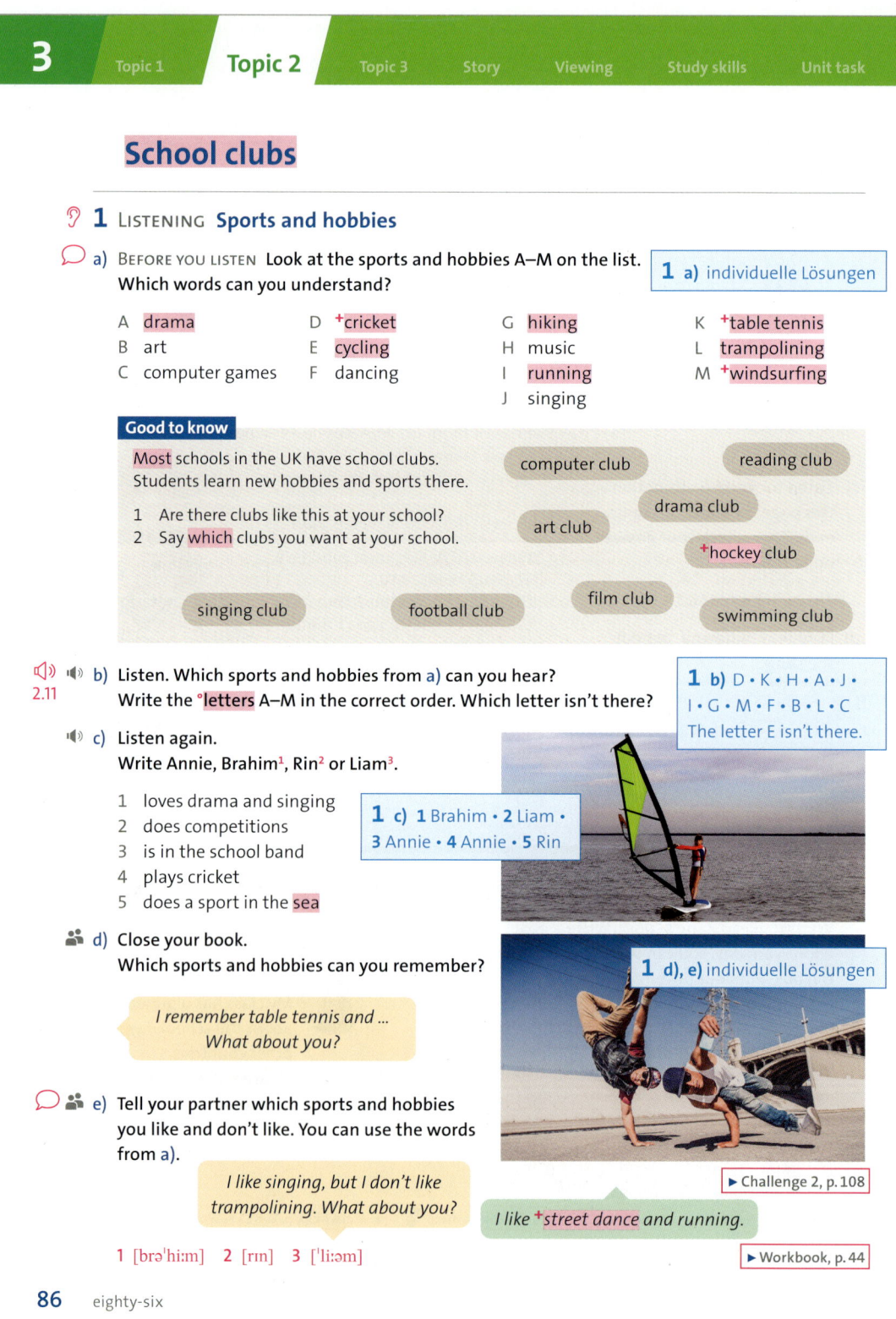

3 | Topic 1 | **Topic 2** | Topic 3 | Story | Viewing | Study skills | Unit task

School clubs

👂 **1** LISTENING **Sports and hobbies**

💬 **a)** BEFORE YOU LISTEN Look at the sports and hobbies A–M on the list. Which words can you understand?

> **1 a)** individuelle Lösungen

A drama
B art
C computer games
D ⁺cricket
E cycling
F dancing
G hiking
H music
I running
J singing
K ⁺table tennis
L trampolining
M ⁺windsurfing

Good to know

Most schools in the UK have school clubs. Students learn new hobbies and sports there.

1 Are there clubs like this at your school?
2 Say which clubs you want at your school.

computer club · reading club · drama club · art club · ⁺hockey club · singing club · football club · film club · swimming club

🔊 2.11 **b)** Listen. Which sports and hobbies from a) can you hear?
Write the °letters A–M in the correct order. Which letter isn't there?

> **1 b)** D · K · H · A · J · I · G · M · F · B · L · C
> The letter E isn't there.

🔊 **c)** Listen again.
Write Annie, Brahim[1], Rin[2] or Liam[3].

1 loves drama and singing
2 does competitions
3 is in the school band
4 plays cricket
5 does a sport in the sea

> **1 c) 1** Brahim • **2** Liam • **3** Annie • **4** Annie • **5** Rin

👥 **d)** Close your book.
Which sports and hobbies can you remember?

> *I remember table tennis and ... What about you?*

> **1 d), e)** individuelle Lösungen

💬👥 **e)** Tell your partner which sports and hobbies you like and don't like. You can use the words from a).

> *I like singing, but I don't like trampolining. What about you?*

> *I like ⁺street dance and running.*

> ▶ Challenge 2, p. 108

1 [brəˈhiːm]   2 [rɪn]   3 [ˈliːəm]

> ▶ Workbook, p. 44

86 eighty-six

Topic 2 Vorbereitung

Material: Ex 1 UMA/CD, Handpuppe Scout, ▶ KV 3.2: GAME Sports and hobbies (je nach Bedarf), vergrößerte Bilder der ▶ KV 3.2 als Flashcards • Ex 2 UMA/CD, von L vorbereitete Wortkarten mit Adverbien • Ex 3 UMA, vergrößertes Bild von S. 87, Handpuppe Scout
Zeitbedarf: ca. 1–2 Std.
Minimalversion: Ex 1d) auslassen
Begleitmedien: WB (S. 44–45), INKL (S. 86–87)

3

2 How often?

🔊 2.11 **a)** Listen again. Choose the correct words.

1 Annie A sometimes B often C never plays cricket,
   but she A always B sometimes C rarely plays table tennis.
2 Brahim A often B rarely C always does drama,
   but he A sometimes B rarely C never goes running.
3 Rin A always B sometimes C often goes hiking,
   and she A rarely B sometimes C never does dancing.
4 Liam A rarely B always C never does art,
   but he A rarely B sometimes C often plays computer games.

> **2 a) 1** often, rarely • **2** often, never • **3** often, sometimes • **4** always, rarely

> ▶ Box: Voc., p. 237

b) Put the words in the correct place.

> **2 b)** never • rarely • often • sometimes • always

never … … … always

3 SPEAKING +Surfing sentences

a) Look at the picture. Make sentences. Your partner checks your verbs.

He sometimes ~~play~~ football. – No, that's wrong. He sometimes plays football.
I never go swimming. – Yes, that's right.
You often … – Yes, that's right. / No, that's wrong. You often …

I often go surfing.

I / You / He / She — often / sometimes / never / rarely — play / plays / go / goes — football. / cycling. / surfing. / hockey. / swimming.

b) Use the words in the picture and say sentences about you.

> **3** individuelle Lösungen

> ▶ Language file 11, p. 187
> ▶ Challenge 3, p. 108
> ▶ Workbook, p. 45

eighty-seven **87**

Ex 2 Einstieg:
• (SB zu) L heftet Wortkarten mit Häufigkeitsadverbien (*never/rarely/sometimes/ often/always*) an die Tafel (in ungeordneter Reihenfolge).
• ▶ Semantisierung

Erarbeitung:
a) (SB auf) S lesen die Sätze. Sie notieren die Zahlen 1–4 und ergänzen die Lösungen beim **3. Hören.**
• **Ausw.:** ▶ Five-minute teacher oder Plenum

b) (SB zu) Die Wortkarten werden an der Tafel gemäß AA geordnet, anschließend übertragen S den TA in ihr Heft.

Ex 3 Einstieg:
• (SB zu) L zeigt vergrößertes Bild von S. 87 (UMA).
• L fragt Handpuppe Scout: *What's your hobby?* Scout: *I often go surfing.* L zur Klasse: *Scout often goes surfing.*
• L verweist auf das Bild: *Can you make more sentences?*
• S bilden einige Beispielsätze, L korrigiert ggf. die Verben.

Erarbeitung:
a) (SB auf) gemäß AA
• **Ausw.:** S bilden Sätze im Plenum.

b) gemäß AA, im ▶ Partner talk
• **Ausw.:** S präsentiert die Ergebnisse des Partners / der Partnerin.
• ▷ L liest mit lernschwächeren S ▶ LF 11, S. 187.
• ▷ ▶ Challenge 3, S. 108

Topic 2 Inhalt

Lernschwerpunkt: einen AG-Aushang verstehen • über die Freizeitgestaltung sprechen und schreiben
Kompetenzen: Mediation wesentliche Inhalte eines AG-Aushangs ins Deutsche vermitteln • Speaking sich zu den eigenen Aktivitäten und denen eines Partners / einer Partnerin äußern • Writing eine Nachricht über die eigene Freizeitgestaltung schreiben
Redemittel: Wortfeld *sports and hobbies* • Häufigkeitsadverbien

---

Ex 4 Einstieg:
• (SB zu) L zeigt zunächst nur die Bilder des Posters (UMA).
L: *What can you see in the pictures?*
S: *I can see students / young people / race cars / ...*
• L deckt ganzes Poster auf.
L: *Look! It's a poster about the Formula 24 Club. Let's get some information about the club.*

Erarbeitung:
a) (SB auf) **1. Lesen** (*Skimming*, ▶ Lesetechniken), dann Klären der AA und Hinweis auf die ▶ Tippbox, S. 88 (▶ Mediation)
• Bearbeitung der Aufgabe in PA: **2. Lesen** für *Partner B*, *Partner A* notiert Antworten im Heft (▶ Note-taking, s. Tipps).

b) Bearbeitung der Aufgabe in PA: **2. Lesen** für *Partner A*, *Partner B* notiert Antworten im Heft.
• **Ausw.:** S-Paare präsentieren die Ergebnisse mithilfe ihrer Notizen im Plenum.

• **Alternative:** L bereitet Karten mit den Fragen aus dem SB vor (*Partner A/B*) und verteilt diese an die S-Paare.
• S notieren sich zunächst in EA Antworten zu den Fragen, dann PA gemäß **Ex 4 a) + b)**.
• ☑/☒ Je nach Leistungsvermögen erhalten S weniger oder mehr als drei Karten mit Fragen.

---

3 | Topic 1 | **Topic 2** | Topic 3 | Story | Viewing | Study skills | Unit task

⤻ 👥 **4** °MEDIATION **A very special school club**

a) Read the poster from Varndean school.

> **4 a) 1** Ein elektrisches Auto • **2** Mr Price und Ms Haffar helfen. • **3** Die Teilnahme ist kostenlos.

Partner A: You can't understand the poster. Ask partner B the questions below.
Partner B: Answer partner A's questions in German.

1 Was baut man in dieser AG?
2 Arbeiten die Schüler/innen allein oder haben sie Hilfe?
3 Kostet die Teilnahme etwas?

> 💡 Du brauchst nicht jedes Wort zu übersetzen. Gib nur das Wichtigste wieder.

b) °Swap roles.

Partner B: You can't understand the poster. Ask partner A the questions below.
Partner A: Answer partner B's questions in German.

1 Welche Eigenschaften sollte man für die AG haben?
2 Wer nimmt am Rennen teil?
3 Wann findet die AG statt?

> **4 b) 1** Man sollte aktiv und ein Teamplayer sein. Man sollte gut in Sport, Mathe, Kunst und Werken sein. • **2** 700 Mannschaften • **3** Freitags um 15.30 Uhr

FORMULA 24 CLUB

Are you active and good in a team?
Are you °good at sports, maths, art or design and technology?
If you want an interesting hobby, then join Formula 24 Club at Varndean!

We plan and make an electric car from old °materials.
Then we °race with 700 other teams from the UK and other countries.
°More than 10,000 students do the °race °every year!

We meet every Friday afternoon at 3.30 for two hours. Mr Price and Ms Haffar sometimes help us, but we work hard too.
It's always a lot of °fun °even if we aren't the winner! It's a free club because we make and °sell °cakes to °get °money for materials.

Topic 2 Vorbereitung

Material: Ex 4 UMA, vergrößertes Poster von S. 88, von L vorbereitete Karten mit den Fragen der Aufgabe (Klassensatz) •
Ex 5 Stuhlkreis für Einstieg, UMA, vergrößerte Abbildung von S. 89 oben (Sätze), Handpuppe Scout • Ex 6 UMA, vergrößertes Foto von S. 89, weißes Papier (A4, Klassensatz)

Zeitbedarf: ca. 2 Std.

Minimalversion: Ex 5a) als HA vorbereiten lassen

Begleitmedien: WB (S. 45–46), App (Digital help, Digital quiz), INKL (S. 88–89), DIFF (3.4)

3

🗨 👥 **5** SPEAKING **Secret sentences**

a) Write three sentences for **1** and three sentences for **2**. Choose words from the blue boxes for each sentence. Don't °**show** them to your partner.

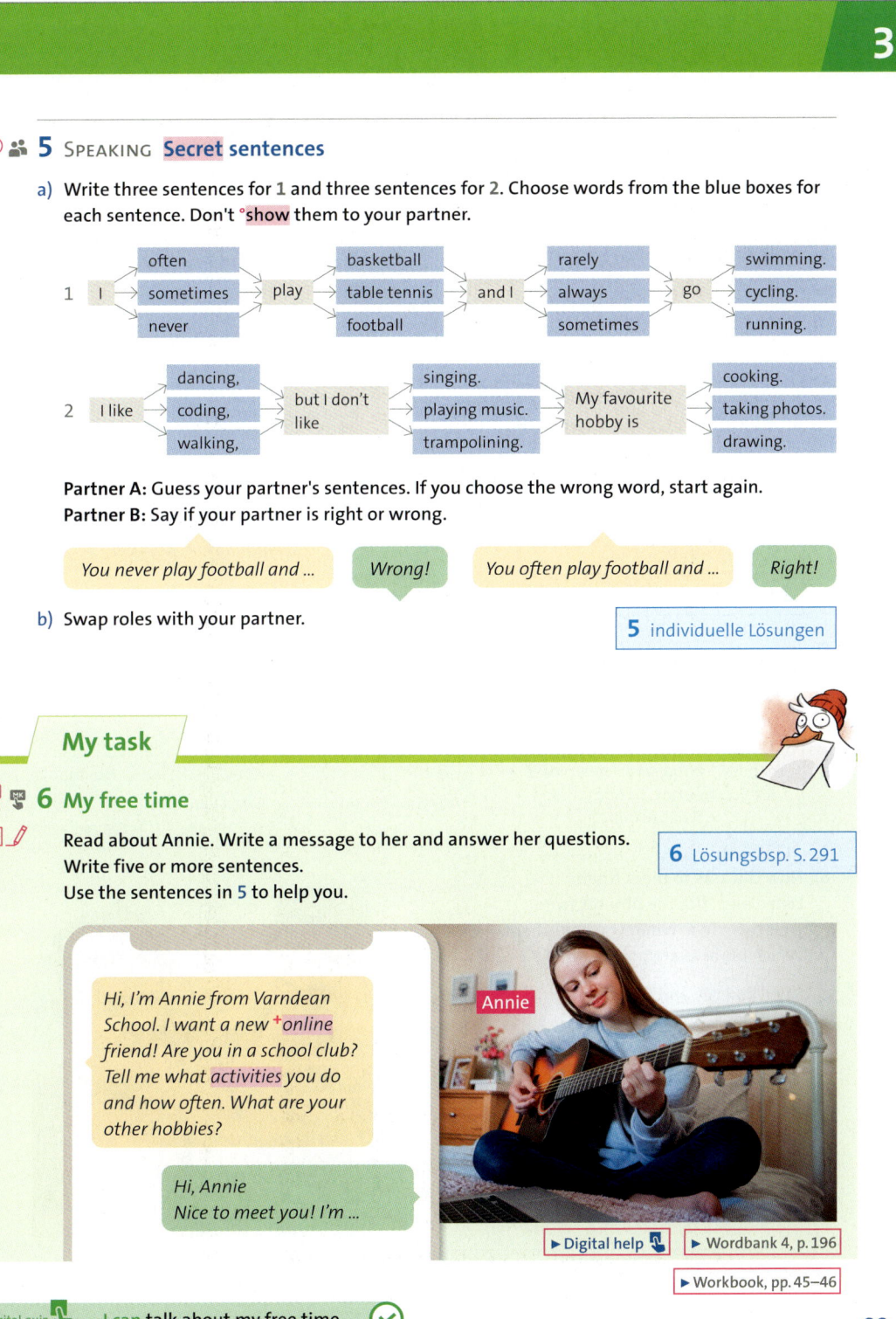

```
          often                basketball              rarely              swimming.
   1   I  sometimes  →  play   table tennis  → and I   always   →  go      cycling.
          never                football                sometimes           running.
```

```
            dancing,                      singing.                           cooking.
   2  I like coding,  →  but I don't  →   playing music.  → My favourite     taking photos.
            walking,        like          trampolining.    hobby is          drawing.
```

Partner A: Guess your partner's sentences. If you choose the wrong word, start again.
Partner B: Say if your partner is right or wrong.

You never play football and … | *Wrong!* | *You often play football and …* | *Right!*

b) Swap roles with your partner.

5 individuelle Lösungen

My task

🔖 ✏ **6 My free time**

📖 ✏ Read about Annie. Write a message to her and answer her questions.
Write five or more sentences.
Use the sentences in **5** to help you.

6 Lösungsbsp. S. 291

Hi, I'm Annie from Varndean School. I want a new +online friend! Are you in a school club? Tell me what activities you do and how often. What are your other hobbies?

Annie

Hi, Annie
Nice to meet you! I'm …

▶ Digital help 🔄 | ▶ Wordbank 4, p. 196

▶ Workbook, pp. 45–46

Digital quiz 🔄   I can **talk about my free time.** ✓

eighty-nine **89**

Ex 5 Einstieg:
- (SB zu) Aktivierung des Wortschatzes: ▶ <u>Fruit salad</u> (abgeleitet auf *hobbies*).
- L zeigt die Sätze von a) mit dem UMA, S bilden mündlich Beispielsätze, L notiert ggf. Sätze an die Tafel.

Erarbeitung:
a) (SB auf) Klären der AA, S notieren Sätze, anschließend Bearbeitung in PA gemäß AA.

b) gemäß AA mit getauschten Rollen
- ▶ <u>Early finisher</u>: Zwei S-Paare tauschen Partner/innen und wiederholen die Aufgabe.
- **Ausw.:** S1 nimmt Rolle von Scout ein (mit Handpuppe) und denkt sich einen Satz aus. Zwei S verlassen den Raum, S1 trägt Satz vor. Die zwei S kommen wieder herein und versuchen im Wettstreit, den Satz zu erraten.

My task Ex 6 Einstieg:
- (SB zu) L zeigt vergrößertes Foto von S. 89 (UMA).
  L: *Look, this is Annie. What can you say about Annie?*
  S: *Annie is a student / at home / plays the guitar / …*
- L präsentiert Annies Nachricht (UMA), oder das SB wird geöffnet, stilles Lesen.

Erarbeitung:
- (SB auf) Klären der AA, L verweist auf Ex 5 und ▶ <u>Wordbank 4, S. 196</u>, Bearbeitung der Aufgabe in EA.
- **Alternative:** S gestalten ein Blatt gemäß der Aufmachung im SB mit eigenem Foto o. Ä.
- **Ausw.:** ▶ <u>English corner</u>

Topic 3 Inhalt

Lernschwerpunkt: sich mit Freunden verabreden • Pläne machen
Kompetenzen: Reading Chat-Nachrichten Details über eine Verabredung entnehmen • Listening eine Verabredung am Telefon verstehen • Speaking sich mit einem Freund / einer Freundin verabreden
Redemittel: Redewendungen für Verabredungen

Ex 1 Einstieg:
- (SB zu) TA: *When do you meet your friends? What do you do?*
- S tauschen sich im ▶ Milling around aus.
  L: *Lily wants to meet Zane. Let's read about it.*

Erarbeitung:
a) (SB auf) **1. Lesen:** S lesen die Nachrichten und erfragen ggf. unbekannten Wortschatz.
- **2. Lesen:** S bringen Nachrichten in die richtige Reihenfolge gemäß AA.
- **Ausw.:** ▶ Partner check

b) S schreiben die Zahlen und die passenden Namen in EA ins Heft.
- **Ausw.:** ▶ Five-minute teacher

Ex 2 Einstieg:
- (SB zu) L mit Handpuppe Scout.
  L: *Scout! You look sad. What's wrong?*
  Scout: *I want to meet George but I don't know what to say.*
  L: *We can help you!*

Erarbeitung:
a) (SB auf) TA der Tabelle. Im Plenum drei Beispiele an der Tafel lösen.
- S schreiben in EA die Lösungen ins Heft oder auf ▶ KV 3.3 (Ex 1).
- **Ausw.:** TA im Plenum ergänzen

b) + c) gemäß AA
- **Ausw.:** im Plenum

- **Zusatz:** ▶ Early finisher: S schreiben einen Dialog für Scouts Anruf bei George.

| 3 | Topic 1 | Topic 2 | **Topic 3** | Story | Viewing | Study skills | Unit task |

Meeting friends

1 READING **Are you busy?**

1 a) 1 d • 2 c • 3 a • 4 e • 5 b

a) Write the letters to put the messages in the correct order. Check with a partner.

1d, 2 …

b) Choose Lily or Zane for each phrase.

1. wants to meet at the weekend   *Lily*
2. is busy on Saturday and Sunday
3. wants to go cycling
4. likes swimming
5. says sorry
6. is sad
7. is always busy

a   Oh, OK. Are you free on Sunday? Let's go cycling!

b   That's a shame. You're always busy, Zane. I never see you now. 😟

c   Sorry, Lily. I'm busy on Saturday.

d   Hi, Zane, let's meet on Saturday!

e   Sorry, I can't. On Sunday I have a swimming competition.

1 b) **1** Lily • **2** Zane • **3** Lily • **4** Zane • **5** Zane • **6** Lily • **7** Zane

2 LISTENING **Let's meet**

a) BEFORE YOU LISTEN **Copy the table. Write the phrases in the correct place.**

Let's … • No, thanks. • I'd love to. • I'm busy. • Good idea! • Yes, please! • Are you free on …? • Sorry, I can't. • What about …?

Ask to meet		Say *yes*		Say *no*	
Let's …	✓	I'd love to.	✓	No, thanks.	(−)
Are you free on …?	✓	Good idea!	✓	I'm busy.	✓
What about …?	✓	Yes, please!	(−)	Sorry, I can't.	✓

🔊 2.12 b) Now Lily asks to meet Noah. Listen and °tick the phrases from your table in a) when you hear them. Which phrases are not in the °dialogue?

c) Say when Lily and Noah meet.

Lily and Noah meet at … on …

at 9 o'clock
at the park
on Saturday
on Sunday

Lily   Noah

2 c) … (at the cafe) at 10.30 a.m. on Sunday.

▶ Workbook, p. 47

90 ninety

Topic 3 **Vorbereitung**

Material: Ex 2 UMA/CD, Handpuppe Scout, ► KV 3.3: Meeting friends (Klassensatz) • Ex 4 ► KV 3.3
Zeitbedarf: ca. 2 Std.
Begleitmedien: WB (S. 47), App (Digital quiz), INKL (S. 90–91), DIFF (3.5)

3

💬 **3** ROLE-PLAY **Can we meet this weekend?**   **3** individuelle Lösungen
Go to p. 104 and act out Lily and Noah's conversation.   ► Challenge 4, p. 109

My task

4 Are you free?

🖊 a) Copy the °calendar.

	Friday	**Saturday**	**Sunday**
9.00	*SCHOOL*	*activity:* *with:*	*activity:* *with:*
1.00	*SCHOOL*	*activity:* *with:*	*activity:* *with:*
5.00	*activity:* *with:*	*activity:* *with:*	*activity:* *with:*

💬 👥 b) DOUBLE CIRCLE
Choose an activity from the box or use your own idea. Talk to a partner and write your plan in your calendar.

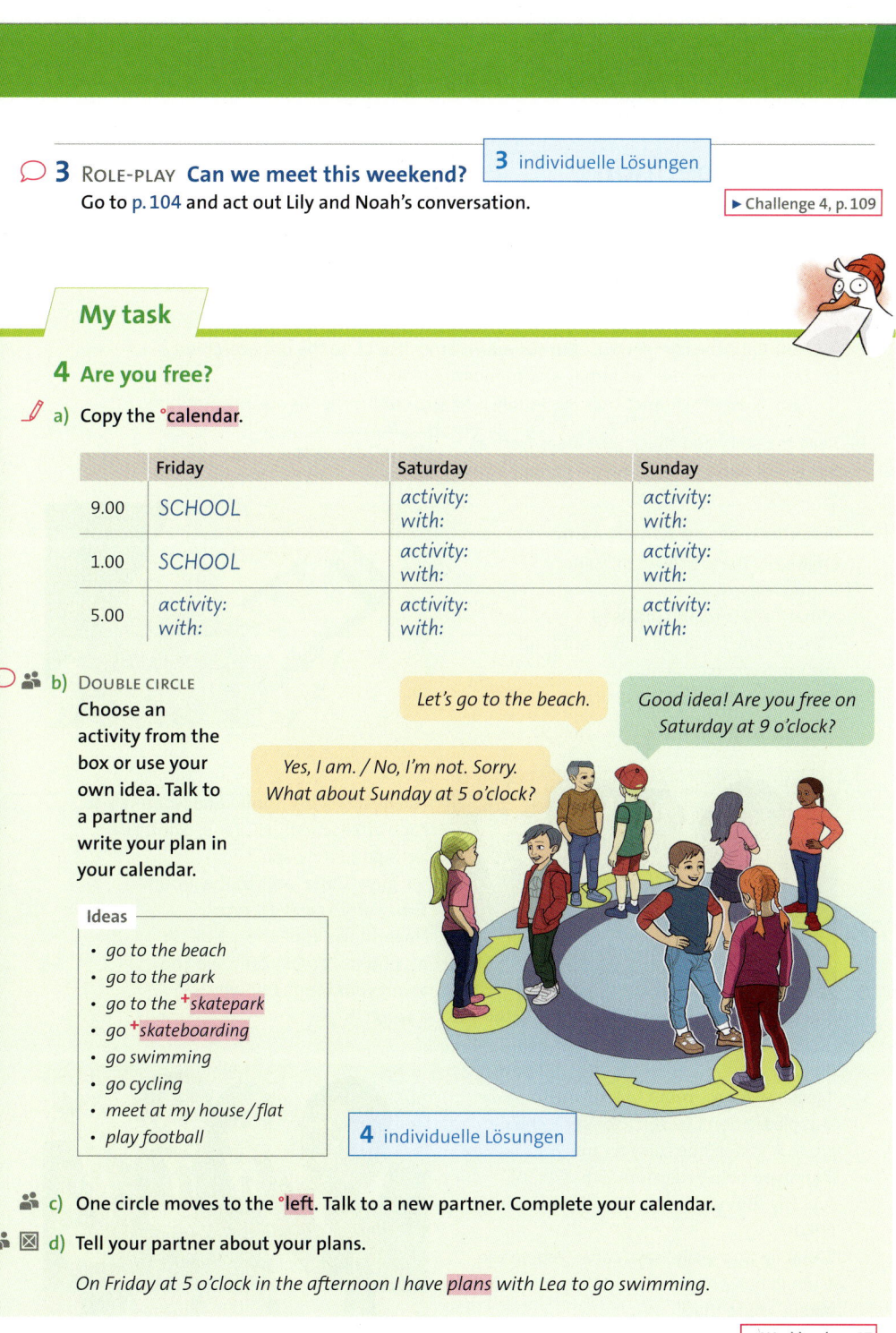

Let's go to the beach.

Good idea! Are you free on Saturday at 9 o'clock?

Yes, I am. / No, I'm not. Sorry. What about Sunday at 5 o'clock?

Ideas
• *go to the beach*
• *go to the park*
• *go to the* +*skatepark*
• *go* +*skateboarding*
• *go swimming*
• *go cycling*
• *meet at my house / flat*
• *play football*

4 individuelle Lösungen

👥 c) One circle moves to the °left. Talk to a new partner. Complete your calendar.

👥 ✉ d) Tell your partner about your plans.

On Friday at 5 o'clock in the afternoon I have plans *with Lea to go swimming.*

► Workbook, p. 47

Digital quiz 🐸   **I can make plans to meet friends.** ✅

Ex 3 **Einstieg:**
• (SB zu) L: *Please walk around the room. Now look …*
• L nennt verschiedene Adjektive und S spielen sie nach.
• mögliche Adjektive: *happy, sad, bored, angry, tired, cold, hot, busy, stressed …*

Erarbeitung:
• (SB auf) S spielen den Dialog auf S. 104 (► Role-play).
• weitere Hinweise s. S. 104
• ✉ Lernstärkere S denken sich einen eigenen Dialog aus (► Challenge 4, S. 109).

My task Ex 4 **Einstieg:**
• (SB zu) TA: Tabelle aus Ex 2
• Wdh.: gemeinsames Sammeln der Phrasen aus Ex 2 in den richtigen Spalten

Erarbeitung:
a) (SB auf) gemäß AA
• ▶ Lernschwächere oder langsamere S nutzen die Tabelle auf ► KV 3.3 (Ex 2) und tragen schon einmal vier Aktivitäten aus der Ideenliste in ihre Tabelle ein. L sollte S darauf hinweisen, dass sie ein paar Slots frei lassen und auch noch keine Namen eintragen sollen.

b) L übt Beispieldialog mit mind. zwei S und zeigt an der Tafel das Eintragen der Aktivitäten.
• S stellen sich im ► Double circle auf und führen ersten Dialog durch.

c) gemäß AA

d) **Ausw.:** gemäß AA, Sprachhilfe s. ► KV 3.3 (Ex 3)

91

Story **Inhalt**

Lernschwerpunkt: eine Geschichte über einen Wettbewerb und damit verbundene Emotionen verstehen
Kompetenzen: Speaking Vermutungen über den Inhalt einer Geschichte äußern • Reading eine Geschichte verstehen und ihr die Gefühle der Lehrwerkspersonen entnehmen • den Textabschnitten Überschriften zuordnen
Redemittel: Adjektive zum Beschreiben von Gefühlen

Ex 1 Einstieg:
- (SB zu) L: *Have you ever won a competition? What for?*
  S: *Yes, a competition in sports/ music/…*
  L: *What can be the prize for a competition?*
- Mögliche Antworten: *money / a football / a cup / …*

Erarbeitung:
a) L zeigt die vergrößerten Bilder von S. 92–93 (UMA) oder verteilt ▶ KV 3.4 (Ex 1).
  L: *Who can you see in the pictures? How do they feel? Talk to a partner.*
- S beschreiben Bilder in PA:
  In picture 1/2/… I can see …
  (▶ Picture duet).
- (SB auf) Bearbeitung gemäß AA, L erfasst die Anzahl der Antworten der S als TA (… x A, … x B, … x C).

b) L: *Let's read the story and find out the correct answer.*
- 1. Lesen im ▶ Mitleseverfahren, anschließend Auswertung im Plenum mit Bezug auf TA aus a).
- ⊠ S nennen die Absätze gemäß AA, S: *Parts 4, 5 and 6 show the correct answer.*
- ☑ Für Lernschwächere Vorentlastung des Wortschatzes: S nutzen Erschließungstechniken (▶ Semantisierung), L semantisiert übrigen Wortschatz.

---

3   Topic 1   Topic 2   Topic 3   **Story**   Viewing   Study skills   Unit task

The competition

💬📖 **1** READING **About the story**

☑ **a)** BEFORE YOU READ **Look at the °title and the pictures. Choose A, B or C.**

> **1 a)** B

A   Zane wins the competition. But his mum is too ill to go to the prize ceremony.
B   Zane is the winner. His family and friends are really happy.
C   Zane wins the competition. His family is happy, but his friends are angry at him.

⊠ **b)** **Read the story and check your ideas from a). Say which parts (1–6) show the correct answer.**

> **1 b)** parts 4–6

🔊 2.13

1
'Hey, Lily! Look at this!' Lily's mum shows Lily the article about Zane in the newspaper.
'What?' Lily is really surprised.
'I know Zane's mum is ill. But not that she's in a wheelchair.'
She takes a photo of the article and sends it to Sunita and Noah.

2
The next day Lily, Sunita and Noah talk to Zane after school. 'Hi, Zane,' Sunita says. 'Let's go to the park.'
'Hi, guys.' Zane looks at the ground. 'Erm, sorry. I can't. I … erm …'
Noah shows Zane the article on his phone. 'It's OK, Zane, we know about your mum. But why is it a secret?'

Zane   Sunita   Noah   Lily

3
'I feel bad for my mum,' says Zane. 'But please don't be sorry for her – she's great. And don't be sorry for me!'
'Zane, you help your mum – that's cool,' says Lily. 'But we're your friends. You can tell us.'
'Don't be angry, Lily,' says Zane. 'People see Mum in her wheelchair and they think she's stupid. I hate that!'

Zane   Sunita   Noah   Lily

92   ninety-two

Story Vorbereitung

Material: Ex 1 UMA, vergrößerte Bilder der Story, UMA/CD, ▶ KV 3.4: The competition (Klassensatz) • Ex 2 UMA, Überschriften aus dem SB, ▶ KV 3.4 • Ex 3 ggf. Requisiten für *Role-play*, UMA/CD/App

Zeitbedarf: ca. 1–2 Std.

Minimalversion: Ex 2 oder Ex 3 auslassen

Begleitmedien: INKL (S. 92–93)

🔊 2.14

4

Later at Zane's home …
'Hello, Louise Adebayo. What? Really? …
That's great! Thank you so much. … Bye'.
'Zane, come here!' His mum is happy.
'You're the *Best Kids Competition* winner!
Well done!'
'Thanks, Mum,' says Zane. 'I love you!'

5

Zane tells his friends. Everybody is happy!
Zane gets ⁺tickets for the prize show for his
family and friends. But Zane's mum is tired
and she is in bed for two days.
'The prize show isn't a good idea, Mum,'
says Zane. Zane's mum looks at him. 'Why
not? I can do it.'
'OK, Mum!' Zane says.

6

At the prize show …
Zane talks to everybody.
'Hello. Thanks for choosing me as the winner.
Mum and Dad and Holly – you're the best!
And thanks to my friends Lily, Sunita and
Noah! There's some prize money for the
winner. I'd like to …'

📖 **2 Headings**   **2** 1 c • 2 b • 3 e • 4 f • 5 d • 6 a

Choose headings from a–f for parts 1–6. Or use your own ideas. *1c, 2 …*

a   Zane says thank you.
b   Zane's friends tell him they know.
c   Zane's friends find out about his mum.

d   Zane tells his friends he's the winner.
e   Zane explains about his mum.
f   Zane's mum is happy.

📖 **3 What happens in the story**

3 1 … a newspaper article to Sunita and Noah. • 2 … to the park with his friends. • 3 … his mum's illness. • 4 … the winner of the competition. • 5 … go to the prize show. • 6 … some prize money.

Read the story again. Complete the sentences.

▶ Parallel exercise, p. 109

1   Lily sends …
2   Zane says he can't go …
3   Zane explains about …

4   Zane's mum tells him that he is …
5   Zane's mum is tired, but she wants to …
6   The competition winner gets …

ninety-three **93**

Ex 2 Einstig:

- (SB zu) L: *Let's find headings for the paragraphs of the story.*
- L zeigt die Überschriften aus Ex 2 (UMA). S lesen laut vor.

Erarbeitung:

- (SB auf) Klären der AA, S ordnen beim **2. Lesen** die Überschriften den Abschnitten zu.
- S notieren die Lösungen im Heft oder nutzen ▶ KV 3.4 (Ex 2).
- **Ausw.:** ▶ Partner check: S vergleichen Ergebnisse und mögliche eigene Ideen, anschließend Präsentation im Plenum.
- **Sich.** von neuem Wortschatz durch ▶ Semantisierung und ▶ Lautschulung, S notieren Vokabeln in ihr *Vocab file* (▶ Vokabelarbeit).

Ex 3 Erarbeitung:

- (SB auf) L klärt AA im Plenum.
- ▶ Parallel ex, S. 109 auf leichterem Niveau
- L kann S individuell zuweisen.
- Ggf. **3. Lesen**, S notieren die Lösungen in ihr Heft.
- **Ausw.:** ▶ Five-minute teacher

- **Zusatz:** Geschichte nachspielen: S bilden Gruppen (▶ Gruppenbildung) und lesen/ spielen die Szenen mit verteilten Rollen (*Lily's mum, Lily, Sunita, Noah, Zane, Zane's mum, narrator*) vor einer anderen Gruppe oder der Klasse vor (dabei auf Mimik und Gestik/Gefühle achten).
- L stellt ggf. die Aufnahme zum Üben der Aussprache zur Verfügung (UMA/CD bzw. App).

Story Inhalt | Vorbereitung

Lernschwerpunkt: Gefühle von Personen beschreiben
Kompetenzen: Speaking Gefühle der Charaktere beschreiben und darstellen • über Zanes Pläne spekulieren •
Listening gehörte Informationen mit eigenen Vermutungen vergleichen • Life skills überlegen, wem man einen Preis verleihen würde
Redemittel: Wortfeld *feelings*

Material: Ex 4 von L vorbereitete Flashcards (Smileys) • Ex 5 Realien (britisches Geld) oder Bilder, UMA/CD
Zeitbedarf: ca. 1 Std.
Minimalversion: Ex 6 auslassen
Begleitmedien: App (Digital quiz), INKL (S. 94), DIFF (3.6)

Ex 4 Einstieg:
• (SB zu) Wdh. *feelings*: Adjektive als TA, Smileys von S. 100 als ▶ Flashcards zeigen. L: *Match the smileys and the adjectives.*

Erarbeitung:
a) (SB auf) gemäß AA

b) Klären der AA, S bilden Gruppen und üben ein Standbild ein (▶ Freeze-frame).

c) Ausw.: Gruppen präsentieren gemäß AA, Klasse gibt Feedback.

Ex 5 Einstieg:
• (SB zu) L bringt britisches Geld mit oder zeigt Bilder (UMA). L: *Do you know the UK's money?*
• Unterrichtsgespräch zum Geld (▶ Good to know, S. 94).

Erarbeitung:
a) (SB auf) GA gemäß AA

b) 1. Hören: S notieren die Lösung.
• **2. Hören:** S prüfen.
• **Ausw.:** Gruppen präsentieren ihre Ergebnisse im Plenum.

Ex 6 Erarbeitung:
a) (SB auf) Klären der AA (▶ Think-Pair-Share)
• Bearbeitung gemäß AA in EA
• ☒ Lernstärkere S formulieren Begründung.
• ▶ More help, S. 109

b) gemäß AA in PA

c) gemäß AA im Plenum

---

3 Topic 1 Topic 2 Topic 3 **Story** Viewing Study skills Unit task

💬 **4** SHOWTIME °**Freeze!**

angry • happy • sad • sorry • surprised • tired

a) Say how people in the story feel in parts 1–6.

In part 1 Lily is surprised.   *In part 2 Zane is …*
In part 3 Zane is … and Lily …   *In part 4/5/6 …*

👥 **b)** Choose one of the six parts of the story.
Show it as a °freeze-frame. Show °feelings with your °body and °face.

c) Show the class. The class says what part it is. Then the class gives feedback.

> *It's part 5. Zane's friends are happy. His mum is tired.*

> *Your freeze-frame is great!*

> **4 a)** In part 2 Zane is sad. • In part 3 Zane is sorry and Lily is angry. • In part 4 Zane's mum is happy. • In part 5 Zane's friends are happy and Zane's mum is tired. • In part 6 Zane is happy.

5 Zane's prize money

💬👥 **a)** Zane's prize money is £500. Guess what Zane does with the money. You can use the ideas in the box or your ideas. °Agree on two ideas.

> **5 a)** individuelle Lösungen

Ideas
• *gets a new video* +*console* / …
• *gets a new TV for his family* / …
• *gives some money to his mum and dad*
• *pays for a big* +*party with family and friends*
• *pays for a cleaner*

Good to know
The UK's money is the pound (£). ▶ Box: Voc., p. 239
In one pound, there are 100 pence (p). How much is £500 in +euros?

> *I think he gets / gives / pays for …*

> *That's a good idea!*

> *I think he …*

🎧 **b)** Listen to Zane's ideas in his °speech. Are they the same as your group's ideas?

🔊 2.15 *Zane wants to …*   *Our ideas are the same / different.*

> **5 b)** Zane wants to pay for a big party with family and friends and to pay for a cleaner.

💬 **6** LIFE SKILLS **Be kind**

> **6** individuelle Lösungen

a) THINK Zane is kind because he helps his mum. You can choose one person for a prize. Who is kind in your group of friends, your family or where you live?
☒ Think about °reasons why.

> ▶ More help, p. 109

My basketball +*trainer is really kind because …*

👥 **b)** PAIR Tell a partner about the person. *My kind person is …*

c) SHARE Tell the class your ideas.

> **4 b)** individuelle Lösungen

94 ninety-four

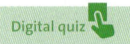 Digital quiz   **I can** understand feelings in a story.

Viewing Inhalt | Vorbereitung

Lernschwerpunkt: Filmszenen über Mutproben verstehen
Kompetenzen: Viewing Filmszenen Informationen entnehmen • Speaking Informationen über die Protagonisten zusammentragen • Brainstorming zu einer neuen Mutprobe
Redemittel: Wortfeld *sports and hobbies*

Material: Ex 2 + Ex 3 UMA/DVD
Zeitbedarf: ca. 1 Std.
Minimalversion: Ex 1b) auslassen
Begleitmedien: WB (S. 48), INKL (S. 95)

| Topic 1 | Topic 2 | Topic 3 | Story | **Viewing** | Study skills | Unit task | **3** |

1 a) ... goes swimming. Emir does drama and he plays football.

The Brighton dares: Sports and hobbies

1 About Daisy and Emir

a) BEFORE YOU WATCH **Look at the lists.**
What are Daisy and Emir's sports and hobbies?

Daisy plays table tennis and she ...

Emir
do drama
play football

Daisy
play table tennis
go swimming

b) What other things do you know about the friends? (Pages 33 and 63 can help you.)

1 b) Daisy is eleven years old. They go to Varndean school. Their teacher is Mr Campbell. Daisy dares Emir every Friday. Emir dares Daisy every Friday. Daisy likes Luke.

2 VIEWING Time for a new dare

Watch the video. Choose the correct picture (A or B) for each dare.

Daisy's dare for Emir is to ...

A
wear underpants[1] on his head.

B
wear pink hair.

Emir's dare for Daisy is to ...

A
make a street drawing.

B
play street music.

2 Daisy's dare for Emir: A • Emir's dare for Daisy: B

3 VIEWING Who helps? Who can't help?

3 a) 1 d • 2 c • 3 a • 4 b

a) Match the people to how they help or can't help. Then watch the video again and check.

1 Gloria helps Emir.
2 Amal can't help Daisy.
3 Gloria can't help Daisy.
4 Jenny helps Daisy.

a She has a trip to London at the weekend.
b Daisy can play her guitar.
c She can't play the violin for six weeks.
d She gives him a good idea.

b) Complete how Emir and Daisy do their dares.

Emir makes a ... from ...   Daisy plays the air[2] ... to her brother's ...

3 b) Emir makes a *beanie* (*a hat*) from *his underpants*. Daisy plays the air *guitar* to her brother's *music*.

4 A new sports or hobby dare   **4** individuelle Lösungen

Brainstorm new sports or hobbies dares for Daisy and Emir. Then choose the best dare!

What about this: play table tennis in the canteen.

[1] **underpants** *Unterhose*   [2] **air** *Luft*

▶ Workbook, p. 48

Ex 1 Einstieg:
• (SB zu) L stellt S Fragen über ihre Hobbys. L: *What are your hobbies? Do you sometimes do something crazy?*

Erarbeitung:
a) (SB auf) S nennen die Hobbys aus der Liste in PA.

b) S nennen Dinge, an die sie sich aus den anderen Videos (S. 33 und 63) erinnern.
• **Ausw.:** im Plenum

Ex 2 Einstieg:
• (SB zu) L: *What do you think is the next dare?*
• L sammelt Ideen in TA.

Erarbeitung:
• (SB auf) L: *Look at the pictures of some more dares. What do you think?*
• S sagen, wie sie die Mutproben finden.
• **1. Sehen**: S wählen jeweils das richtige Bild.
• **Ausw.:** im Plenum

Ex 3 Erarbeitung:
a) (SB auf) gemäß AA in PA. S schreiben Lösungen ins Heft.
• S überprüfen ihre Lösungen beim **2. Sehen**.
• **Ausw.:** ▶ Five-minute teacher

b) S ergänzen die Sätze.
• **Ausw.:** im Plenum

Ex 4 Erarbeitung:
• (SB auf) gemäß AA. S sammeln in GA Ideen in einem ▶ Brainstorming.
• **Ausw.:** im Plenum

Lernschwerpunkt: neuen Wortschatz nachschlagen und lernen

Kompetenzen: Reading einem Text neue Wörter entnehmen und alphabetisch ordnen • Wörter Gruppen zuordnen • Study skills neuen Wortschatz im *Dictionary* nachschlagen und im *Vocab file* systematisieren

Redemittel: Wortfeld *sports and hobbies*

Material: Ex 1 Handpuppe Scout, evtl. Stricknadeln o. Ä. • Ex 4 Handpuppe Scout

Zeitbedarf: ca. 1 Std.

Minimalversion: Ex 3 kann als HA erarbeitet werden

Begleitmedien: App (Digital quiz), INKL (S. 96), DIFF (3.7)

Ex 1 Einstieg:

(SB zu) Handpuppe Scout mit Stricknadeln:
Scout: *Look, this is my favourite hobby. It's knitting.*
L: *Can you spell it?* (Scout buchstabiert).
L: *What is it in German?* (S antworten).
L: *Let's learn some more free-time activities.*

Erarbeitung:

a) (SB auf) Klären der AA
• S notieren die Wörter untereinander.

b) gemäß AA, auf ▶ Tippbox, S. 96 hinweisen

c) gemäß AA, S prüfen und wiederholen die neuen Wörter, dann ▶ Lautschulung.

Ex 2 Erarbeitung:
• (SB auf) gemäß AA
• **Ausw.:** ▶ Five-minute teacher

Ex 3 Einstieg:
• (SB zu) Liste der Wörter aus Ex 1 + 2 als TA, evtl. Wdh. der Aussprache

Erarbeitung:
• (SB auf) gemäß AA
• **Ausw.:** ▶ Partner check, dann Bsp. im Plenum

Ex 4 Einstieg:
• (SB zu) Handpuppe Scout: *Let's play a game.*
• Erklären von *Odd word out* mit Bsp. als TA.

Erarbeitung:

a) + b) (SB auf) gemäß AA

---

3 | Topic 1 | Topic 2 | Topic 3 | Story | Viewing | **Study skills** | Unit task

Look up and remember words

1 Look up free-time activities

A new English friend writes to you about free-time activities. You °need to look up the words in blue.

> I have a lot of free-time activities! I like °crafts. My favourite hobby is °jewellery making. I like °chess and jigsaw puzzles too. I love collecting things with cats and I love °skating.

a) First write the words in a list in °alphabetical order.

b) Look up the words in the English-German Dictionary on pages 255–266.

🔊 2.16 c) Listen and check your answers.

💡 For words with the same first letter, look at the second letter.

> **1** chess - Schach • collecting things - Sammeln • crafts - Basteln • jewellery making - Schmuck machen • jigsaw puzzles - Puzzlespiele • skating - Schlittschuhlaufen

2 Find more free-time activities

Look at Wordbank 4 on free time (p. 196). What are these activities in English?

1 Backen	3 Kajakfahren	5 Nageldesign
2 Boxen	4 Klettern	6 Reiten

> **2** **1** baking • **2** boxing • **3** kayaking • **4** climbing • **5** doing nail art • **6** horse riding

3 Write and remember

Choose five English words from 1 and 2. Write them in your VOCAB FILE.

English	Write a sentence, draw a picture	German & my other languages
collecting	I like collecting rubbers and football cards.	Sammeln, toplamak
jigsaw puzzles	🧩	...

4 Odd word out

a) Find the odd word out.

> **4 a) 1** drawing • **2** cola or fish • **3** monkey or parrot • **4** money • **5** sofa

1 running • swimming • cycling • drawing
2 ⁺cola • ⁺burger • sandwich • fish
3 monkey • parrot • dog • rabbit
4 book • money • words • page
5 kitchen • bathroom • sofa • living room

> It's good to learn words in groups.

b) Make an *Odd word out* with four words for the class.

> **4 b)** individuelle Lösungen

▶ Skills file 4, p. 177

Digital quiz 👆 I can **look up** and learn new words. ✓

Unit task | Inhalt | Vorbereitung

Lernschwerpunkt: die eigenen Highlights der Woche in einem Comic oder Video vorstellen

Kompetenzen: Writing über Höhepunkte der Woche schreiben • Speaking Höhepunkte der Woche vortragen • Feedback geben

Redemittel: Wortfelder *sports and hobbies, days of the week* • Feedback

Material: Step 2 *Task A:* weißes Papier (A3), *Task B:* geeignete Aufnahmegeräte • Step 3 + 4 *Task B:* geeignete Abspielgeräte • Step 4 UMA

Zeitbedarf: 2 Std.

Begleitmedien: App (Digital quiz), INKL (S. 97)

| Topic 1 | Topic 2 | Topic 3 | Story | Viewing | Study skills | **Unit task** | **3** |

Unit task individuelle Lösungen

Share your ⁺highlights of the week

Step 1

°Think about what you do °every week. Write sentences about the best things. Choose three to five activities.

On Wednesday I have a singing lesson. On Saturday I always get up at 10 o'clock. My dad often takes me to a football match.

Or you can be your favourite singer, a ⁺superhero, a TV star, your pet – or me!

► Wordbank 4, p. 196

Step 2

YOU CHOOSE Do °task A or B.

Task A	Task B
Draw a comic of your activities from step 1. Write your sentences from step 1 under your comic pictures. You can add speech bubbles too. 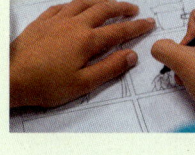	Make a video: °Record your sentences from step 1 on your phone. You can show things, °for example headphones for music. ⁺*Check that the light is good for your video. Speak clearly.* 

Step 3

Task A	Task B
👥 Show your comic to a partner. Get feedback. *I like your pictures. Check your spelling.*	👥 Play your video to a partner. Get feedback. *Your video is really good. Don't speak so fast.* ► Let's talk: Feedback, p. 211

Step 4

👥 Look at the comics and watch the videos. Give feedback.

Your ⁺comic is great! Your pictures are cool!

► Let's talk: Feedback, p. 211

Digital quiz · **I can share the highlights of my week.** ✓

ninety-seven **97**

Unit task Einstieg:
- L erklärt *Unit task* mit den notwendigen Schritten und verweist auf Wahlmöglichkeiten (analog und digital).

Step 1 Erarbeitung:
- (SB auf) S liest Text im SB vor. L: *Do you have more examples for highlights of the week?*
- S nennen Bsp., L notiert sie als TA, anschließend Erarbeitung in EA gemäß AA.

Step 2 Erarbeitung:
- L verweist nochmals auf Wahlmöglichkeit.
- gemeinsames Klären der AA für beide Alternativen
- bei *Task A* auf das Differenzierungsangebot in der AA hinweisen
- für *Task B* notwendige Technik bereitstellen, Belehrung zum Datenschutz
- Bearbeitung in EA gemäß AA

Step 3 Erarbeitung:
- gemäß AA in PA (bei ungerader Anzahl eine Dreiergruppe)
- S geben Feedback.

Step 4 Erarbeitung:
- (SB auf, S. 211) Sätze zum Feedback gemeinsam lesen, ggf. ► Lautschulung
- **Alternative:** L zeigt die Sätze von S. 211 über den UMA.
- Präsentation der Ergebnisse: Comics aushängen (► Gallery walk, ► English corner), Videos zeigen, evtl. auf Homepage der Schule stellen (Datenschutz beachten)

Checkpoint Inhalt

Lernschwerpunkt: Kompetenzen und sprachliche Mittel üben, Lernfortschritte erkennen
Kompetenzen: Reading eine E-Mail lesen und Fragen dazu beantworten • Speaking über den eigenen Schulweg sprechen •
sich zu Freizeitaktivitäten äußern • Writing Sätze über einen Tagesablauf vervollständigen
Strukturen: *simple present*
Redemittel: Wortfelder *school journey* (Transportmittel), *daily routine, sports and hobbies*

Allgemeine Anmerkung:
s. Unit 1, S. 36

Ex 1 Einstieg:
• (SB auf) S lesen das Lernziel
  (*I can ...*) rechts oben auf der
  Seite vor.
• Sie schätzen ihr Können zum
  Lernziel ein, z. B. mit ► Thumbs
  up, und notieren sich das
  Ergebnis.

Erarbeitung:
a) S lesen den Text leise oder
  laut.
  L: *What text is it?*
  S: *It's an email.*

b) gemäß AA in EA
• **Ausw.:** ► Five-minute teacher
  oder ► Meldekette

c) L zeichnet grünen und roten
  Daumen (wie in der orange-
  farbenen Sprechblase) an
  die Tafel und stellt Fragen
  gemäß SB, S halten Daumen
  entsprechend.
• anschließend schriftliche
  Bearbeitung in EA
• **Ausw.:** im Plenum
• **Alternative:** Ausw. von **b)** und
  c) am ► Bus stop (► KV Extra):
  S vergleichen ihre Lösungen
  mithilfe der ► KV 3.5A.

d) ► Klären der AA, Bearbeitung in
  PA
• **Ausw.:** im Plenum, grüner und
  roter Daumen siehe **c)**
• nach der Lösungskontrolle
  erneute Einschätzung des
  Könnens (gleiche Methode
  wie im Einstieg)

---

3 **Checkpoint** Digital checkpoint 🔗

📖 **1** READING **Zara's[1] school journey**   I can **talk about my school journey.** ✓

a) Read the email from Zane's friend Zara.

> 🟢🟡🔴
>
> | to | Zane |
> | from | Zara |
>
> Hi, Zane
> How are you? My new school in London is great. I have lots of friends now and I like most of
> the teachers. But I have a problem and that's the journey to school. London is so big and my
> house isn't near my school. 👎 Sometimes I go to school by car, with my mum, and that's good
> because it's fast. But most days I go by bus. I don't like the bus because the other people are
> really loud! 😠 It's slow too: The journey takes 45 minutes. Sometimes I'm late for school and
> my class teacher isn't happy! What about you? Is your school journey good or bad? Why?
>
> See you later 😄
> Zara

b) Read the sentences. True or false?

1 Zara isn't happy at her school.
2 Her school journey is long.
3 Zara goes to a different school in Brighton.
4 The bus is often quiet.
5 She's sometimes in trouble with her teacher.

> **1 b) 1** false • **2** true • **3** false • **4** false • **5** true

c) Answer the questions.

1 Is Zara's car journey good or bad? – *Zara's car journey is ... because it's ...*
2 Is Zara's bus journey good or bad? – *Zara's bus journey is ... because the bus is ... and ...*

> **1 c) 1** Zara's car journey is good
> because it's fast. • **2** Zara's bus journey
> is bad because the bus is really loud
> and slow too.

💬👥 **d)** SPEAKING **Talk about your school journey with a partner.**

> **1 d)** individuelle Lösungen

> *I go to school by* 🚗/🚲/
> 🚆/🚌/*I* 🚶 *to school.*
> *My school journey is* 👍/👎 *because it's*
> *long / short / loud / quiet / fast / slow.*
> *That's* 👍/👎 *because ...*

1 [ˈzɑːrə]

Check 🔗

Checkpoint Vorbereitung

Material: alle Aufgaben ▸ KV Extra: Bus stop, ▸ KV 3.5A: Checkpoint answers
Zeitbedarf: ca. 2 Std.
Minimalversion: Auswahl der Aufgaben erfolgt aufgrund der zu überprüfenden Lernziele
Begleitmedien: App (Digital checkpoint), INKL (S. 98–99)

Die Übungen kannst du auch digital machen   **3**

✏ **2** WORDS **Sunita's morning**   I can describe my daily routine (simple present). ✓

Sunita talks about her morning routine. Complete her sentences.

1 I ... at six fifteen.

2 At six thirty I ...

3 And I ...

4 After that I ...

5 Then I ...

6 I ... at 8 o'clock.

> **2** **1** get up • **2** have a shower • **3** brush my teeth •
> **4** get dressed • **5** eat breakfast • **6** go to school

✏ **3** LANGUAGE **Sunita's evening**

Complete Sunita's sentences. Use the verbs in the box in the correct form.

do (2 x) • eat • go • make • read • take • tidy • watch

I come home from school at 4 p.m. Sometimes Nish (1) ... a snack for us — we're always hungry after school! Then I (2) ... my homework. That (3) ... thirty minutes. We (4) ... dinner at 7 p.m. and then Ben (5) ... the kitchen. After dinner I (6) ... TV and Nish (7) ... his homework on the computer. Mum and Ben often (8) ... the newspaper. On weekdays I (9) ... to bed at 9 p.m.

> **3** **1** makes • **2** do • **3** takes • **4** eat • **5** tidies • **6** watch • **7** does • **8** read • **9** go

💬 **4** SPEAKING **A conversation with Ryan**   I can talk about my free time. ✓

Ryan asks Lily about her free time. Look at Lily's calendar and say her answers.

Are you in a school club, Lily? Tell me what other activities you do and how often.

Phrases
• (Yes,) I'm in the ... club.
• I °*also* like / do / play / go to / ...
• I (sometimes / often / always) play / walk / do ...

Monday	Tuesday	Wednesday	Thursday	Friday	Saturday	Sunday
5.30 p.m.: table tennis		4.30 p.m.: parkour	After school: art club		10 a.m.: parkour	11 a.m.: walk with Dad

> **4** Yes, I'm in the school art club. I also like parkour. It's really fun. I sometimes play tennis and I sometimes walk with my dad.

Check

Ex 2 **Einstieg:**
• s. Ex 1 (Selbsteinschätzung)
• **Alternative:** (SB zu) L stellt zur Aktivierung des Wortschatzes Fragen zum Tagesablauf, z. B. *When do you get up?*, S antworten entsprechend.

Erarbeitung:
• (SB auf) gemäß AA
• **Ausw.:** ▸ Bus stop (▸ KV Extra): S vergleichen ihre Lösungen mithilfe der ▸ KV 3.5A.
• **Alternative:** ▸ Meldekette (mit TA)

Ex 3 **Erarbeitung:**
• (SB auf) Klären der AA
• S schreiben Sätze in ihr Heft und ergänzen.
• ⏯ Langsamere S notieren nur die Lösungswörter.
• **Ausw.:** ▸ Bus stop (▸ KV Extra): S vergleichen ihre Lösungen mithilfe der ▸ KV 3.5A.
• **Alternative:** ▸ Partner check, anschließend im Plenum (mit TA)
• erneute Selbsteinschätzung zum o. g. Lernziel (s. Ex 2)

Ex 4 **Einstieg:**
• s. Ex 1 (Selbsteinschätzung)

Erarbeitung:
• (SB auf) gemäß AA in PA
• ⊠ Lernstärkere S und ▸ Early finishers ergänzen die Tabelle aus dem SB zunächst mit zusätzlichen Angaben, dann Bearbeitung gemäß AA.
• **Ausw.:** ▸ Bus stop (▸ KV Extra): S vergleichen ihre Antworten mithilfe der Musterlösung auf der ▸ KV 3.5A.
• erneute Selbsteinschätzung

Checkpoint Inhalt

Lernschwerpunkt: Kompetenzen und sprachliche Mittel üben, Lernfortschritte erkennen
Kompetenzen: Listening Dialoge hören und Informationen zuordnen • Study skills Vokabeln im *Dictionary* nachschlagen und Gruppen zuordnen • Writing über die Höhepunkte einer Woche schreiben
Redemittel: Wortfelder *meeting friends, sports and hobbies, feelings and emotions*

Ex 5 Einstieg:
- (SB auf) S lesen das Lernziel (*I can ...*) vor.
- Sie schätzen ihr Können zum Lernziel ein, z. B. mit ▸ Thumbs up, und notieren sich das Ergebnis.

Erarbeitung:
- Gemeinsames Klären der AA, S schreiben die Sätze mit Ergänzung in ihr Heft.
- **Ausw.:** ▸ Bus stop (▸ KV Extra): S vergleichen ihre Lösungen mithilfe der ▸ KV 3.5B.
- erneute Selbsteinschätzung

- **Zusatz:** Dialog mit verteilten Rollen lesen und spielen.
- ☒ Lernstärkere S erarbeiten einen Dialog mit eigenen Informationen und spielen ihn in PA.

Ex 6 Einstieg:
- s. Ex 5 (Selbsteinschätzung)

Erarbeitung:
a) (SB auf) Klären der AA
- S übertragen Tabelle in ihr Heft und ergänzen die Informationen beim **1. Hören**.

b) S notieren Satzanfänge und ergänzen Informationen beim **2. Hören**.
- evtl. **3. Hören** zum Überprüfen der Ergebnisse
- **Ausw.:** ▸ Bus stop (▸ KV Extra): S vergleichen ihre Lösungen mithilfe der ▸ KV 3.5B.
- erneute Selbsteinschätzung

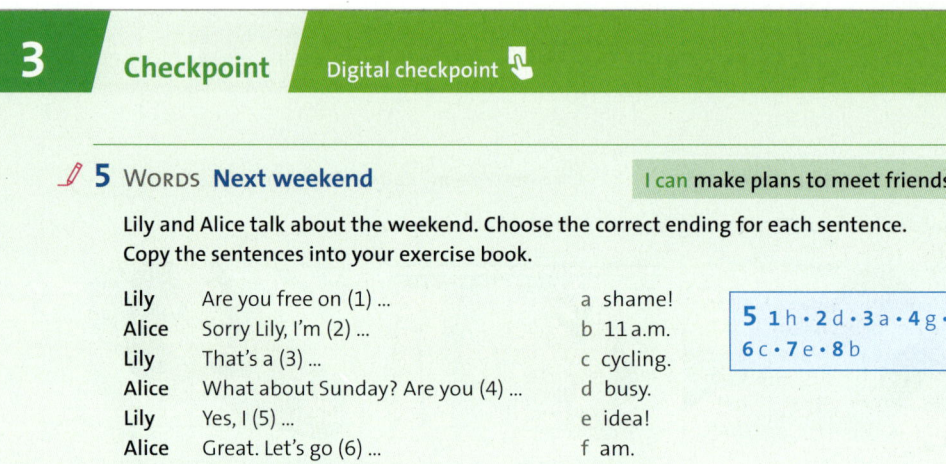

3 / **Checkpoint** Digital checkpoint

🖊 **5** WORDS **Next weekend**   I can **make plans to meet friends.** ✓

Lily and Alice talk about the weekend. Choose the correct ending for each sentence. Copy the sentences into your exercise book.

Lily	Are you free on (1) ...	a	shame!
Alice	Sorry Lily, I'm (2) ...	b	11 a.m.
Lily	That's a (3) ...	c	cycling.
Alice	What about Sunday? Are you (4) ...	d	busy.
Lily	Yes, I (5) ...	e	idea!
Alice	Great. Let's go (6) ...	f	am.
Lily	Good (7) ...	g	free?
Alice	Let's meet at the park at (8) ...	h	Saturday?

> **5** 1 h • 2 d • 3 a • 4 g • 5 f • 6 c • 7 e • 8 b

🎧 **6** LISTENING **Saturday plans**   I can **understand feelings in a story.** ✓

🔊 2.17 **a)** Listen to Noah's conversations. What are the students' plans for Saturday? Copy and complete the table. Use the words in the box.

> homework • free (3 x) • see grandpa • shopping • swimming • yoga

	Saturday morning	Saturday afternoon
1 Zane	see grandpa	swimming
2 Lily	homework	shopping
3 Noah	free	free
4 Sunita	yoga	free

b) Listen again. Say how they feel. Write the correct ending.

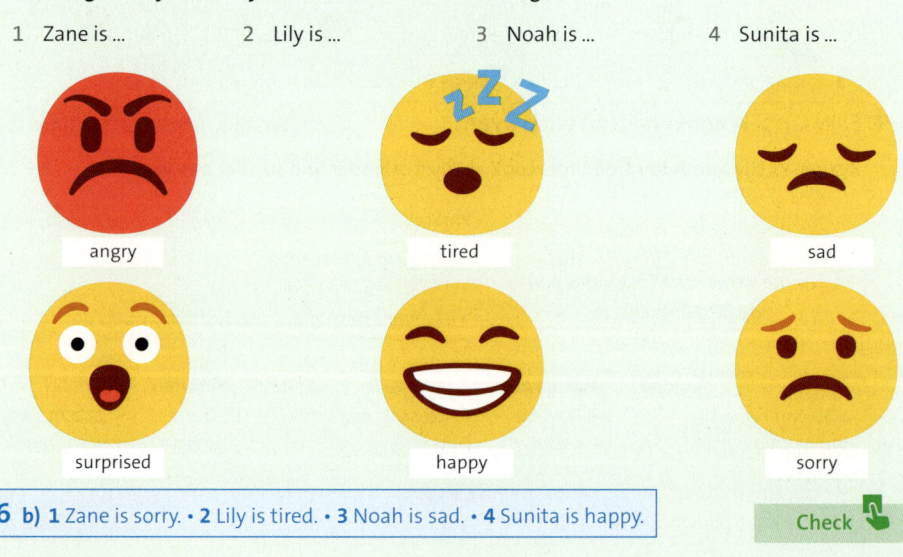

1 Zane is ...	2 Lily is ...	3 Noah is ...	4 Sunita is ...
angry	tired	sad	
surprised	happy	sorry	

> **6 b)** 1 Zane is sorry. • 2 Lily is tired. • 3 Noah is sad. • 4 Sunita is happy.

Check

100 one hundred

Checkpoint Vorbereitung

Material: alle Aufgaben ▸ KV Extra: Bus stop, ▸ KV 3.5B: Checkpoint answers • Ex 6 UMA/CD • Ex 8 UMA
Zeitbedarf: ca. 2 Std.
Minimalversion: Auswahl der Aufgaben erfolgt aufgrund der zu überprüfenden Lernziele
Begleitmedien: App (Digital checkpoint)

Die Übungen kannst du auch digital machen ⬇ **3**

7 STUDY SKILLS The computer club

I can **look up and learn new words.** ✓

a) Read about the computer club at a British school.

b) Look at the text again. Write the blue words in alphabetical order.

c) Look up the words in the Dictionary on **pages 255–266.**

d) Write the words from b) in the correct group.

Hi, we're the computer club! We °swap ideas about technology. We love °memes. We help our °classmates with computer problems. We give them °amazing tips. It's great – we're never °stressed. We meet on Wednesdays at 3.30 p.m. in the computer room.

7 b) amazing • classmates • memes • stressed • swap

°emails	classmates	angry	good	give
headphones	friends	sad	interesting	tell
memes	students	scared	important	share
websites	teachers	stressed	amazing	swap

8 WRITING Fabian's¹ week

I can **share the highlights of my week.** ✓

Fabian shares the highlights of his week. Look at the pictures and write his sentences.

On Monday afternoon I go cycling with my friend. ...

Monday afternoon – cycling

Tuesday – guitar lesson

Wednesday – grandpa's house

Thursday afternoon – school drama club

Friday evening – computer games

Saturday and Sunday – big breakfast

8 Lösung S. 291   1 ['feɪbɪən]

Check ⬇

one hundred and one **101**

Ex 7 Einstieg:
• s. Ex 5 (Selbsteinschätzung)
• (SB auf) ⬚ als Erinnerung:
  L: *Where can you look up new words in your textbook?*
  S: *On pages 255–266.*

Erarbeitung:
a) S lesen den Text möglichst selbstständig in EA.

b) + c) klären der AA für beide Aufgaben, Bearbeitung gemäß AA

d) S übertragen Tabelle in ihr Heft und ergänzen gemäß AA.
• **Ausw.:** ▸ Bus stop (▸ KV Extra): S vergleichen ihre Lösungen mithilfe der ▸ KV 3.5B.
• erneute Selbsteinschätzung

Ex 8 Einstieg:
• s. Ex 5 (Selbsteinschätzung)
• (SB zu) L erinnert evtl. an *Unit task* (s. S. 97):
  L: *Can you remember your highlights of the week?*
• mögliche S-Antworten:
  Yes, I often play ... on ...
  L: *Now let's look at Fabian's highlights of his week.*

Erarbeitung:
• (SB auf) gemäß AA in EA, S notieren Sätze in ihr Heft.
• ⬚ Sätze als TA oder über UMA zeigen.
• **Ausw.:** ▸ Bus stop (▸ KV Extra): S vergleichen ihre Sätze mithilfe der ▸ KV 3.5B.
• erneute Selbsteinschätzung

Lernschwerpunkt: Texte aus einem *school magazine* über besondere Schulwege und Hobbys lesen

Kompetenzen: Reading Texte über verschiedene Schulwege verstehen • Texte über Freizeitaktivitäten verstehen und eigene Ideen daraus entwickeln • Speaking/Writing über ein Sammelhobby berichten • Viewing einen Filmtrailer anschauen

Redemittel: Wortfelder *school journey, sports and hobbies*

Allgemeine Anmerkung:
s. Unit 1, S. 40

School journeys Erarbeitung:

• (SB auf) S lesen Femis Text laut im Plenum oder leise in EA und klären ggf. Verständnisfragen.

• L erklärt, dass die Bilder unten auf der Seite Szenen aus dem Film *On the Way to School* zeigen.

• S lesen und erschließen sich die Texte zu den einzelnen Personen in PA (▶ Leseacht).

• **Alternative:** Vorgabe einer Tabelle als TA (Spalten für alle fünf Namen):

	Femi	Samuel	...
how?			
how long?			
extra information			

• S lesen die Texte und ergänzen in PA die fehlenden Informationen.

• **Ausw.:** ▶ Meldekette

• **Zusatz:** L zeigt den Trailer von *On the Way to School*, der online zum Anschauen frei verfügbar ist.
L: *What do you think about the kids and their school journeys?*

• S antworten optional auf Englisch oder Deutsch.

VARNDEAN Teen Zine

This month's topics: your school journey and free time

Our school magazine: by students for students

School journeys

Hi, I'm **Femi**. I go to school by bike. It only takes ten minutes. I'm lucky! For some kids their school journey takes a long time. There's a great film about four students (10–13) and their school journeys. Read about them here. You can watch the trailer online. Look for the film *On the Way to School*.

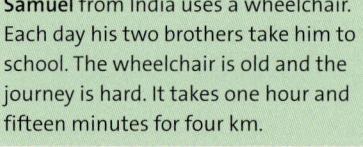

Samuel from India uses a wheelchair. Each day his two brothers take him to school. The wheelchair is old and the journey is hard. It takes one hour and fifteen minutes for four km.

Zahira lives in the mountains[1] in Morocco. Every week Zahira and her friends walk 22 km through[2] the mountains to her school. Her journey takes four hours.

Jackson from Kenya walks 15 km to school with his sister every day. It takes two hours. They need to be careful of dangerous[3] elephants!

Carlito lives in Argentina. He rides his horse to school every day and his little sister sits on the horse too. Their journey is 18 km.

[1] **mountain** *Berg*   [2] **through** *durch*   [3] **dangerous** *gefährlich*

Text file Vorbereitung

Material: School journeys Trailer und Abspielgerät, ggf. Internetzugang • My cool hobby ggf. weißes Papier (A4, Klassensatz) • The International Birdman competition ggf. technische Ausstattung für Internet-Recherche, weißes Papier (A3/A4, Klassensatz)

Zeitbedarf: abhängig davon, welche Texte bearbeitet werden; pro Text ca. 1 Std.

Minimalversion: alle Texte sind optionale Zusatztexte

My cool hobby

Two Varndean students tell Teen Zine about their hobbies.

Adam: I have a cool hobby: I collect toothbrushes. I have two hundred and thirty-seven! They're all new. I like the different colours and the different toothbrushes.

Ming: I collect stones and I draw on them. I draw animals and fruit and other things. I find the stones at the beach here in Brighton. It's a fun hobby!

Tell us if you collect something[1]. Or bring some of your things to school and tell your class!

The International Birdman[2] competition

Each year in a small town[3] near Brighton there's a special competition: People jump off[4] the pier and try to[5] fly!

They often wear funny clothes too. They get money for charity[6] and have great fun!

I'm a bird!

Oh-oh …

Don't try this at home! But why not draw your own Birdman costume? Or think of a cool competition for your school?

---

[1] **something** *etwas*   [2] **birdman** *Vogelmensch*   [3] **town** *Stadt*   [4] **jump off sth.** *von etwas herunterspringen*
[5] **try to do sth.** *versuchen, etwas zu tun*   [6] **charity** *wohltätige Organisation*

My cool hobby Erarbeitung:

- (SB auf) S lesen die beiden Texte in EA oder PA.
- Sie schreiben einen eigenen Text über sich oder eine Person aus der Familie oder dem Freundeskreis (auf 3. Person Singular achten – L verweist auf ► LF 10, S. 187) oder S tauschen sich in PA mündlich aus.
- **Ausw.:** Mündliche Ergebnisse werden im Plenum präsentiert, schriftliche Ergebnisse in der ► English corner.

The International Birdman competition

- Der Lesetext wird handlungsorientiert umgesetzt.

Erarbeitung:

- (SB auf) S lesen den Text und recherchieren ggf. im Internet nach weiteren Informationen.
- Die Kostüme werden in EA oder PA auf weißem Papier gestaltet und über einen ► Gallery walk präsentiert.
- S geben Feedback (► Let's talk: Feedback, S. 211).
- Für einen Wettbewerb in der Schule ist die Unterstützung von L notwendig.

Partner page / Diff bank
Inhalt

Lernschwerpunkt: zusätzliche Übungen, Differenzierungs- und Hilfsangebote
Kompetenzen: Speaking sagen, wie viel Uhr es ist • sich mit einem Freund / einer Freundin verabreden • sich über den Schulweg äußern • besondere Zahlen und deren Bedeutung erraten • Listening kurzen Dialogen die Uhrzeit entnehmen
Redemittel: Wortfelder *meeting friends*, *school journey*, Uhrzeit, Zahlen 10–60

Ex 3 Einstieg:
- (SB zu) TA: ca. 16 verschiedene Uhrzeiten mit *a.m.* und *p.m.*
- Klasse wird in zwei Gruppen geteilt. S stellen sich in zwei Schlangen auf.
- S in der ersten Position bekommen aufgerollte Zeitung oder Fliegenklatsche.
- L liest eine der Uhrzeiten vor.
- S versuchen, schnellstmöglich auf die richtige Zeit zu hauen.
- Das Gewinnerteam bekommt einen Punkt.
- Dann sind die nächsten S an der Reihe.

Erarbeitung:
a) + b) (SB auf) gemäß AA, *Partner B* öffnet das Buch auf S. 106.
- **Ausw.:** S vergleichen ihre Uhrzeiten mit denen im Buch.

Ex 8 s. S. 85

Ex 3 Einstieg: s. S. 91

Erarbeitung:
a) (SB auf) L: *How can you make the dialogue sound good?*
- TA: Klasse sammelt (auf Deutsch), wie man den Dialog besser macht: Gefühle darstellen, Stimme am Ende von Fragen heben, möglichst wenig ablesen etc. (▶ Role-play)
- S üben den Dialog in PA.

b) S ändern in PA die blauen Teile des Dialogs.
- ☒ ▶ Challenge 4, S. 109
- **Ausw.:** Präsentation der Dialoge im Plenum
- Mit-S geben ▶ Feedback.

---

3 | **Partner page**

Partner page

▶Page 82

3 SPEAKING **The time**

Partner A

3 a) 1 9.10 a.m. • **2** 11.45 a.m. • **3** 3.15 p.m. • **4** 3.35 p.m. • **5** 8.50 p.m.

a) Look at the clocks. Tell your partner the time. Use the 12-hour clock with a.m. and p.m.

It's … | 1 **09.10** | 2 **11.45** | 3 **15.15** | 4 **15.35** | 5 **20.50** |

b) Ask the time. Listen and write the five times.   *What's the time?*   ▶ Numbers, p. 277

3 b) 1 6.45 a.m. • **2** 12.05 p.m. • **3** 2.30 p.m. • **4** 6.55 p.m. • **5** 10.40 p.m.

▶Page 85

8 SONG **Good morning!**
2.10 c)

What? (Today is Saturday!)
Is it? Well, then
It's eight o'clock, go back to bed
It's eight o'clock, go back to bed
Who gets up at eight when you can
°sleep in °till late?
It's eight o'clock, go back to bed!

▶Page 91

3 ROLE-PLAY **Can we meet this weekend?**

a) Read Lily and Noah's conversation. Then °act it out.

Lily	Hi, Noah, can we meet this weekend?
Noah	I'd love to, Lily.
Lily	Great! Let's go to the skatepark.
Noah	Sorry, I can't go to the skatepark. It's too loud for me. What about the cafe?
Lily	Good idea! Are you free on Saturday?
Noah	Sorry, I'm busy on Saturday. But I'm free on Sunday.
Lily	OK, let's meet at the cafe at 10.30 a.m.
Noah	Let's ask Sunita too. See you on Sunday!

b) °Change the blue words and make a new conversation. Act it out for °another pair.

3 b) Lösungsbsp. S. 291

104 one hundred and four

Diff bank Vorbereitung

Material: Ex 3 Fliegenklatsche oder Zeitung • MP 3 UMA/CD
Zeitbedarf: abhängig davon, welche Aufgaben bearbeitet werden
Minimalversion: *More practice-* und *Challenge*-Aufgaben sind stets Zusatzaufgaben

---

Diff bank **3**

Diff bank

▶ Page 81

1 **1** bike. • **2** by train. • **3** walk • **4** go to school by bus. • **5** go to school by car.

💬 More practice 1 **On the way to school**

Say how these students go to school.
Complete °their sentences.

1 Ahmed: I go to school by …
2 Ruby: I go to school …
3 Nik: I … to school.
4 Zelal: I …
5 Billy: I …

▶ Page 82

💬 More practice 2 **Your special numbers**

a) Write three special numbers for you.
The ideas in the box can help you.

👥 b) Show your partner your numbers. He/She guesses what the number is. °Take turns.

Ideas
- your °birthday
- your favourite number
- your lucky number
- your house number
- how old you are
- how old your pet is
- your favourite football °shirt number

My first number is 52.

Is 52 your house number?

Yes, it is. / No, it isn't.

52
7
31

2 b) individuelle Lösungen

👂 More practice 3 **What's the time?**

🔊 a) Listen to five conversations. Write the times in numbers.
2.6
👥 b) Check with a partner.

3 a) **1** 8.50 • **2** 10.55 • **3** 12.40 • **4** 3.30 • **5** 4.20

Number 1 is 8.15.

Yes, that's right.

No, that's wrong. It's …

one hundred and five **105**

MP 1
- Diese Aufgabe dient zur Festigung der Vokabeln aus dem Unit-Einstieg (s. S. 80–81).

Erarbeitung:
- (SB auf) S vervollständigen die Sätze.
- **Ausw.:** ▶ Five-minute teacher oder ▶ Partner check (falls nicht mit der ganzen Klasse durchgeführt)

MP 2 Einstieg:
- (SB zu) Spiel: Zwei S gehen vor die Tür, ihre Stühle werden hochgestellt. Die restlichen S bekommen je eine Zahl zugeteilt. TA mit den verteilten Zahlen. S tauschen Plätze.
- Die zwei S von draußen kommen zurück und versuchen, die S an ihren Platz zurückzusetzen, indem sie die richtigen Zahlen nennen. S: *Number … and …, please swap seats.*
- Das Spiel endet, wenn alle S an ihrem Platz sitzen.

Erarbeitung:
a) (SB auf) gemäß AA

b) L sollte einen Beispieldialog vorgeben (TA). S arbeiten in PA.
- **Ausw.:** S stellen die Zahlen ihres Partners / ihrer Partnerin im Plenum vor.

MP 3 Einstieg:
- (SB zu) L erfragt die aktuelle Uhrzeit. Ein/e S antwortet.

Erarbeitung:
a) (SB auf) gemäß AA

b) S vergleichen ihre Lösungen in PA (▶ Partner check).
- **Ausw.:** Vergleich im Plenum

Lernschwerpunkt: zusätzliche Übungen, Differenzierungs- und Hilfsangebote
Kompetenzen: Speaking sagen, wie viel Uhr es ist • lustige Sätze in der 3. Person Singular bilden • Listening einem
Hörtext entnehmen, wer etwas macht • Writing anhand von Bildern Scouts Tagesablauf beschreiben
Strukturen: *simple present*
Redemittel: Uhrzeit, Wortfelder *daily routine, free-time activities*

Ex 3 s. S. 104

MP 4 Erarbeitung:
- (SB auf) L teilt vorbereitete Kärtchen aus (z. B. kleine Karteikarten).
- S entwerfen drei bis vier Kartenpaare gemäß AA.
- Sie überprüfen die Karten eines Partners / einer Partnerin auf Richtigkeit.
- S spielen das Spiel in Vierer- oder Fünfergruppen.

- **Zusatz:** Karten einsammeln und in den nächsten Stunden im *Warm-up* entweder als
  ▶ Swap cards oder für ein
  ▶ Menschen-Memo einsetzen.

MP 5
- In dieser Übung soll den S bewusst werden, dass *he/she* jeweils für einen Namen steht.

Erarbeitung:
- (SB auf) S lesen die Sätze.
- **1. Hören:** S schreiben die korrekten Namen in ihr Heft.
- **Ausw.: 2. Hören:** S überprüfen ihre Lösungen.

MP 6 Erarbeitung:
a) (SB auf) gemäß AA, S schreiben die richtigen Verbformen in ihr Heft.
- **Ausw.:** ▶ Five-minute teacher

b) gemäß AA

- **Alternative:** ▶ Early finishers, die mit **a)** schnell fertig sind, finden am ▶ Bus stop (Einsatz ▶ KV Extra) einen Partner / eine Partnerin und bearbeiten **b)**.

---

3 **Diff bank**

▶Page 82

3 SPEAKING **The time**

Partner B

3 a) **1** 9.10 a.m. • **2** 11.45 a.m. • **3** 3.15 p.m. • **4** 3.35 p.m. • **5** 8.50 p.m.

a) Ask the time. Listen and write the five times.

What's the time?

b) Look at the clocks. Tell your partner the time. Use the 12-hour clock with a.m. and p.m.

It's …

1	2	3	4	5
06.45	12.05	14.30	18.55	22.40

3 b) **1** 6.45 a.m. • **2** 12.05 p.m. • **3** 2.30 p.m. • **4** 6.55 p.m. • **5** 10.40 p.m.

▶ Numbers, p. 277

More practice 4 GAME **Match the times**

- Each student: Make 3–4 pairs of cards like these.
- Put all your cards on the table. Mix them up.
- Take turns to °turn over two cards.
- Is it a °match? Say 'Match!'

16.45

four forty-five

▶ Numbers, p. 277

▶Page 84

More practice 5 **Who is it?**

2.8

5 Lösung S. 291

Say who it is: Zane, Holly, Louise or Eno. Then listen and check.

1 He watches TV.
2 She uses a wheelchair.
3 He meets his sister at her school.
4 She gets up at 7.30.

5 He does his homework.
6 He makes breakfast.
7 He tidies the kitchen.
8 She goes to school with her brother.

More practice 6 **Zane's favourite sport**

a) Find the correct form of the verb.

6 a) **1** goes • **2** walks • **3** have • **4** work • **5** swims • **6** want • **7** loves

Zane (1 go) … to swimming training every week. He (2 walk) … to his °swimming pool. Zane and the other swimmers (3 have) … training for an hour. They (4 work) … really hard. Zane often (5 swim) … in competitions. All the swimmers (6 want) … to be the winner! But Zane is really good. He (7 love) … swimming.

Zane

b) Tell your partner about a sport you do and the sport °somebody in your family does.

6 b) individuelle Lösungen

106 one hundred and six

Diff bank Vorbereitung

Material: MP 4 Blanko-Karteikärtchen (6–8 pro S) • MP 5 UMA/CD • MP 6 ▶ KV Extra: Bus stop • MP 7 UMA, Würfel (ein Würfel pro S-Paar/Gruppe) • Challenge 1 UMA, vergrößerte Bilder von S. 107
Zeitbedarf: abhängig davon, welche Aufgaben bearbeitet werden
Minimalversion: *More practice-* und *Challenge*-Aufgaben sind stets Zusatzaufgaben

More practice 7 Funny sentences

°Throw the °dice and make funny sentences. Make five to eight different sentences.

*he, she, it, das **S** muss mit!*

Step 1	Step 2	Step 3
Throw the dice. Choose a person.	Throw the dice again. Choose an action.	Throw the dice again. Choose a time/place.
1 Zane	1 go/to dancing lessons	1 at 5 a.m.
2 Holly	2 watch/horror films on TV	2 at school.
3 Mr and Mrs Adebayo	3 cook/spaghetti	3 in the car.
4 Sunita	4 draw/manga pictures	4 at lunchtime.
5 Lily and Noah	5 listen/to loud music	5 at 10 p.m.
6 Scout	6 do/yoga	6 on the bus.

 + + = *Sunita cooks °spaghetti on the bus.*

7 individuelle Lösungen

Challenge 1 Scout's °routine

Write about Scout's routine. Use the verbs in the box in the correct form and your own ideas.

eat • get up • go • meet • swim • watch

1 °Every day Scout … 2 She often …

Ch 1 Lösungsbsp. S. 291

MP 7 Erarbeitung:
• (SB zu) L zeigt Aufgabe mit dem UMA.
• Gemeinsames Klären der AA, L demonstriert ein bis zwei Beispiele mit einem/einer S vor der Klasse und weist auf die ▶ Tippbox, S. 107 hin.
• anschließend Bearbeitung in PA/GA gemäß AA
• **Ausw.:** Jede Gruppe bzw. jedes Paar liest ihren/seinen lustigsten Satz vor.
• ☒ **Zusatz:** Lernstärkere S überlegen sich selbst ein Raster, mit dem sie lustige Sätze bilden.

Challenge 1
• Diese Aufgabe kann zur Differenzierung für starke oder schnelle S verwendet werden (s. Vorwort, S. XIII).

Erarbeitung:
• (SB auf) Gemeinsames Klären der AA
• L zeigt ggf. die vergrößerten Bilder (UMA).
• S schreiben Sätze gemäß AA in ihr Heft.
• **Ausw.:** ▶ Partner check und anschließend Plenum oder S schreiben Sätze an die Tafel.
• ☒ **Zusatz:** Lernstärkere S beschreiben zusätzlich den Tagesablauf ihres (Traum-) Haustiers.

Diff bank Inhalt

Lernschwerpunkt: zusätzliche Übungen, Differenzierungs- und Hilfsangebote
Kompetenzen: Writing einen Post zum Tagesablauf verfassen • Mindmaps vervollständigen • Speaking sich mit einem Freund / einer Freundin verabreden • Reading eine Geschichte verstehen und Satzteile verbinden • Life skills überlegen, wem man einen Preis verleihen würde
Strukturen: *simple present* • Wortstellung bei Sätzen mit Häufigkeitsadverbien
Redemittel: Wortfelder *daily routine, sports and hobbies, meetings friends*

MH 9 Erarbeitung: s. S. 85
- Diese Hilfe sollte vor allem lernschwächeren S angeboten werden.
- Unsicheren S könnte L anbieten, dass sie den vorgegebenen Text einmal lesen dürfen, bevor sie ihren eigenen Text schreiben. So haben sie eine gute Idee, was erwartet wird.

Challenge 2
- Diese Aufgabe kann zur Differenzierung für lern-stärkere oder schnelle S verwendet werden.

Einstieg:
- (SB auf) ▶ Semantisierung von *go, do, play*, L schreibt Verben an die Tafel.

Erarbeitung:
- Mindmaps als TA, ggf. Verweis auf S. 34 (Mindmaps als Hilfe beim Vokabellernen)
- Klären der AA, L erarbeitet mit S ein oder zwei Beispiele im Plenum.
- S schreiben Wörter an die Tafel, anschließend übertragen S die Mindmaps in ihr Heft und ergänzen gemäß AA.
- **Ausw.:** ▶ Partner check, anschließend im Plenum (S schreiben Wörter an die Tafel)

Challenge 3 Erarbeitung:
a) (SB auf) ▶ Klären der AA, S übertragen Tabelle in ihr Heft und ergänzen gemäß AA.
- **Ausw.:** im Plenum (mit TA)

b) gemäß AA, L erarbeitet mit S ein Beispiel im Plenum.
- **Ausw.:** ▶ Partner check und Plenum

---

3 **Diff bank**

▶Page 85

✎ More help **9** MY TASK **My school day**

Write a °post about your day.
Put your post in your DOSSIER.

> Hi, Zane
> My name is … and I live in … This is my day:
> In the morning I get up at … I have breakfast at …
> I go to school at … I walk / I go by …
> The journey takes … minutes.
> We start school at … Our first lesson starts at …
> We have lunch at … School ends at …
> In the evening I … I go to bed at …
>
> Bye!

▶Page 86

✎ Challenge 2 **Sports and hobbies**

Ch 2 Lösungsbsp. S. 291

Copy the mind maps.
°Add words from exercise 1a) on p. 86 or your own ideas.

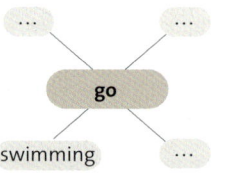
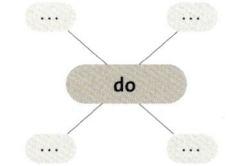
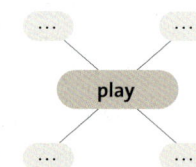

go   do   play
… swimming …

▶Page 87

✎ Challenge 3 **I often play table tennis**

a) LOOKING AT LANGUAGE Complete the table headings 1–4 with the words on the right.

1 …	2 …	3 …	4 …
I	often	play	table tennis.
I	rarely	play	basketball.
I	sometimes	play	music.

adverb of frequency
subject   object
verb
▶ Language file 11, p. 187

b) Write the sentences in the correct order.

Zane

> 1 When I feel °stressed, … (always / I / swimming / go) because it helps me.
> 2 … (play / I / sometimes / basketball) next to the beach when it's °sunny.
> 3 … (football / play / I / rarely), but … (watch / I / often / football matches).
> 4 … (cook / often / I) for my family.
> 5 … (I / walk / always) to school, but … (goes / Sunita / often) by bus.

Ch 3 a), b) Lösung S. 291

Diff bank Vorbereitung

Material: Challenge 4 geeignete Aufnahme- und Abspielgeräte
Zeitbedarf: abhängig davon, welche Aufgaben bearbeitet werden
Minimalversion: *More practice-* und *Challenge*-Aufgaben sind stets Zusatzaufgaben

►Page 91

Challenge 4 **Let's go to the park**

Ch 4 Lösungsbsp. S. 291f.

ROLE-PLAY **Act out a new conversation. Use the emojis to help you.**

 A: ?

 A: ! ?

 B: !

 B: ?

 A: ?

  A: !

 B: ?

 B: !

►Page 93

Parallel exercise **3 What happens in the story**

Read the story again. Match the sentence parts.

1 Lily sends   a his mum's illness.
2 Zane says he can't go   b the winner of the competition.
3 Zane explains about   c some prize money.
4 Zane's mum tells him that he is   d to the park with his friends.
5 Zane's mum is tired, but she wants to go   e a newspaper article to Sunita and Noah.
6 The competition winner gets   f to the prize show.

3 1 e · 2 d · 3 a · 4 b · 5 f · 6 c

►Page 94

More help **6** LIFE SKILLS **Be kind**

a) **Zane is kind because he helps his mum. You can choose one person for a prize.**
Who is kind in your group of friends, your family or where you live?
°**Think about** °**reasons why.**

My teacher is really kind because ...
My friends are ...

6 individuelle Lösungen

teacher trainer		helps / help	me with my homework / with my computer / at sport / with problems / ...
brother sister	he she they	gives / give	me sweets / books / help / ...
friends		sends / send	me funny messages / pictures / °memes / ...
°classmates		shares / share	°their lunch / good ideas / ...

Challenge 4 Erarbeitung:
- (SB auf) L sollte Hinweis geben, dass die Unterhaltung ähnlich zu der auf S. 104 sein kann. S können sich dort Hilfe holen, falls sie die Emojis nicht verstehen.
- S schreiben den Dialog und üben ihn ein.
- **Ausw.:** s. S. 104
- **Zusatz:** S können ihre Dialoge auch filmen und der Klasse später zeigen.

Parallel ex 3 s. S. 93
- Diese Aufgabe ist die einfachere Variante zu Ex 3 auf S. 93 mit dem gleichen Ergebnis.

Erarbeitung:
- (SB auf) gemäß AA
- **Ausw.:** s. S. 93

MH 6 s. S. 94
- Diese Aufgabe bietet Ideen und sprachliche Mittel für lernschwächere S, aber auch für stärkere S, die Begründungen formulieren möchten.

Erarbeitung:
- (SB auf) gemäß AA, vgl. auch S. 94
- S sollten die hier angebotenen Redemittel in der *Think*-Phase zur Formulierung nutzen, um in den nächsten beiden Phasen kommunizieren zu können (►Think-Pair-Share).

Unit-Übersicht

Storyline: Die S lernen Brighton kennen und erfahren mehr über Lily, ihre Familie und ihre Wohngegend. In der Story organisiert Lily einen *Clean-up day*. Es werden Aktivitäten für Jugendliche in Brighton und Umgebung vorgestellt.

Strukturen: *simple present: negative sentences* (S. 113) • *simple present: questions and short answers* (S. 117) • *simple present: wh-questions* (S. 120)

Viewing: verschiedene Orte in Brighton werden vorgestellt (S. 110–111) • Daisy und Emir stellen einander weitere Mutproben, dieses Mal *in town*. (S. 125)

Unit task: eine Präsentation über die besten drei Orte für Kids vorbereiten und halten

---

Unit 4 Einstieg:

- (SB zu) Handpuppe Scout mit Stadtplan:
  L: *Why do you have a map?*
  Scout: *Today I want to show you my city, Brighton. Look, I have some pictures for you.*
- L präsentiert die Brighton-Fotos von S. 110–111 mithilfe des UMA.
- **Alternative:** L zeigt selbst recherchierte Fotos von Brighton.
  L: *What places can you see?*
  S: *I can see a park / a street / ...*
- S antworten und erfragen ggf. fehlende Redemittel:
  S: *What is ... in English?*
- L notiert den erfragten Wortschatz als Liste an die Tafel.
- L steuert, welcher Wortschatz ins *Vocab file* übertragen wird (▶ Vokabeltafel).

Ex 1 Erarbeitung:

a) (SB auf) L führt ein Beispiel mit Scout vor.
- L präsentiert die Fotos aus dem SB (s. **Einstieg**).
- S übernehmen die Rollen von Scout und L und arbeiten gemäß AA in PA.
- **Ausw.:** S präsentieren Beispiele im Plenum, die restliche Klasse rät, welches Bild gemeint ist.

b) S notieren die Zahlen 1–7 in ihr Heft. Das Zuordnen findet beim **1. Sehen** statt.
- **Ausw.:** ▶ Five-minute teacher
- ggf. **2. Sehen** zum Vergleichen

Unit 4
Where I live

This is my **+**city!

1 VIEWING **This is Brighton**[1]

1 a) individuelle Lösungen

💬 👥 **a)** BEFORE YOU WATCH **Choose a photo. Say what you can see. Your partner °guesses the photo.**

| I can see | a beach / a building / a cinema / a lot of people / a pier / a skatepark / shops / ... |
| This place is | busy / cool / interesting / modern / nice / old / quiet / ... |

📺 **b)** **Watch the video. Match the numbers of the photos to the letters of the places:** *1b, 2 ...*

| a Brighton beach | b Brighton Palace Pier | c Duke of York's cinema | d Hove[2] Skatepark |
| e Brighton Marina | f Pavilion[3] Gardens | g North Laine | **1 b) 1** b • **2** f • **3** g • **4** d • **5** c • **6** a • **7** e |

1 [ˈbraɪtn] **2** [həʊv] **3** [pəˈvɪlɪən]

110 one hundred and ten

Lead-in Inhalt

Lernschwerpunkt: Informationen über Brighton verstehen
Kompetenzen: Speaking Fotos von Brighton beschreiben •
sagen, welche Orte in Brighton man mag • Viewing Infos
über Brighton verstehen und korrekt zuordnen
Redemittel: *sights in Brighton • I like … (place) because …*

Vorbereitung

Material: Einstieg UMA, selbst recherchierte Fotos von
Brighton • Ex 1 Handpuppe Scout, Stadtplan, UMA/DVD,
vorbereitete Wortkarten
Zeitbedarf: ca. 1 Std.
Begleitmedien: WB (S. 56), App (Digital quiz), INKL (S. 110–
111)

Nach dieser Unit kann ich … ✓

○ Informationen über Brighton verstehen
○ meine Nachbarschaft beschreiben
○ über meine Stadt oder mein Dorf sprechen
○ über Sehenswürdigkeiten und
  das Wetter reden
○ Präsentationen halten

Unit task ✓

○ die besten Orte in meiner Umgebung
  präsentieren

1 c) **1** North Laine • **2** Pavilion Gardens •
3 Duke of York's cinema • **4** (Hove)
Skatepark • **5** Brighton (Palace) Pier •
6 Brighton Marina • **7** Brighton beach

c) **What are the places in 1–7? Then watch the video again and check.**

1 There are a lot of cool shops and cafes here and they're all different.
2 This is a good place for a picnic. You can hear street music here.
3 You can watch old and new films here.
4 People come here to do skateboarding and practise new skills.
5 You can eat fish and chips and play games here.
6 This is a good place for +bowling and great food.
7 This place is five miles long.

Good to know

1 mile = 1.6 km

▶ Box: Voc., p. 240

d) **Which places in Brighton do you like? Why?**

1 d) individuelle Lösungen

▶ More help, p. 134

▶ Workbook, p. 56

Digital quiz **I can understand information about Brighton.** ✓

one hundred and eleven **111**

Nach dieser Unit …

• L bespricht mit S die Lernziele
  der Unit (s. links) und kündigt
  die *Unit task* an.
• Am Ende der Unit überprüfen
  S das Erreichen der Ziele
  mithilfe des *Checkpoint*
  (S. 128–131) bzw. gemeinsam
  im Plenum.

Ex 1 Erarbeitung (Forts.)
c) L schreibt die Nummern 1–7
  an die Tafel.
• S liest einen Satz vor und
  stellt Vermutung an.
• L notiert Ort an die Tafel (oder
  heftet die passende Wortkarte
  an).
• S vergleichen beim **3. Sehen**.
• **Ausw.:** S korrigieren an der
  Tafel:
  S: *Number … is wrong. The
  correct place is …*
• Satz 7: L verweist auf die Info
  in ▶ Good to know, S. 111.

d) L präsentiert die vergrößerten
  SB-Seiten mithilfe des UMA.
  L: *Which place do you like?
  Why?*
  Scout: *I like the beach because
  there are many people.*
• Scout spielt den Dialog mit S
  weiter.
• anschließend gemäß AA in PA
• ▶ More help, S. 134 für lern-
  schwächere S
• **Ausw.:** S-Paare präsentieren
  ihre Ergebnisse im Plenum.

• **Zusatz:** Wdh. der Zahlen
  Scout: *Now let's do some
  maths. How many km are six
  miles?*
• S antworten und übernehmen Scouts Rolle beim
  Rechnen an der Tafel.

4

Topic 1 | Inhalt

Lernschwerpunkt: die eigene Wohngegend beschreiben
Kompetenzen: Listening erfassen, was jemand sieht, hört und riecht • Reading einem Text über Lilys Wohngegend
Informationen und Adjektive entnehmen • Speaking sagen, was man an seiner Wohngegend (nicht) mag •
Study skills Notizen machen • sprachliche Regelmäßigkeiten entdecken
Strukturen: *simple present*: *negative sentences*
Redemittel: *I can see/hear/smell ...* • *adjectives and their opposites* • *places* • *I don't like ...* • *She doesn't like ...*

Ex 1 Einstieg:
• (SB zu) L zeigt das Foto von
S.112 (UMA):
L: *Who is this?*
S: *This is Lily. / I don't know.*
L: *Look at the photo again,*
please. Let's find out what Lily
can see, hear and smell.
(L semantisiert *smell*.)

Erarbeitung:
a) (SB auf) S übertragen Tabelle
ins Heft.
• S notieren ihre Ergebnisse
nach dem **1. Hören**.
• ☒ L bietet den Wortschatz
von ▶ More help, S.135 auf
einzelnen Wortkarten an.
• S nutzen die Wortkarten, um
ihre Höreindrücke zu sortieren.

b) gemäß AA in PA
• ▶ Scaffolding als TA: *What are*
your ideas? I have ... And you?
• **Ausw.:** im Plenum.
• L/S überträgt die Tabelle an
die Tafel, ergänzt die passen-
den Wörter bzw. heftet die
Wortkarten an.

Ex 2 Einstieg:
• (SB zu) ▶ Semantisierung des
neuen Wortschatzes

Erarbeitung:
a) (SB auf) gemäß AA in EA
• **Ausw.:** L notiert Wortpaare an
die Tafel.

b) nach **1. Lesen/Hören** gemäß
AA in EA (▶ Lesetechniken,
▶ Mitleseverfahren)
• **Ausw.:** ▶ Five-minute teacher

• ☒ **Alternative: Ex 2–4**
können mithilfe von ▶ KV 4.1
A + B bearbeitet werden.
• S können auf der KV u. a. das
Markieren von Wörtern üben.

112

| 4 | **Topic 1** | Topic 2 | Topic 3 | Story | Viewing | Study skills | Unit task |

My neighbourhood

🔊 ⚲ **1 From Lily's window** | **1 a)** Lösung S. 292

🔊 **a)** Look at the photo and listen. You're Lily. What can you see, hear and smell?

👁 I can see ...	👂 I can hear ...	👃 I can smell ...
houses	seagulls	the neighbour's cooking
...	...	...

▶ More help, p.135

👥 **b)** Compare your answers. Take turns to say them. Add new ideas to your table.

1 b) individuelle Lösungen

📖 **2** READING **Lily's homework** | **2 a)** Lösung S. 292

a) BEFORE YOU READ Make six pairs of °opposites to
describe a neighbourhood: *big – small, ...*

~~big~~ • boring • clean • dirty • friendly •
horrible • interesting • loud • nice •
quiet • ~~small~~ • unfriendly

☒ **b)** Read Lily's homework. Say which words (adjectives) from a) Lily uses for:

1 the shop: *small*
2 her neighbours: ...
3 activities at the youth centre: ...
4 the fields: ...
5 some places on the estate: ...
6 the cars: ...

2 b) 1 small • **2** friendly • **3** interesting •
4 big • **5** dirty • **6** loud

🔊 2.19

My neighbourhood

I live in Brighton on the Whitehawk[1] Estate. There are a lot of flats and houses and
a small shop. We don't have a car – we go to the town centre by bike or bus.

I like our neighbours, they're really friendly. I like the youth centre because it has
interesting activities. I sometimes go to the homework club after school because my
5 parents work late. My sister doesn't live with us because she's married.
I like the sports centre. It doesn't have parkour, but I like playing table tennis there.
And I like the big fields near the estate too. I walk there with my dad. But we don't
go very often because he doesn't have a lot of free days.

Some people don't look after our estate. They don't put rubbish in the bins and
10 some places on the estate are really dirty. I don't like all the rubbish. I also don't like
all the cars, they're very loud.

My neighbourhood has some problems. But I think it's nice and I like it.

1 [ˈwaɪthɔːk] | ▶ Workbook, p. 57

Topic 1 Vorbereitung

Material: Ex 1 UMA/CD, vorbereit. Wortkarten (s. Reservoir von ▶ More help, S. 135) • Ex 2 UMA/CD, ▶ KV 4.1A + B: Lily's homework (Klassensatz) • Ex 3 UMA, ▶ KV 4.1A + B • Ex 4 UMA/App (Erklärfilm), ▶ KV 4.1A + B • Ex 5 (bei Bedarf) kleine Zettel (Klassensatz)
Zeitbedarf: ca. 2 Std.
Minimalversion: Ex 5 auslassen
Begleitmedien: WB (S. 57), App (Erklärfilm), INKL (S. 112–113)

4

✏ 3 Lily's notes

a) Copy Lily's table with notes for her homework in 2.
Read her homework again and complete her notes.

☺	☹
the neighbours	the rubbish
...	...

3 a) Lösung S. 292

3 b) Lösungsbsp. S. 292

💬 ☒ b) Say why Lily likes or doesn't like the things in a).

Lily likes ... because ...   She doesn't like ... because ...

▶ Parallel exercise, p. 135

📖 4 LOOKING AT LANGUAGE Simple present: negative sentences

☒ a) Find all the sentences with *don't* and *doesn't* in Lily's homework in 2.

4 a) Lösung S. 292

We *don't* have a car.   My sister *doesn't* live with us. ...

b) Complete the rule.

Wenn wir im *simple present* ausdrücken wollen, dass wir etwas nicht machen, verwenden wir:

I You We They	+ ■ + have, live, like, go, ...
	don't
He She It	+ ■ + have, live, like, go, ...
	doesn't

Scout **likes** rubbish. Lily **doesn't like** rubbish.

▶ Language file 12, p. 188

💬 5 SPEAKING Your neighbourhood

5 individuelle Lösungen

a) °**Brainstorm** neighbourhood words. Collect ideas on the board.

▶ More practice 1, p. 135

b) Think about what you like and don't like about your neighbourhood.

👥 c) SPEED DATING Talk to different partners. Make notes.

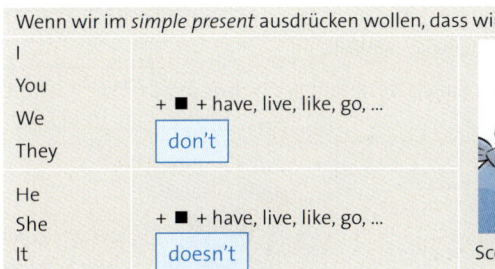

name	likes	doesn't like
Masoud[1]	his friends	all the dogs
Emma	...	...

Hi, Masoud. I like the sports centre. What about you?

d) Tell the class about one student.

Masoud likes his friends. He doesn't like ...

1 [məˈsuːd]

▶ Workbook, p. 57

one hundred and thirteen **113**

Ex 3 Einstieg:
• (SB zu) ▶ Semantisierung von *note*

Erarbeitung:
a) (SB auf) Klären der AA
• S ergänzen die Tabelle beim **2. Lesen** (bzw. Hören) in EA.
• **Ausw.:** ▶ Partner check, dann Plenum (ggf. Tabelle als TA)

b) Lernstärkere S arbeiten auf S. 113, lernschwächere S:
☒ ▶ Parallel ex, S. 135
• L führt ein Bsp. vor, anschl. gemäß AA in EA od. PA.
• **Ausw.:** Alle S präsentieren Ergebnisse im Plenum.
• **Alternative:** ▶ KV 4.1A + B

Ex 4 Einstieg:
• (SB auf) als Wdh: ▶ Buzz reading von Lilys Text (s. Ex 2, S. 112)

Erarbeitung:
a) (SB auf) Klären der AA
• S notieren Sätze im Heft.
• **Ausw.:** ▶ Meldekette

b) gemäß AA im Plenum
• S notieren die Regel im Merkteil (▶ English folder).
• ▶ LF 12, S. 188 lesen, Erklärfilm (UMA/App)
• ☒ **Alternative:** ▶ KV 4.1A + B

Ex 5 Einstieg:
• (SB zu) ▶ Thumbs up: L: *Do you like your neighbourhood?* S: *Yes, I do. / No, I don't.*

Erarbeitung:
a) (SB auf) ▶ Brainstorming

b) gemäß AA

c) (SB auf) L spielt einen Dialog mit S vor.
• ▶ Speed dating (s. a. SB, S. 27)

d) gemäß AA im Plenum

Topic 1 Inhalt

Lernschwerpunkt: die eigene Wohngegend beschreiben
Kompetenzen: Reading Online-Posts verstehen • Speaking über mögliche Aktivitäten im Wohnort sprechen • Plätze in einem Ort verstehen und beschreiben • Writing einen Online-Post über die eigene Wohngegend schreiben
Redemittel: *places* • *my neighbourhood has ...* • *adjectives*

Ex 6 Einstieg:
- (SB zu) L stimmt S ein:
  L: *What can you do in a youth centre?*
  S: *I can meet friends / play football / ...*
  L: *Let's find out more about Lily's youth centre.*

Erarbeitung:
a) (SB auf) Klären der AA: ein Bsp. im Plenum
- S arbeiten gemäß AA in EA und schriftl.
- ▣ ▶ Parallel ex, S. 135
- **Ausw.:** ▶ Partner check, dann im Plenum

b) L führt Bsp. mit S vor.
- anschl. gemäß AA in PA
- **Zusatz:** Einsatz von ▶ KV 4.2: einem Würfelspiel, bei dem die S positive und negative Sätze im *simple present* bilden.

Ex 7 Einstieg:
- ▣ (SB zu) zur Wdh.:
  L: *Do you know these places in your neighbourhood?*
- L zeigt vorbereitete ▶ Flashcards mit den fünf *places* von **Ex 7**.
- S nennen bekannte Vokabeln.

Erarbeitung:
a) (SB auf) gemäß AA in EA
- **Ausw.:** ▶ Meldekette

b) Klären der AA im Plenum
- gemäß AA schriftl. in EA
- ▶ SF 2, S. 174
- **Ausw.:** ▶ Gallery walk

c) Klären der AA
- gemäß AA in EA oder PA
- **Ausw.:** ▶ Gallery walk oder im Plenum (TA)

4	**Topic 1**	Topic 2	Topic 3	Story	Viewing	Study skills	Unit task

📖 6 The youth centre

💬 **a)** Lily tells her friends about the youth centre. Complete what she says.

> 6 a) Lösung S. 292f.

1   *It doesn't open at weekends.*

> *I often go to the youth centre, but not at weekends. It (1 not open) ... at weekends. There are a lot of activities like cooking, boxing and football. There's a girls' group on Tuesday, but I (2 not go) ... there, I (3 not have) ... time then. Sometimes I play +pool at the youth centre with my neighbour Niles. He (4 not go) ... to Varndean and his school (5 not have) ... a lot of clubs. We (6 not pay) ... for the activities – they're all free. A lot of people on our estate (7 not have) ... a lot of money.*

▶ Box: Voc., p. 241

▶ Parallel exercise, p. 135

👥 **b)** Talk about the activities in a) with a partner.

> 6 b) individuelle Lösungen

I go to / I don't go to	a youth centre.
I like / I don't like	pool / cooking / boxing / football.
I play / I don't play	pool / football.

▶ More practice 2, p. 136

📖 7 Words Places (1)

> 7 a) 1 e • 2 d • 3 a • 4 d • 5 c

✏️ **a)** Match the places to the °explanations.

1	shop	a	You swim in the sea here.
2	sports centre	b	You watch films here.
3	beach	c	You go walking here.
4	cinema	d	You do different sports here.
5	field	e	You buy things here.

You can explain words in your VOCAB FILE.

b) Start a page in your VOCAB FILE with a mind map for places. Add the places in a) plus at least four more places from pages 110–114.

▶ Skills file 2, p. 174

> 7 b), c) Lösungsbsp. S. 293

🗙 **c)** Add explanations for all your words in b).

places

shop: You buy things here.

▶ Workbook, pp. 58–59

Topic 1 Vorbereitung

Material: Ex 6 ▶ <u>KV 4.2: GAME Activity cards</u> (pro Spielgruppe), ein Würfel (pro Spielgruppe) • **Ex 7** vorbereitete Flashcards • **Ex 8** UMA, ggf. vorbereitete Bingo-Vorlage (Klassensatz) • **Ex 10** Handpuppe Scout mit Tablet, Computerzugang (mit Schreibprogrammen)
Zeitbedarf: ca. 2 Std.
Minimalversion: Ex 8 bei Zeitmangel auslassen
Begleitmedien: WB (S. 58–59), App (Digital help, Digital quiz), INKL (S. 114–115), DIFF (4.1, 4.2)

4

💬 **8 Places game**

a) Make a table with nine places from your mind map in **7b)**.

b) When the teacher explains a place:
Put up your hand and say the correct place. °Cross it out.
When you have three words →↓↙↘, °shout "Here!".

8 individuelle Lösungen

shop	...	...
...	...	...
...	beach	...

▶ More practice 3, p. 136

📖 **9 READING My neighbourhood**

9 Lösung S. 293

Read the posts. Say what Jing[1] and Alexis[2] think about their neighbourhoods.

Jing likes/doesn't like her neighbourhood because …
Alexis likes/doesn't like his neighbourhood because …

www.my-neighbourhood.example.net

Hi, everybody! What's your neighbourhood like?
I live in a big city. It's very loud in my neighbourhood. There are a lot of cars and people. Everybody is very busy and it's also dirty. I don't like my neighbourhood. I'd like to live in a small town.
Jing, China

www.my-neighbourhood.example.net

▶ Box: Voc., p. 241

I live in a village in the country. Our village doesn't have many interesting places. There's a shop and a lot of fields and animals. It's boring sometimes, but I like living here. Our neighbours are very friendly and there are a lot of other kids.
Alexis, France

My task **10** individuelle Lösungen

✏️ **10 A ⁺post about my neighbourhood**

Write a post like the posts in **9**. Write at least five sentences. Put your text in your DOSSIER.

I live in a village/a town/a city/in the country.
My neighbourhood has/doesn't have …
I like/don't like …

▶ Digital help ▶ More help, p. 137

Digital quiz **I can describe my neighbourhood.** ✓ **1** [dʒɪŋ] **2** [əˈleksɪs] one hundred and fifteen **115**

Ex 8 Erarbeitung:
a) (SB auf) Klären der AA: das Spiel ist eine Bingo-Variante.
• gemäß AA: L präsentiert eine leere Tabelle als Bsp. (UMA/TA) od. teilt vorbereitete Vorlagen an die S aus.
• ⚑ L notiert vorab die *places* von **Ex 7b)** an der Tafel.
b) Klären der AA: L nutzt die Umschreibungen von 7b) u. demonstriert ein Bsp.:
L: *You buy things there.*
S: *It's a shop!*
• Durchführung im Plenum

Ex 9 Einstieg:
• (SB auf) L stimmt S ein:
L: *Let's read about Jing and Alexis, who write about their neighbourhoods.*

Erarbeitung:
• gemäß AA in EA
• S notieren die Antworten in ihr Heft.
• **Ausw.:** ▶ Partner check, anschl. im Plenum

My task Ex 10 Einstieg:
• (SB zu) Scout mit Tablet:
Scout: *Look, I have a post from my friend Blue Bird. She wants to know about your neighbourhood.*
L: *Let's answer your friend.*

Erarbeitung:
• (SB auf) gemäß AA mithilfe der Vorgaben
• ▶ More help, S. 137
• S können ihre *posts* am Computer schreiben und ggf. ausdrucken.
• **Sich.:** im ▶ Dossier
• **Alternative:** präsentieren in der ▶ English corner

Topic 2 Inhalt

Lernschwerpunkt: über eine Stadt bzw. ein Dorf sprechen
Kompetenzen: Listening Orte richtig erkennen und zuordnen • ein Lied über eine Kleinstadt verstehen • Fragen über eine Stadt verstehen und beantworten • Speaking sich über den eigenen Wohnort austauschen • Study skills sprachliche Regelmäßigkeiten entdecken • Intercultural competence Informationen über Städte in UK erhalten
Strukturen: *simple present: questions and short answers*
Redemittel: *places in a town or a village • Do you like/have …? – Yes, I/we do. / No, I/we don't.*

Ex 1 Erarbeitung:

a) (SB zu) L zeigt die acht *places* von S. 116 (UMA od. ▶Flashcards und Wortkarten an Tafel):
L: *Do you know the places?*
• S ordnen die Wörter den Orten zu.
• ▶Good to know, S. 116

b) (SB auf) ▶Lautschulung

c) gemeinsames Klären der AA
• L führt ggf. Bsp. im Plenum vor.
• S arbeiten in Kleingruppen (▶Gruppenbildung).

d) gemäß AA

• **Zusatz:** Festigung des neuen Wortschatzes mithilfe eines ▶Word memory.

Ex 2 Einstieg:

• (SB zu) ▶Brainstorming:
L: *What places does your town/village have?*
S: *It has …*
L: *Let's listen to a song about Kasia's town.*

Erarbeitung:

a) 1. **Hören** gemäß AA
• S können beim Zuhören den Kopf auf die Bank legen.
• **Ausw.:** gemäß AA (▶Thumbs up)

b) 2. **Hören** gemäß AA, ggf. schriftl. mit ▶KV 4.3 (Ex 1a)

c) (SB auf) 3. **Hören** gemäß AA
• ggf. schriftl. mit ▶KV 4.3 (Ex 1b)
• **Ausw.:** ▶Meldekette

d) ▶KV 4.3 (Ex 1c)
• **Ausw.:** S antworten im Plenum.

• **Zusatz:** S schreiben ihren eigenen Song, s. ▶KV 4.3 (Ex 2)

My town or village

📖 **1** WORDS **Places (2)**   1 a) 1 b • 2 c • 3 a • 4 f • 5 e • 6 g • 7 d • 8 h

a) Lily's friend Kasia[1] doesn't live in Brighton, she lives in a small town. Lily tells Kasia about Brighton. Match the places to the pictures.

Lily: Brighton has …
1 a hospital
2 an ice rink
3 a library
4 a supermarket
5 a museum
6 a ⁺shopping centre
7 a stadium
8 a train station

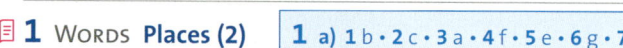

Good to know

Brighton is a city – but it's a small city.
The top three biggest UK cities are:
1 London
2 Birmingham[2]
3 Manchester[3]
Find the places on the UK map in your book.

🔊 📧 **b)** Listen and repeat the places in a).   **1 b)** *Reihenfolge wie in 1 a)*

🔊 2.20 💬 **c)** Write the places from a) on °pieces of paper and put them in a box. °Sit in a circle. The first student takes a piece of paper and °mimes an activity for the place. A student from the group says the place. Then give the box to the next student.

I think it's a hospital / …

d) Add the places to your mind map from p. 114.

🎵 **2** SONG **Kasia's town**   **2 b), c) 1** park • **2** beach • **3** pier • **4** stadium • **5** library

🔊 2.21 **a)** Close your °eyes and listen to Kasia's song. Is Kasia happy or not with her town? Give a 👍 or a 👎.   **2 a)** 👎

🔊 **b)** Listen again. What places do you hear? Collect them on the °board.

🔊 **c)** Listen again. Complete the song with the places.

d) Say what Kasia likes about her town.

2 d) She likes her friends in the neighbourhood.

Kasia's town

*I think that my town is boring
And I don't like living here.
My town doesn't have a (1) …
It doesn't have a (2) … or (3) …
There °isn't anything for me
No (4) …, no (5) …
°The only thing here that is good
Are my friends in the neighbourhood!*

▶Workbook, p. 60

116 one hundred and sixteen   1 [ˈkæʃə] 2 [ˈbɜːmɪŋəm] 3 [ˈmæntʃɪstə]

Topic 2 Vorbereitung

Material: Ex 1 ggf. vorbereitete Flashcards/Wortkarten, UMA/CD • Ex 2 UMA/CD, ▶ KV 4.3: Kasia's song (Klassensatz) •
Ex 3 Handpuppe Scout • Ex 4 UMA/App (Erklärfilm) • Ex 5 UMA
Zeitbedarf: ca. 2 Std.
Minimalversion: Ex 5 als HA
Begleitmedien: WB (S. 60–61), App (Erklärfilm), INKL (S. 116–117)

💬👥 **3 SPEAKING Different places**

> **3 a) Picture A and B:** hospital, library, supermarket, ice rink
> **Picture A:** museum and a train station
> **Picture B:** stadium and a shopping centre.

a) **Partner B:** Look at p. 134.
Partner A: Look at your picture.
Take turns to ask and answer questions.
Use the places in 1a).

Does your town have a hospital?
– Yes, it does./No, it doesn't.
– That's the same./That's different.

b) Now ask and answer questions about your town or village.
▶ Wordbank 11, p. 202

Do you like your town or village?

Yes, I do. / No, I don't.

Do you have a favourite place? (What is it?)

> **3 b)** individuelle Lösungen

📺 **4 LOOKING AT LANGUAGE Simple present: questions and short answers**
Erklär-film

a) Look at the questions in 3a) and 3b). Complete the rule.

> Wenn du eine Entscheidungsfrage stellst, auf die man mit **Ja** oder **Nein** antwortet,
> verwendest du die gebeugte Form des Hilfsverbs *do* (■ oder ■) am Anfang der Frage:
>
> ■ + *I/you/we/they* + *have/like/…*?
> ■ + *he/she/it* + *have/like/…*?

> **4 a)** Do … / Does …

b) Look at 3a) and 3b) again. Complete these short answers:

Yes, it … / No, it …   Yes, I … / No, I …

> **4 b)** does / doesn't • do / don't

▶ Language file 13, p. 188
▶ Language file 14, p. 189

📖 **5 In town with Kasia and Bella**

> **5 a)** Lösung S. 293

a) Lily °interviews her friend Kasia for some homework.
Put the questions in order.

1 with you / go everywhere / does / Bella / ?
2 you / do / know / the town well / ?
3 have / problems / with Bella / you / in shops / do / ?
4 you and Bella / the bus / use / do / ?

b) Match the questions to Kasia's answers.

a Yes, I do. I have a map of it in my head.
b Yes, she does. She comes to school too.
c Yes, we do. Everybody on the bus knows Bella!
d No, I don't. Guide dogs can go everywhere.

> **5 b) 1** b • **2** a • **3** d • **4** c

Kasia and her guide dog Bella

▶ Challenge 1, p. 137
▶ Workbook, pp. 60–61

one hundred and seventeen **117**

Ex 3 Einstig:
• (SB zu) ▶ Scaffolding (TA): *Does your town have …?*
  – *Yes, it does. / No, it doesn't.*
• L spielt den Beispieldialog mit Scout vor.

Erarbeitung:
a) (SB auf) gemäß AA in PA:
  ▶ Partner B, S. 134
• ☑ kurze Wdh. der acht *places* von Ex 1a), ggf. als TA (für *Partner A*)
• **Ausw.:** S-Paare präsentieren ihre Dialoge im Plenum.

b) gemäß AA weiterhin in PA
• Die S-Paare von a) bleiben bestehen.
• ▶ Wordbank 11, S. 202
• **Ausw.:** im Plenum

Ex 4 Erarbeitung:
a) (SB auf) gemäß AA
• L notiert die Fragen als TA.
• **Ausw.:** L/S ergänzen die Regel im Plenum (TA).

b) gemäß AA
• **Ausw.:** L/S ergänzt den TA.
• **Sich.:** S übertragen den kompletten TA (Fragen u. Kurzantworten) in ihren Merkteil (▶ English folder).
• Erklärfilm (UMA/App) ▶ LF 13, S. 188, ▶ LF 14, S. 189

Ex 5 Einstig:
• (SB zu) L zeigt das vergrößerte Bild (UMA).
  L: *What can you say about Kasia?*
  S: *She is blind.*
• ▶ Semantisierung von *guide dog*

Erarbeitung:
a) + b) (SB auf) gemäß AA
• **Ausw.:** ▶ Meldekette

Topic 2 Inhalt

Lernschwerpunkt: über eine Stadt bzw. ein Dorf sprechen
Kompetenzen: Listening Fragen über Brighton verstehen und beantworten • Speaking sich über den eigenen Wohnort und Tourismus austauschen • Orte durch Fragen erraten • Mediation Online-Informationen über Brighton ins Deutsche übertragen
Redemittel: *places in a town or a village • Do you like/have ...? – Yes, I/we do. / No, I/we don't.*

Ex 6 Einstieg:
• (SB zu) L fragt Scout:
  L: *Do you visit other places in England?*
  Scout: *No, I don't. I love Brighton.*
  Scout fragt S: *Do you visit other places in ...?*
  S: *Yes, I do. I visit ...*

Erarbeitung:
a) (SB auf) schriftl. gemäß AA

b) Ausw. von a): S vergleichen Lösungen beim **1. Hören**, ggf. **2. Hören**.

c) PA oder ▶ Milling around
• **Ausw.:** S präsentieren zu zweit Beispiele im Plenum.

Ex 7 Erarbeitung:
a) (SB auf) gemäß AA
• S notieren Ergebnisse beim **1. Hören**.
• ☑ L u. S klären Inhalt der Bilder im Plenum:
  L: *What can you see in picture A? ...*

b) + c) gemäß AA
• **Ausw.** von b) beim **2. Hören**

d) gemäß AA in PA (▶ Role-play),
  s. a. ▶ Tippbox, S. 118
• ☑ ggf. **3. Hören**
• **Ausw.:** gemeinsam im Plenum

Ex 8 Einstieg:
• (SB zu) S aktivieren Vorwissen:
  L: *What questions do you ask when you are a visitor in a town?*
  S: *Does your town ...?*

Erarbeitung:
• (SB auf) gemäß AA in PA
• **Ausw.:** S-Paare präsentieren ihre Ergebnisse im Plenum.

---

4 | Topic 1 | **Topic 2** | Topic 3 | Story | Viewing | Study skills | Unit task

📖 **6 Towns and visitors**

6 a), b) 1 Do • **2** Do • **3** Does • **4** Do • **5** Does

🗨 a) Complete the questions with *do* or *does*.

1 ... visitors ask you questions in English?
2 ... you have a favourite place in another country?
3 ... your town or village have a lot of visitors?
4 ... you visit other places in Germany?
5 ... your town have a visitor information centre?

Do you visit other places in England?

No, I don't. I never visit other places. I love Brighton!

🔊 2.22 🔊 b) Listen and check the questions in a).

✉ 👥 c) Take turns to ask the questions. Answer with short answers. Give extra information.

▶ More practice 4, p. 137

👂 **7 LISTENING Questions from visitors**

7 a) 1 D • **2** E • **3** A • **4** C • **5** B • **6** F

🔊 ✉ a) Listen to six short conversations. Match them to the correct pictures: *1D, 2 ...*
🔊 2.23

👥 b) Complete the questions in your exercise book.

1 Does bus 12A go to the ...?
2 Do you know a good fish and chip ...?
3 Does the Brighton Museum open on ...?
4 Do you have the ...?
5 Does Brighton have a visitor ... centre?
6 Does the ... ⁺get warm in summer?

7 b), c) Lösung S. 293

🔊 c) Listen again and check. Does Lily answer *yes* or *no*? Tick (✓) or cross (✗).

👥 d) ROLE-PLAY Ask the questions in b) and give short answers. Be polite!

💡 When you ask for information, be polite. Use *Excuse me* (before you ask something) and *Thank you*. When people say *Thank you*, say *You're welcome*.

✉ 👥 **8 SPEAKING Questions about your town**

8 individuelle Lösungen

🗨 Take turns to ask for °tips about your partner's town or village.

Does your town / village have a good ...? / Do you know a good ...?

---

118   one hundred and eighteen

Topic 2 Vorbereitung

Material: Ex 6 Handpuppe Scout, UMA/CD • Ex 7 UMA/CD • Ex 9 UMA • Ex 10 Handpuppe Scout
Zeitbedarf: ca. 2 Std.
Minimalversion: Ex 8 ggf. auslassen
Begleitmedien: App (Digital quiz, Digital help), INKL (S. 118–119), DIFF (4.3, 4.4)

4

→ **9** MEDIATION °**Welcome to the pier!**

9 Lösungsbsp. S. 293

Your family wants to go to Brighton. You find a good website about the pier.
Answer your family's questions about it.

1 Wann hat die Seebrücke auf?
2 Muss man dafür Eintritt zahlen?
3 Ich sehe eine Achterbahn und ein Karussell. Was gibt es außerdem?
4 Es gibt Konzerte. Und was noch?
5 Was ist das rosa Zeug auf dem Bild?
6 Was kann man dort essen? Gibt es auch etwas Gesundes?

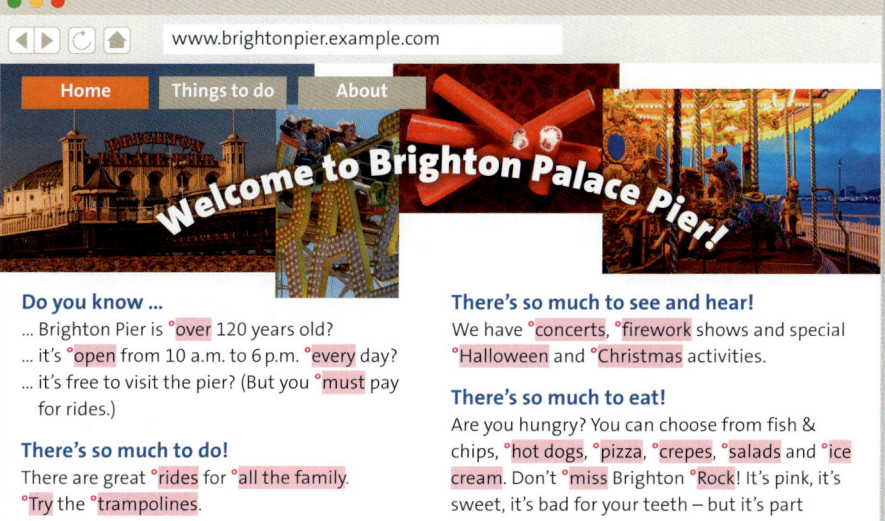

www.brightonpier.example.com

Home | Things to do | About

Welcome to Brighton Palace Pier!

Do you know …
… Brighton Pier is °over 120 years old?
… it's °open from 10 a.m. to 6 p.m. °every day?
… it's free to visit the pier? (But you °must pay for rides.)

There's so much to do!
There are great °rides for °all the family. °Try the °trampolines.
Play games and win prizes.

There's so much to see and hear!
We have °concerts, °firework shows and special °Halloween and °Christmas activities.

There's so much to eat!
Are you hungry? You can choose from fish & chips, °hot dogs, °pizza, °crepes, °salads and °ice cream. Don't °miss Brighton °Rock! It's pink, it's sweet, it's bad for your teeth – but it's part of Brighton!

My task

👥 **10 Five questions about places**

10 individuelle Lösungen

a) Make teams. Choose a place from your mind maps (p. 114).

b) Team 1 asks five yes/no-questions to guess the place. Team 2 gives short answers.

Do you buy food there? – Yes/No, you … – Is it a …?

Team 1 gets one °point for the correct place.

c) The teams swap roles.

 Remember: You can also ask questions with forms of *be*:
Is it free? – No, it isn't.
Are there shops? – Yes, there are.

▶ Digital help 📱 | ▶ More help, p. 138

 Digital quiz 📱 | I can talk about my town or village. ✓

Ex 9 Einstieg:
• (SB zu) L zeigt die vergrößerten Fotos von S. 119 (UMA). L: *What can you see? Where are the pictures from?*
• S beschreiben die Fotos und erkennen, dass diese Teil einer Website sind.

Erarbeitung:
• (SB auf) Klären der AA (▶ Mediation)
• schriftl. in EA, dann ▶ Partner check
• **Ausw.:** Präsentation der Ergebnisse im Plenum

My task Ex 10 Einstieg:
• (SB zu) L fordert S auf, Orte/Geschäfte in einer Stadt zu nennen (▶ Chain game):
L: *My town has a shop.*
S1: *My town has a shop and a cinema.*
S2: *My town has a shop, a cinema and …*
• L/Scout leitet über zum *task*: Scout: *Now let's play a game. You must guess my place. What questions can you ask?*
• S stellen Fragen (ggf. TA).

Erarbeitung:
a) (SB auf) gemäß AA in zwei Gruppen (▶ Gruppenbildung)

b) Klären der AA im Plenum, s. a. ▶ Tippbox, S. 119
• Team 2 wählt den ersten Ort aus, Team 1 stellt Fragen.
• ▶ More help, S. 138: enthält ▶ Scaffolding für beide Teams.

c) gemäß AA

Topic 3 Inhalt

Lernschwerpunkt: über das Wetter und Sehenswürdigkeiten in Brighton sprechen

Kompetenzen: Listening einer Stadtführung Informationen über Brighton und das Wetter entnehmen • Reading einer Online-Bewertung Informationen entnehmen • Speaking Fragen über Aktivitäten bei jedem Wetter stellen und beantworten • Study skills sprachliche Regelmäßigkeiten entdecken

Strukturen: *simple present: wh-questions*

Redemittel: *weather words • sights in Brighton*

Ex 1 Einstieg:
- (SB zu) L mit Scout:
  L: *Today we are on a walking tour and we need these things.* (L zeigt Schirm u. Mütze.)
  Scout: *Why?*
  L: *Because it can be rainy and windy. Do you know other weather words?*
- L sammelt Beispiele als TA.

Erarbeitung:

a) (SB auf) gemäß AA
- L zeigt vergrößerte Bilder (UMA).
- ▶Semantisierung, ▶Vokabeltafel
- **Ausw.:** ▶Five-minute teacher, anschl. ▶Lautschulung

b) S notieren die Ergebnisse beim **1. Hören**.
- **Ausw.:** ▶Meldekette, ggf. **2. Hören**.

c) Klären der AA im Plenum
- S notieren das korrekte Wort beim **1. Hören**.
- ▶Partner check, dann **2. Hören**
- **Ausw.:** ▶Meldekette

Ex 2 Einstieg:
- (SB zu) L zeigt Bild vom i360 Tower in Brighton:
  L: *Look at the tower. Would you go there?*
- S antworten spontan.

Erarbeitung:

a) (SB auf) S notieren die Antworten im Heft.
- **Ausw.:** ▶Meldekette

b) gemäß AA
- **Ausw.:** im Plenum
- L/S vervollständigen die Regel.
- **Sich.:** S übertragen die Regel in ihren Merkteil.
- Erklärfilm (UMA/App), ▶LF 15, S.189

| 4 | Topic 1 | Topic 2 | **Topic 3** | Story | Viewing | Study skills | Unit task |

Brighton in all weathers

1 ▶ LISTENING A walking tour

a) BEFORE YOU LISTEN **Find the correct picture.**

1 It's rainy.   4 It's cloudy.
2 It's sunny.   5 It's windy.
3 It's snowy.   ▶ Box: Voc., p. 243

> **1 a) 1** D • **2** A • **3** E • **4** B • **5** C

> *Hi, Sunita – My uncle Aleksander and my aunt Svetlana from °Russia are here in Brighton on holiday. We're on a walking tour now!*

2.24 b) **Listen to the walking tour. Put the weather pictures in the correct order.**

> **1 b)** E • D • A • C • B

2.25 c) **Listen to Eli's[1] tour from the next day. What's different? Choose the correct words.**

1 Today Eli talks about the Pavilion when it's A snowy B sunny C rainy.
2 He says you can have a A party B ⁺barbecue C picnic outside the Pavilion.
3 Today on the beach it isn't A windy B cold C warm. ▶ Box: Voc., p. 243
4 On the pier it's very A sunny B rainy C windy.
5 Today the wind takes a woman's A hat B sandwich C phone.
6 At the end the tourists can visit the i360 because it isn't A cloudy B cold C snowy.

> ▶ More practice 5, p. 138

> **1 c) 1** B • **2** C • **3** B • **4** C • **5** A • **6** A

2 LOOKING AT LANGUAGE Simple present: *wh*-questions

Erklärfilm

a) **Read the questions about the i360 °tower from people on the tour. Match them to the correct answers (a–d).**

> **2 a) 1** b • **2** a • **3** d • **4** c

1 When does the i360 open today?   a It goes up and down every 30 minutes.
2 How often does it go up and ⁺down?   b It opens at 10 o'clock.
3 How fast does it travel?   c Because you can take great photos from the top.
4 Why do you think it's interesting?   d It travels 16 metres per second.

b) **Look at these yes/no-questions and the questions in a). What's different? Complete the sentences in the box.**

Does the i360 open today?   Ja/Nein-Fragen fangen mit … an.
Do you think it's interesting?   Wh-Fragen fangen mit … an.

> **2 b)** *Ja/Nein*-Fragen fangen mit *Do/Does* … an.
> *Wh*-Fragen fangen mit *einem Fragewort* an.

> ▶ Language file 15, p. 189

> ▶ Workbook, p. 62

1 ['iːlaɪ]

120 one hundred and twenty

Topic 3 Vorbereitung

Material: Ex 1 Handpuppe Scout, Schirm, Mütze, UMA/CD • Ex 2 Bild vom i360 Tower in Brighton, UMA/App (Erklärfilm) •
Ex 4 UMA • Ex 5 Handpuppe Scout, drei vorbereitete Fragekärtchen, weißes A5-Papier (Klassensatz)
Zeitbedarf: ca. 2 Std.
Minimalversion: Ex 4 auslassen
Begleitmedien: WB (S. 62–63), App (Digital quiz, Digital help), INKL (S. 120–121), DIFF (4.5)

---

3 More questions on the tour | 3 Lösung S. 293

Some people on Eli's tour have more questions about Brighton.
Write the questions in the correct order.

1 the shops / when / open / do / ?
2 buy train tickets / do / I / how / ?
3 you / do / why / love Brighton / ?
4 where / stop / the bus / does / ?
5 does / how much / cost / a bus ticket / ?
6 like / do / food / what / you / ?

4 The Upside Down House | 4 a), b) Lösungen S. 294

Lily's aunt and uncle want to visit the Upside Down House.
Partner B: Look at p. 134.

a) **Partner A:** Look at the online °review.
Answer partner B's questions.

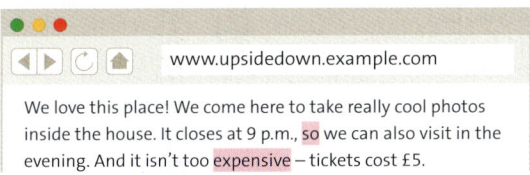

www.upsidedown.example.com

We love this place! We come here to take really cool photos
inside the house. It closes at 9 p.m., so we can also visit in the
evening. And it isn't too expensive – tickets cost £5.

b) **Partner A:** Ask partner B these questions. Add *do* or *does*.

1 When ... the Upside Down House open?
2 Where ... I buy tickets?
3 How ... we take funny photos?

▶ Challenge 2, p. 138

My task

5 +Quiz-quiz-swap | 5 a), b) Lösungsbsp. S. 294

a) Write one question about your town or village and the weather on a card.
Use the notes in the table to help you.

*What do you do
when it's snowy?*

What ... do Where ... go How ... travel	when it's	sunny / rainy / snowy / cloudy / windy / hot / cold / warm?

b) WALK AROUND
Find a partner and ask your question.
Answer your partner's question about your town.

When it's hot, I go swimming.

▶ Digital help   ▶ More help, p. 139

c) Swap cards and °walk around again. Find a new partner and ask your new question.

▶ Workbook, pp. 62–63

Digital quiz   I can **talk about** °**sights in Brighton and the weather.** ✓   one hundred and twenty-one **121**

Ex 3 Erarbeitung:
• (SB auf) gemäß AA schriftl.
in EA
• ▶ L bildet Frage 1 im Plenum
als TA, ggf. 2. Frage.
• **Ausw.:** ▶ Five-minute teacher

Ex 4 Einstieg:
• (SB zu) L präsentiert das
vergrößerte Bild (UMA):
• ▶ Semantisierung von *upside
down*

Erarbeitung:
a) (SB auf) Klären der AA
(*Partner B:* s. S. 134), ▶ Info-gap
activity
• *Partner A u. B* lesen zunächst
ihre jeweiligen Texte.
• ▶ Lernschwächere S
notieren die vollständige
Frage vorab.
b) gemäß AA
• **Ausw.:** Vergleich im Plenum
(▶ Meldekette)

My task Ex 5 Einstieg:
• (SB zu) Scout (mit drei
vorbereiteten Fragekarten):
Scout: *I want to do a quiz.
Look, here are some question
cards.* (Scout stellt Fragen und
L/S antwortet.)
L: *Let's make more question
cards.*

Erarbeitung:
a) (SB auf) L teilt Papier (A5) aus.
• S notieren jeweils eine Frage.

b) + c) gemäß AA (▶ Swap cards,
▶ Milling around)
• ▶ More help, S. 139: ▶ Scaffolding
für mögliche Antworten.
• **Ausw.:** S fragen/antworten im
Plenum.

Lernschwerpunkt: eine Geschichte lesen und verstehen
Kompetenzen: Reading eine Geschichte verstehen • Writing Daten auf einem Plakat ergänzen
Redemittel: *my neighbourhood*

Ex 1 Einstig:
- (SB zu) L zeigt Bilder von Straßen voll mit Müll.
  L: *What can you see in the picture? What do you think about it?*
- S beschreiben das Bild.
  TA (▶ Scaffolding): *I think this neighbourhood is nice/great/ bad/dirty because …*

Erarbeitung:
a) (SB auf) TA: *Lily's neighbour-hood*
- S lesen AA und das *scaffolding*.
- **Ausw.:** L sammelt Ideen der S als TA.

b) gemäß AA
- ☑ L zeigt Bilder vom Einstieg: Was erkennen S?
- Sammeln von Begriffen (TA)

Ex 2 Einstig:
- (SB zu) L leitet ein:
  L: *Lily's neighbourhood is very dirty. She doesn't like it. What can she do?*
- TA: *What can Lily do?*
- L sammelt Ideen der S.
  L: *You have many good ideas. Let's check out Lily's idea.*

Erarbeitung:
a) (SB auf) S lesen Überschrift.
- Vergleich mit TA, ob S die gleiche Idee hatten.
- S lesen den ersten Absatz (bis Ende Zeile 8, „… estate."), dann füllen sie das Poster aus (z. B. am UMA oder TA).

b) S lesen/hören die Story leise in EA (▶ Mitleseverfahren).
- Fokus auf Leseauftrag (*Reading for detail*, s. ▶ Lese-techniken)

Lily's idea

💬 **1 BEFORE YOU READ Where Lily lives**

1 a) Lösungsbsp. S. 294

a) What can you remember about Lily's neighbourhood? Collect information with the class.

She lives on an …   The neighbours are …
The neighbourhood is …   There's a lot of …

b) What rubbish or things can you find on the streets in your neighbourhood?

1 b) individuelle Lösungen

📖 **2 READING ⁺Clean-up day**

a) Lily makes a poster for a clean-up day on her estate. Read the first °paragraph of the story and °complete the poster.

b) Now read all the story.
Say what Buddy finds in the ground.

2 a) Clean-up • On Sunday • 9 o'clock • youth centre • rubbish • estate

HELLO, NEIGHBOURS!
Come to our … day
When? …, 2nd ⁺April at …   Where? At the …
Do you get angry about … everywhere?
Do you want to live on a clean …?
Then help us to clean up!

🔊 2.26   It's 9 o'clock on a Sunday morning and there's a big group in front of the youth centre. 'It's a great idea to have a clean-up day, Lily!' says her sister Chloe[1].
5 'Look at all these people!'
'A lot of people are angry about rubbish everywhere,' says Lily and Chloe's mum, Olga. 'They want to live on a clean estate.'
'I'm happy you're here, Chloe,' says Lily.
10 'I don't see you a lot now because you're married.' 'I know, I'm sorry. But it's great you have new friends!' 'Yes, it is. Noah, Sunita, Zane – this is my sister Chloe.'
'Hi guys! Nice to meet you. And who is
15 this?' 'It's my dog Buddy,' says Noah.
'He's really cute!' says Chloe.

'Hello, everybody. Welcome to Clean-up day!' says Olga. 'We have a lot of rubbish bags.' 'What about things for the Swap
20 Place?' asks Lily's neighbour Dosia. 'So other people can use them.' 'Yes,' Olga

answers. 'Let's put good things over there. And let's meet here at 12 o'clock for lunch.'

2 b) Buddy finds • a dead mouse (l. 25) • an old shoe (l. 27) • a gold ring (ll. 31–32)

1 [ˈkləʊi]   2 [ˈdɒʃə]

Story Vorbereitung

Material: Ex 1 Bilder von Straßen/Orten mit viel Müll, ggf. auch Bilder von sauberen Straßen • Ex 2 UMA/CD •
Ex 3 vergrößertes Bild von S. 122 (UMA)
Zeitbedarf: ca. 1 Std.
Minimalversion. Ex 1, Ex 2a) und Ex 3 auslassen
Begleitmedien: INKL (S. 122–123)

4

🔊 2.27

25 Lily, Chloe and Noah work together. Buddy wants to help too. First he finds a dead mouse. '°Yuck,' says Noah. Next Buddy brings an old shoe to Lily. 'Thanks, Buddy,' says Lily. Then Buddy digs in the ground for a long time. He barks.
30 'What do you have now?' asks Noah. 'Wow! Good dog! Hey, Lily, look at this.' It's a gold ⁺ring. 'It has "Jack and Maria[1]" in it,' Lily finds out. ▶ Box: Voc., p. 245
'So Jack and Maria are married,' says Chloe.
35 'The ring looks old. But who are Jack and Maria? How do we find them?'

The neighbours meet at the youth centre at 12 o'clock. They have over fifty ⁺bags of

⁺rubbish! They also have some old tables
40 and chairs, a bike, shoes and a lot of other things for the Swap Place. They take them to the Swap Place garage. They eat lunch and Lily tells the others about the ring. 'Why don't you put a note in the youth
45 centre?' asks Zane. 'Maybe somebody knows Jack and Maria.' 'Good idea, Zane,' Lily answers.

Two days later a boy phones Lily's mum. 'My name's Davy,' he says. 'I'm Jack and
50 Maria's grandson. My grandma is really happy about her ring! My grandparents want to give the youth centre some money to say thank you.'

✏ 3 People in the story

Who are they? Complete the sentences.

> 3 1 Lily's sister • 2 Lily's mum • 3 Lily's neighbour • 4 Jack / Maria / the ring • 5 Jack and Maria's grandson

1 Chloe is ...
2 Olga is ...
3 Dosia is ...
4 J... and ... are the names in ...
5 Davy is ...

📖 4 Why, what and how?

Answer the questions.

> 4 1 Chloe is married now. (p. 112) • 2 He finds a dead mouse and an old shoe. • 3 The group collects over 50 bags of rubbish. • 4 They put up a notice in the youth centre. • 5 They want to give the youth centre some money.

1 Why doesn't Lily see Chloe very often?
2 What two things does Buddy find before the ring?
3 How many bags of rubbish does the group collect?
4 How do the kids find Jack and Maria?
5 How do Jack and Maria want to say thank you?

1 [məˈriːə]

▶ Parallel exercise, p. 139
▶ More practice 6, p. 139

Ex 2b) (Forts.):
• **Ausw.:** TA: *What does Buddy find?*
• S/L schreiben die drei Dinge an die Tafel.
• ☒ S nennen die Zeilenan- gaben für die Dinge.

Ex 3 Einstieg:
• (SB zu) L zeigt vergrößertes Bild von S. 122 (UMA).
  L: *Look at the picture on p. 122. Who is who in the picture?*
• S nennen die Personen im Bild.
• Neue Personen sind: Chloe (*Lily's sister, next to Lily*), Olga (*Lily's mother, behind Zane*).

Erarbeitung:
• (SB auf) S notieren Sätze im Heft gemäß AA.
• ▶ Early finisher: S schlagen selbstständig ihnen unbe- kannte Vokabeln der Story im *Dictionary* nach und über- tragen sie in ihr *Vocab file*.
• **Ausw.:** ▶ Five-minute teacher
• ▶ Early finisher: S schreiben ihre Vokabeln an die ▶ Vokabel- tafel (▶ Vokabelarbeit).

Ex 4 Erarbeitung:
• (SB auf) schriftl. gemäß AA
• ⊡ Lernschwächere S bearbeiten ▶ Parallel ex, S. 139.
• L leitet ggf. das selbstständige Nachschlagen von unbekann- ten Vokabeln an.
• **Ausw.:** ▶ Five-minute teacher.
• **Sich.** des Lernwortschatzes der Story: S erhalten vorberei- tete Vokabellisten (engl. od. dt. ist vorgegeben).
• In GA vervollständigen S die Listen, ▶ Early finisher fungieren dabei als ▶ Experts.

Story Inhalt | Vorbereitung

Story Inhalt | Vorbereitung

Lernschwerpunkt: eine Geschichte lesen und verstehen
Kompetenzen: Reading Eine Geschichte verstehen •
Writing / Life Skills eine Tauschaktion planen und dafür ein
Plakat erstellen
Redemittel: *my neighbourhood*

Material: Ex 7 ggf. Material für einen eigenen *swap place*,
weißes A3-Papier für Poster (eins pro Gruppe), ggf. Sticker
(drei pro S)
Zeitbedarf: ca. 1 Std.
Minimalversion: Ex 7 auslassen
Begleitmedien: WB (S. 64), App (Digital quiz), INKL (S. 124),
DIFF (4.6)

Ex 5 Erarbeitung:
- (SB auf) Klären der AA:
  L erinnert daran, was die
  Zeilenangaben in Klammern
  bedeuten.
- S suchen das passende Wort
  und übertragen es in ihr
  Vocab file. Sie ergänzen die
  deutsche Bedeutung mit
  Bleistift.
- **Ausw.:** Vergleich im Plenum
- **Sich.:** ► Vokabeltafel.

Ex 6 Einstieg:
- (SB zu) L zeigt Fotos von *swap
  places* in der Umgebung (z. B.
  Mitnehmbücherei).
  L: *Describe the pictures.
  Explain how these places work.*

Erarbeitung:
a) (SB auf) S arbeiten im Heft.

b) gemäß AA
- **Ausw.:** Vergleich im Plenum
  (► Meldekette)

Ex 7 Einstieg:
- (SB zu) ► Thumbs up:
  L: *What do you think about
  the swap place?*
- ☒ S begründen ihre Meinung.

Erarbeitung:
a) (SB auf) Klären der AA
- ► Alphabet game
- ☒ Lernschwächere S nutzen
  das *Dictionary* als Hilfe.
- **Ausw.:** gemeinsam im Plenum

b) gemäß AA
- **Ausw.:** ► Gallery Walk.
- S verteilen max. drei Smileys
  od. Sticker an die Poster, die
  ihnen am besten gefallen.

c) Durchführung eines *swap
place* (z. B. als Schulprojekt)

---

4   Topic 1   Topic 2   Topic 3   **Story**   Viewing   Study skills   Unit task

📖 **5 Words in the ⁺text**

Find words in the story with these meanings.

1   To find something in the ground you ... (line 28)
2   when a dog 'speaks' (line 29)
3   the meal after breakfast (line 43)
4   paper or a card with information (line 44)
5   Your grandma and grandpa are your ... (line 51)

5 1 dig • **2** bark(s) • **3** lunch •
4 a note • **5** grandparents

📖 **6 The Whitehawk Swap Place**

a) True or false?

1   Olga asks about the Swap Place.
2   Things for the Swap Place are things that other people can use.
3   *(To) swap* means to give something to somebody and take another thing.
4   The neighbours don't find many things for the Swap Place.
5   The Swap Place is in the youth centre.

6 a) 1 false • **2** true • **3** true • **4** false • **5** false

☒ **b)** Correct the false sentences.

6 b) 1 *Dosia* asks about the Swap Place. •
4 The neighbours find *a lot of* things for the
Swap Place. • **5** The Swap Place is in *a garage*.

✏ **7** LIFE SKILLS ⁺**Go green!**

👥 **a)** You can °organize a Swap Place in your class or at your school.
Think of things at home and make an A–Z of things for a Swap Place.
Then compare your ideas with the class.

A – animals *(toys)*
B – books

7 a) Lösungsbsp. S. 294

👥 **b)** Make a poster for your Swap Place with information about it.

7 b) individuelle Lösungen

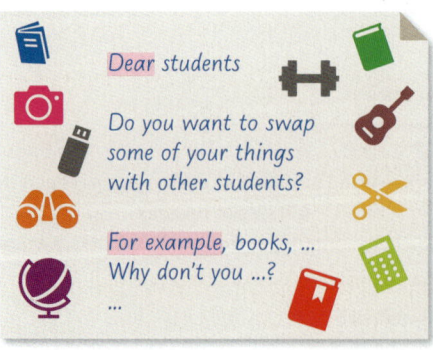

Dear students

Do you want to swap
some of your things
with other students?

For example, books, ...
Why don't you ...?
...

I use a lot of things
from other people.

c) Choose the best poster and start to swap!

► Workbook, p. 64

    Digital quiz   **I can** understand a story about green activities.

Viewing Inhalt | Vorbereitung

Lernschwerpunkt: Filmszenen einer Stadttour verstehen
Kompetenzen: Viewing dem Film Informationen zu den
Mutproben von Emir und Daisy entnehmen • Writing
Wörter in Spiegelschrift schreiben
Redemittel: *Brighton sights*

Material: Ex 2 UMA/DVD
Zeitbedarf: ca. 1 Std.
Minimalversion: Ex 3 auslassen
Begleitmedien: INKL (S. 125)

| Topic 1 | Topic 2 | Topic 3 | Story | **Viewing** | Study skills | Unit task | 4 |

The Brighton dares: In town

1 In Brighton
1 Lösungsbsp. S. 294

BEFORE YOU WATCH **Look at the dares. Answer the questions.**

1 Do you think this dare is hard or easy for Emir? Why?
2 What sights¹ can Daisy show people on her tour of Brighton?

I think the dare is hard/ easy for Emir because …

Daisy can show people …

Daisy's dare for Emir:
Change the time on the
Queen's Park Clock Tower.

Emir's dare for Daisy:
Give a free tour of Brighton to
a tourist (in a swimming cap).

2 VIEWING How they do the dares
2 a) Lösungsbsp. S. 294

a) **Team A: Read the notes about Daisy. Team B: Read the notes about Emir.**
Watch the video and complete the notes about Daisy or Emir.

Daisy …
1 asks people on the …
2 goes to Volk's … Railway.
3 meets Mara, a tourist from the …
4 takes the number … bus.

Emir …
1 takes a mirror from … to the clock.
2 takes a photo of the time on the clock: It's …
3 takes a photo in the mirror. The time is …
4 Emir shows Daisy and Mara the …

b) **Team A: Find another A student and compare notes.**
Team B: Find another B student and compare notes.
2 b), c) individuelle Lösungen

c) Two A students make a group with two B students. Present your notes. Listen and complete
the notes in a) about the other person. Then watch the video again and check.

3 Try Emir's trick
3 individuelle Lösungen

a) Write the name of a Brighton sight.
Look in a mirror and copy it. Or use these mirror letters.

b) Read your partner's sight! Use a mirror or these letters.

ABCDEFGHIJKLM
NOPQRSTUVWXYZ

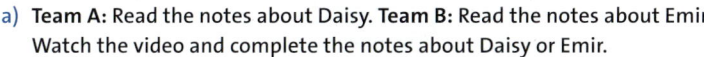

¹ **sight** *Sehenswürdigkeit*

Ex 1 Einstieg:
- (SB zu) TA: *A free tour of (name of nearest city)*
  L: *Which places in your town can you show on a free tour?*
- S sammeln Ideen im ▶ Five-finger brainstorming.

Erarbeitung:
- (SB auf) S beantworten die Fragen 1 und 2 in PA.
- **Ausw.:** L holt Stimmungsbild zu Frage 1 (▶ Thumbs up) ein.
- Einzelne S begründen ihre Meinung mithilfe des ▶ Scaffolding im SB.
- Zu Frage 2: TA: *Daisy's Tour.*
- L sammelt die Orte, die die S vorschlagen u. ergänzt den TA.

Ex 2 Erarbeitung:
a) (SB auf) ▶ Jigsaw gemäß AA: L teilt Klasse in zwei Teams.
- S lesen die Sätze zu ihrer Person (Daisy od. Emir).
- Klären von Verständnisfragen im Team (L hilft bei Bedarf).
- **1. Viewing:** S vervollständigen die Sätze.
- ☒ S prüfen, welche *sights* von der Liste aus **Ex 1** (s. TA) besucht werden.

b) Austausch in PA gemäß AA
- S prüfen und ergänzen ihre Notizen.

c) gemäß AA
- **Sich.:** 2. Viewing und Vergleich aller Sätze im Plenum (▶ Five-minute teacher)

Ex 3 Erarbeitung:
a) (SB auf) gemäß AA
b) **Sich.:** Entziffern der Wörter in PA.

Lernschwerpunkt: Präsentationen selbst erstellen und halten

Kompetenzen: Speaking eine Präsentation halten •
Media skills Folien für eine Präsentation erstellen •
sich filmen

Redemittel: *useful phrases for giving a presentation*

Material: Ex 1 eigene Präsentation über den Lieblingsort zum Einstieg und als Best Practice • Ex 2/4 Folien (Klassensatz) od. Zugang zu digitaler Präsentationssoftware • geeignete Aufnahmegeräte

Zeitbedarf: ca. 1 Std.

Begleitmedien: App (Digital quiz), INKL (S. 126), DIFF (4.7)

Ex 1 Einstieg:
- (SB zu) L zeigt eine kurze Präsentation über den eigenen (od. einen fiktiven) *favourite place* (ca. 3 Folien). L: *Scout wants to give a presentation too. Let's help her!*
- Die L-Präsentation dient den S als Vorbild und erleichtert das Erstellen der eigenen Präsentationen.

Erarbeitung:
- (SB auf) gemäß AA
- **Ausw.:** ▶ Meldekette

Ex 2 Erarbeitung:
- (SB auf) S liest die ▶ Tippbox, S. 126 laut vor.
- S arbeiten gemäß AA (am Computer oder auf Papier).
- **Ausw.:** L hat eine leere Folie (digital) vorbereitet.
- Im Plenum entsteht eine Folie für Scouts Vortrag.

Ex 3 Erarbeitung:
- gemäß AA
- **Ausw.:** TA mit Tabelle

Ex 4 Erarbeitung:
a) S nutzen die Ergebnis-Folie von Ex 2 für ihre eigene Präsentation.
- In PA erstellen S mind. eine weitere eigene Folie (s. Hilfen in Ex 1–3 u. ▶ SF 5, S. 179).
- ▣ S präsentieren ihre Folien aus Scouts Perspektive.
- S präsentieren sich ihre Folien gegenseitig in PA.

b) ▶ Feedback gemäß AA
- **Ausw.:** Austausch im Plenum
- Einzelne S präsentieren.

---

4   Topic 1   Topic 2   Topic 3   Story   Viewing   **Study skills**   Unit task

Give a presentation

1 Plan your presentation

Put °topics A–E in the correct order for Scout's presentation about her favourite places.

A   Talk about other good places in Brighton
B   Explain why it's my favourite place
C   Say hello and what the presentation is about
D   Ask for questions and say thank you
E   Say my favourite place

Help me plan a presentation, please!

> **1** C • E • B • A • D

2 Make a ⁺slide show

Scout's notes are too long on this °slide. Help her choose five words or phrases.

> **2** Brighton beach • Many people • Fish and chips • Sandwiches • I love fish and chips too!

My favourite place
My favourite place in Brighton is the beach because a lot of people come here and they often eat fish and chips or sandwiches. And I love fish and chips too!

Me on the beach!

Make the title big.
Use short notes.
Use some colour.
Choose big pictures.

3 Find useful phrases

> **3** Lösung S. 295

Copy the table. Put the phrases in the correct place.

> In this photo you can see • I'd like to talk about • In the end • Next • Do you have any questions? • Let's look at this picture of • My presentation is about • Thank you for listening.

Start the presentation	Continue the presentation	Talk about pictures	End the presentation
I'd like to talk about	...	...	...

4 Practise your presentation

> **4** individuelle Lösungen

a) Give your presentation on Scout's favourite places to your partner or film °yourself.

b) Give your partner or yourself feedback. Draw one, two or three ☺ or ☹.

Speak loudly: ...   *Speak clearly: ...*   *Look at your partner / group: ...*

▶ Skills file 5, p. 179

Digital quiz 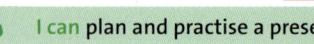   **I can** plan and practise a presentation.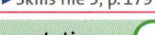

Unit task | Inhalt | Vorbereitung

Lernschwerpunkt: Präsentationen selbst erstellen und halten

Kompetenzen: Speaking eine Präsentation halten

Redemittel: *useful phrases for giving a presentation*

Material: *Placemats* (für 5–6 Gruppen), digitale Endgeräte (z. B. Tablets oder Computer) zur Erstellung einer Bildschirmpräsentation, ▶ KV 4.4: Giving feedback (Klassensatz)

Zeitbedarf: ca. 2 Std.

Begleitmedien: App (Digital help, Digital quiz), INKL (S. 127)

| Topic 1 | Topic 2 | Topic 3 | Story | Viewing | Study skills | **Unit task** | **4** |

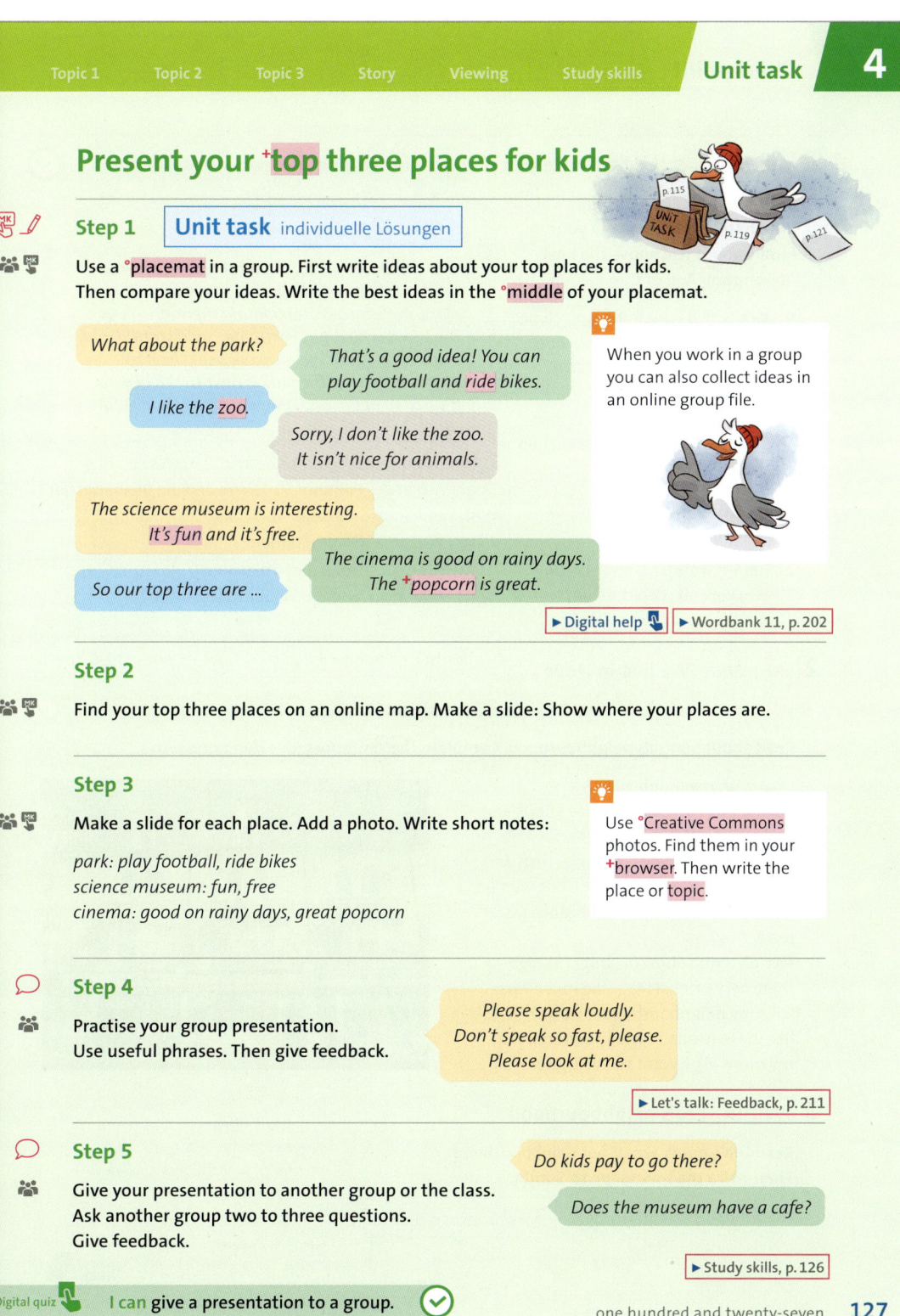

Present your ⁺top three places for kids

Step 1   **Unit task** individuelle Lösungen

Use a °placemat in a group. First write ideas about your top places for kids. Then compare your ideas. Write the best ideas in the °middle of your placemat.

What about the park?

That's a good idea! You can play football and ride bikes.

I like the zoo.

Sorry, I don't like the zoo. It isn't nice for animals.

The science museum is interesting. It's fun and it's free.

The cinema is good on rainy days. The ⁺popcorn is great.

So our top three are ...

When you work in a group you can also collect ideas in an online group file.

▶ Digital help   ▶ Wordbank 11, p. 202

Step 2

Find your top three places on an online map. Make a slide: Show where your places are.

Step 3

Make a slide for each place. Add a photo. Write short notes:

park: play football, ride bikes
science museum: fun, free
cinema: good on rainy days, great popcorn

Use °Creative Commons photos. Find them in your ⁺browser. Then write the place or topic.

Step 4

Practise your group presentation. Use useful phrases. Then give feedback.

Please speak loudly. Don't speak so fast, please. Please look at me.

▶ Let's talk: Feedback, p. 211

Step 5

Give your presentation to another group or the class. Ask another group two to three questions. Give feedback.

Do kids pay to go there?

Does the museum have a cafe?

▶ Study skills, p. 126

Digital quiz   **I can** give a presentation to a group. ✓

one hundred and twenty-seven **127**

Step 1 Einstieg:
- (SB zu)
  L: *Let's find out about your favourite places!*
- TA: *Top places for kids*

Erarbeitung:
- (SB auf) L teilt vorbereitete ▶ Placemats aus (eins pro Kleingruppe).
- S sammeln Ideen und kommentieren auf dem *Placemat* der Gruppe.
- ▶ Scaffolding von Step 1 u. ▶ Wordbank 11, S. 202 als Hilfe
- **Ausw.:** Diskussion der besten Ideen und Sammlung in der Mitte der *Placemat*

Step 2 Erarbeitung:
- L führt S in die Handhabung einer Online-Karte ein. (Wie funktioniert die Suche? etc.)
- L unterstützt beim Erstellen der ersten Folie am Computer.

Step 3 Erarbeitung:
- S erstellen ▶ Cue cards.
- L führt in die Bildsuche ein, erklärt, wie *Creative Commons photos* gefunden werden können (▶ Tippbox, S. 127).
- L zeigt, wie Fotos in *slides* eingefügt werden.

Step 4 Erarbeitung:
- gemäß AA
- S geben ▶ Feedback analog zu ▶ Study skills, S. 127 (Ex 4) ▶ KV 4.4
- S nutzen die Hilfen von ▶ Let's talk, S. 211

Step 5 Erarbeitung:
- gemäß AA
- ▶ KV 4.4 mit *Feedback sheets* für die Präsentationen.

Checkpoint Inhalt

Lernschwerpunkt: Kompetenzen und sprachliche Mittel üben, Lernfortschritte erkennen

Kompetenzen: Mediation eine Textnachricht erfassen • Writing eine Nachricht über die Wohngegend schreiben •
Listening Informationen zu Aktivitäten in einer Stadt entnehmen • Speaking ein Bild beschreiben

Strukturen: *simple present: negative sentences • simple present: questions and short answers • simple present: wh-questions*

Redemittel: *neighbourhood • places and activities in town • sights in Brighton*

Allg. Anmerkung: s. Unit 1, S. 36

Ex 1 Einstieg:
- (SB auf) S lesen das Lernziel zu diesem Abschnitt vor (*I can …*).
- S schätzen ihr Können zum Lernziel ein, z. B. mit ▶Thumbs up, und notieren das Ergebnis.

Erarbeitung:
a) + b) gemäß AA
- S notieren Antworten in ihr Heft.
- **Ausw.:** ▶Bus stop (Einsatz ▶KV Extra): S vergleichen ihre Lösungen mithilfe von ▶KV 4.5A.
- Nach der Lösungskontrolle erneute Einschätzung des Könnens (gleiche Methode wie im **Einstieg**)

Ex 2 + 3 Einstieg:
- (SB auf) s. Ex 1 (Selbsteinschätzung)

Erarbeitung:
- schriftl. gemäß AA
- **Ausw.:** ▶Bus stop (Einsatz ▶KV Extra): S vergleichen ihre Lösungen mithilfe von ▶KV 4.5A.
- **Alternative:** ▶Five-minute teacher **(Ex 2)**
- ▶Partner check, anschl. Präsentation der Ergebnisse im Plenum **(Ex 3)**
- erneute Selbsteinschätzung (s. Ex 1)

---

4 Checkpoint Digital checkpoint 👆

↰ **1** MEDIATION **Jack's favourite place** | I can **understand** information about Brighton. ✓

a) Read the message from your British friend Jack and tell your family about it. Choose the best °description A, B or C. | **1 a)** C

Hi
Your family wants to visit Brighton? Cool! You °must visit Hove Skatepark. It's my favourite place. I often go skateboarding there. It isn't in the town centre, but Portslade[1] train station and Wish Road South bus stop are near the park. And what's best: The park is next to the beach. It's free to get in and it's always open! Have fun!
Jack ✓

A Jack will, dass wir ihn und seine Familie in Brighton besuchen.
B Jacks Familie ist oft im Hove Skatepark.
C Jack meint, dass wir den Hove Skatepark in Brighton besuchen sollten.

1 b) 1 Nein(, er ist nicht im Zentrum). • **2** Neben dem Skatepark ist der Bahnhof Portslade und die Bushaltestelle Wish Road South. • **3** Nein, man muss keinen Eintritt zahlen. • **4** Der Skatepark ist immer offen.

b) Answer your family's questions in German.

1 Ist der Skatepark im Zentrum?
2 Wie kommt man dorthin?
3 Muss man Eintritt zahlen?
4 Bis wann ist der Skatepark offen?

📖 **2** LANGUAGE **We live in Hove** | **2 1** doesn't • **2** don't • **3** don't • **4** don't • **5** doesn't • **6** doesn't

| I can °**describe** my neighbourhood (simple present: negative sentences). ✓

Read about Sunita's neighbourhood. Complete the sentences. Use *don't* or *doesn't*.

I live with my family in Hove. Our neighbourhood has nice shops and parks, but it (1) … have a cinema. There's a great beach in Hove. Nish and I often go there after school, but we (2) … go there at the weekend because it's really busy. There's a museum too, but I (3) … go there very often. I (4) … like museums! I like my neighbourhood, but Nish (5) … like it. He wants to live in London, but my mum (6) … want to live there!

✏ **3** WRITING **Lea's neighbourhood**

Read Lea's notes about her neighbourhood. Then write Lea's message to Sunita.

Hi, Sunita! I live in a … | **3** Lösungsbsp. S. 295

– *small village*
– *clean*
– *fields, 3 shops, nice cinema* ☺
– *no youth centre* ☹
– *boring*

Check ↴

1 [pɔːtˈsleɪd]

Checkpoint Vorbereitung

Material: alle Aufgaben ▶ KV Extra: Bus stop, ▶ KV 4.5A + B: Checkpoint answers • Ex 4 UMA/CD • Ex 5 ggf. Bilder aus der Region (s. Zusatz)

Zeitbedarf: ca. 2 Std.

Minimalversion: Auswahl der Aufgaben erfolgt aufgrund der zu überprüfenden Lernziele

Begleitmedien: App (Digital checkpoint), INKL (S. 128–129)

Die Übungen kannst du auch digital machen 👆   **4**

4 A tour of Chester

> I can **talk about my town or village (simple present: questions and short answers).** ✓

a) LANGUAGE Zane visits his cousin Sophie and asks questions about her town. Complete the sentences.

> **4 a) 1** Do • **2** do • **3** Does • **4** does • **5** Does • **6** doesn't

Zane   (1) ... you like your town?
Sophie Yes, I (2) ... It's a nice place.
Zane   (3) ... your town have a good park?
Sophie Yes, it (4) ... I often go cycling there.
Zane   (5) ... your town have a beach?
Sophie No, it (6) ... It's a shame!

b) WORDS Write the names of the places a–f.

> **4 b) a** stadium • **b** ice rink • **c** supermarket • **d** hospital • **e** train station • **f** library

   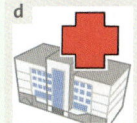  

a   b   c   d   e   f

2.28 c) LISTENING Listen to the tour. Where do Zane and Sophie go? Write the letters a–f from b) in the correct order: *1c, 2 ...*

> **4 c) 1** c • **2** a • **3** e • **4** f • **5** d • **6** b

5 Photos of Brighton

> I can **talk about °sights in Brighton and the weather (simple present: wh-questions).** ✓

a) LANGUAGE Write the questions in the correct order.

1 see / in the picture / what / you / do / ?
2 like / the weather / what's / ?
3 do / like / why / you / the picture / ?

> **5 a) 1** What do you see in the picture? • **2** What's the weather like? • **3** Why do you like the picture?

b) SPEAKING Choose your favourite photo (A or B). Your partner asks you the questions from a). Answer the questions. Then swap roles.

> **5 b)** Lösungsbsp. S. 295

   A

   B

Phrases
- *I can see ...*
- *There's / There are ...*
- *The weather is ...*
- *I like picture A/B because ...*

Check 👆

one hundred and twenty-nine   **129**

Ex 4 Einstieg:
- (SB auf) s. Ex 1 (Selbsteinschätzung)

Erarbeitung:
a) gemäß AA

b) S notieren Vokabeln in ihr Heft.

c) S notieren die Lösungen beim 1. Hören.
- S überprüfen die Lösungen beim 2. Hören.
- **Ausw.:** ▶ Bus stop (Einsatz ▶ KV Extra): S vergleichen ihre Lösungen für a), b) u. c) mithilfe von ▶ KV 4.5A.
- **Alternative:** ▶ Meldekette im Plenum
- erneute Selbsteinschätzung

Ex 5 Einstieg:
- (SB auf) s. Ex 1 (Selbsteinschätzung)

Erarbeitung:
a) schriftlich gemäß AA
- **Ausw.:** gemeinsam im Plenum od. mithilfe von ▶ KV 4.5B
- **Alternative:** ▶ Five-minute teacher

b) gemäß AA in PA
- S-Paare wählen jeweils ein Bild.
- **Ausw.:** ▶ Bus stop (Einsatz ▶ KV Extra): S vergleichen ihre Lösungen mithilfe von ▶ KV 4.5B.
- erneute Selbsteinschätzung
- **Alternative:** Präsentieren der Dialoge im Plenum

- **Zusatz:** L zeigt 2 Bilder aus der Region an der Tafel.
- In PA: S nutzen die gleichen Fragen und ▶ Scaffolding.
- **Ausw.:** S-Paare präsentieren ihre Ergebnisse im Plenum.

Lernschwerpunkt: Kompetenzen und sprachliche Mittel üben, Lernfortschritte erkennen
Kompetenzen: Reading eine Geschichte lesen und verstehen • Study skills eine Präsentation planen und üben •
Speaking eine Präsentation vortragen
Redemittel: *things at home • places in town*

Ex 6 Einstieg:
• (SB auf) S lesen das Lernziel zu diesem Abschnitt vor (*I can …*).
• S schätzen ihr Können zum Lernziel ein, z. B. mit ▶ Thumbs up, und notieren das Ergebnis.

Erarbeitung:
a) gemäß AA
• **Alternative:** (SB zu) L zeigt Titel und Bilder des Lesetextes mithilfe des UMA.
• ein/e S nennt die Lösung im Plenum
• **Ausw.:** s. c)

b) S notieren Antworten in EA beim **1. Lesen** in ihr Heft.
• **Ausw.:** s. c)

c) (SB auf) S notieren Wörter in EA beim **2. Lesen** in ihr Heft
• **Ausw.:** ▶ Bus stop (▶ KV Extra): S vergleichen ihre Lösungen mithilfe von ▶ KV 4.5B.
• **Alternative:** ▶ Five-minute teacher oder ▶ Meldekette
• nach der Lösungskontrolle erneute Einschätzung des Könnens (gleiche Methode wie im **Einstieg**)

---

4 Checkpoint Digital checkpoint

6 READING At the Swap Place I can understand a story about green activities. ✓

a) BEFORE YOU READ **Look at the title and the pictures. Choose the correct answer.**

The story is about A Zane's family B Zane's day at school C Zane's things.

6 a) C

2.29 **At the Swap Place**
It's Saturday morning and Zane wants to meet his friends at the park. 'Dad, where's my scooter?' asks Zane. 'I can't find it. It isn't in the flat and it isn't outside.'
5 'It's at the Swap Place, Zane,' says Eno. 'We have too many things. And you don't need those old toys.'
'But Dad! It's my scooter and I still use it sometimes!' says Zane.
'Ah, I'm really sorry, Zane. Go to the Swap Place now.
10 Maybe it's still there.'

'Excuse me,' says Zane °when he °gets there. 'I think my dad …'
The woman in the Swap Place doesn't say hello. She looks sad.
15 'Are you OK? °What's wrong?' asks Zane.
'Oh yes, I'm OK,' says the woman. 'But we have so many things here. The place is really messy. I want to tidy it, but I don't know where to start.'
'I can help you with that!'

20 Two hours later, Zane goes home. 'Hi, Dad. Sorry I'm late. I don't have my scooter, but I have some other things! Two footballs, a console, a book, and a jigsaw puzzle. The Swap Place is great.'
'Hi, Zane. More things! That's … °erm … great.'

b) Read the story: °true or °false?

1 Zane's scooter isn't in the flat.
2 Eno finds the scooter outside.
3 The Swap Place is very tidy.
4 Zane helps the woman in the Swap Place.
5 Zane finds a lot of things in the Swap Place.

6 b) 1 true • **2** false • **3** false • **4** true • **5** true

c) Find words in the story with these meanings.

1 the day after Friday (line 1)
2 kids play with them (line 6)
3 not tidy (line 17)
4 where someone lives (line 20)
5 a game with a lot of parts (lines 22–23)

6 c) 1 Saturday • **2** toys • **3** messy • **4** home • **5** jigsaw puzzle

Check

Checkpoint Vorbereitung

Material: alle Aufgaben ▶ KV Extra: Bus stop, ▶ KV 4.5B: Checkpoint answers • **Ex 6** UMA • **Ex 8** UMA
Zeitbedarf: ca. 2 Std.
Minimalversion: Auswahl der Aufgaben erfolgt aufgrund der zu überprüfenden Lernziele
Begleitmedien: App (Digital checkpoint)

Die Übungen kannst du auch digital machen    4

💬 **7** STUDY SKILLS **Buddy's favourite places**   *I can plan and practise a presentation.* ✅

👥 **a)** Look at Noah's °slides. Which slide is the best? Why? Talk to your partner.   **7 a)** Lösungsbsp. S. 295

1 The first place is the Pavilion Gardens.

2 **The beach**

– we walk
– the sea

3 Buddy loves our garden too because all his toys are there.

I think slide number 1/2/3 is the best because it has a big title / short notes / a big picture.

I think you're right.

I think you're wrong and slide number 1/2/3 is the best because …

🖊 **b)** Copy and complete Noah's sentences with words from the box.

1 My … is about Buddy's favourite places.
2 In this … you can see the Pavilion Gardens.
3 In the … photo we have the beach.
4 Let's … at these pictures of Buddy's toys in the garden.
5 Thank you for …
6 Do you have any …?

listening • look • next • photo • presentation • questions

7 b) 1 presentation • **2** photo • **3** next • **4** look • **5** listening • **6** questions

---

💬 **8** SPEAKING   **Ideas for a rainy day**   *I can give a presentation to a group.* ✅

Tim wants to talk about places to go on a rainy day. Look at his slides and give his presentation.

Ideas for a rainy day
– hello
– my presentation

the sports centre
– a lot of activities
– not expensive

the ice rink
– costs 10 euros
– fun

the cinema
– interesting films
– nice cafe

Questions?
– thank you
– any questions

8 Lösungsbsp. S. 295

Check 🔽

one hundred and thirty-one **131**

Ex 7 Einstieg:
• (SB auf) s. **Ex 6** (Selbstein-schätzung)

Erarbeitung:
a) Klären der AA im Plenum
• mündlich gemäß AA in PA
• **Ausw.:** s. **b)**
• **Alternative:** S-Paare präsentieren ihre Kurzdialoge im Plenum.

b) schriftl. in EA gemäß AA
• S notieren vollständige Sätze in ihr Heft.
• **Ausw.:** ▶ Bus stop (▶ KV Extra): S vergleichen ihre Lösungen mithilfe von ▶ KV 4.5B.
• **Alternative:** ▶ Meldekette
• erneute Selbsteinschätzung (s. **Ex 6**)

Ex 8 Einstieg:
• (SB auf / UMA) s. **Ex 6** (Selbsteinschätzung)

Erarbeitung:
• Klären der AA
• ☒ Ggf. präsentiert L/S das erste *slide* als Bsp. im Plenum.
• S bereiten die Präsentation in EA vor.
• **Ausw.:** ▶ Bus stop (▶ KV Extra): S vergleichen ihre Präsentationen mithilfe von ▶ KV 4.5B.
• **Alternative:** Einzelne S präsentieren ihre *slides* im Plenum (▶ Feedback im Plenum).
• erneute Selbsteinschätzung (s. **Ex 6**)

Text file Inhalt

Lernschwerpunkt: ein *school magazine* lesen
Kompetenzen: Reading einen Text über ein Essensprojekt in Brighton lesen und verstehen • Rätsel lösen • eine Postkarte lesen • den Klappentext einer Lektüre lesen
Redemittel: *food* • *shopping for young people*

Allg.: s. Unit 1, S. 40

The Real Junk Food Project
Einstieg:
- TA: *junk food – waste food*
  L: *What's the difference? Give some examples.*
- Diskussion im Plenum
  (▶ Semantisierung bei Bedarf)

Erarbeitung:
- S lesen den Text, z. B. in einer ▶ Leseacht.
- **Ausw.:** S äußern ihre eigene Meinung frei od. mithilfe eines ▶ Scaffolding als TA:
  I like / I don't like the project because …
- L erfasst die Ideen an der Tafel.

Puzzle time Erarbeitung:
- gemäß AA

---

4 **Text file**

OPTIONAL

VARNDEAN Teen Zine

This month's topic: Brighton

Our school magazine: by students for students

Questions and answers: The Real Junk Food Project

What is it?
It's a cafe in Brighton.

Why is it different?
The cafe uses waste[1] food and there are no prices[2].

Where does the food come from?
When shops in Brighton don't sell[3] all their food, they don't put the rest in the bin – they give it to the cafe!

How much do meals cost?
People pay what they can. People with more money pay more, and homeless[4] people eat for free. And everybody sits together!

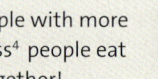

Who are the cooks?
They're volunteers – people who help for no money –, but they're still very good at cooking!

Puzzle time

Where in Brighton am I?

1 I'm not land and I'm not sea
   But to walk on water, you can walk on me!

2 I'm high in the sky
   With a big round[5] eye
   But I'm not a bird and I can't fly!

1 1 Brighton Palace Pier • **2** The i360

Joke[6] time
What do you call it when it's rainy for two days in Brighton?
The weekend!

---

[1] **waste** *überschüssig; hier: Lebensmittel, die weggeworfen werden sollten* [2] **price** *Preis* [3] **sell** *verkaufen*
[4] **homeless** *obdachlos* [5] **round** *rund* [6] **joke** *Witz*

Text file Vorbereitung

Material: What's your favourite shop? weißes Papier (Klassensatz) • Fergal's reading tip ggf. Lektüre *A Brighton birthday* (als Klassensatz), UMA

Zeitbedarf: abhängig davon, welche Texte bearbeitet werden

Minimalversion: alle Beiträge sind optionale Zusatztexte

Begleitmedien: INKL (S. 130–131)

4

OPTIONAL

A postcard from Brighton

Dear Annie

Brighton is great! My favourite place here is Snooper's Paradise. It's a really cool shop and it sells ... everything[1]! Hats, skateboards, photos, guitars, clocks, toys, books, posters ...

It's very big. Even[2] the people who work in the shop don't know everything they sell! But you can always find something different. Wish you were here![3]

Leena xx

TO

SNOOPERS PARADISE

What's your favourite shop?

Fergal's reading tip:

My favourite book is 'A Brighton birthday'. It's a cool story with lots of places in Brighton and I love the puzzles too!

It's Saturday morning and Alice wakes up - it's her birthday! But there are no birthday messages, no presents, and everyone is busy. What's happening? Then she gets a mysterious message with a puzzle ...

lighthouse ● ● ● Zu allen Ausgaben

Rebecca Robb Benne, Zoe Thorne

A Brighton birthday

Lektüre mit Rätseln

1

Cornelsen

A Brighton birthday

ISBN 978-3-06-036258-5

---

[1] **everything** *alles* [2] **even** *sogar* [3] **Wish you were here!** *Ich wünschte, du wärst hier!*

A postcard from Brighton
Einstieg:
- (SB zu)
  L: *What do young people usually buy?*
- S äußern spontan Ideen.

Erarbeitung:
- (SB auf) L stellt Leseauftrag:
  L: *Why do young people like the shop Snooper's Paradise in Brighton?*
- S lesen die Postkarte und antworten:
  S: *Young people like Snooper's Paradise because they can buy ... (everything / hats, skateboards ...)*

What's your favourite shop?
Erarbeitung:
- S gestalten eine Postkarte ihres Lieblingsladens.
- **Sich.:** Ausstellung in der ► English corner bzw. Ablage im ► Dossier

Fergal's reading tip
Einstieg:
- (SB zu) L stellt die Lektüre in der Klasse vor.
- Das Titelbild kann mithilfe des UMA präsentiert werden.
  L: *What can you see in the picture?*
  S: *I can see ...*

Erarbeitung:
- (SB auf) S lesen den Klappentext.
- Falls geplant, beginnt die Klasse an dieser Stelle mit der Lektüre von *A Brighton birthday*.

Partner page / Diff bank **Inhalt**

Lernschwerpunkt: zusätzliche Übungen, Differenzierungs- und Hilfsangebote
Kompetenzen: Speaking Informationen mit einem Partner austauschen • über Brighton sprechen
Strukturen: *simple present: negative sentences*
Redemittel: *places in town • activities for young people*

Ex 3 **Erarbeitung:** s. S.117
a) *Partner B:* gemäß AA

Ex 4 **Erarbeitung:** s. S.121
a) + b) *Partner B:* gemäß AA

MH 1 **Erarbeitung:** s. S.111
• (SB auf) S nutzen das ▸ Scaffolding als Hilfe bei der Satzbildung.

---

4 **Partner page / Diff bank**

Partner page

▸Page 117

3 SPEAKING **Different places**

a) **Partner B:** Look at your picture. °Take turns to ask and answer questions. Use the places in the box.

Does your town have a supermarket?
– Yes, it does. / No, it doesn't.
– That's the same. / That's different.

> **3 a) Picture A and B:** hospital, library, supermarket, ice rink
> **Picture A:** museum and a train station
> **Picture B:** stadium and a shopping centre.

a hospital • an ice rink • a library • a museum • a shopping centre • a stadium • a supermarket • a train station

▸Page 121

4 **The Upside Down House**

a) **Partner B:** Ask partner A these questions. °Add *do* or *does*.

1 What ... people do inside the house?
2 When ... the Upside Down House close?
3 How much ... tickets cost?

b) **Partner B:** Look at the online °review. Answer partner A's questions.

> **4 a), b)** Lösungen S.294

www.upsidedown.example.com

The Upside Down house is great! It's good to be there at 10 a.m. when it opens, so there aren't too many people. You don't need to buy tickets online – you buy tickets at the +kiosk. My tip: take funny photos – put your hands up, then turn the photo upside down!

Diff bank

▸Page 111

More help **1** VIEWING **This is Brighton**

d) **Which places in Brighton do you like? Why?**

> **1 d)** individuelle Lösungen

I like	Brighton Marina Brighton Beach Brighton Palace Pier the Duke of York's cinema Hove Skatepark North Laine the Pavilion Gardens	because	it's they're	cool / different / free / modern / nice / old / ...
			there's there are	a lot of cafes / shops / lights / street music / ...
			you can	have a picnic / hear street music / watch films / do skateboarding / practise new skills / go bowling / eat fish and chips / fast food / ...

Diff bank | Vorbereitung

Material: MH 1 UMA/CD
Zeitbedarf: abhängig davon, welche Aufgaben bearbeitet werden
Minimalversion: *More practice*-Aufgaben sind stets Zusatzaufgaben

---

▸Page 112

More help **1 From Lily's window**

1 a) Lösung S. 292

a) Look at the photo and listen. You're Lily. What can you see, hear and smell?

2.18

I can see …
I can hear …
I can smell …

> babies • buses • cars • °coffee • dogs • doors • flats •
> °grass • houses • kids • loud/nice music •
> my neighbour's TV • a °police car • rubbish • streets

▸Page 113

Parallel exercise **3 Lily's notes**

3 b) *Lily likes* the neighbours • the youth centre • the sports centre • the fields near the estate • her/the neighbourhood
She doesn't like the rubbish • the cars

b) Make sentences from Lily's table in a).

Lily likes …   *She doesn't like …*

More practice 1 **You don't like …**

a) Draw °something to eat that you don't like.

b) Take turns to show your pictures. One student says what the picture shows.

You don't like fish.

3 individuelle Lösungen

c) Tell the class about your group.

Otto doesn't like fish, Mariam doesn't like °pizza, …

▸Page 114

Parallel exercise **6 The youth centre**

6 a) Lösung S. 292

a) Lily tells her friends about the youth centre. Choose *don't* or *doesn't*.

1 It doesn't open at weekends.

> I often go to the youth centre, but not at weekends.
> It (1) *don't/doesn't* open at weekends. There are a lot of
> activities like cooking, boxing and football. There's a girls'
> group on Tuesday, but I (2) *don't/doesn't* go there, I (3) *don't/
> doesn't* have time then. Sometimes I play pool at the youth
> centre with my neighbour Niles. He (4) *don't/doesn't* go to
> Varndean and his school (5) *don't/doesn't* have a lot of
> clubs. We (6) *don't/doesn't* pay for the activities – they're all
> free. A lot of people on our estate (7) *don't/doesn't* have a
> lot of money.

MH 1 s. S. 112

• S erhalten hier sprachliche Hilfen zur Bearbeitung von Ex 1.

Erarbeitung:

a) gemäß AA

• ▸ als Vorentlastung:
▸ Semantisierung u. ▸ Lautschulung des neuen Wortschatzes

Parallel ex 3 s. S. 113

• Diese Aufgabe eignet sich für lernschwächere S.

Erarbeitung:

b) (SB auf) gemäß AA in PA

• **Ausw.:** S lesen ihre Sätze im Plenum vor (wie S. 113, nur ohne Begründung).

MP 1 Diese Aufgabe bietet zusätzliches Üben zur Verneinung im *simple present*.

Erarbeitung:

a) (SB auf) gemäß AA in EA

b) S arbeiten in Kleingruppen (▸ Gruppenbildung) gemäß AA.
• L präsentiert ein Bsp.

c) **Ausw.** gemäß AA im Plenum

Parallel ex 6 s. S. 114
Erarbeitung:

a) (SB auf) gemäß AA
• S notieren Lösungen in ihr Heft.
• **Ausw.:** ▸ Partner check, dann im Plenum (s. S. 114)

Diff bank Inhalt

Lernschwerpunkt: zusätzliche Übungen, Differenzierungs- und Hilfsangebote
Kompetenzen: Writing einen Post über die Nachbarschaft schreiben • Speaking einen Dialog gestalten
Strukturen: *simple present: questions and short answers* • Fragebildung im *simple present*
Redemittel: *places in Brighton* • *neighbourhood*

MP 2 Erarbeitung:
a) (SB auf) Klären der AA
• S schreiben vollständige Sätze in ihr Heft.
• **Ausw.:** ▶ Five-minute teacher

b) schriftl. gemäß AA
• **Ausw.:** S lesen ihre Sätze mehreren Mit-S vor (▶ Milling around).
• Anschl. im Plenum:
L: *What does/doesn't …* (S-Name) *like?*
S: *He/She likes / doesn't like …*
• S nutzen dabei die Info aus ▶ Milling around.

MP 3 Erarbeitung:
• (SB auf) Klären der AA
• L/S führen ein Beispiel im Plenum vor.
• S notieren die vollständigen Sätze im Heft.
• **Ausw.:** ▶ Five-minute teacher

---

4 **Diff bank**

More practice 2 **New activities**

a) The youth centre wants to plan new activities. Look at the questionnaire and Lily's answers. Then complete what the °youth worker says.

1 Lily … °acting.
Lily doesn't like acting.
2 She … dancing.
3 She … cricket.
4 She … °chess.
5 She … °jewellery making.
6 She … reading.

b) Now write the answers for you in your exercise book.

I like acting. I don't like dancing.

2 a) 1 doesn't like • **2** doesn't like • **3** doesn't play • **4** plays • **5** doesn't like • **6** likes

Help us plan new activities!
°Tick (✓) or °cross (✗) for you.
Name: *Lily Hall*
I like acting. ✗
I like dancing. ✗
I play cricket. ✗
I play chess. ✓
I like jewellery making. ✗
I like reading. ✓

2 b) individuelle Lösungen

▶Page 115

More practice 3 **Great places in Brighton**

WORDS Lily tells a new boy at the youth centre about her neighbourhood and Brighton. Complete what she says with the correct places from the box. There are two °extra places.

beach • cafe • cinema • fields • marina • park • pier • shop • sports centre

You can buy °everything at the (1) … on the estate.
There's a small (2) … next to it. They have great hot chocolate!
There's a (3) … here too – you can do a lot of different sports there.
The (4) … is near. You can see the sea from our estate.
You can also see the °boats in the (5) …
The (6) … is near the beach. It looks great in the evening when there are a lot of lights.
°What else? Oh, yes. I often watch films at home, but there's a great (7) … in Brighton.

3 1 shop • **2** cafe • **3** sports centre • **4** beach • **5** marina • **6** pier • **7** cinema
extra places: park, fields

Diff bank Vorbereitung

Material: MH 10 weiße Blätter (Klassensatz) oder digitales Endgerät mit Schreibprogamm • Challenge 1 ggf. digitales Endgerät mit Schreibprogramm
Zeitbedarf: abhängig davon, welche Aufgaben bearbeitet werden
Minimalversion: *More practice-* und *Challenge*-Aufgaben sind stets Zusatzaufgaben

4

 **More help** **10** MY TASK **A post about my neighbourhood**

10 individuelle Lösungen

Write a post like the post in 9. Write °at least five sentences. Put your text in your DOSSIER.

I live in	a village / a town / a city / the country.
My neighbourhood is / isn't	boring / clean / dirty / horrible / interesting / loud / nice / quiet / ....
My neighbourhood has / doesn't have	a cinema / a park / a swimming pool / a youth centre / shops / ...
The neighbours are	friendly / loud / nice / quiet / unfriendly / ...
I like / don't like	my neighbourhood.

▶ Page 117

Challenge 1 **Do you like your neighbourhood?**

a) Write five interview questions for students in your class. You can use the °sentence starters in the box or your own ideas.

> Do you go ...? • Do you play ...? •
> Do you like ...? • Do you have ...? •
> Does your brother/sister ...? •
> Does your mum/dad ...?

b) Find a partner and ask your questions. Answer your partner's questions. Use short answers and add more °information.

c) Write a short article about your partner for your school website.

Ch 1 individuelle Lösungen

▶ Page 118

More practice 4 **I'm lost!**

A visitor asks Lily for help. Complete the questions in the conversation.

Visitor	Excuse me, (1 you / live) ... here?
Lily	Yes, I do. (2 you / °need) ... help?
Visitor	Yes, I do. I'm lost. I want to go to the visitor information centre. Is it in this street?
Lily	Yes, it is. (3 your phone / have) ... a map?
Visitor	Yes, it does, but °my phone is dead.
Lily	OK, let's look on my phone. (4 you / see) ... this place? We're here. And here's the visitor information centre in this building.
Visitor	(5 the building / have) ... a name?
Lily	Yes, it does. It's the Brighton Centre. It isn't °far °down there, on the °right. (6 that / help) ...?
Visitor	Yes, it does. Thank you very much.
Lily	You're welcome.

> **4** **1** do you live • **2** Do you need • **3** Does your phone have •
> **4** Do you see • **5** Does the building have • **6** Does that help

one hundred and thirty-seven **137**

MH 10 s. S.115
• Diese Aufgabe bietet sprachliche Mittel zur Bearbeitung von Ex 10.

Erarbeitung:
• gemäß AA mithilfe des ▶ Scaffolding
• S können Computer/Schreibprogramme nutzen.
• **Sich.:** s. S. 115

Challenge 1
• gut geeignet für lernstärkere S oder ▶ Early finisher

Einstieg:
• (SB zu) L leitet an:
L: *Do you play football?*
S: *Yes, I do.*
L: *Where do you play football?*
S: *In the park ... / ...*

Erarbeitung:
a) (SB auf) S notieren Fragen gemäß AA.

b) gemeinsame Klärung der AA
• ggf. ein Bsp. im Plenum durchführen (in PA)

c) S schreiben Artikel ins Heft oder nutzen ein Schreibprogramm (Computer).
• **Ausw.:** ▶ English corner, ▶ Gallery walk

MP 4 Erarbeitung:
• (SB auf) schriftl. gemäß AA in EA
• S nummerieren ihre Lösungen im Heft.
• **Ausw.:** ▶ Five-minute teacher

• **Zusatz:** S lesen und spielen den Dialog mit verteilten Rollen (▶ Role-play).

Diff bank Inhalt

Lernschwerpunkt: zusätzliche Übungen, Differenzierungs- und Hilfsangebote
Kompetenzen: Speaking einen Ort in einer Stadt erraten • Writing über das Wetter in Brighton oder einem anderen Ort schreiben • ein Gedicht schreiben
Strukturen: Fragebildung im *simple present*
Redemittel: *places in a town/village • weather words • days of the week*

MH 10 s. S. 119
• Diese Aufgabe bietet zusätzliche sprachliche Mittel für lernschwächere S.

Erarbeitung:
b) (SB auf) S nutzen die Redemittel zur Formulierung der Fragen, um den Ort der anderen Gruppe erraten zu können.

MP 5 Erarbeitung:
• (SB auf) Klären der AA
• L erarbeitet 1. Satz mündlich im Plenum, anschl. schriftl. in EA.
• **Ausw.:** ▶ Five-minute teacher
• **Zusatz:** S bilden ähnliche Sätze zum aktuellen Wetter in ihrem Ort und ergänzen die entsprechenden Symbole.
• S gestalten einen inviduellen Wetterbericht auf einem Blatt Papier (z. B. als HA).
• **Sich.:** aushängen der fertigen Wetterberichte in der ▶ English corner
• ▶ Gallery walk mit möglichem Feedback

Challenge 2
• gut geeignet für lernstärkere S oder ▶ Early finisher

Erarbeitung:
• (SB auf) Klären der AA
• S notieren die Fragen im Heft.
• **Ausw.:** ▶ Partner check, anschl. Vergleich im Plenum

---

4 Diff bank

▶ Page 119

More help **10** MY TASK **Five questions about places**   **10** individuelle Lösungen

b) Team 1 asks five yes/no-questions to guess the place. Team 2 gives short answers.

	sell	clothes / drinks / food / something / ...?
Does this place	have	books / films / football matches / games / grass / old things / table tennis / trains / trees / water / ...? a lot of °sick people / ° young people / ...?
Is it the		beach / cinema / hospital / library / museum / park / shopping centre / sports centre / stadium / swimming pool / train station / youth club / ...?

▶ Page 120

More practice 5 **The weather in Brighton**

Lily looks at the weather for next week. Complete the sentences with the words from the box.

1 On M..., it's ... and ...
2 On Tu..., it's ... and ...
3 On W..., it's ...
4 On Th..., it's ... and ...

cloudy • cold • rainy • snowy • sunny • warm • windy

Monday	Tuesday	Wednesday	Thursday
°20°C	18°C	10°C	3°C

5 **1** On Monday, it's warm and sunny. • **2** On Tuesday, it's windy and cloudy. • **3** On Wednesday, it's rainy. • **4** On Thursday, it's cold and snowy.

▶ Page 121

Challenge 2 **Questions for Scout**

Look at Scout's answers. What are the questions? Use the words in the boxes.

how • what • when • where • who • why

eat • feel • like • live • love • °wake up

1 I live in Brighton.

2 I wake up at 5 a.m.

3 I eat sandwiches and chips and fish.

4 I feel happy.

5 I like Noah, Sunita, Zane and Lily.

6 Because I love the sea and the food on the beach.

Ch 2 **1** Where do you live? • **2** When do you wake up? • **3** What do you eat? • **4** How do you feel? • **5** Who do you like? • **6** Why do you love [Brighton]?

138 one hundred and thirty-eight

Diff bank Vorbereitung

Material: MP 5 UMA
Zeitbedarf: abhängig davon, welche Aufgaben bearbeitet werden
Minimalversion: *More practice*-Aufgaben sind stets Zusatzaufgaben

---

More help **5** MY TASK **Quiz-quiz-swap**

b) WALK AROUND
Find a partner and ask your question.
Answer your partner's question about your town.

5 b) Lösungsbsp. S. 294

When it's	sunny / rainy / snowy / cloudy / windy / hot / cold / warm,	I	have a picnic / °stay at home / visit my friends / go to the cinema / go swimming / …
		I go to	the beach / the park / the shops / …
		I travel by	bus / bike / car / train / …
		I walk.	

▶Page 123

Parallel exercise **4** **Why, what and how?**

4 1 c · 2 e · 3 d · 4 a · 5 b

Match the questions to the answers.

1 Why doesn't Lily see Chloe very often?
2 What two things does Buddy find before the ring?
3 How many bags of rubbish does the group collect?
4 How do the kids find Jack and Maria?
5 How do Jack and Maria want to say thank you?

a They put a note in the youth centre.
b They want to give the youth centre some money.
c She's married now.
d Over fifty.
e A dead mouse and an old shoe.

More practice 6 **Name °poems**

a) Complete the name poem about Lily.
Use the ideas in the box or your own ideas.

6 a) Lösungsbsp. S. 294

active · art · Brighton · clever · cool · cycling · great · her family · parkour · quiet · school ·

Likes …
Is …
Loves …
You are …, Lily!

b) Write a name poem for you or somebody in your family.

6 b) individuelle Lösungen

MH 5 s. S. 121
• Die Aufgabe bietet zusätzliche sprachliche Hilfen für lernschwächere S.

Erarbeitung:
b) (SB auf) L präsentiert das ▶Scaffolding mithilfe des UMA während des ▶Milling around.

• ⊠ **Alternative:** L bereitet ▶Cue cards mit den vorgegebenen Antworten von ▶More help, S. 139 vor, die die S beim *Milling around* nutzen können.

Parallel ex 4 (s. S. 123)
• Diese Aufgabe ist vor allem für lernschwächere S geeignet, die beim verstehenden Lesen Unterstützung brauchen.

Erarbeitung:
• (SB auf) S ordnen die Antworten zu, indem sie die passenden Zahlen und Buchstaben im Heft notieren.
• **Ausw.:** ▶Five-minute teacher
• Die Lösungen von S. 123 können u. U. etwas abweichen, da die S sie dort frei formulieren.

MP 6 **Erarbeitung:**
a) (SB auf) S schreiben das fertige Gedicht ins Heft.
• **Ausw.:** Freiwillige S lesen ihre Gedichte im Plenum vor.

b) Lernstärkere S schreiben ein Gedicht z. B. mit den Buchstaben des eigenen Namens.
• ▶Dictionary, S. 255–266, ▶Wordbanks, S. 194–204.
• **Sich.:** ▶English corner, ▶Dossier

Unit-Übersicht

Storyline: Noah plant seine Geburtstagsparty zum Thema Zirkus. Er schreibt die Einladung und erstellt mit seinem Vater eine Einkaufsliste. Seine Freunde überlegen, was sie ihm schenken können. Zane backt Noah einen Kuchen und stellt sein Lieblingsrezept vor. Am Ende wird gefeiert – allerdings mit einigen Hindernissen und anders als Zane es kennt.
Strukturen: *present progressive* (S. 144) • *much, many, a lot of* (S. 147)
Viewing: Maiku backt einen Schokoladenkuchen (S. 150) • Glorias Geburtstagsparty wird vorbereitet und gefeiert (einschließlich weiterer Mutproben) (S. 155)
Unit task: ein Rezeptbuch für die Klasse erstellen

Unit 5 Einstieg:
• (SB zu) ▸ Five-finger brainstorming: S sammeln je fünf bekannte *food words*. L notiert die Wörter (TA *food*, ▸ Vokabelarbeit) in einer ▸ Mindmap.

Ex 1 Einstieg:
• (SB auf)
L: *Look at the pictures. Which foods from our brainstorming can you see?*

Erarbeitung:
a) S lesen in PA die beiden Texte und versuchen, noch unbekannte Wörter zu erschließen.
• **Ausw.:** L sammelt die Wörter an der ▸ Vokabeltafel mit deutscher Übersetzung. S erläutern ihre Strategien zur Erschließung.
• S übertragen den neuen Wortschatz in ihr *Vocab file*.

b) 1. Hören: S wiederholen die Wörter.
• **2. Hören:** S wiederholen die Wörter und zeigen auf das entsprechende Bild.

• **Zusatz:** S ergänzen die Mindmap aus dem Einstieg mit den neuen *Food*-Wörtern.
• S zeichnen kleine Bildchen des jeweiligen *food* in ihr *Vocab file* und ergänzen ggf. Begriffe aus anderen Sprachen.

Unit 5
Enjoy!

My favourite dessert is trifle[1]. Dad always makes it for my birthday and at Christmas. In trifle there is fruit and red jelly, then custard[2] and then cream, and then more fruit. A lot of people put strawberries on trifle, but I'm allergic to strawberries.

▸ Box: Voc., p. 246

Noah

fruit
cream
custard
jelly

Noah's birthday dessert

💬 **1** Words **Food**

👥 a) Look at Noah and Sunita's pages in 7C's class recipe book. Which words in blue do you understand? Use the photos or words from German and other languages.

I think 'fruit' is 'Obst'. It's like 'Frucht' in German and 'frukty' (фрукты) in Russian.

🔊 🔈 b) Listen and °**repeat** the food words in blue.
2.30

1 [ˈtraɪfl] 2 [ˈkʌstəd]

1 a) individuelle Lösungen

1 b) fruit • cream • strawberry • meat • cheese • pea • tomato sauce • spice • bread • rice • vegetable

▸ More practice 1, p. 165

Lead-in Inhalt

Lernschwerpunkt: über verschiedene Gerichte sprechen, Rezepte verstehen

Kompetenzen: Reading / Intercultural competence
Rezeptbuch-Einträge verstehen • Speaking sich über Lebensmittel und Gerichte austauschen

Redemittel: Wortfeld *food and drinks*

Vorbereitung

Material: Ex 1 UMA/CD
Zeitbedarf: ca. 1 Std.
Begleitmedien: WB (S. 70), App (Digital quiz), INKL (S. 140–141), DIFF (5.1)

Nach dieser Unit kann ich ... ✓

- ○ über Essen sprechen
- ○ über Geburtstage und Feste sprechen
- ○ mein Lieblingsgericht beschreiben
- ○ über Unterschiede sprechen
- ○ unbekannte Wörter erklären

Unit task ✓

- ○ ein Rezeptbuch erstellen

A lot of people in the UK go to Indian restaurants. We eat a lot of Indian food at home. There are a lot of Indian dishes with meat, but we eat vegetarian food. This is my favourite dish – °mattar paneer[1]. It's Indian cheese and peas in a tomato sauce with a lot of spices. We usually eat it with bread or rice and some vegetables.

► Box: Voc., p. 247

vegetables · bread · rice · Sunita · tomato sauce · peas · cheese

Sunita's favourite dish

💬 **2** SPEAKING **Our food**

a) Read Noah and Sunita's pages again. Complete the sentences.

1 You make trifle with ...
2 Noah is allergic to ...
3 Sunita doesn't eat ...   She's a ...
4 You make mattar paneer with ...

2 a) 1 fruit, red jelly, custard and cream • **2** strawberries • **3** meat, vegetarian • **4** cheese, peas, tomato sauce and spices

Good to know

A lot of people in the UK eat vegetarian or vegan food. It's very healthy.

b) What about you? Talk about the food on these pages.

I love ...   I don't like ...   I often/never eat ... (because ...)   I'm allergic to ...

2 b) individuelle Lösungen

1 [mʌtr pʌˈnɪə]

► Workbook, p. 70

 Digital quiz I can **talk about food.** ✓

Nach dieser Unit ...

- L bespricht mit S die Lernziele der Unit (s. links) und kündigt die *Unit task* an.
- Am Ende der Unit überprüfen die S das Erreichen der Ziele mithilfe des *Checkpoint* (S. 158–161) bzw. gemeinsam im Plenum.

Ex 2 Einstieg:

- (SB zu)
  L: *What food do you eat on special days? What's in the food?*
- TA: ► Scaffolding: *In ... there's ... / My favourite dish is ... It's ... with ...*
- Ggf. Hinweis von L, dass die Namen der Gerichte nicht übersetzt werden müssen. Stattdessen sollte das Essen und seine Zutaten beschrieben werden.
- S beschreiben in PA und mithilfe der Mindmap Gerichte an besonderen Tagen.
- S stellen ihr Gericht im Plenum vor.

Erarbeitung:

a) (SB auf) gemäß AA, schriftlich in EA

- **Ausw.:** ► Five-minute teacher

b) S tauschen sich im ► Milling around über die beiden Gerichte aus. Sie nutzen ihr Buch für das ► Scaffolding.

- **Ausw.:** L schreibt die Namen der Gerichte auf je eine Tafelseite. S stellen sich zu ihrem Favoriten. Einige S begründen ihre Wahl kurz im Plenum.
- S lesen ► Good to know, S. 141.

141

Topic 1 Inhalt

Lernschwerpunkt: über Geburtstage und Partys sprechen
Kompetenzen: Reading einer Einladung Informationen entnehmen • Speaking sich über Geburtstage austauschen •
Writing eine Einladung schreiben
Redemittel: Wortfelder *months and seasons, dates, ordinal numbers*

Ex 1 Einstieg:
• (SB zu) L zeigt ein vergrößertes Bild einer Geburtstagsparty, z. B. Ex 10, S. 145 (UMA), ▶ Gucklochmethode. S raten, was man sieht, bis der Begriff *birthday party* fällt.

Erarbeitung:
a) (SB auf) S lesen AA und ▶ Scaffolding, PA gemäß AA
• 🖳 L weist lernschwächere S auf ▶ More help, S. 165 hin.
• **Ausw.:** ▶ Meldekette

b) 1. Lesen: S lesen die Einladung.
L: *What can you see in the picture?*
S: *It's an invitation to Noah's birthday party.*
• **2. Lesen:** In EA lesen S AA und schreiben Fragen ins Heft.
• **Ausw.:** ▶ Five-minute teacher

Ex 2 Einstieg:
• (SB zu) L heftet ▶ Flashcards mit Monaten an die Tafel.
L: *Put these into order, please.*
• S ordnen die Karten nach dem Jahresverlauf.
Erarbeitung:
a) 1. Hören: gemäß AA
• **2. Hören:** gemäß AA

b) L zeigt Bilder der Jahreszeiten (UMA). S ordnen die ▶ Flashcards mit den Monaten den Bildern zu.
• (SB auf) S überprüfen ihre Lösungen.
• S lesen ▶ Scaffolding. ▶ Milling around gemäß AA
• **Ausw.:** S nennen aus dem Gedächtnis so viele Geburtsmonate ihrer Mit-S wie möglich: *Lea's birthday is in April. Timo's …*

Time for a party

1 READING Noah's invitation

💬👥 **a)** BEFORE YOU READ **What do you usually do on your birthday? Tell a partner.**

I usually / never have a birthday party.
We usually eat sausages and birthday cake.
We often go bowling. – What about you?

📖 **b) Read Noah's invitation. Answer the questions.**

1 How old is Noah on his birthday? *He's …*
2 What day of the week is his birthday party? *It's on …*
3 What time does the party start? *It starts at …*
4 Where's the party? *It's at …*
5 What activities are there? *There are …*
6 What food is there? *There's …*
7 How can Noah's friends answer the invitation?
   They can … or … him.

1 a) individuelle Lösungen

1 b) 1 12 years old • **2** on Saturday 30th May • **3** 2 o'clock • **4** Hove Park • **5** fun circus party games • **6** great picnic food • **7** They can phone or text him.

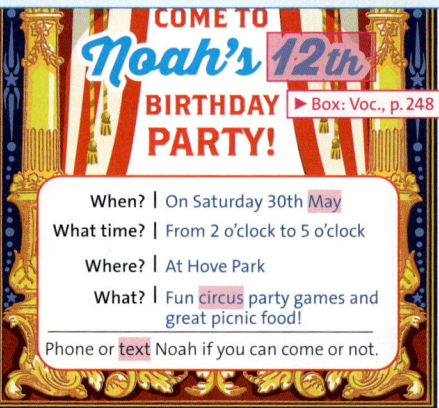

COME TO
Noah's 12th
BIRTHDAY
PARTY!
▶ Box: Voc., p. 248

When?	On Saturday 30th May
What time?	From 2 o'clock to 5 o'clock
Where?	At Hove Park
What?	Fun circus party games and great picnic food!

Phone or text Noah if you can come or not.

▶ More practice 2, p. 165; Challenge 1, p. 166

👂💬 **2 WORDS Months and seasons** ▶ Box: Voc., p. 248

🔊 **a)** SONG **Listen and sing. Then listen again and stand up for your birthday month.**
2.31

👥 **b)** WALK AROUND **Find out from different partners what their birthday month is.**

A When's your birthday?
B It's in spring.
A Is it in March?
B No, it isn't.
A Is it in …?
B Yes, it is. When's your birthday?

2 b) individuelle Lösungen

winter	spring	summer	autumn
December January February	March April May	June July August	September October November

▶ More practice 3, p. 166

142 one hundred and forty-two

Topic 1 Vorbereitung

Material: Ex 1 Bild einer Geburtstagsparty z. B. Ex 10, S. 145 / UMA • Ex 2 Flashcards mit Monatsnamen, UMA/CD •
Ex 3 UMA/CD • Ex 5 ggf. weißes A5-Papier für Einladungen
Zeitbedarf: ca. 2 Std.
Minimalversion: Ex 2b), Ex 4, Ex 5 auslassen
Begleitmedien: WB (S. 71), INKL (S. 142–143), DIFF (5.2)

5

3 Birthday dates   3 a) Numbers S. 277

a) Look at the °list of numbers on p. 277.
Listen and repeat the numbers from 1st to 31st.

b) Look how Scout says and writes her birthday.
Then listen to eight students.
Write their birthdays.   3 b) Lösung S. 295

> My birthday is **on the first of** April.

> My birthday is on 1st April.

1 Noah: 30th May   5 Theo: ... February
2 Lily: ... April   6 Ivy: ... January
3 Zane: ... August   7 Tareq: ... July
4 Sunita: ... March   8 Marta: ... October

c) Check your answers with a partner.   3 c) individuelle Lösungen

Lily's birthday is on the ... of ... – That's right. / That's wrong. I think it's on ...

▶ Numbers, p. 277   ▶ More practice 4 + 5, p. 166

4 SPEAKING My birthday

a) Make two groups.
Make a line in your group
in order of your birthdays.
Which group is °quicker?

b) Check: Are you in the right place
in the line?
Take turns: Say your birthday.

4 individuelle Lösungen

> When's your birthday?

> It's on the 10th of March. So I'm before you in the line.

> It's on the 21st of May. What about you?

5 WRITING My birthday invitation   5 individuelle Lösungen

a) Look at Noah's invitation in 1 again. °Change the parts in blue and write an invitation
to your birthday party. Make it look good!

b) °GALLERY WALK Look at all the invitations. What do you think? Make notes.

Which invitation ...
1 looks the best (colours, photos, ...)?   3 has the best activity?
2 has the best place?   4 has the best food?

▶ Workbook, p. 71

one hundred and forty-three **143**

Ex 3 Einstig:
• (SB zu) ▶ Vokabelrennen. S
stellen sich nach Platzierung
auf.
L: *X, you're first. Well done. Y,
you are second. Great!*
• ▶ Semantisierung von *first,
second, third* und *fourth*.

Erarbeitung:
a) (SB auf, S. 277) **1. Hören:**
gemäß AA
• **Sich.:** TA: Ordnungszahlen. Ein
S zeigt auf die Zahl, S nennen
sie im ▶ Zählen in der Gruppe.

b) gemäß AA

c) ▶ Partner check gemäß AA
• **Ausw.:** ▶ Five-minute teacher

Ex 4 Einstig:
• (SB zu) Wiederholung, wie
man ein Datum schreibt
und sagt.

Erarbeitung:
a) (SB auf) S lesen AA und
▶ Scaffolding, dann gemäß AA

b) **Ausw.:** S der 1. Gruppe
nennen nacheinander ihren
Geburtstag. Die 2. Gruppe
überprüft die Anordnung.

Ex 5 Einstig:
• (SB zu) ▶ Five-finger brainstorming: *good places for a birthday
party* (TA)
• kurze ▶ Blitzlichtrunde

Erarbeitung:
a) (SB auf) gemäß AA

b) ▶ Gallery walk: S notieren sich
zu jeder Kategorie jeweils drei
S-Namen (1.–3. Platz).
• **Ausw.:** S nennen ihre *top 3*.

Topic 1 Inhalt

Lernschwerpunkt: mit dem *present progressive* gerade stattfindende Handlungen beschreiben
Kompetenzen: Speaking sagen, was man gerade macht • beschreiben, was gerade in einem Bild geschieht • Reading ein Telefongespräch lesend verstehen
Strukturen: *present progressive*
Redemittel: *party words*

Ex 6 Einstieg:
- (SB zu) L führt Dinge vor (sitzen, schreiben, …) und sagt dazu einen Satz im *present progressive*.
- S stehen auf, wenn der Satz wahr ist, und hocken sich hin, wenn er falsch ist.

Erarbeitung:
- (SB auf) S finden mit dem Bild die Lösungen für 1 und 2 (TA).
- S hören oder lesen Text in EA.
- **Ausw.:** S beschreiben die Unterschiede.

Ex 7 Hinweis:
- direkter Anschluss an Ex 6

Erarbeitung:
a) TA der Tabelle
- **2. Lesen** des Textes von Ex 6.
- S vervollständigen die Sätze.
- **Ausw.:** L ergänzt Sätze im TA, dabei sollten die *ing*-Form und die Form von *to be* farbig unterstrichen werden.

b) S lesen ▶ Tippbox, S. 144 (s. a. ▶ LF 16, S. 190), schauen ggf. Erklärfilm und beschreiben die Bildung des *present progressive* mithilfe des Regelkastens.
- **Sich.:** S übertragen Regel in den Merkteil.

Ex 8 Einstieg:
- L gibt Bsp., was S gerade tun. L: … *is looking at the board. What is … doing?*
- S beantworten die Frage.

Erarbeitung:
- S spielen Dialog im ▶ Double circle gemäß AA und nutzen SB für das ▶ Scaffolding.
- **Ausw.:** Freiwillige S präsentieren Dialog im Plenum.

144

5 | **Topic 1** | Topic 2 | Topic 3 | Story | Viewing | Study skills | Unit task

📖 **6 Zane calls Noah**

6 1 C · 2 C

Look at the picture and read the phone conversation. What's different? What are Noah and Buddy really doing?

1 Noah is A resting B playing with Buddy C juggling.
2 Buddy is A playing ball B sleeping C watching Noah.

🔊 2.35

Zane	Hi, Noah! What are you doing?
Noah	Hi, Zane. °Erm, I'm not telling you. It's a secret. … Erm, I'm playing with Buddy. Yes, … he's playing ball now.
Zane	Oh, I'm calling to ask: Do you need help with your party?
Noah	Erm, thanks a lot, but no. What are you doing?
Zane	I'm not busy. I'm listening to music at the moment.
Noah	OK. Sorry, I must go, Zane! See you!

💻 **7 LOOKING AT LANGUAGE Present progressive**

Erklärfilm

a) Complete the examples from 6.

What **are** you	…	?
I'm	…	with Buddy.
He's	…	ball now.
I'm not	…	you.

7 a) What are you doing? • I'm playing with Buddy. • He's playing ball now. • I'm not telling you.

💡 Mit dem *present progressive* sprechen wir darüber, was in diesem Moment *(now, at the moment)* geschieht. Wir beschreiben mit dem *present progressive* auch, was auf Bildern passiert.

▶ Language file 16, p. 190

b) Look at the examples in **a)**. Complete the °rule.

Wir bilden das *present progressive* mit …

7 b) einer Form von *to be* + Verb + *-ing*

I	'm / 'm not	
he / she	is / isn't	play + ■
you / we / they	are / aren't	

💬 **8 DOUBLE CIRCLE What are you doing?**

8 Lösungsbsp. S. 295

👥 Have a phone call with different partners. Choose from the ideas in the box.

Hi! What are you doing? Are you free?

Hi! Sorry, no, I'm busy. I'm … What are you doing?

I'm … OK – see you!

cleaning my room • coding • eating a kebab • playing cards • playing with my pet snake • standing on my head • teaching my parrot to sing • watching a film • writing a post

Topic 1 Vorbereitung

Material: Ex 6 UMA/CD • Ex 7 UMA/App (Erklärfilm) • Ex 9 ▶ KV 5.1: Swap cards – Sam's birthday party (zweimal kopieren, ggf. eine Version durchstreichen für verneinte Aussagen) • Ex 10 weiteres Beispielbild mit Kindern, die etwas tun
Zeitbedarf: ca. 3 Std.
Minimalversion: Ex 8 auslassen
Begleitmedien: WB (S. 72–73), App (Digital quiz, Digital help, Erklärfilm), INKL (S. 144–145), DIFF (5.3)

5

9 A birthday photo

Zane is showing his mum a photo of his friend's birthday party. Complete his sentences with the *-ing* form of the words in the box.

draw • ~~eat~~ • lie • listen • play • sit • take • wear

1 I'm *eating* birthday cake.
2 Sunita and Ruby are ... to music.
3 Ju is ... a gold hat.
4 Noah is ... on a chair with a cat.
5 He's ... photos with his phone.
6 Max and Albie have balloons. They're ... with them.
7 Lily is at the table. She's ... a picture.
8 Amina and Vicky are ... on the floor.

9 1 *eating* • 2 listening • 3 wearing • 4 sitting • 5 taking • 6 playing • 7 drawing • 8 lying

The spelling of some verbs with *-ing* is different:
sit – si**tt**ing
take – tak**i**ng
lie – l**y**ing

▶ Parallel exercise, p. 167; More practice 6 + 7, p. 167

---

10 SPEAKING Find the differences

Partner B: Look at p. 164.
Partner A: Look at this picture.
Take turns and find six differences.

In my picture a boy and a girl in blue T-shirts are singing karaoke.

*In my picture they are / aren't ...
In my picture a dog is ...*

10 Lösungsbsp. S. 296

▶ Challenge 2, p. 168

My task

11 My party photos

YOU CHOOSE Do task A or B.

Task A: Bring photos of family parties to class or show them on your phone to your partner. Describe them.
This is my birthday party. It's the 26th of February. Look! I'm wearing ... We're eating / playing / ...

11 Task A individuelle Lösungen

11 Task B Lösungsbsp. S. 296

Task B: Describe the photos on p. 164.

▶ Digital help ▶ More help, p. 168

▶ Workbook, pp. 72–73

 Digital quiz I can **talk about birthdays and parties.** ✓

one hundred and forty-five **145**

Ex 9 Einstig:
- (SB zu) S wiederholen *present progressive* mit den ▶ Swap cards von ▶ KV 5.1.

Erarbeitung:
- (SB auf) gemeinsames Lesen der ▶ Tippbox, S. 145.
- S schreiben die Sätze in ihr Heft ab und ergänzen die Verben.
- ▶ Partner check
- **Ausw.:** ▶ Five-minute teacher
- ☑ Lernschwächere S bearbeiten die ▶ Parallel ex, S. 167.

Ex 10 Einstieg:
- (SB zu) L zeigt ein Bild mit Kindern, die etwas tun.
- S formulieren wahre und falsche (auch verneinte) Aussagen zum Bild (▶ Three truths, two lies).
- S korrigieren falsche Sätze.
- L achtet auf korrekte Verwendung der Verneinung.

Erarbeitung:
- (SB auf) S beschreiben die Bilder in PA gemäß AA (weitere Ideen s. Hinweise S. 164).
- ☑ ▶ More help, S. 168
- **Ausw.:** S nennen die Unterschiede zwischen den Bildern, TA wie in Lösungen, S. 296.
- **Zusatz:** ▶ Three truths, two lies zum Bild formulieren lassen

---

My task Ex 11 Erarbeitung:
- **Task A** S bringen eigene Fotos mit und beschreiben sie in PA.
- **Task B** S, die keine eigenen Bilder mitgebracht haben, beschreiben die von S. 164.
- S überprüfen, ob die *partners* das *present progressive* richtig bilden, und berichtigen sich ggf.
- **Ausw.:** Bilder im Plenum zeigen

Lernschwerpunkt: sich auf ein Geburtstagsgeschenk einigen • Essen und Getränke für eine Party planen

Kompetenzen: *Listening* einem Dialog Informationen entnehmen • *Speaking* Vorschläge für ein Geburtstagsgeschenk machen • ein Geschenk annehmen • *Reading* nach einem Dialog eine Einkaufsliste erstellen

Strukturen: *much, many, a lot of*

Redemittel: Wortfelder *presents, food and drinks* • *shopping list* • Vorschläge machen und darauf reagieren

---

Ex 1 Einstieg:
- (SB zu) L zeigt eine Einladung. L: *I have an invitation to my neighbour's daughter's party and I need a present. She is twelve. Do you have ideas?* S: *You can buy …*
- TA: Liste mit Ideen

Erarbeitung:

a) (SB auf) L: *Let's find a present for Noah.*
- ▶ Buzz groups gemäß AA
- **Ausw.:** L sammelt Noahs Vorlieben und Abneigungen (TA).

b) 1. Hören gemäß AA
- **Ausw.:** S beantworten die Frage im Plenum.
- ☒ S geben eine Begründung.

c) 2. Hören gemäß AA
- **Ausw.:** ▶ Five-minute teacher
- ☒ S nutzen das ▶ Scaffolding, um in ▶ Buzz-groups ein Geschenk für die Nachbarstochter (s. **Einstieg**) zu finden.
- **Ausw.:** im Plenum

Ex 2 Einstieg:
- (SB zu) L: *Think of five cool birthday presents.*
- ▶ Five-finger brainstorming

a) Erarbeitung:
L: *Let's collect your ideas.*
- TA: Liste mit den Geschenken

b) (SB auf) ▶ Klären der AA, L führt einen Bsp.-Dialog mit S.
- ▶ Buzz-groups gemäß AA
- **Ausw.:** Dialoge im Plenum

c) S reagieren gemäß AA.
- ☒ ▶ More help, S. 168

5 Topic 1 **Topic 2** Topic 3 Story Viewing Study skills Unit task

Party shopping

🔊 **1** LISTENING **A present for Noah**

👥 **a)** BEFORE YOU LISTEN Say what things in the box Noah likes or doesn't like.

He likes …   He doesn't like …

🔊 **b)** Sunita and Lily are looking online for a birthday present for Noah. Look at the website. Then listen. Say what they choose. Say why.
2.37 ☒

1 a) Noah likes animals, circus tricks, and walking. • He doesn't like strawberries and cycling.

animals • circus tricks • cycling • strawberries • walking

1 b) Lösungsbsp. S. 296

www.presents.example.com

Do you need an idea for a present? Look here!

animal book

sweatshirt with a name

magic set

cool bike lights

mini-drone

smart hat

🔊 **c)** Listen again. Complete the phrases.

1 c) Lösung S. 296

What about a …?
Why don't we buy …?
Let's get some/a/the …

☹ *I'm n… sure.*
It's too …
Noah already has …

☺ *It's a great …!*
That's a … idea.
That's p…!

💬 **2** SPEAKING **Find a present**

2 individuelle Lösungen

a) °Brainstorm a list of cool birthday presents on the °board.

👥 **b)** Find a birthday present for each student in your group. Use the presents from 1b) and 2a) and phrases from 1c). The 'birthday kid' listens.

First let's find a present for Samir.
OK. Why don't we buy …?
That's a great idea, but Samir already has …

c) The 'birthday kid' says thank you and °comments on the present.

Thanks, guys! A recipe book is a great present. I'm learning to cook, so it's perfect!
Thanks for the sweatshirt. I really like it!

▶ More help, p. 168
▶ Workbook, p. 74

Material: Ex 1 UMA/CD • Ex 3 Realien (für neuen Wortschatz), UMA/CD, ▶ KV 5.2: A ham and cheese sandwich (Klassensatz) •
Ex 4 Tasche, Geld, Einkaufszettel, UMA/CD • Ex 5 UMA/App (Erklärfilm)
Zeitbedarf: ca. 2 Std.
Minimalversion: Ex 2 auslassen
Begleitmedien: WB (S. 74–75), App (Erklärfilm), INKL (S. 146–147)

5

3 LISTENING Party food and drinks

a) BEFORE YOU LISTEN Can you remember …

- What sort of party is Noah's birthday party?
- Where's the party?
- What's his birthday dessert?

2.38 **b)** Look at the party menu.
Listen to Noah and his parents.
What three things are wrong?

> **3 a) 1** It's a "circus games and picnic" party. •
> **2** It's at Hove park • **3** It's trifle.

> **3 b) 1** No ham sandwiches. •
> **2** No cheese sandwiches. • **3** No cola.

★ Noah's party menu ★

Food
ham sandwiches,
cheese sandwiches,
hot dogs, pasta salad,
carrots, trifle, melon

Drinks
cola, lemonade

4 WORDS The shopping list

4 a) Lösung S. 296

2.39 **a)** Read the conversation. Write Noah's shopping list for the party.

Noah I'm writing the shopping list. How much bread do we need?
Dad   For the hot dogs? A lot of bread! Two packets.
Noah OK. And how many sausages?
Dad   Hmm, let's get twenty.
Noah How much pasta?
Dad   A big bag of pasta.
Noah And how many carrots do we need? One bag?
Dad   Yes, we don't need many. And one big melon.
Noah OK. How many lemons do we need for the lemonade? And how much sugar?
Dad   Let's get twelve lemons. We already have sugar.

Noah | Noah's dad

bread: 2 packets
sausages:
…

b) °Compare your list with your partner. Then listen and check.

5 a) Lösung S. 296

5 LOOKING AT LANGUAGE *much, many, a lot of*

Erklär-film **a)** Complete the table with food and drinks from 4a).

How much …?	How many …?
bread	sausages
…	…

b) Complete the box with *much, many* and *a lot of*.

- Zählbare Wörter haben eine Pluralform (Mehrzahl): *twenty sausages, twelve lemons.*
- Nicht zählbare Wörter verwendet man nicht im Plural: *bread, milk, °water.*
- Wir verwenden ■ mit zählbaren Wörtern und ■ mit nicht zählbaren Wörtern.
- ■ kann man in Aussagesätzen mit zählbaren und mit nicht zählbaren Wörtern benutzen.

5 b) Lösung S. 297   ▶ Language file 17, p. 191   ▶ More practice 8, p. 168
▶ Workbook, p. 75

one hundred and forty-seven **147**

Topic 2 Inhalt

Lernschwerpunkt: sich über Essen und Getränke verständigen • ein Fest planen einschließlich Aktivitäten
Kompetenzen: Listening einen Song verstehen • Speaking sich über Einkaufsgewohnheiten austauschen • ein Klassenfest planen • Mediation Spielregeln auf Deutsch wiedergeben
Redemittel: Wortfeld *food and drinks*

Ex 6 Einstieg:
- (SB zu) L wiederholt *much / many / a lot of* mit ▶ Flash-cards (*food and drinks*)

Erarbeitung:
- (SB auf) Klären der AA, S lesen Beispiele, L zeigt das vergrößerte Bild am UMA.
- (SB zu) L schaltet UMA aus u. führt mit guten S ein Bsp. vor.
- (SB auf) S notieren fünf Fragen im Heft.
- S suchen ihre Partner/innen per ▶ Bus stop (▶ KV Extra).
- (SB zu) PA gemäß AA
- S notieren Antworten.
- 🖥 ▶ Scaffolding als TA
- **Ausw.:** (SB auf) S vergleichen in PA die Antworten.
- ggf. Ermittlung des Siegers

Ex 7 Einstieg:
- (SB zu) L berichtet über sich selbst, z. B.: *I often go food shopping. I sometimes go with my family / partner / ... I usually go shopping at the market. And what about you?*

Erarbeitung:
a) (SB auf) L fragt ein oder zwei lernstärkere S, diese antworten
- dann gemäß AA in PA
- **Ausw.:** Einzelne S präsentieren Ergebnisse.

b) (SB auf oder UMA) S notieren Buchstaben während des **1.** Hörens.
- **Ausw.:** s. S. 169, ▶ Five-minute teacher

c) 2. Hören gemäß AA
- L notiert Wörter als TA.
- **Ausw.:** Chorsprechen (▶ Lautschulung)
- S singen das Lied (Text S. 169).

148

5 Topic 1 **Topic 2** Topic 3 Story Viewing Study skills Unit task

✏️ 👥 **6** GAME *How much ...? – How many ...? – A lot of ...!*   **6** Lösungsbsp. S. 297

💬 Look in the °fridge and write five questions. Then close your books.
In turns, ask your questions and write your partner's answers:

How many strawberries are there? – Not many. There are five strawberries.
How much pasta is there? – There's a lot of pasta – four packets.
How much cheese is there? – Not much. One small piece.

Open your books again and check. The partner with more correct answers wins.

7 a) Lösungsbsp. S. 297

🎵 **7** SONG **The shopping song**

💬 👥 a) BEFORE YOU LISTEN Ask and answer the questions about food shopping.

1 How often do you go food shopping?
   I never / sometimes / often go ...
2 Do you usually go with your parents or do you sometimes go alone?
   I usually / sometimes / ... go ...
3 Where do you usually go shopping?
   In the supermarket. / In small shops. / At the market.

🔊 2.41 b) Listen to the song. Write the letters of the foods (A–N) in the order of the song. Check on p. 169.

🔊 c) Listen again and say which food words in the song °rhyme. Then sing!

7 c) Lösungsbsp. S. 297

A  B  C
D  E  F
G  H 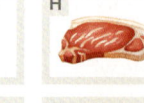 I
J  K  L
M  N

7 b) K – M – C – D – E – G – H – I – J – A – L – B – N – F

▶ Workbook, p. 75

148 one hundred and forty-eight

Topic 2 Vorbereitung

Material: Ex 6 Flashcards (*food and drinks*), UMA, ▶ KV Extra: Bus stop • Ex 7 UMA/CD • Ex 8 Realien
(für das Schokoladenspiel) • Ex 9 ggf. Handpuppe Scout
Zeitbedarf: ca. 1–2 Std.
Minimalversion: Ex 7 auslassen, Ex 8 als HA
Begleitmedien: WB (S. 75), App (Digital quiz, Digital help), INKL (S. 148–149), DIFF (5.4)

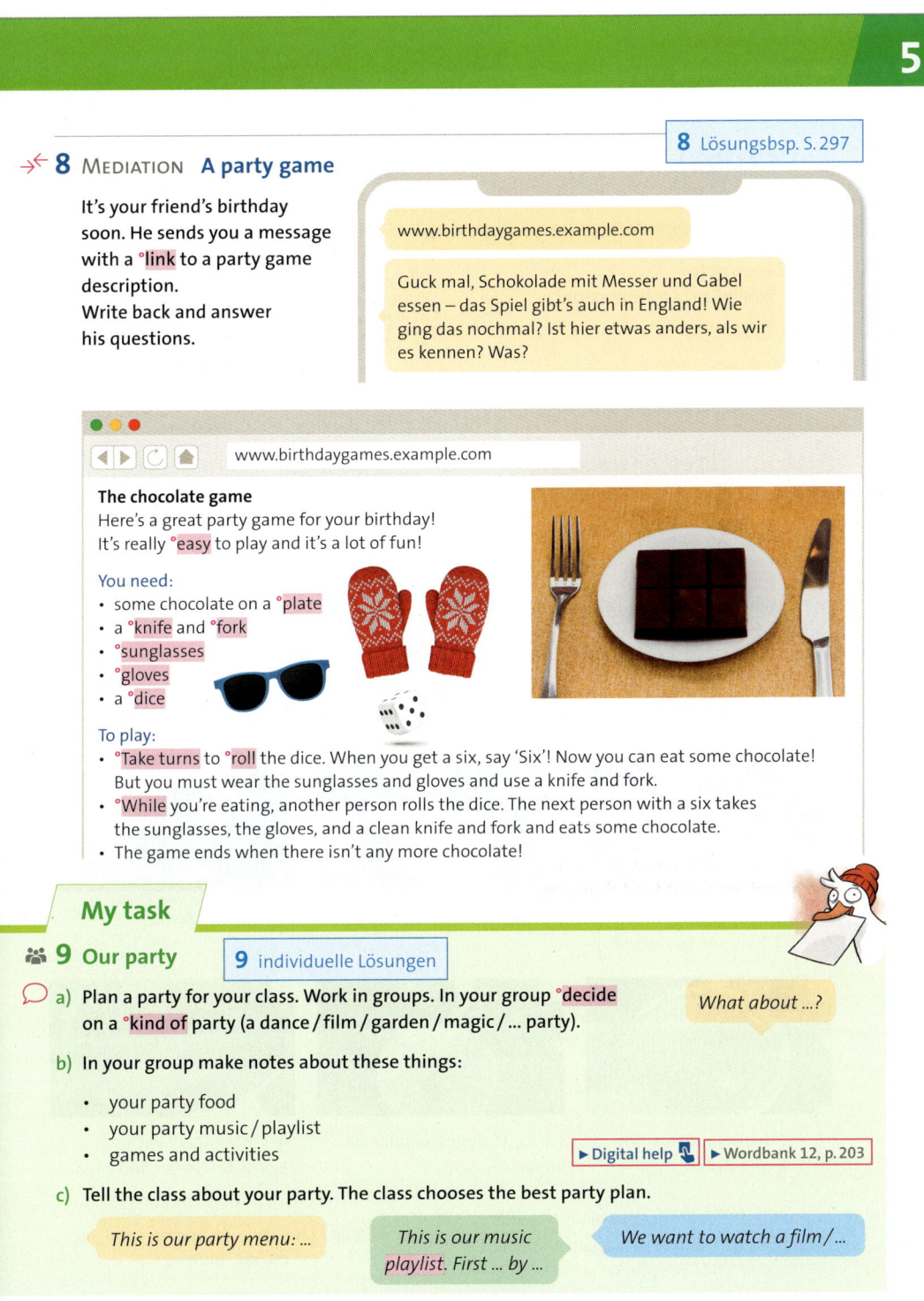

5

→← **8** MEDIATION **A party game**

It's your friend's birthday soon. He sends you a message with a °link to a party game description.
Write back and answer his questions.

8 Lösungsbsp. S. 297

www.birthdaygames.example.com

Guck mal, Schokolade mit Messer und Gabel essen – das Spiel gibt's auch in England! Wie ging das nochmal? Ist hier etwas anders, als wir es kennen? Was?

www.birthdaygames.example.com

The chocolate game
Here's a great party game for your birthday!
It's really °easy to play and it's a lot of fun!

You need:
• some chocolate on a °plate
• a °knife and °fork
• °sunglasses
• °gloves
• a °dice

To play:
• °Take turns to °roll the dice. When you get a six, say 'Six'! Now you can eat some chocolate! But you must wear the sunglasses and gloves and use a knife and fork.
• °While you're eating, another person rolls the dice. The next person with a six takes the sunglasses, the gloves, and a clean knife and fork and eats some chocolate.
• The game ends when there isn't any more chocolate!

My task

👥 **9** **Our party**

💬 a) **Plan a party for your class. Work in groups. In your group °decide on a °kind of party (a dance / film / garden / magic / … party).**

What about …?

b) **In your group make notes about these things:**

• your party food
• your party music / playlist
• games and activities

▶ Digital help ▶ Wordbank 12, p. 203

c) **Tell the class about your party. The class chooses the best party plan.**

This is our party menu: …

This is our music playlist. First … by …

We want to watch a film / …

Digital quiz **I can talk about party food and activities.** ✓

one hundred and forty-nine **149**

Ex 8 Einstieg:
• (SB zu) L bringt Realien für dieses Spiel mit.
  L: *Look, what can you see?*
  S: *I can see …*
  L: *I need these things for a party game. Do you know the game?*
• S antworten oder L nennt den Namen des Spiels.

Erarbeitung:
• (SB auf) S bearbeiten Text gemäß AA (ggf. gibt L Hinweise zur Textform).
• **Ausw.:** ▶ Partner check
• Einzelne S präsentieren Ergebnisse im Plenum.

My task Ex 9 Einstieg:
• (SB zu)
  L: *Now let's plan our own party. What things are important?*
• ▶ Five-finger brainstorming
• S besprechen Ideen in PA und dann im Plenum.

Erarbeitung:
a) (SB auf) ▶ Gruppenbildung, ein Blatt für jede Gruppe
• gemäß AA
• **Sich.:** L stellt sicher, dass sich jede Gruppe für eine Party entschieden hat.

b) L verweist auf ▶ Wordbank 12, S. 203 und ▶ Let's talk 5, S. 210.
• Gruppen machen sich Notizen.

c) gemäß AA
• ☒ L präsentiert ein Beispiel mit Handpuppe Scout.
• **Ausw.:** Gruppen präsentieren ihre Ergebnisse.
• ▶ Feedback von der Klasse (ggf. Scaffolding)

5

Lernschwerpunkt: eine Backanleitung hörend und sehend verstehen • das eigene Lieblingsessen beschreiben
Kompetenzen: Viewing ein authentisches Koch-Video verstehen • Reading/Intercultural competence einen Blogeintrag zu einem nigerianischen Gericht verstehen • (moderne) Essenstraditionen im UK kennenlernen • Writing einen Blogeintrag über das eigene Leibgericht schreiben
Redemittel: Wortfelder *cooking and baking, food and drinks*

Ex 1 Einstieg:
- (SB zu) ▸ Semantisierung der neuen Wörter
- L bringt Realien/Zutaten mit. L: *Today we're making a cake. What do we need?*
- L zeigt Zutat und L/S nennt Vokabel. Wortliste als TA
- ▸ Lautschulung

Erarbeitung:
- (SB auf) S lesen die Nachricht.
- PA gemäß AA
- **Ausw.:** im Plenum
- ⊠ S begründen ihre Entscheidung.
- S liest die Zutatenliste laut vor einschließlich der Mengenangaben.
- ▸ Semantisierung von *gram, millilitre*

Ex 2 Einstieg:
- (SB zu) L: *Who of you bakes? Where do you get your recipes?*
- S antworten. L: *Let's watch a baking video.*

Erarbeitung:
a) (SB auf) S beantworten Frage nach **1. Sehen** (bis 0:40).
- **Ausw.:** im Plenum

b) S notieren Reihenfolge beim **2. Sehen** (komplett).
- **Ausw.:** ▸ Meldekette

c) gemäß AA, Satz 1 im Plenum, Sätze 2–6 notieren die S in ihr Heft.
- **Ausw.:** **3. Sehen** zum Überprüfen der Lösung

| 5 | Topic 1 | Topic 2 | **Topic 3** | Story | Viewing | Study skills | Unit task |

Let's cook!

📖 **1** BEFORE YOU WATCH **What are you cooking?**

👥 Read Zane's notes.
What °kind of cake is he making?

I think it's a … cake.

> Hey, Zane! What are you doing?
>
> Hi, Lily. I'm watching a cooking video. I want to make this for Noah's birthday party.

> **1** It's a *chocolate* cake.

For the cake:

250 g flour	2 eggs
60 ml oil	salt
120 g sugar	½ teaspoon vanilla
50 g cocoa	2 teaspoons baking powder
30 ml milk	

For the icing:

| 200 g butter | 400 g icing sugar |
| 100 g chocolate | |

🎬 **2** VIEWING **A cooking video**

💻 **a)** Watch the first part of the video °until 0:40. Which things in the list in **1** does Maiku °forget to say?

💻 **b)** Watch all the video. Put the photos in the correct order.

> **2 a)** butter, icing sugar

> **2 b)** B • E • D • A • F • C

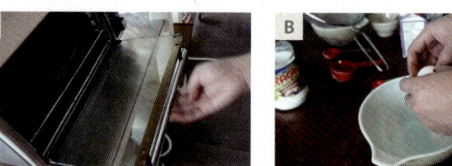
He's … the mixture in the oven (180°C for 50 minutes).

He's … the eggs.

He's … the cake.

He's … the flour, cocoa and baking powder.

He's … the eggs, vanilla, oil, sugar and salt.

He's … the icing with chocolate, butter and sugar.

c) Complete the sentences in **b)** with words from the box. Then watch again and check.

> **2 c)** **B** breaking • **E** adding • **D** mixing • **A** putting • **F** making • **C** decorating

adding • breaking • decorating • making • mixing • putting

▸ Workbook, p. 76

Topic 3 Vorbereitung

Material: Ex 1 Realien (Zutaten) • Ex 2 UMA/DVD • Ex 3 ggf. Bild (Lieblingsessen der Lehrkraft), Flashcards (Zutaten für Zanes Lieblingsgericht und 3–7 weitere Zutaten), UMA/CD • Ex 4 Handpuppe Scout (mit einem Sandwich), weiße A4-Blätter im Klassensatz, Bild von *stir-fry*

Zeitbedarf: ca. 1–2 Std.

Minimalversion: Ex 3 als HA, Ex 4 als HA beenden

Begleitmedien: WB (S. 76–77), App (Digital quiz, Digital help), INKL (S. 150–151), DIFF (5.5, 5.6)

5

📖 3 READING Zane's favourite dish

> **3 1** F (from Nigeria) • **2** T • **3** F (chicken) • **4** T • **5** NT (every week) • **6** F (Zane thinks he cooks it best, not his father)

Read Zane's blog post. Write if these sentences are true (T), false (F), or not in the text (NT).

1 Zane's favourite dish is from India.
2 Jollof rice is a main course.
3 It's a vegetarian dish.
4 Zane likes °plantain[1].

5 Zane's dad cooks jollof[2] rice every Saturday.
6 Zane thinks that his dad cooks it best.

🔊 2.42

www.cooking-with-zane.example.net

We eat it with plantain – it's a kind of banana. It isn't sweet, so we fry it with honey. °Yum!
This is an important dish for my family and my dad cooks it every week. And sometimes I cook it when we have a party – don't tell him, but I think I cook it best! 😊

Zane

This is my favourite dish. It's called jollof rice and it's from °Nigeria.
It's a spicy dish and a main course. You make it with rice, tomatoes, onions, peppers, chicken – and a lot of spices!
It's delicious and I love it!

My task

✏️ **4 My favourite dish**

> **4** individuelle Lösungen

Use Zane's blog post in **3** and these questions to write about your favourite dish. Put your text in your DOSSIER.

- What kind of dish is it? A main course? A dessert?
- Is it sweet?
- What culture or country does it come from?
- What's in the dish?
- When do you eat it? Who cooks it?
- Do you eat it with your family?
- What do you drink with it?

Good to know

Food and drinks in the UK
- Modern food has a lot of traditions. We eat food from everywhere.
- °Chinese stir-fry with vegetables and noodles is the favourite dish in the UK.
- A lot of people drink tea (often with milk and sugar), but a lot of people drink coffee too.

 ▶ Digital help 🔌 ▶ More help, p. 169 ▶ Wordbank 12, p. 203

1 ['plæntɪn], ['plænteɪn] 2 ['dʒɒlɒf]  ▶ Workbook, p. 77

 Digital quiz 🔌 I can describe my favourite dish. ✅

one hundred and fifty-one **151**

Ex 3 Einstieg:
- (SB zu) ▶ Semantisierung von neuem Wortschatz mit ▶ Flashcards von den im Text genannten Lebensmitteln sowie 3–7 weiteren, die nicht im Text vorkommen
- Wortliste als TA und Übernahme ins *Vocab file*
- ☒ S hören die Aufnahme des Textes und identifizieren per ▶ Flashcards die Lebensmittel, von denen Zane spricht.

Erarbeitung:
- (SB auf) gemäß AA in EA
- ☒ S korrigieren die falschen Aussagen.
- **Ausw.:** ▶ Five-minute teacher

My task Ex 4 Einstieg:
- (SB zu) Handpuppe Scout hat ein Sandwich und stellt vor: Scout: *My favourite dish is a sandwich. What's your favourite dish?* S: *My favourite dish is …*

Erarbeitung:
- (SB auf) gemeinsames Lesen des ▶ Good to know, S. 151
- ▶ Semantisierung von *stir-fry* mit Bild
- Fragen vorlesen lassen und gemeinsam klären
- ▶ Wordbank 12, S. 203
- ▶ More help, S. 169
- S schreiben ihren Text auf ein weißes Blatt, das sie ausgestalten (ggf. als HA).
- **Ausw.:** S präsentieren ihre Ergebnisse im ▶ Gallery walk.
- anschließend ▶ English corner
- Ablage im ▶ Dossier

Story Inhalt

Lernschwerpunkt: unterschiedliche Vorlieben verstehen und akzeptieren
Kompetenzen: Reading eine Geschichte bildgestützt verstehen und ihr neuen Wortschatz entnehmen • Speaking Fragen zum Inhalt der Geschichte beantworten
Redemittel: *party words • feelings • That's the same. / That's different.*

Ex 1 Einstieg:
- (SB zu) TA: *Noah's birthday party*
  L: *What can you remember about Noah's party?*
- S sammeln, woran sie sich erinnern (Thema der Party, Ort und Essen).
- L sammelt Ideen an Tafel. Falls S sich nicht erinnern, dürfen sie das Buch zur Hilfe öffnen.

Erarbeitung:
a) (SB auf)
- L zeigt das erste Bild mithilfe des UMA.
- S decken die Story ab und sehen nur Ex 1.
- gemäß AA im ▸ Partner talk
- **Ausw.:** ▸ Five-minute teacher

- ⊠ **Alternative:** (SB zu) L zeigt alle Bilder der Story willkürlich gemischt.
- S hören den Text absatzweise und ordnen jedem Absatz ein Bild zu.

b) ▸ Klären der AA
- TA der unten stehenden Schritte (in Stichwörtern) und des passenden ▸ Scaffolding
- **1. Lesen:** S arbeiten in PA immer die folgenden fünf Schritte ab:
  1) S betrachten erst das Bild und beschreiben es.
  2) S lesen leise den zum Bild gehörenden Abschnitt.
  3) S tauschen sich darüber aus, was sie in dem jeweiligen Absatz verstanden haben.
  (Forts. s. S. 153 oben)

A different kind of party

📖 **1** READING **What's happening in the story?**

> **1 a) 1** are • **2** isn't • **3** are • **4** isn't • **5** isn't • **6** aren't

a) BEFORE YOU READ **Look at the first picture and choose the correct word.**

1 The friends are / aren't meeting Noah.
2 Zane is / isn't bringing a drink.
3 Noah and his family are / aren't sitting in the park.
4 Buddy is / isn't running in the park.
5 It is / isn't raining.
6 The kids are / aren't wearing school uniforms.

b) **Read the story and answer the questions.**

1 Why is it a different kind of party?
2 What three things are problems for Lily and Zane?
3 Does Noah think these are problems too?

> **1 b) 1** no music, no dancing • **2** Noah is allergic to strawberries, no music, Buddy eats the trifle • **3** No, Noah is happy with his party.

🔊 2.43

Lily	This is Hove Park and it's 2 o'clock. But where are Noah and his family?
Zane	Look, there they are! Noah's waving. Oh, and here's Sunita!
5 **Sunita**	Hi! What are you bringing to the party, Zane?
Zane	It's my special chocolate cake. It's for Noah's party.
Lily	It looks delicious! You're so good at baking, Zane.
10 **Zane**	Happy birthday, Noah! Here's a dessert for you!
Noah	Thanks! Mum and Dad, my friends are here.
Mum	Hello! Nice to meet you.
Lily	And here are some strawberries, Noah.
15 **Noah**	Thanks, but I'm allergic to strawberries, remember?
Lily	Oh no, I'm sorry …
Dad	That's OK, Lily — it's very kind of you to bring them. And I love strawberries!
20 **Sunita**	Zane, are you OK? You're very quiet.
Zane	Erm, this is a very different kind of party. I mean, we're just sitting and talking. There's no music, people aren't dancing … It isn't the kind of party I like!
25 **Sunita**	Well, it is a little different. But Noah doesn't like loud music or dancing. So I think this is the kind of party he likes.

Story Vorbereitung

Material: Ex 1 UMA/CD
Zeitbedarf: ca. 2 Std.
Begleitmedien: INKL (S. 152–153)

🔊 2.44

Dad	Do you want to open your presents now, Noah?	
30 Noah	No, let's eat my birthday trifle first!	
Dad	OK, it's in my bag over there ... Oh no! Stop, Buddy!	
Noah	Is Buddy OK?	
Mum	Yes, he's fine. There's no chocolate in the trifle, so it's OK. But we can't eat it now! I'm sorry, Noah.	

35

Noah	Lily, °erm, are you OK?
Lily	It's just ... I feel sad. Your party ...
Noah	What do you mean?
40 Lily	Well, there are so many problems ... You can't eat my strawberries, we don't have music, and now there's no trifle!

Noah	What? This is the best birthday party ever! I'm having a picnic with my family and my best friends and my dog. It isn't too loud, so I'm feeling good. It's sunny, I have presents, and we can eat Zane's chocolate cake. It's the perfect party for me!
Lily	That's true ...
50 Noah	So don't be sad. You know ... I think it's really funny!
Lily	You're right! Hahaha!
Noah	Now you're smiling!

45

Noah	And now – my secret: Watch this!
55 Sunita	°Wow! Noah, that's amazing!
Zane	You're really good at juggling!
Dad	Yes, when Noah wants to learn something, he works really hard.
Noah	Ta-dah! Well, this is a circus birthday party, right? Now it's your turn – I can show you how to juggle too! And then ... my magic show!
Zane	Wow, this is a great party! It's a new kind of party for me, but it's great fun. Thanks, Noah!

60

65

▶ Box: Voc., p. 253

3) TA mit Scaffolding (vorher anschreiben):
In this part of the story, Noah/ Zane/Lily/Sunita/...
– is happy/sad/angry/sorry/ embarrassed/...
– gives/talks/eats/juggles/...

4) S stellen sich gegenseitig Fragen, wenn sie etwas nicht verstanden haben: (TA mit Scaffolding):
I don't understand this part/ sentence.
Can you help me?
What is ... in German?

5) S beantworten nach dem **1. Lesen** der Geschichte die Fragen aus Ex 1 b).

- **Ausw.:** Vergleich der Antworten im Plenum
- **2. Lesen:** S lesen die Geschichte leise und suchen nach unbekannten Wörtern.
  S: *What's ... in English?*
- L semantisiert das Wort (▶ Semantisierung), beschreibt es kurz auf Englisch, führt passende Bewegungen aus oder Ähnliches und schreibt die deutsche und englische Bedeutung an die ▶ Vokabeltafel.
- S ergänzen ihr *Vocab file*.
- ⊠ S üben, einen Teil des Textes vorzulesen. L stellt ihnen die Aufnahme des Textes zur Verfügung, damit sie gezielt die korrekte Aussprache trainieren.

Story Inhalt | Vorbereitung

Lernschwerpunkt: unterschiedliche Vorlieben verstehen und akzeptieren

Kompetenzen: Reading eine Geschichte verstehen und ihr neuen Wortschatz entnehmen • Speaking / Life skills über kulturelle und persönliche Unterschiede sprechen

Redemittel: *party words • feelings • That's the same. / That's different.*

Zeitbedarf: ca. 2 Std.

Minimalversion: Ex 4 auslassen

Begleitmedien: App (Digital quiz), INKL (S. 154), DIFF (5.7)

Ex 2 Hinweis:
- idealerweise im direkten Anschluss an das Lesen der Geschichte

Erarbeitung:
- (SB auf) S lesen die Sätze und notieren die Namen im Heft.
- **Ausw.:** ▶ Meldekette

Ex 3 Einstieg
- zur Auffrischung, falls erst in Folgestunde bearbeitet:
- L macht 5–7 *true/false*-Aussagen zur Geschichte. S entscheiden, ob die Aussage wahr oder falsch ist, und nennen die dazugehörige Textzeile.

Erarbeitung:
- gemäß AA
- **Ausw.:** ▶ Five-minute teacher
- ☒ **Zusatz:** S beschreiben das Bild mit dem *present progressive.*

Ex 4 Einstieg:
- (SB zu) L macht Aussagen. S stehen auf, wenn Aussage zutrifft. Beispiele: *I like football/pizza/meat/…*

Erarbeitung:
- **a)** (SB auf) gemäß AA, S schreiben Lösungen ins Heft.
- **b)** S sollen in PA (mind.) drei Unterschiede und drei Gemeinsamkeiten finden.
- **Alternative:** ▶ Milling around
- S notieren Ergebnisse im Heft.
- **c) Ausw.:** Präsentation im Plenum gemäß AA
- ☒ **Zusatz:** kurze Diskussion, warum es wichtig ist, dass wir Unterschiede akzeptieren

---

| 5 | Topic 1 | Topic 2 | Topic 3 | **Story** | Viewing | Study skills | Unit task |

📖 2 Who is it?

> **2** 1 Zane • 2 Noah • 3 Noah's dad • 4 Zane, Sunita • 5 Buddy • 6 Lily • 7 Noah • 8 Zane

Complete the sentences with a name or names.

1 … makes some food for the party.
2 … can't eat strawberries.
3 … loves eating strawberries.
4 … and … think the party is too quiet at first.

5 … eats the trifle.
6 … feels sad about the party.
7 … thinks the party is perfect.
8 … thinks something different about the party at the end.

▶ More practice 9, p. 169

📖 3 Words in the story

> **3** 1 waving • 2 delicious • 3 picnic • 4 perfect • 5 smiling

Find the words in the story for the °descriptions.

1 moving your hand to say hello (line 3)
2 when food is really good (line 8)
3 eating in the park with friends (line 44)
4 when something is really great (line 48)
5 looking happy (line 53)

Noah

📖 4 °LIFE SKILLS People are different

> **4** individuelle Lösungen

a) Read the sentences about Noah and his friends. Write how you are the same or different.

1 Noah likes quiet parties. *I like quiet parties too. / I don't like quiet parties.*
2 Zane likes loud music.
3 Noah's dad loves strawberries.
4 Sunita doesn't eat meat.
5 Lily likes parkour.

💬 👥 **b)** Talk to your partner. What's the same and what's different?

> *I don't eat ham. What about you?*
>
> *I eat ham, so that's different. I like skateboarding. And you?*
>
> *Cool! I like skateboarding too. That's the same.*

c) Tell the class one thing that is the same for you and your partner. Then say one thing that's different.

   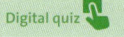 Digital quiz   **I can** understand and talk about differences.

Viewing Inhalt | Vorbereitung

Lernschwerpunkt: Filmszenen verstehen

Kompetenzen: Viewing / Intercultural competence Film-szenen zum Thema Geburtstagsparty verstehen • Speaking über die *Brighton dares* diskutieren

Redemittel: Wortfeld *birthday words* • Diskussionswort-schatz

Material: Ex 2 UMA/DVD

Zeitbedarf: ca. 1 Std.

Minimalversion: Ex 3 auslassen

Begleitmedien: WB (S. 78), INKL (S. 155)

| Topic 1 | Topic 2 | Topic 3 | Story | **Viewing** | Study skills | Unit task | 5 |

The Brighton dares: A birthday

🖉 1 Birthday words   1 a) Lösungsbsp. S. 297

a) BEFORE YOU WATCH **Make a mind map for the word** *birthday*. **Add as many words as you can.**

👥 b) **Compare with a partner and add his/her ideas.**

party

birthday — …

📺 2 VIEWING The party

2 a) 1 Saturday 11th • 2 6 p.m. • 3 dance • 4 parkour • 5 yes, he does • 6 the weather

a) **Watch the video from 00:00 to 04:17. Complete the invitation and the information about Daisy's friend.**

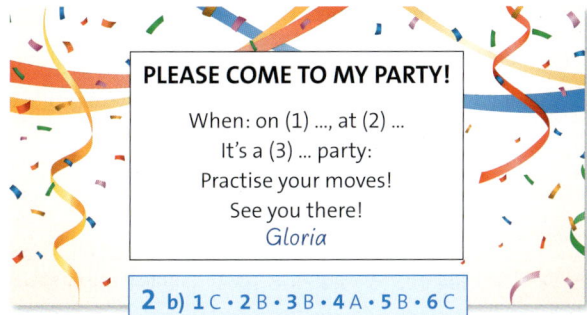

PLEASE COME TO MY PARTY!

When: on (1) …, at (2) …
It's a (3) … party:
Practise your moves!
See you there!
Gloria

2 b) 1 C • 2 B • 3 B • 4 A • 5 B • 6 C

Daisy's imaginary[1] friend

Dare: *Take an imaginary friend to Gloria's party*
Name of friend: *Sota*
From: *Japan*
Hobby: (4) …
Likes England? (5) …
Likes best? (6) …

b) **Now watch the video from 04:18 to 06:27. Choose the correct answers about Emir's dare.**

1 Emir does his dare … A at his home. B at the party. C in the supermarket.
2 Emir feels … A brave. B nervous. C angry.
3 Daisy makes a video of Emir: He's … A dancing. B singing. C singing and dancing.
4 Other people look … A surprised but happy. B angry. C embarrassed[2].
5 The video is … A for dancing at the party. B a present for Gloria. C for a video channel[3].
6 Emir buys a toy dog as a birthday present from … A himself. B Daisy. C Sota.

c) **Watch the video from 06:28 to 09:17 and answer the questions.**

1 Which birthday things from your mind map in 1 can you see and hear? Make notes.
2 What is everybody doing when the video ends?

2 c) 1 Lösung S. 297 • 2 dancing

💬👥 3 All the dares   3 individuelle Lösungen

Think about all the dares in this book (pages 33, 63, 95, 125 and 155).
Which is the best dare and why? Discuss in your group and then tell the class.

---

[1] **imaginary** *Fantasie- (vorgestellt)*   [2] **embarrassed** *verlegen, peinlich berührt*   [3] **video channel** *Video-Kanal*

▶ Workbook, p. 78

one hundred and fifty-five   **155**

Ex 1 Einstig:
• (SB zu) S spielen Galgenraten mit dem Begriff *birthday*.
• S teilen sich in zwei Gruppen auf (▶ Gruppenbildung) und spielen gegeneinander.

Erarbeitung:
a) (SB auf) S beginnen die ▶ Mindmap um das erratene Wort *birthday* im Plenum.
• Ergänzung in EA

b) gemäß AA
• **Ausw.:** S ergänzen Begriffe im TA. Mehrere S schreiben dabei gleichzeitig.

Ex 2 Erarbeitung:
a) S lesen AA und Texte.
• **1. Sehen** (bis 04:17): S schreiben die fehlenden Wörter in ihr Heft.

b) **2. Sehen** (bis 06:27): gemäß AA

c) **3. Sehen** (komplett): S verglei-chen mit ihrer Mindmap aus Ex 1.
• Austausch im ▶ Partner talk
• ☒ S ergänzen weitere *birthday things*.
• **Ausw.** im Plenum

Ex 3 Erarbeitung:
• GA gemäß AA, L teilt Klasse in fünf Gruppen.
• Jede Gruppe fasst eine der Mutproben kurz zusammen.
• Jede Gruppe präsentiert ihre Zusammenfassung im Plenum und begründet ihre Wahl im Plenum.

Lernschwerpunkt: Wörter erklären

Kompetenzen: Speaking Wörter umschreiben und dafür Oberbegriffe, Adjektive usw. nutzen

Redemittel: Wortfeld *food and drinks* • Adjektive • *umbrella words*

Material: Ex 4 drei vorbereitete Beispielkarten für das Spiel (*food, drinks, dishes*) sowie Blankokarten (zwei pro S), von L vorbereitete *swap cards*

Zeitbedarf: ca. 1 Std.

Minimalversion: Ex 1b) auslassen

Begleitmedien: App (Digital quiz), INKL (S. 156), DIFF (5.8)

Ex 1 Einstieg:
- (SB zu) TA: *subject – days of the week – clothes*
  L: *Please give examples for school subjects / clothes / …*
- S nennen Beispiele.
- L ergänzt TA.
- Wiederholung des Konzepts der *umbrella words* anhand der S-Beispiele (s. a. ▶SF 6, S.181)

Erarbeitung:
a) (SB auf) gemäß AA
- **Ausw.:** ▶Five-minute teacher

b) S schreiben Sätze ins Heft.
- **Ausw.:** ▶Meldekette

Ex 2 Einstieg:
- (SB zu) L beschreibt 5–7 *food and drinks*, S raten.
  L: *It's a kind of vegetable. It is red and round.*
  S: *Tomato.*

Erarbeitung:
- (SB auf) gemäß AA in EA
- **Ausw.:** S lesen einen Satz vor, die Klasse rät.

Ex 3 Einstieg:
- (SB zu) Übungsrunde mit 2–3 ähnlichen Bsp. im Plenum.

Erarbeitung:
- (SB auf) schriftl. gemäß AA
- **Ausw.:** ▶Five-minute teacher

Ex 4 Einstieg:
L zeigt drei vorbereitete Karten und erklärt sie, S raten.

Erarbeitung:
- S bereiten Karten vor und verteilen sie gemäß AA.
- **Alternative:** L bringt fertige ▶Swap cards mit.
- **Ausw.:** S spielen in Gruppen.

---

5 | Topic 1 | Topic 2 | Topic 3 | Story | Viewing | **Study skills** | Unit task

Explaining words

🖉 **1 Use umbrella words** | **1 a) 1** e • **2** c • **3** f • **4** b • **5** a • **6** d

a) Match the food and drinks to the correct umbrella words.

1e, 2 …

1	~~watermelon~~	a	It's a kind of pasta.
2	chicken	b	It's a kind of Chinese food.
3	pepper	c	It's a kind of meat.
4	stir-fry	d	It's a kind of drink.
5	spaghetti	e	~~It's a kind of fruit.~~
6	milk	f	It's a kind of vegetable.

Chips are a kind of potato. Potatoes are a kind of vegetable. Vegetables are healthy. So chips are healthy, right?

b) Now describe these food and drinks with umbrella words.

1 ham   2 trifle   3 onion   4 water   5 lemon   6 noodles

1 b) Lösung S. 298

🖉 **2 Describe it** | **2** Lösungsbsp. S. 298

Describe the food and drinks. Think of colours and use words from the box.

watermelon: *It's green outside and red inside. It's big and sweet.*

1 cola   2 carrot   3 curry   4 sugar   5 tea   6 pea

big • cold • hot • long • small • spicy • sweet

🖉 **3 Add more information** | **3 1** spring and in summer • **2** vegetables and spices • **3** dessert

Complete the descriptions in 1–3.

1 **watermelon:** You eat it in summer.
  strawberries: You eat them in …
2 **spaghetti:** You make it with tomato sauce.
  curry: You make it with …
3 **stir-fry:** You eat it as a main dish.
  trifle: You eat it for …

I eat chips in the summer and in the winter. I eat chips with chips or sometimes with fish.

💬👥 **4 GAME Explain it!** | **4** individuelle Lösungen

Start in groups of three. Each student writes two words (food, drinks, dishes) on pieces of paper.
Swap words with another group, but don't show them.
In each group, a student takes a °piece of paper and explains the word.
The group has one minute to °guess it.

▶ Skills file 6, p. 181

Digital quiz **I can explain words.** ✓

Unit task Inhalt | Vorbereitung

Lernschwerpunkt: ein Klassenkochbuch erstellen
Kompetenzen: Writing ein Rezept schreiben, Feedback geben • Media skills im Internet recherchieren
Redemittel: Wortfelder *food, cooking things and activities* • Feedback geben

Material: Einstieg + Step 1 Rezepte von S. 151/163 (UMA) oder andere Rezepte (ggf. von S als HA mitbringen lassen) •
Step 2 + Step 3 ▶ KV 5.3: Make a class recipe book (nach Bedarf) •
Step 5 Blankozettel für das S-Feedback
Zeitbedarf: 2–3 Std.
Begleitmedien: App (Digital quiz), INKL (S. 157)

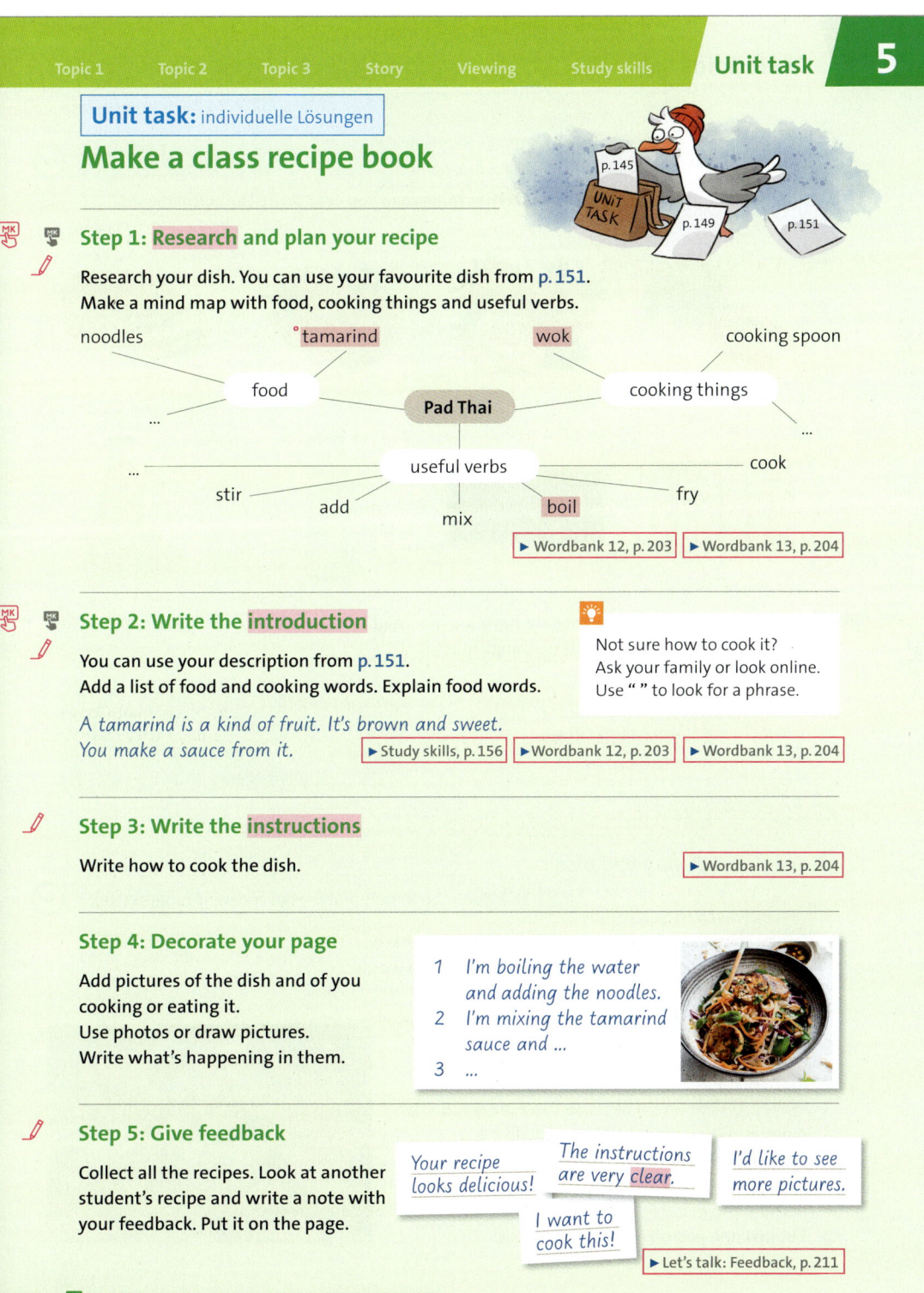

| Topic 1 | Topic 2 | Topic 3 | Story | Viewing | Study skills | | Unit task | 5 |

Unit task: individuelle Lösungen

Make a class recipe book

Step 1: Research and plan your recipe

Research your dish. You can use your favourite dish from **p. 151**.
Make a mind map with food, cooking things and useful verbs.

noodles — tamarind — wok — cooking spoon
food — Pad Thai — cooking things
... — ... — ...
... — useful verbs — cook
stir — add — mix — boil — fry

▶ Wordbank 12, p. 203   ▶ Wordbank 13, p. 204

Step 2: Write the introduction

You can use your description from **p. 151**.
Add a list of food and cooking words. Explain food words.

A tamarind is a kind of fruit. It's brown and sweet.
You make a sauce from it.

> Not sure how to cook it?
> Ask your family or look online.
> Use " " to look for a phrase.

▶ Study skills, p. 156   ▶ Wordbank 12, p. 203   ▶ Wordbank 13, p. 204

Step 3: Write the instructions

Write how to cook the dish.

▶ Wordbank 13, p. 204

Step 4: Decorate your page

Add pictures of the dish and of you cooking or eating it.
Use photos or draw pictures.
Write what's happening in them.

1 *I'm boiling the water and adding the noodles.*
2 *I'm mixing the tamarind sauce and ...*
3 *...*

Step 5: Give feedback

Collect all the recipes. Look at another student's recipe and write a note with your feedback. Put it on the page.

Your recipe looks delicious!
The instructions are very clear.
I'd like to see more pictures.
I want to cook this!

▶ Let's talk: Feedback, p. 211

Digital quiz   **I can research and write a recipe.** ✓

one hundred and fifty-seven **157**

Unit task Einstieg:
- (SB zu) L zeigt ein Rezept als Beispiel, s. S. 151 oder S. 163 (UMA).
- L nennt Ziel der *Unit task* und bespricht mit S die Schritte zum Erreichen dieses Ziels.

Step 1 Erarbeitung:
- (SB auf) S suchen im Internet ein Rezept für ihr Gericht (Tipp: gleiches Gericht wie in *My Task* S. 151), ggf. als vorbereitende HA.
- L erstellt Liste, wer welches Gericht vorstellt (u. achtet auf einfache Gerichte).
- S erstellen ihre ▶ Mindmap.
- **Ausw.:** S stellen in PA ihre Mind-maps vor und ergänzen sie.

Step 2 Erarbeitung:
- Klären der AA, ▶ Tippbox, S. 157
- S nutzen ihre Texte aus *My task* von S. 151 und ergänzen Erklärungen für unbekannte Wörter gemäß AA.
- ☑ S ergänzen den Lücken-text auf ▶ KV 5.3.

Step 3 Erarbeitung:
- TA mit ▶ Scaffolding: *First, ... / Then, ... / Next, ...*
- S beschreiben das Vorgehen.
- ☑ S nehmen ▶ KV 5.3 zur Hilfe.
- **Ausw.:** ▶ Partner check oder Überprüfung durch L

Step 4 Erarbeitung:
- gemäß AA als HA

Step 5 Erarbeitung:
- S geben im ▶ Gallery walk Feedback auf Zetteln.
- S überarbeiten ihr Rezept.
- L sammelt Rezepte als Buch.

Checkpoint Inhalt

Lernschwerpunkt: Kompetenzen und sprachliche Mittel üben, Lernfortschritte erkennen
Kompetenzen: Speaking sich über Essen und Getränke für einen Filmabend verständigen • Reading einem Text Informationen zu einer Geburtstagsparty entnehmen
Strukturen: *present progressive • much, many, a lot of*
Redemittel: *Wortfeld food and drinks • party words*

Allgemeine Anmerkung:
s. Unit 1, S. 36

Ex 1 Einstieg:
- (SB auf) Selbsteinschätzung zum Lernziel *I can talk about food*, ▸ Thumbs up

Erarbeitung:
a) gemäß AA
- **Ausw.:** ▸ Bus stop (▸ KV Extra): S vergleichen ihre Lösungen mithilfe von ▸ KV 5.4 A.
- **Alternative:** ▸ Partner check

b) S entscheiden im ▸ Partner talk, was sie kaufen, und notieren in ganzen Sätzen.
- **Ausw.:** S stellen ihre Wahl kurz im Plenum vor.
- erneute Selbsteinschätzung

Ex 2 Einstieg:
- (SB auf) Freiwillige/r S liest das angegebene Lernziel vor.
- s. Ex 1 (Selbsteinschätzung)

Erarbeitung:
- S schreiben die ergänzten Sätze ins Heft.
- **Ausw.:** ▸ Five-minute teacher
- **Alternative:** L stellt S ▸ KV 5.4 A zur Verfügung. S überprüfen sich selbst oder gegenseitig im ▸ Partner check (ggf. ▸ Bus stop und ▸ KV Extra)
- nach der Lösungskontrolle erneute Einschätzung des Könnens (gleiche Methode wie im **Einstieg**)
- ▸ Early finisher schreiben zwei wahre und drei falsche Sätze zum Bild (▸ Three truths, two lies). Zwei der Sätze sollten verneint sein.
- S stellen ihre Sätze vor. Klasse reagiert mit ▸ Right/wrong cards.

158

---

5 | **Checkpoint** | Digital checkpoint

🖉 **1 A film night**

> **1 a) 1** carrots • **2** strawberries •
> **3** tomatoes • **4** bread • **5** sausages •
> **6** chocolate • **7** milk • **8** lemonade

I can **talk about food.** ✓

a) WORDS Look at the food and drinks. What things can you see? Write the correct word.

b) SPEAKING You and your partner are having a film °night. You talk about what you want to buy for food and drinks. Choose three things from a).

> Let's buy some ... / I want to buy ...
> I love ... / I often eat/drink ...
> Do you like ...?

> Yes, that's a good idea. /
> No, I don't want to buy ..., but let's buy ...
> I don't like ... / I never eat/drink ... /
> I'm allergic to ...

1 b) Lösungsbsp. S. 298

📖 **2** LANGUAGE **A very bad picnic**

> **2 1** wearing • **2** decorating • **3** sitting • **4** barking •
> **5** texting • **6** eating • **7** playing • **8** listening

I can **talk about birthdays and parties (present progressive).** ✓

Sunita shows her friends a photo of a bad family party. Complete her sentences with the *-ing* form of the words in the box.

> bark • decorate • eat • listen •
> play • sit • text • wear

1 Willow's birthday is in August, so we're ... T-shirts, but it's cold and rainy.
2 Mum is ... a tree, but it's very windy.
3 We're ... on the °grass because there are no chairs.
4 A dog is ... because it wants our food.
5 Nish is on his phone. He's ... his friends.
6 A seagull is ... my sandwich.
7 Ben is ... the guitar.
8 But just one person is ... to Ben's music!

Check

Checkpoint Vorbereitung

Material: alle Aufgaben ▶ KV 5.4 A: Checkpoint answers, bei Bedarf ▶ KV Extra: Bus stop • Ex 2 Right/wrong cards (Klassensatz) • Ex 3 UMA/App (Erklärfilm von S. 147) • Ex 4 ggf. digitale Endgeräte für Internetrecherche (Websites mit Informationen zu Geburtstagsfeiern)
Zeitbedarf: ca. 1 Std.
Minimalversion: Auswahl der Aufgaben erfolgt entprechend der zu überprüfenden Lernziele
Begleitmedien: App (Digital checkpoint, Erklärfilm von S. 147), INKL (S. 158–159)

Die Übungen kannst du auch digital machen 🔽   5

3 LANGUAGE After the party

3 a) 1 much • 2 many • 3 much • 4 many • 5 many

✅ **I can** talk about party food and activities *(much, many, a lot of)*.

a) Complete the questions with *much* or *many*.

1 How … lemonade is there?
2 How … sandwiches are there?
3 How … salad is there?
4 How … sausages are there?
5 How … carrots are there?

b) Look at the picture. Answer the questions from a). Use *much, many* or *a lot of*.

1 There isn't … lemonade.
2 There aren't …
3 There's a …
4 There are …
5 There aren't …

3 b) 1 much • 2 many sandwiches. • 3 lot of salad. • 4 many sausages. • 5 many carrots.

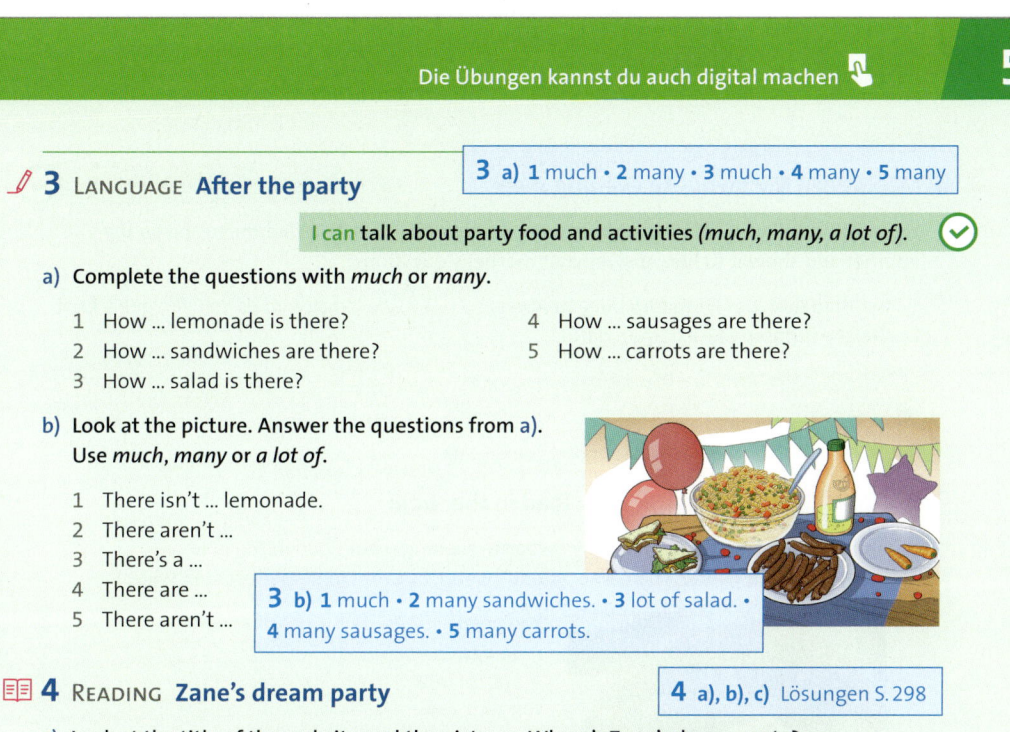

📖 4 READING Zane's dream party

4 a), b), c) Lösungen S. 298

a) Look at the title of the website and the pictures. Where's Zane's dream party?

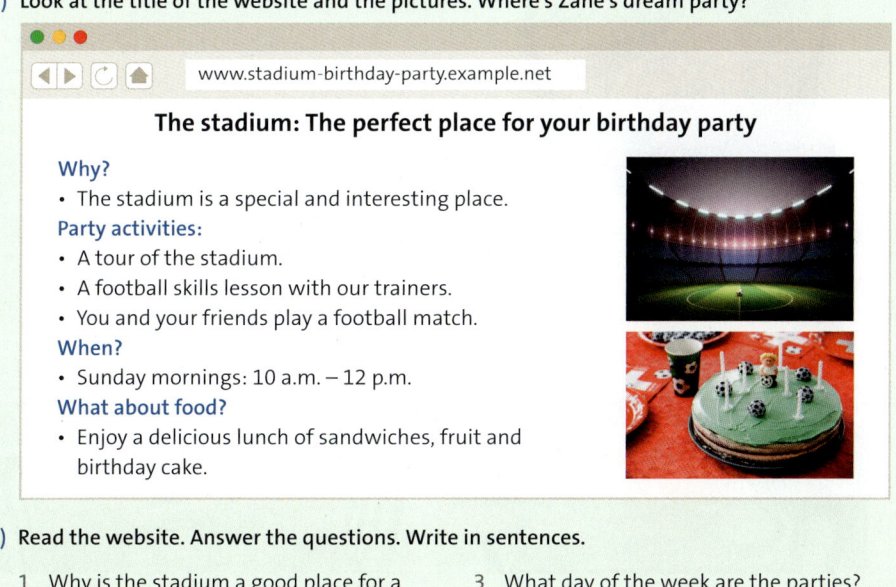

www.stadium-birthday-party.example.net

The stadium: The perfect place for your birthday party

Why?
• The stadium is a special and interesting place.
Party activities:
• A tour of the stadium.
• A football skills lesson with our trainers.
• You and your friends play a football match.
When?
• Sunday mornings: 10 a.m. – 12 p.m.
What about food?
• Enjoy a delicious lunch of sandwiches, fruit and birthday cake.

b) Read the website. Answer the questions. Write in sentences.

1 Why is the stadium a good place for a party?
2 What activities are there?
3 What day of the week are the parties?
4 How long are the parties?
5 What food is there?

c) Where's your dream party? Why? You can use the ideas in the box.

home • ice rink • museum • park • skatepark • stadium • zoo

Check

one hundred and fifty-nine **159**

Ex 3 Einstieg:
• (SB auf) s. Ex 1 (Selbsteinschätzung)
• ▶ Sollten sich die S hier schon als schwach einschätzen, sehen sie sich vorab den Erklärfilm von S. 147 noch einmal an.

Erarbeitung:
a) gemäß AA
• S schreiben die Fragen in ihr Heft und lassen jeweils Platz für die Antwort.

b) gemäß AA
• S schreiben die Antworten neben die passenden Fragen.
• **Ausw.:** ▶ Bus stop (Einsatz ▶ KV Extra): S vergleichen ihre Lösungen mithilfe von ▶ KV 5.4 A.
• **Alternative:** ▶ Five-minute teacher

Ex 4 Einstieg:
• (SB auf) s. Ex 1 (Selbsteinschätzung)

Erarbeitung:
a) gemäß AA in EA
• **Ausw.:** S beantworten Frage im Plenum.

b) 1. Lesen: gemäß AA
• S notieren Antworten in ganzen Sätzen.
• ▶ Partner check
• 2. Lesen: S berichtigen ihre Fehler.
• **Ausw.:** S erhalten ▶ KV 5.4 A und überprüfen ihr Ergebnis.

c) S schreiben einen Text wie in a) über ihre *dream party*.
• ▶ S können auf Websites lokaler Attraktionen (Zoo, Kartbahn, …) nach Infos für eine Geburtstagsparty suchen (ggf. auf Deutsch) und sie vorstellen.

Checkpoint Inhalt

Lernschwerpunkt: Kompetenzen und sprachliche Mittel üben, Lernfortschritte erkennen
Kompetenzen: Mediation Fragen zu einem Rezept beantworten • Listening einem Hörtext Informationen zu einem Abendessen entnehmen • Writing einen Blogeintrag mit einem Rezept verfassen • Study skills Wörter erklären
Redemittel: Wortfelder *food, cooking and baking*

Ex 5 Einstieg:
- (SB auf) Selbsteinschätzung zum Lernziel, ▸ Thumbs up

Erarbeitung:
- S lesen AA.
- **1. Lesen:** S lesen Text in EA und schlagen selbstständig unbekannte Wörter im *Dictionary* (S. 255–266) nach.
- **2. Lesen:** S schreiben die Antworten auf die Fragen in ihr Heft.
- **Ausw.:** Vorstellung im Plenum
- erneute Selbsteinschätzung mit ▸ Thumbs up

Ex 6 Einstieg:
- (SB auf) Selbsteinschätzung zum Lernziel, ▸ Thumbs up
- S beschreiben in PA die Bilder, ▸ Scaffolding: *In picture A/B there's / there are ...*
  S: *In picture A there are three chairs. There's a table.*

Erarbeitung:
a) 1. Hören: gemäß AA
- **Ausw.:** S halten etwas Grünes für Bild A oder etwas Rotes für Bild B hoch (z. B. Farbstifte).
- S begründen ihre Entscheidung.
- 🖵 Falls nötig, wird der Hörtext erneut gehört.

b) 2. Hören: gemäß AA
- 🖵 Ggf. ist für diese Aufgabe ein **3. Hören** erforderlich.
- **Ausw.:** ▸ Bus stop (Einsatz ▸ KV Extra): S vergleichen ihre Lösungen mithilfe von ▸ KV 5.4B.
- **Alternative:** ▸ Five-minute teacher

→ **5** MEDIATION **My favourite evening meal** | I can **describe my favourite dish.** ✓ |

You want to tell your °mother about your new favourite dish. You find the recipe on the internet and show it to her. Answer your mother's questions:

1 Isst man das zum Frühstück oder zu Abend?   3 Wie lange wird es im Ofen gebacken?
2 Welche Zutaten braucht man dafür?

| **5** Lösungsbsp. S. 298 |

www.delicious-dinners.example.net

°Toad in the °hole

Today I want to tell you about my favourite evening meal: Toad in the hole.
I often eat it in winter. The name °sounds weird, but the °ingredients aren't weird!

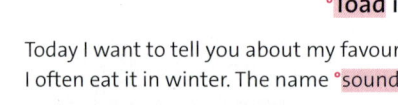

You need:
- 3 eggs
- 300 ml milk
- 8 sausages
- 175 g flour
- oil

How to make it:
1 Mix the eggs, milk and flour.
2 Cook the sausages in oil °until they are brown.
3 Add the mixture to the sausages.
4 Cook in the oven for 30 minutes.

🔊 2.45 🎧 **6** LISTENING **Dinner at Sunita's house** | I can **understand and talk about differences.** ✓ |

a) Zane is at Sunita's house. Listen. Which picture is Sunita's dining room?

| **6 a)** B |

George

b) Listen again. Write 'Zane's family' or 'Sunita's family'.

1 ... eats dinner in a big dining room.   4 ... doesn't eat meat.
2 ... has a small dining room.   5 ... has no animals.
3 ... eats dinner in the living room.

6 b) 1 Sunita's family • **2** Zane's family • **3** Zane's family • **4** Sunita's family • **5** Zane's family

Check ↴

Checkpoint Vorbereitung

Material: alle Aufgaben ▶ KV 5.4 B: Checkpoint answers, bei Bedarf ▶ KV Extra: Bus stop • Ex 6 UMA/CD • Ex 8 digitale Endgeräte für die Arbeit im Internet (dort gibt es Tools mit Blankoseiten für anonyme Blogeinträge)
Zeitbedarf: ca. 1 Std.
Minimalversion: Auswahl der Aufgaben erfolgt entprechend der zu überprüfenden Lernziele
Begleitmedien: App (Digital checkpoint, ggf. Erklärfilme zur Wiederholung), INKL (S. 159)

Die Übungen kannst du auch digital machen 👆   5

📖 **7** STUDY SKILLS **Explaining new words**   I can **explain words.** ✅

a) Daniel is explaining some new words, but there are some °mistakes. Find the mistake in each sentence.

1 carrot: It's a kind of fruit.
2 chicken: It's a kind of cake.
3 dessert: It's the meal before dinner.
4 milk: It's a kind of food.

5 °cornflakes: You eat them with a knife.
6 tea: It's a cold drink.
7 shopping list: You need it at school.
8 vegetables: They're bad for you.

b) Write the correct sentences (1–8).

1 carrot: It's a kind of ...

> **7 a)** Lösung S. 298
> **7 b)** Lösung S. 299

✏️ **8** WRITING **A banana and chocolate °crepe**   I can **research and write a recipe.** ✅

Luisa wants to write a °blog post about her favourite dessert recipe: a banana and chocolate crepe. Look at the pictures and read her notes. Then write her post. Use the sentence starters to help you.

> **8** Lösungsbsp. S. 299

> I want to tell you about ... • You make it with ... • You also need ... •
> First ... • Then ... • After two minutes ... • °Finally ...

125 g flour, 2 eggs, 360 ml milk, 1 tablespoon sugar, chocolate sauce, a banana

need • cooking spoon, °frying pan

mix • flour, eggs, milk and sugar

fry • for two minutes

turn over • fry other °side

put on • °plate • add • chocolate and banana

Check 👆

one hundred and sixty-one   **161**

Ex 7 Einstieg:
• (SB auf) Selbsteinschätzung zum Lernziel, ▶ Thumbs up

Erarbeitung:
a) gemäß AA

b) gemäß AA
• **Ausw.:** ▶ Bus stop (▶ KV Extra): S vergleichen ihre Lösungen mithilfe von ▶ KV 5.4 B.

Ex 8 Einstieg:
• (SB auf) Selbsteinschätzung zum Lernziel, ▶ Thumbs up

Erarbeitung:
• S lesen AA und Kasten mit den Satzanfängen.
• S ordnen die Satzanfänge den Bildern zu.
• Hinweis: Bild 1 hat zwei Satzanfänge (s. Lösungsbsp. S. 299).
• ▶ Partner check: Partner/innen überprüfen, ob sie die Satzanfänge denselben Bildern zugeordnet haben.
• S schreiben ihren Blogbeitrag in EA ins Heft.
• **Ausw.:** ▶ Bus stop (Einsatz ▶ KV Extra): S vergleichen ihre Lösungen mithilfe von ▶ KV 5.4 B.
• **Alternative:** S schreiben und gestalten ihren Blogbeitrag auf einer Blankoseite im Internet.
• Klasse gibt Feedback (▶ Let's talk: Feedback, S. 211)
• erneute Selbsteinschätzung

• **Zusatz:** Auswertung, wie gut sich S bei den Aufgaben dieser Doppelseite selbst eingeschätzt haben, mit ▶ Thumbs up: Stimmen die Einschätzungen vor und nach der Aufgabe überein?

Lernschwerpunkt: Texte im *school magazine* zum Thema Essen lesen
Kompetenzen: Reading einem Text Informationen zum Essen in der Schule entnehmen • ein Rezept lesen und verstehen •
Sprechen Zungenbrecher schnell und richtig nachsprechen
Redemittel: Wortfelder *food, cooking and baking*

Allgemeine Anmerkung:
s. Unit 1, S. 40

Varndean food **Einstieg:**
- (SB zu) TA: *food in school*
- S sammeln Ideen in einer ►Mindmap, was sie in der Schule wo essen.

Erarbeitung:
- (SB auf) S lesen den Text.
- S beantworten die Fragen mündlich oder schriftlich.
- S können einen ähnlichen Text als Artikel für ihre Schülerzeitung verfassen (die zwei besten Beiträge könnten eingereicht werden).

Kian's tongue twisters
Erarbeitung:
- (SB auf) S hören die Zungenbrecher und sprechen sie nach.
- Wettbewerb gemäß AA
- **Zusatz:** S können weitere Zungenbrecher im Internet recherchieren und vortragen.

5

OPTIONAL

Text file

VARNDEAN
Teen Zine

This month's topics: food and parties

Our school magazine: by students for students

Varndean food by Otis
I eat breakfast at school and get a hot lunch every day in the canteen. I'm a vegan so it's great that there is always a vegan menu. In the breaks I get snacks like fruit.

Monday	Tuesday	Wednesday	Thursday	Friday
Sausages / Vegan sausages with potatoes and green vegetables	Beef[1] and vegetable lasagne / Vegan lasagne and garlic[2] bread	Burgers / Vegan burgers with salad	Chicken and pepper burritos / Bean[3] and pepper burritos with brown rice	Fish / Vegan nuggets with chips, baked beans and ketchup

What do you think of our school food?
If you're at a different school: Tell us about your school food. What's on your menu this week?
What can you buy in breaks? What would you like to change[4]?

Kian's tongue twisters

2.46

Listen to my tongue twisters[5]. How fast can you say them? You can have a class competition!

I scream, you scream, we all scream for ice cream!

How many cookies could[6] a good cook cook if a good cook could cook cookies?

Fresh fried fish, fish fresh fried, fried fish fresh, fish fried fresh.

---

[1] **beef** *Rindfleisch* [2] **garlic** *Knoblauch* [3] **bean** *Bohne* [4] **change** *ändern, verändern* [5] **tongue twister** *Zungenbrecher*
[6] **he/she could** *er/sie könnte*

162   one hundred and sixty-two

Text file Vorbereitung

Material: Realien (Zutaten für die Blaubeer-Muffins)
Zeitbedarf: abhängig davon, welche Texte bearbeitet werden; ca. 1 Std. pro Seite
Minimalversion: alle Texte sind optionale Zusatztexte

Baking with Betty

Hi, guys! Today we're making blueberry muffins. Perfect for parties!

You need:

260 g flour	1 egg
2 teaspoons baking powder	150 g sugar
	100 ml sunflower[1] oil
2 teaspoons vanilla sugar	300 ml buttermilk
	250 g blueberries

1 I'm mixing the flour, the baking powder and the vanilla sugar in a bowl[2].

2 In another bowl, I'm mixing the buttermilk, the oil, the egg and the sugar.

3 I'm adding the buttermilk mixture to the flour mixture and mixing everything[3].

4 Now I'm washing the blueberries[4] and I'm adding them to the bowl.

5 I'm making twelve muffins and I'm putting the muffins in the oven.

6 Bake at 180°C for 20–25 minutes. Well done! Twelve blueberry muffins.

---

[1] **sunflower** *Sonnenblume*   [2] **bowl** *Schüssel*   [3] **everything** *alles*   [4] **blueberry** *Blaubeere*

Baking with Betty Erarbeitung:

- Hinweis: Das Rezept kann als Bsp. für das *Unit task* (S. 157) verwendet werden.
- (SB auf) S betrachten Bilder (ohne Lesen).
  L: *What is Betty making?*
  S: *She's making blueberry muffins.*
- **1. Lesen:** S lesen den Text und schreiben ▶ Three truths, two lies zum Rezept, z. B. *In 2 you mix the flour, the baking powder and the buttermilk.*
- **Ausw.:** GA in Vierergruppen: S lesen ihre Sätze vor, die anderen berichtigen die falschen Aussagen.
- Im Plenum: L bespricht mit S das Rezept im Detail. Es besteht aus drei Teilen:
  1) Einleitung: *What do you make?*
  2) Zutaten: *What do you need?* (Jede Zutat wird einzeln genannt. Dazu wird gesagt, wie viel man von der Zutat braucht.)
  3) Zubereitung: *How to make it.* (Zu jedem Schritt gibt es ein Foto.)

Alternative:

- (SB zu) L zeigt Zutatenliste über UMA und Realien der Zutaten. S ordnen die Wörter den Gegenständen zu.
- L zeigt Bilder aus dem UMA und die Texte in anderer Reihenfolge. S lesen die Texte und ordnen sie den Bildern zu.
- Tipp: Wenn möglich Rezept mit der Klasse nachbacken.

Lernschwerpunkt: zusätzliche Übungen, Differenzierungs- und Hilfsangebote

Kompetenzen: Speaking beschreiben, was gerade in einem Bild geschieht • sich über Geburtstage austauschen •
Reading einen Text in die richtige Reihenfolge bringen

Strukturen: *present progressive*

Redemittel: Wortfeld *food* • *birthday parties*

Ex 10 Einstieg: s. S. 145

Erarbeitung:

- *Partner A* verwendet das Bild von S. 145, *Partner B* das Bild von S. 164.
- PA gemäß AA
- ☑ Lernschwächere S markieren sich die Unterschiede, indem sie eine Münze, ein Radiergummi oder Ähnliches an die entsprechende Stelle legen.
- ☑ TA/Wortkarten mit den benötigten Verben:
  sing – sleep – play – read – eat – talk – look at – take pictures – draw
- **Ausw.:** s. S. 145

Ex 11 Erarbeitung:

- Diese Fotos sind für S gedacht, die keine eigenen Fotos für die *My task* von S. 145 mitgebracht haben.
- S beschreiben die Fotos mit dem *present progressive*.
- ☑ L stellt folgendes ▸Scaffolding zur Verfügung:
  The boy / the girl / the children / the man / the woman …
  is / are …
  smile / wear / play / look at / stand behind / sit / hold / dance
- Bilder können außerdem für ein *Warm-up* genutzt werden. S können ▸three truths, two lies zu den Bildern erstellen und sie dann im Plenum vortragen.

---

5 | **Partner page**

Partner page

▶Page 145

💬 **10** SPEAKING **Find the differences**

10 Lösungsbsp. S. 296

Partner B: Look at this picture.
Take turns and find six differences:

> *In my picture the boy and girl in blue T-shirts are singing karaoke.*

> *In my picture they are/aren't …*
> *In my picture a dog is …*

▶Page 145

💬 **11** MY TASK **My party photos**

11 Lösungsbsp. S. 296

Diff bank Vorbereitung

Material: MP 1 ggf. geeignetes digitales Gerät zum Präsentieren • MP 2 ▶ KV Extra: Bus stop
Zeitbedarf: abhängig davon, welche Aufgaben bearbeitet werden
Minimalversion: *More practice*-und *Challenge*-Aufgaben sind stets Zusatzaufgaben
Begleitmedien: INKL (S. 160–161)

Diff bank | 5

Diff bank

▶Page 140

✏ **More practice 1** **Food words** | **1** individuelle Lösungen

Start a new page in your VOCAB FILE. Make lists or a mind map for food words.
You can draw pictures and add words in other languages.

▶Page 142

💬 **More help** **1** READING **Noah's invitation** | **1** individuelle Lösungen

👥 a) What do you usually do on your birthday? Tell a partner.

| We usually / never eat | burgers
°ice cream
fruit
°kebabs
°pizza
sandwiches | We often | go swimming.
go to the cinema / watch a film at home.
play party games.
sing 'Happy Birthday' / sing °karaoke.
take photos. |

📖 **More practice 2** **Thanks for the invitation!**

2 Sunita e – b – (f – d / d – f) – a – c •
Ryan d – f – c – a – e – b

Sunita and Ryan write messages to Noah. Put their messages in the correct order.

Sunita

a *Bye – see you in the park on Saturday!*

b *I'd love to come to your party – thanks!*

c *Love Sunita xox*

d *I love picnics!*

e *Hello, Noah*

f *A circus °theme is a great idea.*

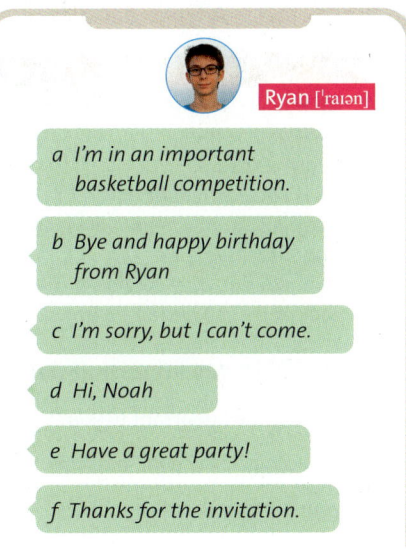

Ryan [ˈraɪən]

a *I'm in an important basketball competition.*

b *Bye and happy birthday from Ryan*

c *I'm sorry, but I can't come.*

d *Hi, Noah*

e *Have a great party!*

f *Thanks for the invitation.*

one hundred and sixty-five **165**

MP 1 Erarbeitung:
- S nutzen die Mindmap aus dem **Einstieg** in die Unit und ergänzen sie (▶ SF 2, S.174–175)
- Sinnvolle *umbrella words: vegetables, fruit, cooked food, breakfast, ...*
- Hier können noch einmal Lernstrategien für neue Vokabeln thematisiert werden.
- **Ausw.:** S präsentieren ihre Mindmap (ggf. über Tablet oder Dokumentenkamera)

MH 1 Erarbeitung: s. S.142
a) Diese Hilfe ist für Lernende geeignet, die viel Unterstützung benötigen. Partner unterschiedlicher Niveaus können zusammenarbeiten. S nutzen ihr Buch während der PA für das ▶ Scaffolding.
- **Ausw.:** s. S.142

MP 2 Erarbeitung:
- S lesen die Textschnipsel und notieren die Buchstaben in der richtigen Reihenfolge.
- **Ausw.:** S finden einen Partner / eine Partnerin über den ▶ Bus stop (▶ KV Extra), ▶ Partner check.
- **Alternative:** S lesen den Text in der richtigen Reihenfolge vor der Klasse vor.

Diff bank **Inhalt**

Lernschwerpunkt: zusätzliche Übungen, Differenzierungs- und Hilfsangebote
Kompetenzen: Reading einer Einladung Informationen entnehmen • Writing eine Antwort auf eine Geburtstagseinladung schreiben • Speaking sich über Kalendertage austauschen
Strukturen: *present progressive*
Redemittel: Wortfelder *months, dates, ordinal numbers*

Challenge 1
• Diese Aufgabe ist besonders für kreative S geeignet.
• Wenn möglich sollte vor Bearbeitung der Aufgabe die Struktur einer Nachricht anhand von MP 2, S. 165 besprochen werden (Fokus auf Begrüßung und Schluss).

Erarbeitung:
• (SB auf) S verfassen ihre eigene Nachricht gemäß AA.
• **Ausw.:** S präsentieren ihren Text im Plenum.

MP 3 Erarbeitung:
a) (SB auf) gemäß AA
• 🗹 S üben das Vortragen des Gedichts.
• **Ausw.:** S präsentieren das Gedicht im Plenum.

b) gemäß AA. S schreiben Frage und Antwort ins Heft.
• **Ausw.:** ▶ Five-minute teacher

MP 4 Erarbeitung:
• (SB auf) S arbeiten in PA gemäß AA.
• ▶ Early finisher bilden zwei bis drei eigene Sätze und notieren sie im Heft.
• **Ausw.:** ▶ Meldekette, ggf. ergänzt mit Fragen der *Early finishers*.

MP 5 Erarbeitung:
a) (SB auf) S sammeln Daten gemäß AA.

b) S tauschen sich über ihre Daten im ▶ Milling around aus.
• L weist auf korrekte Aussprache hin.

---

5 | Diff bank

✏️ **Challenge 1 Ella's party**

Ch 1 individuelle Lösungen

You get this invitation. Write a message to Ella. The messages in More practice 2 on p. 165 can help you. Say *yes* (like Sunita) or *no* (like Ryan).

When?	On Sunday 2nd June
What time?	From 1 p.m. to 4 p.m.
Where?	At Ella's house, 135 Preston Road, Brighton
What?	It's a °cupcake party! We can make a lot of different cupcakes. (But there's other food too!)

Please send me a message if you can come or not.

👂 **More practice 3 A °poem about the months of the year**

🔊 2.32 **a)** Listen to and read the poem. Then say it.

💬 **b)** Answer the questions.
1 Which months have 30 days?
2 Which months have 31 days?
3 Which month has 28 or 29 days?

▶ **Page 143**

3 b) 1 April, June, September, November • **2** January, March, May, July, August, October, December • **3** February

> Thirty days have September,
> April, June and November.
> All the rest have 31.
> February's great with 28
> And a °leap year's fine with 29!

👥 **More practice 4 A °calendar quiz**

4 1 Thursday • **2** the 10th July • **3** Thursday, the 31st July • **4** the 19th July • Tuesday, the 1st July

💬 Look at the calendar for July. Take turns to ask and answer the questions.
1 What day of the week is 3rd July? – *It's ...*
2 What date is the second Thursday in July? – *It's ...*
3 What date is the °last day in July? – *It's ...*
4 Today is 13th July. What date is the next Saturday? – *It's ...*
5 What day and date is Ezra's birthday? (Look at the red circle.) – *It's on ...*

JULY						
Mon	Tue	Wed	Thur	Fri	Sat	Sun
	①	2	3	4	5	6
7	8	9	10	11	12	13
14	15	16	17	18	19	20
21	22	23	24	25	26	27
28	29	30	31			

More practice 5 My important dates

5 individuelle Lösungen

✏️ **a)** What dates are important to you? Write five dates in your exercise book.

💬 *13th December: my dog's birthday*

👥 **b)** Tell your partner about your dates.

> *My dog's birthday is on the 13th of December.*

Diff bank Vorbereitung

Material: MP 3 UMA/CD • MP 6 ggf. Wortkarten • MP 7 UMA/CD
Zeitbedarf: abhängig davon, welche Aufgaben bearbeitet werden
Minimalversion: *More practice-* und *Challenge*-Aufgaben sind stets Zusatzaufgaben
Begleitmedien: INKL (S. 162–163)

5

▶ Page 145

> **3** **1** eating • **2** listening • **3** wearing • **4** sitting •
> **5** taking • **6** playing • **7** drawing • **8** lying

Parallel exercise **9** **A birthday photo**

Zane is showing a photo of his friend's birthday party to his mum. Complete his sentences with the *-ing* form.

1 I'm (eat) *eating* birthday cake.
2 Sunita and Ruby are (listen) … to music.
3 Ju is (wear) … a gold hat.
4 Noah is (sit) … on a chair with a cat.
5 He's (take) … photos with his phone.
6 Max and Albie have balloons. They're (play) … with them.
7 Lily is at the table. She's (draw) … a picture.
8 Amina and Vicky are (lie) … on the floor.

> The spelling of some verbs with *-ing* is different:
> sit – si**tt**ing
> tak**e** – taking
> lie – l**y**ing

More practice 6 **What are they doing?**

> **6 a), b)** Lösungsbsp. S. 299

a) Look at the pictures. What are people doing in different places? Write sentences.

A girl/boy is …   A girl and her dad are …

Mexico City, 6 a.m.

New York, 7 a.m.

London, 12 o'clock

Berlin, 1 p.m.

Tokyo, 8 p.m.

Sydney, 9 p.m.

b) Write what you're doing now. Write what people in your family are doing now.

I'm sitting in the classroom. I'm …   My little brother is playing at home. …

> **7** Lösungsbsp. S. 299

More practice 7 **What's happening?**

Listen to the °sounds. What's happening? Write a sentence. Choose words from the box.

> box • close • cook • dance • drink • eat • play • send • skateboard • swim

---

Parallel ex 9 s. S. 145
• Diese Übung, in der die einzusetzenden Verben bereits zugeordnet sind, ist für lernschwächere S geeignet, die beim verstehenden Lesen Probleme haben.

Erarbeitung:
• (SB auf) gemeinsames Lesen der ▶ Tippbox, S. 167.
• S schreiben die Sätze in ihr Heft und ergänzen die *ing*-Form.
• ▶ Partner check
• Ausw.: ▶ Five-minute teacher

MP 6 Erarbeitung:
a) (SB auf) Die S schreiben zu den Bildern passende Sätze in ihr Heft.
• Für lernschwächere S werden die benötigten Verben als Wortkarten vorgegeben: *wake up – ride a bike – eat – sleep – lie in bed – cook*
• Ausw.: ▶ Five-minute teacher

b) S schreiben Sätze darüber, was sie und ihre Familie gerade tun.
• Ausw.: S präsentieren ihre Sätze im ▶ Milling around und machen dabei eine zum Satz passende Bewegung, ▶ Partner check.

MP 7 Erarbeitung:
• (SB auf) **1. Hören:** S schreiben zu den Geräuschen passende Sätze im *present progressive*.
• **2. Hören / Ausw.:** L hält Aufnahme nach jedem Satz an. S prüfen ihre Sätze und korrigieren wenn nötig.
• S sagen ihre Sätze.

Inhalt

Lernschwerpunkt: zusätzliche Übungen, Differenzierungs- und Hilfsangebote
Kompetenzen: Speaking sich für ein Geschenk bedanken • beschreiben, was gerade in einem Bild geschieht •
Writing einen Blogeintrag über das eigene Leibgericht schreiben
Strukturen: *much, many • present progressive*
Redemittel: Wortfelder *food, cooking and baking*

Challenge 2

• Diese Aufgabe ist für lernstärkere S gedacht.

Erarbeitung:

• (SB auf) S bilden die *present progressive*-Formen und schreiben den vollständigen Text in ihr Heft.
• S vergleichen ihre Lösungen mit einem Partner / einer Partnerin am ▶ Bus stop (▶ KV Extra).
• **Ausw.:** Partner/innen präsentieren ihren Dialog in verteilten Rollen vor der Klasse.

MH 11 Erarbeitung: s. S. 145

• (SB auf) S nutzen die Hilfe, um zu beschreiben, was sie und andere auf ihren Bildern tun. Die Hilfe sollte vor der Bearbeitung der Aufgabe schon einmal gelesen werden.

MH 2 s. S. 146

• Diese Aufgabe bietet Unterstützung für lernschwächere S.

Erarbeitung:

• (SB auf) S nutzen das ▶ Scaffolding zur Bildung entsprechender Sätze.

MP 8 s. S. 147

• Diese Aufgabe bietet eine zusätzliche Übungsmöglichkeit zur Struktur *much/many*.
• Die Aufgabe ist auch für ▶ Early finisher geeignet.

Erarbeitung:

• (SB auf) Klären der AA, S notieren vollständige Sätze in ihr Heft.
• **Ausw.:** ▶ Five-minute teacher

---

5 **Diff bank**

🖉 **A hot day in Brighton**

Ch 2 Lösung S. 299

Write the °conversation.

Scout	Hi, George. (1) What / you / do?
George	(2) I / rest. (3) I / not / feel / good. The sun is too hot and (4) my head / °burn.
Scout	Yes, it's hot. But we're lucky – (5) it / rain / not / now!
George	Yes, you're right. (6) You / wear / a nice hat, Scout.
Scout	Thanks. (7) It / °keep / me °cool. (8) You / not / wear a hat. You need a hat, George!

Scout   George

💬 **11** MY TASK **My party photos**

11 individuelle Lösungen

This is my birthday party.
This is my dad's / grandma's / little sister's / … party.
I'm with my mum and dad / my friends / …

I'm / We're wearing	a party hat / funny °glasses / new clothes / a blue °dress / new trainers / …
I'm / We're eating	birthday cake / cupcakes / pizza / …
I'm / We're playing	a party game / in the garden / with balloons / …

▶ Page 146

💬 **2** SPEAKING **Find a present**

2 individuelle Lösungen

c)
Thanks for the …	It's a great present.	I love …
Thanks, guys!	It's perfect!	I'm learning to …
Thanks very much.	I love it!	It's on my birthday list.
	°Wow!	… is my favourite sport / free time activity / game.

▶ Page 147

📖 **Zane wants to cook**

8 **1** many • **2** much • **3** many • **4** much • **5** much

Complete Zane's questions with *much* or *many*. What dish is he °thinking about?

Zane

How (1) … tomatoes do we need?
And how (2) … meat?
And how (3) … carrots?
How (4) … water do I need for the pasta?
And how (5) … pasta do we need?

(Spaghetti bolognese)

Diff bank Vorbereitung

Material: Challenge 2 ▶ KV Extra: Bus stop • Ex 7 UMA/CD • MP 9 geeignete Requisiten bei Bedarf
Zeitbedarf: abhängig davon, welche Aufgaben bearbeitet werden
Minimalversion: *More practice-* und *Challenge*-Aufgaben sind stets Zusatzaufgaben
Begleitmedien: INKL (S. 164)

▶Page 148

7 SONG The shopping song

I'm going to the supermarket today
Where's my shopping list? I'm on my way.
I have my bags and my money 'cause I
Have a lot of food I need to buy:

Cheese and peas and °aubergines,
°Avocados and tomatoes and °baked beans,
Meat and sweets and °nectarines,
Lemons, melons, ham and °jam and °lamb.
And ...

I'm going to the supermarket today ...

▶Page 151

More help	4 MY TASK My favourite dish		4 individuelle Lösungen

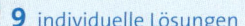

My favourite dish is It's	a dessert / a main course / a cake / a drink / ... cold / delicious / hot / spicy / sweet / ...
It comes from	my dad's / mum's / family's culture °China / Germany / India / °Poland / °Turkey / °South Africa / ...
You make it with	cheese / chocolate / meat / onions / pasta / rice / sugar / tomatoes / ...
I eat / cook it My family eats it My dad / mum cooks it	every day / every week / every Friday / at parties / ...

▶Page 154   9 individuelle Lösungen

| More practice 9 | And this time ... |

a) Choose a °scene from the story and °mime it.

b) One student says a sentence and the group mimes the new scene.

And this time ... Buddy is juggling.

Noah Lily Sunita Zane Noah's mum / dad Buddy	is/are	dancing. eating the cake. juggling. smiling. opening a present. waving.

Ex 7 Erarbeitung:
• Aufgaben zu diesem Lied auf S. 148.
• Mit diesem Text können die S mitsingen.

MH 4 s. S. 151
• Diese Aufgabe bietet sprachliche Mittel für Lernschwächere.

Erarbeitung:
• (SB auf) S nutzen das ▶ Scaffolding für ihren Blogeintrag.

MP 9 s. S. 154
• Diese Übung eignet sich besonders für Klassen mit vielen lernschwächeren S.

Erarbeitung:
a) (SB auf) S wählen selbst, ob sie in der Gruppe oder allein arbeiten wollen.
• S suchen sich eine Szene aus der Geschichte aus und spielen sie pantomimisch vor.
• Tipp: Die Verwendung von Requisiten hilft vielen S, in ihre Rolle zu schlüpfen.
• **Ausw.:** Klasse rät, wer was darstellt und was passiert. Sie formulieren hierzu Sätze im *present progressive* (ggf. ▶ Scaffolding aus b) nutzen).

b) GA gemäß AA
• S verteilen die Rollen (Noah, Lily etc.) in ihrer Gruppe. Wichtig: Rollen sollten mehrmals getauscht werden.

Skills file – Übersicht

Auf den **Skills file**-Seiten findest du Methoden und Tipps, die dir helfen, z. B. Wortschatz zu lernen, Informationen zu sammeln, Wörter zu umschreiben oder kleine Vorträge zu halten.

🔖 Die mit diesem Symbol gekennzeichneten Abschnitte enthalten Hinweise und Tipps, die dir dabei helfen, elektronische Medien beim Englischlernen einzusetzen.

▶️ Dieses Symbol zeigt dir, dass du einen Erklärfilm zu diesem Thema in der App findest.
Erklär-film

Lösungen der Merkaufgaben:

SF 2, Merkaufgabe:
a) Thema: animals • Oberbegriffe: farm animals, wild animals, pets • Unterbegriffe: chicken, snake, dog

SF 3, Merkaufgabe:
- Sea: [es] – [i:] – [eɪ]
- Lanes: [el] – [eɪ] – [en] – [i:] – [es]
- BN2 1PS: [bi:] – [en] – two – one – [pi:] – [es]
- Brighton: [bi:] – [ɑ:] – [aɪ] – [dʒi:] – [eɪtʃ] – [ti:] – [əʊ] – [en]

SF 4, Merkaufgabe 1:
beach, because, bed

SF 4, Merkaufgabe 2:
a) Haupteintrag: opinion
b) Haupteintrag: colour
c) Haupteintrag: shopping

SF 4, Merkaufgabe 3:
a) question: questions   b) mouse: mice
c) potato: potatoes

SF 4, Merkaufgabe 4:
a) drink: 1. das Getränk; 2. trinken
b) love: 1. die Liebe; 2. der Liebling; 3. lieben, sehr mögen
c) mean: 1. gemein, fies; 2. bedeuten; 3. meinen (sagen wollen)

SF 5, Merkaufgabe 1:
a) Karteikarte Nr. 3   b) That's the end of my presentation. Thank you for listening. Do you have any questions?

SF 5, Merkaufgabe 2:
b) I like your presentation. Your pictures are very nice. Please don't speak so fast.

SF 6, Merkaufgabe 1:
a) room   b) fruit

SF 6, Merkaufgabe 2:
It's a place at school. You do sports there.

Erklär-
film

Wörter lernen leichtgemacht

▶ Unit 1 | p. 34

Alle neuen Wörter und Wendungen des Buches findest du im *Vocabulary*, S. 213–253.
Alle fett gedruckten Wörter aus der linken und der rechten Spalte musst du lernen.

Wie kann ich Wörter lernen?

Es gibt viele Möglichkeiten, wie du Wörter lernen kannst.

Hier stellen wir dir einige vor. Probiere sie aus und finde
heraus, welche Methoden am besten zu dir passen.

> Lerne immer nur fünf bis
> zehn Wörter auf einmal.

1 Wörter lernen mit dem *Vocabulary*

Auf S. 213 kannst du sehen, wie das *Vocabulary* aufgebaut ist und welche Symbole und
Abkürzungen dort verwendet werden. Hier ist ein Beispiel von S. 218:

hat	der Hut, die Mütze	hats
(to) **sing**	singen	**singing** = das Singen **singer** = der Sänger, die Sängerin
Sorry. / I'm sorry.	Tut mir leid. / Entschuldigung.	Don't eat my sandwich! – Oh, **I'm sorry.**

- Lies dir zunächst das englische Wort laut vor.

- Lies dann die deutsche Übersetzung und die Beispiele und Hinweise in der rechten Spalte.

- Schreibe das englische Wort auf und präge dir so die Schreibweise ein.

- Wiederhole diese Schritte mehrfach hintereinander, um dir die Wörter gut zu merken.
  Wechsle dabei auch die Leserichtung: Beginne mit der deutschen Übersetzung, sage dann
  das englische Wort.

- Teste dich nun selbst: Decke die deutsche Übersetzung ab, lies das englische Wort. Weißt
  du noch, was es auf Deutsch bedeutet? Kannst du auch die englischen Beispiele nennen?

- Du kannst auch jemanden bitten dich abzufragen.

Merkaufgabe 1

Probiere das gleich einmal aus: Wähle fünf bis zehn Wörter
aus deinem *Vocabulary* und lerne sie wie oben beschrieben.
Lasse dich von deinem Partner oder deiner Partnerin abfragen.

2 Wörter lernen mit digitalen Medien

Vokabeln kannst du auch digital auf deinem Smartphone, Tablet oder PC üben.

Am Ende kannst du dich oft mit einem Quiz testen und bekommst ein Feedback zu deinem Lernergebnis.

Oft kannst du die Wörter auch anhören. So lernst du die richtige Aussprache gleich mit!

Wie kann ich mir Wörter besser merken?

Manche Wörter wollen einfach nicht im Gedächtnis bleiben! Dann können dir Merktechniken helfen:

- Schreibe das Wort auf einen Klebezettel und bringe ihn an einer Stelle an, wo du oft hinschaust.

- Male ein **Bild** zum Wort.

- Verbinde das Wort mit einer passenden **Geste** oder **Bewegung**.

- Suche passende **Reimwörter**: *house – mouse*

- Finde Wörter aus der gleichen **Wortfamilie**:
  dance → dancing
  swim → swimmer

- Erfinde **Bildwörter**.

- Verwende das Wort in einem Satz oder einer typischen **Redewendung**:
  how → How are you?
  ride → ride a bike

- Finde **Gegensatzpaare**:
  big – small
  sunny – rainy

- Finde **Oberbegriffe** *(umbrella words)*:
  football → sport
  monkey → animal

Denke daran, dass du mit deinen Eltern sprichst, bevor du eine kostenpflichtige App herunterlädst.

Das *Vocabulary* (S. 213–253) enthält in der dritten Spalte viele Merkhilfen, die du beim Lernen nutzen kannst.

ein Bild zum Wort

ein Bildwort

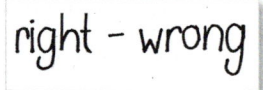

ein Gegensatzpaar

Merkaufgabe 2

Wähle aus deinem *Vocabulary* drei Wörter, die du dir bisher noch nicht merken konntest. Wende drei verschiedene Merktechniken an.

Wörter sammeln und ordnen in einem *Vocab file*

In einem Vokabelordner *(Vocab file)* kannst du Wörter sammeln und in Listen, Mindmaps und Tabellen ordnen.

Dadurch kannst du sie nicht nur besser lernen und behalten, sondern auch noch später nutzen, z. B. wenn du über ein Thema sprechen oder schreiben möchtest.

Zudem kannst du neue Wörter und Seiten an jeder Stelle beliebig ergänzen.

So gestaltest du die Seiten deines *Vocab files*:

- Lege Mindmaps zu bestimmten Themen an, wie z. B. zu *food*. Schreibe das Thema in die Mitte.

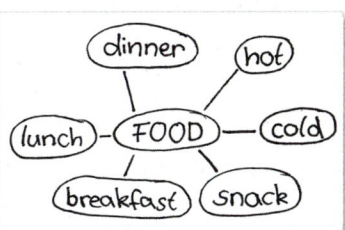

- Ergänze Oberbegriffe *(umbrella words)* und suche passende Wörter oder auch Unterbegriffe dazu (z. B. *lunch: fish and chips, sandwich, salad, …*).

- Erstelle nach und nach weitere Listen, Mindmaps und Tabellen und hefte sie in deinen Ordner. Ergänze deine Listen, wenn du neue Wörter lernst.

Wenn deine Sammlung umfangreicher wird, kannst du ein farbiges Register einfügen, um den Überblick zu behalten.

Merkaufgabe 3

Besorge dir einen Schnellhefter oder Ordner. Lege deine erste Wortliste an und suche im *Vocabulary* passende Wörter dazu, z. B.:

- Reimwörter *(rhyme words)*
- Gegensatzpaare *(opposites)*
- schwierige Wörter *(difficult words)*
- Lieblingswörter *(my favourite words)*

In den *Wordbanks* auf S. 194–204 findest du viele nützliche Wörter, Sätze und Ausdrücke zu bestimmten Themen wie z. B. Schule, Tiere oder Freizeitaktivitäten.

SF 2

Sammeln und ordnen – Mindmaps

▶ Unit 1 | p. 34

Wobei kann mir eine Mindmap helfen?

Eine Mindmap (englisch *mind map*) hilft dir beim Sammeln und Ordnen von Ideen. Du kannst sie bei der Planung von Projekten oder Präsentationen, beim Wörterlernen, bei der Strukturierung von eigenen Texten oder auch bei der Erarbeitung von Lesetexten verwenden.

Wie erstelle ich eine Mindmap?

1 Das Thema

Nimm dir ein leeres Blatt und schreibe das Thema in Großbuchstaben in die Mitte. Umrahme das Thema mit einem Kreis oder einer Wolke.

2 Oberbegriffe

Finde Oberbegriffe zu deinem Thema. Verwende für jeden Oberbegriff eine neue Farbe. Jetzt hat deine Mindmap Hauptäste.

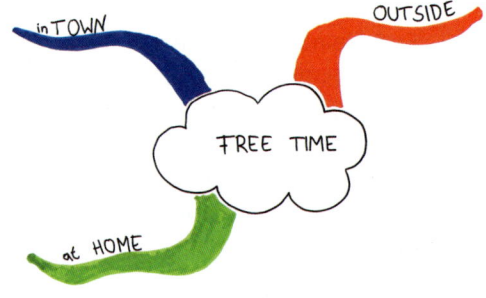

3 Unterbegriffe

Ergänze nun weitere Ideen zu den Oberbegriffen als Unterbegriffe. Verwende dieselbe Farbe wie für den Oberbegriff.

Deine Hauptäste haben nun Nebenäste. An diese kannst du noch weitere Ideen als Unteräste anhängen.

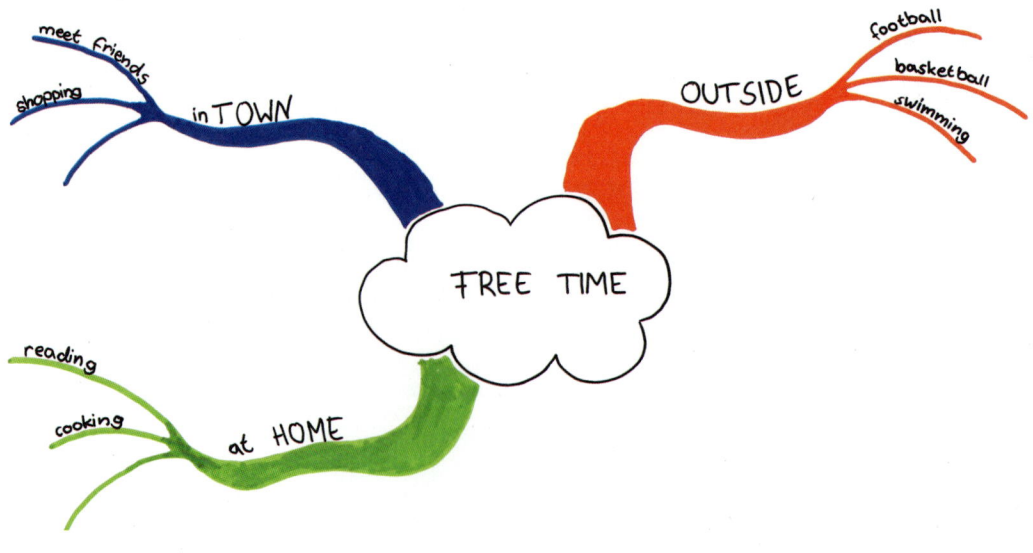

4 Überarbeiten

Gehe alles noch einmal durch und mache deine Mindmap noch anschaulicher: Lassen sich vielleicht Verbindungen zwischen den einzelnen Hauptästen oder den Nebenästen herstellen? Mit Zeichnungen und Symbolen kannst du die Ideen deiner Mindmap weiter verdeutlichen.

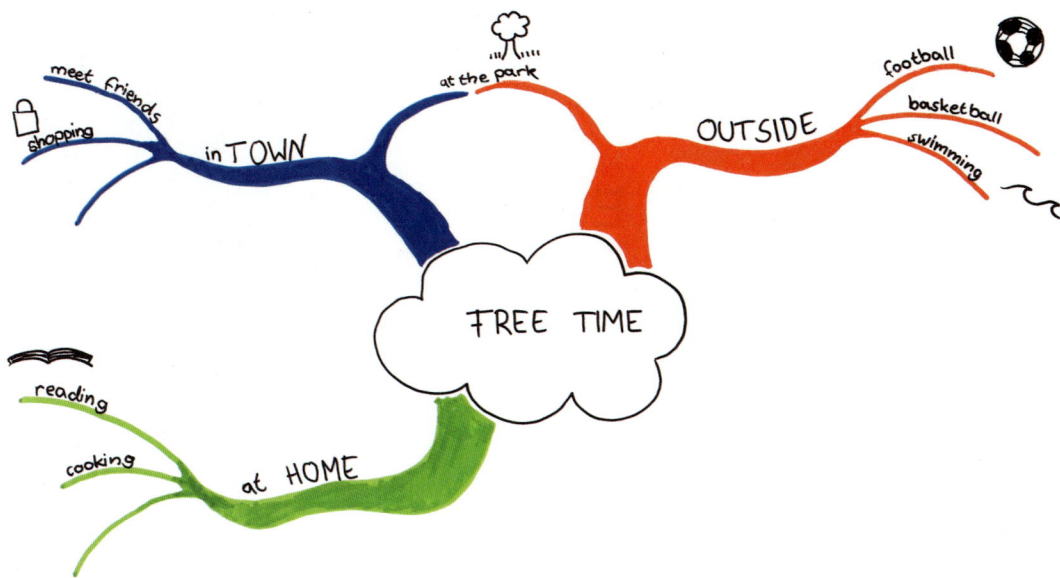

Merkaufgabe

a) Sortiere die folgenden Begriffe:

> *dog • farm animals • pets • wild animals •*
> *snake • animals • chicken*

- Was ist das Thema?
- Was sind die Oberbegriffe?
- Welches sind mögliche Unterbegriffe?

(Die Lösung findest du auf S. 170.)

b) Erstelle eine Mindmap zu diesem Thema.
Gehe wie oben beschrieben (1–4) vor.

SF 3

Buchstabieren

▶ Unit 2 | p. 64

Oft spricht man Wörter oder auch Namen auf Englisch ganz anders aus, als man sie schreibt. Um sie nicht falsch zu schreiben, bittet man darum, sie zu buchstabieren.

Dazu brauchst du das englische Alphabet:

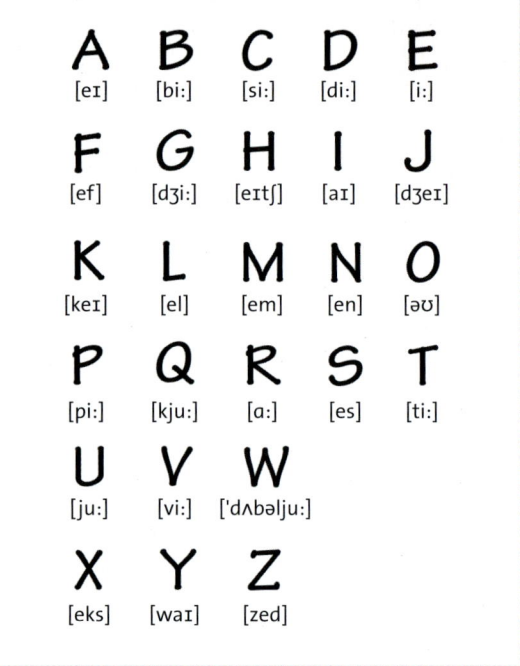

A	B	C	D	E
[eɪ]	[biː]	[siː]	[diː]	[iː]
F	G	H	I	J
[ef]	[dʒiː]	[eɪtʃ]	[aɪ]	[dʒeɪ]
K	L	M	N	O
[keɪ]	[el]	[em]	[en]	[əʊ]
P	Q	R	S	T
[piː]	[kjuː]	[aː]	[es]	[tiː]
U	V	W		
[juː]	[viː]	['dʌbəljuː]		
X	Y	Z		
[eks]	[waɪ]	[zed]		

Can you spell your name, please?

My name is Scout. That's S–C–O–U–T.

💡 Einige Laute haben in der Lautschrift besondere Zeichen, z. B.
- [ʃ] sprichst du wie „sch".
- [dʒ] sprichst du wie „dsch" (z. B. in „Dschungel").
- [ː] Dieses Zeichen sieht wie ein Doppelpunkt aus. Es soll dir sagen, dass der Laut davor lang gesprochen wird.

▶ English sounds, p. 193

Wie übe ich buchstabieren auf Englisch?

🔊 • Höre dir das Alphabet in der App an und lies jeden Buchstaben laut mit, z. B. oben oder auf S. 192.

• Versuche danach, das Alphabet alleine zu sprechen. Die Lautschrift in eckigen Klammern kann dir helfen, dich an die Aussprache zu erinnern.

Merkaufgabe

Buchstabiere Scouts Adresse: *Sea Lanes, BN2 1PS, Brighton*

(Die Lösung findest du auf S. 170.)

💡 Wenn dir jemand etwas buchstabiert, schreibe zuerst die einzelnen Buchstaben auf. Danach lies das ganze Wort oder den ganzen Namen.

Arbeit mit dem Wörterbuch

▶ Unit 3 | p. 96

Wenn du die Bedeutung eines englischen Wortes nicht weißt, kannst du das *English-German Dictionary* deines Englischbuchs (S. 255–266) oder ein Online-Wörterbuch zu Hilfe nehmen.

Wie finde ich Wörter und Ausdrücke im *Dictionary*?

1 In deinem *English-German Dictionary* (und in anderen Wörterbüchern) sind die Wörter alphabetisch geordnet:

g kommt vor h
ga kommt vor ge
gal kommt vor gam

Merkaufgabe 1

Schreibe die folgenden Wörter in der richtigen alphabetischen Reihenfolge untereinander auf:

1 *because*   **2** *beach*   **3** *bed*

Suche die Wörter anschließend in deinem *English-German Dictionary* (S. 255–266). Überprüfe, ob sie in der gleichen Reihenfolge erscheinen wie deine Wörter.

(Die Lösung findest du auch auf S. 170.)

°**furthest** [ˈfɜːðəst] am weitesten (entfernt)
°**fuss** [fʌs]: **make a fuss (of/over)** Theater/Wirbel machen (wegen)

G

°**gallery** [ˈɡæləri] die Galerie
game [ɡeɪm] das Spiel 2 (61)
°**gap** [ɡæp] die Lücke
garage [ˈɡærɑːʒ] die Garage 2 (54)
garden [ˈɡɑːdn] der Garten 2 (54)
geography [dʒiˈɒɡrəfi] die Geografie, die Erdkunde 1 (26)
German [ˈdʒɜːmən] deutsch; Deutsch; der/die Deutsche 1 (27)
Germany [ˈdʒɜːməni] Deutschland 4 (118)
get [ɡet]:
1. bekommen 3 (93)
get sth. *(sich etwas)* holen/besorgen 3 (93)
2. werden 4 (118)
get dressed sich anziehen 3 (83)
get warm warm werden 4 (118)
°**get ready (for)** sich fertig machen

2 Zusammengesetzte Wörter und längere Ausdrücke findest du bei einem Haupteintrag. Der Haupteintrag steht farbig oder **fett** am Anfang, Untereinträge kommen nach dem Haupteintrag. Schaue dir rechts den Eintrag für *name* an.

name [neɪm] der Name (10/11) **family name** der Familienname, der Nachname 2 (64) **first name** der Vorname 2 (64) **What's your name?** Wie heißt du? (10/11)

Merkaufgabe 2

Finde den Haupteintrag zu folgenden Redewendungen:

a) *in my opinion*   **b)** *What colour is ...?*   **c)** *go shopping*

(Die Lösung findest du auf S. 170.)

Was erfahre ich alles aus dem *Dictionary?*

- Im *English-German Dictionary* findest du die deutsche Übersetzung zu den englischen Wörtern aus deinem Buch.

- Außerdem kannst du die richtige Schreibweise eines Wortes überprüfen.

- Du erfährst auch, wie das Wort ausgesprochen wird. Schaue dir dafür die Lautschrift hinter dem Wort an.

- Und du kannst herausfinden, ob ein Wort einen unregelmäßigen Plural hat. Ist die Pluralform regelmäßig, findest du keinen Zusatz.

> **Kingdom** [ˈkɪŋdəm]: the United Kingdom (the UK) das Vereinigte Königreich 3 (82)
> **kiosk** [ˈkiːɒsk] der Kiosk, die Verkaufsbude, der Verkaufsstand 4 (121)
> **kitchen** [ˈkɪtʃɪn] die Küche 2 (55)
> **knife** [naɪf], *pl* **knives** das Messer 5 (150)
> **knives** [naɪvz] *Plural von* **knife**
> **know** [nəʊ] wissen; kennen 1 (20)

Merkaufgabe 3

Finde den Plural von **a)** *question* **b)** *mouse* **c)** *potato*

(Die Lösung findest du auf S. 170.)

- An den Ziffern 1., 2., … kannst du sehen, dass ein Wort mehrere Bedeutungen hat. Lies daher immer den ganzen Eintrag und entscheide dann, welche Bedeutung in deinem Fall die richtige ist.

> **text** [tekst]:
> 1. der Text 4 (124)
> 2. die SMS 5 (142)
> 3. **text sb.** jm. eine SMS schicken 5 (142)

Merkaufgabe 4

Diese Wörter können unterschiedliche Bedeutungen haben:

a) *drink* **b)** *love* **c)** *mean*

Schlage im *English-German Dictionary* nach, was sie bedeuten.

(Die Lösung findest du auf S. 170.)

Wie finde ich Wörter in einem Online-Wörterbuch?

Es gibt sehr viele Online-Wörterbücher im Internet oder als App. Frage deine Lehrkraft, welches Online-Wörterbuch sie dir empfehlen kann. Mit einem Online-Wörterbuch kannst du Wörter sehr schnell finden. So gehst du vor:

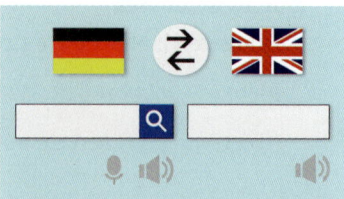

Zunächst musst du die Sprachen und die Suchrichtung eingeben (Englisch – Deutsch oder Deutsch – Englisch) und dann das Wort in das Suchfeld tippen. Gibt es ein Lautsprechersymbol, kannst du dir das gesuchte Wort auch anhören.

Manchmal kannst du das Wort direkt per Spracheingabe suchen. Vielleicht findest du dazu ein Mikrofonsymbol?

Einen Kurzvortrag halten

▶ Unit 4 | p. 126

Ab und zu sollst du vor deiner Klasse etwas vortragen oder präsentieren. Hier erfährst du, wie du dich darauf gut vorbereiten kannst.

Wie bereite ich einen Kurzvortrag vor?

1 Sammeln und aufschreiben

Sammle Ideen und Informationen zu deinem Thema als Stichpunkte und ordne sie, z. B. mithilfe einer Mindmap (SF 2, S. 174) oder in einer Tabelle.

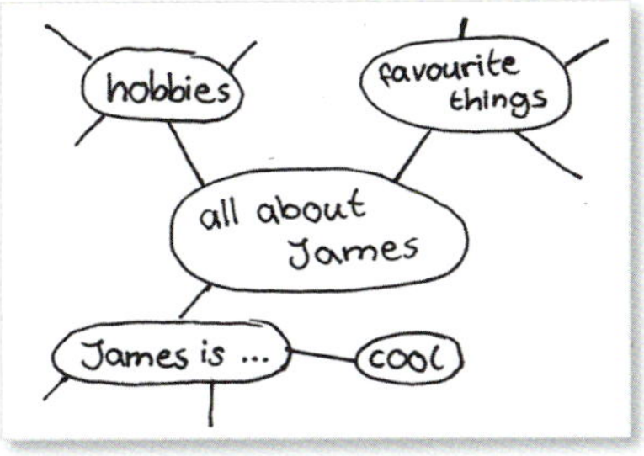

2 Veranschaulichen

Überlege, welche Bilder du zeigen kannst und wie du sie präsentieren möchtest, z. B. als Poster oder am Computer.

Bei einer Präsentation am Computer:

- Wähle ein einfaches Layout.

- Wähle eine gut lesbare Schrift und verwende eine Schriftgröße von mindestens 16 Punkt.

- Schreibe nur wenig Text.

- Wähle nur ein Bild pro Folie. Schreibe dazu, woher du dein Bild hast, z. B. den Namen der Internetseite.

3 Ordnen

Ein Kurzvortrag sollte folgendermaßen aufgebaut sein:

- **Einleitung:** Nenne das Thema.

- **Hauptteil:** Nenne deine Hauptpunkte. Erzähle dann mehr zu jedem Punkt.

- **Abschluss:** Bedanke dich fürs Zuhören. Erkundige dich, ob jemand eine Frage hat.

4 Notizen auf Karteikarten

Mache dir kurze Notizen auf Karteikarten. Du kannst dabei auch Symbole benutzen (z. B. „?" bedeutet: *Do you have any questions?*).

I'd like to talk about …

First I'd like to talk about …
Then I'd like to tell you about …
I'd also like to talk about …
This picture shows …

That's the end of my presentation.
Thank you for listening.
Do you have any questions?

Nummeriere die Karteikarten, damit du beim Vortragen den Überblick behältst.

Merkaufgabe 1

Schaue dir die drei Karteikarten rechts an.

a) Welche Nummer hat die Karte, deren Text du hier lesen kannst? 1, 2 oder 3?

b) Formuliere aus den Notizen vollständige Sätze.

(Die Lösungen findest du auf S. 170.)

5 Üben

Übe deinen Vortrag mithilfe deiner Notizen vor dem Spiegel oder mit einem Partner oder einer Partnerin. Du kannst dich auch selbst mit einem Smartphone aufnehmen. Achte auf die Zeit.

Worauf muss ich beim Vortragen achten?

Überprüfe zu Beginn, ob alles vorbereitet ist: Ist das Poster aufgehängt? Ist der Computer bereit? Liegen die Vortragskarten richtig sortiert? Dann beginne deinen Vortrag:

- Schaue dein Publikum an und warte, bis es ruhig ist.

- Sprich langsam, laut und deutlich.

- Zeige während deines Vortrags auf Bilder oder dein Poster.

Feedback

Hole dir eine Rückmeldung darüber, wie deine Präsentation bei anderen ankommt. Vielleicht ist ein guter Tipp dabei, wie du dich verbessern kannst.

Can you give me some feedback, please?

Bitten dich andere um ein Feedback, sei respektvoll:

- Nenne zuerst Gelungenes, denn Lob tut gut und spornt an! Sage, was dir besonders gefallen hat.

- Dann mache Verbesserungsvorschläge.

Merkaufgabe 2

Die Präsentation eines Mitschülers hat dir gut gefallen. Seine Zeichnungen sind besonders schön, aber er hat etwas zu schnell gesprochen. Welches Feedback ist besser?

a) *Please don't speak so fast. Your pictures are very nice.*

b) *I like your presentation. Your pictures are very nice. Please don't speak so fast.*

Wörter umschreiben

▶ Unit 5 | p. 156

Gerade beim Sprechen kommt es häufig vor, dass dir ein englisches Wort fehlt oder nicht einfällt. Dann kannst du versuchen, es zu umschreiben.

It's a thing. It helps me in the rain.

It's an umbrella, Scout!

Wie umschreibe ich etwas?

1 Erkläre das Wort, indem du zunächst einen passenden Oberbegriff *(umbrella word)* auswählst. In dieser Tabelle findest du besonders häufige Oberbegriffe:

	umbrella words
Personen	boy • child • girl • man • person • woman • ...
Orte	building • country • place • room • ...
Dinge	drink • food • fruit • game • musical instrument • sport • thing • vegetable • ...

Hier ein Beispiel:
- gesuchtes Wort: *waitress*
- passende Oberbegriffe: *person, woman*

Merkaufgabe 1

Finde unter den vier Wörtern den Oberbegriff *(umbrella word)*:

a) *kitchen • hall • room • bedroom*

b) *apple • orange • fruit • banana*

(Die Lösungen findest du auf S. 170.)

2 Nenne dann nähere Details, z. B. wo die Person arbeitet:

It's a woman. She works in a restaurant.

	umbrella word	Umschreibung
waitress	It's a <u>woman</u>.	She works in a restaurant.
kitchen	It's a <u>room</u> in the house.	You make food there.
banana	It's a kind of <u>fruit</u>.	It's long and yellow.

Das sind Redewendungen, die du zum Umschreiben nutzen kannst:

It's a kind of ...
It's a person ...
It's a place ...
It's a thing ...

Merkaufgabe 2

Finde eine passende Umschreibung für *sports hall*.

(Die Lösung findest du auf S. 170.)

Inhalt

Erklär-film Dieses Symbol zeigt dir, dass du einen Erklärfilm zu diesem Thema in der App findest.

LF 1

Der s-Genitiv und die of-Fügung
(The possessive form and the of-phrase)

▶ Hello! + Unit 1

Der s-Genitiv *(The possessive form)*

Noah's phone
Noahs Handy

Scout's hat
Scouts Hut

the dog's colour
die Farbe des Hundes

the girls' bikes
die Fahrräder der Mädchen

Die of-Fügung *(The of-phrase)*

the end of the game
das Ende des Spiels

a kilo of apples
ein Kilo Äpfel

Mit dem s-Genitiv drückst du aus, dass etwas jemandem oder zu jemandem gehört.

Anders als im Deutschen wird im Englischen **bei Personen und Tieren** im Singular das s mit einem Apostroph (') angehängt.

Im Plural enden viele Hauptwörter bereits auf s, dann hängst du kein zweites s, sondern nur einen Apostroph (') an.

Wenn zwei **Sachen** zusammengehören, verwendest du die of-Fügung.
Man gebraucht sie auch bei Mengenbezeichnungen.

Der Artikel *(The article)*

▶ Unit 1 | p. 21

Der unbestimmte Artikel *(The indefinite article)*

a bag
a girl

an apple
an elephant

an hour [ən ˈaʊə]
a uniform [eɪ ˈjuːnɪfɔːm]

Der bestimmte Artikel *(The definite article)*

the [ðə] ruler
the [ðə] classroom

the [ði] elephant
the [ði] English book

Der unbestimmte Artikel (ein, eine) heißt im Englischen *a* oder *an*.
Du verwendest
- *a*, wenn das folgende Wort mit einem Konsonanten (b, c, d, …, z) beginnt,
- *an*, wenn das folgende Wort mit einem Vokal (a, e, i, o, u) beginnt.

! Entscheidend ist die <u>Aussprache</u> des Wortes, nicht die Schreibung.

Der bestimmte Artikel (der, die, das) heißt im Englischen immer nur *the*.
Du sprichst
- [ðə], wenn das folgende Wort mit einem Konsonanten beginnt,
- [ði], wenn das folgende Wort mit einem Vokal beginnt.

Der Plural der Nomen *(The plural of nouns)*

▶ Unit 1 | p. 22

a book	two books
a table	two tables

Bei den meisten Nomen wird im Plural die Endung *-s* angehängt.

a bus	two buses
a beach	two beaches

Nach *-s*, *-x*, *-ch* oder *-sh* wird *-es* angehängt.

a story	two stories
a pony	three ponies

Bei Nomen, die auf Konsonant + *y* enden, wird *y* zu *-ies*.

man	men
woman	women
child	children

Einige Pluralformen sind unregelmäßig. Diese musst du lernen.

jeans	Jeans
trousers	Hose
clothes	Kleidung

Einige Nomen haben keine Singularform und werden nur im Plural gebraucht:
The trousers are new. – Die Hose ist neu.

LF 4

Die Personalpronomen *(The personal pronouns)*

▶ Unit 1 | p. 24

Personalpronomen ersetzen Nomen *(table ⇨ it)* oder Eigennamen *(Ben ⇨ he)*.

Das Pronomen *I (ich)* wird im Englischen immer großgeschrieben.

Das Pronomen *it* steht für Dinge und Tiere und entspricht „er", „sie" oder „es":

   *It's short.*   Er ist kurz.

   *It's blue.*   Sie ist blau.

   *It's new.*   Es ist neu.

Bei Tieren, die du nicht kennst, verwendest du *it*: *It's a dog.*
Über Haustiere, deren Namen du kennst, sprichst du mit *he* oder *she*: *She's my dog.*

LF 5

Die Possessivbegleiter *(The possessive determiners)*

▶ Units 1–2

Is this **your** book?
Ist das dein Buch?

I	**my** room	*mein Zimmer*
you	**your** bike	*dein Fahrrad*
he	**his** drink	*sein Getränk*
she	**her** ball	*ihr Ball*
it	**its** name	*sein/ihr Name*
we	**our** dog	*unser Hund*
you	**your** teacher	*euer Lehrer*
they	**their** class	*ihre Klasse*

Possessivbegleiter zeigen an, wem etwas gehört.

This is my favourite hat.

❗ Nicht verwechseln:
their = ihr/e
they're = sie sind

📺 Das Verb *be* (The verb be)

a) Bejahte Aussagesätze *(Positive statements)* ▶ Unit 1 | p. 24

Kurzform	Langform
I'm eleven.	I am eleven.
You're ten.	You are ten.
He's nice.	He is nice.
She's in my class.	She is in my class.
It's a dog.	It is a dog.
We're here.	We are here.
You're from London.	You are from London.
They're from Hove.	They are from Hove.

Kurzform	
I'm You're He's / She's / It's We're You're They're	from Brighton.

Langform	
Zane is Sunita and Noah are	from Brighton.

Es gibt Kurz- und Langformen. Bei den Kurzformen ist ein Buchstabe weggefallen. Dafür steht ein Apostroph (').

Kurzformen werden eher beim Sprechen und in persönlichen E-Mails oder Chats verwendet.
Sie stehen meist nach Pronomen *(I, you, he, she, it, we, you, they).*

Langformen benutzt du meist nach Eigennamen *(Zane, Sunita)* oder Nomen *(bike, teachers).* Man verwendet sie außerdem bei offiziellen Schreiben.

b) Verneinte Aussagesätze *(Negative statements)* ▶ Unit 1 | p. 29

Kurzform	Langform
I'm not old.	I am not old.
You aren't old.	You are not old.
He isn't old.	He is not old.
She isn't old.	She is not old.
It isn't old.	It is not old.
We aren't old.	We are not old.
You aren't old.	You are not old.
They aren't old.	They are not old.

Bei der Verneinung benutzt du fast immer die Kurzformen.

I'm not mean, I'm nice!

LF 8

Das Verb *be* (*The verb be*)

Erklär-film

c) Fragen und Kurzantworten (*Questions and short answers*)   ▶ Unit 2 | p. 51

Are you eleven?	Yes, I am. / No, I'm not.
Bist du elf?	Ja. / Nein.
Is your room OK?	Yes, it is. / No, it isn't.
Ist dein Zimmer OK?	Ja. / Nein.

Fragen	Kurzantworten
Are you here, Ali?	Yes, I am. No, I'm not.
Are you all OK?	Yes, we are. No, we aren't.
Is Timo at home?	Yes, he is. No, he isn't.
Is Mum tired?	Yes, she is. No, she isn't.
Is your room nice?	Yes, it is. No, it isn't.
Are the cats here?	Yes, they are. No, they aren't.

Antworte auf eine Frage im Englischen nicht einfach mit *yes* oder *no*. Das klingt meist unhöflich. Verwende Kurzantworten.

Are you hungry?

Yes, I am.

LF 9

There is ... / There are ...   ▶ Unit 2 | p. 54

There's a beach in Brighton.
Es gibt einen Strand in Brighton.

There are two girls in the pool.
Da sind zwei Mädchen im Pool.

There's	a man. a bike.

There are	two boys. three dogs.

Mit *there is* (= *there's*) oder *there are* sagst du, dass etwas vorhanden ist.

Im Deutschen heißt es meist:
Es gibt ...
Da sind ...
Es stehen ...
Da liegen ...

LF 10

Erklär-film

Die einfache Form der Gegenwart *(The simple present)*

a) Bejahte Aussagesätze *(Positive statements)* ▶ Unit 3 | p. 84

I often get up at 7 o'clock.
Ich stehe oft um 7 Uhr auf.

Dad always makes breakfast.
Papa macht immer das Frühstück.

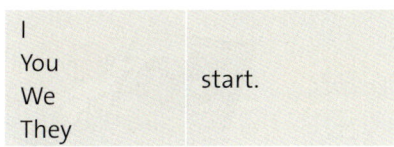

I You We They	start.

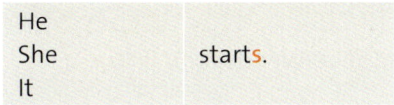

He She It	start**s**.

do [duː] – do**es** [dʌz]
go – go**es**
watch [wɒtʃ] – watch**es** [wɒtʃɪz]
wash – wash**es**
tidy – tid**ies**
have – ha**s**

Mit *simple present* sagst du, was oft oder jeden Tag passiert oder auch selten oder nie geschieht.

Diese Signalwörter findest du oft in Sätzen im *simple present*:
always, often, sometimes, rarely, never.

Mit *he, she* und *it* musst du immer ein *-s* ans Verb anhängen.

He, she, it – ein *-s* muss mit!

! Wenn ein Verb auf *-ss, -x, -sh, -ch* oder *-o* endet, fügst du bei *he/she/it -es* hinzu. Endet ein Verb auf *-y*, fügst du bei *he/she/it -ies* hinzu.

Für das Verb *have* benutzt du bei *he/she/it* die Form **has**.

LF 11

b) Die Wortstellung *(Word order)* ▶ Unit 3 | p. 87, p. 108

s	v	o
Deniz	loves	old cars.

s	a	v	o
Mia	*always*	walks	to school.
Yusuf	*sometimes*	goes	by bike.

In Aussagesätzen ist die Wortstellung wie im Deutschen: *subject – verb – object*.

Mit Häufigkeitsadverbien *(always, often, sometimes, rarely, never)* kannst du sagen, wie oft etwas geschieht.

Anders als im Deutschen stehen sie im Englischen meist direkt vor dem Hauptverb.

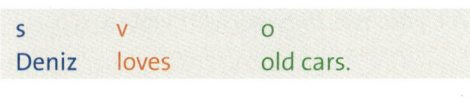

Dad always *makes* breakfast.

Papa *macht* immer das Frühstück.

LF 12

Erklär-film

Die einfache Form der Gegenwart *(The simple present)*

c) Verneinte Aussagesätze *(Negative statements)*   ▶ Unit 4 | p. 113

We don't live in town.
Wir wohnen nicht in der Stadt.

My dad doesn't like snakes.
Mein Papa mag keine Schlangen.

| I
You
We
They | don't start. |

| He
She
It | doesn't start. |

Aussagen im *simple present* kannst du mit *don't* oder *doesn't* verneinen.

Bei *I, you, we, they* verwendest du *don't*.

I don't like cats.

Bei *he, she, it* verwendest du *doesn't*.

LF 13

d) Fragen mit *do/does (Do/Does-questions)*   ▶ Unit 4 | p. 117

Do you like this game?
Magst du dieses Spiel?

Does your sister play football?
Spielt deine Schwester Fußball?

Fragen		
Do	I you we they / your parents	like music?
Does	he / your dad she / Lily it	like music?

Fragen, auf die man mit „ja" oder „nein" antworten kann, heißen Entscheidungsfragen. Sie beginnen mit *Do* oder *Does*.

Mit *I, you, we, they* verwendest du *Do*.

Mit *he, she, it* verwendest du *Does*.

LF 14

![icon] Erklär-film

Die einfache Form der Gegenwart *(The simple present)*

e) Kurzantworten *(Short answers)* ▸ Unit 4 | p. 117

Kurzantworten	
Yes, I do.	No, I don't.
Yes, he does.	No, he doesn't.
Yes, she does.	No, she doesn't.
Yes, it does.	No, it doesn't.
Yes, you do.	No, you don't.
Yes, we do.	No, we don't.
Yes, they do.	No, they don't.

Es ist unhöflich, auf Entscheidungsfragen nur mit *yes* oder *no* zu antworten. Besser ist eine Kurzantwort.

LF 15

f) Fragen mit Fragewörtern *(Questions with question words)* ▸ Unit 4 | p. 120

Where does your pet sleep?
Wo schläft dein Haustier?

What do snakes eat?
Was fressen Schlangen?

Auch Fragen mit Fragewörtern stellst du mit *do* oder *does*. Das Fragewort steht wie im Deutschen am Anfang.

How?	Wie?
What?	Was?
When?	Wann?
Why?	Warum?

Who cooks lunch?
Wer kocht das Mittagessen?

What makes you sad?
Was macht dich traurig?

Wenn mit *Who* oder *What* nach dem Subjekt des Satzes gefragt wird, bildest du die Frage ohne *do* oder *does*.

LF 16

 Erklär-film

Die Verlaufsform der Gegenwart *(The present progressive)*

► Unit 5 | p. 144

I'm reading a comic.
Ich lese gerade einen Comic.

Dad is cooking dinner.
Papa macht gerade das Abendessen.

What are you doing at the moment?
Was machst du jetzt gerade?

Aussagesätze	**Yes**
I'm You're He's She's It's We're They're	working.

Verneinte Sätze	**No**
I'm not You aren't He isn't She isn't It isn't We aren't They aren't	working.

Fragen	**?**
Am I Are you Is he Is she Is it Are we Are they	working?

Mit dem *present progressive* sagst du, was jemand jetzt gerade tut. Damit beschreibst du auch, was auf Bildern passiert.

Diese Zeitangaben findest du oft in Sätzen im *present progressive*:
now, at the moment, today.

Das *present progressive* besteht aus zwei Teilen:

'm oder 're oder 's	+	Verb + *-ing*

I'm having lunch now.

Bei Verben, die auf *-e* enden, fällt das *-e* bei der *ing*-Form weg:

have – having
make – making
ride – riding

Bei einigen Verben wird der letzte Buchstabe verdoppelt:

plan – planning
stop – stopping
sit – sitting

📺
Erklär-
film

Much – many – a lot of

▶ Unit 5 | p. 147

zählbar   nicht zählbar

Bejahte Aussagesätze

We've got a lot of apples.
I eat a lot of fruit.

Verneinte Aussagesätze

My dad doesn't watch many films.
I don't like much sugar in my tea.

Fragen

How many apples do we need?
How much money do you have?

Mit *much, many* oder *a lot of* kannst du über unbestimmte, größere Mengen sprechen.

Dabei ist es wichtig, ob es sich um zählbare oder nicht zählbare Nomen handelt.

Zählbare Nomen haben eine Pluralform: *one apple – two apples.*

Nicht zählbare Nomen kannst du nicht in die Mehrzahl setzen: *cheese, fruit, music, love.*

In bejahten Sätzen verwende *a lot of* – bei zählbaren und nicht zählbaren Nomen.

In verneinten Sätzen und Fragen verwendest du
– *many* bei zählbaren Nomen (viele),
– *much* bei nicht zählbaren Nomen (viel).

Lassen sich die Nomen zählen, musst du eher *many* wählen.

Grammatical terms *(Grammatische Fachbegriffe in diesem Buch)*

adjective	das Adjektiv: *good, old, nice, …*		**positive**	die positive Form: *do, can, …*
adverb (of frequency)	das (Häufigkeits-)Adverb: *often, always, sometimes, rarely, never*		**possessive determiner**	Possessivbegleiter: *my, your, his, her, its, our, their*
article	der Artikel: *a / the* book *an / the* apple		**present progressive**	die Verlaufsform der Gegenwart: *I'm speaking*
form	die Form		**short answer**	die Kurzantwort: *Yes, I do. / No, I'm not. / Yes, she does. / …*
long form	die Langform: *I am, do not, you are*		**short form**	die Kurzform: *I'm, don't*
negative	die negative Form: *don't go, can't go, aren't going, doesn't go, …*		**simple present**	die einfache Gegenwart: *I speak English, he likes it*
noun	das Nomen/Substantiv: *friend, car*		**statement**	Aussage(satz)
object	das Objekt: *I like cats.*		**subject**	das Subjekt: *They eat dinner.*
personal pronoun	Personalpronomen: *I, you, he, she, it, we, they*		**verb**	das Verb: *(to) go, (to) do, (to) have, (to) think, (to) love, …*
plural	Plural, Mehrzahlform: *books, children, potatoes, stories, …*		**wh-question**	die Frage mit Fragewort: *What's this? Who are you?*

Alphabet, Silent letters, English sounds

The English alphabet

a	[eɪ]	h	[eɪtʃ]	o	[əʊ]	v	[viː]
b	[biː]	i	[aɪ]	p	[piː]	w	[ˈdʌbljuː]
c	[siː]	j	[dʒeɪ]	q	[kjuː]	x	[eks]
d	[diː]	k	[keɪ]	r	[ɑː]	y	[waɪ]
e	[iː]	l	[el]	s	[es]	z	[zed]
f	[ef]	m	[em]	t	[tiː]		
g	[dʒiː]	n	[en]	u	[juː]		

Words with silent letters

Manche Wörter enthalten Buchstaben, die du schreibst, aber die entsprechenden Laute sprichst du **nicht**. Deshalb heißen sie auch „stille Buchstaben" *(silent letters)*. Höre dir diese Wörter in der App an und sprich sie nach. So merkst du sie dir leicht.

b lamb

c science

k (to) know, knife

d sandwich, grandma/grandpa/ grandparents/grandson/ granddaughter, Wednesday

l (to) walk, (to) talk

g design

u guitar, building, guide dog

h technology, Christmas, hour

t (to) listen

i fruit

w (to) answer, two, wrong, (to) write

English sounds

> Die Lautschrift zeigt dir die Aussprache von Wörtern und Lauten *(sounds)*.

> Einige dieser Laute kommen im Deutschen nicht vor oder werden anders geschrieben. Sie sind hier mit einem Ausrufezeichen gekennzeichnet: ❗. Übe sie mit Hilfe der App.

	[iː]	green, he, sea	[p]	pen, paper, shop
	[ɑː]	ask, class, car, park	[d]	day, window, good
❗	[ɔː]	or, ball, door, four, morning	[t]	ten, letter, at
	[uː]	ruler, blue, too, two, you	[g]	go, again, bag
	[ɜː]	early, her, girl, work, T-shirt	[k]	kitchen, car, back
	[ɪ]	in, big, expensive	[m]	man, remember, mum
	[e]	yes, bed, again, breakfast	[n]	no, one, ten
	[æ]	animal, apple, black, cat	❗ [ŋ]	wrong, young, uncle, thanks
	[ʌ]	mum, bus, colour	[l]	like, old, small
	[ɒ]	song, on, dog, what	[r]	ruler, friend, sorry
	[ʊ]	book, good, put, bully	❗ [w]	we, where, one
	[u]	shoe, you, to	[j]	yes, you, uniform
	[ə]	again, today, a sister	[f]	family, after, laugh
	[i]	happy, monkey	❗ [v]	very, seven, have
	[eɪ]	name, eight, play, great	[s]	six, poster, yes
	[aɪ]	I, time, right, my	❗ [z]	zoo, quiz, his, music, please
	[ɔɪ]	boy, toilet, noise	[ʃ]	she, station, English
	[əʊ]	old, no, road, yellow	❗ [ʒ]	usually, revision, garage
	[aʊ]	now, house	[tʃ]	chain, teacher, watch
	[eə]	where, pair, share, their	❗ [dʒ]	job, German, project, orange
	[ɪə]	here, material, really, year	❗ [θ]	thing, three, bathroom, north
	[ʊə]	tour	❗ [ð]	the, weather, with
	[b]	bike, table, verb	[h]	house, who, behind

Wordbank 1: Numbers

► Hello! | p. 10

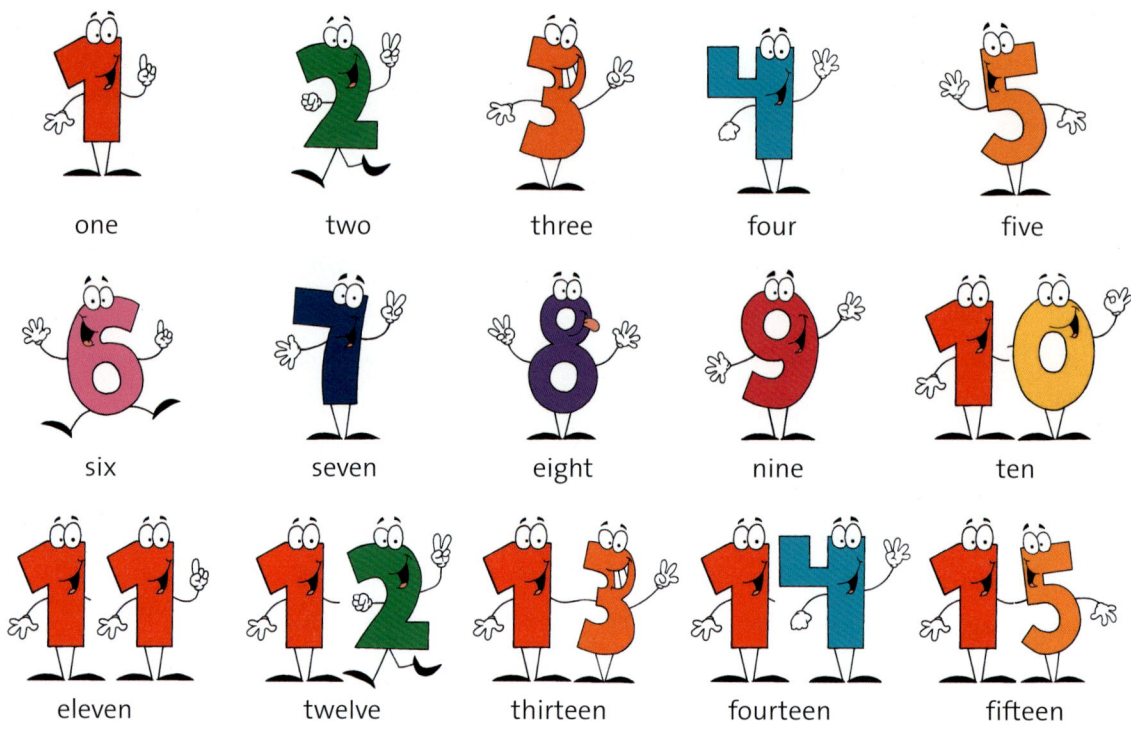

one · two · three · four · five

six · seven · eight · nine · ten

eleven · twelve · thirteen · fourteen · fifteen

Wordbank 2: Colours

► Hello! | p. 12

orange · purple · red · yellow · white · black · green · blue · brown

Wordbank 3: Animals

► Hello! | p. 14

cat, dog, elephant, fish, horse, lion, monkey, parrot, seagull, snake, ...

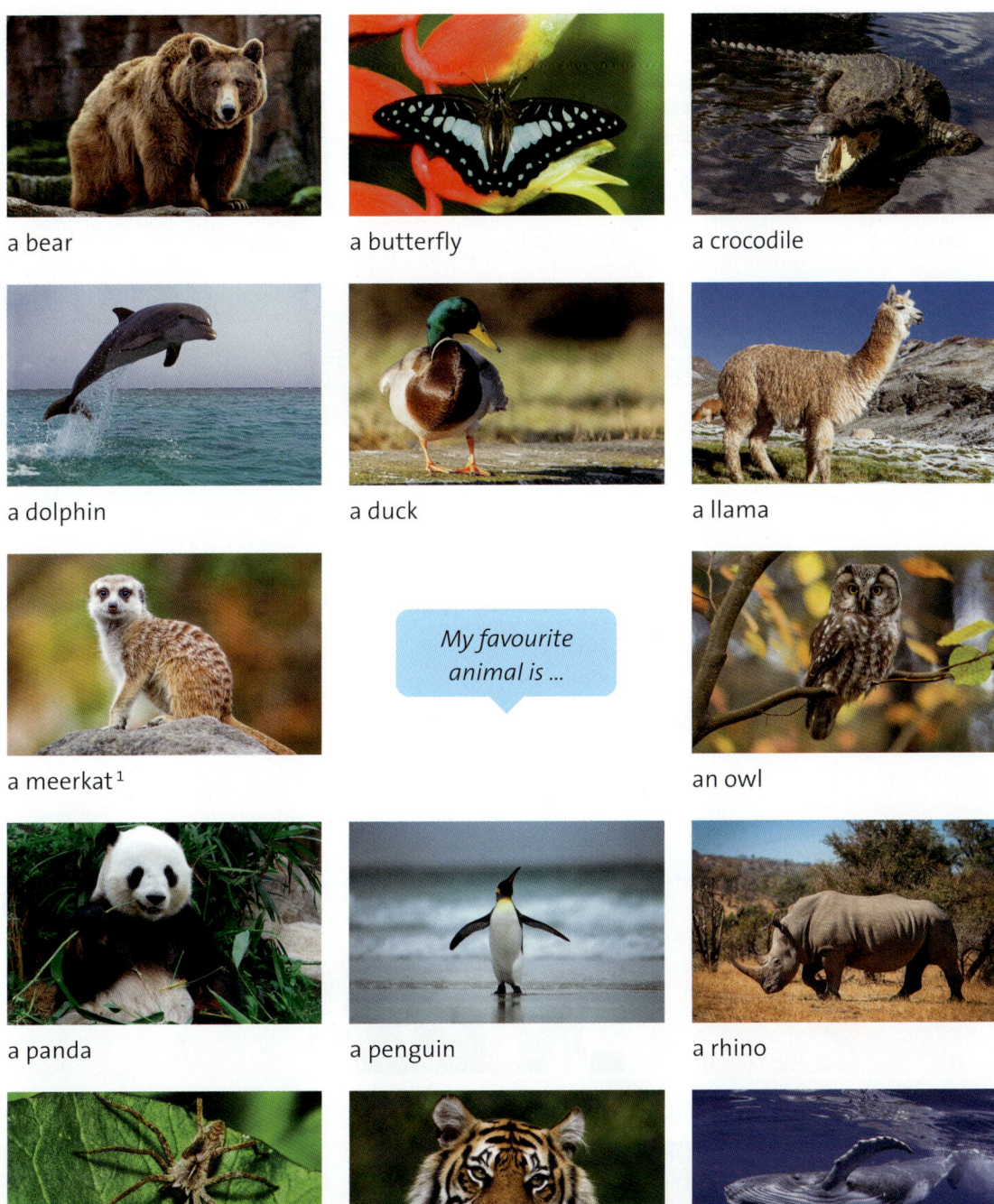

a bear

a butterfly

a crocodile

a dolphin

a duck

a llama

a meerkat [1]

My favourite animal is ...

an owl

a panda

a penguin

a rhino

a spider

a tiger

a whale

---

[1] **meerkat** *Erdmännchen*

Wordbank 4: Free time

▶ Hello! | p. 15

dancing, drawing, football, listening to music, taking photos, swimming, ...

baking

basketball

boxing

climbing

coding

cycling

nail art

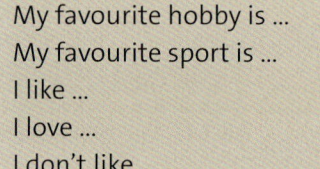
My favourite hobby is ...
My favourite sport is ...
I like ...
I love ...
I don't like ...

gaming

gymnastics

hanging out with friends

judo

kayaking

horse riding

reading

Wordbank 5: School subjects

▶ Unit 1 | p. 27

art, computing, design and technology, English, French, maths, music, PE, …

German (*Deutsch*)

media studies (*Medienkompetenz*)

school club (*AG*)

business and employment studies: technology, economics, home economics (*Arbeitslehre: Technik, Wirtschaft, Hauswirtschaft*)

   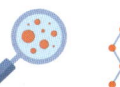 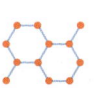

science: biology, chemistry, physics (*Naturwissenschaften: Biologie, Chemie, Physik*)

social studies: history, geography, politics (*Gesellschaftswissenschaften: Geschichte, Geografie, Politik*)

ethics (*Ethik*)

RE: religious education (*Religionslehre*)

philosophy (*Philosophie*)

special needs support (*Förderunterricht*)

study time (*Arbeitsstunde, Eigenarbeit, Hausaufgaben*)

tutor time (*Klassenlehrkraftstunde/Verfügungsstunde*)

one hundred and ninety-seven **197**

Wordbank 6: Places at school

▶ Unit 1 | p. 29

art room, canteen, classroom, computer room, corridor, sports hall, …

cinema

dance studio

drama room

games room

library

music room

office

playground

science lab

sports field

staff room

swimming pool

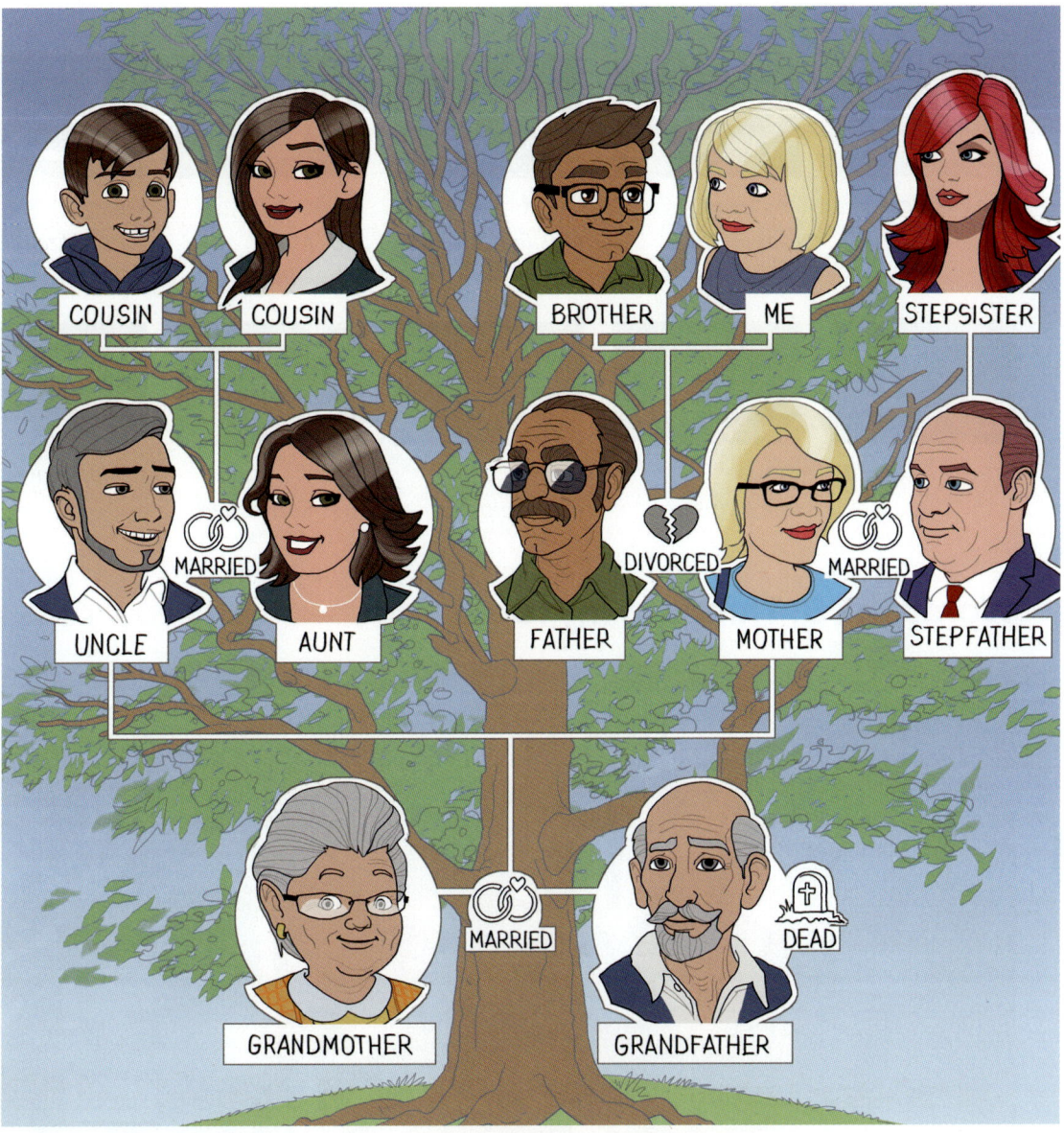

parents / grandparents	die Eltern / die Großeltern
child / children	das Kind / die Kinder
son / daughter	der Sohn / die Tochter
grandson / granddaughter	der Enkel / die Enkelin
blended family	die Patchworkfamilie
separated	getrennt
husband / wife	der Ehemann / die Ehefrau
single	alleinstehend
niece / nephew	Nichte / Neffe

Wordbank 8: Pets

▶ Unit 2 | p. 53

cat, dog, fish, hamster, horse, parrot, snake, …

budgie *(der Wellensittich)* chicken *(das Huhn)* ferret *(das Frettchen)* guinea pig *(das Meer-schweinchen)* kitten *(das Kätzchen)*

lizard *(die Echse)* mouse *(die Maus)* puppy *(der Welpe)* rabbit *(das Kaninchen)* rat *(die Ratte)*

Wordbank 9: Things in my room

▶ Unit 2 | p. 59

Wordbank 10: The times of the day

▶ Unit 3 | p. 82

DAY

in the morning
at 7 o'clock
at 7 a.m.

at noon

in the afternoon
at 4 o'clock
at 4 p.m.

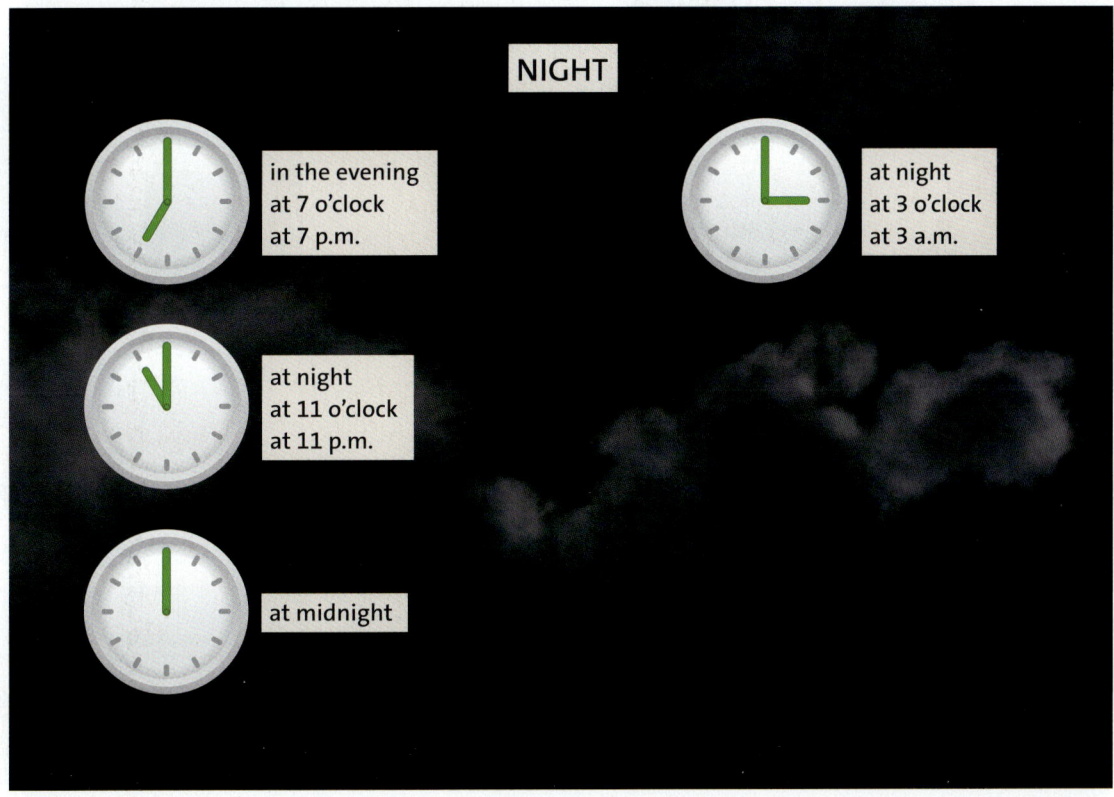

NIGHT

in the evening
at 7 o'clock
at 7 p.m.

at night
at 3 o'clock
at 3 a.m.

at night
at 11 o'clock
at 11 p.m.

at midnight

Wordbank 11: Places in my town or village

▶ Unit 4 | p. 117

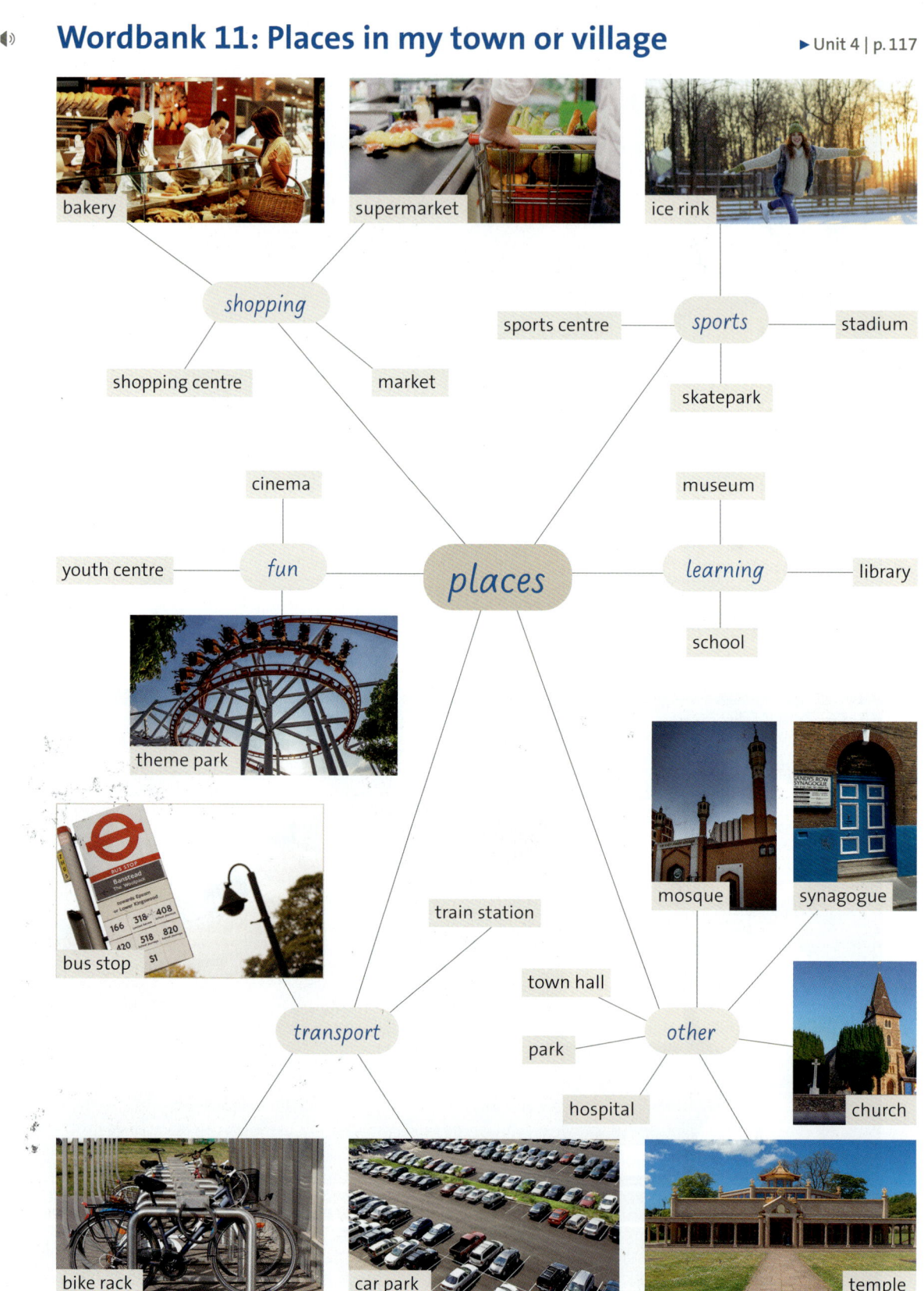

bakery

supermarket

ice rink

shopping

shopping centre

market

sports centre

sports

stadium

skatepark

cinema

museum

youth centre

fun

places

learning

library

school

theme park

bus stop

mosque

synagogue

train station

town hall

other

park

transport

hospital

church

bike rack

car park

temple

Wordbank 12: Food

▶ Unit 5 | p. 151

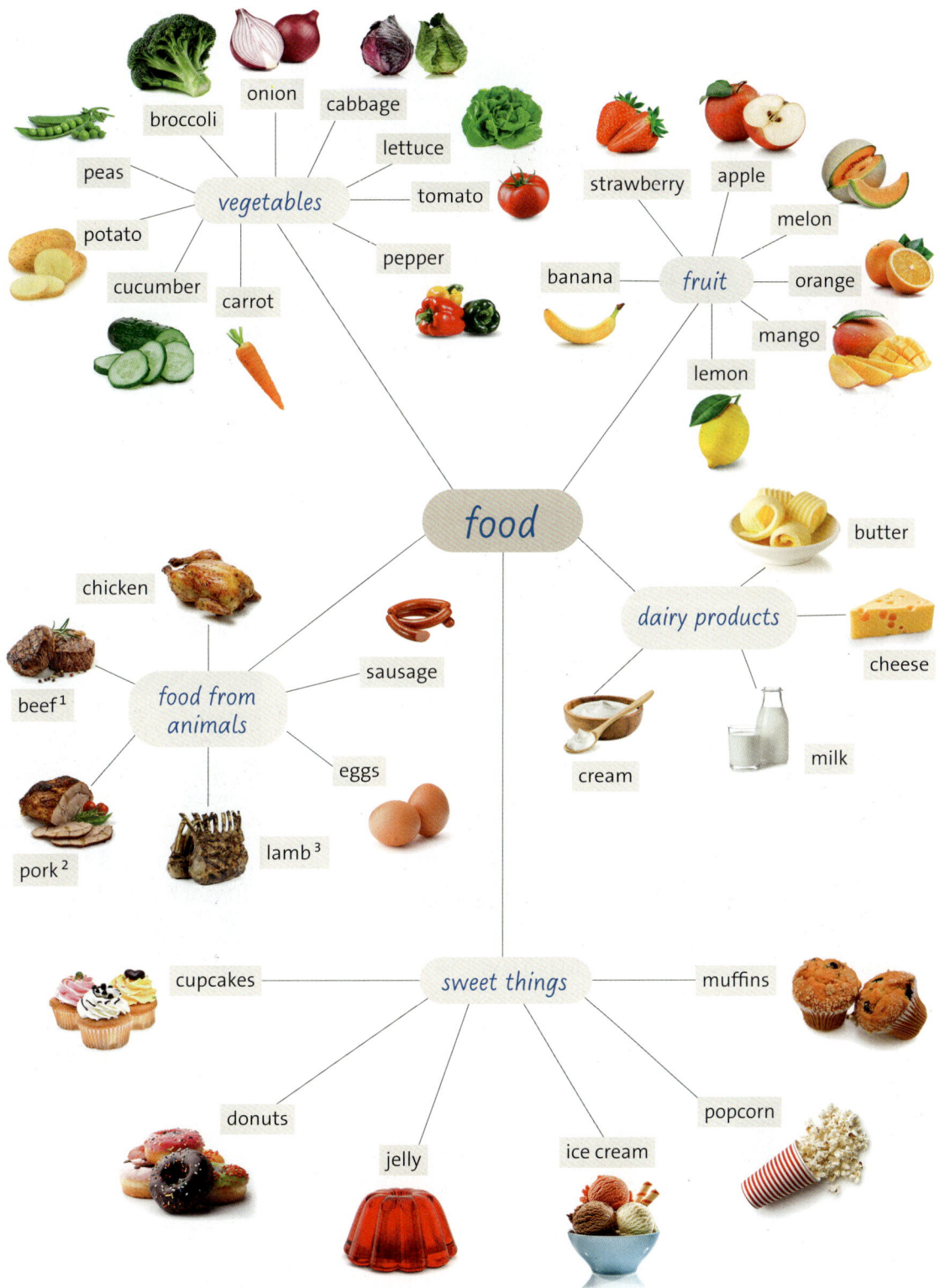

vegetables
- broccoli
- onion
- cabbage
- lettuce
- peas
- tomato
- potato
- pepper
- cucumber
- carrot

fruit
- strawberry
- apple
- melon
- banana
- orange
- mango
- lemon

food

dairy products
- butter
- cheese
- cream
- milk

food from animals
- chicken
- sausage
- beef[1]
- eggs
- pork[2]
- lamb[3]

sweet things
- cupcakes
- muffins
- donuts
- jelly
- ice cream
- popcorn

---

[1] **beef** *Rindfleisch*   [2] **pork** *Schweinefleisch*   [3] **lamb** *Lamm; Lammfleisch*

Wordbank 13: Cooking

▶ Unit 5 | p. 157

(to) add

(to) bake

(to) boil

(to) cut

(to) fry

(to) mix

(to) pour

(to) roll out

(to) stir

baking tray

frying pan

oven

pot

spoon

whisk

Hier findest du englische Sätze mit ihrer deutschen Übersetzung. Höre sie dir in der App an. Da jede Sprache anders funktioniert, ist eine wortwörtliche Übersetzung oft nicht möglich: Achte daher auf die kleinen Unterschiede.

1 Sich und andere vorstellen

Über den Namen und das Alter sprechen

Hello!	Hello, I'm … / Hi! I'm …	Hallo, ich bin …
	What's your name?	Wie heißt du?
	How old are you?	Wie alt bist du?
	I'm … (years old). What about you?	Ich bin … (Jahre alt). Und du?
Unit 1	(Sunita) is 12 years old.	(Sunita) ist 12 Jahre alt.
	I'm 12 too.	Ich bin auch 12.
Unit 5	When's your birthday?	Wann hast du Geburtstag?
	My birthday is on the first of May.	Mein Geburtstag ist am ersten Mai.

Sich begrüßen und verabschieden

Hello!	Hi! / Hello!	Hi! / Hallo!
	Bye!	Tschüs!
	Goodbye.	Auf Wiedersehen. / Servus.
	Nice to meet you.	Freut mich, dich / euch / Sie kennenzulernen.
	Nice to meet you too.	(Freut) Mich auch.
Unit 1	See you soon.	Bis bald.
	See you.	Bis dann. / Tschüs.
Unit 2	Speak later.	Tschüs. / Bis später.
Unit 3	Hello everybody!	Hallo allerseits! / Servus allerseits!
	I'd love / like to meet you.	Ich würde mich (liebend) gerne mit dir / euch treffen.
	See you later / tomorrow.	Bis später / morgen.
Unit 4	Welcome to (our house).	Willkommen in (unserem Haus).

Über die Familie und Freunde sprechen ▶ Wordbank 7, p. 199

Unit 1	This is my best friend (Noah).	Das ist meine beste Freundin / mein bester Freund (Noah).
	We are / aren't friends.	Wir sind / sind keine Freunde.
	These are my new friends (Lily and Harry).	Das sind meine neuen Freunde (Lily und Harry).
	Good friends are always helpful.	Gute Freunde sind immer hilfsbereit.
Unit 2	That's me. / This is me.	Das bin ich.
	That's my family.	Das ist meine Familie.
	This is me and my big sister Rahel.	Das bin ich und meine große Schwester Rahel.
	Next to me is my little brother Nick.	Neben mir ist mein kleiner Bruder Nick.

	These are my parents.	Das sind meine Eltern.
	Grandma and Grandpa live in the neighbourhood.	Großmutter und Großvater leben in der Nachbarschaft.
	My uncle and my aunt are from Russia.	Mein Onkel und meine Tante sind aus Russland.
	They have a daughter and two sons.	Sie haben eine Tochter und zwei Söhne.
	So, I have three cousins.	Also habe ich drei Cousinen und Cousins.
Unit 4	My parents often work late.	Meine Eltern arbeiten oft lange.
	I have a lot of friends at school.	Ich habe viele Freunde in der Schule.
	Do you have brothers and sisters?	Hast du Geschwister?
	No, I don't have brothers and sisters.	Nein, ich habe keine Geschwister.
	But I have three cousins.	Aber ich habe drei Cousinen und Cousins.

Über Hobbys, Vorlieben und Abneigungen sprechen ▶ Wordbank 4, p. 196

Hello!	I like / love sandwiches.	Ich mag / liebe Sandwiches.
	My favourite animal is a fish.	Meine Lieblingstiere sind Fische.
	What's your favourite ...?	Was ist dein Lieblings...?
	My favourite sport / hobby is (tennis). What about you?	Mein Lieblingssport / Lieblingshobby ist (Tennis). Und deins?
	I like / love dancing.	Ich mag / liebe Tanzen.
	I don't like football.	Ich mag Fußball nicht. / Ich mag keinen Fußball.
Unit 1	Let's go to the beach!	Lass uns / Lasst uns an den Strand gehen!
	Let's play football!	Lass uns / Lasst uns Fußball spielen!
Unit 2	My dream pet is a cute little dog.	Mein Traum-Haustier ist ein süßer kleiner Hund.
Unit 3	Let's go cycling!	Lass uns / Lasst uns Fahrrad fahren!
	I hate that.	Ich hasse das.
Unit 4	Which places / things do you like?	Welche Orte / Dinge magst du?
	I like my neighbourhood / friends.	Ich mag meine Nachbarschaft / Freunde.
	I don't like rubbish.	Ich mag Müll nicht.
	Why do you love (Brighton)?	Warum liebst du (Brighton)?
	I love (Brighton) because ...	Ich liebe (Brighton), weil ...
	I like living here because ...	Ich lebe gern hier, weil ...

Das eigene Zuhause/Zimmer beschreiben ▶ Wordbank 9, p. 200

Unit 2	This is my home.	Das ist mein Zuhause.
	I live in a flat / house.	Ich wohne in einer Wohnung / in einem Haus.
	Our house has a garden / balcony.	Unser Haus hat einen Garten / Balkon.
	Where's your room?	Wo ist dein Zimmer?
	It's on the ground / first / top floor.	Es ist im Erdgeschoss / 1. Stock / Obergeschoss.
	What's in your room?	Was ist / gibt es in deinem Zimmer?

	There's / There are (a bed / two chairs).	Da ist / Da sind / Es gibt (ein Bett / zwei Stühle).
	There are a lot of books on the shelves.	Es gibt / Es stehen viele Bücher in den Regalen.
	I have my own room.	Ich habe ein eigenes Zimmer.
	Is your room messy or tidy?	Ist dein Zimmer unordentlich oder aufgeräumt?
	Is it loud or quiet in your room?	Ist es laut oder leise in deinem Zimmer?
	Are you at home?	Bist du zu Hause?
	I'm home.	Ich bin zu Hause.
	My room is small, but it's perfect for me.	Mein Zimmer ist klein, aber es ist perfekt für mich.
	I live with my parents and my brother.	Ich lebe zusammen mit meinen Eltern und meinem Bruder.
	We live in a small house near (Bremen).	Wir leben in einem kleinen Haus bei (Bremen).
	There's a kitchen, a living room, two bedrooms and a bathroom.	Es gibt eine Küche, ein Wohnzimmer, zwei Schlafzimmer und ein Bad.
Unit 5	Do you often clean your room?	Machst du dein Zimmer oft sauber?
	Yes, I do. But it's always messy.	Ja, manchmal. Aber es ist immer unordentlich.

Über den Wohnort und die Nachbarschaft sprechen

Hello!	Where are you from?	Wo kommst du her? / Wo wohnst du?
	I'm from ...	Ich bin / komme aus ...
Unit 2	I live in ...	Ich wohne in ...
	I live with my mum and dad.	Ich wohne zusammen mit meiner Mutter und meinem Vater.
	We live in a flat / a house in ...	Wir wohnen in einer Wohnung / einem Haus in ...
	Tell me about your home!	Erzähl mir etwas über dein Zuhause.
	Where's your home?	Wo bist du zu Hause?
	Who are your neighbours?	Wer sind eure Nachbarn?
Unit 3	Where's your house?	Wo ist dein / euer Haus?
	Our house isn't near my school.	Unser Haus ist nicht in der Nähe meiner Schule.
Unit 4	Where do you live?	Wo wohnst du?
	I live in a village / town / city / in the country.	Ich wohne in einem Dorf / einer (Klein-)Stadt / einer (Groß-)Stadt / auf dem Land.
	What's your neighbourhood like?	Wie sieht deine Nachbarschaft aus?
	It's busy, but nice.	Es ist ziemlich viel los, aber es ist nett.
	I like our neighbours, they're really friendly.	Ich mag unsere Nachbarn. Sie sind wirklich freundlich.
	My neighbourhood has some problems.	Es gibt einige Probleme in der Nachbarschaft.
	A lot of people on our estate don't have a lot of money.	Viele Leute in unserer Wohngegend haben nicht viel Geld.

2 Über Gefühle, Wünsche und Empfindungen sprechen

Hello!	How are you?	Wie geht es dir?
	I'm fine / I'm OK, thanks.	Danke, mir geht es gut.
Unit 1	I'm not scared of school / snakes.	Ich habe keine Angst vor der Schule / vor Schlangen.
	Why are you angry / happy / sad / tired?	Warum bist du wütend / glücklich / traurig / müde?
	I'm happy because I have good friends.	Ich bin glücklich, weil ich gute Freunde habe.
	I'm not alone.	Ich bin nicht alleine.
	Go away!	Hau ab! / Haut ab!
	You're in trouble now!	Jetzt bekommst du Ärger!
	If I'm in trouble, my friends help me.	Wenn ich Ärger habe, helfen mir meine Freunde.
	Who's scared?	Wer hat Angst?
	We aren't scared of (them / the bullies)!	Wir haben keine Angst vor (denen / den Mobbern)!
	Sometimes people are mean to me.	Manchmal sind Leute echt fies zu mir.
	They think I'm different or difficult.	Sie glauben, ich bin anders oder schwierig.
	But I'm just quiet / clever.	Dabei bin ich nur ruhig / schlau.
Unit 2	I'd like to go away.	Ich würde am liebsten weggehen.
	I'd like to be back at home.	Ich wäre am liebsten wieder zurück zu Hause.
	Don't be so rude!	Sei nicht so unhöflich / frech!
	How do you feel?	Wie fühlst du dich?
Unit 3	Sometimes people think I'm stupid.	Manchmal denken Leute, ich bin blöd.
	Well, I'm not!	Bin ich aber nicht!
	I'm really surprised.	Ich bin echt überrascht.
	Sometimes I'm in trouble with my parents.	Ich habe manchmal Ärger mit meinen Eltern.
	Don't be sorry for me.	Du brauchst kein Mitleid mit mir zu haben.
Unit 4	Why are you angry?	Warum bist du wütend?
	I'm angry because my neigbourhood is really dirty.	Ich bin wütend, weil es in meiner Nachbarschaft so dreckig ist.
	Sometimes school is boring.	Manchmal ist es langweilig in meiner Schule.
Unit 5	I feel sad / great.	Ich bin traurig / Ich fühle mich toll.

3 Über den Schulalltag sprechen ▶ Wordbank 5, 6, pp. 197–198

Unit 1	We're in the same class.	Wir sind in der gleichen Klasse.
	Mr Lee is my class teacher and English teacher.	Herr Lee ist mein Klassenlehrer und Englischlehrer.
	I'm at a new school.	Ich bin an einer neuen Schule.
	What about your new school?	(Sag mal) Wie ist es an der neuen Schule?
	I'm lucky. The students in my class are really nice.	Ich habe Glück. Meine Mitschülerinnen / Mitschüler in meiner Klasse sind echt nett.

	Where are your English lessons?	Wo finden deine / eure Englischstunden statt?
	They're in room 2.	Die sind in Raum 2.
	On Monday morning I have (maths).	Montagmorgen habe ich (Mathematik).
	The next lesson is …	Die nächste Stunde ist …
	I'm in class 7B.	Ich bin in Klasse 7b.
	Where's the canteen?	Wo ist die Kantine?
	The name of my school is …	Meine Schule heißt …
	I'm at … school.	Ich bin auf der … Schule.
	My timetable is great.	Mein Stundenplan ist super.
	The classrooms aren't near the canteen.	Die Klassenräume sind nicht in der Nähe der Kantine.
Unit 2	Is it hard to do your homework?	Fällt es dir schwer, deine Hausaufgaben zu machen?
	The (English) homework is hard.	Die (Englisch-)Hausaufgaben sind schwer.
Unit 3	Our first lesson starts at …	Unsere erste Stunde fängt um … an.
	Lunchtime at school is at twelve thirty.	Mittagessen in der Schule ist um halb eins.
	After school I do my homework.	Nach der Schule mache ich meine Hausaufgaben.
	I have a lot of homework.	Ich habe viele Hausaufgaben auf.
	Me too.	Ich auch.
	My school journey is short.	Mein Schulweg ist kurz.
	I go to school (by bus).	Ich fahre (mit dem Bus) zur Schule.
	The start of school is at 9 a.m. / School starts at 9 a.m.	Die Schule fängt um 9 Uhr an.
	I come home from school at 4 p.m.	Ich komme um 16 Uhr aus der Schule nach Hause.
	My homework takes 30 minutes.	Ich brauche 30 Minuten für die Hausaufgaben.
Unit 5	Are you good at (sports / maths)?	Bist du gut in (Sport / Mathematik)?

4 Über den Tagesablauf sprechen, sich verabreden

Unit 3	My parents work long days.	Meine Eltern arbeiten sehr lang.
	In the morning I get up at (7 o'clock), have a shower and get dressed.	Morgens stehe ich um (7 Uhr) auf, dusche und ziehe mich an.
	Sometimes I meet my friends in the afternoon.	Manchmal treffe ich mich nachmittags mit meinen Freunden.
	We meet every Friday afternoon at 3.30.	Wir treffen uns jeden Freitagnachmittag um halb vier.
	In the evening I often play computer games.	Abends spiele ich oft Computerspiele.
	On weekdays I always go to bed at (9 o'clock).	An Wochentagen gehe ich immer um (9 Uhr) ins Bett.
	How often do you play (tennis)?	Wie oft spielst du (Tennis)?
	I never / rarely play (tennis).	Ich spiele nie / selten (Tennis).

	Let's meet in the afternoon.	Lass uns nachmittags / am Nachmittag treffen.
	Let's meet on Saturday!	Lass uns am Samstag treffen!
	Sorry, I'm busy on Saturday.	Tut mir leid, ich bin am Samstag beschäftigt.
	Are you free on Sunday?	Hast du Sonntag Zeit?
	I'd love to, but I can't.	Ich würde gerne, aber ich kann nicht.
	What do you do in your free time?	Was machst du in deiner Freizeit?
Unit 4	I practise the guitar every day.	Ich übe jeden Tag auf der Gitarre.
	On Saturday mornings I always look after my little sister.	Samstagvormittags passe ich immer auf meine kleine Schwester auf.
Unit 5	What are you doing?	Was machst du gerade?
	What do you usually do at the weekend?	Was machst du / macht ihr normalerweise am Wochenende?
	We usually stay at home.	Normalerweise bleiben wir zu Hause.
	Where's the party?	Wo findet die Party statt?
	Thanks for the invitation.	Danke für die Einladung.
	Send me a message if you can come or not.	Sende mir eine Nachricht, ob du kommen kannst oder nicht.

5 Seine Meinung äußern und diskutieren

Unit 1	Sorry, can you say that again?	Entschuldigung. Kannst du das noch einmal sagen?
	Listen, (Tony)!	Hör zu, (Tony)!
	Listen to (Gina).	Hör / Hört (Gina) zu.
	You're welcome.	Bitte, gern geschehen. / Nichts zu danken.
	I think …	Ich denke / glaube …
	Let me think.	Lass mich nachdenken.
	I don't know.	Das weiß ich nicht.
Unit 2	Good / Great / Clever idea!	Gute / Tolle / Schlaue Idee!
	We can talk about problems.	Wir können über Probleme reden.
	Please be polite.	Sei bitte höflich.
Unit 3	Yes, that's right.	Ja, das stimmt.
	No, that's wrong.	Nein, das ist falsch.
	I think you're right / wrong.	Ich glaube, da hast du recht / unrecht.
	I think that's false.	Ich glaube, das ist falsch.
Unit 4	Do you think it's interesting?	Denkst du, es ist interessant?
	Why do you think it's interesting?	Warum denkst du, es ist interessant?
	Do you have any questions?	Hast du / Habt ihr Fragen?
Unit 5	What do you think?	Was denkst du?
	What do you mean?	Was meinst du?

6 Über Essen und Lebensmittel sprechen ▸ Wordbank 12, 13, pp. 203–204

Unit 1	I'm really hungry.	Ich habe echt Hunger. / Ich bin echt hungrig.
	We're always hungry.	Wir haben immer Hunger.
Unit 4	Are you hungry?	Hast du Hunger?
	Try the pizza.	Probier mal die Pizza.
	No, I'm not hungry.	Nein, ich habe keinen Hunger.
	Where do you buy your food?	Wo kaufst du / kauft ihr Essen / Lebensmittel ein?
	We buy our food in the supermarket / at the market.	Wir kaufen unser Essen im Supermarkt / auf dem Markt.
Unit 5	What food do you eat?	Was isst du so?
	We eat a lot of fruit and vegetables.	Wir essen viel Obst und Gemüse.
	I'm not vegan, but I eat vegan food sometimes.	Ich bin kein/e Veganer/in, aber ich esse manchmal vegan.
	I like vegetarian food because it's healthy.	Ich mag vegetarisches Essen, weil es gesund ist.
	Eating too much meat is not healthy.	Zu viel Fleisch ist ungesund.
	My favourite dish is (pizza).	Mein Lieblingsgericht ist (Pizza).
	I'm allergic to …	Ich bin allergisch gegen …
	Enjoy your food.	Guten Appetit. / Genieß dein Essen. / Lass es dir schmecken.

7 Feedback geben

Unit 1	I like the photos in your poster.	Ich mag die Bilder auf deinem Poster.
	Your poster is really good / great.	Dein Poster ist wirklich gut / toll.
	You can use more words or pictures.	Du kannst mehr Wörter oder Bilder verwenden.
Unit 2	Your presentation about (your dream room) is cool / very nice.	Deine Präsentation zu (deinem Traumzimmer) ist cool / sehr schön.
	Your presentation was too long.	Deine Präsention war zu lang.
Unit 3	Please speak more loudly.	Sprich bitte ein bisschen lauter.
	Don't speak so fast.	Sprich nicht so schnell.
	Speak clearly, please.	Sprich bitte deutlich.
	Well done!	Gut gemacht!
	Great job!	Tolle Arbeit!
Unit 4	That was useful information.	Das waren nützliche Informationen.
	Please check that again.	Überprüfe das bitte noch einmal.
	Remember to make notes.	Denk daran, Notizen zu machen.
	Your notes are helpful.	Deine Notizen sind nützlich.
Unit 5	I'd like to see more pictures.	Ich würde gerne mehr Bilder sehen.
	The instructions are very clear.	Die Anweisungen sind sehr klar.

Classroom English

You and your teacher

Du und deine Lehrerin / dein Lehrer

Good morning, Mr / Mrs / Ms ... (bis 12 Uhr)	Guten Morgen, Herr / Frau ...
Good afternoon, Mr / Mrs / Ms ... (ab 12 Uhr)	Guten Tag, Herr / Frau ...
Sorry, I'm late.	Entschuldigung, dass ich zu spät komme.
Can I open / close the window, please?	Kann ich bitte das Fenster öffnen / zumachen?
Can I go to the toilet, please?	Kann ich bitte zur Toilette gehen?

Homework and exercises

Hausaufgaben und Übungen

Sorry, I have no exercise book.	Es tut mir leid, ich habe mein Schulheft nicht dabei.
I don't understand this exercise.	Ich verstehe diese Übung nicht.
I can't do number 3.	Ich kann Nummer 3 nicht lösen.
Sorry, I haven't finished.	Entschuldigung, ich bin noch nicht fertig.
I have ... Is that right?	Ich habe ... Ist das richtig?
Sorry, I don't know.	Es tut mir leid, das weiß ich nicht.
What's for homework?	Was haben wir (als Hausaufgabe) auf?

You need help

Du brauchst Hilfe

Can you help me, please?	Können Sie / Kannst du mir bitte helfen?
What page is it, please?	Auf welcher Seite sind wir / steht das?
What's ... in English / German?	Was heißt ... auf Englisch / Deutsch?
Can you write it on the board, please?	Können Sie das bitte an die Tafel schreiben?
Can I say it in German?	Kann ich das auf Deutsch sagen?
Can you speak louder, please?	Können Sie / Kannst du bitte lauter sprechen?
Can you say / play that again, please?	Können Sie das bitte noch einmal sagen / abspielen?

Work with a partner

Partnerarbeit

Can I work with Julian?	Kann ich mit Julian arbeiten?
Can I use your (pen), please?	Kann ich deinen (Stift) benutzen?
Yes, here you are.	Hier, bitte.
It's my / your turn.	Ich bin / Du bist dran.
Let's make / draw a ...	Lass uns ein ... machen / zeichnen.
Let's act out the story / dialogue.	Lass uns die Geschichte / den Dialog spielen.

What your teacher says

Was deine Lehrerin / dein Lehrer sagt

Let's go.	Lasst uns anfangen. / Los geht's.
Listen, please. / Quiet, please.	Hört bitte zu. / Ruhe bitte.
Open your books at page 24, please.	Schlagt bitte Seite 24 auf.
Do exercise 5 for homework, please.	Macht bitte Übung 5 als Hausaufgabe.
Write the correct words.	Schreibt die richtigen Wörter (hin).
Correct the false sentences.	Korrigiert die falschen Sätze.
Where's your book, David?	Wo ist dein Buch, David?
Try again!	Versuche es noch einmal!
That's all for today. You can go.	Das ist alles für heute. Ihr könnt gehen.

Im *Vocabulary* findest du alle neuen Wörter und Wendungen, die du lernen musst. Sie stehen in der Reihenfolge, in der sie im Buch zum ersten Mal vorkommen. Höre dir in der App jedes Wort beim Lernen genau an und sprich es nach.

Inhalt

Symbole und Abkürzungen

► p. 12 ► pp. 18/19	Die Seitenzahl in der linken Spalte zeigt dir, wo das Wort zum ersten Mal in diesem Buch vorkommt (*p.* = *page*, Seite; *pp.* = *pages*, Seiten).
►► Hello	Die doppelten Pfeile weisen auf ein Wort mit gleicher Bedeutung hin, das du gelernt hast. Blaue Wörter kennst du aus der Grundschule.
(to) **close** ◄ ► (to) **open**	Das „Gegenteil"-Zeichen bedeutet: *(to) close* ist das Gegenteil von *(to) open*.
❗ *English:* I'm **at** school. *German:* Ich bin **in** der Schule.	Das ❗ zeigt: Vorsicht, hier keinen Fehler machen!
a – an **a d**og **an e**lephant **a n**ice picture **an o**ld picture	In den Merkboxen findest du wichtige Hinweise zu den neuen Wörtern und Wendungen.
sb./sth.	*somebody* (jemand) / *something* (etwas)
infml.	*informal* (informell, umgangssprachlich)
pl.	*plural* (Plural, Mehrzahlform)

Hinweise

Tipps zum Vokabellernen findest du im Skills file auf S. 171–173. Die Wordbanks (S. 194–204) bieten dir nach Themen sortierten Wortschatz. Let's talk (S. 205–212) enthält Wendungen für wichtige Situationen, z.B.: seine Meinung äußern und diskutieren.
Englische Wörter, die Wörtern im Deutschen ähnlich sind, findest du auf S. 254.
Im Dictionary (S. 255–276) kannst du englische und deutsche Wörter nachschlagen.

Hello! Nice to meet you

▶ pp. 10/11

Hello.	Hallo. / Servus.
Nice to meet you.	Freut mich, dich/euch/Sie kennenzulernen.
nice	nett, schön
(to) meet	kennenlernen; (sich) treffen
you	du; dich; dir; ihr; euch; Sie; Ihnen
I'm (= I am)	ich bin

I = ich
❗ "I" wird immer großgeschrieben – auch wenn es nicht am Satzanfang steht.

hungry	hungrig

I'm hungry. = Ich habe Hunger.

careful	vorsichtig

Careful, Leo! = Vorsicht, Leo! (*wörtlich:* (Sei) vorsichtig!)

a seagull	eine Möwe

a computer	**ein** Computer
a show	**eine** Show
a baby	**ein** Baby

it's (= it is)	es ist *(bei Sachen und Tieren auch: er ist; sie ist)*

it = es *(bei Sachen und Tieren auch: er; sie)*
is = ist

the	der, die, das

the computer	**der** Computer
the show	**die** Show
the baby	**das** Baby

What's your name?	Wie heißt du? *(wörtlich:* Was ist dein Name?)

What ...? = Was ...?
name = der Name

you	du, dir *(Dativ)*, dich *(Akkusativ)*	ihr, euch *(Dativ)*, euch *(Akkusativ)*
your	dein, deine	euer, eure

Hi.	Hallo.	▶▶ Hello.
number	die Zahl, die Ziffer, die Nummer

1 one	**2** two	**3** three	**4** four	**5** five	**6** six	**7** seven
8 eight	**9** nine	**10** ten	**11** eleven	**12** twelve	**13** thirteen	**14** fourteen

▶ Numbers, p. 277

year	das Jahr; der Jahrgang

one **year** – two, three, four **year**s

old	alt
How old are you?	Wie alt bist du?

How ...? = Wie ...?
you are = du bist / ihr seid

Where are you from?	Wo kommst du her?

Where ...? = Wo ...?
from Hove = aus Hove

(to) like	mögen
football	der Fußball
you're (= you are)	du bist; ihr seid; Sie sind
thank you, thanks	danke (schön)
colour	die Farbe

❗ *English:* What colour **is** ...? – It's white.
German: Welche Farbe **hat** ...?

colours					
black schwarz	**blue** blau		**brown** braun	**green** grün	**grey** grau	**pink** pink, rosa
purple violett, lila	**orange** orange; die Orange			**red** rot	**yellow** gelb	**white** weiß

and	und	
right	richtig	
wrong	falsch	right ◄ ► wrong
What about you?	Und du? / Was ist mit dir?	
class	die Klasse; der Unterricht; der Kurs	**!** one **class** – two **classes**
too	auch	**!** *English:* I'm from Bamberg **too**. *German:* Ich bin **auch** aus Bamberg.
Bye. **Goodbye.**	Tschüs. Auf Wiedersehen. / Servus.	**Hello.** ◄ ► **Bye. / Goodbye.**

Goodbye, holidays!

► p. 12	**holiday(s)**	der Urlaub; die Ferien; Urlaubs-	**!** on **holiday** = **im/in den** Urlaub
	in the picture	auf dem Bild	**picture** = Bild **in** = in; auf
	mum	die Mama, die Mutti	
	dad	der Papa, der Vati	
	Leo's mum	Leos Mama/Mutti	
	animal	das Tier	
	drink	das Getränk	noun: **drink** – verb: (to) **drink** (trinken)
	thing	das Ding, die Sache	
	(to) eat	essen; fressen	
	things **to** eat	Dinge zum Essen	**to** = (um) zu Nice **to** meet you! = Schön, dich/euch/Sie kennen**zu**lernen!
	other	andere(r, s)	the **others** = die anderen
	here	hier; hierher	**Here's** (= **Here is**) Scout.
	I can see … **I can't (= cannot) see …**	ich kann … sehen ich kann … nicht sehen	(to) **see** = sehen **can** = können **can't** (= **cannot**) = nicht können

I can see Scout. What about you?

(to) remember	sich erinnern an; daran denken, nicht vergessen	Can you **remember** my name? (dich erinnern an) **Remember**, seagulls like sandwiches too! (Denk dran!)

	dog	der Hund	
▶ p. 13	**How are you?**	Wie geht's? / Wie geht es dir/euch/ Ihnen?	
	I'm fine. / Leo is fine.	Mir/Leo geht es gut.	I'm **fine**. = I'm **OK**.
	I'm not ...	ich bin nicht ...; ich bin kein/e ...	I'm **not** ten. And I'm **not** a seagull. Ich bin **nicht** zehn. Und ich bin **keine** Möwe.
	so good	so gut	Are you OK? – I'm not **so good**. I'm hungry!

About me

▶ p. 14	**about me/you/...**	über mich/dich/...	❗ me = **1.** mir; **2.** mich; **3.** ich *(in bestimmten Wendungen)*

Hello, Ms Palmer, it's me, Tim.

Hi, Tim.

	my	mein/e	**my** name (**mein** Name) **my** class (**meine** Klasse)
	favourite animal	das Lieblingstier	adjective: **favourite** – noun: **favourite** (der Liebling, der Favorit, die Favoritin)
	there's (= there is) **there are**	es ist ... / es gibt ... es sind ... / es gibt ...	**there** = da, dort; dahin, dorthin
	cat	die Katze	
	an elephant	ein Elefant	**a – an** **a d**og **an e**lephant **a n**ice picture **an o**ld picture
	horse	das Pferd	
	lion	der Löwe	
	monkey	der Affe	
	parrot	der Papagei	
	snake	die Schlange	
	fish, *pl* **fish**	der Fisch, die Fische	❗ one **fish** two **fish**
▶ p. 15	**hobby**	das Hobby	❗ *English:* one **hobby** – two,three **hobbies** *German:* ein **Hobby** – zwei,drei **Hobbys**
	sport	der Sport; die Sportart	
	(to) listen (to)	(sich etwas) anhören; zuhören	**Listen,** Scout! Hör zu, Scout! **Listen to** Leo. Hör(t) Leo zu. **Listen to** the song. Hört euch das Lied an.

music	die Musik	❗ Betonung auf der 1. Silbe: **mu**sic
(to) **draw**	zeichnen	**drawing** = das Zeichnen
(to) **dance**	tanzen	nouns: **dance** (der Tanz); *(hobby:)* **dancing** (das Tanzen); *(person:)* **dancer** (der Tänzer, die Tänzerin)
(to) **swim**	schwimmen	nouns: **swimming** (das Schwimmen); *(person:)* **swimmer** (der Schwimmer, die Schwimmerin)
photo	das Foto	❗ **in** the photo = **auf** dem Foto
(to) **take photos**	Fotos machen	❗ *English:* Can you **take** a **photo** of us? *German:* ... ein **Foto** von uns **machen?**
(to) **love**	lieben, sehr mögen	verb: (to) **love** – noun: **love** (die Liebe)
I don't like football.	Ich mag Fußball nicht. / Ich mag keinen Fußball.	
guitar	die Gitarre	(to) **play** = spielen (to) **play** the **guitar** = Gitarre spielen **player** = der Spieler, die Spielerin guitar
bike	das Fahrrad	bike
cap	die (Schirm-)Mütze, die Kappe	cap
chain	die Kette	chain
book	das Buch	
phone	das Handy, das Telefon	noun: **phone** – verb: (to) **phone** (anrufen; telefonieren) **phone number** = die Telefonnummer ❗ "Handy" klingt zwar englisch, aber für das (Mobil-)Telefon heißt es auf Englisch immer **phone**.
scooter	der (Tret-)Roller	
small	klein	
new	neu	**new** ◄ ► **old**
big	groß	**big** ◄ ► **small**
this	dies; diese(r, s)	**This** is Scout. – Hello, Scout! Nice to meet you.
gold	das Gold; goldfarben	gold

silver	das Silber; silberfarben	silver
with	mit; bei	**!** 1. Is Max the kid **with** the red bike? (mit) 2. Where's Scout? – Scout is **with** Leo. (bei)
(to) **read**	lesen	**reader** = der Leser, die Leserin
(to) **put**	*(etwas wohin)* tun, legen, stellen, stecken	**Put** your books and your sandwich in your rucksack.
▶ p. 16 **hat**	der Hut, die Mütze	hats
(to) **sing**	singen	**singing** = das Singen **singer** = der Sänger, die Sängerin
Sorry. / I'm sorry.	Tut mir leid. / Entschuldigung.	Don't eat my sandwich! – Oh, **I'm sorry.**
that	das (dort)	**that's** (= **that is**) = das (da) ist **Is that** a seagull? – Yes, **that's** Scout.

Ready for school

▶ p. 17 **ready**	fertig, bereit	Are you **ready**? Where's your rucksack?
for	für	Is that drink **for** me? – No, it's my drink!
school	die Schule	This is my new **school**, and I'm in class 5C.
please	bitte	Sing that song for me, **please**.
quiet	ruhig, still, leise	It's **quiet** and I can read my book. Super!
(to) **stand up**	aufstehen	
(to) **sit down**	sich hinsetzen	(to) **sit down** ◄ ► (to) **stand up**
(to) **look at** sb./sth.	jn. anschauen; sich etwas anschauen	(to) **look** = sehen, schauen
(to) **open**	öffnen; aufschlagen *(Buch)*	verb: (to) **open** – adjective: **open** (offen, geöffnet)
(to) **put your hand(s) up**	die Hand / die Hände hochstrecken	**hand** = die Hand
(to) **close**	schließen, zumachen	(to) **close** ◄ ► (to) **open**

Unit 1: My new school

▶ pp. 18/19 (to) **code**	programmieren *(Computer)*; kodieren	**coding** = das Programmieren verb: (to) **code** – noun: **code** (der Code; die Vorwahl(nummer))
(to) **walk**	(zu Fuß) gehen, wandern	**walking** = das Wandern verb: (to) **walk** – noun: **walk** (der Spaziergang)

(to) **cook**	kochen	**cooking** = das Kochen verb: (to) **cook** – noun: **cook** (der Koch, die Köchin)
student	der Schüler, die Schülerin; der Student, die Studentin	❗ Betonung auf der 1. Silbe: <u>stu</u>dent
at	an; in; bei; auf	❗ **at** school = **In** der Schule **at** this school = **auf/an** dieser Schule
but	aber	I like cooking, **but** I like parkour too.

Topic 1

▶ p. 20 **time**	die Zeit; die Uhrzeit	I'm hungry! Is it **time** to eat?
friend	der Freund, die Freundin	Scout the seagull is Leo's **friend**.
... **are** friends.	... sind Freunde/Freundinnen.	Scout and Leo **are** friends.
(to) **be busy**	beschäftigt sein, (viel) zu tun haben	Sorry, Scout, I can't play with you. I'm **busy**. **busy** = (viel)beschäftigt (to) **be** = sein
tired	müde	Are you two **tired**? 
tie	die Krawatte	
(to) **be scared (of)**	Angst haben (vor)	Scout, be quiet! I'm not **scared of** you.
of	von	• the colour **of** my bike (... meines Rades) • the names **of** the animals (... der Tiere)
(school) uniform	die (Schul-)Uniform	**school uniforms**  tie
the same	gleich; derselbe/dieselbe/dasselbe; dieselben	Sunita and Noah are in **the same** class.
(to) **know**	wissen; kennen	I'm from Hove, not from Brighton. – I **know**!
British	britisch	adjective: **British** – noun: **(Great) Britain** (Großbritannien)
(to) **have**	haben	Are you hungry? You can **have** my sandwich!
often	oft	I love cooking. I **often** cook nice things to eat.
great	großartig, toll	I like my new school. It's **great**!

	horrible	schrecklich	horrible ◄ ► great
► p. 21	glue stick	der Klebestift	glue = der Kleber, der Klebstoff
	pencil case	das Federmäppchen	pencil = der Bleistift case = das Etui, der Behälter, der Kasten
	pen	der Kugelschreiber, der Stift; der Füller	
	rubber	das Radiergummi	
	pencil sharpener	der Bleistift(an)spitzer	
	exercise book	das Schulheft, das Übungsheft	exercise = die Übung, die Aufgabe
	English	Englisch; englisch	**!** Ländernamen, -adjektive und Sprachen werden im Englischen immer großgeschrieben: **England, English** **!** in English = auf Englisch
	apple	der Apfel	
	ruler	das Lineal	
	desk	der Schreibtisch	
► p. 22	different (to)	verschieden; anders (als)	six different colours
	Mr Lee	Herr Lee	Mr Lee Ms Lee / Mrs Lee **!** Ms = allgemeine Anrede für Frauen Mrs = Anrede für verheiratete Frauen
	teacher	der Lehrer, die Lehrerin	class teacher = der/die Klassenlehrer/in
	I'm late.	Ich habe mich verspätet.	late = (zu) spät
	Don't be late.	Verspäte dich nicht.	Scout! Don't eat my sandwiches!
	again	wieder, noch einmal	Stand up. – Thanks, you can sit down again.
	window	das Fenster	
	yes	ja	yes ◄ ► no (nein)
	(to) go	gehen; fahren	Can I go to the toilet, please? (gehen) I often go to Plymouth. (fahren)
	to	zu, nach	**!** to = 1. (um) zu: things to eat; 2. zu, nach: I go to school.
	toilet	die Toilette	
	now	nun, jetzt	Ah, great! I love sport. But now I'm hungry.

(to) **take**	(mit)nehmen; bringen	Please **take** your book and read exercise 10. (nehmen) Remember: **Take** your sandwiches with you! (mitnehmen) Can you **take** the new kids to the toilet? (bringen)
(to) **say**	sagen	Be quiet! – Listen, it's nice to **say** "please".
(to) **talk (to)**	sprechen, reden (mit)	**Talk to** your friends **about** your hobbies. verb: (to) **talk** – noun: **talk** (das Gespräch; die Rede, der Vortrag)
Let's ..., Let us ...	Lass uns ... / Lasst uns ...	**Let us** go now.
us	uns	Do you want to go with **us**? Please talk to **us**.
(to) **start**	beginnen, anfangen (mit)	verb: (to) **start** – noun: **start** (der Anfang, der Start)
first	erste(r, s)	**at first** = zuerst, am Anfang **!** **first** = **1.** erste/r/s; **2.** zuerst, als Erstes
secondary school	die weiterführende Schule	I'm 11. I go to **secondary school** now.
▶ p. 23 **in class**	im Unterricht	Please don't eat your sandwiches **in class**.
What page ...?	Welche Seite ...?	**!** **what?** = **1.** welche(r, s)?; **2.** was?
page (p.)	die (Buch-/Heft-)Seite	**on page 15 / on p. 15** = auf Seite 15 / auf S. 15 *but* Open your books **at page** 23. (... **auf** Seite 23.)
(to) **understand**	verstehen	In English, please. I don't **understand** German.
(to) **help**	helfen	verb: (to) **help** – noun: **help** (die Hilfe)
question	die Frage	"What's this?" is a **question**.
answer	die Antwort	**question** ◄ ► **answer** noun: **answer** – verb: (to) **answer** (antworten (auf), beantworten)
the answer **to the question**	die Antwort auf die Frage	**!** **to** = **1.** auf: the answer **to** the question; **2.** (um) zu: things **to** eat; **3.** zu, nach: I go **to** school.
(to) **use**	benutzen, verwenden	noun: **user** = der (Be-)Nutzer, die (Be-)Nutzerin
Here you are.	Bitte schön. / Hier, bitte.	Can I use your book, please? Yes, here you are.
You're welcome.	Bitte, gern geschehen. / Nichts zu danken.	

<table>
<tr><td colspan="3">"bitte"</td></tr>
<tr><td>• in Aufforderungen und Bitten:</td><td>please</td><td>Close the window, please. / Where's the toilet, please?
(Schließ das Fenster, bitte. / Wo ist die Toilette, bitte?)</td></tr>
<tr><td>• wenn du jemandem etwas gibst:</td><td>Here you are.</td><td>Can I use your pen, please? – Yes, here you are.
(Kann ich deinen Stift benutzen? – Hier, bitte.)</td></tr>
<tr><td>• wenn sich jemand bedankt hat:</td><td>You're welcome.</td><td>I can help you. – Thanks. – You're welcome.
(Ich kann dir helfen. – Danke. – Bitte, gern geschehen.)</td></tr>
</table>

(to) **ask**	fragen	What page is it? – Don't **ask** me. I don't know. ❗ *English*: Can I **ask** you a **question**? *German*: Kann ich dir eine **Frage** stellen?
classroom	das Klassenzimmer	

Topic 2

▶ p. 24 **timetable**	der Stundenplan	Look at your **timetable**, please. Can you see your English **lessons**?
lesson	die (Unterrichts-)Stunde	**lessons** *(pl)* = Unterricht(sstunden)
they're (= they are) **they aren't**	sie sind sie sind nicht	**they** = sie *(Plural)*
room	der Raum, das Zimmer	The English lessons are in **room** number 201.
(to) **be asleep**	schlafen	My cat is **asleep**.
he's (= he is) **he isn't (= he is not)**	er ist er ist nicht	**he** = er
(to) **think**	denken, meinen, glauben	**I think ...** = Ich denke/meine/glaube/finde, ...
(to) **be right**	Recht haben	**You're right.** = Du hast Recht. (to) **be right** ◀ ▶ (to) **be wrong** (Unrecht haben)
we're (= we are)	wir sind	you're (you are) — du bist; ihr seid we're (we are) — wir sind they're (they are) — sie sind
all	alle(s)	Are **all** your school things in your rucksack?
break	die Pause	My favourite time at school is the **break**!
soon	bald	Don't eat in class. It's time for break **soon**!
minute	die Minute	❗ Betonung auf der 1. Silbe: **min**ute
she's (= she is)	sie ist	**she** = sie *(weibliche Person)*

's (is) (= ist)
he's (he is) — He's my dad. — it's (it is) / that's (that is) — It's/That's nice.
she's (she is) — She's my mum. — what's (what is) — What's your name?

people *(pl)*	die Leute, die Menschen	four **people**

► p. 25
after lesson 1 / **after** school	nach der ersten Unterrichtsstunde / nach der Schule	I don't have time for all my hobbies **after** school.
girl	das Mädchen	girl boy
boy	der Junge	
message	die Nachricht, die Mitteilung	I have this **message** on my phone from Zane: "My new school uniform is great!"
(to) **be lucky**	Glück haben	**You're lucky.** = Du hast Glück. **lucky** (number) = Glücks-(zahl) my **lucky** colour = meine Glücksfarbe ❗ Sie **hat Glück.** = She's **lucky.** Sie **ist glücklich.** = She's **happy.**
See you.	Bis dann. / Tschüs.	**See you soon.** = Bis bald!
day	der Tag	
week	die Woche	Oh no! School starts this **week.** (diese Woche)
on Monday	am Montag	**on Sundays** = an jedem Sonntag, sonntags ❗ **on** = **1.** an/am: We don't go to school **on** Sunday.; **2.** auf: My books are **on** my desk.

Monday (der) Montag	**Tuesday** (der) Dienstag	**Wednesday** (der) Mittwoch
Thursday (der) Donnerstag	**Friday** (der) Freitag	**Saturday** (der) Samstag
Sunday (der) Sonntag	❗ Die Wochentage werden immer großgeschrieben.	

► p. 26
subject	das (Schul-)Fach	What's your favourite **subject** at school?
assembly	die Schulversammlung	All my days at school start with **assembly.**
history	die Geschichte *(vergangene Zeiten)*	
geography	die Geografie, die Erdkunde	❗ Betonung auf der 2. Silbe: ge**o**graphy
lunch	das Mittagessen	What's **for lunch**? = Was gibt es zum Mittagessen?
maths	die Mathe(matik)	a **maths** exercise
art	die Kunst	I like drawing pictures. I love **art** lessons!

science	die Naturwissenschaft	a **science** lesson

French	Französisch; französisch	
design and technology	das Werken, der Werkunterricht	**design** = Gestaltung, Design **technology** = Technik(unterricht); Technologie
computing	die Informatik	
PE (physical education)	der (Schul-)Sport	
▶ p. 27 **biology**	die Biologie	❗ Betonung auf der 2. Silbe: b**io**logy
because	weil	I'm happy **because** now we have PE.
hard	schwer, schwierig; hart	This exercise is so **hard**. Help me, please!
German	deutsch; Deutsch; Deutsche/r	Xaver is **German**. He's from Würzburg.

Topic 3

▶ p. 28 **place**	der Ort, der Platz	Put it there. That's the right **place**.
alone	allein	I often walk **alone** and think.
our	unser/e	**our** poster (**unser** Poster) **our** class (**unsere** Klasse)
bag	die Tasche	**bags**

canteen	die Kantine, die (Schul-)Mensa	Time for lunch! Let's go to the **canteen**.
corridor	der Korridor	
map	die Landkarte, der Stadtplan	
building	das Gebäude	What's that **building**, Mum? – My old school!
hall	die Halle, der Saal	**sports hall** = Sporthalle ❗ **hall** = **1.** die Halle, der Saal; **2.** der Flur, die Diele
near	nahe (bei), in der Nähe von	Hove is **near** Brighton.
maybe	vielleicht	Let me think – **maybe** this is the answer: …
really	wirklich	Our teachers are **really** nice.
always	immer	You're a great friend. You're **always** so nice!
▶ p. 29 **food**	das Essen, das Lebensmittel; das Futter	▶▶ things to eat

bad	schlecht; schlimm	**bad ◄ ► good**
grandma	die Oma	

grandpa   grandma

very big	sehr groß	London is **very** big. You can't see all nice places there in one day.

Story

► p. 30

brave	mutig	**!** **brave** = mutig – Sunita is **brave**. **good** = brav – **Good** dog!
friendly	freundlich, nett	Don't be scared. They're **friendly** dogs. 
helpful	hilfsbereit; hilfreich, nützlich	You often help other people. You're very **helpful**. (hilfsbereit) This exercise is hard, but there are **helpful** tips on page 85. (hilfreiche/nützliche Tipps)
kind	nett, freundlich	► ► friendly
mean	gemein, fies	**mean ◄ ► kind, friendly** They're horrible people. They're really **mean**.
who	wer	**how?** wie? **where?** wo? **what?** was? **who?** wer?
sad	traurig	**sad ◄ ► happy**
then	dann, danach	Now it's assembly time, **then** we have maths.
free	frei; kostenlos	**free time** = Freizeit, freie Zeit **Are you free** after school? = Hast du nach der Schule Zeit?
today	heute	What's our first lesson **today**? – French.
beach	der Strand	Let's go **to the beach**. = zum Strand, an den Strand **!** **on** the beach = **am** Strand

(to) **move**	(sich) bewegen	Please don't **move** now …
slow	langsam	This animal is very **slow**.
too slow	zu langsam	Let's go to the beach. – Sorry, I'm **too** busy.
weird	seltsam, komisch	That's **weird**. My sandwich isn't in my bag, but Scout is very happy …
trouble	der Ärger, Schwierigkeiten	He is **in trouble**. = Er hat Ärger. / Er ist in Schwierigkeiten.
those	die dort, jene (dort)	**!** **Those** kann mit Nomen stehen: I don't like **those** people. They're mean. Oder es kann alleine stehen: Hey! **Those** are my things!
bully	der Mobber, die Mobberin; der Tyrann, die Tyrannin	noun: **bully** – verb: (to) **bully** (tyrannisieren, mobben)
him	ihm, ihn	There's Tom. Can you see **him**? (ihn) Let's talk to **him**. (mit ihm)
them	sie, ihnen	I – me he – him we – us they – them
some	einige, ein paar; etwas, ein wenig	There are **some** books in my bag. (einige) I understand **some** French. (etwas, ein wenig)
▶ p. 31 **still**	(immer) noch; trotzdem	It's 4.30 and Joe **still** isn't here. (noch) I know you're tired! **Still** – please listen. (trotzdem)
away	weg, fort	(to) **walk/go away** = weggehen
her friends	ihre Freunde/Freundinnen	I – my we – our she – her you – your he – his they – their (ihr/e)
his friends	seine Freunde/Freundinnen	
These are my friends.	Das hier sind meine Freunde/ Freundinnen.	

this, that – these, those

- Wenn etwas näher beim Sprecher oder bei der Sprecherin ist, verwendet man eher **this** und **these**.

  This dog is so nice, and I love **these** cats.

- Wenn etwas weiter entfernt ist, verwendet man eher **that** und **those**.

  That snake and **those** seagulls … no, I'm really scared.

▶ p. 32	opinion	die Meinung	**in my opinion** = meiner Meinung nach
	best	beste(r, s); am besten	You're my **best** friend!
	when	wenn *(zeitlich)*	❗ **when** = **1.** wann: **When**'s lunch? **2.** wenn: I eat a sandwich **when** I'm hungry.

Study skills

▶ p. 34	(to) learn	lernen	It's hard to **learn** all these new words. Can I **learn** to play the guitar, Mum?
	vocabulary, *infml auch* **vocab**	der Wortschatz, das Vokabular; das Vokabelverzeichnis	Reading English books is good for your **vocabulary**. (Wortschatz) Learn the new words on these **vocabulary** pages. (Vokabeln, Vokabelverzeichnis)
	mind map	die Gedankenkarte, das Wörternetz, die Mindmap	
	way	der Weg; die Art und Weise	You're in the **way**. (im Weg) Do it **(in) this way**! (auf diese Art/Weise) You can do it **in different ways**. (**auf** unterschiedliche Art/Weise)
	file	die Datei; der Ordner, die Liste	I have a **file** on my computer with all the new words from my French lessons.
	word	das Wort	What's the English **word** for "Handy"? – The right **word** is "phone".
	or	oder; sonst	Do you like cats **or** dogs? – I love cats!
	(from) A to Z	(von) A bis Z	We go to school **from** Monday **to** Friday. ❗ **to** = **1.** bis: from Monday **to** Friday; **2.** (um) zu: things **to** eat; **3.** zu, nach: I go **to** school.; **4.** auf: the answer **to** your question

Unit task

| ▶ p. 35 | (to) make | machen, herstellen | Let's **make** music! I play the guitar and you can sing. |
| | step | die Stufe; der Schritt | Let's sit down on the **steps** and look at the map. |

| | useful | nützlich, hilfreich | These exercises are too hard? Here are some **useful** tips. (= these tips can help you) |
| | difficult | schwierig, schwer | This exercise is really **difficult**. (= really hard) |

Unit 2: My family and home

▶ pp. 48/49	**family**	die Familie	❗ Betonung auf der 1. Silbe: **fam**ily
	home	das Heim, das Zuhause	(to) go **home** = nach Hause gehen **at home** = zu Hause
	aunt	die Tante	**aunt ◀ ▶ uncle**
	uncle	der Onkel	
	brother	der Bruder	**brother ◀ ▶ sister**
	sister	die Schwester	
	cousin	der Cousin, die Cousine	❗ Betonung auf der 1. Silbe: **cou**sin
	daughter	die Tochter	Do they have kids? – Yes, they have one
	son	der Sohn	**daughter,** Jane, and one **son,** Jack.
	circle	der Kreis	drawing a **circle** 
	neighbour	der Nachbar, die Nachbarin	**neighbourhood** = die Nachbarschaft, die Gegend, das Viertel There's a bike shop in my **neighbourhood.**
	stepmum	die Stiefmutter	step- ("Stief-") **stepmum** **stepdad** **stepsister** **stepbrother** **stepdaughter** **stepson**

Topic 1

▶ p. 50	**pet**	das (Haus-)Tier	Are seagulls good **pets?** – No, they aren't!
	a lot (of) **lots (of)**	viel/e; sehr viel/e	I have **a lot of** books in my room. (viele) I like the breaks at school **a lot.** (sehr)
	rabbit	das Kaninchen	rabbit —— hamster
	hamster	der Hamster	
	Are you lost?	Hast du dich verlaufen/verirrt?	**Are you lost?** – Yes, I am. Where's Room 3?
	angry	wütend	Scout has my sandwich. I'm so **angry!**
	vet	der Tierarzt, die Tierärztin	a **vet** with a dog 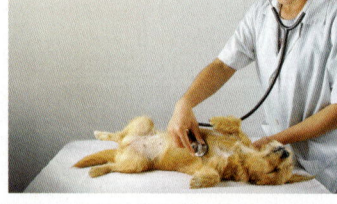

weekend	das Wochenende	❗ **at** the **weekend** = **am** Wochenende **at weekends** = **an** den Wochenenden (= an vielen/allen Wochenenden)

work	die Arbeit	**at work** = **bei** der Arbeit, **am** Arbeitsplatz
		noun: **work** –
		verb: (to) **work** =
		    1. arbeiten: **Work** with a partner.
		    2. funktionieren: My old laptop **works** OK.

house	das Haus	
loud	laut	Quiet, please. You're too **loud.**
messy	unordentlich	adjective: **messy** – noun: **mess** (das Chaos, die Unordnung)
▶ p. 51 **polite**	höflich	
only	nur, bloß; erst	I **only** have one pet. (nur) My sister is **only** two. (erst)
▶ p. 52 **homework**	die Hausaufgabe(n)	What's for **homework?** = Was haben wir als Hausaufgabe(n) auf? ❗ *English:* (to) **do** your **homework** *German:* **(deine) Hausaufgaben machen** **homework** hat <u>keinen Plural</u>: **Homework is** horrible. **Hausaufgaben <u>sind</u>** schrecklich.
(to) do	machen, tun	my favourite thing to **do** = das, was ich am liebsten tue
missing	vermisst	We can help you to find your **missing** pet.
(to) fly	fliegen	Seagulls and parrots can **fly.**
(to) call	nennen; rufen; anrufen	• This is Fiona, but we **call** her Fi. (nennen) • It's time for a snack – **call** the kids! (rufen) • **Call** me on this phone number: … (anrufen) verb: (to) **call** – noun: **(phone) call** (der Ruf; der (Telefon-)Anruf)

if	wenn, falls	What **if** …? =Was wäre, wenn …?
		❗ **if** =
		    1. falls: **If** you see our missing cat, please phone us.
		    2. ob: I don't know **if** this is the right answer.

(to) find	finden	I can't **find** my bag. Where is it?

▶ p. 53 **(to) want**	wollen	❗ • **want** sth. = etwas (haben) wollen
		    I **want** a new computer.
		   • **want <u>to do</u>** sth. = etwas tun wollen
		    I **want to have** it now.

active	aktiv	**active** ◄ ► **passive** (passiv)
cute	niedlich, süß	Our rabbit is still very small and he's so **cute!**

fast	schnell	I like my bike, but it isn't very **fast.**
interesting	interessant	Books about animals are very **interesting.**
special	besondere(r, s)	... **is special** = ... ist etwas Besonderes What's **special about** this place? = Was ist das Besondere **an** diesem Ort?
lizard	die Eidechse	
quite	ziemlich, ganz	My homework is **quite** hard. (ziemlich schwer) My maths teacher is **quite** nice. (ganz nett)
dream	der Traum	I'm a vet. It's my **dream** job. I love it. noun: **dream** – verb: (to) **dream (of/about sth.)** (träumen (von etwas))

Topic 2

▶ p. 54	tree	der Baum	
	garden	der Garten	tree garden
	ground floor	das Erdgeschoss	**ground** = der (Erd-)Boden ❗ **floor** = **1.** die Etage, das Stock(werk); **2.** der Fußboden
	top	die Spitze, das obere Ende	**at the top (of** sth.) = oben; am oberen Ende (von etwas); an der Spitze (von etwas) **top floor** = das Dach-/Obergeschoss, das oberste Stockwerk, die oberste Etage
	flat	die Wohnung	some **flats** with **balconies**
	balcony	der Balkon	
	garage	die Garage	❗ Betonung auf der 1. Silbe: **ga**rage
	he/she/it has	er/sie/es hat	I **have** he **has** you **have** she **has** we **have** it **has** they **have**
	each	jede(r, s) (einzelne), jeweils	**Each** student can ask one question. = You can ask one question **each.** (jeweils eine Frage)
	lamp	die Lampe	
▶ p. 55	tour (of)	die Tour, die Reise, der Rundgang / die Rundfahrt (durch)	❗ a **tour of** Brighton = ein Rundgang / eine Rundfahrt / eine Reise **durch** Brighton
	bedroom	das Schlafzimmer	

bathroom	das Bad(ezimmer)	
dining room	das Esszimmer	
kitchen	die Küche	
living room	das Wohnzimmer	
shoe	der Schuh	
(to) live	leben, wohnen	Leo **lives** in Hove.
(to) tell	erzählen, sagen	**Tell** the class about your hobbies. Please **tell** me how I can help you.

Topic 3

▶ p. 56	bed	das Bett	❗ (to) **go to bed** = **ins** Bett gehen
	cushion	das Kissen	
	wardrobe	der Kleiderschrank	cushions bed mirror wardrobe
	mirror	der Spiegel	
	clothes *(pl)*	die Kleidung, die Kleidungsstücke	❗ *English:* **All** her **clothes are** black. *German:* Ihre gesamte **Kleidung ist** schwarz.
	shelf, *pl* shelves	das Regal(brett)	❗ one **shelf** – two **shelves**
	robot	der Roboter	Hello, **robot!**
	chair	der Stuhl	
	chocolate	die Schokolade	❗ Betonung auf der 1. Silbe: **choc**olate
	under	unter	**on ◀ ▶ under**
	table	der Tisch	a **table** a **desk**
	in front of	vor	
	behind	hinter	
	next to	neben	
▶ p. 57	door	die Tür	
	tidy	ordentlich	• adjective: **tidy** • My room is always very **tidy.** • verb: (to) **tidy** (aufräumen) • I often **tidy** my room. **tidy ◀ ▶ messy**

▶ p. 58	person	die Person	❗ Nur selten wird der Plural **persons** benutzt. Normalerweise: one **person** – five **people**
▶ p. 59	sweets *(pl)*	die Bonbons, die Süßigkeiten	noun: **sweets** – adjective: **sweet** (süß)
	its terrarium	sein Terrarium / ihr Terrarium	❗ I have a pet. **It's** (= **It is**) a hamster. **Its** name is Joe. (= the hamster's name)

I – **my** name	we – **our** names
you – **your** name	you – **your** names
he – **his** name	they – **their** names
she – **her** name	it – **its** name

	wall	die Wand, die Mauer	❗ **on** the wall = **an** der Wand; **an** die Wand
	my own room	mein/ein eigenes Zimmer	❗ *English:* Do you have **your own** room? *German:* Hast du **ein eigenes** Zimmer?

Story

▶ p. 60	**problem**	das Problem	❗ Betonung auf der 1. Silbe: **prob**lem
	parents *(pl)*	die Eltern	▶▶ your mum and dad
	of course	natürlich, selbstverständlich	Where's my phone? Oh, in my bag, **of course**!
	at her mum's **(house)**	bei ihrer Mutter (zu Hause/daheim)	Can we meet **at Lily's** / **at Lily's house?** Our house is too loud and too messy.
	funny	witzig, lustig; seltsam	• All those animals in the house – it's not **funny!** (witzig, lustig) • What's so **funny about** a horse in the living room? (Was ist so lustig **an** …?) • That's **funny** … my phone isn't in my bag … where is it? (seltsam)
	(to) **speak (to)**	sprechen (mit)	I can **speak** English. Can I **speak to** you after the lesson, Mr Lee? **speaking** = das Sprechen
	later	später	**Speak later.** = Tschüs. / Bis später.
▶ p. 61	**dinner**	das Abendessen	I'm hungry! **What's for** dinner, dad? = Was gibt es zum Abendessen? ❗ **for** lunch / **for** dinner = **zum** Mittagessen / **zum** Abendessen
	love	der Liebling	❗ **love** = 1. der Liebling; 2. die Liebe; 3. lieben
	rude	unhöflich, frech	**polite ◀▶ rude**
	little	klein	▶▶ small We have a cute **little** rabbit.
	perfect	perfekt	❗ Betonung auf der 1. Silbe: **per**fect
	part (of)	der Teil (von)	What **part of** England are you from? = Aus welchem Teil Englands …? A pet is always **part of** the family.
	electric	elektrisch, Elektro-	I play the **electric** guitar in our band.

headphones *(pl)*	der Kopfhörer	❗ *English:* These **are** my new **headphones.** *German:* Dies **ist** mein neuer **Kopfhörer**.
game	das Spiel	Let's meet at Jo's and play some nice **games**.
back	zurück	Mum is **back** at home. (wieder zu Hause)
▶ p. 62 **on the phone**	am Telefon	❗ **on** = **1.** auf: **on** the desk **2.** an/am: **on** Monday, **on** the phone
noise	das Geräusch; der Lärm	Listen! What's that **noise**? (Geräusch) All that **noise!** I can't do my homework. (Lärm)
idea	die Idee	Can't we do it this way? – Of course! Good **idea**.
important	wichtig	Listen, please. This is very **important**.
long	lang	**(for) a long time** = lange, (für) eine lange Zeit Sorry, I can't talk to you **for a long time**.

Study skills

▶ p. 64 **(to) spell**	buchstabieren	verb: (to) **spell** – noun: **spelling** (die Schreibweise, die Rechtschreibung)
alphabet	das Alphabet	❗ Betonung auf der 1. Silbe: **al**phabet
address	die Adresse	Where do you live? What's your **address?** ❗ Beachte die Schreibweise: a**dd**ress
like this	so, auf diese Art	▶▶ (in) this way Look, it's not hard if you do it **like this**. ❗ **1.** it's always **like this** (so) **2.** a story **like this** (so/solch eine Geschichte)
oh	Null *(im gesprochenen Englisch)*	

15 fifteen	21 twenty-one	40 forty	100 a/one hundred
16 sixteen	22 twenty-two	50 fifty	101 a/one hundred and one
17 seventeen	(...)	60 sixty	102 a/one hundred and two
18 eighteen	30 thirty	70 seventy	103 a/one hundred and three
19 nineteen	31 thirty-one	80 eighty	(...)
20 twenty	(...)	90 ninety	▶ Numbers, p. 277

(to) write	schreiben	First **write** your text, then check the spelling!

Unit task

▶ p. 65 **(to) present** sth. **(to sb.)**	(jm.) etwas präsentieren, vorstellen	verb: (to) **present** sth. **to** sb. – noun: **presentation** (das Referat, die Präsentation) (to) **give a presentation** = ein Referat halten ❗ *English:* **Present** your idea **to** your friends. *German:* Stelle deinen Freunden deine Idee vor. (*nicht:* ~~Present them your idea~~.)
modern	modern	❗ Betonung auf der 1. Silbe: **mo**dern
photographer	der Fotograf, die Fotografin	❗ Betonung auf der 2. Silbe: pho**to**grapher

Unit 3: My day

▶ pp. 80/81

journey	die Reise, die Fahrt; der Weg	It's not a long **journey** from here to Hove. You can walk or take the bus.
(to) come	(mit)kommen	**Come** to our disco on Saturday! (kommen) Your friends can **come** too! (mitkommen)
bus	der Bus	**!** *English:* **on** the bus *German:* **im Bus**
by bike/bus/…	mit dem Fahrrad/Bus/…	Let's not walk there, let's go **by** bus.
car	das Auto	
train	der Zug, die Eisenbahn	**!** *English:* **on** the train *German:* **im Zug**
short	kurz; klein *(Person; Körpergröße)*	**short ◄ ► long** It's a **short** walk. (= not a long walk) My little brother is still **short.** (klein *(Körpergröße)*)

Topic 1

▶ p. 82

weekday	der Werktag, der Wochentag	Monday to Friday are **weekdays.** **weekdays ◄ ► weekend**
at 8 o'clock	um 8 Uhr	It's **1 o'clock** now.
4 p.m.	4 Uhr nachmittags, 16 Uhr	**9 p.m.** = 9 Uhr abends, 21 Uhr
4 a.m.	4 Uhr (früh)morgens	**9 a.m.** = 9 Uhr vormittags
the United Kingdom (= the UK)	das Vereinigte Königreich	**► ►** England, Scotland, Wales and Northern Ireland
hour	die Stunde	**!** Das "h" wird nicht gesprochen. Das Wort klingt genau wie "our".
clock	die (Wand-, Stand-, Turm-)Uhr	
morning	der Morgen	**!** **in** the morning = morgens, **am** Morgen
evening	der Abend	**!** **in** the evening = abends, **am** Abend
lunchtime	die Mittagszeit	**!** **at** lunchtime = **zur** Mittagszeit
end	das Ende, der Schluss	noun: **end** – verb: (to) **end** (enden; beenden)
in the end **at** the end (of)	schließlich; zum Schluss am Ende (von)	Walk or take the bus? **In the end** I often go by bus. **At the end of** a long school day I'm always tired.

▶ p. 83

before (school / the lesson)	vor (der Schule / der Unterrichtsstunde)	**before** the lesson ◄ ► **after** the lesson

	before		after	
preposition *(plus noun)*	**before** school	(**vor** der Schule)	◄ ►	**after** school	(**nach** der Schule)
conjunction *(plus sentence)*	**before** you read	(**bevor** du liest)	◄ ►	**after** you read	(**nachdem** du liest)

why	warum	

what?	was?	**when**	wann?
where?	wo(hin)?	**why?**	warum?
who?	wer?	**how?**	wie?

newspaper (*kurz auch:* **paper**)	die (Tages-)Zeitung	**paper** = **1.** dle (Tages-)Zeitung I read the **paper** / **newspaper** in the morning. **2.** das Papier I can draw an elephant. Do you have a pen and some **paper?**
letter	der Brief	I often write **letters** to my grandma.
competition	der Wettbewerb	One of my photos is in an art **competition.**
(to) choose	(aus)wählen	Walk or go by bike? You can **choose.**
winner	der Gewinner, die Gewinnerin / der Sieger, die Siegerin	Lucie is the **winner** of the photo competition! (= Her photo is the best photo.)
illness	die Krankheit	noun: **illness** – adjective: **ill** (krank)
wheelchair	der Rollstuhl	a **wheelchair**
husband	der Ehemann	Zoe and Carl are our parents. Carl is Zoe's **husband.**
cafe	das Café	**!** Betonung auf der 1. Silbe: **ca**fe
(to) get up	aufstehen	On weekdays I **get up** at 7 a.m.
shower	die Dusche	(to) **have a shower** = (sich) duschen
(to) get dressed	sich anziehen	You're late! **Get dressed!** Where are your clothes?
breakfast	das Frühstück	

(to) take	dauern, *(Zeit)* brauchen, in Anspruch nehmen	The journey from London to Brighton **takes** an hour by train.
		! (to) **take** =
		  1. dauern, *(Zeit)* brauchen, in Anspruch nehmen;
		  2. (mit)nehmen; bringen;
		  3. (to) **take photos** = Fotos machen

(to) watch (sth.)	(sich etwas) anschauen; (etwas) beobachten	(to) **look** • (to) **see** • (to) **watch** • **Look! Look** at the picture. (schauen, anschauen) • Can you **see** me? (sehen) • Can I **watch** the football game? (anschauen) Let's **watch** the dogs. (beobachten)

▶ p.84	line	die Zeile; die Reihe	a **line** of houses
	shopping	das Einkaufen; die Einkäufe	(to) **do the shopping** = die Einkäufe erledigen, einkaufen gehen (to) **go shopping** = einkaufen gehen
	afternoon	der Nachmittag	

• **in** the morning	morgens, am Morgen	• **on** Monday	am Montag
in the afternoon	nachmittags, am Nachmittag	**on** Tuesdays	dienstags, an Dienstagen
in the evening	abends, am Abend	**on** Friday morning	freitagmorgens, am Freitagmorgen

▶ p.85	(to) **brush**	bürsten	verb: (to) **brush** – noun: **brush** (die Bürste)
	tooth, *pl* teeth	der Zahn	(to) **brush your teeth** = (sich) die Zähne putzen
	everybody	jeder; alle	**Hello everybody!** = Hallo/Servus allerseits! Mr Lee is really nice. **Everybody** likes him.
	project	das Projekt	❗ Betonung auf der 1. Silbe: **pro**ject
	country	das Land, *(auch:)* die ländliche Gegend	❗ **in** the country = **auf** dem Land

Topic 2

▶ p.86	(school) club	die AG *(in der Schule)*	**club** = **1.** der Klub, der Verein; **2. school club** = die AG
	drama	das Schauspiel, die darstellende Kunst	
	(to) **cycle**	Rad fahren	**cycling** = das Radfahren
	(to) **hike**	wandern	**hiking** = das Wandern We often go **hiking** at the weekend.
	(to) **run**	rennen, laufen	**running** = das Laufen *(Sport)*
	trampolining	das Trampolinspringen/-turnen	**trampoline** = das Trampolin
	most schools	die meisten Schulen	**Most** students in my class go to school clubs.
	Which clubs ...?	Welche AGs ...?	**Which** school club do you like?
	sea	das Meer, die See	❗ **by** the sea = **am** Meer, **an** der See
▶ p.87	sentence	der Satz	"I like you." is a short English **sentence.**

sometimes	manchmal	
never	nie, niemals	always often sometimes rarely never
rarely	selten *(Adv.)*	adverb: **rarely** (I **rarely** read old books.) adjective: **rare** (a **rare** old book)
▶ p.89 secret	das Geheimnis; geheim	This is a **secret** message. (geheim) It's our **secret**. (Geheimnis)
activity	die Aktivität, die Tätigkeit	❗ Betonung auf der 2. Silbe: ac**tiv**ity

Topic 3

▶ p.90 a shame	schade; eine Schande	You're not free this afternoon? **That's a shame!** (Das ist schade!) **What a shame!** (Wie schade!)
I'd love to. **(= I would love to.)**	Sehr gerne. / Das würde ich sehr gerne.	**Would you like** a drink? – Oh yes, please, **I'd love** some cola! **I'd like/love ...** (= **I would like/love ...**) = Ich hätte (liebend) gern ... / Ich möchte (liebend gern) ... **I'd love/like to meet** Zane. = Ich würde mich (liebend) gerne mit Zane treffen.
(to) **ask** sb. **to do** sth.	jn. bitten, etwas zu tun	Can I **ask** you **to help** me? = Can I **ask** you **for** some help? ❗ (to) **ask** = **1.** fragen; 　　　　**2.** (to) **ask** sb. **for** sth. = jn. **um** etwas bitten
▶ p.91 plan	der Plan	noun: **plan** – verb: (to) **plan** (planen) I'm **planning** dinner with my friends. – Oh, nice! What do you **plan to cook?** (... planst du / plant ihr, zu kochen?)

Story

▶ p.92 (to) **win**	gewinnen	I feel good when my football team **wins.**
prize	der Preis, der Gewinn	The **prize** for the winner of this competition is a weekend in Paris.
ceremony	die Feier, die Zeremonie	**prize ceremony** = die Preisverleihung ❗ Betonung auf der 1. Silbe: **ce**remony
(to) **show**	zeigen	**Show** your teacher your story. = **Show** your story **to** your teacher. (Zeige deinem Lehrer / deiner Lehrerin deinen Text.) verb: (to) **show** – noun: **show** (die Show, die Aufführung; die Ausstellung)
article	der Artikel	❗ Betonung auf der 1. Silbe: **ar**ticle
surprised	überrascht	This bike for only £150? I'm really **surprised.**

(to) **send**	senden, schicken	I'd like to **send** my sister a message. = I'd like to **send** a message **to** my sister. = ... meiner Schwester eine Nachricht schicken
next	nächste(r, s)	**the next day** = am nächsten Tag
guys *(pl)*	Leute *(als Anrede verwendet)*	Hey, **guys,** great to see you!
(to) **feel**	sich fühlen; fühlen	I **feel** great when I make music.
(to) **be/feel sorry for** sb.	Mitleid haben mit jm.	**I'm** / I **feel sorry for** him. = Ich habe Mitleid mit ihm. / Er tut mir leid.

her	sie; ihr	❗ **her** = **1.** sie; ihr:
		      I can see **her**. (sie) / I can help
		      her. (ihr)
		2. ihr/e (wessen?): **her** dog, **her**
		      room

stupid	dumm, blöd; albern	That's a **stupid** idea. (= not a clever idea)
(to) **hate**	hassen	verbs: (to) **love** ◀ ▶ (to) **hate** nouns: **love** ◀ ▶ **hate** (der Hass)
▶ p.93 **much**	viel; sehr	**How much** time do we have? (viel) I like Zane so **much.** (so sehr) **Thank you very much.** = Vielen Dank. / Danke vielmals.
Well done.	Gut gemacht!	**well** = gut *(Adv.)* adjective: **good** Your English is very **good.** – adverb: **well** You speak English very **well.**
news	die Nachrichten	**news** hat keinen Plural: **That is** good news. Das **sind** gute **Nachrichten.**
(to) **get**	*(sich etwas)* holen/besorgen; bekommen	Where can I **get** help? (bekommen) Let's **get** some sandwiches. (holen/besorgen)
as the winner	als Gewinner/in	❗ *English:* **as the** winner / **as a** teacher *German:* **als** Gewinner/in / **als** Lehrer/in
money	das Geld	Nice bike ... how much **money** do I have?
heading	die Überschrift	The **heading** is at the top of a page or where a new part or unit of a book starts.
(to) **find out (about)**	herausfinden; sich informieren (über)	Let's **find out** when the show starts. (herausfinden) **Find out about** the cricket club at our school and tell your friends. (sich informieren über)
(to) **explain** sth. **to** sb.	jm. etwas erklären	❗ *English:* Please **explain** it **to me.** *German:* **Erkläre** es **mir** bitte.
(to) **happen (to** sb.)	(jm.) geschehen, passieren	Tell us what **happen**s in the story.
▶ p.94 (to) **give**	geben	Can you **give** me that book, please?

(to) **pay (for** sth.**)**	zahlen; (etwas) bezahlen	**!** *English:* Let me **pay for** the pizzas. *German:* Lass mich die Pizzas **bezahlen.**
cleaner	die Reinigungskraft	
pound (£)	das Pfund *(britische Währung)*	**!** you write: **£ 5** – you say: five **pounds**
penny (= p), *pl* **pence**	der Penny, Pence *(Plural)*	

Pounds and euros
In **England** you have **pounds** and **pence.**

You say:	*You write:*
fifty p / fifty pence	**50 p**
one pound / a pound	**£ 1**
two pounds fifty	**£ 2.50**

In **Germany** you have **euros** and **cents.**

You say:	*You write:*
fifty cents	**€ 0.50**
one euro / a euro	**€ 1**
two euros fifty	**€ 2.50**

Study skills

▶ p. 96	(to) **look** sth. **up**	etwas nachschlagen, nachschauen	What's "Möwe" in English? – Sorry, I don't know. Let's **look** it **up.**
	jigsaw (puzzle)	das Puzzle	**puzzle** = das Rätsel
	(to) **collect**	(ein)sammeln	My friend Jamie **collects** old clocks.
	letter	der Buchstabe	**!** **letter** = **1.** der Buchstabe; **2.** der Brief
	card	die Karte	playing **cards** = die Spielkarten
	language	die Sprache	She speaks three **languages:** English, German and French.
	group	die Gruppe	Please work in **groups** of 3 or 4 students.

Unit task

▶ p. 97	(to) **share**	teilen	I **share** a room **with** my brother. = My brother and I **share** a room. (Wir teilen uns ein Zimmer.) verb: (to) **share** – noun: **share** (der (An-)Teil)
	match	das Spiel, der Wettkampf	a football **match** ▶▶ a football game
	light	das Licht; die Lampe	I have good **lights** on my bike. **car light** = der Autoscheinwerfer
	(to) **speak clearly/loudly**	deutlich/laut sprechen	

Unit 4: Where I live

pp. 110/111	**cinema**	das Kino	**!** **at** the cinema = **im** Kino
	pier	der Pier, die Seebrücke	
	shop	das Geschäft, der Laden	(to) **be at the shops** = Einkäufe erledigen
	busy	hektisch, belebt	It's too **busy** in the shops. Let's go home. **!** **busy** = **1.** hektisch, belebt; **2.** (viel) beschäftigt

palace	der Palast, das Schloss	❗ Betonung auf der 1. Silbe: **pal**ace
duke	der Herzog	
marina	der Jachthafen	
north	der Norden; nördlich; Nord-	York is in the **north** of England.
picnic	das Picknick	(to) **have a picnic** = ein Picknick machen
(to) **hear**	hören	❗ (to) **hear** = hören (können) (to) **listen** (to) = zuhören, horchen **Listen!** Can you **hear** that noise?
street	die Straße *(in Ortschaften)*	**street music** = die Straßenmusik **street dance** = der Streetdance *(Tanzstil)* ❗ **in the street** = **auf** der Straße
(to) **practise**	üben	I **practise** the guitar every day. verb: (to) **practise** – noun: **practice** (die Übung(en))
skill	die Fähigkeit, die Fertigkeit	
chips *(pl)*	die Pommes frites	**fish and chips** = Fisch mit Pommes frites
mile	die Meile *(ca. 1,6 km)*	**per** = pro ❗ **at** 30 **miles per hour** = **mit** 30 Meilen pro Stunde
kilometre (km)	der Kilometer	1,000 **metres** = 1 **kilometre** **1 mile = 1.6 km**
1.6 (one point six)	1,6 (eins Komma sechs)	

Im Englischen steht ein **Punkt,** im Deutschen ein **Komma.**

English: 1.6 = one **point** six   *German:* 1,6 = eins **Komma** sechs

Topic 1

▶ p. 112

(to) **smell**	riechen; schlecht riechen	verb: (to) **smell** – noun: **smell** (der Geruch; der Gestank)
cooking	das Kochen, das *(gekochte)* Essen	my **cooking** = mein (gekochtes) Essen verb: (to) **cook** – nouns: *(person)* **cook**; *(what you cook/eat; a hobby)* **cooking**
boring	langweilig	Maths isn't **boring!** I think it's very interesting.
clean	sauber	adjective: **clean** – verb: (to) **clean** (sauber machen, putzen)
dirty	schmutzig	**dirty ◀ ▶ clean**
unfriendly	unfreundlich	**friendly ◀ ▶ unfriendly**

youth centre	das Jugendzentrum	**youth** = die Jugend; der Jugendliche **centre** = das Zentrum; die Mitte
field	das Feld; die Weide	❗ the horses **in** the field = die Pferde **auf** der Weide
estate	die Wohnsiedlung; das Gewerbegebiet	❗ **on** our estate = **in** unserer (Wohn-) Siedlung
town	die Stadt	**in town** = in der Stadt **town centre** = das Stadtzentrum
married (to)	verheiratet (mit)	Jack is **married to** Jill. = Jack is Jill's husband.
(to) look after	sich kümmern um; aufpassen auf	I sometimes **look after** my baby sister. People don't **look after** our town well: there's a lot of rubbish in the streets.
rubbish	der (Haus-)Müll, der Abfall	Please put your **rubbish** in the **bin.**
bin	der (Müll-)Eimer	
also	auch	I like music, and I **also** like dancing. = I like music and I like dancing too.
▶ p. 113 **note**	die Notiz; der kurze Brief	**(to) make notes** = (sich) Notizen machen *(zur Vorbereitung)*
▶ p. 114 **like**	wie; wie zum Beispiel	My bike is **like** your bike. (wie) I like team sports **like** cricket, basketball or football. (wie zum Beispiel) What's your new school **like**? (Wie ist …?)
(to) box	boxen	**boxing** = das Boxen
a girls' group	eine Mädchengruppe, eine Gruppe für Mädchen	

Apostroph + s: Etwas gehört (zu) jemandem. Aber beachte die **Stellung des** Apostrophs!

Singular + Apostroph + s: **eine** Person

the **girl's** dog
der Hund **des Mädchens**

Plural -s + Apostroph: **mehrere** Personen

the **girls'** dogs
die Hunde **der Mädchen**

(to) buy	kaufen	▶▶ (to) get sth. I'm hungry. Let's **buy** some sandwiches.
▶ p. 115 **village**	das Dorf	a very small town in the country
many	viele	You have **many** fish in your aquarium! **How many** are there?

much („viel") – **many** („viele")

How much time do we have?
Wie viel Zeit …?

How many shops are in your village?
Wie viele Geschäfte …?

We don't have **much** time, but we have **a lot of / lots of** work.
    nicht viel Zeit   **viel** Arbeit

There aren't **many** shops, but there are **a lot of / lots of** fields.
    nicht viele Geschäfte   **viele** Felder

Topic 2

▶ p. 116	**hospital**	das Krankenhaus	When you're very ill, you go **to hospital.** (ins Krankenhaus) Is he very ill? Is he **in hospital?** (im Krankenhaus)
	ice rink	die Schlittschuhbahn	
	library	die Bücherei, die Bibliothek	I don't always buy books, I often get them from the **library.** ❗ **at** the library = **in** der Bücherei/Bibliothek
	supermarket	der Supermarkt	❗ **at** the **supermarket** = **im** Supermarkt
	museum	das Museum	❗ **at** the **museum** = **im** Museum
	stadium	das Stadion	❗ **at** the **stadium** = **im** Stadion
	(train) station	der Bahnhof	❗ Betonung auf der 1. Silbe: **sta**tion
	biggest	der/die/das größte; am größten	What's the **biggest** building in this town? (das größte Gebäude) Which city is **biggest:** London, Berlin, Madrid? (am größten)
▶ p. 117	**everywhere**	überall	There's rubbish **everywhere** here in the park. It's horrible!
	head	der Kopf	a snake with three **heads**
	guide dog	der Blindenhund	I have a **guide dog** because I can't see very well, and my dog helps me. noun: **(tour) guide** (der Reiseleiter, die Reiseleiterin / der Fremdenführer, die Fremdenführerin) – verb: (to) **guide** (führen, leiten)
▶ p. 118	**visitor**	der Besucher, die Besucherin; der Gast	nouns: **visitor** / **visit** (der Besuch) – verb: (to) **visit** (besuchen) Can we **visit** grandpa on Sunday? He loves having **visitors.**
	another	ein/e andere/r/s; noch ein/e	! don't like this game. Can't we play **another** (= a different) game? Do you really want to buy **another** (= a new, an extra) bag? You have so many!
	Germany	Deutschland	noun/country: **Germany** – adjective/language: **German**
	information	die Information(en)	**visitor information centre** = die Touristeninformation, das Fremdenverkehrsbüro
			information hat keinen Plural: **That is** interesting information. Das **sind** interessante **Informationen.**
	fish and chip shop	*die Imbissstube, die Fisch mit Pommes frites verkauft*	
	warm	warm	(to) **get warm** = warm werden

summer	der Sommer	**summer** ◀ ▶ **winter** (der Winter)
Excuse me, …	Entschuldigung, … / Entschuldigen Sie, …	**Excuse me,** please. Where's the train station?
something	etwas	Can I ask you **something?** I'm hungry! Can I have **something** to eat?

Topic 3

▶ p. 120

weather	das Wetter, die Witterung	What's the **weather** like? Can we go to the beach?
rainy	regnerisch	It's a **rainy** day. = It's **raining.** adjective: **rainy** – noun: **rain** (der Regen) – verb: (to) **rain** (regnen)
sunny	sonnig	It's **sunny.** = Die Sonne scheint. adjective: **sunny** – noun: **sun** (die Sonne)
snowy	schneebedeckt; verschneit	adjective: **snowy** – noun: **snow** (der Schnee) – verb: (to) **snow** (schneien)

Verben und Nomen, die dieselbe Form haben

answer	1. (be)antworten	2. die Antwort	phone	1. anrufen	2. das Telefon
cook	1. kochen	2. der Koch, die Köchin	plan	1. planen	2. der Plan
dance	1. tanzen	2. der Tanz	rain	1. regnen	2. der Regen
drink	1. trinken	2. das Getränk	snow	1. schneien	2. der Schnee
help	1. helfen	2. die Hilfe	walk	1. (zu Fuß) gehen	2. der Spaziergang
love	1. lieben	2. die Liebe	work	1. arbeiten	2. die Arbeit

cloudy	wolkig, bewölkt	adjective: **cloudy** – noun: **cloud** (die Wolke)
windy	windig	It's **windy.** adjective: **windy** – noun: **wind** (der Wind)
outside the Pavilion	außerhalb des Pavilion	**outside** ◀ ▶ **inside**

	preposition (+ noun)	**adverb** (Where?)
inside	Do your rabbits live **inside your house?** (innerhalb (von))	They're never **inside.** (= in the house) ((nach) (dr)innen)
outside	No, they live **outside the house.** (außerhalb (von))	They're always **outside.** (= in the garden) ((nach) draußen)

cold	kalt	(to) **be cold** = frieren adjective: **cold** – noun: **cold** (die Kälte; die Erkältung) (to) **have a cold** = erkältet sein

woman, *pl* **women**	die Frau	❗ one **woman** – two **women** one **man** – two **men** (ein Mann – zwei Männer)
up	hinauf, hoch	**up** ◄ ► **down** (hinunter, herunter)
(to) travel	reisen, fahren	verb: (to) **travel** – noun: **travel** (das Reisen)
every	jede(r, s)	I go to the drama club **every** Tuesday. **every 30 minutes** = alle 30 Minuten
second	die Sekunde	**for 30 seconds** = für 30 Sekunden, 30 Sekunden lang
► p. 121 **more**	mehr, weitere	I only go to the cycling club. I don't have time for **more** clubs. Please write **three more** words into the mind map. (noch drei Wörter, drei weitere Wörter)
(to) stop	(an)halten; stoppen; aufhören (mit)	**(to) start** ◄ ► **(to) stop** The bus **stops** here. (hält an) Please **stop** talking and listen. (aufhören mit) verb: (to) **stop** – noun: **stop** (der Halt, der Haltepunkt; die Unterbrechung) **bus stop** = die Bushaltestelle
(to) cost	kosten	How much does this phone **cost?** verb: (to) **cost** – noun: **cost** (die Kosten; der Preis)
upside down	verkehrt herum, auf dem Kopf	the **upside down house** = das Haus, das auf dem Kopf steht
so	also, daher	It's Sunday, **so** we don't go to school. ❗ **so** = 1. **so** big/cold/… = so groß/kalt/… 2. also, daher
expensive	teuer	£5 for this comic? That's very **expensive!** (= it costs a lot of money)
swap	der Tausch	noun: **swap** My friends and I like to have **clothes swaps**. (der Kleidertausch, die Kleidertauschparty) – verb: (to) **swap** (tauschen) I **swap** clothes with my friends.
hot	heiß, warm	**cold – warm – hot** **hot chocolate** = der Kakao, die heiße (Trink-)Schokolade
(to) need sth. **(to) need to do** sth.	etwas brauchen etwas tun müssen	I **need** money. I **need to buy** a new bike.
tip	der Tipp	Thanks for those **tips!** They're very helpful.
(to) turn sth. **(over)**	etwas umdrehen	**Turn** it upside down. = Dreh/Stell es auf den Kopf. (to) **turn** = (sich) umdrehen

Story

► p. 122 **(to) clean** sth. **up**	etwas aufräumen, sauber machen	verb: (to) **clean up** – noun: **clean-up** (die Säuberung) **clean-up day** = der Dreck-weg-Tag *(Aktionstag zum Müllsammeln)*

Welcome to ...	Willkommen in/an ...	**Welcome to** our house! Here's my room.
so (that)	sodass	❗ **so** = 1. (*auch* **so that**) = sodass; 2. **so** big/cold/... = so groß/kalt/... 3. also, daher
over there	da drüben, dort drüben	**over here** ◀ ▶ **over there**
together ▶ p. 123	zusammen	Work in groups and find answers to these questions **together.**
dead	tot	Fish and chips? No, I don't eat **dead** animals.
mouse, *pl* **mice**	die Maus	two **mice**
Next ...	Als Nächstes ...	**Next** I'd like to look at some photos with you. ❗ **next** = 1. der/die/das nächste; 2. als Nächstes
(to) bring	bringen, mitbringen	Daisy, **bring** me the shoe!
(to) dig	graben	My dog likes **digging** in the sand.
(to) bark (at sb.)	(jn. an)bellen	My dog never **barks at** you: he knows you!
(to) look	aussehen	What does it **look** like? (Wie sieht es aus?)
Look at the pictures. Sieh dir die Bilder an.	**Look,** Noah. There's a seagull. Schau mal, Noah. Da ist eine Möwe.	Your school uniform **looks** great. Deine Schuluniform sieht toll aus.
over 50	über / mehr als 50	Seagulls can fly **over** the sea. (über (*räumlich*)) It's a big school with **over** 1000 students. (mehr als)
somebody **someone**	jemand	❗ **somebody** *or* **someone** = jemand **everybody** *or* **everyone** = jeder; alle There's **someone/somebody** at the door.
grandson **granddaughter**	der Enkel die Enkelin	your son's or your daughter's son your son's or your daughter's daughter
grandparents *(pl)*	die Großeltern	▶▶ your parents' parents
meal ▶ p. 124	die Mahlzeit, das Essen	Do you eat a hot **meal** at lunchtime? (warme Mahlzeit)
things **that** people can use	Dinge, die Menschen gebrauchen/ benutzen können	❗ Kein Komma im Englischen: *English:* **sports that** I don't like *German:* **Sportarten, die** ich nicht mag
(to) mean	bedeuten; meinen (*sagen wollen*)	What does this word **mean?** (bedeuten) What do you **mean?** (meinen) verb: (to) **mean** – noun: **meaning** (die Bedeutung)
toy	das Spielzeug	Little Emma likes to play with **toy** cars.

Dear ...	Liebe/r ...	DEAR DAD WE LOVE YOU
example	das Beispiel	**!** **for example** = **zum** Beispiel

Study skills

▶ p. 126	**title**	der Titel, die Überschrift	I like the band and their music, but some of their song **titles** are really weird.
	phrase	der Ausdruck, die (Rede-)Wendung	A **phrase** is a group of words with a special meaning, for example "for seven seconds".
	Do you have any questions?	Habt ihr / Hast du (irgendwelche) Fragen?	**Are there any** cats in your photo? – No, **there aren't any** cats in my photo. There aren't **any** .... / I don't have **any** .... = Es gibt/sind kein/e ... / Ich habe kein/e ....
	(to) continue	fortfahren, weitermachen; (sich) fortsetzen, weitergehen	Let's stop now and **continue** later. / ... and **continue to write** our presentation later. (to) **continue to do** sth. = etwas weiterhin tun, (mit) etwas weitermachen, fortfahren

Unit task

▶ p. 127	**zoo**	der Zoo	Do you like going to the **zoo** and looking at all the animals?
	(to) ride (a bike)	(mit dem Fahrrad) fahren	▶▶ (to) cycle
	(to) be fun	Spaß machen; lustig sein	**fun** = Spaß (to) **have fun** = Spaß haben Swimming is **fun.** = ... macht Spaß. That's a **funny** story! = Das ist eine lustige Geschichte!
	topic	das Thema	The **topic** of my presentation is "animals in zoos".

Unit 5: Enjoy!

▶ pp. 140/141	**(to) enjoy**	genießen	**enjoy** doing sth. = genießen, etwas zu tun **Enjoy!** = Viel Vergnügen! / Guten Appetit!
	dessert	die Nachspeise, das Dessert	**!** Weiches -s- in der Wortmitte **dessert** **for** dessert = **zum/als** Nachtisch
	birthday	der Geburtstag	**!** **on** my birthday = **an** meinem Geburtstag
	Happy **birthday**! Herzlichen Glückwunsch zum Geburtstag.	When's your **birthday**? Wann hast du Geburtstag?	My **birthday** is in April. Ich habe im April Geburtstag.
	Christmas	(das) Weihnachten	**Christmas Day** = der 1. Weihnachtstag (25. 12.)
	fruit	das Obst	
	jelly	das Gelee; der Wackelpudding	

5

cream	die Sahne	**strawberries** and **cream**
strawberry	die Erdbeere	
allergic (to)	allergisch (gegen)	It's sad, but I can't eat strawberries. I'm **allergic to** them.
Russian	russisch, Russisch; der Russe, die Russin	This is a **Russian** dessert. Yum! (russisch) I speak English, French and **Russian.** (Russisch) Sergej is **Russian.** He's from St. Petersburg. (... ist Russe.)
Indian	indisch; der Inder, die Inderin	adjective/person: **Indian** – noun/country: **India** (Indien)
restaurant	das Restaurant	Let's eat **at a restaurant** this evening. (= **in** einem Restaurant)
dish	das Gericht *(die Mahlzeit)*	This is my favourite Indian **dish.** ►► meal
meat	das Fleisch	I don't eat **meat.**
vegetarian, *infml auch:* **veggie**	vegetarisch; der/die Vegetarier/in	I'm a **vegetarian.**
cheese	der Käse	
pea	die Erbse	**peas**
tomato, *pl* **tomatoes**	die Tomate	**tomato sauce** (die Tomatensoße) **tomato**
spice	das Gewürz	noun: **spice** – adjective: **spicy** (würzig)

noun + -y → adjective

cloud	→ cloudy	*but:*	
mess	→ messy	fun	→ funny
rain	→ rainy	sun	→ sunny
snow	→ snowy	spice	→ spicy

usually	normalerweise, meistens	Do you often go to work by car? – No, never. I **usually** cycle. When it rains, I take the bus.
bread	das Brot	**white bread** **black bread**
rice	der Reis	**rice** with **vegetables**
vegetables *(pl)*	das Gemüse	

! *English:* **Vegetables are** good for you. *German:* **Gemüse ist** gut für dich.

vegan	vegan; der Veganer, die Veganerin	**!** Betonung auf der 1. Silbe: **ve**gan
healthy	gesund	Stay fit and **healthy** – go jogging with us! adjective: **healthy** – noun: **health** (die Gesundheit)

Topic 1

▶ p. 142

invitation (to)	die Einladung (zu, nach)	I have an **invitation to** Jill's party.
sausage	das (Brat-, Bock-)Würstchen, die Wurst	
cake	der Kuchen, die Torte	
twelfth (12th) birthday	der zwölfte Geburtstag	

1st first erste(r, s)	2nd second zweite(r, s)	3rd third dritte(r, s)	4th fourth vierte(r, s)	5th fifth fünfte(r, s)	8th eighth achte(r, s)	9th ninth neunte(r, s)	12th twelfth zwölfte(r, s)

▶ Numbers, p. 277

circus	der Zirkus	
(to) **text** sb.	jm. eine SMS schicken	**Text** me when you're back from London, OK? **!** **text** = **1.** der Text; **2.** die SMS; **3.** (to) **text** sb. = jm. eine SMS schicken

The **months** (die Monate)			
1 January der Januar **2 February** der Februar **3 March** der März	**4 April** der April **5 May** der Mai **6 June** der Juni	**7 July** der Juli **8 August** der August **9 September** der September	**10 October** der Oktober **11 November** der November **12 December** der Dezember

season	die Jahreszeit; die Saison	There are four seasons: **spring** (der Frühling), **summer** (der Sommer), **autumn** (der Herbst), **winter** (der Winter).

▶ p. 143

date	das Datum	**birthday date** = das Datum des Geburtstags
the first of April (1st April)	der erste April	

▶ p. 144

(to) **rest**	ruhen; sich ausruhen	verb: (to) **rest** – noun: **rest** (Ruhe, Pause, Erholung) (to) **take** a **rest** = eine Pause machen
(to) **juggle**	jonglieren	He's **juggling** with **balls**.
ball	der Ball	
(to) **sleep**	schlafen	verb: (to) **sleep** – noun: **sleep** (der Schlaf)
moment	der Moment	**!** Betonung auf der 1. Silbe: **mo**ment **at** the **moment** = **im** Moment, zurzeit
must	müssen	**I must go.** = Ich muss Schluss machen. (am Telefon/Briefschluss) **!** Kein **-s** bei he/she/it: Noah **must** go.

(to) **stand**	stehen; sich (hin)stellen	Sit down! You don't need to **stand.** (stehen) **Stand** here, please. (sich hinstellen)
(to) **teach**	lehren, unterrichten	Mr Schwarz is a teacher. He **teaches** English. My sister is **teaching** me to play the guitar. (... bringt mir das Gitarrespielen bei.)
▶ p. 145 (to) **lie**	liegen	❗ *-ing*-Form. **lying** – I'm **lying** on the sofa.
(to) **sit**	sitzen; sich setzen	You can **sit** on this chair.
(to) **wear**	tragen, anhaben *(Kleidung)*	At English schools students **wear** uniforms.
balloon	der Ballon	
difference	der Unterschied	noun: **difference** – adjective: **different**

Topic 2

▶ p. 146 **present**	das Geschenk	a **present**
magic set	der Zauberkasten	**magic** = magisch, Zauber-; die Zauberei Let me show you a **magic** trick. (Zaubertrick) Can you **do magic?** (Kannst du zaubern?)
What about a ... ?	Wie wäre es mit einer/einem ... ?	❗ **What about ...?** = **1. What about another sandwich?** Wie wär's mit noch einem Sandwich? **2. What about you?** Und du? / Was ist mit dir?
sure	sicher	The next lesson is art. – Are you **sure?** Can you help me? – **Sure.** (Sicher! / Na klar!)
already	schon	Get up! It's 7 o'clock **already!** – Go away! It's Sunday! ❗ Wortstellung: Noah **already has** bike lights. – Noah hat schon Fahrradleuchten.
recipe book	das Kochbuch	**recipe** = das (Koch-)Rezept
▶ p. 147 **sort (of)**	die Art (von)	What **sort of** music do you like? all **sorts of** things (lauter Dinge, alles mögliche) *English:* a **sort** of ... – *German:* eine **Art** (von) ... *English:* **art** – *German:* **Kunst**
menu	die Speisekarte	What can we eat at this restaurant? Let's look at the **menu.**
ham	der Schinken	**salad** with **ham**
salad	der Salat *(als Gericht oder Beilage)*	
carrot	die Möhre, die Karotte	
melon	die Melone	❗ Betonung auf der 1. Silbe: **me**lon

	lemonade	die Limonade	**Lemonade** is a sweet cold drink.
	shopping list	die Einkaufsliste	What do we need to buy at the supermarket? Let's make a **shopping list.** noun: **list** (die Liste) – verb: (to) **list** ((auf)listen)
	packet	die Packung, das Päckchen	a **packet** of **bread** (eine Packung Brot)
	lemon	die Zitrone	**lemons**
	sugar	der Zucker	There's a lot of **sugar** in these sweets.
	milk	die Milch	Cheese? **Milk** chocolate? No thanks, not for me. I'm vegan.
▶ p. 148	**piece**	das Stück, der/das Teil	Your cake is great! Can I have another **piece,** please? **piece of paper** = das Stück Papier, der Zettel
	market	der Markt	**!** **at** the **market** = **auf** dem Markt

Topic 3

▶ p. 150	**gram (g)**	das Gramm	100 **gram**s **of** rice = 100 Gramm Reis
	flour	das Mehl	You need **flour,** sugar and lemons to make these muffins.
	millilitre (ml)	der Milliliter	You need 200 **millilitres of** milk. (200 ml Milch)
	oil	das Öl	Oh no, look, now there's **oil** everywhere!
	cocoa	der Kakao	**!** Beachte Aussprache und Schreibung! • Betonung auf der 1. Silbe: **co**coa • *English:* **co**coa *German:* Ka**ka**o

egg	das Ei	**eggs, milk, flour, sugar**
salt	das Salz	I always put **salt** on my chips, but too much.
teaspoon	der Teelöffel	**spoon** = der Löffel **knife,** *pl* **knives** = das Messer **fork** = die Gabel **tablespoon** = der Esslöffel **teaspoon** = der Teelöffel
vanilla	die Vanille	I like this dessert with custard or **vanilla** sauce.
baking powder	das Backpulver	(to) **bake** = backen **powder** = das Pulver
icing	die Glasur, der Zuckerguss	**icing sugar** = der Puderzucker
butter	die Butter	You need milk to make **butter** or cream.
mixture	die Mischung	noun: **mixture** – verb: (to) **mix** = mischen
oven	der Backofen	Put the cake in the **oven** and bake it for 45 minutes.
degree (°)	das/der Grad	It's very cold today, only 5 **degrees**! (= 5°)
(to) add	hinzufügen; addieren	When you **add** blue to yellow, you get green.
(to) break sth.	etwas zerbrechen	Let's **break** the chocolate **up,** then each of us can have some pieces.
(to) decorate	dekorieren, schmücken	❗ Betonung auf der 1. Silbe: (to) **de**corate
▶ p. 151 **culture**	die Kultur	❗ Betonung auf der 1. Silbe: **cul**ture
main course	das Hauptgericht	▶▶ **main dish** **main** = Haupt-, wichtigste(r, s)
be called	heißen	Our dog **is called** Fido. (= Its name is Fido.)
onion	die Zwiebel	an **onion**
pepper	die Paprika, die Peperoni; der Pfeffer	
chicken	das Huhn; das (Brat-)Hähnchen	What a question! I'm a vegetarian, so of course I don't eat **chicken.**
delicious	köstlich, lecker	This dessert with strawberries and cream is **delicious!** Can I have some more, please?
banana	die Banane	I love fruit like **bananas,** strawberries or melons.
honey	der Honig	**Honey** is sweet. Most vegan people don't eat it because it comes from animals.

tradition	die Tradition	noun: **tradition** – adjective: **traditional** (traditionell) ❗ Betonung auf der 2. Silbe: tra<u>di</u>tion / tra<u>di</u>tional
stir-fry	*das Gericht aus kurz angebratenen Zutaten, z.B. kleinen Stücken Fleisch, Fisch und/oder Gemüse*	noun: **stir-fry** verb: (to) **stir-fry** sth. (etwas unter Rühren scharf anbraten) I often **stir-fry** vegetables and eat the **stir-fry** with a delicious sauce. (to) **stir** = (um)rühren (to) **fry** = braten; frittieren
noodles *(pl)*	die Nudeln	❗ In China people have **noodles** in their meals. In Italy people eat **pasta.**
tea	der Tee	Let's make **tea** or **coffee,** sit down and talk.
coffee	der Kaffee	

tea   coffee

Story

▶ p. 152	**kind (of)**	die Art (von), die Sorte (von)	**What kind of** shoes do you usually wear? all **kinds of** things (lauter Dinge, alles mögliche) ▶▶ sort (of)
	(to) **wave** (**to** sb.)	(jm. zu)winken	Oh, there they are, but they don't see us! **Wave to** them!
	(to) **be good at** sth. **/ at doing** sth.	etwas gut können; gut in etwas sein	You speak French, English and Russian? You're **good at** learning languages!
	just	nur, bloß; einfach	**Just** listen to me for five minutes, please. Don't **just** sit there! Get up and help me.
	no	kein, keine; verboten	I have **no** brothers or sisters. Sorry, **no** dogs! (Hunde verboten!) ❗ **no** = 1. kein/e; verboten; 2. nein
	Well, …	Nun, …/ Also, …/ Na ja, …	❗ **well** = 1. Nun, …/ Also, …/ Na ja, … Cycle to school in the rain? **Well,** I'm not sure … 2. gut *(Adv.)* You speak English really **well.**
	a little	ein wenig, ein bisschen	Would you like sugar in your tea? – Yes, please, but only **a little.** (= not much) ❗ **little** = klein **a little** = ein wenig, ein bisschen
▶ p. 153	**true**	wahr, richtig	Is it **true** that you're the winner of the competition? Wow! Well done!
	(to) **smile**	lächeln	(to) **smile at** sb. = jn. anlächeln verb: (to) **smile** – noun: **smile** (das Lächeln)

amazing	erstaunlich; großartig	24,000,000 people live in Shanghai? **Amazing!** (erstaunlich) This museum is so great – really **amazing.** (großartig)
it is sb.**'s turn (to do** sth.**)**	jm. ist dran / an der Reihe (etwas zu tun)	

When is (it) my turn (to play)?	Wann bin ich dran / an der Reihe (zu spielen)?
We're **taking turns** to play. = We're **taking it in turns** to play.	Wir wechseln uns (beim Spielen) ab. / Wir wechseln uns dabei ab, zu spielen.
Now **it's your turn** (to play).	Jetzt bist du dran / an der Reihe (zu spielen). / Jetzt bist du (beim Spielen) dran / an der Reihe.

how to do sth.	wie man etwas tut / tun kann / tun soll	I don't know … **… what to do / what to say. … how to answer. … where to go.**

Study skills

▶ p. 156

watermelon	die Wassermelone	**water** = das Wasser
potato, *pl* **potatoes**	die Kartoffel	
(to) describe	beschreiben	verb: (to) **describe** – noun: **description** (die Beschreibung) ! *English:* **Describe** the picture **to** him/her. *German:* **Beschreibe** ihm/ihr das Bild.

Unit task

▶ p. 157

(to) research	erforschen, untersuchen, recherchieren	verb: (to) **research** I'd like to **research** this topic. – noun: **research** (die Forschung(en), die Recherche(n)) I'd like to **do** some **research.** (recherchieren)
(to) boil	kochen *(in Wasser);* sieden	! *German* „kochen": Let's **cook** a nice curry. (Mahlzeit zubereiten) Let's **boil** some eggs. (in Wasser kochen) The water is **boiling.** (sieden)
introduction	die Einführung, die Einleitung	the first part of a presentation, a text, a book etc. where you tell people what you want to talk/write about
instruction	die Anweisung	Do you always read the **instructions** when you get a new phone?
clear	klar, deutlich	adjective: **clear** **clear** instructions (deutliche Anweisungen) – adverb: **clearly** speak **clearly** (deutlich sprechen)

Ähnliche Wörter im Englischen und Deutschen

Viele englische Wörter ähneln deutschen Wörtern: *a cowboy* = ein Cowboy.
Beachte aber die Unterschiede 1–3!

(1) Nomen werden im Deutschen großgeschrieben, aber im Englischen klein.

(2) Verben haben im Deutschen andere Endungen, aber einen ähnlichen Stamm, z.B. planen – *(to) plan*.

(3) Oft unterscheidet sich die Aussprache. Höre dir die blau markierten Wörter in der App an und sprich sie nach.

active / activity	dance / (to) dance	millilitre	snack
address	December	mini	sofa
allergic (to)	drama	minute	software
alphabet	drink / (to) drink	modern	song
app	electric	moment	sport
April	elephant	Monday	star
article	end / (to) end	museum	stop
August	England / English	music	story
badminton	family	name	street dance
balcony	fan	November	student
ball	February	number	summer
banana	feedback	October	Sunday
band	film	online	supermarket
barbecue	(to) find	park	surfing
basketball	fish	parkour	sweatshirt
biology	football	partner	(to) swim
blazer	Friday	party	swimmer
bowling	friend / friendly	pasta	test / (to) test
box	garage	perfect	text / (to) text
(to) bring	garden	person	ticket
British	gold	photo	tip
browser	group	picnic	title
burger	hamster	plan / (to) plan	toilet
bus	happy	playlist	tomato
butter	Hello	pool	top
cafe	highlight	popcorn	tourist
card	hockey	post	tradition
check	hot dog	poster	trainer / training
chocolate	house	problem	trick
circus	hungry	project	T-shirt
city	idea	restaurant	uniform
class	information	ring	vanilla
classroom	internet	robot	vegan
clever	January	room	vegetarian / veggie
club	July	rucksack	video
coffee	June	salad	warm
cola	karaoke	sandwich	website
comic	kebab	sauce	wind
computer	kid	school	winner
console	kilometre (km)	(to) send	winter
cool	kiosk	September	word
corridor	lamp	shopping centre	yoga
cost / (to) cost	market	silver	zoo
cousin	maths	skateboard	
culture	melon	skatepark	
curry	milk	smart	

Im *English-German Dictionary* kannst du nachschlagen, was ein Wort bedeutet oder wie es ausgesprochen wird.

Es werden folgende **Abkürzungen und Symbole** verwendet:

infml = informal (umgangssprachlich)	*pl = plural* (Mehrzahl)
sb. = somebody (jemand)	*sth. = something* (etwas)
jd. – jemand jm. = jemandem	jn. = jemanden

° Mit diesem Kringel sind Wörter markiert, die nicht zum Lernwortschatz gehören.

Die **Fundstellenangaben** zeigen, wo ein Wort zum ersten Mal vorkommt. Die Ziffern in Klammern bezeichnen Seitenzahlen.

1 (26) = Unit 1, Seite 26

A

a [ə] ein, eine (10/11)
about [əˈbaʊt]: **about me/you/...** über mich/dich/... (14) **What about a ... ?** Wie wäre es mit einer/einem ... ? 5 (146) **What about you? Und du? /** Was ist mit dir? (10/11)
°**act** [ækt] aufführen, spielen **act out** aufführen, vorspielen
°**action** [ˈækʃn] die Aktion, die Handlung
active [ˈæktɪv] aktiv 2 (53)
activity [ækˈtɪvəti] die Aktivität, die Tätigkeit 3 (89)
add [æd] hinzufügen; addieren 4 (150)
address [əˈdres] die Adresse 2 (64)
after [ˈɑːftə]:
  1. after (school) nach (der Schule) 1 (25)
  °**Repeat after me: ....** Sprich mir nach: .... / Wiederhole: ....
  2. after (you read) nachdem (du liest) 3 (83)
afternoon [ɑːftəˈnuːn] der Nachmittag 3 (84) **in the afternoon** nachmittags, am Nachmittag 3 (84)
again [əˈgen] wieder, noch einmal 1 (22)
°**agree on** [əˈgriː ɒn] sich einigen auf
all [ɔːl] alle(s) 1 (24) °**all the family** die ganze Familie °**all the time** die ganze Zeit, ständig °**(not) at all** überhaupt (nicht)
allergic (to) [əˈlɜːdʒɪk] allergisch (gegen) 5 (140/141)
°**almost** [ˈɔːlməʊst] fast, nahezu, beinahe
alone [əˈləʊn] allein 1 (28)
alphabet [ˈælfəbet] das Alphabet 2 (64)
°**alphabetical** [ælfəˈbetɪkl] alphabetisch
already [ɔːlˈredi] schon 5 (146)
also [ˈɔːlsəʊ] auch 4 (112)
always [ˈɔːlweɪz] immer 1 (28)
am [æm]: **I'm (= I am)** ich bin (10/11)
a.m. [eɪˈem]: **4 a.m.** 4 Uhr (früh) morgens 3 (82) **9 a.m.** 9 Uhr vormittags 3 (82)
amazing [əˈmeɪzɪŋ] erstaunlich; großartig 5 (153)
an [ən] ein/e *(vor Vokalen)* (14)
and [ænd], [ənd] und (10/11)

angry [ˈæŋgri] wütend 2 (50)
animal [ˈænɪml] das Tier (12)
another [əˈnʌðə] ein/e andere/r/s; noch ein/e 4 (118)
answer [ˈɑːnsə]:
  1. die Antwort 1 (23)
  2. (be)antworten 1 (23)
any [ˈeni]: **Do you have any questions?** Habt ihr / Hast du (irgendwelche) Fragen? 4 (126) **there aren't any ...** es gibt keine ... 4 (126)
°**anything** [ˈeniθɪŋ]: **not (...) anything** nichts
app [æp] die App 1 (34)
apple [ˈæpl] der Apfel 1 (21)
April [ˈeɪprəl] der April 4 (122)
are [ɑː] bist, sind, seid (10/11) **we/they are** wir/sie sind 1 (24) **we/they aren't** wir/sie sind nicht 1 (24) **you are** du bist / ihr seid (10/11)
art [ɑːt] die Kunst 1 (26)
article [ˈɑːtɪkl] der Artikel 3 (92)
as [æz], [əz]: **as the winner** als Gewinner/in 3 (93)
ask [ɑːsk]:
  1. fragen 1 (23)
  ask a question eine Frage stellen 1 (23)
  2. ask sb. for sth. jn. um etwas bitten 3 (90)
  ask sb. to do sth. jn. bitten, etwas zu tun 3 (90)
asleep [əˈsliːp]: **be asleep** schlafen 1 (24)
assembly [əˈsembli] die Schulversammlung 1 (26)
at [æt], [ət] an; in; bei; auf 1 (18/19) **at 8 o'clock** um 8 Uhr 3 (82) **at her mum's (house)** bei ihrer Mutter (zu Hause/daheim) 2 (60) **at the cinema** im Kino 4 (110/111) **at the top (of)** oben, am oberen Ende (von); an der Spitze (von) 2 (54) **at work** bei der Arbeit, am Arbeitsplatz 2 (50) **be good at sth. / at doing sth.** etwas gut können; gut in etwas sein 5 (152) **Open your books at page 10.** Schlagt eure Bücher auf Seite 10 auf. (17) °**at least** wenigstens, zumindest °**at night** nachts, in der Nacht
°**aubergine** [ˈəʊbəʒiːn] die Aubergine
August [ˈɔːgəst] der August 5 (142)
aunt [ɑːnt] die Tante 2 (48/49)
autumn [ˈɔːtəm] der Herbst 5 (142)

°**avocado** [ævəˈkɑːdəʊ] die Avocado
away [əˈweɪ] weg, fort 1 (31)

B

back [bæk]:
  1. zurück 2 (61)
  back at home wieder zu Hause 2 (61)
  °**2.** der Rücken; die Rückseite, der hintere Teil
  °**at the back** hinten °**at the back of your book** hinten in deinem Buch °**on the back of the card** auf der Rückseite der Karte
bad [bæd] schlecht; schlimm 1 (29)
badminton [ˈbædmɪntən] das Badminton, der Federball *(Spiel)* 1 (18/19)
bag [bæg] die Tasche 1 (28)
bake [beɪk] backen 5 (150)
°**baked beans** *(pl)* [beɪkt ˈbiːnz] die gebackenen Bohnen *(in Tomatensoße gekochte weiße Bohnen)*
baking powder [ˈbeɪkɪŋ paʊdə] das Backpulver 5 (150)
balcony [ˈbælkəni] der Balkon 2 (54)
ball [bɔːl] der Ball 5 (144)
balloon [bəˈluːn] der Ballon 5 (145)
banana [bəˈnɑːnə] die Banane 5 (151)
band [bænd] die Band, die Musikgruppe 1 (30)
barbecue [ˈbɑːbɪkjuː] das Grillfest, das Grillen 4 (120)
bark (at sb.) [bɑːk] (jn. an)bellen 4 (123)
basketball [ˈbɑːskɪtbɔːl] der Basketball 1 (18/19)
bathroom [ˈbɑːθruːm] das Bad(ezimmer) 2 (55)
be [biː] sein 1 (20) **Don't be late.** Verspäte dich nicht. 1 (22)
beach [biːtʃ] der Strand 1 (30) **on the beach** am Strand 1 (30) **to the beach** zum Strand, an den Strand 1 (30)
because [bɪˈkɒz] weil 1 (27)
bed [bed] das Bett 2 (56) **go to bed** ins Bett gehen 2 (56)
bedroom [ˈbedruːm] das Schlafzimmer 2 (55)
before [bɪˈfɔː]:
  1. before (school / the lesson) vor (der Schule / der Unterrichtsstunde) 3 (83)
  2. before (you read) bevor (du liest) 3 (83)

behind [bɪˈhaɪnd] hinter 2 (56)
°**below** [bɪˈləʊ] unten; unter(halb von)
best [best] beste(r, s); am besten 1 (32)
big [bɪg] groß (15)
biggest [ˈbɪgɪst] der/die/das größte; am größten 4 (116)
bike [baɪk] das Fahrrad (15)
bin [bɪn] der (Müll-)Eimer 4 (112)
biology [baɪˈɒlədʒi] die Biologie 1 (27)
°**bird** [bɜːd] der Vogel
birthday [ˈbɜːθdeɪ] der Geburtstag 5 (140/141) **Happy birthday!** Herzlichen Glückwunsch zum Geburtstag! 5 (140/141) **My birthday is in April.** Ich habe im April Geburtstag. 5 (140/141) **on my birthday** an meinem Geburtstag 5 (140/141) **When's your birthday?** Wann hast du Geburtstag? 5 (140/141)
black [blæk] schwarz (10/11)
blazer [ˈbleɪzə] der Blazer *(das Jackett, oft Teil der Schuluniform)* 1 (20)
blue [bluː] blau (10/11)
°**board** [bɔːd]:
  1. die Tafel
  2. das Spielbrett
°**board game** [ˈbɔːd geɪm] das Brettspiel
°**boat** [bəʊt] das Boot; das Schiff
°**body** [ˈbɒdi] der Körper
boil [bɔɪl] kochen *(in Wasser);* sieden 5 (157)
book [bʊk] das Buch (15)
boring [ˈbɔːrɪŋ] langweilig 4 (112)
bowling [ˈbəʊlɪŋ] das Bowling, das Kegeln 4 (110/111)
°**box** [bɒks] die Box, der Kasten
box [bɒks] boxen 4 (114)
boxing [ˈbɒksɪŋ] das Boxen 4 (114)
boy [bɔɪ] der Junge 1 (25)
°**brainstorm** [ˈbreɪnstɔːm] Ideen (ungeordnet) sammeln
brave [breɪv] mutig 1 (30)
bread [bred] das Brot 5 (140/141)
break [breɪk] die Pause 1 (24)
break sth. [breɪk] etwas zerbrechen 5 (150)
breakfast [ˈbrekfəst] das Frühstück 3 (83)
bring [brɪŋ] bringen, mitbringen 4 (123)
Britain [ˈbrɪtn] Großbritannien 1 (20)
British [ˈbrɪtɪʃ] britisch 1 (20)
°**bro** [brəʊ] *(infml für brother)* der Bruder, der Kumpel
brother [ˈbrʌðə] der Bruder 2 (48/49)
brown [braʊn] braun (10/11)
browser [ˈbraʊzə] der Browser *(Computerprogramm zum Finden und Lesen von Websites)* 4 (127)
brush [brʌʃ]:
  1. bürsten 3 (85)
  brush your teeth (sich) die Zähne putzen 3 (85)
  2. die Bürste 3 (85)
building [ˈbɪldɪŋ] das Gebäude 1 (28)
bully [ˈbʊli]:
  1. der Mobber, die Mobberin; der Tyrann, die Tyrannin 1 (30)
  2. tyrannisieren, mobben 1 (30)
burger [ˈbɜːgə] der Hamburger *(die Frikadelle)* 3 (96)

°**burn** [bɜːn] brennen
bus [bʌs] der Bus 3 (80/81)
  by bus mit dem Bus 3 (80/81)
  on the bus im Bus 3 (80/81) °**catch the bus** den Bus nehmen, erwischen
bus stop [ˈbʌs stɒp] die Bushaltestelle 4 (121)
busy [ˈbɪzi]:
  1. (viel)beschäftigt 1 (20)
  you're busy du bist beschäftigt, du hast (viel) zu tun 1 (20)
  2. hektisch, belebt 4 (110/111)
but [bʌt], [bət] aber 1 (18/19)
butter [ˈbʌtə] die Butter 5 (150)
buy [baɪ] kaufen 4 (114)
by [baɪ]: **by bus** mit dem Bus 3 (80/81) **by the sea** am Meer, an der See 3 (86)
Bye. [baɪ] Tschüs. (10/11)

C

cafe [ˈkæfeɪ] das Café 3 (83)
cake [keɪk] der Kuchen, die Torte 5 (142)
°**calendar** [ˈkælɪndə] der Kalender
call [kɔːl]:
  1. nennen; rufen; anrufen 2 (52)
  be called heißen 5 (151)
  2. der Ruf 2 (52)
  3. *(kurz für: phone call)* der (Telefon-)Anruf 2 (52)
can [kæn], [kən] können (12) **I can see ….** Ich kann … sehen. (12) **I can't (= cannot) see ….** Ich kann … nicht sehen. (12)
canteen [kænˈtiːn] die Kantine, die (Schul-)Mensa 1 (28)
cap [kæp] die (Schirm-)Mütze, die Kappe (15)
car [kɑː] das Auto 3 (80/81)
car light [ˈkɑː laɪt] der Autoscheinwerfer 3 (97)
card [kɑːd] die Karte 3 (96) **playing card** die Spielkarte 3 (96)
careful [ˈkeəfl] vorsichtig (10/11)
carrot [ˈkærət] die Möhre, die Karotte 5 (147)
case [keɪs] das Etui, der Behälter, der Kasten 1 (21)
cat [kæt] die Katze (14)
°**catch the bus** [kætʃ] den Bus nehmen, erwischen
°**'cause** [kɔːz] *(infml)* weil (= because)
°**Celsius** [ˈselsiəs]: **°C = degree Celsius** der Grad Celsius
cent [sent] der Cent 3 (94)
centre [ˈsentə] das Zentrum; die Mitte 4 (112)
ceremony [ˈserəməni] die Feier, die Zeremonie 3 (92)
chain [tʃeɪn] die Kette (15)
chair [tʃeə] der Stuhl 2 (56)
°**challenge** [ˈtʃælɪndʒ] die Herausforderung
°**change** [tʃeɪndʒ] (sich) (ver)ändern; wechseln
°**characteristic** [kærəktəˈrɪstɪk] die Eigenschaft, das (charakteristische) Merkmal

check [tʃek]:
  1. (über-)prüfen, kontrollieren 3 (97)
  2. die (Über-)Prüfung, die Kontrolle 3 (97)
°**checkpoint** [ˈtʃekpɔɪnt] der Kontrollpunkt
cheese [tʃiːz] der Käse 5 (140/141)
°**chess** [tʃes] das Schach
chicken [ˈtʃɪkɪn] das Huhn; das (Brat-)Hähnchen 5 (151)
°**China** [ˈtʃaɪnə] China
°**Chinese** [tʃaɪˈniːz] chinesisch; Chinesisch
chips *(pl)* [tʃɪps] die Pommes frites 4 (110/111) **fish and chips** der Fisch mit Pommes frites 4 (110/111)
chocolate [ˈtʃɒklət] die Schokolade 2 (56) **hot chocolate** Kakao, heiße (Trink-)Schokolade 4 (121)
choose [tʃuːz] (aus)wählen 3 (83)
Christmas [ˈkrɪsməs] (das) Weihnachten 5 (140/141)
Christmas Day [krɪsməs ˈdeɪ] der 1. Weihnachtstag (25. 12.) 5 (140/141)
cinema [ˈsɪnəmə] das Kino 4 (110/111) **at the cinema** im Kino 4 (110/111)
circle [ˈsɜːkl] der Kreis 2 (48/49)
circus [ˈsɜːkəs] der Zirkus 5 (142)
city [ˈsɪti] die (Groß-)Stadt 4 (110/111)
°**clap** [klæp] klatschen
class [klɑːs] die Klasse; der Unterricht; der Kurs (10/11) **in class** im Unterricht 1 (23)
class teacher [ˈklɑːs tiːtʃə] der Klassenlehrer, die Klassenlehrerin 1 (22)
°**classmate** [ˈklɑːsmeɪt] der Mitschüler, die Mitschülerin
classroom [ˈklɑːsruːm] das Klassenzimmer 1 (23)
clean [kliːn]:
  1. sauber 4 (112)
  2. sauber machen, putzen 4 (112)
  clean sth. up etwas aufräumen, sauber machen 4 (122)
clean-up [ˈkliːn ʌp] das Säubern, das Saubermachen 4 (122)
clean-up day [ˈkliːn ʌp deɪ] der Dreck-weg-Tag *(Aktionstag zum Müllsammeln)* 4 (122)
cleaner [ˈkliːnə] die Reinigungskraft 3 (94)
clear [klɪə] klar, deutlich 5 (157)
clearly [ˈklɪəli]: **speak clearly** deutlich sprechen 3 (97)
clever [ˈklevə] schlau, klug (10/11)
clock [klɒk] die (Wand-, Stand-, Turm-)Uhr 3 (82)
close [kləʊz] schließen, zumachen (17)
°**closed** [kləʊzd] geschlossen
clothes *(pl)* [kləʊðz] die Kleidung, die Kleidungsstücke 2 (56)
clothes swap [ˈkləʊðz swɒp] der Kleidertausch, die Kleidertauschparty 4 (121)
cloud [klaʊd] die Wolke 4 (120)
cloudy [ˈklaʊdi] wolkig, bewölkt 4 (120)

club [klʌb] der Klub, der Verein 3 (86) **school club** die AG *(in der Schule)* 3 (86) °**join a club** in einen Klub eintreten

cocoa [ˈkəʊkəʊ] der Kakao 5 (150)

code [kəʊd]:
1. programmieren *(Computer)*; codieren 1 (18/19)
2. der Code 1 (18/19)
3. die Vorwahl(nummer) 1 (18/19)

coding [ˈkəʊdɪŋ] das Programmieren 1 (18/19)

coffee [ˈkɒfi] der Kaffee 5 (151)

cola [ˈkəʊlə] die Cola 3 (96)

cold [kəʊld]:
1. kalt 4 (120) **be cold** frieren 4 (120)
2. die Kälte 4 (120)
3. die Erkältung 4 (120) **have a cold** erkältet sein 4 (120)

collect [kəˈlekt] (ein)sammeln 3 (96)

colour [ˈkʌlə] die Farbe (10/11) **What colour is ...?** Welche Farbe hat ...? (10/11)

°**column** [ˈkɒləm] die Spalte

come [kʌm] (mit)kommen 3 (80/81)

comic [ˈkɒmɪk] der Comic 3 (97)

°**comment on sth.** [ˈkɒment] etwas kommentieren

°**compare** [kəmˈpeə] vergleichen

competition [kɒmpəˈtɪʃn] der Wettbewerb 3 (83)

°**complete** [kəmˈpliːt] vervollständigen

computer [kəmˈpjuːtə] der Computer 1 (28)

computing [kəmˈpjuːtɪŋ] die Informatik 1 (26)

°**concert** [ˈkɒnsət] das Konzert

console [kɒnˈsəʊl] die Konsole 3 (94)

continue [kənˈtɪnjuː] fortfahren, weitermachen; (sich) fortsetzen, weitergehen 4 (126) **continue to do sth.** etwas weiterhin tun, (mit) etwas weitermachen, fortfahren 4 (126)

°**conversation** [kɒnvəˈseɪʃn] das Gespräch

cook [kʊk]:
1. kochen 1 (18/19)
2. der Koch, die Köchin 1 (18/19)

cooking [ˈkʊkɪŋ]:
1. das Kochen 1 (18/19)
2. das *(gekochte)* Essen 4 (112)

cool [kuːl]:
1. cool (15)
°2. kühl

°**copy** [ˈkɒpi] kopieren, abschreiben

°**correct** [kəˈrekt]:
1. korrekt
2. korrigieren

corridor [ˈkɒridɔː] der Korridor 1 (28)

cost [kɒst]:
1. die Kosten; der Preis 4 (121)
2. kosten 4 (121)

°**count** [kaʊnt] zählen

country [ˈkʌntri] das Land, *(auch:)* die ländliche Gegend 3 (85)

course [kɔːs]:
1. **main course** das Hauptgericht 5 (151)
°2. der Kurs(us)

cousin [ˈkʌzn] der Cousin, die Cousine 2 (48/49)

°**crafts** *(pl)* [krɑːfts] das Kunsthandwerk, das Basteln

cream [kriːm] die Sahne 5 (140/141)

°**creative commons** [krieitɪv ˈkɒmənz] „schöpferisches Gemeingut" *(gemeinnützige Organisation, die das einfache Verbreiten von Nutzungsrechten zum Ziel hat)*

cricket [ˈkrɪkɪt] das Kricket *(Mannschaftssportart)* 3 (86)

°**cross** [krɒs] mit einem Kreuz versehen **cross sth. out** etwas durchstreichen

culture [ˈkʌltʃə] die Kultur 5 (151)

curry [ˈkʌri] das Curry *(Gewürz und auch Gericht)* 5 (156)

cushion [ˈkʊʃn] das Kissen 2 (56)

custard [ˈkʌstəd] der Custard *(Vanillesoße)* 5 (140/141)

cute [kjuːt] niedlich, süß 2 (53)

cycle [ˈsaɪkl] Rad fahren 3 (86)

cycling [ˈsaɪklɪŋ] das Radfahren 3 (86)

D

dad [dæd] der Papa, der Vati (12)

°**daily** [ˈdeɪli] täglich

dance [dɑːns]:
1. tanzen (15)
2. der Tanz (15)
do a dance einen Tanz tanzen (15)

dancer [ˈdɑːnsə] der Tänzer, die Tänzerin (15)

dancing [ˈdɑːnsɪŋ] das Tanzen (15)

date [deɪt] das Datum 5 (143) **birthday date** das Datum des Geburtstags 5 (143)

daughter [ˈdɔːtə] die Tochter 2 (48/49)

day [deɪ] der Tag 1 (25) **work long days** lange arbeiten, lange Arbeitstage haben 3 (83)

dead [ded] tot 4 (123) °**My phone is dead.** Mein Telefon-Akku ist leer.

Dear ... [dɪə] Liebe/r ... 4 (124)

December [dɪˈsembə] der Dezember 5 (142)

°**decide** [dɪˈsaɪd] beschließen, sich entscheiden

decorate [ˈdekəreɪt] dekorieren, schmücken 5 (150)

degree [dɪˈgriː] das/der Grad 5 (150) °**degree Celsius** der Grad Celsius

delicious [dɪˈlɪʃəs] köstlich, lecker 5 (151)

describe [dɪˈskraɪb] beschreiben 5 (156)

description [dɪˈskrɪpʃn] die Beschreibung 5 (156)

design [dɪˈzaɪn] die Gestaltung, das Design 1 (26)

design and technology [dɪzaɪn ən tekˈnɒlədʒi] das Werken, der Werkunterricht 1 (26)

desk [desk] der Schreibtisch 1 (21)

dessert [dɪˈzɜːt] die Nachspeise, das Dessert 5 (140/141) **for dessert** zum/als Nachtisch 5 (140/141)

°**dialogue** [ˈdaɪəlɒg] der Dialog

°**dice** [daɪs], *pl* **dice** der Würfel **throw the dice** würfeln

°**dictionary** [ˈdɪkʃənri] das Wörterbuch, das *(alphabetische)* Wörterverzeichnis

difference [ˈdɪfrəns] der Unterschied 5 (145)

different (to) [ˈdɪfrənt] verschieden; anders (als) 1 (22)

difficult [ˈdɪfɪkəlt] schwierig, schwer 1 (35)

dig [dɪg] graben 4 (123)

°**digital** [ˈdɪdʒɪtl] digital

dining room [ˈdaɪnɪŋ ruːm] das Esszimmer 2 (55)

dinner [ˈdɪnə] das Abendessen 2 (61) **for dinner** zum Abendessen 2 (61)

dirty [ˈdɜːti] schmutzig 4 (112)

dish [dɪʃ] das Gericht *(die Mahlzeit)* 5 (140/141) **main dish** das Hauptgericht 5 (151)

do [duː] machen, tun 2 (52) °**do sport** Sport treiben °**he doesn't like ...** er mag ... nicht

dog [dɒg] der Hund (12)

done [dʌn]: **Well done.** Gut gemacht! 3 (93)

door [dɔː] die Tür 2 (57)

°**double** [ˈdʌbl] doppelt, Doppel-

down [daʊn] hinunter, herunter 4 (120)

°**down there** [daʊn ˈðeə] dort runter, dort hinunter; dort unten

drama [ˈdrɑːmə] das Schauspiel, die darstellende Kunst 3 (86)

draw [drɔː] zeichnen (15)

drawing [ˈdrɔːɪŋ] das Zeichnen (15)

dream [driːm]:
1. der Traum 2 (53)
2. **dream (of/about sth.)** träumen (von etwas) 2 (53)

°**dress** [dres]:
1. das Kleid
2. **dress up (as)** sich schick anziehen; sich verkleiden (als)

dressed [drest]: **get dressed** sich anziehen 3 (83)

drink [drɪŋk]:
1. das Getränk (12)
2. trinken (12)

drone [drəʊn] die Drohne 5 (146)

duke [djuːk] der Herzog 4 (110/111)

E

each [iːtʃ] jede(r, s) (einzelne), jeweils 2 (54)

°**early** [ˈɜːli] früh

°**easy** [ˈiːzi] einfach, leicht

eat [iːt] essen; fressen (12)

egg [eg] das Ei 5 (150)

eight [eɪt] acht (10/11)

eighteen [eɪˈtiːn] achtzehn 2 (64)

eighty [ˈeɪti] achtzig 2 (64)

electric [ɪˈlektrɪk] elektrisch, Elektro- 2 (61)

elephant [ˈelɪfənt] der Elefant (14)

eleven [ɪˈlevən] elf (10/11)

°**else** [els]: **What else?** Was sonst noch?

end [end]:
1. das Ende, der Schluss 3 (82)
at the end (of) am Ende (von)
3 (82) **in the end** schließlich; zum
Schluss 3 (82)
2. enden; beenden 3 (82)
°**ending** [ˈendɪŋ] die Endung; das Ende
(Text, Geschichte)
England [ˈɪŋɡlənd] England 1 (21)
English [ˈɪŋɡlɪʃ] Englisch; englisch 1 (21)
enjoy [ɪnˈdʒɔɪ] genießen 5 (140/141)
enjoy doing sth. es genießen, etwas
zu tun 5 (140/141) **Enjoy!** Viel
Vergnügen! / Guten Appetit!
5 (140/141)
°**enough** [ɪˈnʌf] genug
°**erm** [ɜːm] äh (Verlegenheitslaut)
°**especially** [ɪˈspeʃəli] insbesondere
estate [ɪˈsteɪt] die Wohnsiedlung; das
Gewerbegebiet 4 (112)
euro [ˈjʊərəʊ], pl **euros** der Euro 3 (94)
°**even** [ˈiːvn] sogar, selbst
evening [ˈiːvnɪŋ] der Abend 3 (82)
in the evening abends, am
Abend 3 (82)
ever [ˈevə]: **the best son ever** der beste
Sohn überhaupt / der beste Sohn, den
man sich wünschen kann 3 (83)
every [ˈevri] jede(r, s) 4 (120) **every
30 minutes** alle 30 Minuten 4 (120)
everybody [ˈevribɒdi] jeder;
alle 3 (85) **Hello everybody!** Hallo/
Servus allerseits! 3 (85)
°**everything** [ˈevriθɪŋ] alles
everywhere [ˈevriweə] überall 4 (117)
example [ɪɡˈzɑːmpl] das Beispiel
4 (124) **for example** zum Beispiel
4 (124)
Excuse me, ... [ɪksˈkjuːz miː]
Entschuldigung, ... / Entschuldigen
Sie, ... 4 (118)
exercise [ˈeksəsaɪz] die Übung, die
Aufgabe 1 (21)
exercise book [ˈeksəsaɪz bʊk] das
Schulheft, das Übungsheft 1 (21)
expensive [ɪkˈspensɪv] teuer 4 (121)
explain sth. to sb. [ɪkˈspleɪn] jm.
etwas erklären 3 (93)
°**explanation** [ekspləˈneɪʃn] die
Erklärung
°**eye** [aɪ] das Auge

F

°**face** [feɪs] das Gesicht
°**fact** [fækt] die Tatsache
°**false** [fɔːls] falsch, unrichtig
family [ˈfæməli] die Familie 2 (48/49)
family name [ˈfæməli neɪm] der
Familienname, der Nachname 2 (64)
fan [fæn] der Fan 2 (51)
°**far** [fɑː] weit (entfernt)
fast [fɑːst] schnell 2 (53)
favourite [ˈfeɪvərɪt]:
1. Lieblings- (14)
2. der Liebling, der Favorit, die
Favoritin (14)
February [ˈfebruəri] der Februar 5 (142)
°**feed** [fiːd] **Don't feed the seagulls.**
Füttert / Füttern Sie nicht die Möwen.

feedback (no pl) [ˈfiːdbæk] das
Feedback (die Rückmeldung) 1 (35)
feel [fiːl] fühlen; sich fühlen 3 (92)
feel sorry for sb. Mitleid haben mit
jm. 3 (92)
°**feeling** [ˈfiːlɪŋ] das Gefühl
field [fiːld] das Feld; die Weide 4 (112)
in the field auf der Weide 4 (112)
fifteen [fɪfˈtiːn] fünfzehn 2 (64)
fifty [ˈfɪfti] fünfzig 2 (64)
file [faɪl] die Datei; der Ordner, die
Liste 1 (34)
film [fɪlm] der Film (16)
°**finally** [ˈfaɪnəli] schließlich, endlich
find [faɪnd] finden 2 (52) **find out
(about)** herausfinden; sich
informieren (über) 3 (93)
fine [faɪn]: **I'm fine.** Mir geht es
gut. (13)
°**finger** [ˈfɪŋɡə] der Finger
°**finish** [ˈfɪnɪʃ]:
1. das Ende, das Ziel
2. enden; beenden, zu Ende machen
°**firework** [ˈfaɪəwɜːk] der
Feuerwerkskörper **fireworks** (pl)
das Feuerwerk
first [fɜːst]:
1. erste(r, s) 1 (22)
2. zuerst, als Erstes 1 (22)
at first zuerst, am Anfang 1 (22)
first name [ˈfɜːst neɪm] der
Vorname 2 (64)
fish [fɪʃ], pl **fish** der Fisch (14)
fish and chip shop [fɪʃ ən ˈtʃɪp ʃɒp]
die Imbissstube, die Fisch mit Pommes
frites verkauft 4 (118)
five [faɪv] fünf (10/11)
flat [flæt] die Wohnung 2 (54)
floor [flɔː]:
1. der Fußboden 2 (54)
2. die Etage, der Stock, das
Stockwerk 2 (54)
flour [ˈflaʊə] das Mehl 5 (150)
fly [flaɪ] fliegen 2 (52)
food [fuːd] das Essen, das
Lebensmittel; das Futter 1 (29)
football [ˈfʊtbɔːl] der Fußball (10/11)
for [fɔː] für (17) **for 30 seconds** für 30
Sekunden, 30 Sekunden lang 4 (120)
What's for homework? Was haben
wir als Hausaufgabe(n) auf? 2 (52)
What's for lunch? Was gibt es zum
Mittagessen? 1 (26)
°**forget** [fəˈɡet] vergessen
fork [fɔːk] die Gabel 5 (150)
°**form** [fɔːm] das Formular
°**formula** [ˈfɔːmjələ] die Formel
forty [ˈfɔːti] vierzig 2 (64)
four [fɔː] vier (10/11)
fourteen [fɔːˈtiːn] vierzehn (10/11)
free [friː]:
1. frei 1 (30)
free time die Freizeit, die freie
Zeit 1 (30) **Are you free after
school?** Hast du nach der Schule
Zeit? 1 (30)
2. kostenlos 1 (30)
°**freeze** [friːz] (ge)frieren; erstarren
°**freeze-frame** [ˈfriːz freɪm] das
Standbild (Film)

Friday [ˈfraɪdeɪ], [ˈfraɪdi] der
Freitag 1 (25)
°**fridge** [frɪdʒ] der Kühlschrank
fried [fraɪd] frittiert, gebraten 5 (151)
friend [frend] der Freund, die
Freundin 1 (20)
friendly [ˈfrendli] freundlich, nett 1 (30)
°**friendship** [ˈfrendʃɪp] die
Freundschaft
from [frɒm] von, aus (10/11) **Where
are you from?** Wo kommst du
her? (10/11)
front [frʌnt]: **in front of** vor 2 (56)
fruit [fruːt] das Obst 5 (140/141)
fry [fraɪ] braten; frittieren 5 (151)
°**frying pan** [ˈfraɪŋ pæn] die
Bratpfanne
°**full (of ...)** [fʊl] voll; voller ...
fun [fʌn] der Spaß 4 (127) **be
fun** Spaß machen; lustig sein 4 (127)
have fun Spaß haben 4 (127)
funny [ˈfʌni]:
1. seltsam 2 (60)
2. witzig, lustig 2 (60)
What's funny about ...? Was ist lustig
an ...? 2 (60)
°**further** [ˈfɜːðə] weiter (entfernt)
°**furthest** [ˈfɜːðəst] am weitesten
(entfernt)
°**fuss** [fʌs]: **make a fuss (of/over)**
Theater/Wirbel machen (wegen)

G

°**gallery** [ˈɡæləri] die Galerie
game [ɡeɪm] das Spiel 2 (61)
°**gap** [ɡæp] die Lücke
garage [ˈɡærɑːʒ] die Garage 2 (54)
garden [ˈɡɑːdn] der Garten 2 (54)
geography [dʒiˈɒɡrəfi] die Geografie,
die Erdkunde 1 (26)
German [ˈdʒɜːmən] deutsch; Deutsch;
der/die Deutsche 1 (27)
Germany [ˈdʒɜːməni] Deutschland
4 (118)
get [ɡet]:
1. bekommen 3 (93)
get sth. (sich etwas) holen/besorgen
3 (93)
2. werden 4 (118)
get dressed sich anziehen 3 (83)
get warm warm werden 4 (118)
°**get ready (for)** sich fertig machen
(für), sich vorbereiten (auf)
3. **get up** aufstehen 3 (83)
°**get (there)** (dort) hinkommen
girl [ɡɜːl] das Mädchen 1 (25)
give [ɡɪv] geben 3 (94)
°**glasses** (pl) [ˈɡlɑːsɪz] die Brille
°**glove** [ɡlʌv] der Handschuh
glue [ɡluː] der Kleber, der
Klebstoff 1 (21)
glue stick [ˈɡluː stɪk] der
Klebestift 1 (21)
go [ɡəʊ]:
1. gehen; fahren 1 (22)
I must go. Ich muss Schluss machen.
(am Telefon/Briefschluss) 5 (144)
2. **go green** grün/umweltfreundlich
werden 4 (124)

°goat [gəʊt] die Ziege
gold [gəʊld]:
1. das Gold (15)
2. goldfarben (15)
good [gʊd]:
1. gut (13)
be good with ... gut umgehen können mit ... 1 (31) °good for you gesund (z.B. Nahrung, Lebensgewohnheiten)
2. brav 1 (30)
Goodbye. [gʊdˈbaɪ] Auf Wiedersehen! / Servus. (10/11)
gram (g) [græm] das Gramm 5 (150)
granddaughter [ˈgrændɔːtə] die Enkelin 4 (123)
grandma [ˈgrænmɑː] die Oma 1 (29)
grandpa [ˈgrænpɑː] der Opa 1 (29)
grandparents (pl) [ˈgrænpeərənts] die Großeltern 4 (123)
grandson [ˈgrænsʌn] der Enkel 4 (123)
°grass [grɑːs] das Gras; der Rasen
great [greɪt] großartig, toll 1 (20)
Great Britain [greɪt ˈbrɪtn] Großbritannien 1 (20)
green [griːn]:
1. grün (10/11)
2. umweltbewusst 4 (124)
go green grün/umweltfreundlich werden 4 (124)
grey [greɪ] grau (10/11)
ground [graʊnd] der (Erd-)Boden 2 (54)
ground floor [graʊnd ˈflɔː] das Erdgeschoss 2 (54)
group [gruːp] die Gruppe 3 (96)
°guess [ges] (er)raten
guide [gaɪd]:
1. führen, leiten 4 (117)
2. (= tour guide) der Reiseleiter, die Reiseleiterin / der Fremdenführer, die Fremdenführerin 4 (117)
guide dog [ˈgaɪd dɒg] der Blindenhund 4 (117)
guitar [gɪˈtɑː] die Gitarre (15)
guys (pl) [gaɪz] Leute (Anrede) 3 (92)

H

hall [hɔːl]:
1. der Flur, die Diele 1 (28)
2. die Halle, der Saal 1 (28)
sports hall die Sporthalle 1 (28)
°Halloween [hæləʊˈiːn] (das) Halloween (der Abend des 31. Oktober)
ham [hæm] der Schinken 5 (147)
hamster [ˈhæmstə] der Hamster 2 (50)
hand [hænd] die Hand (17)
happen (to sb.) [ˈhæpən] (jm.) geschehen, passieren 3 (93)
happy [ˈhæpi] glücklich, froh 1 (20) Happy birthday! Herzlichen Glückwunsch zum Geburtstag! 5 (140/141)
hard [hɑːd] schwer, schwierig; hart 1 (27)
has [hæz], [həz]: he/she/it has er/sie/es hat 2 (54)
hat [hæt] der Hut, die Mütze (16)

hate [heɪt]:
1. hassen 3 (92)
2. der Hass 3 (92)
have [hæv] haben 1 (20)
he [hiː] er 1 (24) he's (= he is) er ist 1 (24)
head [hed] der Kopf 4 (117)
heading [ˈhedɪŋ] die Überschrift 3 (93)
°headline [ˈhedlaɪn] die Überschrift
headphones (pl) [ˈhedfəʊnz] der Kopfhörer 2 (61)
health [helθ] die Gesundheit 5 (140/141)
healthy [ˈhelθi] gesund 5 (140/141)
hear [hɪə] hören 4 (110/111)
Hello. [həˈləʊ] Hallo. / Servus. (10/11) Hello everybody! Hallo/Servus allerseits! 3 (85)
help [help]:
1. helfen 1 (23)
2. die Hilfe 1 (23)
helpful [ˈhelpfl] hilfsbereit; hilfreich, nützlich 1 (30)
her [hɜː], [hə]:
1. sie; ihr 3 (92)
2. her friends ihre Freunde/Freundinnen 1 (31)
here [hɪə] hier; hierher (12) Here you are. Bitte schön. / Hier, bitte. 1 (23)
Hi. [haɪ] Hallo. (10/11)
°high [haɪ] hoch
highlight [ˈhaɪlaɪt]:
1. das Highlight (der Höhepunkt) 3 (97)
2. hervorheben, markieren, unterstreichen 3 (97)
hike [haɪk] wandern 3 (86)
hiking [ˈhaɪkɪŋ] das Wandern 3 (86)
him [hɪm] ihm, ihn 1 (30)
his friends [hɪz] seine Freunde/Freundinnen 1 (31)
history [ˈhɪstri] die Geschichte (vergangene Zeiten) 1 (26)
hobby [ˈhɒbi] das Hobby (15)
hockey [ˈhɒki] das Hockey 3 (86)
°hole [həʊl] das Loch
holiday [ˈhɒlədeɪ] der Urlaub (12) holidays (pl) die Ferien (12) on holiday im/in den Urlaub (12)
home [həʊm]:
1. das Heim, das Zuhause 2 (48/49) at home zu Hause 2 (48/49)
2. nach Hause 2 (48/49) go home nach Hause gehen 2 (48/49)
homework [ˈhəʊmwɜːk] die Hausaufgabe(n) 2 (52) do your homework Hausaufgaben machen 2 (52) What's for homework? Was haben wir als Hausaufgabe(n) auf? 2 (52)
honey [ˈhʌni] der Honig 5 (151)
horrible [ˈhɒrəbl] schrecklich 1 (20)
horse [hɔːs] das Pferd (14)
hospital [ˈhɒspɪtl] das Krankenhaus 4 (116)
hot [hɒt] heiß, warm 4 (121)
hot chocolate [hɒt ˈtʃɒklət] der Kakao, die heiße (Trink-)Schokolade 4 (121)
hot dog [ˈhɒt dɒg] der Hotdog (heißes Würstchen in einem Brötchen) 5 (147)
hot meal [hɒt ˈmiːl] die warme Mahlzeit 4 (124)

hour [ˈaʊə] die Stunde 3 (82) per hour pro Stunde 4 (110/111)
house [haʊs] das Haus 2 (50)
how [haʊ] wie (10/11) How are you? Wie geht's? / Wie geht es dir/euch/Ihnen? (13)
hundred [ˈhʌndrəd] a/one hundred (ein)hundert 2 (64)
hungry [ˈhʌŋgri] hungrig (10/11) I'm hungry. Ich habe Hunger. (10/11)
husband [ˈhʌzbənd] der Ehemann 3 (83)

I

I [aɪ] ich (10/11) I'm (= I am) ich bin (10/11)
°ice cream [aɪs ˈkriːm] das (Speise-)Eis
ice rink [ˈaɪs rɪŋk] die Schlittschuhbahn 4 (116)
icing [ˈaɪsɪŋ] die Glasur, der Zuckerguss 5 (150)
icing sugar [ˈaɪsɪŋ ʃʊgə] der Puderzucker 5 (150)
idea [aɪˈdɪə] die Idee 2 (62)
if [ɪf]:
1. wenn, falls 2 (52) What if? Was wäre, wenn? 2 (52)
2. ob 2 (52)
ill [ɪl] krank 3 (83)
illness [ˈɪlnəs] die Krankheit 3 (83)
important [ɪmˈpɔːtnt] wichtig 2 (62)
in [ɪn] in; auf (12) in English auf Englisch 1 (21) in the afternoon nachmittags, am Nachmittag 3 (84) in the country auf dem Land 3 (85) in the evening abends, am Abend 3 (82) in the field auf der Weide 4 (112) in the morning morgens, am Morgen 3 (82) in the picture auf dem Bild (12) in town in der Stadt 4 (112) °in the sky am Himmel
India [ˈɪndiə] Indien 5 (140/141)
information [ɪnfəˈmeɪʃn] die Information(en) 4 (118) visitor information centre die Touristeninformation, das Fremdenverkehrsbüro 4 (118)
°ingredient [ɪnˈgriːdiənt] die Zutat
inside [ɪnˈsaɪd]:
1. (dr)innen; nach (dr)innen 4 (120)
2. innerhalb (von) 4 (120) inside the house im Haus 4 (120)
instruction [ɪnˈstrʌkʃn] die Anweisung 5 (157)
interesting [ˈɪntrəstɪŋ] interessant 2 (53)
internet [ˈɪntənet] das Internet 2 (65)
°interview [ˈɪntəvjuː] befragen, interviewen
°into [ˈɪntu], [ˈɪntə] in (... hinein)
introduction [ɪntrəˈdʌkʃn] die Einführung, die Einleitung 5 (157)
invitation (to) [ɪnvɪˈteɪʃn] die Einladung (zu, nach) 5 (142)
is [ɪz] (er/sie/es) ist (10/11) he isn't (= is not) er ist nicht 1 (24) he's (= he is) er ist 1 (24)
it [ɪt] es (10/11) it's (= it is) es ist (bei Sachen und Tieren auch: er ist; sie ist) (10/11)
°Italy [ˈɪtəli] Italien

its [ɪts] sein/seine, ihr/ihre *(besitzanzeigend: Dinge und Tiere)* 2 (59)

J

°**jam** [dʒæm] die Marmelade
January [ˈdʒænjuəri] der Januar 5 (142)
jelly [ˈdʒeli] das Gelee; der Wackelpudding 5 (140/141)
°**jewellery** [ˈdʒuːəlri] der Schmuck
jewellery making Schmuck herstellen *(als Hobby)*
jigsaw (puzzle) [ˈdʒɪgsɔː] das Puzzle 3 (96)
°**join a club** [dʒɔɪn] in einen Klub eintreten
journey [ˈdʒɜːni] die Reise, die Fahrt; der Weg 3 (80/81)
juggle [ˈdʒʌgl] jonglieren 5 (144)
July [dʒuˈlaɪ] der Juli 5 (142)
June [dʒuːn] der Juni 5 (142)
just [dʒʌst] nur, bloß; einfach 5 (152)

K

°**kangaroo** [kæŋgəˈruː] das Känguru
karaoke [kæriˈəʊki] das Karaoke 5 (145)
kebab [kɪˈbæb] der Kebab 5 (144)
kid [kɪd] das Kind, der/die Jugendliche 3 (83)
kilometre (km) [ˈkɪləmiːtə] der Kilometer 4 (110/111)
kind [kaɪnd] nett, freundlich 1 (30)
kind (of) [kaɪnd] die Art (von), die Sorte (von) 5 (152)
Kingdom [ˈkɪŋdəm]: **the United Kingdom (the UK)** das Vereinigte Königreich 3 (82)
kiosk [ˈkiːɒsk] der Kiosk, die Verkaufsbude, der Verkaufsstand 4 (121)
kitchen [ˈkɪtʃɪn] die Küche 2 (55)
knife [naɪf], *pl* **knives** das Messer 5 (150)
knives [naɪvz] *Plural von* **knife**
know [nəʊ] wissen; kennen 1 (20)

L

°**lab** [læb] *siehe* **laboratory**
°**laboratory** [ləˈbɒrətri], *infml auch* **lab** das Labor
°**lamb** [læm] das Lamm(fleisch)
lamp [læmp] die Lampe 2 (54)
°**lane** [leɪn] die Gasse, der Weg *(oft als Teil von Straßennamen)*
°**language** [ˈlæŋgwɪdʒ] die Sprache
°**last** [lɑːst] letzte(r, s)
late [leɪt] (zu) spät 1 (22) **I'm late.** Ich habe mich verspätet. 1 (22)
later [ˈleɪtə] später 2 (60) **Speak later.** Tschüs. / Bis später. 2 (60)
°**leap year** [ˈliːp jɪə] das Schaltjahr
learn [lɜːn] lernen 1 (34)
°**least** [liːst]: **at least** wenigstens, zumindest
°**left** [left] links; nach links **on the left** auf der linken Seite **to the left** nach links
lemon [ˈlemən] die Zitrone 5 (147)

lemonade [leməˈneɪd] die Limonade 5 (147)
lesson [ˈlesn] die (Unterrichts-)Stunde 1 (24)
let's (= let us) [lets] lass(t) uns 1 (22)
letter [ˈletə]:
1. der Brief 3 (83)
2. der Buchstabe 3 (96)
library [ˈlaɪbrəri] die Bücherei, die Bibliothek 4 (116)
lie [laɪ] liegen 5 (145)
°**life** [laɪf], *pl* **lives** das Leben
°**life skills** *(pl)* [ˈlaɪf skɪlz] die Alltagskompetenzen, die lebenswichtigen Fertigkeiten
light [laɪt] das Licht; die Lampe 3 (97) **car light** der Autoscheinwerfer 3 (97)
like [laɪk] mögen (10/11) **I'd (= I would) like ...** Ich hätte gern ... / Ich möchte ... 3 (90) **I'd (= I would) like to meet ...** Ich würde mich gerne mit ... treffen. 3 (90) °**I like to be ...** Ich bin gerne ...
like [laɪk] wie; wie zum Beispiel 4 (114) **like this** so, auf diese Art 2 (64) **a story like this** so/solch eine Geschichte 2 (64) **What's ... like?** Wie ist ...? / Wie sieht ... aus? 4 (114)
line [laɪn]:
1. die Reihe 3 (84)
2. die Zeile 3 (84)
°**link** [lɪŋk] die Verbindung; der Link
lion [ˈlaɪən] der Löwe (14)
list [lɪst]:
1. die Liste 5 (147)
2. (auf)listen 5 (147)
listen [ˈlɪsn] zuhören (15) **listen to sth.** sich etwas anhören (15)
little [ˈlɪtl]:
1. klein 2 (61)
2. **a little** ein wenig, ein bisschen 5 (152)
live [lɪv] leben, wohnen 2 (55)
°**lives** [laɪvz] *Plural von* **life**
living room [ˈlɪvɪŋ ruːm] das Wohnzimmer 2 (55)
lizard [ˈlɪzəd] die Eidechse 2 (53)
long [lɒŋ] lang 2 (62) **(for) a long time** lange, (für) eine lange Zeit 2 (62) **work long days** lange arbeiten, lange Arbeitstage haben 3 (83)
look [lʊk]:
1. aussehen 4 (123)
2. sehen, schauen (17)
look after sich kümmern um; aufpassen auf 4 (112) **look at sb./sth.** jn. anschauen; sich etwas anschauen (17) **look sth. up** etwas nachschlagen, nachschauen 3 (96) °**Look out!** Vorsicht! / Pass(t) auf!
lost [lɒst]: **Are you lost?** Hast du dich verlaufen/verirrt? 2 (50)
lot [lɒt]:
1. **a lot (of) / lots (of)** viel/e 2 (50)
2. **a lot** sehr 2 (50)
loud [laʊd] laut 2 (50)
loudly [ˈlaʊdli]: **speak loudly** laut sprechen 3 (97)

love [lʌv]:
1. die Liebe (15)
2. der Liebling 2 (61)
3. lieben, sehr mögen (15)
I'd (= I would) love ... Ich hätte liebend gern ... / Ich möchte liebend gern... 3 (90) **I'd (= I would) love to meet ....** Ich würde mich liebend gerne mit ... treffen. 3 (90)
lucky [ˈlʌki] Glücks-, glücklich 1 (25) **be lucky** Glück haben 1 (25)
lucky number [lʌki ˈnʌmbə] die Glückszahl 1 (25)
lunch [lʌntʃ] das Mittagessen 1 (26) **What's for lunch?** Was gibt es zum Mittagessen? 1 (26)
lunchtime [ˈlʌntʃtaɪm] die Mittagszeit 3 (82) **at lunchtime** zur Mittagszeit 3 (82)

M

magic [ˈmædʒɪk]:
1. magisch 5 (146)
2. die Zauberei 5 (146)
do magic zaubern 5 (146)
magic set [ˈmædʒɪk set] der Zauberkasten 5 (146)
magic trick [ˈmædʒɪk trɪk] der Zaubertrick 5 (146)
main [meɪn] Haupt-, wichtigste(r, s) 5 (151) **main course/dish** das Hauptgericht 5 (151)
make [meɪk] machen, herstellen 1 (35)
many [ˈmæni] viele 4 (115) **how many?** wie viele? 4 (115)
map [mæp] die Landkarte, der Stadtplan 1 (28)
March [mɑːtʃ] der März 5 (142)
marina [məˈriːnə] der Jachthafen 4 (110/111)
market [ˈmɑːkɪt] der Markt 5 (148)
married (to) [ˈmærid] verheiratet (mit) 4 (112)
°**match** [mætʃ]:
1. (passend) zusammenfügen **match to** zuordnen
2. das Gegenstück, das (zusammenpassende) Paar
match [mætʃ] das Spiel, der Wettkampf 3 (97)
°**material** [məˈtɪəriəl] das Material; der Stoff
maths [mæθs] die Mathe(matik) 1 (26)
°**mattar paneer** [mʌtr pʌˈnɪə] das Mattar Paneer *(nordindisches Gericht)*
May [meɪ] der Mai 5 (142)
maybe [ˈmeɪbi] vielleicht 1 (28)
me [miː]:
1. mich; mir (14)
2. **It's me.** Ich bin's. (14) **Not me!** Ich nicht! (= Ich bin/war/habe/... es/das nicht!) (14)
meal [miːl] die Mahlzeit, das Essen 4 (124) **hot meal** die warme Mahlzeit 4 (124)

mean [miːn]:
1. gemein, fies 1 (30)
2. bedeuten 4 (124)
3. meinen *(sagen wollen)* 4 (124)

meaning [ˈmiːnɪŋ] die Bedeutung 4 (124)

meat [miːt] das Fleisch 5 (140/141)

°**medlation** [miːdiˈeɪʃn] die Vermittlung, die Sprachmittlung

meet [miːt] kennenlernen; (sich) treffen (10/11) **Nice to meet you.** Freut mich, dich/euch/Sie kennenzulernen. (10/11)

melon [ˈmelən] die Melone 5 (147)

°**meme** [miːm] das Internet-Mem, das Internetphänomen

menu [ˈmenjuː] die Speisekarte 5 (147)

mess [mes] das Chaos, die Unordnung 2 (50)

message [ˈmesɪdʒ] die Nachricht, die Mitteilung 1 (25)

messy [ˈmesi] unordentlich 2 (50)

metre [ˈmiːtə] der Meter 4 (110/111)

mice [maɪs] *Plural von* **mouse**

°**middle** [ˈmɪdl] die Mitte **in the middle (of)** in der Mitte (von)

mile [maɪl] die Meile *(ca. 1,6 km)* 4 (110/111)

miles per hour (mph) [maɪlz pər ˈaʊə] Meilen pro Stunde 4 (110/111) **at 30 miles per hour** mit 30 Meilen pro Stunde 4 (110/111)

milk [mɪlk] die Milch 5 (147)

millilitre (ml) [ˈmɪliliːtə] der Milliliter 5 (150)

°**mime** [maɪm] vorspielen, pantomimisch darstellen

mind map [ˈmaɪnd mæp] die Gedankenkarte, das Wörternetz, die/das Mindmap 1 (34)

mini [ˈmɪni] Mini- 5 (146)

mini-drone [mɪni ˈdrəʊn] die Minidrohne 5 (146)

minute [ˈmɪnɪt] die Minute 1 (24) °**Wait a minute.** Warte mal. / Einen Moment.

mirror [ˈmɪrə] der Spiegel 2 (56)

°**miss** [mɪs] verpassen, versäumen, auslassen

missing [ˈmɪsɪŋ] vermisst 2 (52) °**the missing parts** die fehlenden Teile

°**mistake** [mɪˈsteɪk] der Fehler

mix [mɪks] (ver)mischen 5 (150) °**mix sth. up** etwas (durcheinander) mischen

mixture [ˈmɪkstʃə] die Mischung 5 (150)

modern [ˈmɒdn] modern 2 (65)

moment [ˈməʊmənt] der Moment 5 (144) **at the moment** im Moment, zurzeit 5 (144)

Monday [ˈmʌndeɪ], [ˈmʌndi] der Montag 1 (25)

money [ˈmʌni] das Geld 3 (93)

monkey [ˈmʌŋki] der Affe (14)

month [mʌnθ] der Monat 5 (142)

more [mɔː] mehr, weitere 4 (121) **speak more loudly** lauter sprechen 3 (97) **three more** noch drei, drei weitere 4 (121)

morning [ˈmɔːnɪŋ] der Morgen 3 (82) **in the morning** morgens, am Morgen 3 (82)

most [məʊst]: **most schools** die meisten Schulen 3 (86) °**most important** der/die/das wichtigste; am wichtigsten

°**mother** [ˈmʌðə] die Mutter

mouse [maʊs], *pl* **mice** die Maus 4 (123)

°**movie** [ˈmuːvi] der Film, der Spielfilm

Mr Lee [ˈmɪstə] Herr Lee 1 (22)

Mrs Lee [ˈmɪsɪz] Frau Lee *(Anrede für verheiratete Frauen)* 1 (22)

Ms Lee [mɪz] Frau Lee 1 (22)

much [mʌtʃ] viel; sehr 3 (93) **Thank you very much.** Vielen Dank. / Danke vielmals. 3 (93)

mum [mʌm] die Mama, die Mutti (12)

museum [mjuˈziːəm] das Museum 4 (116)

music [ˈmjuːzɪk] die Musik (15)

must [mʌst] müssen 5 (144) **I must go.** Ich muss Schluss machen. *(am Telefon/Briefschluss)* 5 (144)

my [maɪ] mein/e (14)

N

name [neɪm] der Name (10/11) **family name** der Familienname, der Nachname 2 (64) **first name** der Vorname 2 (64) **What's your name?** Wie heißt du? (10/11)

near [nɪə] nahe (bei), in der Nähe von 1 (28)

°**nectarine** [ˈnektəriːn] die Nektarine

need [niːd] brauchen 4 (121) **need to do sth.** etwas tun müssen 4 (121)

neighbour [ˈneɪbə] der Nachbar, die Nachbarin 2 (48/49)

never [ˈnevə] nie, niemals 3 (87)

new [njuː] neu (15)

news [njuːz] die Nachrichten 3 (93)

newspaper [ˈnjuːspeɪpə] die (Tages-)Zeitung 3 (83)

next [nekst]:
1. nächste(r, s) 3 (92) **the next day** am nächsten Tag 3 (92)
2. **Next ...** Als Nächstes ... 4 (123)

next to [ˈnekst tə] neben 2 (56)

nice [naɪs] nett, schön (10/11) **Nice to meet you.** Freut mich, dich/euch/Sie kennenzulernen. (10/11) °**Have a nice weekend/day.** Schönes Wochenende / Schönen Tag!

°**Nigeria** [naɪˈdʒɪəriə] Nigeria

°**Nigerian** [naɪˈdʒɪəriən] nigerianisch; der Nigerianer, die Nigerianerin

°**night** [naɪt] die Nacht **at night** nachts, in der Nacht

nine [naɪn] neun (10/11)

nineteen [naɪnˈtiːn] neunzehn 2 (64)

ninety [ˈnaɪnti] neunzig 2 (64)

no [nəʊ]:
1. nein 1 (22)
2. kein/e; verboten 5 (152)

noise [nɔɪz] das Geräusch; der Lärm 2 (62)

noodles *(pl)* [nuːdlz] die Nudeln 5 (151)

north [nɔːθ] der Norden; nördlich; Nord- 4 (110/111)

north-east [nɔːθˈiːst] der Nordosten, nordöstlich 4 (110/111)

north-west [nɔːθˈwest] der Nordwesten, nordwestlich 4 (110/111)

not [nɒt] nicht (13) **I'm not a boy.** Ich bin kein Junge. (13)

note [nəʊt] die Notiz; der kurze Brief 4 (113) **make notes** (sich) Notizen machen *(zur Vorbereitung)* 4 (113)

November [nəʊˈvembə] der November 5 (142)

now [naʊ] nun, jetzt 1 (22)

number [ˈnʌmbə] die Zahl, die Ziffer, die Nummer (10/11)

O

o'clock [əˈklɒk]: **at 8 o'clock** um 8 Uhr 3 (82)

October [ɒkˈtəʊbə] der Oktober 5 (142)

°**odd word out** [ɒd wɜːd ˈaʊt] das Wort, das nicht zu den anderen passt

of [ɒv], [əv] von 1 (20) **bags of rubbish** Tüten/Säcke mit/voller Müll 4 (123)

of course [əv ˈkɔːs] natürlich, selbstverständlich 2 (60)

often [ˈɒfn], [ˈɒftən] oft 1 (20)

oh [əʊ] Null *(im gesprochenen Englisch)* 2 (64)

oil [ɔɪl] das Öl 5 (150)

OK [əʊˈkeɪ]: **I'm OK.** Es geht mir gut. (13)

old [əʊld] alt (10/11) **How old are you?** Wie alt bist du? (10/11)

on [ɒn]:
1. auf 1 (25) **on holiday** im/in den Urlaub (12) **on Monday** am Montag 1 (25) **on Mondays** an jedem Montag, montags 1 (25) **on my birthday** an meinem Geburtstag 5 (140/141) **on the beach** am Strand 1 (30) **on the bus** im Bus 3 (80/81)
2. **on the phone** am Telefon 2 (62)

one [wʌn] eins (10/11)

onion [ˈʌnjən] die Zwiebel 5 (151)

online [ɒnˈlaɪn] online, Online- 3 (89)

only [ˈəʊnli]:
1. nur, bloß; erst 2 (51)
°2. **the only thing(s)** die einzige Sache / die einzigen Dinge

open [ˈəʊpən]:
1. öffnen; aufschlagen *(Buch)* (17)
2. offen, geöffnet (17)

opinion [əˈpɪnjən] die Meinung 1 (32) **in my opinion** meiner Meinung nach 1 (32)

°**opposite** [ˈɒpəzɪt] das Gegenteil

or [ɔː] oder; sonst 1 (34)

orange [ˈɒrɪndʒ]:
1. orange (farben) (10/11)
2. die Orange (10/11)

°**order** [ˈɔːdə] Reihenfolge **put in the right order** in die richtige Reihenfolge bringen

°**organize** [ˈɔːgənaɪz] organisieren

other [ˈʌðə] andere(r, s) (12) **the others** die anderen (12)

our [ˈaʊə] unser/e 1 (28)

outside [aʊtˈsaɪd]:
  1. draußen; nach draußen 4 (120)
  2. außerhalb (von) 4 (120)

oven [ˈʌvn] der Backofen 5 (150)

over [ˈəʊvə]:
  1. über (*räumlich*) 4 (123) **over here** hier herüber; hier drüben 4 (122) **over there** da drüben, dort drüben 4 (122) °**over the sea** über dem Meer
  2. **over 50** über / mehr als 50 4 (123)

own [əʊn]: **my own room** mein/ein eigenes Zimmer 2 (59)

P

packet [ˈpækɪt] die Packung, das Päckchen 5 (147)

page (p.) [peɪdʒ] die (Buch-/Heft-) Seite 1 (23)

°**pair** [peə] das Paar

palace [ˈpæləs] der Palast, das Schloss 4 (110/111)

°**pan** [pæn] die Pfanne

paper [ˈpeɪpə]:
  1. die (Tages-) Zeitung 3 (83)
  2. das Papier 3 (83)
  piece of paper das Stück Papier, der Zettel 5 (148)

°**paragraph** [ˈpærəgrɑːf] der (Text-) Abschnitt

°**parallel** [ˈpærəlel] parallel, Parallel-

parents (*pl*) [ˈpeərənts] die Eltern 2 (60)

park [pɑːk] der Park 3 (84)

parkour [pɑːˈkʊə] der Parkour (*akrobatischer Hindernislauf in der Stadt*) 1 (18/19)

parrot [ˈpærət] der Papagei (14)

part (of) [pɑːt] der Teil (von) 2 (61)

partner [ˈpɑːtnə] der Partner, die Partnerin 1 (34)

party [ˈpɑːti] die Party 3 (94)

passive [ˈpæsɪv] passiv 2 (53)

pasta [ˈpæstə] die Pasta (*italienische Bezeichnung für Teigwaren*) 5 (147)

pay (for sth.) [peɪ] zahlen; (etwas) bezahlen 3 (94)

PE (= physical education) [piː ˈiː] der (Schul-)Sport 1 (26)

pea [piː] die Erbse 5 (140/141)

pen [pen] der Kugelschreiber, der Stift; der Füller 1 (21)

pence [pens] *Plural von* **penny**

pencil [ˈpensl] der Bleistift 1 (21)

pencil case [ˈpensl keɪs] das Federmäppchen 1 (21)

pencil sharpener [ˈpensl ʃɑːpnə] der Bleistift(an)spitzer 1 (21)

penny (p) [ˈpeni] der Penny (*kleinste britische Münze*) 3 (94)

people (*pl*) [ˈpiːpl] die Leute, die Menschen 1 (24)

pepper [ˈpepə]:
  1. der Pfeffer 5 (151)
  2. die Paprika, die Peperoni 5 (151)

per [pɜː], [pə] pro 4 (110/111) **miles per hour (mph)** Meilen pro Stunde 4 (110/111)

perfect [ˈpɜːfɪkt] perfekt 2 (61)

perfectly (still) [ˈpɜːfɪktli] ganz/völlig (still) 2 (61)

person [ˈpɜːsn] die Person 2 (58)

pet [pet] das (Haus-)Tier 2 (50)

phone [fəʊn]:
  1. anrufen; telefonieren (15)
  2. das Handy, das Telefon (15) **on the phone** am Telefon 2 (62)

phone call [ˈfəʊn kɔːl] der (Telefon-) Anruf 2 (52)

phone number [ˈfəʊn nʌmbə] die Telefonnummer (15)

photo [ˈfəʊtəʊ] das Foto (15) **in the photo** auf dem Foto (15) **take photos** Fotos machen (15)

photographer [fəˈtɒgrəfə] der Fotograf, die Fotografin 2 (65)

phrase [freɪz] der Ausdruck, die (Rede-)Wendung 4 (126)

physical education (PE) [fɪzɪkl edʒuˈkeɪʃn] der (Schul-)Sport 1 (26)

picnic [ˈpɪknɪk] das Picknick 4 (110/111) **have a picnic** ein Picknick machen 4 (110/111)

picture [ˈpɪktʃə] das Bild (12)

piece [piːs] das Stück, der/das Teil 5 (148) **piece of paper** das Stück Papier 5 (148)

pier [pɪə] der Pier, die Seebrücke 4 (110/111)

pink [pɪŋk] rosa (10/11)

°**pizza** [ˈpiːtsə] die Pizza

place [pleɪs] der Ort, der Platz 1 (28)

°**placemat** [ˈpleɪsmæt] das Platzdeckchen

plan [plæn]:
  1. der Plan 3 (91)
  2. planen 3 (91)
  plan to do sth. planen, etwas zu tun 3 (91)

°**plantain** [ˈplæntɪn] die Kochbanane

°**plate** [pleɪt] der Teller

play [pleɪ] spielen (15)

player [ˈpleɪə] der Spieler, die Spielerin (15)

°**playground** [ˈpleɪgraʊnd] der Spielplatz

playing card [ˈpleɪɪŋ kɑːd] die Spielkarte 3 (96)

playlist [ˈpleɪlɪst] die Playlist 5 (149)

please [pliːz] bitte (17)

p.m. [piːˈem]: **4 p.m.** 4 Uhr nachmittags, 16 Uhr 3 (82) **9 p.m.** 9 Uhr abends, 21 Uhr 3 (82)

°**poem** [ˈpəʊɪm] das Gedicht

point [pɔɪnt]:
  1. das Komma (*Dezimalzeichen*) 4 (110/111)
  1.6 (one point six) 1,6 (eins Komma sechs) 4 (110/111)
  °**2.** der Punkt

°**point (at/to)** [pɔɪnt] zeigen, deuten (auf)

°**Poland** [ˈpəʊlənd] Polen

°**police car** [pəˈliːs kɑː] das Polizeiauto

polite [pəˈlaɪt] höflich 2 (51)

pool [puːl] das Pool(billiard) 4 (114)

popcorn [ˈpɒpkɔːn] das Popcorn 4 (127)

post [pəʊst]:
  1. der Post (*Teil eines Blogs*) 4 (115)
  2. posten (*im Internet veröffentlichen*) 4 (115)

poster [ˈpəʊstə] das Poster 1 (35)

potato [pəˈteɪtəʊ], *pl* **potatoes** die Kartoffel 5 (156)

pound (£) [paʊnd] das Pfund (*britische Währung*) 3 (94)

powder [ˈpaʊdə] das Pulver 5 (150)

practice [ˈpræktɪs] die Übung(en) 4 (110/111)

practise [ˈpræktɪs] üben 4 (110/111)

present [ˈpreznt] das Geschenk 5 (146)

present sth. (to sb.) [prɪˈzent] (jm.) etwas präsentieren, vorstellen 2 (65)

presentation [preznˈteɪʃn] das Referat, die Präsentation 2 (65) **give a presentation** ein Referat halten 2 (65)

prize [praɪz] der Preis, der Gewinn 3 (92)

prize ceremony [ˈpraɪz serəməni] die Preisverleihung 3 (92)

problem [ˈprɒbləm] das Problem 2 (60)

°**profile** [ˈprəʊfaɪl] das Profil; die Beschreibung, das Portrait

project [ˈprɒdʒekt] das Projekt 3 (85)

purple [ˈpɜːpl] violett, lila (10/11)

put [pʊt] (*etwas wohin*) tun, legen, stellen, stecken (15) **put your hand/ hands up** die Hand / die Hände hochstrecken (17) °**put in the right order** in die richtige Reihenfolge bringen

puzzle [ˈpʌzl] das Rätsel 3 (96)

Q

question [ˈkwestʃən] die Frage 1 (23) **ask a question** eine Frage stellen 1 (23)

°**questionnaire** [kwestʃəˈneə] der Fragebogen

°**quick** [kwɪk] schnell

°**quicker** [ˈkwɪkə] schneller

quiet [ˈkwaɪət] ruhig, still, leise (17)

quite [kwaɪt] ziemlich, ganz 2 (53)

quiz [kwɪz], *pl* **quizzes** das Quiz, das Ratespiel; der Test 4 (121) **do a quiz** ein Quiz / ein Ratespiel / einen Test machen 4 (121)

quizzes [ˈkwɪzɪz] *Plural von* **quiz**

R

rabbit [ˈræbɪt] das Kaninchen 2 (50)

°**race** [reɪs]:
  1. Rennen fahren; um die Wette laufen/reiten/...
  2. das (Wett-)Rennen

rain [reɪn]:
  1. regnen 4 (120)
  2. der Regen 4 (120)

rainy [ˈreɪni] regnerisch 4 (120)
rare [reə] selten *(Adj.)* 3 (87)
rarely [ˈreəli] selten *(Adv.)* 3 (87)
read [riːd] lesen (15)
reader [ˈriːdə] der Leser, die Leserin (15)
ready [ˈredi] fertig, bereit (17)
  °**Ready, steady, go!** Auf die Plätze, fertig, los! °**get ready (for)** sich fertig machen (für), sich vorbereiten (auf)
really [ˈriːəli], [ˈrɪəli] wirklich 1 (28)
°**reason** [ˈriːzn] der Grund, die Begründung
°**reception** [rɪˈsepʃn] der Empfang *(auch beim Telefon)*; die Rezeption
recipe [ˈresəpi] das (Koch-)Rezept 5 (146)
recipe book [ˈresəpi bʊk] das Kochbuch 5 (146)
°**record** [rɪˈkɔːd] aufnehmen, aufzeichnen
red [red] rot (10/11)
°**registration** [redʒɪˈstreɪʃn] *die Anwesenheitskontrolle und Ankündigung aktueller Ereignisse vor dem Unterricht*
remember [rɪˈmembə]:
  1. daran denken, nicht vergessen (12) **remember to do sth.** daran denken, etwas zu tun (12)
  2. sich erinnern an (12) **remember doing sth.** sich daran erinnern, etwas getan zu haben (12)
°**repeat** [rɪˈpiːt] wiederholen
research [rɪˈsɜːtʃ]:
  1. erforschen, untersuchen, recherchieren 5 (157)
  2. die Forschung(en), die Recherche(n) 5 (157)
  do research recherchieren 5 (157)
rest [rest]:
  1. ruhen; sich ausruhen 5 (144)
  2. die Ruhe, die Pause, die Erholung 5 (144)
  take a rest Pause machen 5 (144)
restaurant [ˈrestrɒnt] das Restaurant 5 (140/141)
°**review** [rɪˈvjuː] der Bericht, die Rezension *(kritische Besprechung)*
°**rhyme** [raɪm] (sich) reimen
°**rhythm** [ˈrɪðəm] der Rhythmus
rice [raɪs] der Reis 5 (140/141)
ride [raɪd]:
  1. **ride a bike** mit dem Fahrrad fahren 4 (127)
  °2. die Fahrt; das Fahrgeschäft *(auf Volksfesten, in Vergnügungsparks)*
right [raɪt]:
  1. richtig (10/11)
  be right Recht haben 1 (24)
  °2. rechts; nach rechts
  °**on the right** rechts, auf der rechten Seite °**to the right** nach rechts
  °3. **right by the sea** direkt an der See, direkt am Meer
ring [rɪŋ] der Ring 4 (123)
robot [ˈrəʊbɒt] der Roboter 2 (56)
°**rock** [rɒk] die Zuckerstange
°**role** [rəʊl] die Rolle *(Film, Theater)*
°**role-play** [ˈrəʊlpleɪ] das Rollenspiel

°**roll the dice** [rəʊl ðə ˈdaɪs] würfeln
room [ruːm] der Raum, das Zimmer 1 (24)
°**routine** [ruːˈtiːn] die Routine, der (Tages-/Übungs-)Ablauf
rubber [ˈrʌbə] das Radiergummi 1 (21)
rubbish [ˈrʌbɪʃ] der (Haus-)Müll, der Abfall 4 (112)
rucksack [ˈrʌksæk] der Rucksack (15)
rude [ruːd] unhöflich, frech 2 (61)
°**rule** [ruːl] die Regel
ruler [ˈruːlə] das Lineal 1 (21)
running [ˈrʌnɪŋ] das Laufen *(Sport)* 3 (86)
°**Russia** [ˈrʌʃə] Russland

S

sad [sæd] traurig 1 (30)
salad [ˈsæləd] der Salat *(als Gericht oder Beilage)* 5 (147)
salt [sɔːlt] das Salz 5 (150)
same [seɪm]: **the same** gleich; derselbe/dieselbe/dasselbe; dieselben 1 (20)
sandwich [ˈsænwɪtʃ], [ˈsænwɪdʒ] das Sandwich (10/11)
Saturday [ˈsætədeɪ], [ˈsætədi] der Samstag 1 (25)
sauce [sɔːs] die Soße 5 (140/141)
sausage [ˈsɒsɪdʒ] das (Brat-, Bock-)Würstchen, die Wurst 5 (142)
say [seɪ] sagen 1 (22)
scared [skeəd]: **be scared (of)** Angst haben (vor) 1 (20)
°**scene** [siːn] die Szene
school [skuːl] die Schule (17) **at school** in der Schule 1 (18/19)
school club [ˈskuːl klʌb] die AG *(in der Schule)* 3 (86)
school uniform [skuːl ˈjuːnɪfɔːm] die Schuluniform 1 (20)
science [ˈsaɪəns] die Naturwissenschaft 1 (26)
scooter [ˈskuːtə] der (Tret-)Roller (15)
sea [siː] das Meer, die See 3 (86) **by the sea** am Meer, an der See 3 (86) °**right by the sea** direkt an der See, direkt am Meer
seagull [ˈsiːgʌl] die Möwe (10/11)
season [ˈsiːzn] die Jahreszeit; die Saison 5 (142)
second [ˈsekənd]:
  1. die Sekunde 4 (120)
  2. **(2nd)** zweite(r, s) 5 (142)
secondary school [ˈsekəndri skuːl] die weiterführende Schule 1 (22)
secret [ˈsiːkrət]:
  1. geheim 3 (89)
  2. das Geheimnis 3 (89)
see [siː] sehen (12) **See you soon.** Bis bald! 1 (25) **See you.** Bis dann. / Tschüs. 1 (25)
°**sell** [sel] verkaufen
send [send] senden, schicken 3 (92)
sentence [ˈsentəns] der Satz 3 (87)
°**sentence starter** [ˈsentəns stɑːtə] der Satzanfang
September [sepˈtembə] der September 5 (142)

seven [ˈsevn] sieben (10/11)
seventeen [sevnˈtiːn] siebzehn 2 (64)
seventy [ˈsevnti] siebzig 2 (64)
shame [ʃeɪm]: **a shame** schade; eine Schande 3 (90)
share [ʃeə]:
  1. der (An-)Teil 3 (97)
  2. teilen 3 (97)
sharpener [ˈʃɑːpnə] der Anspitzer 1 (21)
she [ʃiː] sie *(weibliche Person)* 1 (24) **she's (= she is)** sie ist 1 (24)
shelf [ʃelf], *pl* **shelves** das Regal(brett) 2 (56)
shelves [ʃelvz] *Plural von* **shelf**
shoe [ʃuː] der Schuh 2 (55)
shop [ʃɒp] das Geschäft, der Laden 4 (110/111) **be at the shops** Einkäufe erledigen 4 (110/111)
shopping [ˈʃɒpɪŋ] das Einkaufen; die Einkäufe 3 (84) **do the shopping** die Einkäufe erledigen, einkaufen gehen 3 (84) **go shopping** einkaufen gehen 3 (84)
shopping centre [ˈʃɒpɪŋ sentə] das Einkaufszentrum 4 (116)
shopping list [ˈʃɒpɪŋ lɪst] die Einkaufsliste 5 (147)
short [ʃɔːt] kurz; klein *(Person; Körpergröße)* 3 (80/81)
°**shout** [ʃaʊt] rufen
show [ʃəʊ]:
  1. die Show, die Aufführung; die Ausstellung 3 (92)
  2. zeigen 3 (92)
shower [ˈʃaʊə] die Dusche 3 (83) **have a shower** (sich) duschen 3 (83)
°**sick** [sɪk] krank
°**side** [saɪd] die Seite
°**sight** [saɪt] die Sehenswürdigkeit
silver [ˈsɪlvə]:
  1. das Silber (15)
  2. silberfarben (15)
sing [sɪŋ] singen (16)
singer [ˈsɪŋə] der Sänger, die Sängerin (16)
singing [ˈsɪŋɪŋ] das Singen (16)
°**Sir** [sɜː] *Anrede für einen Lehrer (GB)*
sister [ˈsɪstə] die Schwester 2 (48/49)
sit [sɪt] sitzen 5 (145) **sit down** sich hinsetzen (17)
six [sɪks] sechs (10/11)
sixteen [sɪksˈtiːn] sechzehn 2 (64)
sixty [ˈsɪksti] sechzig 2 (64)
°**size** [saɪz] die Größe
skateboard [ˈskeɪtbɔːd]:
  1. das Skateboard 3 (91)
  2. Skateboard fahren 3 (91)
skateboarding [ˈskeɪtbɔːdɪŋ] das Skateboardfahren 3 (91)
skatepark [ˈskeɪtpɑːk] der Skatepark 3 (91)
°**skating** [ˈskeɪtɪŋ] das Schlittschuhlaufen; das (Inline-)Skaten
skill [skɪl]:
  1. die Fähigkeit, die Fertigkeit 4 (110/111)
  °2. die Lern- und Arbeitstechnik
°**sky** [skaɪ] der Himmel **in the sky** am Himmel

sleep [sliːp]:
1. der Schlaf 5 (144)
2. schlafen 5 (144)
°**sleep in** ausschlafen
°**slide** [slaɪd] das Dia; die Folie (*Präsentationssoftware*)
slide show [ˈslaɪd ʃəʊ] die Slideshow, die Bildschirmpräsentation 4 (126)
slow [sləʊ] langsam 1 (30)
small [smɔːl] klein (15)
smart [smɑːt]:
1. schick 5 (146)
2. intelligent, clever 5 (146)
smell [smel]:
1. der Geruch; der Gestank 4 (112)
2. riechen; schlecht riechen 4 (112)
smile [smaɪl]:
1. das Lächeln 5 (153)
2. lächeln 5 (153)
smile at sb. jn. anlächeln 5 (153)
snack [snæk] der Snack, die kleine Mahlzeit 3 (83)
snake [sneɪk] die Schlange (14)
snow [snəʊ]:
1. der Schnee 4 (120)
2. schneien 4 (120)
snowy [ˈsnəʊi] schneebedeckt; verschneit 4 (120)
so [səʊ]:
1. so (13)
so good so gut (13) **so that** sodass, damit 4 (121)
2. also, daher 4 (121)
3. **so (that)** sodass 4 (122)
sofa [ˈsəʊfə] das Sofa 2 (56)
software [ˈsɒftweə] die Software 3 (83)
some [sʌm], [səm] einige, ein paar; etwas, ein wenig 1 (30)
somebody [ˈsʌmbədi] jemand 4 (123)
someone [ˈsʌmwʌn] jemand 4 (123)
something [ˈsʌmθɪŋ] etwas 4 (118)
sometimes [ˈsʌmtaɪmz] manchmal 3 (87)
son [sʌn] der Sohn 2 (48/49)
song [sɒŋ] das Lied (13)
soon [suːn] bald 1 (24)
sorry [ˈsɒri]: **Sorry. / I'm sorry.** Tut mir leid. / Entschuldigung. (16) **be/feel sorry for sb.** Mitleid haben mit jm. 3 (92) **I'm / I feel sorry for him.** Er tut mir leid. 3 (92)
sort (of) [sɔːt] die Art (von) 5 (147)
°**sound** [saʊnd]:
1. das Geräusch; der Klang, der Laut
2. klingen (*sich ... anhören*)
°**South Africa** [saʊθ ˈæfrəkə] Südafrika
spaghetti [spəˈɡeti] die Spaghetti 5 (156)
speak (to) [spiːk] sprechen (mit) 2 (60) **Speak later.** Tschüs. / Bis später. 2 (60)
speaking [ˈspiːkɪŋ] das Sprechen 2 (60)
special [ˈspeʃl] besondere(r, s) 2 (53)
°**speech** [spiːtʃ] die Rede, die Ansprache
°**speech bubble** [ˈspiːtʃ bʌbl] die Sprechblase
spell [spel] buchstabieren 2 (64)

spelling [ˈspelɪŋ] die Schreibweise, die Rechtschreibung 2 (64)
spice [spaɪs] das Gewürz 5 (140/141)
spicy [ˈspaɪsi] würzig 5 (140/141)
spoon [spuːn] der Löffel 5 (150)
sport [spɔːt] der Sport; die Sportart (15) °**do sport(s)** Sport treiben
sports hall [ˈspɔːts hɔːl] die Sporthalle 1 (28)
spring [sprɪŋ] der Frühling 5 (142)
stadium [ˈsteɪdiəm] das Stadion 4 (116)
stand [stænd] stehen; sich (hin) stellen 5 (144) **stand up** aufstehen (17)
star [stɑː] der (Film-/Pop-)Star 1 (30)
start [stɑːt]:
1. der Anfang, der Start 1 (22)
2. beginnen, anfangen (mit) 1 (22)
station [ˈsteɪʃn] der Bahnhof 4 (116)
°**stay** [steɪ] bleiben; übernachten
°**steady** [ˈstedi]: **Ready, steady, go!** Auf die Plätze, fertig, los!
step [step] die Stufe; der Schritt 1 (35)
stepbrother [ˈstepbrʌðə] der Stiefbruder 2 (48/49)
stepdad [ˈstepdæd] der Stiefvater 2 (48/49)
stepdaughter [ˈstepdɔːtə] die Stieftochter 2 (48/49)
stepfather [ˈstepfɑːðə] der Stiefvater 2 (48/49)
stepmother [ˈstepmʌðə] die Stiefmutter 2 (48/49)
stepmum [ˈstepmʌm] die Stiefmutter 2 (48/49)
stepsister [ˈstepsɪstə] die Stiefschwester 2 (48/49)
stepson [ˈstepsʌn] der Stiefsohn 2 (48/49)
still [stɪl] (immer) noch; trotzdem 1 (31)
stir [stɜː] (um)rühren 5 (151)
stir-fry [ˈstɜː fraɪ]:
1. *das Gericht aus unter Rühren kurz angebratenen Zutaten, z.B. kleine Stücke Fleisch, Fisch und/oder Gemüse* 5 (151)
2. (Gemüse- oder Fleischstücke) unter Rühren scharf anbraten 5 (151)
stop [stɒp]:
1. (an)halten; stoppen; aufhören (mit) 4 (121)
2. der Halt, der Haltepunkt; die Unterbrechung 4 (121)
bus stop die Bushaltestelle 4 (121)
story [ˈstɔːri] die Geschichte (Erzählung) 1 (30)
strawberry [ˈstrɔːbəri] die Erdbeere 5 (140/141)
street [striːt] die Straße (*in Ortschaften*) 4 (110/111)
street dance [ˈstriːt dɑːns] der Streetdance (*Tanzstil*) 3 (86)
street music [ˈstriːt mjuːzɪk] die Straßenmusik 4 (110/111)
°**stressed** [strest] gestresst
student [ˈstjuːdnt] der Schüler, die Schülerin; der Student, die Studentin 1 (18/19)

°**study** [ˈstʌdi] lernen (*auch z.B. für Prüfungen*)
°**study skills** *(pl)* [ˈstʌdi skɪlz] die Lerntechniken
stupid [ˈstjuːpɪd] dumm, blöd; albern 3 (92)
subject [ˈsʌbdʒɪkt] das (Schul-)Fach 1 (26)
sugar [ˈʃʊɡə] der Zucker 5 (147)
summer [ˈsʌmə] der Sommer 5 (118)
sun [sʌn] die Sonne 4 (120)
Sunday [ˈsʌndeɪ], [ˈsʌndi] der Sonntag 1 (25)
°**sunglasses** *(pl)* [ˈsʌnɡlɑːsɪz] die Sonnenbrille
sunny [ˈsʌni] sonnig 4 (120) **It's sunny.** Die Sonne scheint. 4 (120)
superhero [ˈsuːpəhɪərəʊ], *pl* **superheroes** der Superheld, die Superheldin 3 (97)
supermarket [ˈsuːpəmɑːkɪt] der Supermarkt 4 (116)
sure [ʃʊə], [ʃɔː] sicher 5 (146)
surfing [ˈsɜːfɪŋ] das Surfing 3 (87)
surprised [səˈpraɪzd] überrascht 3 (92)
swap [swɒp]:
1. tauschen 4 (121)
2. der Tausch 4 (121)
clothes swap der Kleidertausch, die Kleidertauschparty 4 (121)
sweatshirt [ˈswetʃɜːt] das Sweatshirt 5 (146)
sweet [swiːt]:
1. süß 2 (59)
2. das Bonbon 2 (59)
sweets *(pl)* [swiːts] die Süßigkeiten 2 (59)
swim [swɪm] schwimmen (15)
swimmer [ˈswɪmə] der Schwimmer, die Schwimmerin (15)
swimming [ˈswɪmɪŋ] das Schwimmen (15)
°**swimming pool** [ˈswɪmɪŋ puːl] das Schwimmbad

T

T-shirt [ˈtiː ʃɜːt] das T-Shirt 5 (145)
table [ˈteɪbl]:
1. der Tisch 2 (56)
°**2.** die Tabelle
table tennis [ˈteɪbl tenɪs] das Tischtennis 3 (86)
tablespoon [ˈteɪblspuːn] der Esslöffel 5 (150)
take [teɪk]:
1. (mit)nehmen; bringen 1 (22)
take photos Fotos machen (15)
2. dauern, (*Zeit*) brauchen, in Anspruch nehmen 3 (83)
talk [tɔːk]:
1. das Gespräch; die Rede, der Vortrag 1 (22)
2. **talk (to)** sprechen, reden (mit) 1 (22)
talk about sprechen, reden über 1 (22)

°tamarind [ˈtæmərɪnd] die Tamarinde
°task [tɑːsk] die Aufgabe **do a task** eine Aufgabe machen
tea [tiː] der Tee 5 (151)
teach [tiːtʃ] lehren, unterrichten 5 (144) **teach sb. to do sth.** jm. beibringen, etwas zu tun 5 (144)
teacher [ˈtiːtʃə] der Lehrer, die Lehrerin 1 (22)
teaspoon [ˈtiːspuːn] der Teelöffel 5 (150)
tech [tek] *siehe* **technology**
technology [tekˈnɒlədʒi], *infml auch* **tech** die Technik, der Technikunterricht; die Technologie 1 (26)
teeth [tiːθ] *Plural von* **tooth brush your teeth** (sich) die Zähne putzen 3 (85)
tell [tel] erzählen, sagen 2 (60)
ten [ten] zehn (10/11)
°ten thousand [ten ˈθaʊznd] zehntausend (10.000)
tennis [ˈtenɪs] das Tennis 3 (86)
terrarium [teˈreəriəm] das Terrarium 2 (59)
test [test]:
  1. der Test; die Klassenarbeit 1 (34)
  2. testen 1 (34)
text [tekst]:
  1. der Text 4 (124)
  2. die SMS 5 (142)
  3. **text sb.** jm. eine SMS schicken 5 (142)
°than [ðən]: **more than 100** mehr als 100
thank you [ˈθæŋk juː] danke (schön) (10/11) **Thank you very much.** Vielen Dank. / Danke vielmals. 3 (93)
thanks [θæŋks] danke (schön) (10/11)
that [ðæt]:
  1. das (dort) (16)
  that's (= that is) das (da) ist (16) °**That's where I like to be.** Dort / Genau dort bin ich gerne.
  2. der, die, das *(Relativpronomen)* 4 (124)
  things that people can use Dinge, die ich gebrauchen/benutzen kann 4 (124)
  3. **so that** sodass 4 (122)
the [ðə] der, die, das (10/11)
their [ðeə] ihr/e *(Plural)* 1 (31)
them [ðem], [ðəm] sie, ihnen 1 (30)
°theme [θiːm] das Thema
then [ðen] dann, danach 1 (30)
there [ðeə] da, dort; dahin, dorthin (14) **there are** es sind … / es gibt … (14) **there's (= there is)** es ist … / es gibt … (14)
these [ðiːz] diese (hier) 1 (31) **These are my friends.** Das hier sind meine Freunde/Freundinnen. 1 (31)
they [ðeɪ] sie *(Plural)* 1 (24) **they're (= they are)** sie sind 1 (24)
thing [θɪŋ] das Ding, die Sache
think [θɪŋk] denken, meinen, glauben 1 (24) **I think …** Ich denke/meine/glaube/finde, … 1 (24) °**think about** nachdenken über
third (3rd) [θɜːd] dritte(r, s) 5 (142)

thirteen [θɜːˈtiːn] dreizehn (10/11)
thirty [ˈθɜːti] dreißig 2 (64)
this [ðɪs] dies; diese(r, s) (15)
those [ðəʊz] die dort, jene (dort) 1 (30)
°thousand [ˈθaʊznd] tausend
three [θriː] drei (10/11)
°throw [θrəʊ] werfen
Thursday [ˈθɜːzdeɪ], [ˈθɜːzdi] der Donnerstag 1 (25)
°tick [tɪk] ankreuzen, abhaken
ticket [ˈtɪkɪt] die Eintrittskarte, die Fahrkarte, das Ticket 3 (93)
tidy [ˈtaɪdi]:
  1. ordentlich 2 (57)
  2. aufräumen 2 (57)
tie [taɪ] die Krawatte 1 (20)
°till [tɪl] bis
time [taɪm] die Zeit; die Uhrzeit 1 (20) **(for) a long time** lange, (für) eine lange Zeit 2 (62) **What's the time?** Wie spät ist es? 3 (82) °**all the time** die ganze Zeit, ständig
timetable [ˈtaɪmteɪbl] der Stundenplan 1 (24)
tip [tɪp] der Tipp 4 (121)
tired [ˈtaɪəd] müde 1 (20)
title [ˈtaɪtl] der Titel, die Überschrift 4 (126)
to [tu], [tə]:
  1. zu, nach 1 (22)
  the answer to the question die Antwort auf die Frage 1 (23)
  °**different to you** anders als du
  2. bis 1 (34)
  (from) A to Z (von) A bis Z 1 (34)
  3. (um) zu (12)
  how to do sth. wie man etwas tut / tun kann / tun soll 5 (153) **things to eat** Dinge zum Essen (12)
°toad [təʊd] die Kröte
today [təˈdeɪ] heute 1 (30)
together [təˈgeðə] zusammen 4 (123)
toilet [ˈtɔɪlət] die Toilette 1 (22)
tomato [təˈmɑːtəʊ], *pl* **tomatoes** die Tomate 5 (140/141)
tomato sauce [təˈmɑːtəʊ sɔːs] die Tomatensoße 5 (140/141)
too [tuː]:
  1. auch (10/11) **from Berlin too** auch aus Berlin (10/11)
  2. **too slow** zu langsam 1 (30)
tooth [tuːθ], *pl* **teeth** der Zahn 3 (85)
top [tɒp] die Spitze, das obere Ende 2 (54) **at the top (of)** oben, am oberen Ende (von); an der Spitze (von) 2 (54) **the top six films** die sechs besten Filme (16)
top floor [tɒp ˈflɔː] das Dach-/Obergeschoss, das oberste Stockwerk, die oberste Etage 2 (54)
topic [ˈtɒpɪk] das Thema 4 (127)
tour (of) [tʊə] die Tour, die Reise, der Rundgang / die Rundfahrt (durch) 2 (55)
tour guide [ˈtʊə gaɪd] der Reiseleiter, die Reiseleiterin / der Fremdenführer, die Fremdenführerin 4 (117)
tourist [ˈtʊərɪst] der Tourist, die Touristin 4 (120)
°tower [ˈtaʊə] der Turm

town [taʊn] die Stadt 4 (112)
town centre [taʊn ˈsentə] das Stadtzentrum 4 (112)
toy [tɔɪ] das Spielzeug 4 (124)
tradition [trəˈdɪʃn] die Tradition 5 (151)
traditional [trəˈdɪʃənl] traditionell 5 (151)
train [treɪn] der Zug, die Eisenbahn 3 (80/81)
train station [ˈtreɪn steɪʃn] der Bahnhof 4 (116)
trainer [ˈtreɪnə] der Trainer, die Trainerin 3 (94)
training [ˈtreɪnɪŋ] das Training 3 (83)
trampoline [ˈtræmpəliːn] das Trampolin 3 (86)
trampolining [ˈtræmpəliːnɪŋ] das Trampolinspringen/-turnen 3 (86)
°transport *(no pl)* [ˈtrænspɔːt] das Fortbewegungsmittel; die Beförderung
travel [ˈtrævl]:
  1. das Reisen 4 (120)
  2. reisen, fahren 4 (120)
tree [triː] der Baum 2 (54)
trick [trɪk] der Trick, das Kunststück 5 (146)
trifle [ˈtraɪfl] das Trifle *(britischer Nachtisch)* 5 (140/141)
trouble [ˈtrʌbl] der Ärger, Schwierigkeiten 1 (30) **be in trouble** Ärger haben, in Schwierigkeiten sein 1 (30)
true [truː] wahr, richtig 5 (153)
°try [traɪ] versuchen, (aus)probieren
Tuesday [ˈtjuːzdeɪ], [ˈtjuːzdi] der Dienstag 1 (25)
°Turkey [ˈtɜːki] die Türkei
turn [tɜːn] (sich) (um)drehen 4 (121) **Turn it upside down.** Dreh/Stell es auf den Kopf. 4 (121) **turn sth. (over)** etwas umdrehen 4 (121)
turn [tɜːn]: **it is sb.'s turn (to do sth.)** jd. ist dran / an der Reihe (etwas zu tun) 5 (153) **take turns / take it in turns (to do sth)** sich abwechseln; sich dabei abwechseln, etwas zu tun 5 (153) **When is (it) my turn (to do sth.)?** Wann bin ich dran / an der Reihe (etwas zu tun)? 5 (153)
TV [tiːˈviː] der Fernseher; das Fernsehen 3 (83)
twelfth (12th) [twelfθ] zwölfte(r, s) 5 (142)
twelve [twelv] zwölf (10/11)
twenty [ˈtwenti] zwanzig 2 (64)
two [tuː] zwei (10/11)

U

°Ugh! [ɜː] Bah!
UK (= United Kingdom) [juː ˈkeɪ] das Vereinigte Königreich 3 (82)
°umbrella [ʌmˈbrelə] der (Regen-)Schirm
°umbrella word [ʌmˈbrelə wɜːd] der Oberbegriff, der Sammelbegriff
uncle [ˈʌŋkl] der Onkel 2 (48/49)
under [ˈʌndə] unter 2 (56)
understand [ʌndəˈstænd] verstehen 1 (23)

unfriendly [ʌnˈfrendli] unfreundlich 4 (112)
uniform [ˈjuːnɪfɔːm] die Uniform 1 (20)
unit [ˈjuːnɪt] die Unit *(die Lerneinheit)* 1 (18/19)
United Kingdom (UK) [junaɪtɪd ˈkɪŋdəm] das Vereinigte Königreich 3 (82)
°**until** [ənˈtɪl] bis *(zeitlich)*
up [ʌp] hinauf, hoch 4 (120)
upside down [ʌpsaɪd ˈdaʊn] verkehrt herum, auf dem Kopf 4 (121)
us [ʌs], [əs] uns 1 (22) **It's just us.** Es sind nur wir. 5 (152)
use [juːz] benutzen, verwenden 1 (23)
useful [ˈjuːsfl] nützlich, hilfreich 1 (35)
user [ˈjuːzə] der (Be-)Nutzer, die (Be-)Nutzerin 1 (23)
usually [ˈjuːʒuəli] normalerweise, meistens 5 (140/141)

V

vanilla [vəˈnɪlə] die Vanille 5 (150)
vegan [ˈviːɡən] vegan; der Veganer, die Veganerin 5 (140/141)
vegetables *(pl)* [ˈvedʒtəblz] das/die Gemüse 5 (140/141)
vegetarian [vedʒəˈteəriən], *infml auch* **veggie:**
1. der/die Vegetarier/in 5 (140/141)
2. vegetarisch 5 (140/141)
veggie [ˈvedʒi] *siehe* **vegetarian**
°**verse** [vɜːs] der Vers, die Strophe *(Lied)*
very [ˈveri] sehr 1 (29)
vet [vet] der Tierarzt, die Tierärztin 2 (50)
video [ˈvɪdiəʊ] das Video; Video- 2 (55)
°**viewing** [ˈvjuːɪŋ] das Fernsehen, das Betrachten *(von DVDs, Filmen usw.)*
village [ˈvɪlɪdʒ] das Dorf 4 (115)
visit [ˈvɪzɪt]:
1. der Besuch 4 (118)
2. besuchen 4 (118)
visitor [ˈvɪzɪtə] der Besucher, die Besucherin; der Gast 4 (118)
visitor information centre [vɪzɪtə ɪnfəˈmeɪʃn sentə] die Touristeninformation, das Fremdenverkehrsbüro 4 (118)
vocab [ˈvəʊkæb] *siehe* **vocabulary**
vocabulary [vəˈkæbjələri], *infml auch* **vocab** der Wortschatz, das Vokabular; das Vokabelverzeichnis 1 (34)

W

°**wait (for)** [weɪt] warten (auf) **Wait a minute.** Warte mal. / Einen Moment.
°**wake up** [weɪk ˈʌp] aufwachen
walk [wɔːk]:
1. der Spaziergang 1 (18/19)
2. (zu Fuß) gehen, wandern 1 (18/19)
°**walk around** umhergehen
walking [ˈwɔːkɪŋ] das Wandern 1 (18/19)
wall [wɔːl] die Wand, die Mauer 2 (59) **on the wall** an der Wand; an die Wand 2 (59)
want [wɒnt] wollen 2 (53) **want to do sth.** etwas tun wollen 2 (53)

wardrobe [ˈwɔːdrəʊb] der Kleiderschrank 2 (56)
warm [wɔːm] warm 4 (118)
watch (sth.) [wɒtʃ] (sich etwas) anschauen; (etwas) beobachten 3 (83)
water [ˈwɔːtə] das Wasser 5 (156)
watermelon [ˈmelən] die Wassermelone 5 (156)
wave (to sb.) [weɪv] (jm. zu-) winken 5 (152)
way [weɪ]:
1. der Weg 1 (34)
2. die Art und Weise 1 (34) **(in) this way** auf diese Art/Weise 1 (34) **in different ways** unterschiedlich *(Adv.)*, auf unterschiedliche Art/Weise 1 (34)
we [wiː] wir 1 (24) **we're (= we are)** wir sind 1 (24)
wear [weə] tragen, anhaben *(Kleidung)* 5 (145)
weather [ˈweðə] das Wetter, die Witterung 4 (120)
website [ˈwebsaɪt] die Website 2 (65)
Wednesday [ˈwenzdeɪ], [ˈwenzdi] der Mittwoch 1 (25)
week [wiːk] die Woche 1 (25)
weekday [ˈwiːkdeɪ] der Werktag, der Wochentag 3 (82)
weekend [wiːkˈend] das Wochenende 2 (50) **at the weekend** am Wochenende 2 (50)
weird [wɪəd] seltsam, komisch 1 (30)
welcome [ˈwelkəm]:
1. **Welcome to …** Willkommen in/an … 4 (122)
2. **You're welcome.** Bitte, gern geschehen. / Nichts zu danken. 1 (23)
well [wel]:
1. gut *(Adv.)* 3 (93) **Well done.** Gut gemacht! 3 (93)
2. **Well, …** Nun, …/ Also, …/ Na ja, … 5 (152)
what [wɒt]:
1. was (10/11)
2. welche(r, s) 1 (23) **What about a … ?** Wie wäre es mit einer/einem … ? 5 (146) **What about you?** Was ist mit dir? (10/11) **What's your name?** Wie heißt du? (10/11)
wheelchair [ˈwiːltʃeə] der Rollstuhl 3 (83)
when [wen]:
1. wann 1 (32)
2. wenn *(zeitlich)* 1 (32)
°3. als *(zeitlich)*
where [weə] wo; wohin (10/11) **Where are you from?** Wo kommst du her? (10/11)
which [wɪtʃ] welche(r, s) 3 (86) **Which clubs …?** Welche AGs …? 3 (86)
°**while** [waɪl] während
white [waɪt] weiß (10/11)
who [huː] wer 1 (30) °**someone who …** jemand, der/die …
why [waɪ] warum 3 (83) °**the reason why …** der Grund dafür, dass … / der Grund, weshalb …
win [wɪn] gewinnen 3 (92)

wind [wɪnd] der Wind 4 (120)
window [ˈwɪndəʊ] das Fenster 1 (22)
windsurfing [wɪndsɜːfɪŋ] das Windsurfing 3 (86)
windy [ˈwɪndi] windig 4 (120)
winner [ˈwɪnə] der Gewinner, die Gewinnerin / der Sieger, die Siegerin 3 (83)
winter [ˈwɪntə] der Winter 5 (118)
with [wɪð]:
1. mit (15)
2. bei (15)
wok [wɒk] der Wok *(chinesischer Kochtopf)* 5 (157)
woman [ˈwʊmən], *pl* **women** die Frau 4 (120)
women [ˈwɪmɪn] *Plural von* **woman**
word [wɜːd] das Wort 1 (34)
°**wordbank** [ˈwɜːdbæŋk] die Wortbank *(die Sammlung von Wörtern zu einem Thema)*
work [wɜːk]:
1. die Arbeit 2 (50) **at work** bei der Arbeit, am Arbeitsplatz 2 (50)
2. arbeiten; funktionieren 2 (50) **work long days** lange arbeiten, lange Arbeitstage haben 3 (83)
°**workbook** [ˈwɜːkbʊk] das Arbeitsheft
would [wʊd] **I'd (= I would) like/love …** Ich hätte (liebend) gern … / Ich möchte (liebend gern)… 3 (90) **I'd love/like to meet** ….Ich würde mich (liebend) gerne mit … treffen. 3 (90)
°**Wow!** [waʊ] Wow! / Mensch!
write [raɪt] schreiben 2 (64) °**write it down** es aufschreiben
wrong [rɒŋ] falsch (10/11) **be wrong** Unrecht haben 1 (24) °**What's wrong?** Was ist los? / Was ist das Problem?

Y

year [jɪə] das Jahr; der Jahrgang (10/11) °**leap year** das Schaltjahr
yellow [ˈjeləʊ] gelb (10/11)
yes [jes] ja 1 (22)
yoga [ˈjəʊɡə] das Yoga 1 (18/19)
you [juː] du; dich; dir; ihr; euch; Sie; Ihnen (10/11) **you're (= you are)** du bist; ihr seid; Sie sind (10/11)
°**young** [jʌŋ] jung
your [jɔː], [jə] dein/e; euer/eure; Ihr/e (10/11)
°**yourself** [jəˈself] du/dir/dich (selbst)
youth [juːθ] die Jugend; der Jugendliche 4 (112)
youth centre [ˈjuːθ sentə] das Jugendzentrum 4 (112)
°**youth worker** [ˈjuːθ wɜːkə] der Jugendarbeiter, die Jugendarbeiterin
°**Yuck!** [jʌk] Igitt!
°**yum** [jʌm] *(infml)* lecker

Z

zoo [zuː] der Zoo 4 (127)

Das *German-English Dictionary* enthält den **Lernwortschatz** deines Schulbuchs. Es kann dir eine erste Hilfe sein, wenn du vergessen hast, wie etwas auf Englisch heißt.

Wenn du wissen möchtest, wo das englische Wort zum ersten Mal in deinem Schulbuch vorkommt, dann kannst du im *English-German Dictionary* (Seiten 255–266) nachschlagen.

Es werden folgende **Abkürzungen und Symbole** verwendet:

infml = informal (umgangssprachlich)
sb. = somebody (jemand)
jd. = jemand   *jm. = jemandem*

pl = plural (Mehrzahl)
sth. = something (etwas)
jn. = jemanden

A

Abend evening [ˈiːvnɪŋ] **am Abend** in the evening
Abendessen dinner [ˈdɪnə] **zum Abendessen** for dinner
abends in the evening [ˈiːvnɪŋ] **9 Uhr abends** *(21 Uhr)* 9 p.m. [piːˈem]
aber but [bʌt], [bət]
A bis Z: (von) A bis Z *(from)* A to Z [eɪ tu zed]
Abfall rubbish [ˈrʌbɪʃ]
abwechseln: sich abwechseln take turns [tɜːn] **sich dabei abwechseln, etwas zu tun** take it in turns (to do sth.)
acht eight [eɪt]
achtzehn eighteen [eɪˈtiːn]
achtzig eighty [ˈeɪti]
addieren add [æd]
Adresse address [əˈdres]
Affe monkey [ˈmʌŋki]
AG *(in der Schule)* school club [skuːl klʌb]
aktiv active [ˈæktɪv]
Aktivität activity [ækˈtɪvəti]
albern stupid [ˈstjuːpɪd]
alle(s) all [ɔːl] **alle 30 Minuten** every 30 minutes [ˈevri]
allein alone [əˈləʊn]
allergisch (gegen) allergic (to) [əˈlɜːdʒɪk]
Alphabet alphabet [ˈælfəbet]
also so [səʊ] **Also, ...** Well, ... [wel]
alt old [əʊld] **Wie alt bist du?** How old are you?
am: am Anfang at first [æt], [ət] **am Arbeitsplatz** at work **am besten** best [best] **am Ende (von)** at the end (of) **am größten** biggest [ˈbɪɡɪst] **am Meer** by the sea [baɪ] **am Montag** on Monday [ɒn] **am Morgen** in the morning [ɪn] **am Nachmittag** in the afternoon **am nächsten Tag** the next day **am oberen Ende (von)** at the top (of) **am Strand** on the beach **am Telefon** on the phone **am Wochenende** at the weekend
an at [æt], [ət]
anbraten: *(Gemüse- oder Fleischstücke)* **unter Rühren scharf anbraten** stir-fry [ˈstɜː fraɪ]
andere(r, s) other [ˈʌðə] **die anderen** the other **ein/e andere(r, s)** another [əˈnʌðə]

anders different [ˈdɪfrənt]
Anfang start [stɑːt] **am Anfang** at first [æt], [ət]
anfangen (mit) start [stɑːt]
Angst: Angst haben be scared (of) [skeəd]
anhaben *(Kleidung)* wear [weə]
anhalten stop [stɒp]
anhören: sich etwas anhören listen to sth. [ˈlɪsn]
anlächeln: jn. anlächeln smile at sb. [smaɪl]
Anruf *(phone)* call [ˈfəʊn kɔːl]
anrufen call [kɔːl]; phone [fəʊn]
anschauen: etwas/jn. anschauen look at sth./sb. [lʊk] **sich etwas anschauen** watch sth. [wɒtʃ]
Anspitzer sharpener [ˈʃɑːpnə]
Anteil share [ʃeə]
Antwort answer [ˈɑːnsə] **Antwort auf die Frage** the answer to the question
antworten answer [ˈɑːnsə]
Anweisung instruction [ɪnˈstrʌkʃn]
anziehen: sich anziehen get dressed [drest]
App app [æp]
Appetit: Guten Appetit! Enjoy! [ɪnˈdʒɔɪ]
April April [ˈeɪprəl]
Arbeit work [wɜːk] **bei der Arbeit, am Arbeitsplatz** at work
arbeiten work [wɜːk] **lange arbeiten** work long days [lɒŋ]
Ärger trouble [ˈtrʌbl] **Ärger kriegen** be in trouble
Art way [weɪ] **auf diese Art** (in) this way, like this [laɪk] **auf unterschiedliche Art** in different ways **eine Art (von) ...** a kind (of) ... [kaɪnd], sort (of) [sɔːt]
Artikel article [ˈɑːtɪkl]
auch also [ˈɔːlsəʊ]; too [tuː] **auch aus Berlin** from Berlin too
auf at [æt], [ət]; in [ɪn]; on [ɒn] **auf dem Bild, auf dem Foto** in the picture **auf dem Kopf** upside down [ʌpsaɪd ˈdaʊn] **auf dem Land** in the country **auf der Weide** in the field **auf Englisch** in English **Auf Wiedersehen!** Goodbye. [ɡʊdˈbaɪ]
Aufführung show [ʃəʊ]
Aufgabe exercise [ˈeksəsaɪz]
aufhören (mit) stop [stɒp]
auflisten list [lɪst]
aufpassen auf look after [lʊk]

aufräumen tidy [ˈtaɪdi] **etwas aufräumen** clean sth. up [kliːn]
aufschlagen *(Buch)* open [ˈəʊpən] **Schlagt eure Bücher auf Seite 10 auf.** Open your books at page 10.
aufstehen *(aus dem Bett)* get up [ɡet ˈʌp]; *(sich hinstellen)* stand up [stænd ˈʌp]
August August [ɔːˈɡʌst]
aus from [frɒm]
Ausdruck phrase [freɪz]
ausruhen: sich ausruhen relax [rɪˈlæks]
aussehen look [lʊk]
außerhalb (von) outside [aʊtˈsaɪd]
Ausstellung show [ʃəʊ]
auswählen choose [tʃuːz]
Auto car [kɑː]
Autoscheinwerfer car light [ˈkɑː laɪt]

B

backen bake [beɪk]
Backofen oven [ˈʌvn]
Backpulver baking powder [ˈbeɪkɪŋ paʊdə]
Bad(ezimmer) bathroom [ˈbɑːθruːm]
Badminton badminton [ˈbædmɪntən]
Bahnhof *(train)* station [ˈtreɪn steɪʃn]
bald soon [suːn]
Balkon balcony [ˈbælkəni]
Ball ball [bɔːl]
Ballon balloon [bəˈluːn]
Banane banana [bəˈnɑːnə]
Band band [bænd]
Basketball basketball [ˈbɑːskɪtbɔːl]
Basteln crafts *(pl)* [krɑːfts]
Baum tree [triː]
beantworten answer [ˈɑːnsə]
bedeuten mean [miːn]
Bedeutung meaning [ˈmiːnɪŋ]
beenden end [end]
beginnen start [stɑːt]
Behälter case [keɪs]
bei at [æt], [ət]; with [wɪð] **bei der Arbeit** at work **bei ihrer Mutter (zu Hause/daheim)** at her mum's (house)
beibringen: jm. beibringen, etwas zu tun teach sb. to do sth. [tiːtʃ]
Beispiel example [ɪɡˈzɑːmpl] **zum Beispiel** for example **wie zum Beispiel** like [laɪk]
bekommen get [ɡet]
belebt busy [ˈbɪzi]
bellen: (jn. an)bellen bark (at sb.) [bɑːk]

benutzen use [juːz]
Benutzer/in user [ˈjuːzə]
beobachten: (etwas) beobachten
  watch (sth.) [wɒtʃ]
bereit ready [ˈredi]
beschäftigt: (viel) beschäftigt busy
  [ˈbɪzi] **du bist beschäftigt** you're
  busy
beschreiben describe [dɪˈskraɪb]
Beschreibung description [dɪˈskrɪpʃn]
besondere(r, s) special [ˈspeʃl]
besorgen: (sich etwas) besorgen
  get sth. [get]
beste(r, s) best [best] **der beste Sohn
  überhaupt / der beste Sohn, den man
  sich wünschen kann** the best son
  ever [ˈevə]
Besuch visit [ˈvɪzɪt]
besuchen visit [ˈvɪzɪt]
Besucher/in visitor [ˈvɪzɪtə]
Bett bed [bed] **ins Bett gehen** go to
  bed
bevor before [bɪˈfɔː] **bevor du
  liest** before you read
bewegen: sich bewegen move [muːv]
bewölkt cloudy [ˈklaʊdi]
Bibliothek library [ˈlaɪbrəri]
Bild picture [ˈpɪktʃə] **auf dem Bild** in
  the picture [ɪn]
Bildschirmpräsentation slide
  show [ˈslaɪd ʃəʊ]
Biologie biology [baɪˈɒlədʒi]
bis to [tu], [tə] **Bis bald!** See you
  soon. [ˈsiː juː], [ˈsiː jə] **Bis dann.** See
  you. **Bis später.** Speak later. [ˈleɪtə]
bisschen: ein bisschen a little [ˈlɪtl]
bitte please [pliːz] **Bitte schön. / Hier,
  bitte.** Here you are. [hɪə juˈɑː]
  Bitte, gern geschehen. You're
  welcome. [ˈwelkəm]
bitten: jn. bitten, etwas zu tun ask sb.
  to do sth. [ɑːsk] **jn. um etwas bitten**
  ask sb. for sth.
blau blue [bluː]
Blazer (das Jackett, oft Teil der
  Schuluniform) blazer [ˈbleɪzə]
Bleistift pencil [ˈpensl]
Bleistift(an)spitzer pencil sharpener
  [ˈpensl ʃɑːpnə]
Blindenhund guide dog [ˈɡaɪd dɒɡ]
blöd stupid [ˈstjuːpɪd]
bloß just [dʒʌst]; only [ˈəʊnli]
Bockwurst sausage [ˈsɒsɪdʒ]
Boden ground [ɡraʊnd]
Bonbon sweet [swiːt]
Bowling bowling [ˈbəʊlɪŋ]
Boxen boxing [ˈbɒksɪŋ]
boxen box [bɒks]
braten fry [fraɪ] **gebraten** fried
  [fraɪd]
Brathähnchen chicken [ˈtʃɪkɪn]
Bratwurst sausage [ˈsɒsɪdʒ]
brauchen need [niːd]; (Zeit)
  take [teɪk]
braun brown [braʊn]
brav good [ɡʊd]
Brief letter [ˈletə] **der kurze
  Brief** note [nəʊt]

bringen bring [brɪŋ]; take [teɪk]
britisch British [ˈbrɪtɪʃ]
Brot bread [bred]
Browser (Computerprogramm zum
  Finden und Lesen von Websites)
  browser [ˈbraʊzə]
Bruder brother [ˈbrʌðə]
Buch book [bʊk]
Buchseite page (p.) [peɪdʒ]
Bücherei library [ˈlaɪbrəri]
Buchstabe letter [ˈletə]
buchstabieren spell [spel]
Bürste brush [brʌʃ]
bürsten brush [brʌʃ]
Bus bus [bʌs] **im Bus** on the bus
  mit dem Bus by bus
Bushaltestelle bus stop [ˈbʌs stɒp]
Butter butter [ˈbʌtə]

C

Café cafe [ˈkæfeɪ]
Cent cent [sent]
Chaos mess [mes]
clever smart [smɑːt]
Code code [kəʊd]
codieren code [kəʊd]
Cola cola [ˈkəʊlə]
Comic comic [ˈkɒmɪk]
Computer computer [kəmˈpjuːtə]
cool cool [kuːl]
Cousin/e cousin [ˈkʌzn]
Cricket (Mannschaftssportart) cricket
  [ˈkrɪkɪt]
Curry (Gewürz und auch Gericht)
  curry [ˈkʌri]
Custard (Vanillesoße) custard
  [ˈkʌstəd]

D

da there [ðeə] **da drüben** over there
Dachgeschoss top floor [tɒp ˈflɔː]
daher so [səʊ]
dahin there [ðeə]
damit so that [səʊ ðæt]
danach then [ðen]
Dank: Vielen Dank. Thank you very
  much. [ˈθæŋk juː]
Danke(schön). Thank you. [ˈθæŋk
  juː]; thanks [θæŋks] **Danke vielmals.**
  Thank you very much. [mʌtʃ]
danken: Nichts zu danken. You're
  welcome. [ˈwelkʌm]
dann then [ðen]
das
  1. (Artikel) the [ðə]
  2. (Relativpronomen) that [ðæt]
das (dort) that [ðæt] **das
  (da)** that's (= that is)
dasselbe the same [seɪm]
Datei file [faɪl]
Datum date [deɪt] **Datum des
  Geburtstags** birthday date
  [ˈbɜːθdeɪ]
dauern take [teɪk]
dein/e your [jɔː], [jə]
dekorieren decorate [ˈdekəreɪt]

denken think [θɪŋk] **daran denken
  (etwas zu tun)** remember (to do
  sth.) [rɪˈmembə] **Ich denke, ...** I think
  ...
der
  1. (Artikel) the [ðə]
  2. (Relativpronomen) that [ðæt]
derselbe the same [seɪm]
Design design [dɪˈzaɪn]
Dessert dessert [dɪˈzɜːt]
deutlich clear [klɪə] **deutlich
  sprechen** speak clearly [spiːk ˈklɪəli]
Deutsch; deutsch German [ˈdʒɜːmən]
Deutsche German [ˈdʒɜːmən]
Deutschland Germany [ˈdʒɜːməni]
Dezember December [dɪˈsembə]
die
  1. (Artikel) the [ðə]
  2. (Relativpronomen) that [ðæt]
die dort those [ðəʊz]
Diele hall [hɔːl]
Dienstag Tuesday [ˈtjuːzdeɪ]
diese (hier) these [ðiːz]
diese(r, s) this [ðɪs]
dieselbe(n) the same [seɪm]
Ding thing [θɪŋ] **Dinge, die Menschen gebrauchen/benutzen können**
  things that people can use **Dinge
  zum Essen** things to eat
Donnerstag Thursday [ˈθɜːzdeɪ]
Dorf village [ˈvɪlɪdʒ]
dort there [ðeə] **dort drüben** over
  there [ˈəʊvə]
dorthin there [ðeə]
dran: jd. ist dran it is sb.'s
  turn [tɜːn] **Wann bin ich dran (etwas
  zu tun)?** When is (it) my turn
  (to do sth.)?
draußen; nach draußen outside
  [aʊtˈsaɪd]
Dreck-weg-Tag (Aktionstag zum
  Müllsammeln) clean-up day
  [ˈkliːn ʌp deɪ]
drehen turn [tɜːn] **Dreh etwas auf
  den Kopf.** Turn it upside
  down. [ʌpsaɪd ˈdaʊn] **etwas
  umdrehen** turn sth. (over)
drei three [θriː]
dreißig thirty [ˈθɜːti]
dreizehn thirteen [θɜːˈtiːn]
drinnen; nach drinnen inside
  [ɪnˈsaɪd]
dritte(r, s) third (3rd) [θɜːd]
Drohne drone [drəʊn]
du you [juː] **du bist** you're (= you
  are) [jɔː] **du bist beschäftigt** you're
  busy [ˈbɪzi]
dumm stupid [ˈstjuːpɪd]
Dusche shower [ˈʃaʊə]
duschen: (sich) duschen have a
  shower [ˈʃaʊə]

E

Ehemann husband [ˈhʌzbənd]
Ei egg [eg]
Eidechse lizard [ˈlɪzəd]
eigene(r, s): mein/ein eigenes Zimmer
  my own room [əʊn]

Eimer *(Mülleimer)* bin [bin]
ein(e) *(Artikel)* a [ə]; *(vor Vokalen)* an [ən] **ein paar** some [sʌm], [səm] **ein wenig** some; a little [ˈlɪtl] **noch ein(e)** another [əˈnʌðə]
einfach just [dʒʌst]
Einführung introduction [ɪntrəˈdʌkʃn]
einhundert a/one hundred [ˈhʌndrəd]
einige some [sʌm], [səm]
Einkäufe shopping [ˈʃɒpɪŋ] **Einkäufe erledigen** do the shopping, be at the shops [ʃɒp]
Einkaufen shopping [ˈʃɒpɪŋ]
einkaufen gehen do the shopping [ˈʃɒpɪŋ]; go shopping
Einkaufsliste shopping list [ˈʃɒpɪŋ lɪst]
Einkaufszentrum shopping centre [ˈʃɒpɪŋ sentə]
Einladung (zu, nach) invitation (to) [ˌɪnvɪˈteɪʃn]
Einleitung introduction [ɪntrəˈdʌkʃn]
einmal: noch einmal again [əˈgen]
eins one [wʌn]
einsammeln collect [kəˈlekt]
Eintrittskarte ticket [ˈtɪkɪt]
Eisenbahn train [treɪn]
Elefant elephant [ˈelɪfənt]
elektrisch, Elektro- electric [ɪˈlektrɪk]
elf eleven [ɪˈlevən]
Eltern parents *(pl)* [ˈpeərənts]
Ende end [end] **das obere Ende** top [tɒp] **am oberen Ende** at the top (of)
enden end [end]
England England [ˈɪŋglənd]
Englisch; englisch English [ˈɪŋglɪʃ] **auf Englisch** in English [ɪn]
Enkel grandson [ˈgrænsʌn]
Enkelin granddaughter [ˈgrændɔːtə]
Entschuldigung. Sorry / I'm sorry. [ˈsɒri] **Entschuldigung, … / Entschuldigen Sie, …** Excuse me, … [ɪkˈskjuːz miː]
entspannen: sich entspannen relax [rɪˈlæks]
er he [hiː] **er ist** he's (= he is) **er ist nicht** he isn't (= is not)
Erbse pea [piː]
Erdbeere strawberry [ˈstrɔːbəri]
Erdboden ground [graʊnd]
Erdgeschoss ground floor [graʊnd ˈflɔː]
Erdkunde geography [dʒiˈɒgrəfi]
erforschen research [rɪˈsɜːtʃ]
Erholung rest [rest]
erinnern: sich erinnern an remember [rɪˈmembə] **sich daran erinnern, etwas getan zu haben** remember doing sth.
erklären: jm. etwas erklären explain sth. to sb. [ɪkˈspleɪn]
erst only [ˈəʊnli]
erstaunlich amazing [əˈmeɪzɪŋ]
erste(r, s) first [fɜːst] **als Erstes** first
erzählen tell [tel]
es it [ɪt] **es ist** *(bei Sachen und Tieren auch: er ist; sie ist)* it's (= it is) **es ist … / es gibt …** there's [ðeəz] **es sind … / es gibt …** there are [ˈðeər ɑː]

Essen cooking [ˈkʊkɪŋ]; food [fuːd]; meal [miːl]
essen eat [iːt] **Dinge zum Essen** things to eat
Esslöffel tablespoon [ˈteɪblspuːn]
Esszimmer dining room [ˈdaɪnɪŋ ruːm]
Etage floor [flɔː] **die oberste Etage** top floor [tɒp ˈflɔː]
Etui case [keɪs]
etwas some [sʌm], [səm]; something [ˈsʌmθɪŋ]
euer/eure your [jɔː], [jə]
Euro euro, *pl* euros [ˈjʊərəʊ]

F

Fach subject [ˈsʌbdʒɪkt]
Fähigkeit skill [skɪl]
fahren go [gəʊ]; travel [ˈtrævl] **mit dem Fahrrad fahren** ride a bike [raɪd] **Rad fahren** cycle [ˈsaɪkl] **Skateboard fahren** skateboard [ˈskeɪtbɔːd]
Fahrkarte ticket [ˈtɪkɪt]
Fahrrad bike [baɪk]
Fahrt journey [ˈdʒɜːni]
Fakt fact [fækt]
falls if [ɪf]
falsch wrong [rɒŋ]
Familie family [ˈfæməli]
Familienname family name [ˈfæməli neɪm]
Fan fan [fæn]
Farbe colour [ˈkʌlə] **Welche Farbe hat …?** What colour is …?
Favorit/in favourite [ˈfeɪvərɪt]
Februar February [ˈfebruəri]
Federball badminton [ˈbædmɪntən]
Federmäppchen pencil case [ˈpensl keɪs]
Feedback *(Rückmeldung)* feedback *(no pl)* [ˈfiːdbæk]
Feier ceremony [ˈserəməni]
Feld field [fiːld]
Fenster window [ˈwɪndəʊ]
Ferien holidays *(pl)* [ˈhɒlədeɪz]
Fernsehen, Fernseher TV [ˌtiːˈviː]
fertig ready [ˈredi]
Fertigkeit skill [skɪl]
fies mean [miːn]
Film film [fɪlm] **die sechs besten Filme** the top six films [tɒp]
Filmstar star [stɑː]
finden find [faɪnd] **Ich finde, …** I think … [θɪŋk]
Finger finger [ˈfɪŋgə]
Fisch fish, *pl* fish [fɪʃ] **Fisch mit Pommes frites** fish and chips [fɪʃ ən ˈtʃɪps] **Imbissstube, die Fisch mit Pommes frites verkauft** fish and chip shop [ʃɒp]
Fleisch meat [miːt]
fliegen fly [flaɪ]
Flur hall [hɔːl]
Forschungen research [rɪˈsɜːtʃ]
fort away [əˈweɪ]
fortfahren continue [kənˈtɪnjuː] **(mit) etwas fortfahren** continue to do sth. [duː]

fortsetzen: (sich) fortsetzen continue [kənˈtɪnjuː]
Foto photo [ˈfəʊtəʊ] **auf dem Foto** in the photo **ein Foto machen** take a photo
Fotograf/in photographer [fəˈtɒgrəfə]
Frage question [kwestʃən] **Antwort auf die Frage** the answer to the question [ˈɑːnsə] **eine Frage stellen** ask a question **Habt ihr / Hast du (irgendwelche) Fragen?** Do you have any questions?
fragen ask [ɑːsk]
Frau woman, *pl* women [ˈwʊmən], [ˈwɪmɪn] **Frau Lee** *(Anrede für verheiratete Frauen)* Mrs Lee [ˈmɪsɪz] *(allgemeine Anrede für Frauen)* Ms Lee [mɪz]
frech rude [ruːd]
frei free [friː] **freie Zeit** free time [taɪm]
Freitag Friday [ˈfraɪdeɪ], [ˈfraɪdi]
Freizeit free time [ˈfriː taɪm]
Fremdenverkehrsbüro tourist information centre [tʊərɪst ɪnfəˈmeɪʃn sentə]
fressen eat [iːt]
freuen: Freut mich, dich/euch/ Sie kennenzulernen. Nice to meet you. [naɪs]
Freund/in friend [ˈfrend] **Das hier sind meine Freunde/Freundinnen.** These are my friends. [ðiːz] **ihre Freunde/Freundinnen** her friends [hɜː], [hə] **seine Freunde/ Freundinnen** his friends [hɪz]
freundlich friendly [ˈfrendli]; kind [kaɪnd]
frieren be cold [kəʊld]
frittieren fry [fraɪ] **frittiert** fried [fraɪd]
froh happy [ˈhæpi]
Frühling spring [sprɪŋ]
Frühstück breakfast [ˈbrekfəst]
fühlen: sich fühlen feel [fiːl]
Füller pen [pen]
für for [fɔː] **für 30 Sekunden** for 30 seconds
fünf five [faɪv]
fünfzehn fifteen [fɪfˈtiːn]
fünfzig fifty [ˈfɪfti]
Fußball football [ˈfʊtbɔːl]
Fußboden floor [flɔː]
Futter food [fuːd]

G

ganz quite [kwaɪt] **ganz (still)** perfectly (still) [ˈpɜːfiktli]
Garage garage [ˈgærɑːʒ]
Garten garden [ˈgɑːdn]
Gast visitor [ˈvɪzɪtə]
Gebäude building [ˈbɪldɪŋ]
geben give [gɪv] **es gibt …** there's (= there is) … [ðeəz]; there are … [ˈðeər ɑː] **es gibt keine …** there aren't any … [ˈeni] **Was gibt es zum Mittagessen?** What's for lunch? [lʌntʃ]

Geburtstag birthday [ˈbɜːθdeɪ] **an meinem Geburtstag** on my birthday **Datum des Geburtstags** birthday date [deɪt] **Herzlichen Glückwunsch zum Geburtstag!** Happy birthday! [ˈhæpi] **Ich habe im April Geburtstag.** My birthday is in April. **Wann hast du Geburtstag?** When's your birthday?

Gedankenkarte mind map [ˈmaɪnd mæp]

Gegend: ländliche Gegend country [ˈkʌntri]

geheim secret [ˈsiːkrət]

Geheimnis secret [ˈsiːkrət]

gehen go [ɡəʊ] **ins Bett gehen** go to bed [bed] **nach Hause gehen** go home [həʊm] **Wie geht's? / Wie geht es dir / euch / Ihnen?** How are you? [haʊ] **(zu Fuß) gehen** walk [wɔːk]

gelb yellow [ˈjeləʊ]

Geld money [ˈmʌni]

Gelee jelly [ˈdʒeli]

gemein mean [miːn]

Gemüse vegetables (pl) [ˈvedʒtəblz]

genießen enjoy [ɪnˈdʒɔɪ] **es genießen, etwas zu tun** enjoy doing sth.

Geografie geography [dʒiˈɒɡrəfi]

Geräusch noise [nɔɪz]

Gericht (Mahlzeit) dish [dɪʃ] das Gericht aus unter Rühren kurz angebratenen Zutaten, z. B. kleine Stücke Fleisch, Fisch und/oder Gemüse stir-fry [ˈstɜː fraɪ]

gern: ich hätte gern ... I'd (= I would like ... [laɪk] **Ich hätte liebend gern ... / Ich möchte liebend gern...** I'd (= I would) love ... [lʌv] **Ich würde mich (liebend) gerne mit ... treffen.** I'd (= I would) like/love to meet ...

Geruch smell [smel]

Geschäft shop [ʃɒp]

geschehen: (jm.) geschehen happen (to sb.) [ˈhæpən] **Bitte, gern geschehen.** You're welcome. [ˈwelkʌm]

Geschenk present [ˈpreznt]

Geschichte (Erzählung) story [ˈstɔːri]; (vergangene Zeiten) history [ˈhɪstri] **so/solch eine Geschichte** a story like this [laɪk]

Gespräch talk [tɔːk]

Gestaltung design [dɪˈzaɪn]

Gestank smell [smel]

gesund healthy [ˈhelθi]

Gesundheit health [helθ]

Getränk drink [drɪŋk]

Gewerbegebiet estate [ɪˈsteɪt]

Gewinn prize [praɪz]

gewinnen win [wɪn]

Gewinner/in winner [ˈwɪnə] **als Gewinner/in** as the winner

Gewürz spice [spaɪs]

Gitarre guitar [ɡɪˈtɑː]

Glasur icing [ˈaɪsɪŋ]

glauben think [θɪŋk] **Ich glaube, ...** I think ...

gleich the same [seɪm]

Glück: Glücks-, lucky [ˈlʌki] **Glück haben** be lucky

glücklich happy [ˈhæpi]; lucky [ˈlʌki]

Glückszahl lucky number [lʌki ˈnʌmbə]

Gold gold [ɡəʊld]

goldfarben gold [ɡəʊld]

graben dig [dɪɡ]

Gramm gram (g) [ɡræm]

Grad degree [dɪˈɡriː]

grau grey [ɡreɪ]

Grillen barbecue [ˈbɑːbɪkjuː]

Grillfest barbecue [ˈbɑːbɪkjuː]

groß big [bɪɡ] **der/die/das größte, am größten** biggest

großartig amazing [əˈmeɪzɪŋ]; great [ɡreɪt]

Großbritannien (Great) Britain [ˈbrɪtn]

Großeltern grandparents (pl) [ˈɡrænpeərənts]

Großstadt city [ˈsɪti]

grün green [ɡriːn] **grün/ umweltfreundlich werden** go green [ɡəʊ]

Gruppe group [ɡruːp]

gut good [ɡʊd]; (Adv.) well [wel] **Es geht mir gut.** I'm OK. [əʊˈkeɪ] **etwas gut können; gut in etwas sein** be good at sth. / at doing sth. **Guten Appetit!** Enjoy! [ɪnˈdʒɔɪ] **Gut gemacht.** Well done. [dʌn] **gut umgehen können mit ...** be good with ... **Mir geht es gut.** I'm fine. [faɪn] **so gut** so good [səʊ]

H

haben have [hæv] **er/sie/es hat** he/she/it has [hæz], [həz]

Hähnchen chicken [ˈtʃɪkɪn]

Halle hall [hɔːl]

Hallo. Hello. [həˈləʊ]; Hi. [haɪ] **Hallo allerseits!** Hello everybody! [ˈevribɒdi]

halten stop [stɒp]

Hamburger (Frikadelle) burger [ˈbɜːɡə]

Hamster hamster [ˈhæmstə]

Hand hand [hænd] **Hand / Hände hochstrecken** put your hand / hands up [pʊt]

Handy phone [fəʊn]

hart hard [hɑːd]

Hass hate [heɪt]

hassen hate [heɪt]

Haupt- main [meɪn]

Hauptgericht main course [ˈkɔːs]; main dish [dɪʃ]

Haus house [haʊs] **nach Hause gehen** go home [həʊm] **im Haus** inside the house [ɪnˈsaɪd] **wieder zu Hause** back at home [bæk] **zu Hause** at home

Hausaufgabe(n) homework [ˈhəʊmwɜːk] **Hausaufgaben machen** do your homework **Was haben wir als Hausaufgabe(n) auf?** What's for homework? [wɒts fɔː]

Hausmüll rubbish [ˈrʌbɪʃ]

Haustier pet [pet]

heben lift [lɪft]

Heftseite page (p.) [peɪdʒ]

Heim home [həʊm]

heiß hot [hɒt] **heiße (Trink-) Schokolade** hot chocolate [ˈtʃɒklət]

heißen: Wie heißt du? What's your name? [wɒts jɔː ˈneɪm]

hektisch busy [ˈbɪzi]

helfen help [help]

herausfinden find out (about) [ˌfaɪnd ˈaʊt]

Herbst autumn [ˈɔːtəm]

Herr Lee Mr Lee [ˈmɪstə]

herstellen make [meɪk]

herunter down [daʊn]

hervorheben highlight [ˈhaɪlaɪt]

Herzog duke [djuːk]

heute today [təˈdeɪ]

hier here [hɪə] **Hier, bitte.** Here you are. **hier herüber; hier drüben** over here [ˈəʊvə]

hierher here [hɪə]

Highlight (Höhepunkt) highlight [ˈhaɪlaɪt]

Hilfe help [help]

hilfreich helpful [ˈhelpfl]; useful [ˈjuːsfl]

hilfsbereit helpful [ˈhelpfl]

hinauf up [ʌp]

hinsetzen: sich hinsetzen sit down [sɪt ˈdaʊn]

hinter behind [bɪˈhaɪnd]

hinunter down [daʊn]

hinzufügen add [æd]

Hobby hobby [ˈhɒbi]

hoch up [ʌp]

Hockey hockey [ˈhɒki]

höflich polite [pəˈlaɪt]

holen: (sich etwas) holen get sth. [get]

Honig honey [ˈhʌni]

hören hear [hɪə]

Hotdog (heißes Würstchen in einem Brötchen) hot dog [ˈhɒt dɒɡ]

Huhn chicken [ˈtʃɪkɪn]

Hund dog [dɒɡ]

hundert a/one hundred [ˈhʌndrəd]

Hunger: Ich habe Hunger. I'm hungry. [ˈhʌŋɡri]

hungrig hungry [ˈhʌŋɡri]

Hut hat [hæt]

I

ich I [aɪ] **Ich bin** I'm (= I am) [æm] **Ich bin's.** It's me. **Ich nicht!** (= Ich bin/war/habe/... es/das nicht!) Not me! [nɒt]

Idee idea [aɪˈdɪə]

ihm, ihn him [hɪm]

Ihnen (höfliche Anrede) you [juː]

ihnen them [ðem], [ðəm]

ihr (Plural von „du") you [juː] **ihr seid** you're (= you are) [ɑː]

Ihr/e ... (besitzanzeigend zur höflichen Anrede „Sie") your [jɔː], [jə]

ihr/e ... *(vor Nomen; besitzanzeigend)*
  1. *(zu „she")* her ... [hɜ:, hə]
  2. *(zu „it")* its ... [ɪts]
  3. *(zu „they")* their ... [ðeə]
immer always [ˈɔ:lweɪz]
immer noch still [stɪl]
in at [æt], [ət]; in [ɪn] **in den Urlaub** on holiday [ˈhɒlədeɪ] **in der Nähe von** near [nɪə] **in der Schule** at school [sku:l] **in der Stadt** in town [taʊn]
Indien India [ˈɪndiə]
Informatik computing [kəmˈpju:tɪŋ]
Information information [ɪnfəˈmeɪʃn]
informieren: sich informieren (über) find out (about) [faɪnd ˈaʊt]
innen; nach innen inside [ɪnˈsaɪd]
innerhalb (von) inside [ɪnˈsaɪd]
intelligent smart [smɑ:t]
interessant interesting [ˈɪntrəstɪŋ]
Internet internet [ˈɪntənet]

Ja. Yes. [jes] **Na ja, ...** Well, ... [wel]
Jachthafen marina [məˈri:nə]
Jahr year [jɪə] **Ich bin elf Jahre alt.** I'm eleven years old. [jɪəz]
Jahreszeit season [ˈsi:zn]
Jahrgang year [jɪə]
Januar January [ˈdʒænjuəri]
jede(r, s) every [ˈevri] **jede(r, s) einzelne** each [i:tʃ]
jeder everybody [ˈevribɒdi]
jemand somebody [ˈsʌmbədi]; someone [ˈsʌmwʌn]
jene (dort) those [ðəʊz]
jetzt now [naʊ]
jeweils each [i:tʃ]
jonglieren juggle [ˈdʒʌgl]
Jugend youth [ju:θ]
Jugendliche kid [kɪd]; youth [ju:θ]
Jugendzentrum youth centre [ˈju:θ sentə]
Juli July [dʒuˈlaɪ]
Junge boy [bɔɪ] **Ich bin kein Junge.** I'm not a boy. [nɒt]
Juni June [dʒu:n]

Kaffee coffee [ˈkɒfi]
Kakao cocoa [ˈkəʊkəʊ]; hot chocolate [hɒt ˈtʃɒklət]
kalt cold [kəʊld] **kalt werden** get cold [get]
Kälte cold [kəʊld]
Kaninchen rabbit [ˈræbɪt]
Kantine canteen [kænˈti:n]
Kappe cap [kæp]
Karaoke karaoke [kæriˈəʊki]
Karotte carrot [ˈkærət]
Karte card [kɑ:d]
Kartoffel potato, *pl* potatoes [pəˈteɪtəʊ]
Käse cheese [tʃi:z]
Kasten case [keɪs]
Katze cat [kæt]
kaufen buy [baɪ]

Kebab kebab [kɪˈbæb]
Kegeln bowling [ˈbəʊlɪŋ]
kein/e no [nəʊ] **es gibt keine ...** there aren't any [ˈeni]
kennen know [nəʊ]
kennenlernen meet [mi:t] **Freut mich, dich/euch/Sie kennenzulernen.** Nice to meet you. [naɪs]
Kette chain [tʃeɪn]
Kilometer kilometre (km) [ˈkɪləmi:tə]
Kind kid [kɪd]
Kino cinema [ˈsɪnəmə] **im Kino** at the cinema
Kiosk kiosk [ˈki:ɒsk]
Kissen cushion [ˈkʊʃn]
klar clear [klɪə]
Klasse class [klɑ:s]
Klassenarbeit test [test]
Klassenlehrer/in class teacher [ˈklɑ:s ti:tʃə]
Klassenzimmer classroom [ˈklɑ:sru:m]
Kleber glue [glu:]
Klebestift glue stick [ˈglu: stɪk]
Klebstoff glue [glu:]
Kleiderschrank wardrobe [ˈwɔ:drəʊb]
Kleidertausch(party) clothes swap [ˈkləʊðz swɒp]
Kleidung clothes *(pl)* [kləʊðz]
Kleidungsstücke clothes *(pl)* [kləʊðz]
klein little [ˈlɪtl]; short [ʃɔ:t]; small [smɔ:l] **kleine Mahlzeit** snack [snæk]
Klub club [klʌb]
klug clever [ˈklevə]
Koch, Köchin cook [kʊk]
Kochbuch recipe book [ˈresəpi]
kochen cook [kʊk]; *(in Wasser)* boil [bɔɪl]
Kochen cooking [ˈkʊkɪŋ]
Kochrezept recipe [ˈresəpi]
komisch weird [wɪəd]
Komma *(Dezimalzeichen)* point [pɔɪnt] **1,6 (eins Komma sechs)** 1.6 (one point six)
kommen come [kʌm] **Wo kommst du her?** Where are you from?
können can [kæn], [kən] **etwas gut können** be good at sth. / at doing sth. [æt], [ət] **gut umgehen können mit ...** be good at ... [gʊd] **Ich kann ... sehen.** I can see ... **Ich kann ... nicht sehen.** I can't (= cannot) see ... [kɑ:nt]
Konsole console [kənˈsəʊl]
Kontrolle check [tʃek]
kontrollieren check [tʃek]
Kopf head [hed] **Dreh/Stell es auf den Kopf.** Turn it upside down. [ʌpsaɪd ˈdaʊn]
Kopfhörer headphones *(pl)* [ˈhedfəʊnz]
Korridor corridor [ˈkɒrɪdɔ:]
Kosten cost [kɒst]
kosten cost [kɒst]
kostenlos free [fri:]
köstlich delicious [dɪˈlɪʃəs]
krank ill [ɪl]
Krankenhaus hospital [ˈhɒspɪtl]

Krankheit illness [ˈɪlnəs]
Krawatte tie [taɪ]
Kreis circle [ˈsɜ:kl]
Küche kitchen [ˈkɪtʃɪn]
Kuchen cake [keɪk]
Kugelschreiber pen [pen]
Kultur culture [ˈkʌltʃə]
kümmern: sich kümmern um look after [lʊk]
Kunst art [ɑ:t] **darstellende Kunst** drama [ˈdrɑ:mə]
Kunsthandwerk crafts *(pl)* [krɑ:fts]
Kunststück trick [trɪk]
Kurs class [klɑ:s]
kurz short [ʃɔ:t]

Lächeln smile [smaɪl]
lächeln smile [smaɪl]
Laden shop [ʃɒp]
Lampe lamp [læmp]; light [laɪt]
Land country [ˈkʌntri] **auf dem Land** in the country
Landkarte map [mæp]
lang(e) long [lɒŋ] **30 Sekunden lang** for 30 seconds [fɔ:] **(für) eine lange Zeit** (for) a long time [taɪm] **lange arbeiten, lange Arbeitstage haben** work long days [wɜ:k]
langsam slow [sləʊ] **zu langsam** too slow [tu:]
langweilig boring [ˈbɔ:rɪŋ]
Lärm noise [nɔɪz]
lassen: lass(t) uns let's (= let us) [lets]
Laufen *(Sport)* running [ˈrʌnɪŋ]
laut loud [laʊd] **lauter sprechen** speak more loudly [mɔ:]
leben live [lɪv]
Lebensmittel food [fu:d]
lecker delicious [dɪˈlɪʃəs]
legen: (etwas wohin) legen put [pʊt]
lehren teach [ti:tʃ]
Lehrer/in teacher [ˈti:tʃə]
leidtun: Er tut mir leid. I'm / I feel sorry for him. [ˈsɒri]
leise quiet [ˈkwaɪət]
lernen learn [lɜ:n]
lesen read [ri:d]
Leser/in reader [ˈri:də]
Leute people *(pl)* [ˈpi:pl]; *(Anrede)* guys *(pl)* [gaɪz]
Licht light [laɪt]
Liebe love [lʌv]
Liebe/r Dear ... [dɪə]
lieben love [lʌv] **Ich hätte liebend gern ... / Ich möchte liebend gern ...** I'd (= I would) love ... **Ich würde mich liebend gerne mit ... treffen.** I'd (= I would) love to meet ... [mi:t]
Liebling favourite [ˈfeɪvərɪt]; love [lʌv]
Lieblings- favourite [ˈfeɪvərɪt]
Lied song [sɒŋ]
liegen lie [laɪ]
lila purple [ˈpɜ:pl]
Limonade lemonade [leməˈneɪd]
Lineal ruler [ˈru:lə]
Liste file [faɪl]; list [lɪst]

listen list [lɪst]
Löffel spoon [spuːn]
Löwe lion [ˈlaɪən]
lustig (be) funny [ˈfʌni] **Was ist lustig an ...?** What's funny about ...?

M

machen do [duː]; make [meɪk]
Mädchen girl [gɜːl]
magisch magical [ˈmædʒɪkl]
Mahlzeit meal [miːl] **kleine Mahlzeit** snack [snæk] **warme Mahlzeit** hot meal [hɒt]
Mai May [meɪ]
Mama mum [mʌm]
manchmal sometimes [ˈsʌmtaɪmz]
markieren highlight [ˈhaɪlaɪt]
Markt market [ˈmɑːkɪt]
März March [mɑːtʃ]
Mathe(matik) maths [mæθs]
Mauer wall [wɔːl]
Maus mouse, pl mice [maʊs], [maɪs]
Meer sea [siː] **am Meer** by the sea
Mehl flour [ˈflaʊə]
mehr more [mɔː] **mehr als 50** over 50 [ˈəʊvə]
Meile (ca. 1,6 km) mile [maɪl] **mit 30 Meilen pro Stunde** at 30 miles per hour [pər ˈaʊə] **Meilen pro Stunde** miles per hour (mph)
mein/e my [maɪ]
meinen (sagen wollen) mean [miːn]; (denken, glauben) think [θɪŋk] **Ich meine, ...** I think ...
meiste(r, s): die meisten Schulen most schools [məʊst]
meistens usually [ˈjuːʒuəli]
Melone melon [ˈmelən]
Mensa canteen [kænˈtiːn]
Menschen people (pl) [ˈpiːpl]
Messer knife, pl knives [naɪf], [naɪvz]
Meinung opinion [əˈpɪnjən] **meiner Meinung nach** in my opinion
Meter metre [ˈmiːtə]
mich me [miː]
Milch milk [mɪlk]
Milliliter millilitre (ml) [ˈmɪlɪliːtə]
Mindmap mind map [ˈmaɪnd mæp]
Mini- mini [ˈmɪni]
Minidrohne mini-drone [mɪni ˈdrəʊn]
Minute minute [ˈmɪnɪt]
mir me [miː]
mischen mix [mɪks]
Mischung mixture [ˈmɪkstʃə]
mit with [wɪð]
mitbringen bring [brɪŋ]
mitkommen come [kʌm]
Mitleid: Mitleid haben mit jm. be/feel sorry for sb. [ˈsɒri]
mitnehmen take [teɪk]
Mittagessen lunch [lʌntʃ] **Was gibt es zum Mittagessen?** What's for lunch?
Mittagszeit lunchtime [ˈlʌntʃtaɪm] **zur Mittagszeit** at lunchtime
Mitte centre [ˈsentə]
Mitteilung message [ˈmesɪdʒ]

Mittwoch Wednesday [ˈwenzdeɪ], [ˈwenzdi]
mobben bully [ˈbʊli]
Mobber/in bully [ˈbʊli]
möchten: Ich möchte ... I'd (= I would) like ... [laɪk]
modern modern [ˈmɒdn]
mögen like [laɪk] **sehr mögen** love [lʌv]
Möhre carrot [ˈkærət]
Moment moment [ˈməʊmənt] **in diesem Moment** at the moment
Monat month [mʌnθ]
Montag Monday [ˈmʌndeɪ], [ˈmʌndi] **an jedem Montag** on Mondays
montags on Mondays [ˈmʌndeɪ], [ˈmʌndi]
Morgen morning [ˈmɔːnɪŋ] **am Morgen** in the morning
morgens in the morning [ˈmɔːnɪŋ] **4 Uhr (früh) morgens** 4 a.m. [eɪˈem]
Möwe seagull [ˈsiːgʌl]
müde tired [ˈtaɪəd]
Museum museum [mjuˈziːəm]
Musik music [ˈmjuːzɪk]
Musikgruppe band [bænd]
müssen must [mʌst] **etwas tun müssen** need to do sth. [niːd] **Ich muss Schluss machen.** (am Telefon/ Briefschluss) I must go.
Müll rubbish [ˈrʌbɪʃ] **Tüten/Säcke voller Müll** bags of rubbish [bægz]
Mülleimer bin [bɪn]
mutig brave [breɪv]
Mutti mum [mʌm]
Mütze cap [kæp]; hat [hæt]

N

na: Na ja, ... Well, ... [wel]
nach
1. (örtlich) to [tu], [tə] **nach draußen** outside [ˌaʊtˈsaɪd] **nach (dr)innen** inside [ˌɪnˈsaɪd]
2. (zeitlich) after [ˈɑːftə] **nach der Schule** after school
Nachbar/in neighbour [ˈneɪbə]
nachdem: nachdem du liest after you read [ˈɑːftə]
Nachmittag afternoon [ˌɑːftəˈnuːn] **am Nachmittag** in the afternoon
nachmittags in the afternoon [ɑːftəˈnuːn] **4 Uhr nachmittags** (16 Uhr) 4 p.m. [piːˈem]
Nachname family name [ˈfæməli neɪm]
Nachricht message [ˈmesɪdʒ]
Nachrichten news [njuːz]
nachschauen look sth. up [lʊk ˈʌp]
nachschlagen: etwas nachschlagen look sth. up [lʊk ˈʌp]
nächste(r, s) next [nekst] **Als nächstes ...** Next ...
Nachtisch dessert [dɪˈzɜːt] **zum/als Nachtisch** for dessert
nahe (bei) near [nɪə]
Nähe: in der Nähe von near [nɪə]
Name name [neɪm]

natürlich of course [əv ˈkɔːs]
Naturwissenschaft science [ˈsaɪəns]
neben next to [ˈnekst tə]
nehmen, in Anspruch nehmen take [teɪk]
nein no [nəʊ]
nennen call [kɔːl]
nett friendly [ˈfrendli]; kind [kaɪnd]; nice [naɪs]
neu new [njuː]
neun nine [naɪn]
neunzehn nineteen [naɪnˈtiːn]
neunzig ninety [ˈnaɪnti]
nicht not [nɒt]
nie never [ˈnevə]
niedlich cute [kjuːt]
niemals never [ˈnevə]
noch: (immer) noch still [stɪl] **noch drei** three more [mɔː] **noch ein/e** another [əˈnʌðə] **noch einmal** again [əˈgen]
Norden north [nɔːθ]
nördlich; Nord- north [nɔːθ]
Nordosten; nordöstlich north-east [nɔːθˈiːst]
Nordwesten; nordwestlich northwest [nɔːθˈwest]
normalerweise usually [ˈjuːʒuəli]
Notiz note [nəʊt]
Notizen: (sich) Notizen machen (zur Vorbereitung) make notes
November November [nəʊˈvembə]
Nudeln noodles (pl) [nuːdlz]
Null (im gesprochenen Englisch) oh [əʊ]
Nummer number [ˈnʌmbə]
nun now [naʊ] **Nun, ...** Well, ... [wel]
nur just [dʒʌst]; only [ˈəʊnli] **Es sind nur wir.** It's just us.
Nutzer/in user [ˈjuːzə]
nützlich helpful [ˈhelpfl]; useful [ˈjuːsfl]

O

ob if [ɪf]
oben at the top (of) [tɒp]
Obergeschoss top floor [tɒp ˈflɔː]
Obst fruit [fruːt]
oder or [ɔː]
öffnen open [ˈəʊpən]
oft often [ˈɒfn], [ˈɒftən]
Oktober October [ɒkˈtəʊbə]
Öl oil [ɔɪl]
Oma grandma [ˈgrænmɑː]
Onkel uncle [ˈʌŋkl]
online; Online- online [ˌɒnˈlaɪn]
Opa grandpa [ˈgrænpɑː]
orange orange [ˈɒrɪndʒ]
Orange orange [ˈɒrɪndʒ]
ordentlich tidy [ˈtaɪdi]
Ordner file [faɪl]
Ort place [pleɪs]

P

paar: ein paar some [sʌm], [səm]
Päckchen packet [ˈpækɪt]
Packung packet [ˈpækɪt]
Palast palace [ˈpæləs]

Papa dad [dæd]
Papagei parrot [ˈpærət]
Papier paper [ˈpeɪpə] **Stück Papier** piece of paper [piːs]
Paprika pepper [ˈpepə]
Park park [pɑːk]
Parkour (akrobatischer Hindernislauf in der Stadt) parkour [pɑːˈkʊə]
Partner/in partner [ˈpɑːtnə]
Party party [ˈpɑːti]
passieren happen (to sb.) [ˈhæpən]
passiv passive [ˈpæsɪv]
Pasta (italienische Bezeichnung für Teigwaren) pasta [ˈpæstə]
Pause break [breɪk]; rest [rest] **Pause machen** take a rest [teɪk]
Penny (kleinste britische Münze) penny (p), pl pence [ˈpeni], [pens]
Peperoni pepper [ˈpepə]
perfekt perfect [ˈpɜːfɪkt]
Person person [ˈpɜːsn]
Pfeffer pepper [ˈpepə]
Pferd horse [hɔːs]
Pfund (britische Währung) pound (£) [paʊnd]
Picknick picnic [ˈpɪknɪk] **ein Picknick machen** have a picnic [hæv]
Pier pier [pɪə]
Plan plan [plæn]
planen plan [plæn] **planen, etwas zu tun** plan to do sth. [duː]
Platz place [pleɪs]
Playlist playlist [ˈpleɪlɪst]
Pommes frites chips (pl) [tʃɪps] **Fisch mit Pommes frites** fish and chips [fɪʃ ən ˈtʃɪps] **Imbissstube, die Fisch mit Pommes frites verkauft** fish and chip shop [ʃɒp]
Pool(billiard) pool [puːl]
Popcorn popcorn [ˈpɒpkɔːn]
Popstar star [stɑː]
Post (Teil eines Blogs) post [pəʊst]
posten (im Internet veröffentlichen) post [pəʊst]
Poster poster [ˈpəʊstə]
Präsentation presentation [prezn̩ˈteɪʃn]
präsentieren: (jm.) etwas präsentieren present sth. (to sb.) [prɪˈzent]
Preis (Kosten) cost [kɒst]; (Gewinn) prize [praɪz]
Preisverleihung prize ceremony [ˈpraɪz serəməni]
pro per [pɜː], [pə] **Meilen pro Stunde** miles per hour (mph) [maɪlz] **pro Stunde** per hour [ˈaʊə]
Problem problem [ˈprɒbləm]
Programmieren coding [ˈkəʊdɪŋ]
programmieren (Computer) code [kəʊd]
Projekt project [ˈprɒdʒekt]
prüfen check [tʃek]
Prüfung check [tʃek]
Puderzucker icing sugar [ˈaɪsɪŋ ʃʊgə]
Pulver powder [ˈpaʊdə]
putzen clean [kliːn] **(sich) die/deine Zähne putzen** brush your teeth [brʌʃ]
Puzzle jigsaw (puzzle) [ˈdʒɪgsɔː]

Q

Quiz quiz, pl quizzes [kwɪz], [ˈkwɪzɪz] **ein Quiz machen** do a quiz [duː]

R

Rad: Rad fahren cycle [ˈsaɪkl]
Radfahren cycling [ˈsaɪklɪŋ]
Radiergummi rubber [ˈrʌbə]
Ratespiel quiz, pl quizzes [kwɪz], [ˈkwɪzɪz] **ein Ratespiel machen** do a quiz [duː]
Rätsel puzzle [ˈpʌzl]
Raum room [ruːm]
Recherche(n) research [rɪˈsɜːtʃ]
recherchieren (do) research [rɪˈsɜːtʃ]
Recht: Recht haben be right [raɪt]
Rechtschreibung spelling [ˈspelɪŋ]
Rede talk [tɔːk]
reden (mit) talk (to) [tɔːk] **reden über** talk about [əˈbaʊt]
Redewendung phrase [freɪz]
Referat presentation [prezn̩ˈteɪʃn] **ein Referat halten** give a presentation [gɪv]
Regal shelf, pl shelves [ʃelf], [ʃelvz]
Regen rain [reɪn]
regen rain [reɪn]
regnerisch rainy [ˈreɪni]
Reihe line [laɪn]; turn [tɜːn] **Wann bin ich an der Reihe (etwas zu tun)?** When is (it) my turn (to do sth.)?
Reinigungskraft cleaner [ˈkliːnə]
Reis rice [raɪs]
Reise journey [ˈdʒɜːni]; tour [tʊə]
Reisen travel [ˈtrævl]
reisen travel [ˈtrævl]
Restaurant restaurant [ˈrestrɒnt]
Rezept recipe [ˈresəpi]
richtig right [raɪt]; true [truː]
riechen; schlecht riechen smell [smel]
Ring ring [rɪŋ]
Roboter robot [ˈrəʊbɒt]
Roller scooter [ˈskuːtə]
Rollstuhl wheelchair [ˈwiːltʃeə]
rosa pink [pɪŋk]
Rucksack rucksack [ˈrʌksæk]
Ruf call [kɔːl]
Ruhe rest [rest]
ruhen rest [rest]
ruhig quiet [ˈkwaɪət]
rühren stir [stɜː]
Rundfahrt (durch) tour (of) [tʊə]
Rundgang (durch) tour (of) [tʊə]

S

Saal hall [hɔːl]
Sache thing [θɪŋ]
Sack: Säcke voller Müll bags of rubbish [bægz]
sagen say [seɪ]; tell [tel]
Saison season [ˈsiːzn]
Salat (als Gericht oder Beilage) salad [ˈsæləd]
Salz salt [sɔːlt]
sammeln collect [kəˈlekt]

Samstag Saturday [ˈsætədeɪ], [ˈsætədi]
Sandwich sandwich [ˈsænwɪtʃ], [ˈsænwɪdʒ]
Sänger/in singer [ˈsɪŋə]
Satz sentence [ˈsentəns]
sauber clean [kliːn]
sauber machen clean (sth. up) [kliːn]
Saubermachen clean-up [ˈkliːn ʌp]
Säubern clean-up [ˈkliːn ʌp]
schade a shame [ʃeɪm]
Schande a shame [ʃeɪm]
schauen look [lʊk]
Schauspiel drama [ˈdrɑːmə]
schick smart [smɑːt]
schicken send [send]
Schinken ham [hæm]
Schirmmütze cap [kæp]
Schlaf sleep [sliːp]
schlafen be asleep [əˈsliːp]; sleep [sliːp]
Schlafzimmer bedroom [ˈbedruːm]
Schlange snake [sneɪk]
schlau clever [ˈklevə]
schlecht bad [bæd]
schließen close [kləʊz]
schließlich in the end [end]
schlimm bad [bæd]
Schlittschuhbahn ice rink [ˈaɪs rɪŋk]
Schloss palace [ˈpæləs]
Schluss end [end] **Ich muss Schluss machen.** (am Telefon/ Briefschluss) I must go. [mʌst gəʊ] **zum Schluss** in the end
schmücken decorate [ˈdekəreɪt]
schmutzig dirty [ˈdɜːti]
Schnee snow [snəʊ]
schneebedeckt snowy [ˈsnəʊi]
schneien snow [snəʊ]
Schokolade chocolate [ˈtʃɒklət] **heiße (Trink-)Schokolade** hot chocolate [hɒt]
schon already [ɔːlˈredi]
schön nice [naɪs]
schrecklich horrible [ˈhɒrəbl]
schreiben write [raɪt]
Schreibtisch desk [desk]
Schreibweise spelling [ˈspelɪŋ]
Schritt step [step]
Schuh shoe [ʃuː]
Schule school [skuːl] **Hast du nach der Schule Zeit?** Are you free after school? **in der Schule** at school **nach der Schule** after school **weiterführende Schule** secondary school [ˈsekəndri]
Schüler/in student [ˈstjuːdnt]
Schulfach subject [ˈsʌbdʒɪkt]
Schulheft exercise book [ˈeksəsaɪz bʊk]
Schulmensa canteen [kænˈtiːn]
Schulsport PE (= physical education) [piːˈiː], [fɪzɪkl edʒuˈkeɪʃn]
Schuluniform school uniform [skuːl ˈjuːnɪfɔːm]
Schulversammlung assembly [əˈsembli]
schwarz black [blæk]
schwer difficult [ˈdɪfɪkəlt]; hard [hɑːd]

Schwester sister [ˈsɪstə]
schwierig difficult [ˈdɪfɪkəlt]; hard [hɑːd]
Schwierigkeiten trouble [ˈtrʌbl] **in Schwierigkeiten sein** be in trouble
Schwimmen swimming [ˈswɪmɪŋ]
schwimmen swim [swɪm]
Schwimmer/in swimmer [ˈswɪmə]
sechs six [sɪks]
sechzehn sixteen [sɪksˈtiːn]
sechzig sixty [ˈsɪksti]
See *(Meer)* sea [siː] **an der See** by the sea [baɪ]
Seebrücke pier [pɪə]
sehen look [lʊk]; see [siː]
sehr lot [lɒt]; much [mʌtʃ]; very [ˈveri]
sein be [biː] **bist, sind, seid** are [ɑː] *(er/sie/es)* **ist** is [ɪz]
sein/e its [ɪts]
Seite page (p.) [peɪdʒ]
Sekunde second [ˈsekənd] **für 30 Sekunden** for 30 seconds [fɔː]
selbstverständlich of course [əv ˈkɔːs]
selten *(Adj.)* rare [reə]; *(Adv.)* rarely [ˈreəli]
seltsam funny [ˈfʌni]; weird [wɪəd]
senden send [send]
September September [sepˈtembə]
Servus. Goodbye. [gʊdˈbaɪ]; Hello. [həˈləʊ] **Servus allerseits.** Hello everybody. [ˈevribɒdi]
Show show [ʃəʊ]
sicher sure [ʃʊə], [ʃɔː]
Sie *(höfliche Anrede)* you [juː] **Sie sind** you're (= you are)
sie
1. *(weibliche Person)* her [hɜː], [hə]; she [ʃiː] **sie ist** she's (= she is)
2. *(bei Dingen und Tieren)* it [ɪt]
3. *(Plural)* them [ðem], [ðəm]; they [ðeɪ] **sie sind** they're (= they are) **sie sind nicht** they aren't
sieben seven [ˈsevn]
siebzehn seventeen [sevnˈtiːn]
siebzig seventy [ˈsevnti]
sieden boil [bɔɪl]
Sieger/in winner [ˈwɪnə]
Silber silver [ˈsɪlvə]
silberfarben silver [ˈsɪlvə]
Singen singing [ˈsɪŋɪŋ]
singen sing [sɪŋ]
sitzen sit [sɪt]
Skateboard (fahren) skateboard [ˈskeɪtbɔːd]
Skateboardfahren skateboarding [ˈskeɪtbɔːdɪŋ]
Skatepark skatepark [ˈskeɪtpɑːk]
Slideshow slide show [ˈslaɪd ʃəʊ]
SMS text [tekst] **jm. eine SMS schicken** text sb.
Snack snack [snæk]
so like this [laɪk]; so [səʊ]
sodass so that [səʊ ðæt]
Sofa sofa [ˈsəʊfə]
Software software [ˈsɒftweə]
Sohn son [sʌn]
Sommer summer [ˈsʌmə]

Sonne sun [sʌn] **Die Sonne scheint.** It's sunny. [ˈsʌni]
sonnig sunny [ˈsʌni]
Sonntag Sunday [ˈsʌndeɪ], [ˈsʌndi]
sonst or [ɔː]
Sorte (von) kind (of) [kaɪnd]
Soße sauce [sɔːs]
Spaghetti spaghetti [spəˈgeti]
Spaß fun [fʌn] **Spaß haben** have fun [hæv] **Spaß machen** be fun [biː]
spät: (zu) spät late [leɪt]
später later [ˈleɪtə]
Spaziergang walk [wɔːk]
Speisekarte menu [ˈmenjuː]
Spiegel mirror [ˈmɪrə]
Spiel game [geɪm]; match [mætʃ]
spielen play [pleɪ]
Spieler/in player [ˈpleɪə]
Spielkarte playing card [ˈpleɪɪŋ kɑːd]
Spielzeug toy [tɔɪ]
Spitze top [tɒp] **an der Spitze (von)** at the top (of) [æt], [ət]
Sport sport [spɔːt]; *(Schulsport)* PE (= physical education) [piː ˈiː], [fɪzɪkl edʒuˈkeɪʃn]
Sportart sport [spɔːt]
Sporthalle sports hall [ˈspɔːts hɔːl]
Sprechen speaking [ˈspiːkɪŋ]
sprechen (mit) speak (to) [spiːk] **deutlich sprechen** speak clearly [ˈklɪəli] **lauter sprechen** speak more loudly [mɔː] **sprechen über** speak about [əˈbaʊt]
Stadion stadium [ˈsteɪdiəm]
Stadt city [ˈsɪti]; town [taʊn]
Stadtplan map [mæp]
Stadtzentrum town centre [taʊn ˈsentə]
Standuhr clock [klɒk]
Star star [stɑː]
Start start [stɑːt]
stecken: (etwas wohin) stecken put [pʊt]
stehen stand [stænd]
stellen: (etwas wohin) stellen put [pʊt]; **sich (hin)stellen** stand [stænd]
Stiefbruder stepbrother [ˈstepbrʌðə]
Stiefmutter stepmother [ˈstepmʌðə]; stepmum [ˈstepmʌm]
Stiefschwester stepsister [ˈstepsɪstə]
Stiefsohn stepson [ˈstepsʌn]
Stieftochter stepdaughter [ˈstepdɔːtə]
Stiefvater stepdad [ˈstepdæd]; stepfather [ˈstepfɑːðə]
Stift pen [pen]
still quiet [ˈkwaɪət]
Stock(werk) floor [flɔː] **das oberste Stockwerk** top floor [tɒp ˈflɔː]
Strand beach [biːtʃ] **an den/zum Strand** to the beach [tu], [tə]
Straße *(in Ortschaften)* street [striːt]
Straßenmusik street music [ˈstriːt mjuːzɪk]
Streetdance *(Tanzstil)* street dance [ˈstriːt dɑːns]
Stück piece [piːs] **Stück Papier** piece of paper [ˈpeɪpə]

Student/in student [ˈstjuːdnt]
Stufe step [step]
Stuhl chair [tʃeə]
Stunde hour [ˈaʊə]; *(Unterrichtsstunde)* lesson [ˈlesn] **pro Stunde** per hour [pɜː], [pə]
Stundenplan timetable [ˈtaɪmteɪbl]
Superheld/in superhero, *pl* superheroes [ˈsuːpəhɪərəʊ]
Supermarkt supermarket [ˈsuːpəmɑːkɪt]
Surfing surfing [ˈsɜːfɪŋ]
süß cute [kjuːt]; sweet [swiːt]
Süßigkeiten sweets *(pl)* [swiːts]
Sweatshirt sweatshirt [ˈswetʃɜːt]

T

Tag day [deɪ]
Tageszeitung newspaper [ˈnjuːspeɪpə]; paper [ˈpeɪpə]
Tante aunt [ɑːnt]
Tanz dance [dɑːns]
Tanzen dancing [ˈdɑːnsɪŋ]
tanzen dance [dɑːns]
Tänzer/in dancer [ˈdɑːnsə]
Tasche bag [bæg]
Tätigkeit activity [ækˈtɪvəti]
Tausch swap [swɒp]
tauschen swap [swɒp]
Technik technology [tekˈnɒlədʒi], *infml auch* tech
Technikunterricht technology [tekˈnɒlədʒi], *infml auch* tech
Technologie technology [tekˈnɒlədʒi], *infml auch* tech
Tee tea [tiː]
Teelöffel teaspoon [ˈtiːspuːn]
Teil part (of) [pɑːt]; piece [piːs]; share [ʃeə]
teilen share [ʃeə]
Telefon phone [fəʊn] **am Telefon** on the phone [ɒn]
Telefonanruf (phone) call [ˈfəʊn kɔːl]
telefonieren phone [fəʊn]
Telefonnummer phone number [ˈfəʊn nʌmbə]
Tennis tennis [ˈtenɪs]
Terrarium terrarium [teˈreəriəm]
Test test [test]; quiz, *pl* quizzes [kwɪz], [ˈkwɪzɪz] **Test machen** do a quiz [duː]
testen test [test]
teuer expensive [ɪkˈspensɪv]
Text text [tekst]
Thema topic [ˈtɒpɪk]
Ticket ticket [ˈtɪkɪt]
Tier animal [ˈænɪml]; pet [pet]
Tierarzt/Tierärztin vet [vet]
Tipp tip [tɪp]
Tisch table [ˈteɪbl]
Tischtennis table tennis [ˈteɪbl tenɪs]
Titel title [ˈtaɪtl]
Tochter daughter [ˈdɔːtə]
Toilette toilet [ˈtɔɪlət]
toll great [greɪt]
Tomate tomato, *pl* tomatoes [təˈmɑːtəʊ]

Tomatensauce tomato sauce [təˈmɑːtəʊ sɔːs]
Torte cake [keɪk]
tot dead [ded]
Tour tour [tʊə]
Tourist/in tourist [ˈtʊərɪst]
Touristeninformation tourist information centre [tʊərɪst ˌɪnfəˈmeɪʃn sentə]
Tradition tradition [trəˈdɪʃn]
traditionell traditional [trəˈdɪʃənl]
tragen wear [weə]
Trainer/in trainer [ˈtreɪnə]
Training training [ˈtreɪnɪŋ]
Trampolin trampoline [ˈtræmpəliːn]
Trampolinspringen/-turnen trampolining [ˈtræmpəliːnɪŋ]
Traum dream [driːm]
träumen (von etwas) dream (of/about sth.) [driːm]
traurig sad [sæd]
treffen: (sich) treffen meet [miːt]
Tretroller scooter [ˈskuːtə]
Trick trick [trɪk]
Trifle *(englischer Nachtisch)* trifle [ˈtraɪfl]
trinken drink [drɪŋk]
trotzdem still [stɪl]
Tschüs. Bye. [baɪ]; See you. [siː]; Speak later. [spiːk ˈleɪtə]
T-Shirt T-shirt [ˈtiː ʃɜːt]
tun do [duː]; **(etwas wohin) tun** put [pʊt] **du hast (viel) zu tun** you're busy [ˈbɪzi] **es genießen, etwas zu tun** enjoy doing sth. [ɪnˈdʒɔɪ] **etwas weiterhin tun** continue to do sth. [kənˈtɪnjuː] **wie man etwas tut / tun kann / tun soll** how to do sth. [haʊ]
Tür door [dɔː]
Turmuhr clock [klɒk]
Tüte: Tüten voller Müll bags of rubbish [bægz]
Tyrann/in bully [ˈbʊli]
tyrannisieren bully [ˈbʊli]

U

üben practice [ˈpræktɪs]
über
1. *(räumlich)* over [ˈəʊvə]
2. *(mehr als)* **über 50** over 50
3. about [əˈbaʊt] **über mich/dich/...** about me/you/...
überall everywhere [ˈevriweə]
überprüfen check [tʃek]
Überprüfung check [tʃek]
überrascht surprised [səˈpraɪzd]
Überschrift heading [ˈhedɪŋ]; title [ˈtaɪtl]
Übung(en) exercise [ˈeksəsaɪz]; practice [ˈpræktɪs]
Übungsheft exercise book [ˈeksəsaɪz bʊk]
Uhr clock [klɒk]
Uhrzeit time [taɪm]
um: um 8 Uhr at 8 o'clock [æt], [ət]
umdrehen turn [tɜːn]
umrühren stir [stɜː]

umweltbewusst green [griːn]
umweltfreundlich werden go green [gəʊ griːn]
und and [ænd], [ənd] **Und du?** What about you? [əˈbaʊt]
unfreundlich unfriendly [ʌnˈfrendli]
unhöflich rude [ruːd]
Uniform uniform [ˈjuːnɪfɔːm]
unordentlich messy [ˈmesi]
Unordnung mess [mes]
Unrecht: Unrecht haben be wrong [rɒŋ]
uns us [ʌs], [əs]
unser/e our [ˈaʊə]
unter under [ˈʌndə]
Unterricht class [klɑːs] **im Unterricht** in class
unterrichten teach [tiːtʃ]
Unterrichtsstunde lesson [ˈlesn]
Unterschied difference [ˈdɪfrəns]
unterstreichen highlight [ˈhaɪlaɪt]
untersuchen research [rɪˈsɜːtʃ]
Urlaub holiday [ˈhɒlədeɪ] **im/in den Urlaub** on holiday

V

Vanille vanilla [vəˈnɪlə]
Vati dad [dæd]
vegan vegan [ˈviːgən]
Veganer/in vegan [ˈviːgən]
Vegetarier/in vegetarian [vedʒəˈteəriən], *infml auch* veggie [ˈvedʒi]
vegetarisch vegetarian [vedʒəˈteəriən], *infml auch* veggie [ˈvedʒi]
verboten no [nəʊ]
Verein club [klʌb]
Vereinigtes Königreich the United Kingdom (the UK) [junaɪtɪd ˈkɪŋdəm], [juː ˈkeɪ]
vergessen: nicht vergessen remember [rɪˈmembə]
verirren: Hast du dich verirrt? Are you lost? [lɒst]
Verkaufsbude kiosk [ˈkiːɒsk]
Verkaufsstand kiosk [ˈkiːɒsk]
verkehrt herum upside down [ʌpsaɪd ˈdaʊn]
verlaufen: Hast du dich verlaufen? Are you lost? [lɒst]
vermischen mix [mɪks]
vermisst missing [ˈmɪsɪŋ]
verschieden different [ˈdɪfrənt]
verschneit snowy [ˈsnəʊi]
verspäten: Ich habe mich verspätet. I'm late. [leɪt] **Verspäte dich nicht.** Don't be late.
verstehen understand [ʌndəˈstænd]
verwenden use [juːz]
Video; Video- video [ˈvɪdiəʊ]
viel/e a lot of [ə ˈlɒt əv], lots of [ˈlɒts əv]; many [ˈmæni]; much [mʌtʃ] **wie viele?** how many? [haʊ]
vielleicht maybe [ˈmeɪbi]
vier four [fɔː]
vierzehn fourteen [fɔːˈtiːn]
vierzig forty [ˈfɔːti]

violett purple [ˈpɜːpl]
Vokabelverzeichnis vocabulary [vəˈkæbjələri], *infml auch* vocab [ˈvəʊkæb]
Vokabular vocabulary [vəˈkæbjələri], *infml auch* vocab [ˈvəʊkæb]
völlig (still) perfectly (still) [ˈpɜːfɪktli]
von from [frɒm]; of [ɒv], [əv]
vor
1. *(zeitlich)* before [bɪˈfɔː] **vor der Schule / der Unterrichtsstunde** before school / the lesson [skuːl], [ˈlesn]
2. *(räumlich)* in front of [ɪn ˈfrʌnt əv]
vormittags: 9 Uhr vormittags 9 a.m. [eɪˈem]
Vorname first name [ˈfɜːst neɪm]
vorsichtig careful [ˈkeəfl]
vorstellen: (jm.) etwas vorstellen present sth. (to sb.) [prɪˈzent]
Vortrag talk [tɔːk]
Vorwahl(nummer) code [kəʊd]

W

Wackelpudding jelly [ˈdʒeli]
wählen choose [tʃuːz]
wahr true [truː]
Wand wall [wɔːl] **an der/die Wand** on the wall [ɒn]
Wandern hiking [ˈhaɪkɪŋ]; walking [ˈwɔːkɪŋ]
wandern hike [haɪk]; walk [wɔːk]
Wanduhr clock [klɒk]
wann when [wen]
warm hot [hɒt]; warm [wɔːm] **warm werden** get warm [get]
warum why [waɪ]
was what [wɒt] **Was ist mit dir?** What about you? [əˈbaʊt]
Wasser water [ˈwɔːtə]
Wassermelone water melon [ˈmelən]
Website website [ˈwebsaɪt]
Weg journey [ˈdʒɜːni]; way [weɪ]
weg away [əˈweɪ]
Weide field [fiːld] **auf der Weide** in the field
Weihnachten Christmas [ˈkrɪsməs]
Weihnachtstag Christmas Day [krɪsməs ˈdeɪ]
weil because [bɪˈkɒz]
Weise: Art und Weise way [weɪ] **auf diese Weise** (in) this way **auf unterschiedliche Weise** in different ways [ˈdɪfrənt]
weiß white [waɪt]
weitere more [mɔː] **drei weitere** three more [θriː]
weitermachen continue [kənˈtɪnjuː] **(mit) etwas weitermachen** continue to do sth. [duː]
welche(r, s) which? [wɪtʃ]; what [wɒt] **Welche AGs ...?** Which clubs ...? [klʌb]
Wendung phrase [freɪz]
wenn
1. *(falls)* if [ɪf] **Was wäre, wenn?** What if? [wɒt]
2. *(zeitlich)* when [wen]

wer who [huː]
werden get [get]
Werken design and technology [dɪzaɪn ən tekˈnɒlədʒi]
Werktag weekday [ˈwiːkdeɪ]
Werkunterricht design and technology [dɪzaɪn ən tekˈnɒlədʒi]
Wetter weather [ˈweðə]
Wettkampf competition [kɒmpəˈtɪʃn]; match [mætʃ]
wichtig important [ɪmˈpɔːtnt]
wichtigste(r, s) main [meɪn]
wie *(ähnlich/so wie)* like [laɪk]
wie how [haʊ] **Wie alt bist du?** How old are you? **Wie geht es dir/euch/ Ihnen?** How are you? **Wie heißt du?** What's your name? [wɒts] **Wie ist ...? / Wie sieht ... aus?** What's ... like? **wie viele?** how many? **Wie wäre es mit einer/einem ... ?** What about a ... ?
Willkommen in/an ... Welcome to ... [ˈwelkəm]
Wind wind [wɪnd]
windig windy [ˈwɪndi]
Windsurfen windsurfing [wɪndsɜːfɪŋ]
winken: (jm. zu-)winken wave (to sb.) [weɪv]
Winter winter [ˈwɪntə]
wir we [wiː] **Es sind nur wir.** It's just us. [ʌs], [əs] **wir sind** we're (= we are) **wir sind nicht** we aren't
wirklich really [ˈriːəli], [ˈrɪəli]
wissen know [nəʊ]
Witterung weather [ˈweðə]
witzig funny [ˈfʌni]
wo where [weə] **Wo kommst du her?** Where are you from?

Woche week [wiːk]
Wochenende weekend [wiːkˈend] **am Wochenende** at the weekend
Wochentag weekday [ˈwiːkdeɪ]
wohnen live [lɪv]
Wohnsiedlung estate [ɪˈsteɪt]
Wohnung flat [flæt]
Wohnzimmer living room [ˈlɪvɪŋ ruːm]
Wok *(chinesischer Kochtopf)* wok [wɒk]
Wolke cloud [klaʊd]
wolkig cloudy [ˈklaʊdi]
wollen want [wɒnt] **etwas tun wollen** want to do sth. [duː]
Wort word [wɜːd]
Wörternetz mind map [ˈmaɪnd mæp]
Wortschatz vocabulary [vəˈkæbjələri], *infml auch* vocab [ˈvəʊkæb]
Wurst, Würstchen sausage [ˈsɒsɪdʒ]
würzig spicy [ˈspaɪsi]
wütend angry [ˈæŋgri]

Y

Yoga yoga [ˈjəʊgə]

Z

Zahl number [ˈnʌmbə]
zahlen: (etwas be-)zahlen pay (for sth.) [peɪ]
Zahn tooth, *pl* teeth [tuːθ], [tiːθ]
Zauberei magic [ˈmædʒɪk]
Zauberkasten magic set [ˈmædʒɪk set]
zaubern do magic [duː ˈmædʒɪk]
Zaubertrick magic trick [ˈmædʒɪk trɪk]
zehn ten [ten]
zeichnen draw [drɔː]

Zeichnen drawing [ˈdrɔːɪŋ]
zeigen show [ʃəʊ]
Zeile line [laɪn]
Zeit time [taɪm] **(für) eine lange Zeit** (for) a long time [lɒŋ]
Zeitung newspaper [ˈnjuːspeɪpə]; paper [ˈpeɪpə]
Zentrum centre [ˈsentə]
zerbrechen: etwas zerbrechen break sth. [breɪk]
Zeremonie ceremony [ˈserəməni]
Zettel piece of paper [piːs ɒv ˈpeɪpə]
ziemlich quite [kwaɪt]
Ziffer number [ˈnʌmbə]
Zimmer room [ruːm]
Zirkus circus [ˈsɜːkəs]
Zitrone lemon [ˈlemən]
Zoo zoo [zuː]
zu; um zu to [tu], [tə]
Zucker sugar [ˈʃʊgə]
Zuckerguss icing [ˈaɪsɪŋ]
zuerst (at) first [fɜːst]
Zug train [treɪn]
Zuhause home [həʊm]
zuhören listen [ˈlɪsn]
zumachen close [kləʊz]
zurück back [bæk]
zurzeit at the moment [ˈməʊmənt]
zusammen together [təˈgeðə]
zwanzig twenty [ˈtwenti]
zwei two [tuː]
zweite(r, s) second (2nd) [ˈsekənd]
Zwiebel onion [ˈʌnjən]
zwölf twelve [twelv]
zwölfte(r, s) twelfth (12th) [twelfθ]

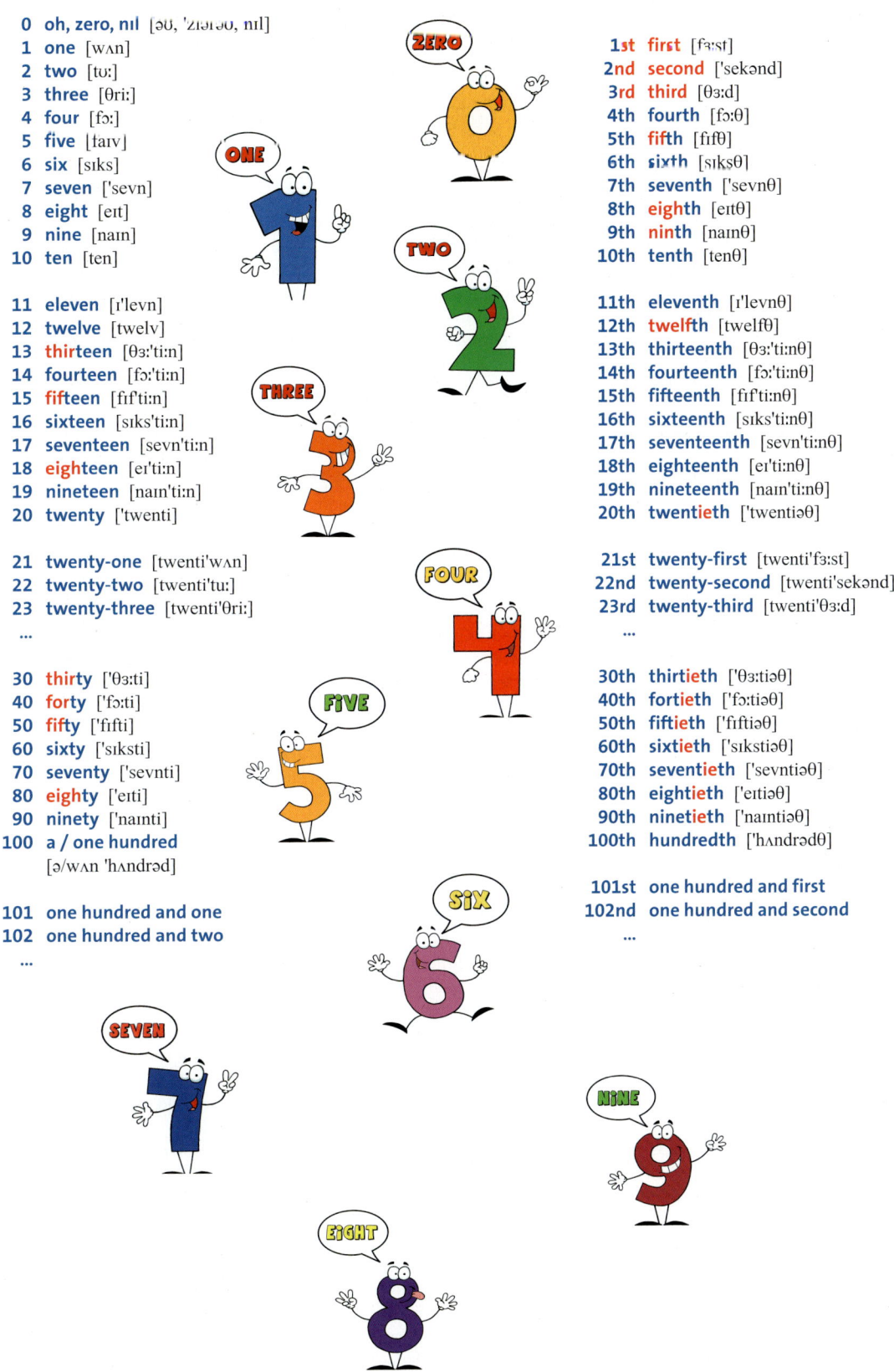

0 oh, zero, nil [əʊ, 'zɪərəʊ, nɪl]
1 one [wʌn]
2 two [tʊ:]
3 three [θri:]
4 four [fɔ:]
5 five [faɪv]
6 six [sɪks]
7 seven ['sevn]
8 eight [eɪt]
9 nine [naɪn]
10 ten [ten]

11 eleven [ɪ'levn]
12 twelve [twelv]
13 thirteen [θɜ:'ti:n]
14 fourteen [fɔ:'ti:n]
15 fifteen [fɪf'ti:n]
16 sixteen [sɪks'ti:n]
17 seventeen [sevn'ti:n]
18 eighteen [eɪ'ti:n]
19 nineteen [naɪn'ti:n]
20 twenty ['twenti]

21 twenty-one [twenti'wʌn]
22 twenty-two [twenti'tu:]
23 twenty-three [twenti'θri:]
...

30 thirty ['θɜ:ti]
40 forty ['fɔ:ti]
50 fifty ['fɪfti]
60 sixty ['sɪksti]
70 seventy ['sevnti]
80 eighty ['eɪti]
90 ninety ['naɪnti]
100 a / one hundred
      [ə/wʌn 'hʌndrəd]

101 one hundred and one
102 one hundred and two
...

1st first [fɜ:st]
2nd second ['sekənd]
3rd third [θɜ:d]
4th fourth [fɔ:θ]
5th fifth [fɪfθ]
6th sixth [sɪksθ]
7th seventh ['sevnθ]
8th eighth [eɪtθ]
9th ninth [naɪnθ]
10th tenth [tenθ]

11th eleventh [ɪ'levnθ]
12th twelfth [twelfθ]
13th thirteenth [θɜ:'ti:nθ]
14th fourteenth [fɔ:'ti:nθ]
15th fifteenth [fɪf'ti:nθ]
16th sixteenth [sɪks'ti:nθ]
17th seventeenth [sevn'ti:nθ]
18th eighteenth [eɪ'ti:nθ]
19th nineteenth [naɪn'ti:nθ]
20th twentieth ['twentiəθ]

21st twenty-first [twenti'fɜ:st]
22nd twenty-second [twenti'sekənd]
23rd twenty-third [twenti'θɜ:d]
...

30th thirtieth ['θɜ:tiəθ]
40th fortieth ['fɔ:tiəθ]
50th fiftieth ['fɪftiəθ]
60th sixtieth ['sɪkstiəθ]
70th seventieth ['sevntiəθ]
80th eightieth ['eɪtiəθ]
90th ninetieth ['naɪntiəθ]
100th hundredth ['hʌndrədθ]

101st one hundred and first
102nd one hundred and second
...

Quellenverzeichnis

Titelbild
Cornelsen/Personen: Anja Poehlmann, Brighton Pier: mauritius images/Steve Vidler

Illustrationen
Cornelsen/**Harald Ardeias:** (S. 4 unten re.; S. 17 1 A–H; S. 21 oben; S. 26 unten (1–11); S. 27 mi. re.; S. 29 oben mi. + 1–6; S. 30; S. 31; S. 33 1–6; S. 36 unten; S. 37; S. 38; S. 42; S. 43 1–6; S. 46; S. 47; S. 50 oben; S. 55 (Sunita's house); S. 56; S. 57 oben; S. 58 unten re.; S. 59 oben; S. 60 1–3; S. 61 4–7; S. 62; S. 63 2; S. 66; S. 67; S. 68; S. 69 unten re.; S. 76–78; S. 82; S. 84 Mitte re.; S. 85 (morning song); S. 91 unten; S. 92; S. 93; S. 95; S. 99; S. 104; S. 105; S. 106; S. 116; S. 117; S. 118 A–F; S. 120 A–E; S. 122 unten re.; S. 123; S. 129 a–f; S. 130; S. 134 oben; S. 142 unten; S. 143 Mitte; S. 144 oben re.; S. 145 Mitte; S. 146; S. 147 oben; S. 148 oben; S. 151 links oben; S. 152–154; S. 158 unten re.; S. 159 oben re.; S. 160 unten; S. 161; S. 164 oben; S. 167 1–6; S. 169; S. 184 links oben + mi.; S. 199; S. 200 unten). Cornelsen/**Inhouse/Josephine Bienert-Köhler:** (S. 101; S. 102; S. 173 oben; S. 176 Alphabet; S. 178 Online-Wörterbuch; S. 179 Bildschirm; S. 180). Cornelsen/**Karen Donnelly:** (S. 133 Cover unten ‚A Brighton Birthday'). Cornelsen/**Michael Fleischmann:** (S. 250 unten). Cornelsen/**Klara Luise Frankenberg:** (S. 172, S. 173 Mitte und unten; S. 174; S. 175; S. 179 oben). Cornelsen/**Irina Zinner:** (Umschlaginnenseite vorne (U2): Möwe, S. 4–9 Möwe; S. 10; S. 11; S. 12 oben; S. 13; S. 14 unten li.; S. 15; S. 16; S. 17 Möwen; S. 18 unten re.; S. 23 unten re.; S. 27 Möwen; S. 29 Möwen; S. 32 oben re.; S. 34; S. 35 Möwen; S. 43 unten re.; S. 45; S. 50 Mitte re.; S. 51 Möwe; S. 53 unten re.; S. 55 Möwe; S. 58 1–6; S. 59 Möwe; S. 64; S. 65; S. 84 Möwe; S. 85 Möwe; S. 87; S. 89 Möwe; S. 90 Möwe; S. 91 Möwe; S. 94; S. 96; S. 97 Möwen; S. 107 1–6; S. 110 Möwe; S. 113; S. 114; S. 115; S. 118 Möwen; S. 119 Möwe; S. 121 Mitte re.; S. 124 oben re. und unten re.; S. 126 oben re.; S. 127; S. 133 Möwe; S. 138 Möwe; S. 143 Möwen; S. 144 Möwe; S. 145 Möwen; S. 149 Möwe; S. 151 Möwe; S. 156; S. 157 oben re.; S. 167 oben re.; S. 168 oben; S. 170; S. 171; S. 176 oben re.; S. 177; S. 178 unten re.; S. 181 Möwen; S. 182; S. 183 Möwe; S. 184 unten re.; S. 185; S. 186; S. 188; S. 189; S. 190; S. 205–214; S. 254; S. 255; Umschlaginnenseite hinten (U3): Möwe).

Abbildungen
Umschlagseite vorne (U2): s. S. 18, 20 und 30; **S. 1** s. S. 34, 35, 36; **S. 4–8:** Cornelsen/Anja Poehlmann; **S. 12:** unten re. Shutterstock.com/New Africa; un.li. Shutterstock.com/Pete Pahham, un.Mi. Shutterstock.com/Djomas; **S. 14:** 1 stock.adobe.com/Arija, 2 Panther Media GmbH/Gertrud Böttcher, 3 Shutterstock.com/Dmitrijs Mihejevs, 4 Shutterstock.com/Iakov Filimonov, 5 Shutterstock.com/Eric Isselee, 6 Shutterstock.com/Alex Staroseltsev, 7 Shutterstock.com/bluedog studio, 8 Shutterstock.com/Susan Schmitz; **S. 15** Emoticons: Shutterstock.com/Chaim Devine; **S. 18** Cornelsen/Anja Poehlmann**; S. 19** Cornelsen/Anja Poehlmann; **S. 20** oben: Cornelsen/Anja Poehlmann, unten re.: Shutterstock.com/AnnaStills; **S. 21** unten: Shutterstock.com/Monkey Business Images; **S. 22** oben mi.: Shutterstock.com/Pavlo S, oben re.: Shutterstock.com/Photo Melon, 7 Cornelsen/Anja Poehlmann; **S. 23:** Shutterstock.com/AnnaStills; **S. 24** oben re.+ 2 b) 1+3+5: Cornelsen/Anja Poehlmann, 2 b) 2: Shutterstock.com/zzveillust, 2 b) 4: Shutterstock.com/JRP Studio; **S. 25** oben re. + mi. li.: Cornelsen/Anja Poehlmann, unten li.: Shutterstock.com/antoniodiaz; **S. 26** Tintenkleckse: mauritius images/alamy stock photo/Daniil Chaban; **S. 28** 1+3+5: Cornelsen/Anja Poehlmann, 2: mauritius images/alamy stock photo/Greg Balfour Evans, 4: mauritius images/alamy stock photo/James Winspear-VIEW; **S. 32** unten: Cornelsen/Anja Poehlmann; **S. 33:** oben re.: Cornelsen/Grasshopper Films (Filmstill); **S. 35** Schirme: Shutterstock.com/chuyuss; **S. 36** A Shutterstock.com/file404, B Shutterstock.com/Quinn Martin, C Shutterstock.com/Monkey Business Images, D Shutterstock.com/guig120; **S. 39** oben re. + B + D: Cornelsen/Anja Poehlmann, A: mauritius images/alamy stock photo/Nigel Cattlin; **S. 40** li. Oben + unten: Cornelsen/Anja Poehlmann, Varndean goat logo: Varndean School Brighton, Handysymbole: Shutterstock.com/MARII1, Mitte re.: mauritius images/alamy stock photo/Nigel Cattlin, re. unten: stock.adobe.com/susan flashman; **S. 41** Jagvir: stock.adobe.com/AJay, Adam: stock.adobe.com/Stuart Monk, Lara: stock.adobe.com/contrastwerkstatt, Nia: shutterstock.com/Monkey Business Images, Holly: stock.adobe.com/denys_kuvaiev, Krawatten: Varndean School Brighton; **S. 44** mi. li.: Cornelsen/Anja Poehlmann, unten li.: Shutterstock.com/antoniodiaz; **S. 48** Sunita (ob. li.): Cornelsen/Anja Poehlmann, A: Shutterstock.com/insta_photos, B: Shutterstock.com/V.S.Anandhakrishna, C: Shutterstock.com/Txema Gerardo, D: Shutterstock.com/JacquiMoore, E-J: Shutterstock.com/StockImageFactory.com, Mitte li.: Cornelsen/Anja Poehlmann; **S. 49:** Cornelsen/Anja Poehlmann; **S. 51** unten: Shutterstock.com/all_about_people; **S. 52** A: Shutterstock.com/Cristi Matei, B: Shutterstock.com/Volodymyr Plysiuk, C: mauritius images/alamy stock photo/Maximilian Weinzierl, D: Shutterstock.com/cbpix, unten re.: Shutterstock.com/Bilal Kocabas; **S. 53** Rex: Shutterstock.com/Ga_photo, Axel: Shutterstock.com/FlavoredPixels, Maude: Shutterstock.com/D.Bond, unten li.: Cornelsen/Anja Poehlmann; **S. 54:** A: mauritius images/alamy stock photo/Natalie Jezzard, B: mauritius images/Novarc Images, C: mauritius images/alamy stock photo/Edward Simons, D: mauritius images/alamy stock photo/Paul Thompson Images; **S. 55** Lily: Cornelsen/Anja Poehlmann; **S. 57** Sunita: Cornelsen/Anja Poehlmann; **S. 59** unten re.: Shutterstock.com/Aluna1; **S. 60 + 61** Emoticon: Shutterstock.com/Chaim Devine; **S. 63** oben re.: Cornelsen/Grasshopper Films (Filmstill), hug: Shutterstock.com/AKalenskyi, postbox: stock.adobe.com/lineartestpilot, ‚from'+'to': stock.adobe.com/SKphotographer, cards: Shutterstock.com/SpicyTruffel, string: Shutterstock.com/Igor Kovalchuk;

Shutterstock.com/Treter; **S.157** unten re.: photoCuisine; **S.158** 1: Shutterstock.com/Nattika, 2: Shutterstock.com/Maks Narodenko, 3: Shutterstock.com/PixaHub, 4: Shutterstock.com/V.S.Anandhakrishna, 5: Shutterstock.com/DenisMArt, 6: Shutterstock.com/baibaz, 7: Shutterstock.com/studiovin, 8: Shutterstock.com/Evgeny Karandaev,; **S.159** Stadion: Shutterstock.com/ktsdesign, Torte: Shutterstock.com/Natalia Ruedisueli; **S.160** Mitte li.: Shutterstock.com/nelea33; **S.162** oben li.: stock.adobe.com/grinchh, oben mi.: Shutterstock.com/Africa Studio, oben re.: Shutterstock.com/Monkey Business Images, cookies: Shutterstock.com/Tetiana Peliustka, ice cream: Shutterstock.com/Yurlick, fish: Shutterstock.com/jorgen mcleman; **S.163** oben li.: stock.adobe.com/DenisProduction.com, muffin: stock.adobe.com/Moving Moment, 1 bis 6: Cornelsen/Inhouse/Katrin Heinecke; **S.164** Mitte li.: Shutterstock.com/Robert Kneschke, Mitte re.: Shutterstock.com/Olesia Bilkei, un.li.: Shutterstock.com/Monkey Business Images, un.re.: Shutterstock.com/Gulcin Ragiboglu; **S.165:** Sunita: Anja Poehlmann, Ryan: Shutterstock.com/Tuzemka; **S.168** unten: Cornelsen/Anja Poehlmann; **S.171** siehe S.218; **S.179** Mitte re. (Montage): Cornelsen/Josephine Bienert-Köhler/Möwe: mauritius images/Nature in Stock, Bildschirm: Shutterstock.com/Passatic; **S.181** Regenschirm: Shutterstock.com/chuyuss; **S.183** Buch: Shutterstock.com/robuart, Hose: Shutterstock.com/DenisProduction.com, Menschen: Shutterstock.com/hisa_nishiya, Pferd: Shutterstock.com/YIK2007; **S.184** Fahrrad: Shutterstock.com/stockphoto-graf, Stift: Shutterstock.com/OrangeVector, Tasche: Shutterstock.com/dashadima; **S.191** oben li.: Shutterstock.com/owatta; **S.192** Shutterstock.com/Laurie Barr; **S.194** Zahlen: Shutterstock.com/HitToon, unten: Shutterstock.com/Africa Studio; **S.195** Bär: stock.adobe.com/perpis, Delfin: stock.adobe.com/slowmotiongli, Ente: Shutterstock.com/Luka Hercigonja, Eule: stock.adobe.com/martinkubik, Krokodil: stock.adobe.com/katrin sauerwein/EyeEm, Lama: stock.adobe.com/Daniel Prudek, Meerkatze: Shutterstock.com/Mrinal Pal, Nashorn: Shutterstock.com/Stu Porter, Panda: stock.adobe.com/leungchopan, Pinguin: stock.adobe.com/www.dgwildlife.com/giedriius, Schmetterling: ClipDealer GmbH/yuliang11, Spinne: ClipDealer GmbH/Vitolef, Tiger: stock.adobe.com/bertie10, Wal: stock.adobe.com/© Seal Photographs/Craig Lambert Photo; **S.196** baking: stock.adobe.com/DragonImages, basketball: stock.adobe.com/Viacheslav Lakobchuk, boxing: Shutterstock.com/LightField Studios, climbing: stock.adobe.com/zhukovvvlad, coding: stock.adobe.com/DragonImages, cycling: Shutterstock.com/Jacek Chabraszewski, nail art: Shutterstock.com/Lapina, gaming: mauritius images/Masterfile RM, gymnastics: Shutterstock.com/Aleksey Mnogosmyslov, friends: stock.adobe.com/Jacob Lund, judo: Shutterstock.com/Kaderov Andrii, kayaking: Shutterstock.com/CroMary, horse riding: Shutterstock.com/Fotokostic, reading: Shutterstock.com/LightField Studios; **S.197** oben li.: Shutterstock.com/buabunya, oben mi.: Shutterstock.com/Draftfolio, oben re.: Shutterstock.com/Lorelyn Medina, 2. Zeile li.: Shutterstock.com/SpicyTruffel, 2. Zeile mi.: Shutterstock.com/mentalmind, 2. Zeile re.: Shutterstock.com/ekler, 3. Zeile li.: Shutterstock.com/Tasha Vector, 3. Zeile mi.: Shutterstock.com/Peter Hermes Furian, 3.Zeile re.: Shutterstock.com/Olga Krichevtseva, unten li.: Shutterstock.com/Merfin, unten mi.: Shutterstock.com/Glinskaja Olga, unten re.: Shutterstock.com/ProStockStudio; **S.198** cinema: stock.adobe.com/Mr. Music/Mr., dance studio: Shutterstock.com/vipman; drama room: stock.adobe.com/Daisy Daisy, games room: stock.adobe.com/Ivan, library: Shutterstock.com/wavebreakmedia, music room: stock.adobe.com/Monkey Business, office: Shutterstock.com/goodluz, playground: stock.adobe.com/S ROBIN/OceanProd, lab: Shutterstock.com/Rawpixel.com, sports field: Shutterstock.com/Rawpixel.com, staff room: Shutterstock.com/DGLimages, pool: Panther Media GmbH/Benis Arapovic; **S.200** Wellensittich: stock.adobe.com/dieter76, Huhn: Shutterstock.com/Moonborne, Frettchen: Shutterstock.com/Couperfield, Meerschweinchen: Shutterstock.com/Tettania, Katze: Shutterstock.com/Nils Jacobi, Echse: Shutterstock.com/Michaelpuche, Maus: Shutterstock.com/Ziga Camernik, Welpe: stock.adobe.com/arezin.com/Aleksey, Kaninchen: Shutterstock.com/Victoria Paladiy, Ratte: Shutterstock.com/George Dolgikh; **S.201** Tag+Nacht: Shutterstock.com/Apple_Mac, Uhren: Shutterstock.com/Skocko; **S.202** bakery: Shutterstock.com/milanzeremski, supermarket: Shutterstock.com/LizardfIms, ice rink: Shutterstock.com/begalphoto, theme park: Shutterstock.com/SIHASAKPRACHUM, bus stop: stock.adobe.com/Kay Ransom, mosque: Shutterstock.com/Victor Moussa, synagogue: mauritius images/alamy stock photo/Peter Llewellyn, church: Shutterstock.com/Jono Photography, bike rack: Shutterstock.com/Aliaksander Karankevich, car park: stock.adobe.com/© Sai Chan/Zoe, temple: mauritius images/alamy stock photo/Edward Herdwick; **S.203** apple: Shutterstock.com/Roman Samokhin, banana: Shutterstock.com/bergamont, beef: Shutterstock.com/MaraZe, broccoli: Shutterstock.com/smspsy, butter: Shutterstock.com/bigacis, cabbage: Shutterstock.com/JIANG HONGYAN, carrot: Shutterstock.com/Valentina Razumova, cheese: Shutterstock.com/Tanya Sid, chicken: Shutterstock.com/JIANG HONGYAN, cream: Shutterstock.com/grey_and, cucumber: Shutterstock.com/Maks Narodenko, cupcakes: Shutterstock.com/Wealthylady, donut: Shutterstock.com/Sergey Sklezner, eggs: Shutterstock.com/Nattika, ice cream: Shutterstock.com/stockcreations, jelly: Shutterstock.com/cigdem, lamb: Shutterstock.com/TheBusinessMan, lemon: Shutterstock.com/Maks Narodenko, lettuce: Shutterstock.com/PotaeRin, mango: Shutterstock.com/Valentyn Volkov, melon: Shutterstock.com/Boonchuay1970, milk: Shutterstock.com/New Africa, muffin: Shutterstock.com/Binh Thanh Bui, onion: Shutterstock.com/Yeti studio, orange: Shutterstock.com/Valentyn Volkov, peas: Shutterstock.com/WIPHARAT CHAINUPAPHA, pepper: Shutterstock.com/DronG, popcorn: Shutterstock.com/Jiri Hera, pork: Shutterstock.com/GSDesign, potato: Shutterstock.com/Anna Kucherova, sausage: Shutterstock.com/Einsteinstudio, strawberry: Shutterstock.com/Tim UR, tomato:

Shutterstock.com/Tim UR; **S. 204** add: Shutterstock.com/Nitr, bake: Shutterstock.com/IC Production, boil: Shutterstock.com/Gorlov-KV, cut: Shutterstock.com/husjur02, fry: Shutterstock.com/fotopai, mix: stock.adobe.com/Africa Studio, pour: Shutterstock.com/Deer worawut, roll out: Shutterstock.com/Igor Zvencom, stir: Shutterstock.com/Nebojsa Markovic, baking tray: Shutterstock.com/goh seok thuan, frying pan: Shutterstock.com/grey_and, oven: Shutterstock.com/taist2, pot: Shutterstock.com/Lipskiy, spoon: Shutterstock.com/Sanit Fuangnakhon, whisk: Shutterstock.com/nevodka; **S. 215** Shutterstock.com/wee dezign; **S. 216** Tim: Shutterstock.com/karelnoppe, Mrs Palmer: Shutterstock.com/Andresr, Elefant + Schlange: Shutterstock.com/Teguh Mujiono, Fische: Shutterstock.com/Tatyana Vyc; **S. 217** Guitar + bike: Shutterstock.com/OneLineStock.com, Kette: Shutterstock.com/Le_Mon, Gold: Shutterstock.com/Paket; **S. 218** Silber: Shutterstock.com/Paket; Hut: Shutterstock.com/MicroOne, Hand: Shutterstock.com/Adam Gregor; **S. 219** müde: Shutterstock.com/Lapina, Uniform: Shutterstock.com/miniwide; **S. 220** Klebestift, Stift, Radiergummi, Bleistiftanspitzer + Lineal: Shutterstock.com/jottaonni, bunte Socken: Shutterstock.com/Paleka, Mr and Ms/Mrs Lee: Shutterstock.com/jakkapan; **S. 221** Shutterstock.com/EugeneEdge; **S. 222** Shutterstock.com/haru; **S. 223** people: Shutterstock.com/Rawpixel.com, girl + boy: Shutterstock.com/bsd, maths: Shutterstock.com/Lyudmyla Ishchenko; **S. 224** Naturwissenschaft: Shutterstock.com/Monkey Business Images, Taschen: Shutterstock.com/Anna Tyukhmeneva; **S. 225** grandpa + grandma: Shutterstock.com/Oguz Aral, dogs: Shutterstock.com/Pixel-Shot; **S. 226** oben: Shutterstock.com/Standret, slow: Shutterstock.com/Outsider321; **S. 227** Shutterstock.com/4 PM production; **S. 228** oben: Shutterstock.com/ChristianChan, Mitte: Shutterstock.com/Pavel L Photo and Video, unten: Shutterstock.com/Noi1990; **S. 229** Shutterstock.com/Studio Harmony; **S. 230** oben: Shutterstock.com/krolya25, Mitte: Shutterstock.com/brgfx, unten: Shutterstock.com/dedi57; **S. 231** Schuhe: Shutterstock.com/pikepicture, Tisch li.: Shutterstock.com/donatas1205, Tisch re.: Panther Media GmbH/Valentyna Chukhlyebova/Vac, Stühle: Shutterstock.com/photka, Bett: Shutterstock.com/Pavel Adashkevich, Roboter: Shutterstock.com/Lecter; **S. 233** Shutterstock.com/dantess; **S. 234** Shutterstock.com/Gemenacom; **S. 235** Rollstuhl: Shutterstock.com/Nerthuz, Dusche: Shutterstock.com/Sashkin; **S. 236** line of houses: Shutterstock.com/Alastair Wallace, cycling: Shutterstock.com/Ljupco Smokovski; **S. 238** Shutterstock.com/pjcross; **S. 239** Shutterstock.com/Michael D Brown; **S. 240** Shutterstock.com/AlyoshinE; **S. 241** rubbish: Shutterstock.com/siam.pukkato, Mädchen mit Hund li.: Shutterstock.com/Zhiganova Dariaa, Mädchengruppe re.: Shutterstock.com/ONYXprj; **S. 242** Shutterstock.com/NextMarsMedia; **S. 243** Shutterstock.com/Helga Khorimarko; **S. 245** mice: Shutterstock.com/Utekhina Anna, Daisy: Shutterstock.com/Tienuskin; **S. 246** Dear Dad: Shutterstock.com/Blue.Poppy.Art; **S. 247** strawberries and cream: Shutterstock.com/Tanya Sid, peas: Shutterstock.com/valzan, tomato sauce: Shutterstock.com/Indigo Photo Club, white bread: Shutterstock.com/Dan Kosmayer, black bread: Shutterstock.com/de2marco, vegetables: Shutterstock.com/Anna Shepulova; **S. 248** sausage: Shutterstock.com/stockcreations, juggling: Shutterstock.com/dompr; **S. 249** present: Shutterstock.com/Rustle, salad: Shutterstock.com/kochabamba; **S. 250** packet: Shutterstock.com/JocularityArt, lemons: Shutterstock.com/Roman Samokhin, grams of rice: Shutterstock.com/Ekaterina_Minaeva; **S. 251** eggs, milk, flour, sugar: Shutterstock.com/paulista, spoon, knife, fork: Shutterstock.com/PolinaPersikova, onion: Shutterstock.com/Lubava; **S. 252** coffee: Shutterstock.com/igra.design; **S. 253** potato: Shutterstock.com/Nataly Studio; **S. 277** Zahlen: Shutterstock.com/HitToon; **Umschlaginnenseite hinten (U3)** Karte: stock.adobe.com/lesniewski

So lernst du mit Lighthouse

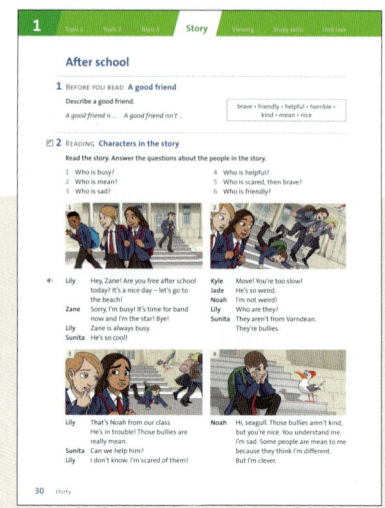

Dein Buch hat fünf Units

Jede Unit beginnt mit zwei Seiten *Lead-in*. Hier bekommst du einen ersten Eindruck von dem, was du in der Unit lernen wirst.

Eine Unit – drei *Topics*

Auf diesen Seiten übst du Lesen, Hören, Schreiben, Sprechen sowie Wortschatz und Grammatik. Jedes *Topic* schließt mit einer *My task* ab. Hier erstellst du z. B. ein kleines Produkt wie einen kurzen Text.

Spannende Storys

Nach den *Topics* kannst du spannende Geschichten über Kinder in Großbritannien lesen sowie Filme sehen.

Diese Symbole geben dir Orientierung in den Units

Partnerarbeit	Partner-Check	Gruppenarbeit	
einfache Aufgabe	schwierige Aufgabe	Medienkompetenz	Wahlaufgabe

Dein Buch findest du auch in der Cornelsen Lernen App

Siehst du eines dieser Symbole in deinem Buch, kannst du in deiner App …

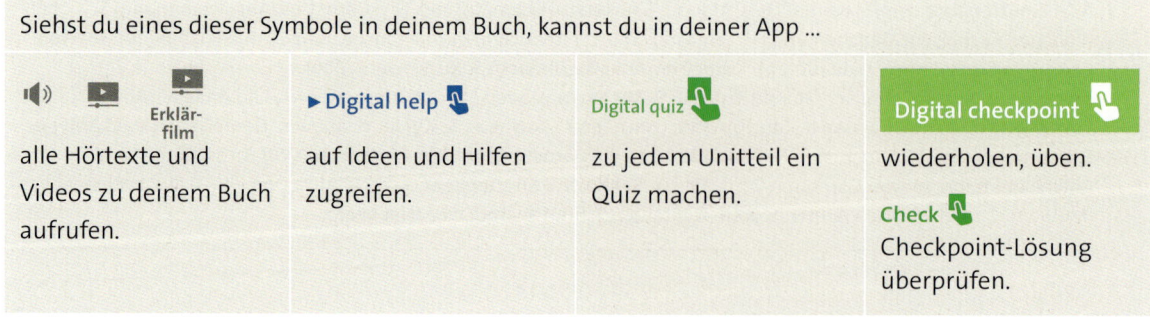

	▶ Digital help	Digital quiz	Digital checkpoint
alle Hörtexte und Videos zu deinem Buch aufrufen.	auf Ideen und Hilfen zugreifen.	zu jedem Unitteil ein Quiz machen.	wiederholen, üben. Check Checkpoint-Lösung überprüfen.

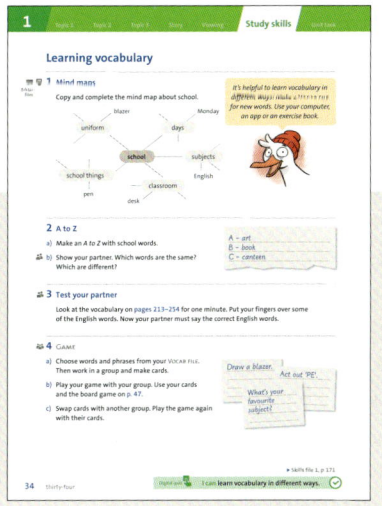

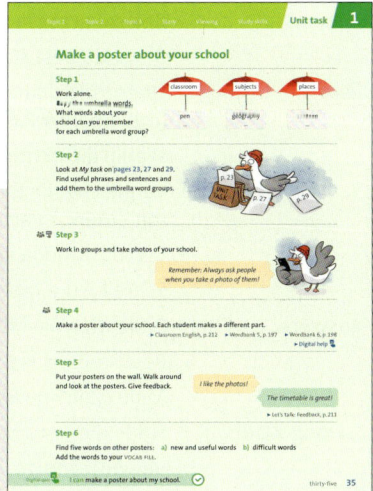

Lern- und Arbeitstechniken

Auf der *Study skills*-Seite übst du wichtige Lern- und Arbeitstechniken, z. B. wie du neue Wörter am besten lernst.

Eine Aufgabe am Unit-Ende

In der *Unit task* erstellst du ein größeres Produkt, z. B. eine Präsentation. Dabei wendest du das Gelernte aus der Unit an.

Im *Checkpoint* wiederholst du

Hier überprüfst du, wie gut du die Lernziele der Unit schon erreicht hast.

Im Anschluss findest du ein *Text file* mit interessanten Texten zum Thema der Unit.

Diese Verweise führen dich in die *Diff bank* am Ende der Unit

▶ More help	▶ Parallel exercise	▶ More practice	▶ Challenge
Hilfen zu den Aufgaben	einfachere Variante einer Übung	weitere Übungen	weitere Übungen mit höherem Schwierigkeitsgrad

Diese Lernangebote findest du im hinteren Teil des Buches

▶ Skills file	▶ Language file	▶ Wordbank
eine Übersicht über die Lern- und Arbeitstechniken	die wichtigsten Sprachregeln	zusätzliche Wörter zu bestimmten Themen

Let's talk	Vocabulary	Dictionary
Redewendungen nach wichtigen Themen und Situationen geordnet	eine Liste der neuen Vokabeln einer Unit mit hilfreichen Tipps	alphabetische Wörterlisten zum Nachschlagen (Englisch – Deutsch, Deutsch – Englisch)

Typical tasks	Häufige Arbeitsanweisungen
Act out the conversation / song / story.	Führt das Gespräch / das Lied / die Geschichte vor.
Answer the questions / partner B's questions.	Beantworte die Fragen / Partner Bs Fragen.
Before you read / listen / watch	Bevor du liest / (zu-)hörst / anschaust ...
Check the spelling / your answers / ideas (with a partner).	Überprüfe deine Rechtschreibung / Antworten / Ideen (mit einem/r Partner/in).
Choose the correct answer / word.	Wähle die richtige Antwort / das richtige Wort aus.
Compare the pictures / your answers / ... with a partner.	Vergleiche die Bilder / deine Antworten / ... mit einem/r Partner/in.
Complete the table / list / sentences / ...	Vervollständige die Tabelle / Liste / Sätze / ...
Copy the table / list / notes.	Schreibe die Tabelle / die Liste / Notizen ab.
Correct the false / wrong sentences / answers.	Berichtige die falschen Sätze / Antworten.
Describe the picture / your room / ...	Beschreibe das Bild / dein Zimmer / ...
Draw pictures.	Male / Zeichne Bilder.
Find the answers / the correct / right / wrong words.	Finde die Antworten / die richtigen / falschen Wörter.
Finish the sentences.	Vervollständige die Sätze.
Give feedback.	Gib Feedback / eine Einschätzung.
Interview your partner.	Stelle deinem/r Partner/in Fragen.
Look at the board / at page ...	Schaue an die Tafel / auf Seite ...
Look at the photos / pictures / map / title.	Sieh dir die Fotos / Bilder / Karte / die Überschrift an.
Listen and check / practise / repeat / guess.	Höre zu und überprüfe / übe / wiederhole / rate.
Listen again.	Höre nochmals zu.
Listen to the story / conversation / dialogue.	Höre dir die Geschichte / das Gespräch / den Dialog an.
Make groups (of six / ... students).	Bildet Gruppen (zu je sechs / ... Schüler/innen).
Make sentences / notes / lists / a mind map.	Fertige Sätze / Notizen / Listen / eine Mindmap an.
Match the sentence parts / what the friends say.	Verbinde die Satzhälften / das, was die Freunde sagen.
Practise with a partner.	Übe mit einem/r Partner/in.
Put it in your Dossier.	Hefte es in deinem Dossier ab.
Put the sentences / dialogue in the correct order.	Bringe die Sätze / den Dialog in die richtige Reihenfolge.
Read about ...	Lies über ...
Read the conversation / text / story / article.	Lies den Dialog / Text / die Geschichte / den Artikel.
Stand up when you hear ...	Wenn du ... hörst, stehe auf.
Swap (cards) with a partner.	Tausche (die Karten) mit einem/r Partner/in.
Take turns.	Wechselt euch ab.
Talk about ...	Sprich / Sprecht über ...
Talk to a partner.	Sprich mit einem/r Partner/in.
Tell your partner / the class.	Erzähle / Sage es deinem/r Partner/in / der Klasse.
True or false? / True, false or not in the text?	Wahr oder falsch? / Wahr, falsch oder nicht im Text?
Say the four / ... sentences.	Sage die vier / ... Sätze.
Use your notes / the words in a).	Benutze deine Notizen / die Wörter aus Aufgabe a).
Walk around.	Gehe (im Raum) herum.
Watch part / scene 1 / all the film.	Sieh dir Teil / Szene 1 / den ganzen Film an.
Watch again.	Sieh es / sie / ihn nochmals an.
Work alone / with a partner / in groups.	Arbeite allein / mit einem/r Partner/in / in Gruppen.
Write the correct answers / sentences / questions / words.	Schreibe die richtigen Antworten / Sätze / Fragen / Wörter (auf).
Write (more) about ...	Schreibe (mehr) über ...

Anhänge zur Lehrkräftefassung Plus

– Lösungsbeispiele

– Methodisch-didaktisches Glossar

– Kopiervorlagen

Hinweis

Lösungen zu geschlossenen Aufgaben finden Sie auf den Unitseiten, direkt bei den Aufgaben.
Auf sehr umfangreiche Lösungen sowie auf Lösungsbeispiele zu halboffenen Aufgaben wird von der
Unitseite hier in den Anhang verwiesen. Zu komplett individuellen Lösungen gibt es keine Muster.

Hello! Nice to meet you

▶ 12, Ex 1 b)   **Lösungsbeispiel**

Scout the seagull, Leo's mum, Ben's dad: s. Bild S. 12/13

Possible numbers: one *(Schild am Imbiss)* • eight *(auf dem T-Shirt des Mädchens)*

Possible animals: a cat *(am Imbiss)* • seagulls *(auf dem Imbiss, vor dem Pier, beim Volleyballfeld, beim Frisbee spielen)* • a dog *(am Wasser, beim Kind mit dem Eis, neben Leos Mutter)* • an alligator/crocodile *(das Schwimmtier auf dem Meer)* • a mouse *(unter dem Poster am Imbiss)*

Possible colours: yellow *(Sonnenschirm, Kleid der Frau rechts)* • red *(Jacke der Frau am Meer, T-Shirt mit der Zahl, Frisbee)* • blue *(das Meer, die meisten Hosen, Rucksack beim Basketballplatz)* • white *(Möwen, T-Shirt der Badmintonspielerin)* • …

Possible drinks: orange juice *(rothaariges Mädchen ganz rechts oben)* • cola *(Junge ganz rechts)* • water *(im Sand beim Basketballkorb)* • smoothie *(beim Imbiss auf dem Schild, Frau neben dem Schild)*

Possible things to eat: a burger *(auf dem Poster des Imbisses, die Möwe rechts unten klaut einen)* • a hot dog *(auf dem Poster des Imbisses)* • a lollipop *(das Kind bei den Bandmintonspielern hat einen)* • bananas and tomatoes *(auf der Picknickdecke von Leo)* • an ice cream *(bei dem schwarzen Hund)*

Possible other things: a basketball *(beim Basketballkorb)* • a football *(bei Leo)* • a volleyball *(beim Volleyballnetz)* • a bag *(beim Basketballplatz)* • a book *(der Junge in der Mitte liest)* • a beach chair *(neben Leos Picknickdecke)* • …

▶ 16, Ex 4 b)   **Lösungsbeispiel**

What's your favourite animal?
My favourite animal is a *dog/cat/tiger/bear/…*
What's your favourite colour?
My favourite colour is *red/yellow/green/pink/…* What about you?

I like *blue/yellow/green* and I don't like *black/white/purple*.
Ten/Eleven is my favourite number 'cause I'm *ten/eleven* years old.
I like my *bike/phone/rucksack/book* and I love my *cat/dog/cap/guitar/…*
But my *scooter/computer/bike* is my favourite thing of all.

What's your favourite hobby?
Listening to music / Swimming / … is my favourite thing to do.
What's your favourite sport?
I like *playing football / dancing / …* too. What about you?

▶ 17, Ex 1 a)   **Lösung**

Quiet please. (G) • Listen (A) • Stand up. (E) • Sit down. (D) • Look at the board. (H) • Open your books.
(F) • Put your hand up. (B) • Close your books. (C)

▶ 17, Ex 1 c)   **Lösung**

Look at the board. (H) • Listen (A) • Put your hand up. (B) • Stand up, please. (E) • Sit down. (D) • Stand
up. (E) • Sit down. (D) • Open your books. (F) • Look at the board. (H) • Put your hand up. (B) • Close
your books. (C) • Stand up. (E) • Sit down. (D) • Thank you!

▶ 17, Ex 3   **Lösung**

A Let's talk (p. 205) • **B** Dictionary (p. 255) • **C** Skills file (p. 170) • **D** So lernst du mit Lighthouse
(vorderer Umschlag innen / p. 282) • **E** Language file (p. 182) • **F** Ähnliche Wörter (p. 254) •
G Vocabulary (p. 213)

Unit 1 My new school

▶18, Ex 1 a) **Lösungsbeispiel**

• Hello, I'm Scout. I'm six years old. I like sandwiches. My favourite hobby is listening to music / drawing / taking photos. My favourite sport is football/swimming/dancing. What about you?

• Hello, I'm *Marie*. I'm *ten* years old. I like *horses*. My favourite hobby is *drawing*. My favourite sport is *horse riding*. What about you?

▶19, Ex 1 c) **Lösungsbeispiel**

Sunita is eleven years old. But I'm *ten years old*.

I don't like *coding*.

Sunita's favourite hobby is *coding*. My favourite hobby is *drawing*.

Sunita's favourite sport is *yoga*. My favourite sport is *handball*.

▶20, Ex 2 **Lösungsbeispiele**

• I like the uniform. The uniform is nice. I like the colour.

• I don't like the school uniform. A uniform is horrible. I don't like the colour. I like jeans and T-shirts.

▶22, Ex 6 **Lösung**

▶42, Ex 6 A In my picture I can see one brown pencil.

B In my picture I can see two brown pencils. (1 different thing)

A In my picture I can see one grey exercise book.

B In my picture I can see two grey exercise books. (2)

A In my picture I can see one green English book.

B In my picture I can see one green English book too. (-)

[...]

A: an orange ruler – B: a red ruler (3)

A: a blue pencil case – B: a black pencil case (4)

A: a red pencil sharpener – B: a blue pencil sharpener (5)

A: a pink pen – B: a green pen (6)

A: an apple / an orange – B: I can't see an apple / an orange (...)

▶23, Ex 9 a) **Lösungsbeispiel**

1 What page is it? – It's page 13.

2 I don't understand *exercise 2*. – Let's ask Ms Bach.

3 Can you help me with *exercise 2*? – Yes, I can.

4 What's the answer to *question 4*? – The answer is c.

5 Can I use your *ruler*? – Yes, here you are.

6 Thanks. – You're welcome.

▶24, Ex 3 **Lösung**

long form	short form	long form	short form
I am	*I'm*	we are	*we're*
you are	*you're*	you are	*you're*
he is	*he's*	they are	*they're*
she is	*she's*		
it is	*it's*		

▶27, Ex 10 a) **Lösungsbeispiel**

1 My favourite subject is PE because sport is cool.

2 I don't like maths because it's horrible.

3 My favourite subject is geography because I like holidays.

▶ **29, Ex 3** **Lösung**

singular	plural
I'm not	*we aren't*
you aren't	*you aren't*
he isn't she isn't it isn't	*they aren't*

▶ **31, Ex 3** **Lösung**

1 Zane *isn't* free after school.
2 Kyle and Jade *aren't* nice to Noah.
3 Sunita and Lily *are* scared of the bullies at first.
4 Lily and Sunita *are* Noah's friends.
5 The seagulls *aren't* nice to Kyle and Jade.
6 Noah's dog *isn't* mean.

▶ **33, Ex 2 b)** **Lösung**

1 Mr Campbell, the teacher, has a *brown* beard.
2 Mrs Collins has Emily's *pencil case*.
3 *Emir* looks for Emily.
4 Emily is in *the school garden*.
5 Mr Campbell *is OK with* Emir's beard.
6 Mrs Collins *can see fine*.

▶ **33, Ex 3** **Lösungsbeispiel**

1 I think the beard dare is weird.
2 I think the backwards dare is clever.
3 I think Mr Campbell is cool.
4 I think Mrs Collins is friendly.

▶ **34, Ex 1** **Lösungsbeispiel**

uniform: blazer, tie, *(shoes, trousers, skirt, blouse, shirt)**
days: Monday, Tuesday, Wednesday, Thursday, Friday, Saturday, Sunday, *(weekday)**
subjects: history, geography, maths, science, French, design and technology, computing, PE, ...
classroom: timetable, desk, *(chair, board)**
school things: glue stick, pen, pencil, pencil case, rubber, pencil sharpener, exercise book, ...
* noch nicht gelernte Wörter

▶ **34, Ex 2 a)** **Lösungsbeispiele**

A – art, answer, ask, assembly, *alphabet**
B – book, *board**
C – canteen, computing, class, corridor, *club**
D – desk, design and technology, *drama**
E – English, exercise book
F – French
G – geography, German, glue stick
H – history, holidays, *homework**
I – in English
J – *join a club**
K – *kids*, kiosk**
L – learn, listen, *lab*, library**
M – maths, mind map, Mr Lee

N – *notes**
O – open your books, opinion
P – PE, pen, pencil, pencil case, pencil sharpener
Q – question
R – remember, right, *rule**
S – school, science, sharpener, sport, student
T – teacher, technology, test
U – uniform, unit
V – vocabulary, *viewing**
W – window, wrong
X – ?
Y – year, you, yes
Z – ?

* noch nicht gelernte Wörter

Unit 2 My family and home

▶51, Ex 4 a) **Lösung**
1 Are you good with animals? • 2 Is your favourite animal friendly? • 3 Is it loud in your house? • 4 Are your favourite animals monkeys? / Are monkeys your favourite animals? • 5 Are you scared of snakes? • 6 Are you and your family cat fans?

▶51, Ex 4 b) **Lösung**
1 Yes, I am. / No, I'm not. • 2 Yes. it is. / No, it isn't. • 3 Yes. it is. / No, it isn't. • 4 Yes, they are. / No, they aren't. • 5 Yes, I am. / No, I'm not. • 6 Yes, we are. / No, we aren't.

▶54, Ex 1 a) **Lösungsbeispiel**
The home in photo A is a house. It's old and big. It has a garden.
The home in photo B is a house. It's old. It has a ground floor and a top floor.
The home in photo C is a flat. The flat is on the top floor. It's small. It has a balcony.
The home in photo D is a house. It's new. It's big. It has a garage.

▶55, Ex 4 a) **Lösungsbeispiel**
Sunita has a brother, Nish. Sunita's mum is Meera. Meera is a vet. Meera has a partner, Ben, a musician. Ben has a daughter, her name is Willow. She's 15. Sunita's grandparents are from India. Her aunt and uncle, Priya and Jay, live in Birmingham. They have two children, Anika and Jay – Sunita's cousins. • George, a parrot, is Sunita's pet. • Sunita lives in a house in Hove. The house is old and it's very big. There's a big garden and there are lots of trees. And the house is loud and messy, there are a lot of animals!

▶55, Ex 5 a) **Lösung**
1 Meera's bedroom • 2 Nish's bedroom • 3 Sunita's bedroom • 4 bathroom • 5 kitchen • 6 hall • 7 dining room • 8 living room

▶55, Ex 5 c) **Lösungsbeispiel**
hall: coats, shoes, bags • **kitchen:** fruit, eggs, fridge, toaster, no biscuits! • **living room:** TV, sofa, pictures, table, books, lamp • **Meera's bedroom:** (double) bed, cushions, a lamp, big windows, wardrobes, a desk, a computer ("home office base"), TV

▶56, Ex 1 a) **Lösungsbeispiel**
I can see a bed. There are three cushions on the bed. There are two blue shoes. I can see clothes in a wardrobe. There's a chair and a desk with a computer. I can see chocolate on the desk. There's a sofa with two cushions. I can see a robot. I can see a yellow lamp. There are three shelves with books. There's a mirror. I can see Scout.

▶56, Ex 1 b) **Lösung**
1 wrong (there are three *blue* cushions) • 2 wrong (there are *shoes* under the bed) • 3 wrong (there's a *small* table with a yellow lamp) • 4 right • 5 wrong (there are a computer, *chocolate* and *a robot* on the desk) • 6 right • 7 right • 8 wrong (the mirror is next to *the wardrobe*)

▶56, Ex 2 b) **Lösungsbeispiel**
things in and on my wardrobe: clothes, shoes, mirror, boxes with things
things on, under and next to my bed: cushions, table, lamp, shoes
things on and next to my desk: computer, chair, shelves, pen, pencil (… more school things)

▶62, Ex 5 **Lösungsbeispiele**
A I have a problem when you *play loud music*.
B I'm sorry. I can *be quiet*.
A That's a good idea. Thanks.
B You're welcome.
[…]

A I have a problem when you *put shoes on the floor in the hall.*
B I'm sorry. I can *put my shoes away.*
A That's a good idea. Thanks.
B You're welcome.

▶ 63, Ex 3 **Lösungsbeispiel**

I think Emir's tree is great. Emir's 3D tree is a nice, big tree with cards.

▶ 64, Ex 3 a) **Lösungsbeispiele**

daughter • neighbour • homework • interesting • wardrobe • chocolate • headphones

▶ 65, Step 1 a) **Lösungsbeispiel**

things in the room: bed, table, wardrobe, chairs, sofa, shelves, mirror, computer, lamp, cushions, …
where: on, under, next to, in front of, behind, in, near
colours: black, blue, red, green, yellow, brown, grey, orange, pink, white, purple, silver, gold, …
pets: dog, cat, hamster, parrot, fish, rabbit, lizard, …
the room is: modern, big, old, small, messy, tidy, nice, cool, …

▶ 67, Ex 4 **Lösungsbeispiel**

I live with my parents and my brother. We live in a small house near Bremen. It's a modern house and it's always tidy. There is a kitchen, a living room, two bedrooms and a bathroom. There's a big garden too. Our neighbours are friendly.

▶ 69, Ex 9 **Lösungsbeispiel**

This is Zane's dream room. It's very big and quite messy. The walls are yellow. There are football posters on the walls. There's a cat on the bed. There's a guitar on the sofa. There's a desk with a computer.

▶ 76, MP 3 a) **Lösungsbeispiel**

1 In this picture there's a small house. There are a lot of trees, the house is in a tree. The house is brown and it has a red door.
2 In this picture there's a big, old house. The house is grey. There are two trees in the garden.
3 In this picture there's a big building. The building is red. There are three trees in front of the house. There are six balconies.
4 In this picture there's an old house. There's a garden, the house is red.
5 In this picture there's a small, brown house. There are a lot of trees. There's a balcony on the top floor.
6 In this picture there's a big building. The building is grey and it has big windows. I can't see trees. There are three balconies.

▶ 78, MP 4 **Lösungsbeispiele**

I see a brown animal under the desk. – It's a rabbit!
I see an animal on a chair. – It's a parrot! / It's George!
I see a black animal next to the bed. – It's a dog!
I see a white animal on the bed. – It's a cat!
I see two green things in front of the desk. – They're shoes!
I see a green thing on the bed. – It's a book!
…

Unit 3 My day

▶ 89, Ex 6 | **Lösungsbeispiel**

Hi, Annie! Nice to meet you! I'm *Jasmin* from *Oberschule West*. I'm in the music and drama club. I'm in the school band and play the guitar. I sometimes do art when I'm stressed because it's relaxing. I often play table tennis and I am in the school club. We meet every Tuesday at 3 o'clock.
See you, ...

▶ 101, Ex 8 | **Lösung**

On Monday afternoon I go cycling with my friend. • On Tuesday I have a guitar lesson. • On Wednesday I go to my grandpa's house. • On Thursday afternoon I go to the school drama club. • On Friday evening I play computer games. • On Saturday and Sunday I have a big breakfast.

▶ 104, Ex 3 b) | **Lösungsbeispiel**

Sunita   Hi, Zane, can we meet *this week*?
Zane   I'd love to, Sunita.
Sunita   Great! Let's go to *the cafe*.
Zane   Sorry, I can't go to *the cafe*. It's too *quiet* for me. What about *cycling*?
Sunita   Good idea! Are you free *on Monday*?
Zane   Sorry, I'm busy *on Monday*. But I'm free *on Wednesday*.
Sunita   OK, let's meet at the cafe at *4.00 p.m.*
Zane   Let's ask Lily too. See you *on Wednesday*!

▶ 106, MP 5 | **Lösung**

1 *Zane* watches TV.
2 *Louise* uses a wheelchair.
3 *Zane* meets his sister at her school.
4 *Holly* gets up at 7.30.
5 *Zane* does his homework.
6 *Eno* makes breakfast.
7 *Zane* tidies the kitchen.
8 *Holly* goes to school with her brother.

▶ 107, Ch 1 | **Lösungsbeispiel**

1 Every day Scout gets up at 7.00 a.m. • 2 She often goes to the sea. • 3 Scout always swims with a friend. • 4 In the afternoon she sometimes watches the people at the beach. • 5 Scout often eats a burger. • 6 She always meets friends!

▶ 108, Ch 2 | **Lösungsbeispiel**

go: swimming • cycling • hiking • running • windsurfing • dancing
do: drama • art • dancing • singing • trampolining
play: computer games • music • table tennis • cricket • the guitar

▶ 108, Ch 3 a) | **Lösung**

1 subject • 2 adverb of frequency • 3 verb • 4 object

▶ 108, Ch 3 b) | **Lösung**

1 When I feel stressed, *I always go swimming* because it helps me.
2 *I sometimes play basketball* next to the beach when it's sunny.
3 *I rarely play football*, but *I often watch football matches*.
4 *I often cook* for my family.
5 *I always walk* to school, but *Sunita often goes* by bus.

▶ 109, Ch 4 | **Lösungsbeispiel**

A Hi B, can we meet this weekend?
B I'd love to, A.

A Great! What about the beach?

B Sorry, I don't like the beach. Can we meet in the park?

A Good idea! Are you free on Saturday?

B Sorry, I'm busy on Saturday. But I'm free on Sunday.

A OK, let's meet at the park at 10.30 am.

B OK. See you on Sunday!

Unit 4 Where I live

►112, Ex 1 a)
►135, Ex 1 a) **Lösungsbeispiel**

I can see ...	I can hear ...	I can smell ...
houses	*seagulls*	*the neighbour's cooking*
trees	a baby	cars
streets	loud/nice/piano music	coffee
cars	kids in school break	grass
buses	a car	rubbish
the sea	a police car / an ambulance	dogs
	my neighbour's TV/radio	
	kids in the street	

►112, Ex 2 a) **Lösung**

big – small • boring – interesting • clean – dirty • friendly – unfriendly • horrible – nice • loud – quiet

►113, Ex 3 a) **Lösung**

☺	☹
the neighbours	*the rubbish*
the youth centre	the cars
the sports centre	
playing table tennis	
the big fields	
the neighbourhood	

►113, Ex 3 b) **Lösungsbeispiel**

Lily likes the neighbours because they are friendly.

She likes the sports centre because she can play table tennis there.

She likes the youth centre because it has interesting activities.

She doesn't like all the cars because they're very loud.

She doesn't like the rubbish because it's not nice.

►113, Ex 4 a) **Lösung**

We don't have a car. • *My sister doesn't live with us* ... • It doesn't have parkour ... • But we don't go very often ... • ... because he doesn't have a lot of free days. • Some people don't look after our estate. • They don't put rubbish in the bins ... • I don't like all the rubbish. • I also don't like all the cars, ...

►114, Ex 6 a)
►135, Ex 6 a) **Lösung**

I often go to the youth centre, but not at weekends. It (**1**) *doesn't open* at weekends. There are a lot of activities like cooking, boxing and football. There's a girls' group on Tuesday, but I (**2**) *don't go* there, I (**3**) *don't have* time then. Sometimes I play pool at the youth centre with my neighbour Niles.

He (4) *doesn't go* to Varndean and his school (5) *doesn't have* a lot of clubs. We (6) *don't pay* for the activities – they're all free. A lot of people on our estate (7) *don't have* a lot of money.

▶114, Ex 7 b), c) **Lösungsbeispiel**

places: shop, sports centre, beach, cinema, field
more places:
marina – you can see the boats here
pier – you can eat fish and chips and play games here
park – you can meet your friends here, it's always open
skatepark – you do skating here
cafe – you can eat breakfast here
gardens – you can hear street music here
estate – there are houses, you live here
town centre – you can go shopping here
youth centre – you can do a lot of activities here like cooking, boxing, girls' group …

▶115, Ex 9 **Lösung**

Jing doesn't like her neighbourhood because it's very loud. • Jing doesn't like her neighbourhood because there are a lot of cars and people. • Jing doesn't like her neighbourhood because everybody is busy. • Jing doesn't like her neighbourhood because it's also dirty.
Alexis likes his neighbourhood because his neighbours are very friendly and there are a lot of kids.

▶117, Ex 5 a) **Lösung**

1 Does Bella go everywhere with you?
2 Do you know the town well?
3 Do you have problems with Bella in shops?
4 Do you and Bella use the bus?

▶118, Ex 7 b), c) **Lösung**

1 Does bus 12A go to the *beach*? ✓
2 Do you know a good fish and chip *shop*? ✓
3 Does the Brighton Museum open on *Monday*? ✗
4 Do you have the *time*? ✓
5 Does the town have a visitor *information* centre? ✓
6 Does the *sea* get really warm in summer? ✗

▶119, Ex 9 **Lösungsbeispiel**

1 Die Seebrücke hat täglich von 10 bis 18 Uhr geöffnet.
2 Der Eintritt ist frei, aber für die Fahrgeschäfte muss man zahlen.
3 Es gibt auch noch ein Trampolin und verschiedene Spiele, bei denen es etwas zu gewinnen gibt.
4 Sie veranstalten außer den Konzerten auch Feuerwerk-Shows und spezielle Aktivitäten zu Halloween und Weihnachten.
5 Das nennt sich „Brighton Rock", das ist pink und süß – und sehr schlecht für die Zähne. Aber es gehört einfach zu Brighton dazu.
6 Man kann dort Fish & Chips essen, außerdem Pizza, Crepes, Hot Dogs und Eis. Wirklich gesund ist wohl nur ein Salat.

▶121, Ex 3 **Lösung**

1 When do the shops open?
2 How do I buy train tickets?
3 Why do you love Brighton?
4 Where does the bus stop?
5 How much does a bus ticket cost?
6 What food do you like?

▶121, Ex 4 a)
▶134, Ex 4 a)

Lösung

1 B What *do* people do inside the house?
   A *They come here to take really cool photos inside the house.*
2 B When *does* the Upside Down House close?
   A *It closes at 9 p.m.*
3 B How much *do* tickets cost?
   A *Tickets cost £5.*

▶121, Ex 4 b)
▶134, Ex 4 b)

Lösung

1 A When *does* the Upside Down House open?
   B *It opens at 10 a.m.*
2 A Where *do* I buy tickets?
   B *You buy tickets at the kiosk.*
3 A How *do* we take funny photos?
   B *Put your hands up, then turn the photo upside down!*

▶121, Ex 5 a), b)
▶139, Ex 5 b)

Lösungsbeispiele

What do you do when it's snowy? – When it's snowy, I go to the Pavilion Gardens.
Where do you go when it's hot? – When it's hot, I go swimming.
How do you travel when it's windy? – When it's windy, I travel by car.

▶122, Ex 1 a)

Lösungsbeispiel

Lily lives on the Whitehawk Estate. There are a lot of flats and houses and
a small shop. The neighbours are friendly. There are a youth centre and a sports centre. Near the
estate there are big fields. The estate is dirty because people don't put their rubbish in the bins.
There are many cars in the estate, it's very loud.
(*Information from p. 112, "My neighbourhood"*)

▶124, Ex 7 a)

Lösungsbeispiele

A – animals (toys), art
B – bags, *balloons**, blazers, books, boxes
C – *calendars**, caps, cars (toys), clocks,
     clothes, chairs, computers
D – desks, dresses
E – exercise books, electric cars (toy)
F – films, *fridges**, *frying pans**
G – *glasses**, *gloves**, guitars
H – headphones, *hockey sticks**
I – *ice skates**
J – *jam**, jigsaw puzzles
K – karaoke sets, *knives**
L – lamps, *lemonade**
M – *magic sets**, maps, *mini-drones**,
     mirrors, music

N – newspapers, noodles
O – *oven gloves**, *opera tickets**
P – phones, *printers**, pens
Q – quizzes
R – *recipe books**, rings, robots
S – school uniforms, silver, skateboards,
     *sweatshirts**
T – *T-shirts**, tables, *teaspoons**, toys, *TV-sets**
U – *umbrella**, *unicorns (toy)**
V – *vegetables**, videos
W – wardrobes
X – *xylophones**
Y – *yoyos**
Z – zoo tickets

* noch nicht gelernte Wörter

▶125, Ex 1

Lösungsbeispiel

1 The Queen's Park Clock is always right. I think the dare is hard.
2 Daisy can show people the beach, the Pier, the Pavilion, the Marina, …

▶125, Ex 2 a)

Lösung

Daisy 1 street • **2** Electric • **3** US • **4** 910
Emir   1 his kitchen • **2** 11.15 • **3** 12.45 • **4** photos

▶126, Ex 3   **Lösung**

Start the presentation	Continue the presentation	Talk about pictures	End the presentation
I'd like to talk about My presentation is about	Next In the end	In this photo you can see Let's look at this picture of	Do you have any questions? Thank you for listening.

▶128, Ex 3   **Losungsbelspiel**

Hi Sunita,

I live in a small village. My neighbourhood is clean. My neighbourhood has fields, three shops and a nice cinema. It doesn't have a youth centre. I don't like my neighbourhood because it's boring. See you!

▶129, Ex 5 b)   **Lösungsbeispiele**

Picture A: I can see a big park. There are some trees and there are a lot of children. The weather is cold and snowy. I like the picture because I love the snow.

Picture B: I can see the beach and the sea. There is the pier and there are many people. The weather is warm and sunny. I like the picture because I like the beach.

▶131, Ex 7 a)   **Lösungsbeispiel**

Slide number 2 is the best because it has a big title, short notes and a big picture.

▶131, Ex 8   **Lösungsbeispiel**

Hello everybody! My presentation is about ideas for a rainy day.

When it's rainy, I like to go to the sports centre. It has lots of activities and it's not expensive. Next, we have the ice rink. It costs ten euros but it's really fun! The cinema is great too. It has interesting films and a nice cafe. Thank you for listening. Do you have any questions?

▶139, MP 6 a)   **Lösungsbeispiel**

L ikes parkour and cycling

I s active and clever

L oves her family and art

Y ou are great and cool, Lily!

Unit 5 Enjoy!

▶143, Ex 3 b)   **Lösung**

1 Noah: 30th May

2 Lily: 15th April

3 Zane: 3rd August

4 Sunita: 2nd March

5 Theo: 11th February

6 Ivy: 19th January

7 Tareq: 31st July

8 Marta: 2nd October

▶144, Ex 8   **Lösungsbeispiel**

– Hi! What are you doing? Are you free?

– Hi! Sorry, no, I'm busy. I'm *playing with my cat*. What are you doing?

– I'm *watching a film*. OK – see you!

► 145, Ex 10
► 164, Ex 10

Lösungsbeispiel

6 Differences:

Partner A: *In my picture a boy and a girl in blue T-shirts are singing Karaoke.*

Partner B: In my picture the boy and the girl in blue T-shirts aren't singing, they are talking.

Partner A: ... the girl on the sofa is playing with her mobile.

Partner B: ... the girl on the sofa isn't playing, she's taking a photo with her mobile.

Partner A: ... the boy in the white shirt is reading a magazine.

Partner B: ... the boy in the white shirt isn't reading, he's drawing a picture.

Partner A: ... the boy and the girl in the middle are eating strawberries.

Partner B: ... they're eating apples.

Partner A: ... the dog is sleeping.

Partner B: ... the dog isn't sleeping.

Partner A: ... the girls in purple clothes are talking.

Partner A: ... they aren't talking, they're eating popcorn.

► 145, Ex 11
► 164, Ex 11

Lösungsbeispiel Task B

In this picture, there are five children in a garden. They're wearing funny hats. They're playing with balloons in their hands. In the middle of them, there's a table. On the table, there's a plate with a cake or a trifle. There's also lemonade and more drinking glasses. In the middle of the cake a firework is burning. I think it's a photo of a birthday party.

► 146, Ex 1 b)

Lösungsbeispiel

Sunita and Lily choose a magic set, because Noah likes doing tricks. (They don't buy a mini-drone because it's too expensive, they don't buy bike lights because Noah doesn't like cycling.)

► 146, Ex 1 c)

Lösung

	☹	☺
What about a smart hat for Noah? Why don't we buy a book? I'm looking at the mini-drone – that's cool. We could get some cool bike lights. Let's get a magic set.	Noah doesn't like music. I'm not sure. It's too expensive. Noah already has bike lights.	It's a great present. That's cool. That's a good idea. That's perfect!

► 147, Ex 4 a)

Lösung

2 packets of bread
20 sausages
a big bag of pasta
1 bag of carrots
1 big melon
12 lemons

► 147, Ex 5 a)

Lösung

How much?	How many?
bread	*sausages*
pasta	carrots
sugar	one (big) melon
	lemons

▶147, Ex 5 b) **Lösung**

Wir verwenden *many* mit zählbaren Wörtern und *much* mit nicht zählbaren Wörtern. • *A lot of* kann man in Aussagesätzen mit zählbaren und mit nicht zählbaren Wörtern benutzen.

▶148, Ex 6 **Lösungsbeispiel**

In the fridge, there are

7 apples • 2 packets of carrots • 2 jugs of lemonade • 3 lemons • 1 lettuce • 2 melons • 1 sausage • 1 sandwich • 12 tomatoes • 4 packets of pasta • 5 strawberries • 1 piece of cheese

How many tomatoes are there? – There are twelve tomatoes in the fridge.

How much pasta is there? – There's a lot of pasta – four packets.

How many lettuces are there? – Not many, just one.

How much lemonade is there? – There's a lot of lemonade – two jugs.

How many apples are there? – There are seven apples.

▶148, Ex 7 a) **Lösungsbeispiel**

1 *How often do you go food shopping?* – I sometimes go shopping.

2 *Do you usually go with your parents or do you sometimes go alone?* – I usually go shopping with my parents.

3 *Where do you usually go shopping?* – In a supermarket.

▶148, Ex 7 c) **Lösungsbeispiel**

Cheese – peas • (avocados – tomatoes) • (meet – sweets) • aubergines – baked beans – nectarines • (lemons – melons) • ham – jam – lamb

▶149, Ex 8 **Lösungsbeispiel**

Für das Schokoladenspiel benötigst du Schokolade auf einem Teller, Messer und Gabel, Sonnenbrille, Handschuhe und einen Würfel. Alle würfeln abwechselnd. Wenn du eine sechs würfelst, musst du „sechs" rufen. Dann darfst du Schokolade essen, aber du musst vorher die Sonnenbrille aufsetzen, Handschuhe anziehen und du musst Messer und Gabel benutzen. Du darfst so lang essen, bis die nächste Person eine sechs würfelt. Dann ist diese Person dran. Das Spiel ist beendet, wenn die ganze Schokolade aufgegessen ist. – Bei uns ist die Schokolade auch noch in Zeitungspapier verpackt. Und man muss noch weitere Winterklamotten (Schal, Mütze, Mantel) anziehen, bevor man mit der Schokolade anfangen darf.

▶155, Ex 1 a) **Lösungsbeispiel**

party – party hats – presents – candles – balloons – napkins – party decorations – party games – music – dancing – friends

invitation – guests – theme – day, time

party food – sandwiches – birthday cake – birthday trifle – strawberries – apples – melons – hot dogs – sausages – chocolate ...

drinks – cola – lemonade – juice – water ...

presents – a toy – a sweatshirt – a cap – a book – a game – a magic set – a drone – bike lights ...

▶155, Ex 2 c) **Lösungsbeispiel**

party – party hats – presents – candles – balloons – napkins – party decorations – music – dancing – friends

invitation – guests – theme – day, time

party food – birthday cake – chocolate

drinks – no drinks!

presents – a toy

► 156, Ex 1 b) **Lösung**

1 ham: It's a kind of meat.
2 trifle: It's a kind of dessert.
3 onion: It's a kind of vegetable.
4 water: It's a kind of drink.
5 lemon: It's a kind of fruit.
6 noodles: It's a kind of pasta.

► 156, Ex 2 **Lösungsbeispiel**

1 cola: It's a drink. It's black and cold and very sweet.
2 carrot: It's a vegetable. It's orange and long. The top is green.
3 curry: It's spicy and hot. It can be vegetarian.
4 sugar: It's white and sweet. You can put it in your tea.
5 tea: It's a hot drink. It's brown. You can drink it with sugar or with milk.
6 pea: It's a vegetable. It's very small and round. It's green.

► 158, Ex 1 b) **Lösungsbeispiel**

A: Let's buy some chocolate.
B: Yes, that's a good idea.
A: I love strawberries. Do you like strawberries?
B: I'm allergic to strawberries. Let's buy some bread.
A: Yes, let's buy some bread and some tomatoes.
B: No, I don't want to buy tomatoes. Do you like carrots?
A: Yes, let's buy some carrots.

► 159, Ex 4 a) **Lösung**

Zane's dream party is in the stadium.

► 159, Ex 4 b) **Lösungsbeispiel**

1 It's special and interesting.
2 There's a tour of the stadium, a football lesson and a football match.
3 They are on Sunday mornings.
4 They are two hours long.
5 There are sandwiches, there's fruit and there's cake.

► 159, Ex 4 c) **Lösungsbeispiel**

I want to have my dream party at the skatepark. I love skateboarding and it's fun.

► 160, Ex 5 **Lösungsbeispiel**

1 Man isst dieses Gericht zu Abend.
2 Man braucht dafür (3) Eier, (300 ml) Milch, (8) Würstchen, (175 g) Mehl und Öl.
3 Es wird 30 Minuten im Ofen gebacken.

► 161, Ex 7 a) **Lösung**

1 carrot: It's a kind of ~~fruit~~.
2 chicken: It's a kind of ~~cake~~.
3 dessert: It's the meal ~~before~~ dinner.
4 milk: It's a kind of ~~food~~.
5 cornflakes: You eat them with a ~~knife~~.
6 tea: It's a ~~cold~~ drink.
7 shopping list: You need it at ~~school~~.
8 vegetables: They're ~~bad~~ for you.

► 161, Ex 7 b) **Lösung**

1 carrot: It's a kind of *vegetable*.
2 chicken: It's a kind of *meat*.
3 dessert: It's the meal *after* dinner.
4 milk: It's a kind of *drink*.
5 cornflakes: You eat them with a *spoon*.
6 tea: It's a *hot* drink.
7 shopping list: You need it at *a/the supermarket*.
8 vegetables: They're *good* for you.

► 161, Ex 8 **Lösungsbeispiel**

1 (Today) I want to tell you about my favourite dessert recipe: A banana and chocolate crepe. You make it with 125 g flour, 2 eggs, 360 ml milk, 1 tablespoon sugar, chocolate sauce and a banana.
2 You also need a cooking spoon and a frying pan.
3 First, you mix the flour, eggs, milk, and sugar.
4 Then you fry it for two minutes.
5 After two minutes you turn the crepe over and fry the other side.
6 Finally, you put it on a plate. You add the chocolate and banana.

► 167, MP 6 a) **Lösungsbeispiel**

1 A girl is sleeping in Mexico City at 6 a.m.
2 A boy is waking up in New York at 7 a.m.
3 A girl and her father are cooking in London at 12 o'clock.
4 A boy is riding his bike in Berlin at 1 p.m.
5 A family is eating in Tokyo at 8 p.m.
6 A girl and a boy are lying in bed in Sydney at 9 p.m.

► 167, MP 6 b) **Lösungsbeispiele**

I'm sitting in the classroom. My little brother is playing at home. My mother is travelling to Berlin. My father is working in the garden. My big brother is doing his homework at school. My cousin is playing football at the stadium.

► 167, MP 7 **Lösungsbeispiele**

1 Someone is eating toast. • 2 Two people are playing table tennis. • 3 A car door is closing. • 4 Someone is sending a message. • 5 Two people are drinking tea. • 6 Someone is boxing.

► 168, Ch 2 **Lösung**

Scout   Hi, George. (**1**) What are you doing?
George (**2**) I'm resting. (**3**) I'm not feeling good. The sun is too hot and (**4**) my head is burning.
Scout   Yes, it's hot. But we're lucky – (**5**) it's raining not now!
George Yes, you're right. (**6**) You're wearing a nice hat, Scout.
Scout   Thanks. (**7**) It's keeping me cool. (**8**) You're not wearing a hat. You need a hat, George!

Methodisch-didaktisches Glossar

Acrostic
(Akrostichon) Das Akrostichon (griechisch *akros*: Spitze, *stichos*: Vers) ist eine Versform, bei der die Zeilenanfänge hintereinander gelesen einen Sinn, z. B. einen Namen oder einen Satz, ergeben. Dies können Buchstaben bei reinen Wortfolgen oder Worte bei Versfolgen sein.

Im Unterricht wird meist folgende vereinfachte Form eingesetzt: Die Buchstaben eines Wortes werden senkrecht untereinandergeschrieben. Jeder Buchstabe kommt auch in einem anderen Wort vor (häufig als Anfangsbuchstabe), diese Wörter werden waagerecht um das senkrechte Startwort angeordnet.

Alphabet game Die S spielen das *Alphabet game* in Kleingruppen à 4–5 S. Ein/e S schreibt das Alphabet auf einen Zettel. Allen Gruppen wird das Thema genannt, dann beginnen sie gleichzeitig, zu jedem Buchstaben ein zum Thema passendes Wort aufzuschreiben.

Variante 1: L stoppt die Gruppen nach einer vorgegebenen Zeit (z. B. 2 Minuten).

Variante 2: Die Gruppe, die als Erstes zu jedem Buchstaben ein Wort gefunden hat, ruft Stopp. Da es besonders schwer ist, Begriffe mit den Buchstaben k, q und x zu finden, sollten diese besonders für Variante 2 ausgeklammert werden. Es kann aber vereinbart werden, dass diese Extrapunkte liefern.

Auswertung: Die Vokabeln können gemeinsam, z. B. an der Tafel, gesammelt werden, um eine Vokabelliste zu einem Thema zu erstellen. Alternativ kann eine Gruppe ihre Liste kurz vorstellen und die anderen ergänzen diese. Um den Wettbewerbsfaktor und die Aufmerksamkeit beim Vergleichen zu erhöhen, kann außerdem die Regel aufgestellt werden, dass Gruppen nur dann einen Punkt für ein Wort erhalten, wenn keine andere Gruppe dieses Wort benutzt hat.

Antwortkärtchen ▸ Right/wrong cards

Appointments Die kooperative Lernform *Appointments* ist eine gesteuerte Form von wechselnder PA in vier Phasen:
1. Die S schreiben drei vorgegebene Uhrzeiten in eine Tabelle. Dann gehen sie zu drei Mit-S, bitten jeweils um ein *Appointment* (*Can we meet at 1/2/3 o'clock?*) und tragen die Namen der Mit-S bei der entsprechenden Uhrzeit in ihrer Tabelle ein.
2. Im zweiten Schritt bearbeiten die S die Aufgabenstellung zunächst für sich und halten ihre Antwort in der Tabelle fest.
3. Auf das Signal von L (*It's 1/2/3 o'clock.*) gehen die S zum jeweiligen *Appointment* mit ihrem Mit-S, befragen ihn und notieren die Antwort in der Tabelle.
4. In der letzten Phase berichten die S im Plenum über ihre Umfrageergebnisse.

Thema	Me:	1 o'clock Name: _____	2 o'clock Name: _____	3 o'clock Name: _____
Frage 1				
Frage 2				
Frage 3				

Arbeitsanweisung,
Aufgabenstellung ▸ Klären der Arbeitsanweisung (AA)

Bewegtes Lernen Insbesondere die Ausweitung von Ganztagsschulen führt dazu, dass S länger im Unterricht sitzen und sich weniger bewegen. Neben gesundheitlichen Auswirkungen ist dies auch aus lernpsychologischer Sicht nicht förderlich für den Lernprozess. Der Faktor Bewegung verhilft S u. a. durch die Verknüpfung beider Hirnhälften, ihre Aufnahme- und Konzentrationsfähigkeit zu erhalten bzw. wiederherzustellen.

Im Sinne eines effektiven Fremdsprachenlernens sollten Bewegungselemente daher ein integrativer Bestandteil des Unterrichts sein. Dazu zählen neben dem Prinzip der ▸ Total Physical Response, bei dem

Formulierungen in der Zielsprache mit passenden Bewegungen assoziiert werden, auch kooperative Lernformen (z. B. ▶ Bus stop), bei denen dem Aspekt Bewegung in einem inhaltlichen Kontext Rechnung getragen wird.

Binnendifferen-ziertes Arbeiten

Heterogene Lerngruppen erfordern einen individualisierten Unterricht, in dem differenziert auf lern-stärkere sowie lernschwächere S eingegangen wird. Das Potenzial lernstärkerer S kann z. B. genutzt werden, indem diese aufstehen, sobald sie eine Aufgabe fertig bearbeitet haben. S, die sich mit der Aufgabe schwertun, können sich melden und von den stehenden S Unterstützung holen (*students as experts*). Dieses Vorgehen gewährleistet einen weitestgehend ruhigen Arbeitsablauf.

Da es in vielen Situationen nicht nötig ist, allen S der Lerngruppe Differenzierungshilfen zu geben, bietet es sich oftmals an, diese verdeckt zu geben (▶ Optional help). Je nach Gegebenheiten im Unter-richtsraum können Hilfen z. B. auf ein verdecktes Flipchart geschrieben oder kopiert in Briefumschläge gelegt werden, die sich die S an ihren Tisch holen und nach Gebrauch wieder zurücklegen.

Blitzlichtrunde

Die Methode der Blitzlichtrunde ermöglicht es allen S, eine kurze, persönliche Stellungnahme zu ei-nem bestimmten Impuls (z. B. Fragen, Themen, Zitate) mündlich abzugeben. Dabei strukturieren die S ihre Gedanken in jeweils nur einem Satz und äußern diesen einer nach dem anderen (meist im Sitz-kreis). Die Beiträge der S werden nicht gewertet oder kommentiert. Die Einsatzmöglichkeiten der Methode umfassen den Einstieg in ein neues Thema, als Ritual für die Stundeneröffnung (z. B. Rück-meldungen oder Austausch zum letzten Lernstoff) oder für Evaluationen (z. B. als Reflexion für Grup-penarbeiten oder zu Aufgabenstellungen).

Brainstorming

Brainstorming ist eine Methode, bei der durch freies Assoziieren möglichst viele – auch ungewöhn-liche und zunächst scheinbar abwegige – Ideen und/oder Lösungsmöglichkeiten zu einem bestimmten Thema gefunden werden sollen. In der ersten Phase werden Ideen gesammelt, erweitert, kombiniert und schriftlich festgehalten. In der zweiten Phase stehen das Kommentieren und die Bewertung der einzelnen Ideen im Mittelpunkt, um zu einer Entscheidung zu gelangen. Verschiedene Techniken kön-nen beim Brainstorming zum Einsatz kommen:

- Listensystem: Alle Ideen werden untereinander aufgelistet; dabei bekommt jede Idee eine eigene Zeile. Wichtige Ideen werden dann unterstrichen und ggf. nach Wichtigkeit nummeriert, unwichti-ge gestrichen.
- Mindmap: Das Thema wird in der Mitte des Blattes festgehalten. Dann werden Oberbegriffe, die zu diesem Thema passen, mithilfe von Hauptästen hinzugefügt. Schließlich kommen Ideen, die zu den Oberbegriffen passen, auf Nebenäste. Die Mindmap erfordert bereits bei der Erstellung eine Strukturierung.
- *Wh*-Fragen: *Who? What? When? Where? Why?* Diese Fragewörter werden in eine Tabelle geschrie-ben. Die Ideen zur jeweiligen Frage werden darunter festgehalten.

Buddy book

Das *Buddy book* ist ein kleines Buch mit 8 bzw. 16 Seiten. Die S können es selbst herstellen, denn es kann in wenigen Schritten aus einem DIN-A4-Blatt gebastelt werden. Als kompakter selbstgemachter Lernbegleiter wird es unter anderem eingesetzt als Notizbuch zu einem Thema, ähnlich wie Karteikar-ten zum Vokabellernen, sowie als Gedankenstütze für einen Vortrag oder auch als Medium zur Refle-xion von Lernfortschritten. Bastelanleitungen finden sich leicht online.

Bus stop (Lerntempoduett)

Die Methode des Lerntempoduetts ermöglicht es den S, gemäß ihrer individuellen Arbeitsgeschwin-digkeit zu arbeiten und ihre Arbeitsergebnisse eigenverantwortlich in PA zu kontrollieren. S, die eine Aufgabe fertig bearbeitet haben, stehen auf. Sobald ein zweiter S aufsteht, kontrollieren sie die Aufga-be im ▶ Partner check.

Vorteil: Es arbeiten nicht immer dieselben S (Freunde, Tischnachbarn) zusammen und schnellere S müssen nicht warten, bis alle Mit-S die Aufgabe gelöst haben und diese im Plenum ausgewertet wird.

In gestuften Übungsarrangements bietet sich auch die erweiterte Form *Bus stop* an. Dabei ist es nicht das Ziel, alle Aufgaben zeitlich zu schaffen, sondern je nach individuellem Lernstand das eigene Pensum zu erledigen (Ermöglichen zieldifferenten Arbeitens). Um jederzeit auf diese kooperative Lernform zurückgreifen zu können, empfiehlt es sich, dass L im Klassenraum – z. B. in den vier Raumecken –

Schilder mit dem Symbol einer Bushaltestelle anbringt, die entsprechend durchnummeriert sind (A–D oder 1–4). Hierfür kann L die ▸ KV Extra: Bus stop nutzen. Die Schilder können für alle Fächer genutzt werden. Ablauf:

1. Die S bearbeiten die erste Aufgabe ihrer Wahl in EA.
2. Wenn ein/e S fertig ist, begibt er/sie sich zum jeweiligen *Bus stop* im Klassenraum und wartet auf eine/n Mit-S, der/die die gleiche Aufgabe bearbeitet hat. Um evtl. Wartezeiten zu überbrücken, kann L dort kleinere (spielerische) Aufgaben mit hohem Aufforderungscharakter bereitlegen. Die S besprechen ihre Ergebnisse in PA. Um zu gewährleisten, dass der Austausch auf Englisch stattfindet, kann L im Vorfeld Redemittel zur Verfügung stellen. Alternativ (z. B. wenn keine Schilder zur Verfügung stehen) kann die Methode auch durchgeführt werden, indem S, die fertig sind, aufstehen und durch vorher vereinbarte Handzeichen, z. B. das Hochhalten von Fingern (1 Finger: Aufgabe 1 usw.) eine/n Mit-S finden, der/die die gleiche Aufgabe bearbeitet hat und für die PA bereit ist.
3. Nach erfolgtem Lösungsvergleich begeben sich die S wieder an ihre Plätze und arbeiten an der nächsten Aufgabe weiter. Die Kontrolle erfolgt am nächsten *Bus stop*, i. d. R. mit einem/einer anderen Mit-S, der/die ebenfalls die Aufgabe schon bearbeitet hat. Eine abschließende Kontrolle aller Aufgaben im Zusammenhang kann schließlich im Plenum oder mithilfe eines Lösungsblattes erfolgen und durch eine Reflexion der Methode ergänzt werden.

Buzz group
(Murmelgruppe)

Die *Buzz group* ist eine variabel einsetzbare Methodik, um S zu eigenen Stellungnahmen anzuregen oder auch Verständnisfragen zu klären.
1. L bittet S, mit den Nachbarn spontane Kleingruppen zu bilden und sich in den nächsten (z. B. 2) Minuten leise über die Frage / das Thema zu unterhalten.
2. L sorgt wieder für Ruhe (akustisches Signal) und animiert einige Gruppen dazu, die Klasse kurz über die Inhalte ihres Gesprächs zu informieren.

Tipp: Bei schwierigeren Themen ist es sinnvoll, Moderationskarten bereitzustellen, um offene Fragen an Pinnwänden auszuhängen und damit weiterzuarbeiten.

Buzz reading
(Lesegemurmel)

Das *Buzz reading* dient dazu, den Redeanteil aller S zu erhöhen und Sprachhemmungen abzubauen. Alle S lesen einen bekannten Text gleichzeitig und leise murmelnd vor sich hin. Die Methode kann flexibel im Unterricht eingesetzt werden. Es empfiehlt sich, diese Phase kurz zu halten und sie z. B. zur Vorbereitung auf einen Lesevortrag einzusetzen. In Kombination mit dem ▸ Mitleseverfahren trägt diese Methode besonders zur Festigung von Aussprache und Intonation bei.

Chain game

Den meisten S ist das *Chain game* sicher als „Ich packe meinen Koffer ...“ bekannt. Bei diesem einfachen Spiel fügt jede/r S der „Kette“ ein neues Glied hinzu. Die Regeln lassen sich dabei variieren, sodass der Schwierigkeitsgrad an die Leistungsstärke der S angepasst werden kann. So kann z. B. festgelegt werden, ob das zuvor Genannte komplett wiederholt werden muss oder ob der letzte Teil ausreicht. Das *Chain game* kann unterschiedlich eingesetzt werden; es lässt sich als Buchstabierspiel, Wort- oder Satzkette und auch als *Story chain* spielen. Häufig wird das *Chain game* zum Festigen oder Wiederholen von Vokabular verwendet.

Beispiel: Ein/e S oder L beginnt mit dem Einstiegssatz *My town has a shop ...* Der/Die nächste S wiederholt den Satz und fügt hinzu: *My town has a shop and a library ...* Der/Die wiederum nächste S wiederholt erneut den kompletten Satz und ergänzt ihn: *My town has a shop, a library and an ice rink ...* So wird das Spiel entsprechend fortgesetzt. Die Klasse passt auf, ob alles richtig gemacht wird. Sagt ein/e S etwas Falsches oder kommt nicht weiter, gibt er/sie z. B. ein Pfand ab.

Continue my story

Nach Vorgabe eines spannenden/interessanten Einstiegssatzes erstellen die S mündlich eine fortlaufende Geschichte, wobei die S nacheinander einen semantisch passenden Satz zur Geschichte ergänzen.

Correcting circle
(Schreibkonferenz)

Bei der Methode *Correcting circle* (auch *Peer correction*) handelt es sich um die gegenseitige Textkorrektur und Hilfe der S untereinander. Diese Form des Feedbacks ist für manche S weniger einschüchternd als die Fehlerkorrektur durch L. Die Methode eignet sich besonders für die Arbeit in Kleingruppen. Es sollte ein Kriterienkatalog für die Textkorrektur vorliegen, der vorher gemeinsam erarbeitet werden kann. Ablauf:

1. Jede/r S erhält ein spezielles Gebiet (z. B. *content, structure, spelling, tenses, word order*).
2. Die S geben ihre Texte reihum weiter und nehmen Korrekturen zu ihrem Gebiet vor, bis der Text wieder bei seinem Verfasser / seiner Verfasserin angekommen ist.
3. Zum Abschluss fertigen die S eine Reinschrift des eigenen Textes an.

L sammelt nach dem Zufallsprinzip einige Ergebnisse zur Bewertung ein. Im Sinne des selbstständigen Lernens kann vereinbart werden, dass S eine DOs-and-DON'Ts-Liste anlegen, die in der Klassenarbeit verwendet werden darf. Dies hilft S bei der Selbstkorrektur und motiviert, an den eigenen Fehlern zu arbeiten.

Cue cards

Cue cards sind Kärtchen, die S als Impuls bzw. als Gedankenstütze während des freien Sprechens nutzen können. Sie bieten die Möglichkeit, die Sprechfertigkeit der S gelenkt zu trainieren und so das längere freie Sprechen einzuüben. Zudem kann L sie lernschwächeren S als Hilfsmittel für *speaking activities* zur Verfügung stellen. *Cue cards* können sowohl Arbeitsaufträge als auch Redemittel oder kleine Zeichnungen abbilden. Sie eigenen sich für das dialogische Sprechen ebenso wie für das Üben von Prüfungssituationen oder von Präsentationen. Eine Möglichkeit *Cue cards* dafür einzusetzen, ist die folgende:

Um sich Notizen für Präsentationen zu machen, hilft es besonders schwachen S, sich vorher ihren Text zu überlegen. Die S knicken von einem Blatt ca. 1/3 des Rands ab. Dann schreiben sie den Text für ihre Präsentation o. ä. auf die breitere Seite und schreiben schließlich die wichtigsten Stichwörter aus ihrem Text auf den Rand. Bei der Präsentation sollten die S nach Möglichkeit die Seite mit den Stichwörtern benutzen. Wenn sie jedoch ihren Text vergessen, können sie die Seite mit dem ausgeschriebenen Text kurz zu Hilfe nehmen.

Daumenabfrage

▶ Thumbs up

Democratic vote

Davon ausgehend, dass bei Gruppenarbeiten häufig die Frage aufkommt, welches Gruppenmitglied das Ergebnis präsentiert, stellt die *Democratic vote* ein Zufallsprinzip zur Auswahl eines/einer S aus einer Gruppe dar. Um möglichst alle S in den Arbeitsprozess einzubinden, sollte erst am Ende der Arbeitsphase ein/e S bestimmt werden, der/die das Ergebnis vorstellt. Dazu stellen sich alle Gruppenmitglieder in einem Kreis auf und zeigen auf ein Signal hin auf eine/n S der Gruppe. Auf den die meisten oder die wenigsten Finger zeigen, trägt das Ergebnis vor. Damit sich jedoch die S nicht schon vorher eine/n Mit-S aussuchen, sollte regelmäßig zwischen beiden Varianten gewechselt werden.

Didaktische Folge

Für den effektiven Spracherwerb ist es bei der Einführung von neuem Wortschatz wichtig, die didaktische Folge zu beachten. Dabei ist die Reihenfolge der Fertigkeiten, die im Zusammenhang mit einem neuen Lexem gefordert sind, genau festgelegt:

1. Hören: Die S hören ein neues Wort mehrfach (Sprachvorbild L oder Audio).
2. Sprechen: Die S sprechen das neue Wort mehrfach nach (▶ Lautschulung).
3. Lesen: Die S sehen das Schriftbild und lesen das neue Lexem.
4. Schreiben: Erst in diesem Schritt produzieren die S das neue Wort schriftlich.

Mit zunehmendem Lernstand können S in verstärktem Maße, vor allem in der Textarbeit, auf erworbene Erschließungstechniken zurückgreifen.

Discussion tickets

Die S erhalten vor einer *Speaking activity* (z. B. *discussion, role play*) jeweils 3 bis 4 *discussion tickets*, mit denen sie während der Diskussion für jede Äußerung bezahlen. Dadurch müssen alle S mindestens drei- bis viermal reden, dürfen aber auch nicht mehr beitragen, sodass die Diskussion gleichmäßig von allen getragen wird.

Variante: Die *Discussion tickets* können auch bestimmte Redemittel enthalten, die von den S an passenden Stellen in der *Speaking activity* verwendet werden müssen. Sie können auch Angaben für den Diskussionsprozess enthalten, die im Laufe der Diskussion befolgt werden müssen (z. B. *In the course of the discussion ask one of the students in your group for his/her opinion. / In the course of the discussion use the following phrase: I see what you mean but …*).

Dossier

Die S sammeln ihre kreativen Beiträge, wie z. B. illustrierte Texte, selbst verfasste Gedichte oder Poster, in einem Dossier. Zusammen mit ihren Selbsteinschätzungsbögen kann daraus zum Schuljahresende eine Präsentationsmappe erstellt werden, die ein umfangreiches Bild der Sprachkompetenz der S bietet.

Double circle
(Doppelter Stuhl-
kreis, Kugellager)

Die kooperative Lernform *Double circle* ist eine Form von wechselnder PA, die sich zum Üben von Diskussionsstrategien eignet. Sie ermöglicht einen hohen Sprachumsatz bei niedriger Hemmschwelle zur aktiven Teilnahme. Ablauf:

1. Die S sitzen (oder stehen) sich in einem Innen- und einem Außenkreis gegenüber. Sie diskutieren ein vorgegebenes Thema oder eine Fragestellung mit ihrem Gegenüber und machen sich ggf. Notizen.
2. Auf ein (akustisches) Signal von L hin bewegen sich entweder die S im Innen- oder im Außenkreis um einige Plätze weiter, damit neue Paarungen entstehen. L bestimmt sowohl die Länge der Gesprächszeit als auch die Anzahl der weiterzurückenden Plätze.
3. In einem zweiten Durchgang berichten sich die S über das Gehörte, wobei die Partner/innen jeweils korrigieren und ergänzen. So sind die S zum aktiven Zuhören gezwungen.

Als Variante bietet es sich an, Innen- und Außenkreis verschiedene Themen oder Fragestellungen zu geben, die sich die S gegenseitig erklären oder beantworten.

Early finisher

Early finisher-Aufgaben sind für besonders lernstarke S, die schneller als andere S die im Unterricht gestellten Aufgaben fertigstellen. Diese S können zur Zeitüberbrückung zusätzliche Aufgaben bearbeiten, die zur ▶ Binnendifferenzierung und Kreativität beitragen.

English corner

Die *English corner* ist eine Pinnwand bzw. ein Teil einer Pinnwand im Klassenzimmer, die ganz dem Fach Englisch vorbehalten ist. In der *English corner* werden z. B. Unterrichtsergebnisse (Texte, Poster etc.) ausgestellt. Der Bereich wird von den S grafisch-visuell gestaltet, sodass er leicht erkennbar ist. Zum einen ergibt sich hierdurch die Möglichkeit, z. B. an Elternabenden oder sonstigen Schulveranstaltungen die Unterrichtsprodukte zu veröffentlichen. Zum anderen können in der *English corner* weitere Lernangebote für ▶ Early finishers dargeboten werden.

Im Sinne des ▶ Binnendifferenzierten Arbeitens können zudem lernstärkere S die ausgestellten Produkte korrigieren bzw. den Mit-S nach vorgegebenen Kriterien ▶ Feedback geben.

English folder

Für den Englischunterricht eignen sich am besten schmale Ringordner. So können die S die Blätter in den verschiedenen Teilen einheften, ohne dabei alle Seiten herausnehmen zu müssen.
Eine mögliche Unterteilung ist:
- *Exercises* (für alle Übungen zur Festigung der Kompetenzen)
- *Looking at language* (der Merkteil für sprachliche Strukturen)
- *Vocab file* (für Wortschatz)
- *My tasks* (für eigene Texte, Geschichten, … ▶ Dossier)

English-only-Karte

Die *English-only*-Karte ist ein nützliches Hilfsmittel, um S einen Anreiz zu geben, Hemmungen zu überwinden und auch in GA mit den Mit-S Englisch zu sprechen. Zu Beginn einer einsprachigen Arbeitsphase wird ein Symbol (z. B. eine Karte mit *Union Jack*) an Tafel oder (Pinn-)Wand geheftet. Die *English-only*-Karte fungiert dann wie ein „Schwarzer Peter": Wer Deutsch spricht, erhält diese Karte und darf sie erst abgeben, wenn ein/e andere/r S Deutsch spricht. Wer bei Beendigung der Arbeitsphase die Karte besitzt, muss eine kleine Pflicht erfüllen, wie z. B. einen Zungenbrecher oder Limerick vortragen oder einen spontanen Kurzvortrag (z. B. *My life as a chair*) halten.

Evaluations-zielscheibe Die Evaluationszielscheibe ist für nahezu alle Feedback-Themen einsetzbar. Zum Zwecke der Rückmeldung über Unterricht, Präsentationen u. Ä. erhält jede/r S von L eine vorbereitete Zielscheibe. Vor dem Ausfüllen wird die Form der vorzunehmenden Markierung auf der Zielscheibe (innen = trifft voll zu, außen = trifft nicht zu) besprochen. Die Markierung kann mit Filzstiften oder Klebepunkten erfolgen. Die Zielscheibe kann in mehrere Bereiche (empfohlen: Quadranten), die wiederum bestimmten thematisch-inhaltlichen Schwerpunkten entsprechen, aufgeteilt werden.

Die Auswertung der Zielscheiben sollte unmittelbar erfolgen. Die S lesen ihre Ergebnisse vor. Diese werden auf eine große Zielscheibe übertragen. Dadurch entstehen reichlich Anlässe zur Diskussion/ Auseinandersetzung mit dem Thema.

Alternative: L stellt eine große Zielscheibe zur Verfügung, die von allen S markiert wird. Nachteil: S neigen dazu, sich an Eintragungen ihrer Vorgänger zu orientieren.

Feedback Die Durchführung von Feedback-Phasen ist von grundlegender Bedeutung für die Entwicklung von methodischen Kompetenzen wie beispielsweise Vortragstechniken. Als Grundlage werden im Vorfeld klare Kriterien definiert, an denen sich das Feedback orientiert. Folgende Regeln sollten dabei beachtet werden:

1. Das Feedback wird so konkret wie möglich formuliert. Dabei werden immer zuerst positive Dinge genannt, bevor in einer zweiten Runde optimierungswürdige Aspekte angeführt werden – am besten mit Handlungsalternativen.
2. Zunächst hat der Präsentierende Gelegenheit, sich zu äußern, danach die übrigen S und zuletzt ergänzt L.
3. Wer ein Feedback gibt, sollte versuchen, das Gesehene zu beschreiben, anstatt zu bewerten. Dabei redet man den Angesprochenen am besten direkt an (also 2. Person, nicht 3.), wobei Meinungen in der Ich-Form vorgetragen werden sollten.

Die Person, die das Feedback erhält, sollte zuhören und es vermeiden, sich zu verteidigen. Letztlich geht es darum, sich selbst durch die Kritik der anderen zu verbessern. Hierzu ist es auch sinnvoll die Rückmeldungen in einer Art DOs-and-DON'Ts-Liste zu notieren.

Film dice Den Zahlen 1–6 eines Würfels werden Satzanfänge zugeordnet, mit deren Hilfe die S den Film oder Filmausschnitt kommentieren. Alternativ basteln die S einen Würfel, auf dem die Satzanfänge stehen. Die Methode ist in PA oder in Viergergruppen möglich. Falls ein/e S einen Satzanfang ein zweites Mal würfelt, muss der Wurf wiederholt werden.

Fishbowl discussion Bei der *Fishbowl discussion* handelt es sich um eine dynamische Diskussionsform, die eine Mischung aus Podiumsdiskussion und Diskussion im Plenum darstellt. In einem Innenkreis sitzend tauschen fünf S ihre Argumente aus, während die übrigen S im Außenkreis sitzend oder stehend die Diskussion beobachten. Ein Stuhl im Innenkreis ist frei. Auf diesen kann sich jederzeit ein Beobachter aus dem Außenkreis setzen, um selbst aktiv an der Diskussion teilzunehmen. Nach seinem Beitrag kehrt dieser S wieder in den Außenkreis zurück und der nächste Beobachter kann teilnehmen. Auf diese Weise können auch stillere S ihre Sprechhemmungen abbauen, da sie sich zunächst als Beobachter in die Diskussion einfinden können, bevor sie selbst aktiv werden. Gleichzeitig haben sie die Sicherheit, dass sie jederzeit wieder in ihre Beobachterrolle im Außenkreis zurückkehren können.

Vor Beginn der Diskussion sollte bestimmt werden, welche Positionen (Ansichten) die fünf S im Innenkreis in der Diskussion einnehmen. Ggf. werden Rollenkarten verteilt. Die S im Außenkreis beobachten den inhaltlichen und formalen Verlauf. Über gezielte und differenzierte Beobachtungsaufträge (z. B. Verwendung von Redemitteln, Beitragshäufigkeit, Gesprächsverhalten, Argumentationstiefe, Sprechlautstärke) kann anschließend der Diskussionsverlauf reflektiert werden.

Five-finger brainstorming Das *Five-finger brainstorming* intendiert eine begrenzte Sammlung von Informationen zu einem Thema bzw. Sachverhalt. Die S zeichnen dazu ihre eigene Hand auf ein Blatt Papier und notieren in jedem Finger einen Aspekt zur vorgegebenen Frage- oder Themenstellung. Einsatzort ist insbesondere die Einstiegsphase zur Reaktivierung oder zur Sammlung des Wortschatzes als Grundlage für den weiteren Ablauf der Unterrichtsstunde (z. B. die Sammlung von Vor- und Nachteilen für eine sich anschließende Diskussion oder die Sammlung von eigenen Interessen für eine folgende kurze Mini-Präsentation).

Five-minute teacher

Bei dieser Methode übernimmt ein/e S für eine kurze Zeit die Rolle von L. Sie eignet sich besonders für das Vergleichen geschlossener Aufgaben oder für immer wiederkehrende Situationen, wie z. B. die Begrüßung und mögliche Stundenrituale. Der *Five-minute teacher* nimmt selbstständig Mit-S dran, vergleicht deren Lösungen und gibt eine Rückmeldung dazu.

Die S sollten besonders zu Beginn dieser Methode das notwendige ▸Scaffolding bekommen, welches am besten als Poster im Klassenraum angebracht wird. Für das Vergleichen von Aufgaben bietet sich als ▸Scaffolding an: *Who wants to do the next task? / I think that is right. / I think that is wrong.*

Flashcards

Flashcards sind Bildkarten, die den S helfen, das Laut- bzw. Schriftbild eines Wortes nachhaltig mit seiner Bedeutung zu verknüpfen. Sie nutzen den auditiven und visuellen Lernkanal parallel (*Dual Code Theory*), wenn ihnen ein Wort mit dem entsprechenden Bild präsentiert wird und damit im Gehirn verknüpft werden kann. Als Applikationen an der Tafel eignen sich Flashcards auch zur schüleraktivierenden Wortschatzarbeit, z. B. indem in einer Reorganisationsphase die Bilder den entsprechenden Wörtern zugeordnet werden.

Four corners

Die vier Ecken des Klassenzimmers werden einer bestimmten Position zu einem Thema zugeordnet und es werden dort Symbole oder gut lesbare schriftliche Statements aufgehängt. Dann trägt L die Frage oder das Problem vor. Nach einer kurzen Nachdenkphase ruft L *Corner!*, woraufhin die S sich einer der vier Positionen zuordnen. Die S in den einzelnen Ecken sollen Ihre Meinungen oder Begründungen in kleinen Gruppen oder zu zweit zusammentragen. Zum Schluss werden die Meinungen auch im Plenum vorgestellt.

Variante: Die vier Ecken werden mit den Buchstaben A, B, C und D (oder 1, 2, 3, 4) versehen. L liest jeweils vier verschiedene Optionen vor, für die die S sich durch Zuordnung zu einer Ecke entscheiden müssen. Da diese Aufgabe auch Hörverstehen und Konzentration fordert, sollten die Optionen zweimal vorgelesen werden, ehe L *Corner!* ruft und eine Entscheidung erforderlich ist. Nach jedem Durchgang erfragt L Begründungen oder Details von einzelnen S.

Beispiel: *What type of holiday would you choose?* (A) *Camping at the seaside*, (B) *a luxury hotel in the mountains*, (C) *a cycling tour staying in B&Bs*, (D) *a city-trip staying in a youth hostel?*

Freeze-frame (Standbildmethode)

Die S erfassen Facetten von textlichen Figurenkonstellationen auf darstellerische Weise. In Gruppen tauschen sich die S zunächst über die darzustellende Situation aus, dann werden Rollen verteilt. Der „Baumeister" bringt die „Modelle" in ein zuvor abgesprochenes Standbild und schöpft körperlichräumliche Ausdrucksmöglichkeiten aus: Abstände zueinander, Körperhaltung, Gestik und Mimik spiegeln die Situation im Text auf intensive Weise wider. Beim Ausruf *Freeze!* verharren die Modelle regungslos. Jetzt können zusätzliche Fotos aus verschiedenen Perspektiven gemacht werden.

Als Auswertung bietet sich eine kurze Erläuterung der jeweiligen Gruppe an, es erscheint jedoch oft didaktisch sinnvoller, wenn die anderen Gruppen den *Freeze frame* zunächst mithilfe von Leitfragen interpretieren: *How are the characters presented? What can we tell about their relationships?* Ein Abgleich mit den Intentionen der präsentierenden Gruppe ist ratsam, um herauszuarbeiten, an welchen Stellen Ideen der Gruppe nicht verständlich waren. Diese kreative und körperbezogene Methode bringt Abwechslung in die oftmals einseitig kognitive Interpretationsarbeit.

Fruit salad

Die S sitzen im Stuhlkreis, ein/e S steht in der Mitte. L nennt jedem/jeder S eine Obstsorte, wobei jede Obstsorte mehrfach genannt werden sollte. Wenn nun der/die S in der Mitte eine Obstsorte nennt, tauschen alle S, die diese Sorte haben, schnell die Plätze. Wenn *Fruit salad!* gerufen wird, tauschen alle S schnell die Plätze. Der/Die S in der Mitte versucht nun auch, einen Platz zu bekommen. Der/Die S ohne Sitzplatz bleibt nun in der Mitte und das Spiel beginnt erneut.

Das Spiel kann thematisch verändert werden, indem z. B. *hobbies, subjects* etc. genannt werden.

Gallery walk (Galeriespaziergang)	Die kooperative Lernform *Gallery walk* bietet eine gute Möglichkeit, Arbeitsergebnisse zu präsentieren und zu diskutieren. Ablauf:

- Die S sind in EA oder GA zu einem Arbeitsergebnis gelangt (z. B. Text, Bild, Poster), das im Raum ausgestellt wird.
- Die S gehen einzeln oder in Gruppen im Uhrzeigersinn von Station zu Station und schauen sich die Ergebnisse der anderen an.

Wenn alle S alle Arbeitsergebnisse gesehen haben, präsentieren sie entweder nacheinander ihre Eindrücke oder besprechen sie gemeinsam in der Klasse.

Als Variante der GA bietet es sich an, die S neu aufzuteilen. In jeder neuen Gruppe sollte jeweils ein/e S aus den ursprünglichen Gruppen sein. Wer aus der neuen Gruppe an dem ausliegenden Produkt mitgewirkt hat, präsentiert es den anderen. Die Gruppen wechseln im Uhrzeigersinn so lange die Tische, bis jede/r S jedes Gruppenergebnis einmal erklärt bekommen hat und das eigene Gruppenprodukt einmal erklären musste.

Gruppenbildung Eine Einteilung der S in Gruppen kann mithilfe folgender Methoden erfolgen:

1. Methoden mit gelenktem Zufall: L bereitet Elemente vor, die zusammen ein Ganzes ergeben. Dies können z. B. Puzzleteile sein, die ein Bild ergeben, oder Wortkarten, die einem Oberbegriff zugeordnet werden können. Die S ziehen ein solches Element und finden sich in den jeweils entsprechenden Gruppen zusammen.
2. Gruppen können durch Auszählen, Würfeln oder nach dem *Line-up*-Verfahren gebildet werden. Bei diesem stellen sich S in der aufsteigenden Reihenfolge ihrer Geburtstage oder Hausnummern auf. L zählt dann die benötigten Gruppen ab, z. B. die ersten drei S, die gemeinsam eine Gruppe bilden, usw.
3. L teilt Gruppen ein und gibt die Namen der Gruppenmitglieder bekannt. Dabei sollten Leistungsniveau, Arbeitstempo und Sozialverhalten der S berücksichtigt werden.

Gucklochmethode Bei dieser Methode der Bildpräsentation schneidet L aus einem Blatt Papier ein Loch aus und legt das Blatt auf eine Abbildung (Foto, Stadtplan etc.) die L z. B. per Dokumentenkamera präsentiert. Anschließend fährt L mit dem Blatt über die Abbildung, sodass die S immer einen anderen kleinen Ausschnitt mit Details des Bildes sehen. L fragt, worum es sich bei der Abbildung handeln könnte. Die S spekulieren, bis L schließlich das ganze Bild präsentiert.

Die Methode lässt sich auch digital mithilfe von Präsentationsprogrammen anwenden, wobei über das Bild eine halbtransparente Folie bzw. Füllung gelegt wird, aus der mithilfe eines Zeichentools ein Guckloch eingefügt wird.

Herringbone technique Diese Technik fungiert als *graphic organizer* und ermöglicht es den S, Informationen aus einem Text (in der Regel zu den fünf *wh*-Fragen und *how*) in übersichtlicher Form zusammenzufassen. Zu diesem Zweck zeichnen die S eine schematische Fischgräte mit sechs Abzweigungen für die Fragewörter in ihr Heft und notieren dazu die entsprechenden Informationen.

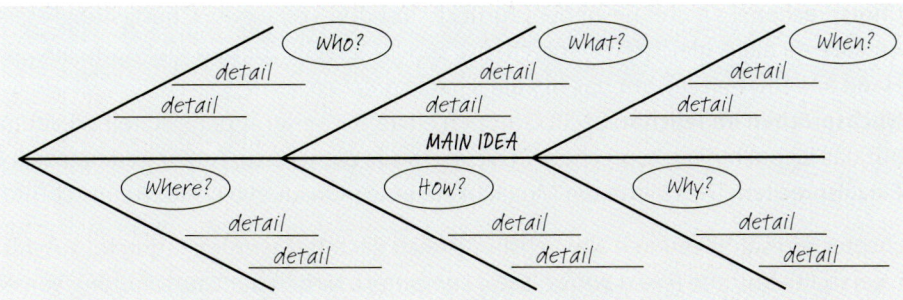

Hot seat *Hot seat* ist eine Methode, bei der ein/e S von den Mit-S auf einem *hot seat* befragt wird oder diese ihre (kontroverse) Meinung wiedergeben. Auf diese Weise können zuvor erarbeitete Unterrichtsinhalte zur Diskussion gestellt bzw. genutzt werden.

Variante: L stellt fünf Stühle vor der Klasse auf. Vier Stühle werden von S besetzt. Jeweils zwei vertreten den gleichen Standpunkt (z. B. *We like the film because … / We don't like it because …*). Der freie Stuhl kann von Mit-S, die die Diskussion verfolgen, belegt werden, um fehlende Gesichtspunkte zu ergänzen.

Info-gap activity

Bei der *Info-gap activity* handelt es sich um eine kooperative Lernform, die den aktiven Umsatz der Fremdsprache erfordert und schult. Den S fehlen Informationen zum Lösen einer Aufgabe, die ihren Partnern/Partnerinnen vorliegen und die sie durch gegenseitiges Befragen herausfinden. Es empfiehlt sich PA in einem festen Team (*Partner A, Partner B*).

Für die Durchführung müssen den S die Informationen und die zu füllenden Lücken vorliegen (Kopiervorlage, Arbeitsblatt, Tabelle im SB etc.). Es ist sinnvoll, den S eine Zeitvorgabe für die Bearbeitung zu geben. Eine Auswertung der Ergebnisse kann zunächst mit einem anderen S-Paar und anschließend im Plenum erfolgen.

Jigsaw (Gruppenpuzzle)

Als *Jigsaw* wird eine arbeitsteilige Gruppenarbeit in zwei Phasen bezeichnet.

Phase 1: Die S bilden Expertengruppen (Gruppe A, B, C etc.), innerhalb derer jedem Gruppenmitglied eine Nummer zugeteilt wird (1, 2, 3 etc.). Alle S einer Expertengruppe (A1, A2, A3 etc.) bearbeiten innerhalb einer vorgegebenen Zeitspanne die gleiche Aufgabe in EA. Anschließend diskutieren die S ihre Arbeitsergebnisse und halten die wichtigsten Informationen fest. Bei Abschluss der 1. Phase verfügen somit alle Mitglieder der Expertengruppe über die gleichen Informationen.

Phase 2: Es werden nun Querschnittsgruppen gebildet, in denen alle S mit der gleichen Nummer zu einer neuen Gruppe zusammenkommen (A1, B1, C1 etc.). Die S berichten den neuen Gruppenmitgliedern über die Ergebnisse ihrer Expertenrunde und beantworten Fragen. Alle S machen sich hierbei Notizen, sodass sie abschließend in der Lage sind, die Ergebnisse sowohl in ihrer Stammgruppe als auch ggf. im Plenum zu präsentieren.

Klären der Arbeitsanweisung (AA)

Für das Klären von Arbeitsanweisungen (AA) gibt es unterschiedliche Möglichkeiten. Im Hinblick auf selbstständiges Arbeiten sollten S möglichst früh dazu befähigt werden, AA ohne Hilfe von L zu erschließen. Damit S sich aktiv mit der AA auseinandersetzen, empfiehlt sich folgendes Vorgehen:

1. Stilles Lesen der AA
2. Verständnisklärung in PA
3. Erklärung der AA durch eine/n S im Klassenverband
4. Bestätigung und oder Korrektur durch L

Andere Möglichkeiten sind:
5. L demonstriert die Vorgehensweise (ggf. mit einem/r S) anhand von Gesten, einem Produkt oder Beispielen.
6. Die AA wird gemeinsam im Plenum gelesen und erläutert.

Kugellager

▶ Double circle

Lautschulung

Für die Lautschulung bieten sich verschiedene Techniken an:
1. **Chorsprechen:** Es bietet besonders zurückhaltenden S eine gute Übungsmöglichkeit. Hoher Sprachumsatz, da alle S gleichzeitig sprechen. L spricht jeweils vor und gibt dann ein Zeichen (z. B. Gestik: Hand ans Ohr halten), auf das hin die S nachsprechen.
2. **Nachsprechen im Teilchor:** L teilt Gruppen ein (z. B. Tischgruppen, Sitzreihen, Jungen/Mädchen), die auf das Signal hin nachsprechen. Diese Methode dient dazu, Fehler genauer zu lokalisieren.
3. **Einzelsprechen:** Dies bietet die Möglichkeit, eine individuelle Korrektur durchführen zu können.

Nachsprechen sollte generell abwechslungsreich gestaltet werden – durch Lautstärke, Geschwindigkeit, verstellte Stimme (*like a parrot, like a computer*). Neben der Lautschulung von einzelnen Wörtern können auch ganze Sätze nachgesprochen werden, um das Intonationsmuster der Fremdsprache zu üben.

Lernen an Stationen	Bei dieser Form des offenen Unterrichts wird der Lernstoff auf mehrere Stationen aufgeteilt, die die S eigenständig in ihrem Tempo nach ihren Interessen bearbeiten. Normalerweise gibt es Pflichtstationen und Wahlstationen, die zu einem übergeordneten Thema gehören, aber unterschiedliche Schwerpunkte setzen. Sie sprechen durch verschiedene Materialien, Medien, Sozialformen und Aufgabenarten möglichst alle Lerntypen an. Diese handlungsorientierte Methode bietet sich zur differenzierten Vertiefung von Wissen oder auch im fächerübergreifenden Unterricht besonders an.
Lerntempoduett	▶ Bus stop
Leseacht	Die Methode Leseacht ermöglicht den S ein kooperatives Erschließen eines Sachtextes, indem sie sich den Text absatzweise abwechselnd vorlesen und sich beim Erfassen des Textinhaltes gegenseitig unterstützen können. Dabei werden zwei Stühle so aufgestellt, dass die S in entgegengesetzte Richtungen blicken. Mit der „20-cm-Stimme" klappt der verbale Austausch untereinander ohne Mit-S zu stören.
Lesegemurmel	▶ Buzz reading
Lesetechniken	Die Leseintention legt fest, wie tief die S in einen Text eindringen müssen, um die gewünschten Informationen zu erhalten. Die S müssen lernen, dass die Tiefe des Textverständnisses eng an die gestellten Aufgaben gebunden ist, und abhängig davon eine passende Lesetechnik auswählen und anwenden. Für L bedeutet dies sorgfältig zu prüfen, welche Intention die Aufgaben zum Leseverstehen haben und welche Leseleistungen die S zur Lösung jeweils erbringen müssen.

Die folgenden Lesetechniken eignen sich für unterschiedliche Aufgabenstellungen. Als überfliegende Lesetechniken stehen sie dem vollständigen Lesen eines Textes, dem *Reading for detail*, gegenüber:

Skimming: Das *Skimming* stellt eine erste, oberflächliche Beschäftigung mit dem Text dar. S überfliegen Überschriften, Fotos/Zeichnungen oder die Aufmachung des Textes. Dies gibt ihnen z. B. Aufschluss über das Thema oder den möglichen Inhalt und zeigt, ob der Text für sie interessant ist oder ihnen zum Lösen einer Aufgabe nützt.

Speed reading: Beim *Speed reading* geht es darum, einen Text zu überfliegen, einen groben Eindruck zu gewinnen und nach *key words* zu suchen. *Speed reading* bedeutet, mit einem Blick mehr Wörter zu erfassen als gewöhnlich, um eine höhere Lesegeschwindigkeit zu erreichen (siehe auch ausführlicher Eintrag zum ▶ Speed Reading).

Scanning: Das *Scanning* ist eine suchende Lesetechnik, die auf Schlüsselwörter und -gedanken ausgerichtet ist. Dabei gehen die S von einer Frage oder Aufgabe aus und überfliegen den Text, bis sie die gesuchte Information gefunden haben. Auch hier ist es nicht das Ziel, den Inhalt des gesamten Textes oder jedes unbekannte Wort zu verstehen.

Weitere Lesetechniken: *Reading between* und *Reading beyond the lines* beziehen sich auf Verstehensprozesse beim Lesen von Texten, die über die reine Informationsentnahme hinausgehen.

Unter *Reading between the lines* versteht man die Fähigkeit des Lesers, die gegebenen Informationen zu interpretieren und so Antworten auf Fragen zu finden. Beispiele hierfür sind das Antizipieren des Ausgangs oder das Ziehen von Schlüssen. Mögliche Fragen des *Reading between the lines* sind z. B.: *Why did …? • What do you think about …? • Can you explain …? • How was this similar to …?*

Beim *Reading beyond the lines* stellt der Leser Zusammenhänge zwischen dem Gelesenen und seinem Vorwissen her, um Antworten auf Fragen zu finden. Um dieses vertiefte Verständnis zu erreichen, muss der Leser in der Lage sein, zu vergleichen, zu generalisieren, zu beurteilen oder das Gelesene weiterzuentwickeln. Beispiele für Fragen auf dieser Ebene sind: *How would you …? • Do you agree …? • What would have happened if …? • How might …? • What effect does …? • If you were … what would you …?*

Line-up-**Verfahren**	▶ Gruppenbildung

Market-place activity
(Marktplatz)

Bei der kooperativen Lernform *Market-place activity* sprechen die S mit verschiedenen Partnern/Partnerinnen über ein vorgegebenes Thema. Ablauf:

1. Die S bewegen sich frei im Klassenraum. L stellt eine Aufgabe, die S in einem vorgegebenen Zeitrahmen bearbeiten. Dieser kann durch ein akustisches Signal wie z. B. das Abspielen und Anhalten von Musik begrenzt werden.
2. Auf das vereinbarte Signal hin bleiben die S stehen und tun sich mit dem/der vor ihnen stehenden zusammen. Die Partner/innen tauschen sich über das Thema bzw. die Aufgabe aus. Je nach Aufgabenart machen sich die S Notizen.
3. Auf das erneute Signal durch L wechseln die S ihren Partner / ihre Partnerin, sodass sie in einem begrenzten Zeitraum mit möglichst vielen S sprechen.
4. Die Ergebnisse können in einem anschließenden Unterrichtsgespräch ausgewertet werden.

Die *Market-place activity* ist eine Form des ▶ Milling around.

Mediation
(Sprachmittlung)

Vermittlungsstrategie zwischen Gesprächspartnern, die sich nicht direkt sprachlich verständigen können. Im Englischunterricht bedeutet dies die zusammenfassende, paraphrasierende Wiedergabe eines Hör- oder Lesetextes in der jeweils anderen Sprache. Bei der *Mediation* werden von dem/der Sprachmittelnden sowohl rezeptive Kompetenzen (einen Ausgangstext zu verstehen) als auch produktive Kompetenzen (einen Ausgangstext in der anderen Sprache wiederzugeben) und häufig auch interkulturelle Kenntnisse verlangt.

L kann den S zur Unterstützung folgende Leitregeln geben:
- Keine Wort-für-Wort-Übersetzung!
- Freie Wiedergabe der wichtigsten Informationen!
- Nicht alle Details wiedergeben!

Meinungsbarometer

Im Gruppenraum wird eine Linie gezogen, die beiden Eckpunkte werden mit 0 % und 100 % markiert, alternativ mit der Farbe rot für Ablehnung und grün für Zustimmung. L erläutert, dass die beiden Eckpunkte für *I fully agree* bzw. *I totally disagree* stehen, dass aber auch Zwischenpositionen möglich sind. L (oder S) liest dann *statements*, Meinungen oder Ideen vor, die S positionieren sich entlang der Linie je nach Grad der Zustimmung. Wenn alle Position bezogen haben, kann L Begründungen von einzelnen S erfragen. Danach kann noch ein weiterer Durchgang erfolgen, um festzustellen, ob S aufgrund der Äußerungen ihre Meinung geändert haben. Diese Möglichkeit sorgt außerdem für mehr Aufmerksamkeit während der Besprechung.

Variante 1: Statt den Grad der Zustimmung zu zeigen, ordnen die S sich einem von drei Bereichen im Klassenzimmer zu, die für *agree*, *disagree* und *unsure* stehen.
Variante 2: Ebenso können in den vier Ecken des Klassenzimmers Schilder mit *strongly agree*, *agree*, *disagree*, *strongly disagree* aufgehängt werden und die S beziehen dort jeweils Stellung.
Variante 3: Der Raum kann auch einfach in zwei Hälften für *yes* und *no* eingeteilt werden.

Egal in welcher Variante sollten die S ihre Meinungen im Anschluss begründen.

Meldekette

Die Meldekette dient der Förderung der S-Interaktion. Sie ist in Plenumsphasen universell einsetzbar, z. B. zur Auswertung von Ergebnissen oder zur Besprechung von Aufgaben. Die S rufen sich gegenseitig auf, wobei jede/r S einen Satz oder eine Antwort nennt. L greift nur bei Bedarf korrigierend ein.

Menschen-Domino

Das Menschen-Domino ist eine gute Methode für ein *Warm-up* zu Stundenbeginn, bei dem z. B. Zeitformen wiederholt und geübt werden können. Jede/r S erhält eine Dominokarte mit Motiven bzw. Informationen. Dazu schreibt L ein oder zwei passende Fragen an, die die zu übende Zeitform vorgeben. Beispiel für Aktivitäten im *simple present*: *What do you usually do on Saturdays?* Die S versuchen dann, im ▶ Milling around ihren Partner / ihre Partnerin zu finden, indem sie sich gegenseitig die Fragen stellen und sie mit den Motiven ihrer Karte beantworten, z. B. S1: *What do you usually do on Saturdays?* S2: *I usually do arts and drama. And you?* S1: *I usually go running and trampolining.* S2: *We aren't partners. Good bye.* Wenn sich Partner/innen finden, laufen sie zusammen herum, bis sie weitere Partner/innen finden (jede/r S hat je zwei). Am Ende sollte eine Schlange entstehen.

Menschen-Memo	L legt ein Oberthema fest, z. B. Verben, Tiere, Körperteile, etc. Es ist für die S einfacher, wenn ihnen die Begriffe vorgegeben werden und sie sich keine ausdenken müssen. Dazu können die Wörter auch auf Karteikarten ausgeteilt werden.

Menschen-Memo

L legt ein Oberthema fest, z. B. Verben, Tiere, Körperteile, etc. Es ist für die S einfacher, wenn ihnen die Begriffe vorgegeben werden und sie sich keine ausdenken müssen. Dazu können die Wörter auch auf Karteikarten ausgeteilt werden.

Zwei S werden ausgewählt und verlassen den Raum, um anschließend die einzelnen Paare zu erraten. Während die zwei S draußen warten, suchen sich die anderen S eine/n Partner/in und überlegen sich eine passende Bewegung. Anschließend kommen die zwei „Ratekinder" wieder herein. Die zwei ratenden S spielen nun gegeneinander und suchen jeweils zwei S aus, die ihr Wort nennen und die Bewegung vormachen. Wurde ein Paar zusammen „aufgedeckt", stellt es sich hinter dem „Ratekind" auf, welches dann noch einmal raten darf. Wurden alle Paare erraten, ist das Spiel vorbei.

Differenzierungsmöglichkeiten:
* Es wird nur eine bestimmte Zeit gespielt und nicht bis alle Paare gefunden wurden.
* Es können Beispielbegriffe genutzt werden.
* Es kann in Teams geraten werden.

Metakognition

Metakognition bedeutet, dass S über ihr Lernen nachdenken, Strategien und Methoden reflektieren und daraus die für sie geeigneten Lernstrategien ableiten. Bereits zu Beginn des Sprachenlernens ist es wichtig, dass S hinterfragen, warum sie in einer Lernsituation so vorgehen, wie sie es tun. Die Erkenntnis dieses Prozesses soll den S helfen, das Sprachenlernen bewusst zu erlernen.

Milling around

Bei dieser Methode bewegen die S sich innerhalb einer vorgegebenen Zeitspanne frei im Klassenraum und begeben sich wieder auf ihren Platz, sobald sie die relevanten Informationen erfragt haben. Auswertung im Plenum. ▶ Market-place activity

Mindmap

Eine Mindmap dient den S als „Gedankenkarte". Sie ordnen darin ihre Ideen übersichtlich an, wobei Zusammengehöriges beieinandersteht, alle Ideen vernetzt werden können und Farben sowie Zeichnungen Wichtiges hervorheben. Mindmaps können individuell und in der Gruppe erstellt werden und eignen sich als Anregung für mündliche und schriftliche Äußerungen. Mögliches Vorgehen:

1. Die Ideen werden zuerst ungeordnet gesammelt (z. B. auf Kärtchen).
2. Im zweiten Schritt werden Oberbegriffe für die Ideen gefunden (z. B. auf farbigen Kärtchen).
3. Im letzten Schritt visualisieren die S diese Grundlagen systematisch in einer Mindmap.

Mini saga

Die S schreiben zu einem bestimmten Thema eine Geschichte, wobei die exakte Wortzahl von 50 erreicht werden muss. Aufgrund der begrenzten Wortzahl setzen sich die S lexikalisch, textlich und inhaltlich aktiv mit der Geschichte auseinander (z. B. *Write a mini saga about your best school day so far.*).

Mitleseverfahren

Beim Mitleseverfahren hören die S während des Lesens eines neuen Textes diesen zugleich. Die Aktivierung des visuellen und des auditiven Kanals (Mehrkanallernen) ermöglicht eine enge Verknüpfung von Laut- und Schriftbild, sodass unbekannte Lexeme nachhaltiger verarbeitet werden können. Das Mitleseverfahren ist didaktisch dem Leseverstehen zugeordnet, da die primäre Sprachaufnahme über die Textvorlage erfolgt. Das laute Lesen dient der Ausspracheschulung und nicht dem Leseverstehen, da durch die Konzentration auf die phonologische Oberfläche das Erfassen des Textinhalts erschwert wird. Als Faustregel gilt: Das laute Lesen sollte immer erst eingesetzt werden, nachdem ein Text bereits inhaltlich erarbeitet worden und unbekannter Wortschatz erschlossen worden ist.

Mnemotechniken

Unter dem Begriff Mnemotechniken werden verschiedene Methoden des Gedächtnistrainings zusammengefasst. Im Fremdsprachenunterricht eingesetzt, helfen sie S, sich Worte und Informationen über die Schritte des Rekodierens, Assoziierens und schließlich des Abrufens besser einprägen zu können. Häufig verwendete Mnemotechniken sind das ▶ Akrostichon, das Finden von Ersatzwörtern, das Einprägen von Merkversen, die Assoziation von Begriffen/Schriftbild und Bildkarten (▶ Flashcards) und das Memo-Spiel.

Mothering

Mothering beschreibt ein Korrekturverhalten von L, das mit dem Korrekturverhalten der Mutter bzw. der Eltern beim Mutterspracherwerb vergleichbar ist. Fehlerhafte Aussagen der S werden dabei z. B. durch Wiederholung, übertriebene Intonation oder übertrieben langsames Sprechtempo korrigiert.

Note-making Das Anfertigen von Notizen ist eine Methodenkompetenz, die auch im Alltag bedeutsam ist. Das *Note-making* ist für die S eine wichtige Fertigkeit zum Generieren und Organisieren von Informationen und Ideen. Die dazu notwendigen Arbeitsschritte reichen vom Sammeln, Sichten und Ordnen der Notizen bis zum Überarbeiten und Anwenden von Stichwörtern, Themen etc. Für das Ordnen von Notizen eignet sich auch eine ▶ Mindmap.

Note-taking Das *Note-taking* ist eine Strategie des Hörverstehens. Wenn möglich, versuchen die S zunächst aus Titel oder Überschrift und ggf. aus Fotos, Bildern oder Grafiken erste Informationen über den Hörtext abzuleiten. Sie stellen sich darauf ein und bauen inhaltliche Erwartungen auf. Während des Hörens machen sie sich Notizen. Diese dienen ihnen dazu, wichtige *key words* oder Ideen aus dem Hörtext festzuhalten. Grundlegendes in Form von Stichpunkten aufzuschreiben, ermöglicht nicht nur einen besseren Zugang zu einem Text, sondern den Zugriff auf das Notierte an späterer Stelle. Insgesamt wird dadurch das Lernen effektiver.

L kann folgende Tipps geben:
- Höre auf das, was gesagt wird und wie es gesagt wird.
- Halte einen Stift bereit und schreibe mit. Nicht jedes Wort ist wichtig.
- Nutze Abkürzungen und Symbole beim Notieren (z. B. Sternchen, Ausrufezeichen, Fragezeichen).

Achte auf Schlüsselwörter und -sätze, besonders solche, die wiederholt werden.

Numbered heads together Diese kooperative Lernform ermöglicht eine hohe Schüleraktivierung, da die S, die das Gruppenergebnis präsentieren, per Zufallsprinzip ausgewählt werden und somit jede/r S Verantwortung für das Gruppenergebnis übernehmen muss. Zunächst bildet L Gruppen (▶ Gruppenbildung). Innerhalb dieser Gruppen erhält jede/r S eine Zahl (abhängig von der Gruppengröße). L (oder auch eine der Gruppen) stellt nun eine Aufgabe, die die Gruppen gemeinsam bewältigen. Das Startsignal für die Beratungsphase ist *Numbered heads together*! Nach Ablauf einer zuvor festgelegten Zeit beendet L die Beratung und wählt durch Nennung einer Zahl die Person aus, die aufsteht und für die Gruppe antwortet. Pro richtige Antwort erhält die Gruppe einen Punkt.

Die einzelnen Gruppen können unterschiedliche, aber auch gleiche Aufgaben bearbeiten. Um bei gleichen Aufgaben zu verhindern, dass die ausgewählten S mit der gleichen Zahl die Antworten der anderen Gruppe mithören, verlassen sie zunächst den Klassenraum.

One-minute presentation Eine *One-minute presentation* ist ein Mini-Referat, in dem einzelne S die Klasse über ein zuvor besprochenes/gewähltes Thema informieren. Der Vortrag erfolgt möglichst frei. Der Zeitrahmen von ca. einer Minute dient zur Beschränkung auf wesentliche Punkte (kann aber bei Bedarf beliebig variiert und z. B. auch auf zwei Minuten ausgeweitet werden: ▶ Two-minute talk). Gleichzeitig ermöglicht die Zeitbeschränkung das Halten von mehreren Vorträgen, ohne dass es für die zuhörenden S langweilig wird.

In fortgeschritteneren Lerngruppen achten die S auf eine kurze Anmoderation und geeignete Überleitungen zwischen den vorgetragenen Aspekten.

Optional help Bei der *Optional help* handelt es sich um eine Form der Differenzierung (▶ Binnendifferenziertes Arbeiten), bei der die S individuell bei Bedarf eine zusätzliche Lernhilfe verwenden können. Dies kann z. B. ein Hilfsblatt sein, das auf dem Pult bereitliegt und dort eingesehen oder mitgenommen werden kann. Es kann zudem eine zusätzliche Hilfe auf den Arbeitsmaterialien sein. Ideal ist es, wenn die *Optional help* zunächst nicht für S sichtbar ist (z. B. als umgeknickter Wort-/Lösungspool am unteren Blattrand) und sie nur dann darauf zurückgreifen, wenn sie Hilfe benötigen.

Partner check Die Methode des *Partner check* ist eine Form der ▶ Peer correction. Sie fördert einerseits die Eigenverantwortung der S für ihre Lernergebnisse und ermöglicht andererseits eine breite Aktivierung der S und einen hohen Sprachumsatz. Auch kann damit in gestuften Aufgabenstellungen den unterschiedlichen Lerntempi der S Rechnung getragen werden, z. B. mithilfe der Methode ▶ Bus stop. Beim *Partner check* tauschen sich die S nach Bearbeitung einer Aufgabe bzw. eines Aufgabenteils mündlich zu den Ergebnissen aus und korrigieren mögliche Fehler. Dieses Vorgehen gibt besonders lernschwächeren S zusätzliche Sicherheit für die anschließende Auswertung im Plenum und ist schnell und flexibel einsetzbar.

Partner talk Die Methode des *Partner talk* ist eine einfache Methode, die sich an vielen Stellen des Lernprozesses einsetzen lässt und die dazu dient, Schüleraktivität und Sprechzeit der Lernenden zu erhöhen. S tauschen sich dabei kurz (oft sind ein bis zwei Minuten ausreichend) zu zweit über einen vorgegebenen Sprechanlass (bestimmte Fragestellung, Vorerfahrungen etc.) aus. Die Fragestellungen sollten – wenn nicht im SB enthalten – an der Tafel oder auf Folie festgehalten werden, damit S darauf zurückgreifen können. In lernschwächeren Gruppen sollte L zusätzlich einige situationsbezogene Redemittel anbieten.

Partnerpuzzle Das Partnerpuzzle ist eine Variante des ▸Jigsaw mit dem Unterschied, dass bei dieser Aktivität insgesamt vier S (A, B, C, D) in unterschiedlichen Schritten kooperativ miteinander arbeiten. So erhalten die S-Paare A+B sowie C+D jeweils eine andere Aufgabe, die zunächst von allen S alleine bearbeitet wird. Anschließend tauschen sich die S-Paare A+B sowie C+D, die die identische Aufgabe hatten, untereinander aus. In der letzten Phase informieren sich S-Paare A+C und B+D gegenseitig über die Inhalte ihrer Aufgaben und nehmen so nach der Rolle des Lernenden, die des Lehrenden ein.

Peer correction ▸ Correcting circle

Phasen des Zur nachhaltigen Schreibförderung sollten S bei der Textproduktion grundsätzlich folgende drei Pha-
Schreibprozesses sen durchlaufen:

1. Entwerfen (▸Brainstorming): Die S sammeln Ideen, z. B. in einer Mindmap oder bei einem ▸stummen Schreibgespräch
2. Schreiben: Die S verfassen auf dieser Grundlage einen ersten Entwurf. Dieser sollte entweder von L oder in höheren Klassenstufen durch Mit-S, z. B. in Form eines ▸Correcting circle, korrigiert werden.
3. Überarbeiten: Auf der Grundlage der Korrekturanmerkungen fertigen die S eine Reinschrift an. Im Sinne einer Differenzierung (▸Binnendifferenziertes Arbeiten) ist es oftmals hilfreich oder sogar notwendig, entsprechende Schreibhilfen oder Sprachmuster bereitzustellen.

Picture dictation Die S malen bzw. zeichnen nach den genauen Anweisungen von L ein Bild (z. B. *In the middle of the picture there is a big house ...*). Alternativ kann auch ein/e S die Rolle von L übernehmen und Bildanweisungen geben.

Picture duet Bei einem *Picture duet* beschreiben die S einander in PA ein vorgegebenes Bild, indem sie jeweils abwechselnd einen Satz dazu formulieren. (L kann eine Mindestzahl an Sätzen pro Bild und S vorgeben.)

Placemat Bei einer *Placemat activity* sitzen vier oder fünf S um ein Blatt Papier (DIN A3 oder DIN A4), welches in einen Schreibbereich pro S sowie einen zusätzlichen Bereich für die Gruppe in der Blattmitte eingeteilt ist.

1. *Placemat* in Gruppen à vier S: 2. *Placemat* in Gruppen à fünf S:

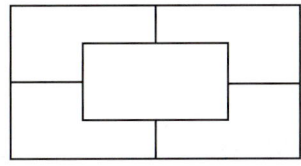 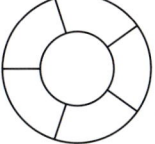

Zu Beginn der Gruppenarbeit schreibt jede/r S zunächst seine Ideen in den eigenen Schreibbereich. Anschließend wird die *Placemat* so lange gedreht, bis jedes Gruppenmitglied die Ideen der anderen S kommentieren und zudem die Kommentare der anderen zu den eigenen Ideen lesen konnte. Um zu verdeutlichen, wer welche Kommentare verfasst hat, sollten die S verschiedenfarbige Stifte verwenden. Im nächsten Schritt diskutiert die Gruppe die notierten Gedanken und schreibt die wichtigsten Punkte oder Argumente in die Mitte der *Placemat*. Auch kontroverse Positionen sollten dabei aufgenommen werden. Abschließend werden die Ergebnisse im Plenum ausgewertet.

Der Zeitbedarf variiert je nach Komplexität des Themas von zehn bis 30 Minuten. Die Vorgabe eines Zeitlimits für die einzelnen Phasen kann sinnvoll sein.

Pro-und-Kontra-Debatte

Eine Debatte ist eine genau geregelte Diskussion. Ziel einer Debatte ist es, zu einer Entscheidung in einer Streitfrage / bei einer Problemstellung zu kommen. Dabei stehen sich klar abgegrenzte Pro- und Kontra-Positionen gegenüber, denen sich die S zuordnen. Zur Untermauerung ihrer jeweiligen Positionen suchen die S in ihren Gruppen nach Gründen, Argumenten und Beispielen, um diese zu belegen. Falls gewünscht kann L die jeweiligen Gruppen auf eine Größe von 3–5 S beschränken.

Ein Moderator (*chairperson*) leitet die Debatte, überwacht die Einhaltung der Reihenfolge, ruft ggf. zur Ordnung und überwacht die festgelegte Redezeit für die einzelnen Gruppen (diese Rolle kann ggf. auch von L übernommen werden). Die an der Debatte nicht direkt beteiligten S agieren als Beobachter. Sie erhalten Beobachtungsaufgaben, stellen Fragen an die beiden Gruppen und stimmen am Ende darüber ab, welche Gruppe überzeugender argumentiert hat. Die Sitzordnung muss ggf. umorganisiert werden.

Die Debatte folgt festen Regeln:

1. Der Moderator eröffnet die Debatte, indem er das Problem vorstellt und die Regeln erklärt.
2. Die erste Gruppe (Pro-Gruppe) stellt ihren Standpunkt dar.
3. Die zweite Gruppe (Kontra-Gruppe) stellt ihren Standpunkt dar.
4. Die Gruppen befragen sich gegenseitig zu ihren Positionen und auch die Beobachter können nun Fragen an die Gruppen richten. Mögliche Regeln zur Steuerung: Wenn Beobachter etwas sagen wollen, müssen sie die Hand heben. Wenn sie direkt etwas entgegnen wollen, müssen sie beide Hände heben. Die Redner beziehen sich auf die Vorredner, signalisieren Zustimmung oder Ablehnung und nennen ihr Argument, das sie durch ein Beispiel untermauern.

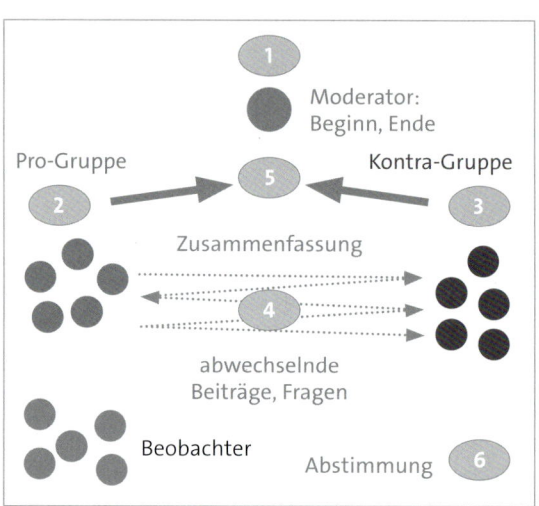

5. Jede Gruppe fasst ihre Argumente noch einmal abschließend zusammen.
6. Die Beobachter stimmen über die Argumente/Standpunkte ab und der Moderator beendet die Debatte.

Pyramidendiskussion

Die Pyramidendiskussion (wachsende Gruppe) ist eine Methode, bei der S ein Thema zunächst in Einzel-, dann in Partner- und schließlich in Gruppenarbeit bearbeiten, um sich darüber zu informieren und aus vielen Perspektiven die zentralsten Ideen, Aspekte und Meinungen dazu in der Diskussion zu ermitteln. Die Erarbeitung, bei der die Auseinandersetzung mit Thema und Sprache durch die stetig wachsende Gruppe immer intensiver wird, erfolgt in folgenden Schritten:

1. Die Aufgabe wird von den S in EA erarbeitet. S machen sich Notizen zum Thema und halten eine vorgegebene Anzahl an Vorschlägen am besten ranglistenartig fest.
2. L gibt nach vorgegebener Zeit ein Signal zum Bilden von Paaren und die Aufgabe wird in PA fortgeführt. Die Partner/innen müssen ihre Listen vergleichen und in der Diskussion eine neue Liste mit gleicher Anzahl an Aspekten erstellen.
3. Nach erneutem Signal finden sich Vierergruppen zusammen, die wiederum ihre Listen vergleichen und auf die anfangs festgelegte Anzahl vereinheitlichen und priorisieren.
4. Nach Ablauf der festgelegten Zeit bilden sich Achtergruppen, in denen der Vorgang wiederholt wird und durch Priorisierung und Abwägen die endgültige Liste erstellt wird.
5. Die Gruppen oder L wählen je einen Sprecher, der das Ergebnis im Plenum vorstellt. In erneuter Diskussion kann sich auch noch im Plenum auf ein Klassenergebnis geeinigt werden.
6. Zum Abschluss wird die Methode im Plenum reflektiert.

Question pot Die Methode des *Question pot* eignet sich besonders gut zur Sicherung des Hör-/Sehverstehens von Filmen oder des Leseverstehens von längeren (fiktionalen) Texten. In einem Gefäß sammelt L Fragen oder (*True-/False-*)Aussagen zu einem gezeigten Film oder einem Lesetext auf Papierstreifen. Anschließend ziehen die S einen Streifen, beantworten die Frage oder sagen, ob die Aussage richtig oder falsch ist. Wird die Methode zur Sicherung des Hör-/Sehverstehens eingesetzt, so sollten sich die Aufgaben nicht nur auf das Gesagte, sondern besonders auch auf Gesehenes beziehen. Die Fragen und Aussagen können je nach Leistungsstand der Klasse entweder von L vorgegeben oder von (lernstärkeren) S formuliert werden.

Read-and-look-up technique Diese Lesetechnik dient der Förderung des freien Sprechens und bildet für die S einen behutsamen Übergang zwischen dem Ablesen und Vortragen von Texten, Informationen und Inhalten. Der/Die präsentierende S hält die Vorlage in den Händen und liest sich einen (Teil-)Satz still durch, bevor er/sie die Klasse oder den/die Partner/in anschaut und den Satz aus dem Gedächtnis wiedergibt. Dabei ist es wichtig, dass S erst dann spricht, wenn er/sie Blickkontakt hergestellt hat. Diese Technik bereitet den freien Vortrag bzw. die Präsentation (auch mithilfe von Stichwortzetteln) vor und hilft unsicheren S, Inhalte vor dem Plenum darzustellen.

L kann die *Read-and-look-up technique* zunächst anhand eines beliebigen Textes demonstrieren. Die S üben danach mit geeigneten kurzen Texten, wobei die zuhörenden Partner/innen darauf achten, dass nicht abgelesen, sondern vor dem Sprechen Blickkontakt hergestellt wird.

Reading circle Beim *Reading circle* lesen alle S den gleichen Text oder die gleichen Texte (z. B. S-Produkte), wobei jede/r S eine andere Rolle übernehmen oder sich auf einen bestimmten Aspekt des Textes konzentrieren kann. Die S schreiben dazu jeweils Informationen, Aussagen oder Assoziationen auf ein Blatt, das anschließend ausgelegt oder bei dem Text aufgehängt wird. Sie gehen herum, lesen die Beiträge der anderen S und tragen ihre Kommentare dazu ein. Die Eindrücke der S werden anschließend im Plenum diskutiert.

Reading club (Reciprocal/Guided reading) Der *Reading club* ist eine kooperative Lernform, bei der die Erschließung eines Textes in 4er-Gruppen arbeitsteilig in verschiedenen Rollen erfolgt. Pro Kapitel/Abschnitt etc. übernimmt jede/r S im Wechsel eine der folgenden Aufgaben:

Der *Clarifier* klärt unbekannten Wortschatz (schlägt diesen nach) und erklärt den Mit-S die neuen Begriffe.

Der *Summarizer* fasst die Inhalte des Abschnitts zusammen und beantwortet die 5 *Wh*-Fragen (*Who? What? When? Where? Why?*).

Wenn der Lesetext Illustrationen zu mehreren Abschnitten enthält, kann statt des *Summarizer* alternativ auch ein *Describer* eingesetzt werden, der die Bilder beschreibt und daraus Rückschlüsse auf den Handlungsverlauf zieht.

Der *Questioner* formuliert Fragen an den Text, die von den Mit-S beantwortet werden.

Der *Predictor* stellt anhand des bisherigen Inhalts Hypothesen zum weiteren Verlauf der Handlung an. Nach jedem Textabschnitt tauschen die S ihre Arbeitsergebnisse aus und rotieren für den nächsten Abschnitt in der Aufgabenverteilung. Durch die arbeitsteilige Vorgehensweise werden metakognitive Textverarbeitungsstrategien gezielt und effektiv angebahnt; zugleich herrscht ein hohes Maß an Kommunikation und Sprachumsatz. Die S müssen an die Methode des *Reading club* (*Reciprocal reading*) schrittweise herangeführt werden. Dazu können entsprechende *Role cards* mit Hinweisen zur jeweiligen Aufgabe hilfreich sein.

Reading log (Lesetagebuch) Ein *Reading log* dient als Unterstützung beim Lesen einer Ganzschrift (Lektüre) oder von längeren Texten. Der Text wird dabei in entsprechende Abschnitte aufgeteilt, z. B. Kapitel oder Sinneinheiten. Zu diesen Abschnitten gibt L Aufgaben und Arbeitsaufträge – im besten Fall bereits als *Reading log*-Heftchen zusammengestellt – vor, die die S nach dem Lesen des entsprechenden Teils bearbeiten.

Kernbereiche eines *Reading log* sind grundlegende Informationen zu den fünf *Wh*-Fragen *Who? When? Where? What? Why?* sowie eine kurze Inhaltsangabe des jeweiligen Kapitels. Eine vertiefende Charakterisierung der Protagonisten kann den S dabei helfen, ein tieferes Verständnis für die Handlungszusammenhänge und -motive zu erlangen.

Zusätzlich kann ein Lesetagebuch den S Raum geben, um vor dem Lesen des Abschnitts jeweils ihre Erwartungen zu notieren; diese werden dann anschließend mit den Leseerfahrungen verglichen und können am Ende so eine Bewertung des gelesenen Buchs/Texts unterstützen.

Für L bietet sich der Vorteil, dass durch den Einsatz eines *Reading log* besser kontrolliert werden kann, ob die S die Lektüre tatsächlich lesen oder nicht.

Right/wrong cards (Antwortkärtchen)

Der Einsatz von *Right/wrong cards* eignet sich besonders zur Überprüfung von Aussagen zum Textverständnis. Die Karten können sowohl zur Lese- als auch Hörverstehenskontrolle eingesetzt werden. Ihr Einsatz ermöglicht eine valide Erfassung des Detailverständnisses und erfordert dabei keine eigene Sprachproduktion der S.

L stellt den S Karten aus farbigem Karton zur Verfügung (alternativ auch farbige Gegenstände, z. B. Stifte). Es wird vereinbart, dass grün für *right* und rot für *wrong* sowie ggf. blau für *not in the text* steht. Nachdem L eine Aussage zum Text vorgelesen hat, halten die S auf Kommando eine Karte in die Höhe. L erhält auf diese Weise auf einen Blick eine breite Rückmeldung darüber, ob der jeweilige Textinhalt von den S verstanden wurde. Wenn sich hier größere Abweichungen zeigen, sollte L dies zum Anlass nehmen, einen erneuten Lese-/Hörauftrag zu stellen, um das gesuchte Detail zu erfassen (selektives Lese-/Hörverstehen).

Das synchrone Ausführen auf Kommando ist wichtig, damit sich unsichere S nicht an ihren Mit-S orientieren. Wenn die Methode mehrfach eingesetzt wurde, können lernstärkere S die L-Rolle übernehmen.

Role-play

Role-plays dienen der Förderung des freien Sprechens und Reagierens in klar umrissenen Gesprächssituationen. Die S schlüpfen in die Rolle einer anderen Person und orientieren sich bei der Ausgestaltung an den Rollenvorgaben bzw. füllen ein vorgegebenes Dialoggerüst mit eigenen Ideen. Dürfen leistungsschwächere bzw. unsichere S Notizen zu Hilfe nehmen, sollte L die ▶ Read-and-look-up technique einsetzen und darauf achten, dass S nicht „am Blatt kleben", um das freie Sprechen zu schulen.

Für die Präsentation ist es vorteilhaft, einen Tisch zwischen die Klasse und die Präsentierenden zu stellen, um somit v. a. für verunsicherte S einen „geschützten Raum" zu schaffen. Bei relativ frei zu gestaltenden *Role-plays* sollte vor der Einübung auf jeden Fall eine Kontrolle und Korrektur stattfinden, um ein Einschleifen von fehlerhaften Sprachmustern zu verhindern.

Running competition

Die Methode *Running competition* ist eine Form der *Whole-class activity* mit Wettbewerbscharakter. Sie vereint das Festigen von Vokabeln oder Strukturen mit Bewegung und kommt daher insbesondere jüngeren S sehr entgegen. Ablauf:

L platziert eine Liste (z. B. mit unregelmäßigen Verben, wobei die Anzahl der Hälfte der Klassengröße entspricht) auf dem Pult, ohne dass diese für die S von ihrem Platz aus einzusehen ist. Die Klasse wird in zwei Gruppen eingeteilt und jeder Gruppe wird eine Tafelseite zugeteilt.

Die Teams legen fest, in welcher Reihenfolge die S „aktiv" werden (am besten von vorne nach hinten). Pro Gruppe geht ein/e S zum Pult und schaut nach, welches Verb dort steht. Er oder sie bildet die entsprechende unregelmäßige Form des *simple past* und schreibt diese an die Tafelseite seines Teams. Ähnlich wie bei einem Staffellauf, kehrt S möglichst schnell zu seiner Gruppe zurück und übergibt die Kreide an den Nächsten in der Reihe. Dabei darf weder gerannt, noch dürfen Hinweise von den nicht agierenden S gegeben werden. Die Gruppe, die als erste die Liste abgearbeitet hat, bekommt einen Punkt.

Im Anschluss erhält jede Gruppe die Möglichkeit ihre Ergebnisse zu verbessern. Dabei sollte L die Zahl der S, die verbessernd eingreifen dürfen, sowie die zur Verfügung stehende Zeit begrenzen (z. B. zwei

Minuten). Die festgelegten S kommen an die Tafel und greifen korrigierend in das Ergebnis ein. Es folgt eine Auswertung im Plenum, bei der pro richtige Form ein Punkt vergeben wird. Die Gruppe mit den meisten Punkten hat gewonnen.

Diese Form der Wiederholung und Festigung von sprachlichen Mitteln ist auf zahlreiche Inhalte, wie z. B. Vokabeln, Adjektive, Steigerungsformen und Wortfelder, übertragbar.

Scaffolding

Das *Scaffolding* ist eine Form der Hilfestellung. Dabei gibt L den S Grundgerüste mit Wortelementen vor, mit denen sie einen Text konstruieren, z. B. *My name is ... There is/are ... in my bag.* Solche Wortgerüste können sowohl für alle Lernenden einer Gruppe gegeben werden oder als individuelle Differenzierung für lernschwächere S.

Scenic play
(Szenisches Spielen)

Durch die Methode des *Scenic play* werden kognitive Fähigkeiten, emotionale und körperliche Ausdruckskräfte sowie manuelle und künstlerische Fertigkeiten der S entwickelt und geschult. Das szenische Spielen von Geschichten bettet die Fremdsprache in einen Kontext ein, an dem die S selbst mit allen Sinnen beteiligt sind. L sollte vorher mit den S besprechen, was für das Nachspielen benötigt wird, und dann die Rollen verteilen. Benötigte Requisiten können oft als Zeichnungen an der Tafel dargestellt werden oder es finden Gegenstände aus dem Klassenraum Verwendung.

Schreibgespräch

Ein Schreibgespräch ist eine schriftliche Form der Kommunikation, bei der zwei S in Stillarbeit auf einem Blatt und mit nur einem Stift einen Dialog führen. Beide S schreiben abwechselnd und in Reaktion auf den vorherigen Beitrag ihre Gedanken auf, wobei sie einander nicht beobachten dürfen. Es entsteht somit ein Text, in dem sich beide Partner/Partnerinnen intensiv und konzentriert mit den Gedanken der/des anderen auseinandersetzen und welcher im Anschluss mündlich diskutiert und kommentiert werden kann.

Schreibkonferenz

▶ Correcting circle

Semantisierung

Neuer Wortschatz sollte grundsätzlich nicht isoliert, sondern stets im Zusammenhang eingeführt werden. Hierbei bieten sich verschiedene Verfahrensweisen an:

1. Deiktische Semantisierungstechniken: Hierunter versteht man bildhafte, nonverbale Verfahren, die sich besonders in der Orientierungsstufe eignen. Zum Einsatz kommen:
- Realia: Realgegenstände eignen sich vorrangig zur anschaulichen Vermittlung konkreter Begriffe. Geht es z. B. um das Wort *pencil case*, so hält L ein Federmäppchen hoch und sagt: *This is a pencil case*. Wort und Bedeutung können so nachhaltig miteinander verknüpft werden.

- Flashcards: ▶ Flashcards

- *Vocab file*: ▶ Vokabelarbeit

- Mimik, Gestik, Demonstration: Lebendiges Handeln der L kann den S die Bedeutung entsprechender Lexeme nachhaltig vermitteln. Dies kann geschehen durch:
  a) Mimik: L demonstriert ein Wort mithilfe des entsprechenden Gesichtsausdrucks, z. B. *angry*, *happy*, *sad*. Dies kann auch verbal unterstützt werden, z. B. *angry*: *Hey, stop that!*
  b) Gestik: Wenn es um das Wort *first* geht, streckt L den Daumen nach oben und sagt: *It's the first morning in London.*
  c) Demonstration: Das Verb *open* wird eindeutig demonstriert, indem L das Fenster öffnet und dabei sagt: *Let's open the window*. Noch lernwirksamer ist es, wenn dazu das gegenteilige Lexem *close* demonstriert und eingeführt wird: *Now let's close the window.*

2. Verbal-definitorische Semantisierungstechniken: Mit zunehmendem Lernstand spielen verbal-definitorische Semantisierungstechniken in der Zielsprache eine stärkere Rolle. Den S sollten alle zur Semantisierung herangezogenen Wortschatzelemente bekannt sein. Zum Einsatz kommen:

- Ganzheitliche Verfahren: Verwendung des Wortes in einem typischen Kontext: *We wash our hands with soap and water.*

- Logische Bezüge: Einführung eines Lexems durch:
  a) Definition: *A dog is an animal with four legs and a tail. It barks.*
  b) *Rule of three* (Dreisatz): *A man has a mouth, a bird has a beak, ...*
  c) *Part – whole* (Rückschluss vom Ganzen aufs Einzelne): *a week = seven days*

- Lexikalische Bezüge: Einführung eines Lexems mithilfe von:
  a) Synonymen: *shop – store*
  b) Antonymen: *young ≠ old*
  c) Über-/Unterordnung: *Dogs, cats and rabbits are pets.*
  d) Herleitung: *happy – happiness*

- Der Rückgriff auf die Muttersprache sollte nur sehr selten erfolgen. In einigen Ausnahmefällen kann dieser allerdings hilfreich sein:
- um auf orthografische Ähnlichkeiten aufmerksam zu machen: *theatre* – Theater
- um phonetische Ähnlichkeiten hervorzuheben: *shoe* – Schuh
- wenn die fremdsprachliche Erklärung sehr umständlich wäre (z. B. *although*)

3. Erschließungstechniken: Mit zunehmendem Lernstand sollten wichtige Erschließungstechniken (Kontext, Vorwissen aus der Fremdsprache, Ähnlichkeiten im Schrift- oder Lautbild zur Muttersprache etc.) trainiert werden. Ein neues Wort sollte v. a. dann semantisiert werden, wenn:
   a) es sich um ein Schlüsselwort für das Textverständnis handelt,
   b) eine hohe Diskrepanz zwischen Laut- und Schriftbild besteht, die Aussprachefehler bewirken kann,
   c) es nicht aus dem Kontext oder auf andere Weise erschließbar ist.

Situativer Wortschatz, der keine zentrale Bedeutung für das Textverständnis hat, muss nicht semantisiert werden. Den S wird auf diese Weise verdeutlicht, dass sie einen Text auch dann verstehen können, wenn sie nicht jedes einzelne Wort kennen (= Training der Toleranz im Umgang mit „Verständnislücken").

Seven letters — Die S wählen sieben Buchstaben des Alphabets und nutzen diese als Anfangsbuchstaben für das Schreiben von Wörtern zu einem bestimmten Thema. Anschließend wird aus diesen Wörtern ein zusammenhängender Text geschrieben.

Simon says — Beim Spiel *Simon says* geht es um eine ▶ Total Physical Response (TPR). Ein/e S oder L steht vor der Klasse, fordert die Lernenden auf, eine Aktion durchzuführen und führt diese direkt vor. Sagt S/L dabei vor der Aktion *Simon says*, so sollen die Lernenden die Aktion nachahmen. Sagt S dies nicht, dürfen die Lernenden sie nicht nachahmen. Lernende, die dies trotzdem tun, scheiden für diese Runde aus. Beispiel: L: *Simon says jump.* (S hüpfen.) L: *Sit.* (Lernende bleiben stehen.)

Small talk — Innerhalb des *Small talk* äußern sich die S zu verschiedenen interessanten, persönlichen und aktuellen Themen im Plenum. Dabei werden die S-Antworten immer wieder erneut von L aufgegriffen und vertieft, an weitere Mit-S weitergegeben bzw. ausführlicher behandelt.

Snowball-Verfahren — Die S arbeiten zunächst paarweise und diskutieren ein Thema, stellen ein Schreibprodukt vor o. Ä. Beide müssen sich innerhalb einer vorgegebenen Zeit auf eine Meinung, eine Idee, ein Schreibprodukt etc. einigen. Dann diskutieren zwei S-Paare miteinander und müssen sich wiederum einigen. Im nächsten Schritt diskutieren zwei Vierer-Teams und müssen sich wieder einig werden. Zuletzt erfolgt der Austausch der Meinungen oder Ergebnisse im Plenum.

Speed dating — Entspricht im Prinzip der Idee des ▶ Double circle mit dem Unterschied, dass die S nicht in einem Kreis sondern in zwei sich anschauenden Linien interagieren.

Speed reading	Um das *Scanning* zu üben bzw. um zu lernen, dass man auch dem Layout bzw. der grafischen Gestaltung grundlegende Informationen entnehmen kann, bietet sich das *Speed reading*-Verfahren an. Die S arbeiten individuell. L erklärt, dass sie in einem Wettbewerb stehen und die erforderlichen Informationen (3–4 Fragen werden an Tafel notiert) so schnell wie möglich finden sollen. Alle S beginnen auf ein Signal hin gleichzeitig zu lesen. Wer alle Antworten gefunden hat, lehnt sich zurück bzw. gibt ein Handzeichen, sodass L erkennt, wer schon fertig ist und den schnellsten S ermitteln kann.

Alternativ blendet L einen gut lesbaren, überschaubaren Text über Smartboard oder Beamer für kurze Zeit ein. Die S nennen die Hauptaussage und/oder möglichst viele Details und tauschen sich darüber im Plenum aus. Die kurze Lesephase kann mehrmals wiederholt werden.

Split viewing	L teilt das Plenum in zwei Gruppen ein. Die eine Hälfte sieht und hört das Video, die andere Gruppe hört nur den Soundtrack, da diese S sich zur Rückwand drehen. L erklärt, dass die sehende Gruppe nach dem *viewing* den anderen die Handlung erklären muss und dass die hörende Gruppe spekulieren soll, was geschieht bzw. sich Fragen überlegt. Nach dem Anschauen des Videoclips beginnen zunächst die „Hörer" mit dem Austausch von Ideen, dann erklären oder ergänzen die „Seher", was genau passiert ist. Für den Austausch bietet sich im Sinne der Erhöhung der individuellen Sprechzeit PA an.

Variante: Man kann durch die Verwendung von Kopfhörern die Klasse auch in reine „Seher" und „Hörer" einteilen. Die „Hörer" drehen sich wie oben einfach um. Die „Seher" blockieren den Soundtrack durch das Hören von Musik und sehen das Video nur. Bei dieser Variante haben beide Gruppen ein Informationsdefizit und können sich über die Bedeutungen, die sie entweder aus dem Gesehenen oder aus dem Gehörten erschlossen haben, vergleichen.

Sprachmittlung	▶ Mediation
Standbildmethode	▶ Freeze-frame
Stimmungs-barometer	Diese Methode wird i.d.R. zu Beginn oder zum Abschluss einer Gruppenarbeit angewandt, um die anfängliche bzw. abschließende Stimmungslage der Mitglieder zu erfassen und zu veranschaulichen. Die moderierende Person stellt hierzu ein Plakat bereit, auf welchem z. B. eine Sonne, Nebel und Gewitterwolken abgebildet sind. Die Gruppenmitglieder erhalten die Gelegenheit, je einen Punkt neben diejenige Abbildung zu kleben bzw. zeichnen, die ihrer Stimmung am ehesten entspricht. Das entstandene Stimmungsbild dient der Gruppe als Diskussionsgrundlage und sofern die Methode regelmäßig durchgeführt wird, kann eine langfristige Entwicklung der Gruppenstimmung protokolliert werden.
Students as experts	▶ Binnendifferenziertes Arbeiten
Stummer Impuls	Ein stummer Impuls kann ein Bild, ein Gegenstand oder ein angeschriebenes Wort bzw. mehrere Wörter sein. L gibt den stummen Impuls, ohne zu sprechen und wartet auf die Äußerungen der S. So kann beispielsweise ein neues Thema gut eingeleitet werden, zu dem die S schon erste Ideen äußern.
Stummes Schreibgespräch	Hierbei kommunizieren zwei oder mehrere S schriftlich und bei absolutem Schweigen miteinander. Die S geben ein Blatt herum und jede/r von ihnen schreibt nacheinander eine These zu einem Thema, eine Antwort auf eine Frage, einen Kommentar o. Ä. auf und gibt das Blatt dann weiter. Der/Die Nächste schreibt eine Ergänzung oder eine neue Stellungnahme dazu, die wichtig für das Thema ist. Auch Schlagworte, Zeichnungen oder Symbole sind erlaubt.

Auf diese Weise lassen sich Ideen und Antworten zu einem Thema entwickeln, Beziehungen aufbauen und vertiefen sowie ein Gedankenaustausch entwickeln. Falls die Ergebnisse im Plenum präsentiert werden sollen, bietet es sich an, dass die beteiligten S sich auf eine festgelegte Anzahl von Ideen oder Thesen einigen, die ihnen am wichtigsten oder prägnantesten erscheinen.

Variante: Es besteht auch die Möglichkeit, dass jede/r S auf einem eigenen Blatt anfängt und die Blätter reihum zur Kommentierung weitergegeben werden. Wenn am Ende alle jedes Blatt kommentiert haben, lesen alle die Kommentare auf ihrem eigenen Blatt.

Swap cards	Bei der Methode *Swap cards* bewegen sich die S im Raum. Dabei haben sie eine Karte mit einer Frage, einer Wendung, Wortschatz etc. in der Hand. Nach einem akustischen Signal durch L finden die S mit-

hilfe einer ▶ Market-place activity einen Partner / eine Partnerin. Dann bearbeiten sie die Aufgaben (S1 fragt S2, S2 fragt S1). Die Karten werden getauscht und die Lernenden suchen sich neue Partner/innen. Um einen zügigen Verlauf zu gewährleisten, werden die Lernenden darauf hingewiesen, immer eine/n Mit-S in ihrer unmittelbaren Nähe zu wählen.

Szenisches Spielen	▶ Scenic play
Think-Pair-Share	Diese kooperative Lernform dient den S dazu, von einer individuellen zu einer gemeinsamen Lösung zu gelangen. Ablauf:

1. EA: Die S denken allein über die Aufgabenstellung nach und machen sich ggf. Notizen.
2. PA: Zwei S besprechen ihre Notizen und kommen zu einer gemeinsamen Lösung.
3. GA: Zwei Paare bilden eine Vierergruppe, die gemeinsam ihre Lösungen bespricht. Eine andere Möglichkeit ist, dass die Paare ihre Lösungen im Plenum vorstellen.

L sollte für jeden Arbeitsschritt ein Zeitlimit setzen.

Three truths, two lies Die S formulieren Sätze, z. B. über ein Bild oder einen Text. Dabei achten sie darauf, mindestens zwei inhaltlich falsche Sätze zu bilden. Die Anzahl an falschen und richtigen Sätzen kann von L variiert werden, sollte aber immer klar vorgegeben sein.

Es empfiehlt sich, diese Sätze aufschreiben zu lassen, da es den S oft schwerfällt, sich die falschen Sätze zu merken. Anschließend können die Sätze im Plenum vorgestellt werden und die Klasse rät, welche Sätze falsch sind.

Thumbs up (Daumenabfrage) Bei dieser Feedback-Methode geben alle S auf Zeichen von L hin mit geschlossenen Augen mit ihrem Daumen eine i.d.R. dreistufige Wertung (*thumbs up* – "neutral" – *down*) zu einer Fragestellung ab (z. B. *Were you able to understand the text/presentation?*). Wenn alle ihre Wertung abgegeben haben, bittet L die S, die Augen wieder zu öffnen und sich die Bewertungen der Klasse anzusehen. Wer möchte, darf sich zu seiner eigenen Bewertung anschließend verbal äußern (z. B. begründen, warum die Bewertung so abgegeben wurde). Auf diese Weise lassen sich Auswertungsprozesse effektiv nonverbal und unter Einbeziehung aller S initiieren.

Ticket vote Die Methode des *Ticket vote* dient dazu, eine Einschätzung der Lerngruppe zu einem Film zu erhalten. Zu diesem Zweck erhält jede/r S eine (imaginäre) Eintrittskarte, die nach dem Sehen in vorbereitete Schachteln geworfen wird. Die Schachteln können zwei (+, -) oder drei (+, 0, -) Kategorien haben. Das Ergebnis kann als Grundlage zu einer Diskussion über den Film dienen, die z. B. als ▶ Hot seat organisiert werden kann.

Total Physical Response (TPR) Das Konzept der *Total Physical Response* (*TPR*) beruht auf der Einbeziehung von Körpersprache und Bewegung, um das Hörverstehen der S zu fördern. *TPR* spricht in besonderem Maße S mit Sprechhemmungen oder geringem Sprachinventar an, die mithilfe der Methode die Fremdsprache handelnd umsetzen und so Erfolgserlebnisse erzielen.

Die S reagieren auf eine Anweisung von L oder einem anderen S nonverbal, indem sie diese in Bewegung umsetzen. Die Anweisungen sollten z. B. durch Gestik oder den Einsatz von Realgegenständen verständlich gemacht werden. Durch mehrfache Wiederholung kann die Behaltensleistung gesteigert werden, indem Handlung und Sprache nachhaltig miteinander verknüpft werden.

Two-minute talk ▶ One-minute presentation

Two stars and a wish Diese Feedback-Methode birgt einen hohen Grad an Wertschätzung und sprachlicher Würdigung, da grundsätzlich die erbrachte Leistung mit mehr Positiva im Vordergrund steht. Es werden zunächst zwei positive Aspekte benannt (= *stars*) und anschließend ein Optimierungswunsch (= *wish*).

Uniform day Um zu erfahren, wie sich das Tragen einer Uniform anfühlen kann, lohnt es sich, einen *Uniform day* durchzuführen. Hierzu spricht sich die Klasse auf Englisch ab, was sie am *Uniform day* anziehen kann. Z. B. eine schwarze Hose und ein weißes T-Shirt, wobei das Ziel ist, eine einheitliche Kleidungsfarbe jeweils für ein Oberteil und ein Unterteil zu finden. Es lohnt sich, die S darauf hinzuweisen, dass die

Kleidung möglichst schick/gepflegt sein sollte, gleichzeitig wird darauf hingewiesen, dass keine neue Kleidung gekauft werden soll. Ob eine Krawatte getragen wird, sollte im Einzelfall entschieden werden.

Der *Uniform day* sollte an einem Tag sein, an dem auch Englischunterricht stattfindet. So können Klassenfotos in Uniform gemacht und die Eindrücke gemeinsam reflektiert werden. Es bietet sich hier z. B. an, über die Gefühle zu sprechen, die man beim Tragen der Uniform hat. Da sich diese Gefühle oft von Unsicherheit (zu Hause) zu Freude (in der Schule) verwandeln, lohnt es sich auch, die S reflektieren zu lassen, wie sie sich vor der Schule gefühlt haben. Die authentischste Uniform kann gekürt werden, um den Mut der S zu belohnen, die besonders schicke Kleidung tragen. Es sollte hierbei jedoch unbedingt sensibel auf das soziale Gefüge in der Klasse geachtet werden.

Vokabelarbeit	Die S sollten möglichst früh damit beginnen, sich eine Vokabelsammlung anzulegen. Dies kann z. B. mithilfe eines Vokabelhefts oder eines selbst angelegten *Vocab files* geschehen, in das die S auch kleine Bilder und Skizzen zur Verdeutlichung der Bedeutung einfügen. Neues Vokabular übertragen die S von der ▶ Vokabeltafel sofort in ihre Vokabelsammlung. Für bestimmte Wortgruppen bzw. thematischen Wortschatz empfiehlt es sich zusätzlich, *Wordwebs* ähnlich einer ▶ Mindmap anzulegen. Dabei sammeln die S Vokabeln, die sie durch Verbinden in Beziehung zueinander setzen bzw. thematisch gruppieren. Die *Wordwebs* können dem *Vocab file* hinzugefügt werden.
Vokabelrennen	Für das Spiel *Vokabelrennen* bilden die S zunächst Kleingruppen. Die S einer Gruppe spielen gegeneinander. L bestimmt, welche Gruppe beginnt und gibt dieser Gruppe eine Vokabel. Der/Die S aus der Gruppe, welche/r die Vokabel am schnellsten errät, darf sich zum nächsten Tisch bewegen. Dort tritt S nun gegen die S dieser Gruppe an. Wieder wird eine Vokabel erfragt und nur der/die schnellste S darf zur nächsten Tischgruppe weitergehen. Dies wird wiederholt, bis ein/e S wieder am Ursprungstisch ankommt.
Vokabeltafel	Wird mithilfe einer Tafel gelehrt, bietet es sich an, eine feste Tafelseite für Vokabeln zu reservieren, die die S immer abschreiben, sobald L dort neue Vokabeln anschreibt. Beim Semantisieren von Wortschatz (▶ Semantisierung) sollte L stets die Übersetzung mit anschreiben, die die S dann ebenfalls übertragen.
Voting finger	▶ Democratic vote
Wachsende Gruppe	▶ Pyramidendiskussion
Word memory	Der Wortschatz (einzelne Wörter, Wortgruppen) wird senkrecht an der Tafel notiert und nacheinander im Chor gesprochen. Nach jedem Chorsprechen wird ein Wort / eine Wortgruppe von der Tafel gewischt. Die abgewischten Wörter werden jedoch beim Chorsprechen weiterhin (auswendig) mit aufgesagt. Am Ende ist der gesamte Wortschatz von der Tafel gewischt worden und wird komplett auswendig (nacheinander) im Chor gesprochen. Zusätzlich kann der verwendete Wortschatz anschließend im Kontext versprachlicht werden (z. B. indem Beispiele oder Definitionen genannt werden).
Words in the air	Bei der Methode *Words in the air* arbeiten die S in PA. Sie schreiben ein Wort in die Luft, das der Partner / die Partnerin erraten soll. Es empfiehlt sich, den zu verwendenden Wortschatz einzuschränken, sodass das Raten leichter fällt und der richtige Wortschatz geübt wird. Diese Aktivität eignet sich besonders gut als *Warm-up* und zur Vokabelwiederholung. Sie kann mit weiteren Bewegungen verknüpft werden, wenn der/die ratende S das Wort z. B. nachspielen oder mit einer Aktivität verknüpfen soll.
World Cafe	Bei dieser Methode gibt es je nach Themen in der Klasse mehrere Gruppentische, die wahlweise mit Flipchartbögen, Packpapier und Stiften ausgestattet sind. Das jeweilige Thema der Gruppe steht in der Mitte der Bögen. Ein/e S fungiert als *host* (Gastgeber/in), d. h. S moderiert die Diskussion und verbleibt bei dem Wechsel der anderen Gruppenmitglieder am Tisch, um die nächste Gruppe über die bisherigen Ergebnisse zu informieren und den weiteren Prozess zu moderieren. Der *host* stellt das Thema vor, die anderen Gruppenmitglieder haben nun Zeit, nachzudenken, zu diskutieren und anschließend ihre Überlegungen auf die Bögen zu schreiben. Diese dienen nun im weite-

ren Verlauf als Diskussionsgrundlage. Der *host* hält ggf. weitere Ergebnisse fest. Auf ein Signal von L wechseln die Gäste den Tisch und werden an dem neuen Tisch vom *host* über die bisherigen Ergebnisse informiert. Nun beginnt der oben beschriebene Ablauf erneut. Zum Abschluss der Diskussionsrunden kehren die S an ihren Ausgangstisch zurück, tauschen ihre Erfahrungen aus und berichten dem Plenum von den Ergebnissen ihrer Gruppe.

Wortschatz-semantisierung

▶ Semantisierung

Zählen in der Gruppe

Ziel dieses kooperativen Spiels ist es, bis zu einer bestimmten Zahl zu zählen, die von L festlegt wird. Diese Zahl sollte nicht zu hoch sein, also etwa 20–25. Das Zählen erfolgt nach folgenden Regeln:

1. Die S dürfen sich nicht austauschen oder vorher absprechen. Dazu kann vereinbart werden, dass sie die Augen schließen.
2. Jede/r S darf zählen.
3. Es darf immer nur eine Zahl genannt werden, d. h. kein/e Mitspieler/in darf zwei aufeinanderfolgende Zahlen nennen. Erst nachdem ein/e andere/r S dran war, darf man erneut mitzählen.
4. Wenn zwei S gleichzeitig eine Zahl nennen, muss die Gruppe vorn vorne mit dem Zählen beginnen.

Zufallsgenerator

Mithilfe dieser Methode kann L nach Zufallskriterien S auswählen, die eine Aufgabe, ein Projekt o. Ä. präsentieren sollen. Zu diesem Zweck stehen zunächst alle S auf und L nennt ein Kriterium. Falls S dieses erfüllen, setzen sie sich hin. Die Person, die am Ende noch steht, präsentiert die Aufgabe.

Tipp: Um zu verhindern, dass sich am Ende alle S setzen können, wählt L Sätze mit Superlativen (z. B. *The youngest / the tallest / ...*).

Bus stop

Lighthouse 1 | Lehrkräftefassung Plus
Illustration: Shutterstock.com/Nemanja Cosovic

1 WALK AROUND Find out about other students.

a) Talk to three different students like this:

You:

1 Hello! I'm … What's your name?

3 I'm … (years old). I'm from …
   Where are you from?

5 I like …
   Nice to meet you.

Your partner:

2 Hi! I'm … I'm … (years old).
   How old are you?

4 I'm from … (too).
   I like … What about you?

6 Nice to meet you too. Bye!

b) Write the answers in the table[1].

Name?			
How old?			
From?			
Likes?			

c) Early finisher Look at your table again. Can you find two or more students with the same answers?

How old? _____ and _____ are _____ years old.

From? _____ and _____ are from _____.

Like? _____ and _____ like _____.

2 What about Scout?

My name is _____.

I'm from _____.

I like _____.

I'm _____ years old.

I'm a _____.

3 What about you?

Make a poster about you. Write sentences. Find some photos or pictures if you like[2].

---

[1] table *Tabelle*   [2] if you like *wenn du möchtest*

Lighthouse 1 | Lehrkräftefassung Plus
Illustration: Cornelsen/Irina Zinner
Fotos: stock.adobe.com/wong stock (Brighton); stock.adobe.com/titelio (Möwe);
stock.adobe.com/robyn mac (Sandwich)

PREPARATION Cut out the activity cards (this page) and the animal cards (next page).

INSTRUCTIONS: Play in two teams. First choose an activity card. Then choose an animal card.
Now mime, draw or make a noise like the animal on your card. Can your partners guess your animal?

HELP You can use *Wordbank 3*, p. 195 in your English book.

Activity cards

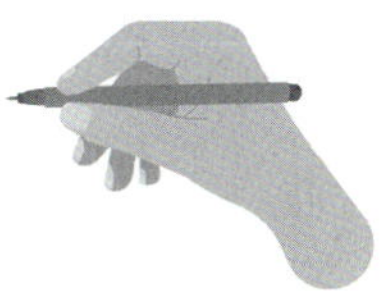 Draw an animal!	 WOOF! Make an animal noise!	 Mime an animal!
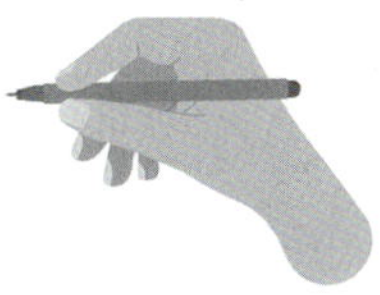 Draw an animal!	 WOOF! Make an animal noise!	 Mime an animal!
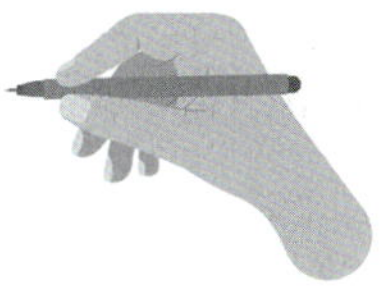 Draw an animal!	 WOOF! Make an animal noise!	 Mime an animal!
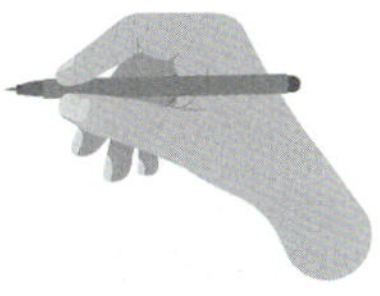 Draw an animal!	 WOOF! Make an animal noise!	 Mime an animal!
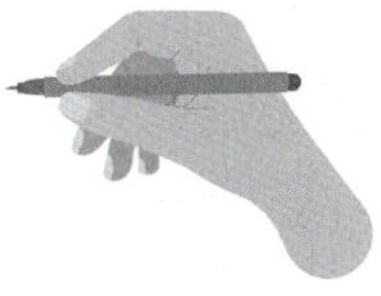 Draw an animal!	 WOOF! Make an animal noise!	 Mime an animal!
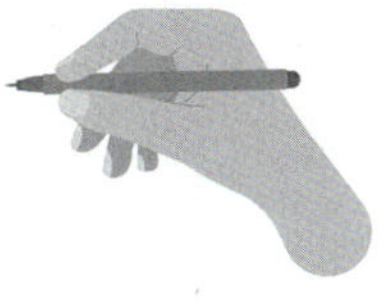 Draw an animal!	 WOOF! Make an animal noise!	 Mime an animal!
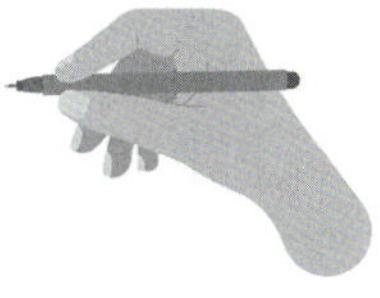 Draw an animal!	 WOOF! Make an animal noise!	 Mime an animal!

Lighthouse 1 | Lehrkräftefassung Plus
Illustrationen: stock.adobe.com/Aletheia Shade (WOOF); Shutterstock.com/WinWin artlab (Hand);
Shutterstock.com/Vector_KIF (Pantomime)

PREPARATION Cut out the animal cards (this page) and the activity cards (next page).

INSTRUCTIONS: Play in two teams. First choose an activity card. Then choose an animal card.
Now mime, draw or make a noise like the animal on your card. Can your partners guess your animal?

HELP You can use *Wordbank 3*, p. 195 in your English book.

Animal cards

a lion	a cat	a horse
a parrot	a dog	a snake
an elephant	a monkey	a crocodile
a rhino	a bear	an owl
a seagull	a meercat	a duck
a tiger	a butterfly	a spider
a whale	a dolphin	a penguin

Cornelsen

Lighthouse 1 | Lehrkräftefassung Plus
Illustrationen: Shutterstock.com/Nadya_Art (cat, dog, butterfly); Shutterstock.com/Andrew Krasovitckii (alle anderen)

1 More hobbies

a) `Early finisher` Find three more[1] hobbies and sports.
Draw the pictures and write a code.
Swap with your partner and find the correct words.

My code

a	e	i	o	u

In code: _____   _____   _____

The word is _____   _____   _____

▼
- -
▲ *fold here*

`More help` You can use *Wordbank 4*, p. 196 in your English Book.

2 DOUBLE CIRCLE Your free time

a) Write sentences about your hobbies and sports.

My favourite hobby/sport is _____.

😊 I like / I love _____ too.

☹ I don't like _____.

b) Stand in two circles. Talk to a partner. One circle moves to find a new partner.

My favourite sport is … What about you?	😊 I like / I love …	☹ I don't like …

3 True or false?

Work in a group of four. Say a right and a wrong sentence about you. Let your partners guess.

I like broccoli.   *Yes, that's right/true.*   *No, that's wrong/false.*

---

[1] three more *drei weitere*

1 Where's Scout?

a) Find these pictures of Scout in your book. Write the page number in the table[1].

b) Write the name of the part of the book in the table.

c) Write a sentence in German about what you can find in this part of the book.

Scout's hats	Page	Title of the part	Was kannst du in diesem Teil deines Buches finden?
	_____	_____ _____	_____ _____
	_____	_____ _____	_____ _____
	_____	_____ _____	_____ _____
	_____	_____ _____	_____ _____
	_____	_____ _____	_____ _____
	_____	_____ _____	_____ _____
	_____	_____ _____	_____ _____

✂---

More help You can use these sentences for **c)**.

In diesem Teil finde ich alle neuen Vokabeln nach Units geordnet. • Das ist das alphabetische Wörterverzeichnis. • Hier finde ich englische Sätze und ihre deutschen Übersetzungen. • Hier finde ich eine Übersicht über alle Teile des Buchs. • Hier finde ich englische Wörter, die deutschen Wörtern sehr ähnlich sind. • In diesem Teil finde ich Hinweise zur Grammatik / zu den Regeln der englischen Sprache. • Auf diesen Seiten bekomme ich wichtige Tipps, wie ich z. B. Wortschatz lernen kann.

[1] table *Tabelle*

1 LISTENING Four students at Varndean school

a) Make groups of three partners. Each partner chooses one category[1] (How old? / Hobby / Sport).

🔊 Listen to four students from Brighton and tick (✓) the right answers.

Name	Sunita Chandra		
How old?	☐ 10	☐ 11	☐ 12
Hobby	☐ coding	☐ drawing	☐ reading
Sport	☐ badminton	☐ dancing	☐ yoga

Name	Noah Williams		
How old?	☐ 10	☐ 11	☐ 12
Hobby	☐ listening to music	☐ reading	☐ taking photos
Sport	☐ basketball	☐ football	☐ walking

Name	Zane Adebayo		
How old?	☐ 10	☐ 11	☐ 12
Hobby	☐ coding	☐ cooking	☐ listening to music
Sport	☐ basketball	☐ football	☐ swimming

Name	Lily Hall		
How old?	☐ 10	☐ 11	☐ 12
Hobby	☐ drawing	☐ reading	☐ listening to music
Sport	☐ dancing	☐ parkour	☐ yoga

b) Tell your answers to your two partners. Then tick (✓) your partners' answers in the table.

> *Sunita is … years old. Noah …*

> *Zane's favourite sport is …*

> *Noah's favourite hobby is …*

2 Choose Sunita, Noah, Zane or Lily. What's the same or what's different for you?

a) Write sentences about you and one of the four students. Use the phrases in the box.

> Sunita / Noah / Zane / Lily is … years old. I'm … too. / But I'm …
> I like … too. / I don't like …
> Sunita's / Noah's / Zane's / Lily's favourite hobby / sport is … My favourite hobby / sport is …

_____

_____

_____

_____

b) Read the sentences to a partner.

_____

[1] category *Kategorie*

My timetable – partner A

Complete the timetable. Walk around the room and ask the students.

What's lesson 4 on Tuesday? → I don't know. It's history.

Lesson	Monday	Tuesday	Wednesday	Thursday	Friday
registration and assembly					
1		computing	art	science	French
2	maths		PE	geography	
break					
3	PE	English		maths	English
4		history	computing	maths	art
lunch					
5	science	French	maths		music
6	history	geography		French	design and technology

My timetable – partner B

Complete the timetable. Walk around the room and ask the students.

What's lesson 4 on Tuesday? → I don't know. It's history.

Lesson	Monday	Tuesday	Wednesday	Thursday	Friday
registration and assembly					
1	English		art	science	French
2	maths	computing		geography	maths
break					
3	PE	English		maths	
4	PE	history	computing		art
lunch					
5		French	maths	French	music
6	history	geography	history	French	design and technology

My timetable – partner C

Complete the timetable. Walk around the room and ask the students.

What's lesson 4 on Tuesday? → I don't know. It's history.

Lesson	Monday	Tuesday	Wednesday	Thursday	Friday
registration and assembly					
1	English	computing	art	science	French
2		computing	PE	geography	maths
break					
3			design and technology	maths	
4	PE	history		maths	art
lunch					
5	science	French	maths	French	music
6	history	geography	computing	French	

My timetable – partner D

Complete the timetable. Walk around the room and ask the students.

What's lesson 4 on Tuesday? → I don't know. It's history.

Lesson	Monday	Tuesday	Wednesday	Thursday	Friday
registration and assembly					
1		computing	art	science	French
2	maths			geography	maths
break					
3	PE	English	design and technology	maths	English
4	PE	history	computing	maths	art
lunch					
5	science	French		French	music
6		geography	history	French	

INSTRUCTIONS:

1 Every student gets a card and translates[1] the adjective.
2 The students walk around the room.
3 When they hear a signal, they find a partner.
4 They exchange information.
5 When they hear a signal, they swap cards.

Start again …

> What's **hungry** in German?

> It's **hungrig**.

What's **brave** in German? It's "_____".	What's **cool** in German? It's "_____".	What's **clever** in German? It's "_____".
What's **friendly** in German? It's "_____".	What's **happy** in German? It's "_____".	What's **helpful** in German? It's "_____".
What's **kind** in German? It's "_____".	What's **nice** in German? It's "_____".	What's **mean** in German? It's "_____".
What's _____ in German? It's "_____".	What's _____ in German? It's "_____".	What's _____ in German? It's "_____".

[1] (to) translate *übersetzen*

Vocabulary cards

a) **PREPARATION:** Choose words and phrases from your VOCAB FILE.
INSTRUCTIONS: Work in a group and make cards. Cut them out.

Draw a ... _____

_____

Open ... _____

_____

Act out ... _____

_____

What's your favourite ... _____

_____

b) Play your game with your group. Use your cards and the board on **p. 47** in your textbook.

Take a card.

Whose turn is it?

It's your turn.

Move to the next room.

Sorry, that's wrong.

c) Swap cards with another group. Play the game again with their cards.

1 LISTENING **At break**

a) D • B • C • A

(4 points)

(6 points)

b)

Name	Favourite lesson today	Why?
Zane	geography	The teacher is nice.
Sunita	computing	It's cool.
Lily	PE	It's fun.

10–9	8–7	6–5	4–0

2 SPEAKING **Mr Lee's desk**

(3 points)

In the picture I can see a white computer, **five red glue sticks, four green exercise books and three rulers.**

3 WORDS **In the classroom**

1. Can you **help** me?
2. Can I **open** the window?
3. Can you **say** that again, please, Ms Miller?
4. **Sorry** I'm late, Ms Miller.
5. I don't **understand** the question.
6. Can I **go** to the toilet, please?

(6 points)

9–8	7–6	5	4

4 LANGUAGE **Sunita's email**

(8 points)

Hi, Jasmine!

How (1) **are** you? I (2) **'m/am** now in class 7C at Varndean School. My timetable (3) **is** great! English lessons (4) **are** on Mondays, Tuesdays and Fridays. I have two music lessons. One (5) **is** in lesson 4 on Tuesdays and one (6) **is** in lesson 1 on Fridays. Science lessons (my favourite lessons) (7) **are** on Tuesdays and Wednesdays. And PE (8) **is** in lessons 5 and 6 on Thursdays. Is your timetable OK? What's your favourite day?

See you

Sunita

8–7	6	5–4	3–0

5 LANGUAGE **Jasmine's school**

(7 points)

This is my school in Hove. The students (1) **aren't / are not** in the building because it's break.
The uniform is nice – the blazer (2) **is** red and the tie (3) **is** blue.
There are two seagulls – they (4) **are** friendly. But they like our sandwiches!
The canteen (5) **is** very big and the food there is great. But the classrooms are in building 1 – they (6) **aren't / are not** near the canteen. The sports hall (7) **isn't / is not** in building 1 – it's near the canteen.

6 WRITING **Seb's school**

(5 points)

(Lösungsbeispiel) Hi, Lily! My school is Schiller School. It's **in Bochum. It isn't big. The students are friendly. My class teacher is Ms Lang. My favourite place is the sports hall. (See you, Seb)**

12–11	10–8	7–6	5–0

7 READING Zane's homework

(5 points)

b) 1 Mr King is **busy**.
2 Sunita is **helpful/clever** and **clever/helpful**.
3 Zane is **sad** then **happy**.

c) 1 Mr King is the **music teacher**.
2 Mr King can talk **at break**.
3 Zane likes **music**.
4 Zane's computer isn't **new**.
5 Sunita is good with **computers**.

(5 points)

😄	🙂	😏	😫
10–9	8–7	6–5	4–0

8 STUDY SKILLS All about Lily

(9 points)

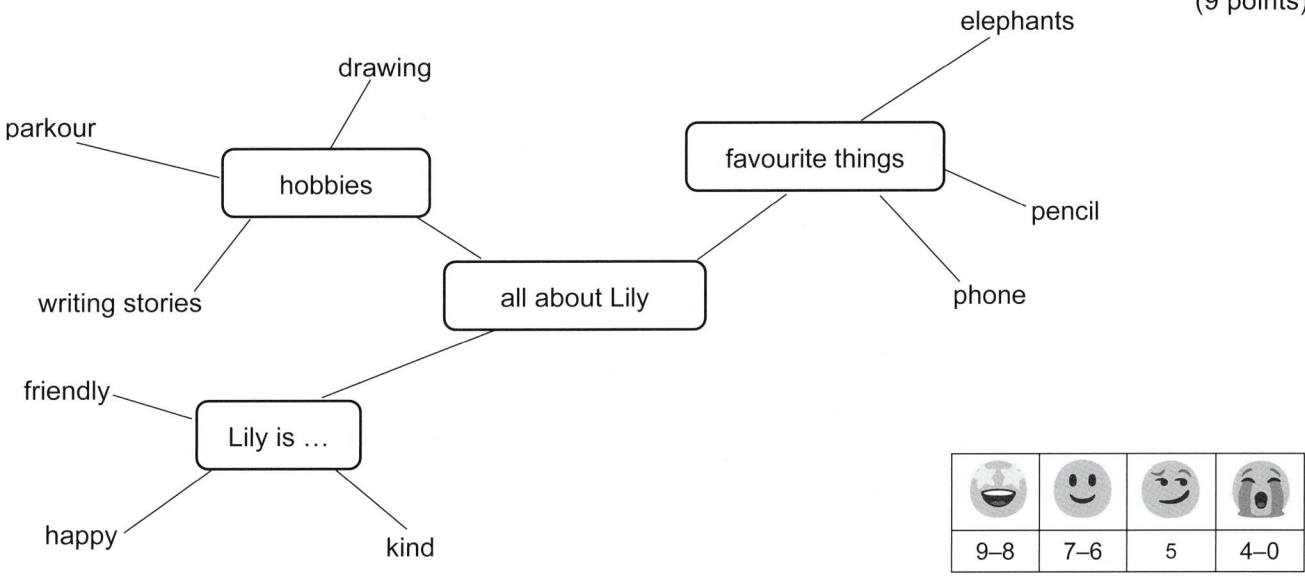

😄	🙂	😏	😫
9–8	7–6	5	4–0

9 READING AND WORDS Noah's poster

a) 1 C • 2 A • 3 D • 4 B

(4 points)

b) 1 This is my timetable. My favourite **subject/lesson** is maths.
2 This is the goat club. It's my favourite **place/club**.
3 This is my uniform. The **tie** is red.
4 This is Mr Lee. He's my class **teacher**. He's nice!

(4 points)

😄	🙂	😏	😫
8–7	6	5–4	3–0

Make your circle of important people

a) Write the names of your important people on the lines. You don't need to write a name on every line. You can draw pictures of your important people. Or you can stick[1] photos of the important people on your circle.

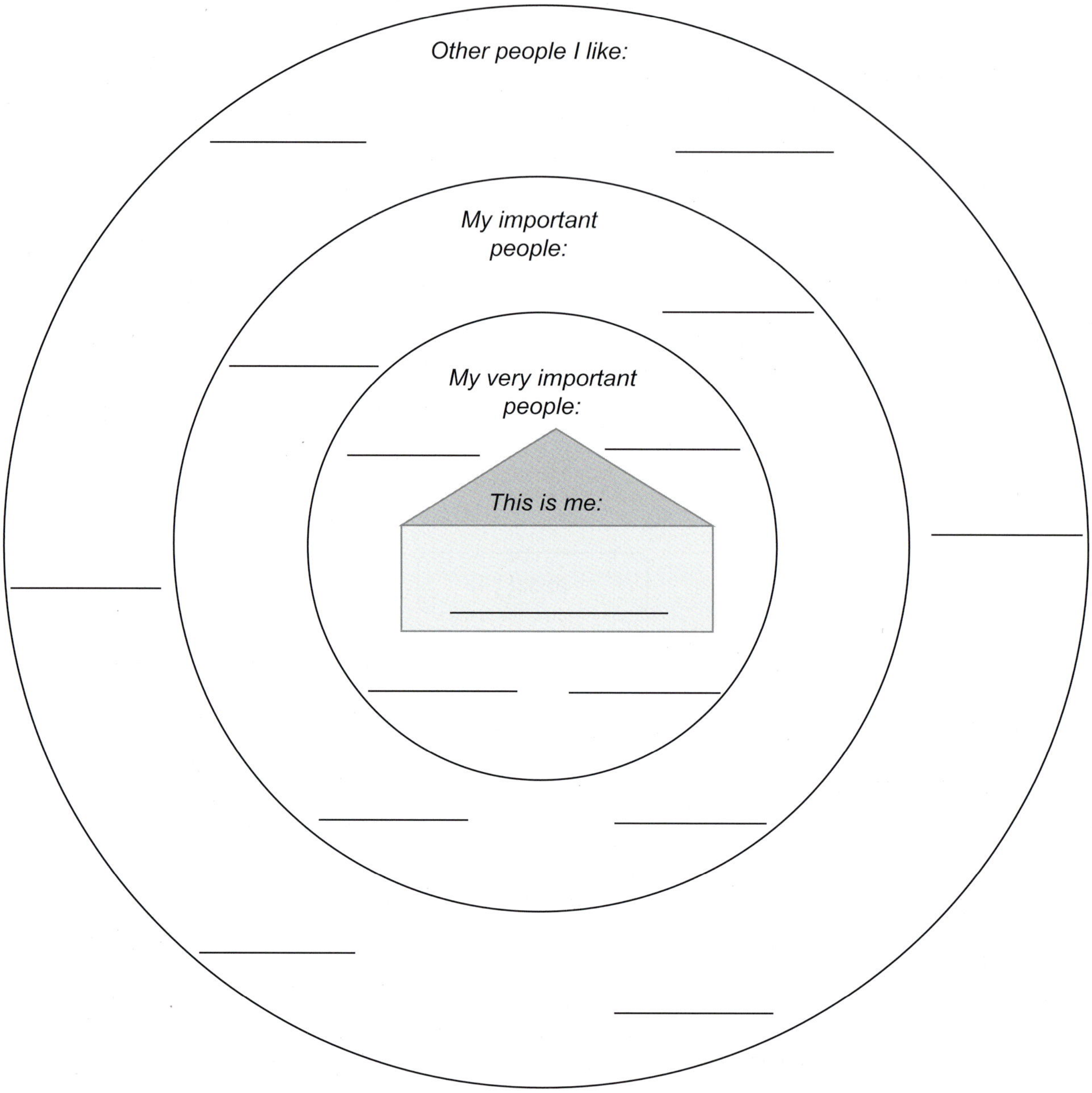

Other people I like:

My important people:

My very important people:

This is me:

b) Tell a partner about your circle of important people.

> *This is _____.*
> *He is my father / brother / grandfather / …*

> *This is _____.*
> *She is my mother / sister / grandmother / …*

> *He / She is important to me because …*
> *… he / she is very nice. /*
> *… he / she is always there for me. /*
> *… I like her / him.*

[1] (to) stick *kleben*

Partner A

Read the first three sentences of the poster to partner B. Your partner completes the missing words in his/her poster. Then listen to your partner and complete your missing words.

MISSING

Our friendly parrot is missing. He's blue and

orange and he's ten years old. He likes talking

and flying, and he's very nice.

But we think he _____ happy because

we have a lot of _____ in our

_____.

It's very _____.

_____ call **07700 900426** if you find him.

✂ -

Partner B

Listen to partner A and complete the missing words in the first three sentences of your poster. Then read the next sentences to your partner and he/she completes the missing words in his/her poster.

MISSING

Our friendly _____ is missing.

He's _____ and orange and he's

_____ years old. He likes _____

and flying, and he's very _____.

But we think he isn't happy because we have

a lot of animals in our home.

It's very loud.

Please call **07700 900426** if you find him.

Lighthouse 1 | Lehrkräftefassung Plus
Foto: Shutterstock.com/Bilal Kocabas

Word and picture cards

PREPARATION Cut out the word and picture cards.

INSTRUCTIONS Play with a partner. Put the cards face down on the table. Turn over two cards. When you have a pair (word and picture), say the word and play again. When you don't have a pair, it's your partner's turn.

lamp	clothes		
wardrobe	sofa		
cushion	computer		
bed	robot		
chocolate	mirror		
shelf	floor		

Lighthouse 1 | Lehrkräftefassung Plus
Illustrationen: Cornelsen/Karen Donnelly

Talk to your partner about your room

a) What is in your partner's room? Listen, then cut out the right things.

b) Listen again. Then put the things in the right place.

c) Show your room to your partner. Does it look right?

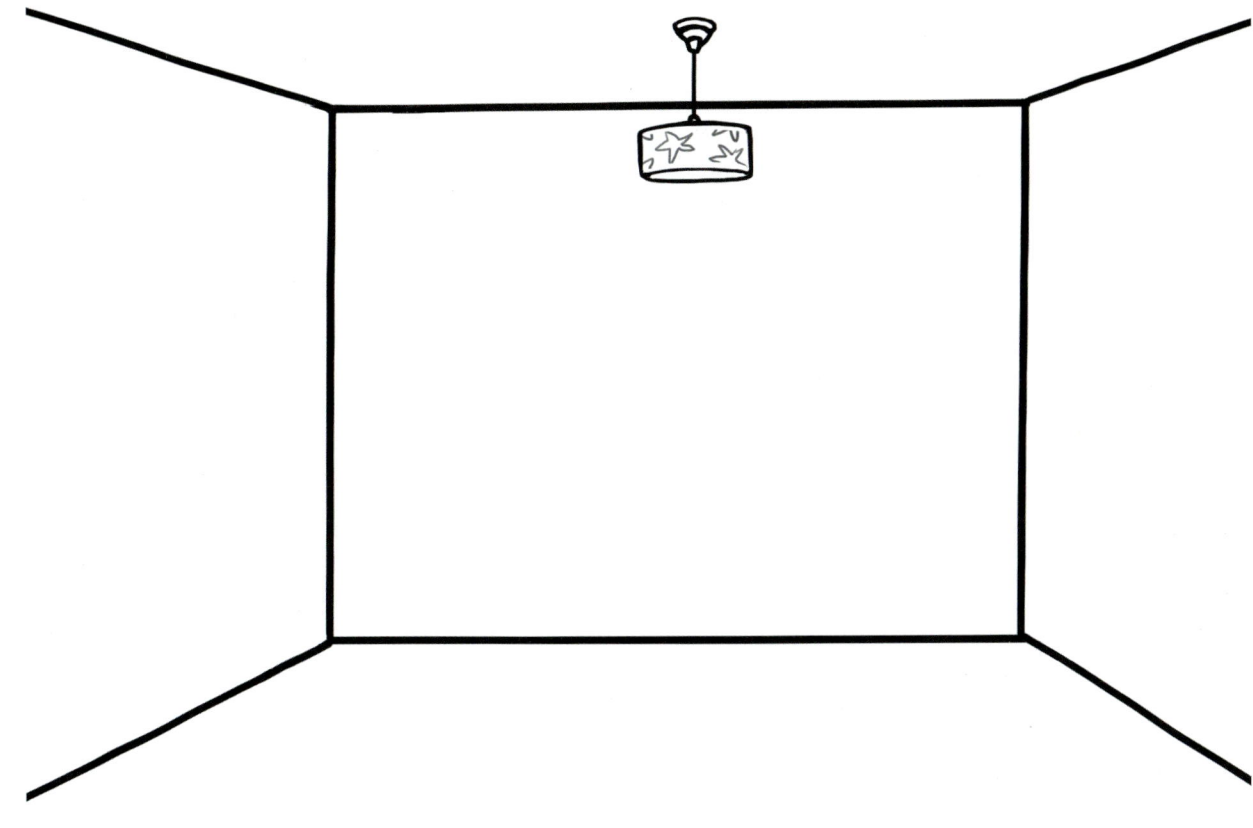

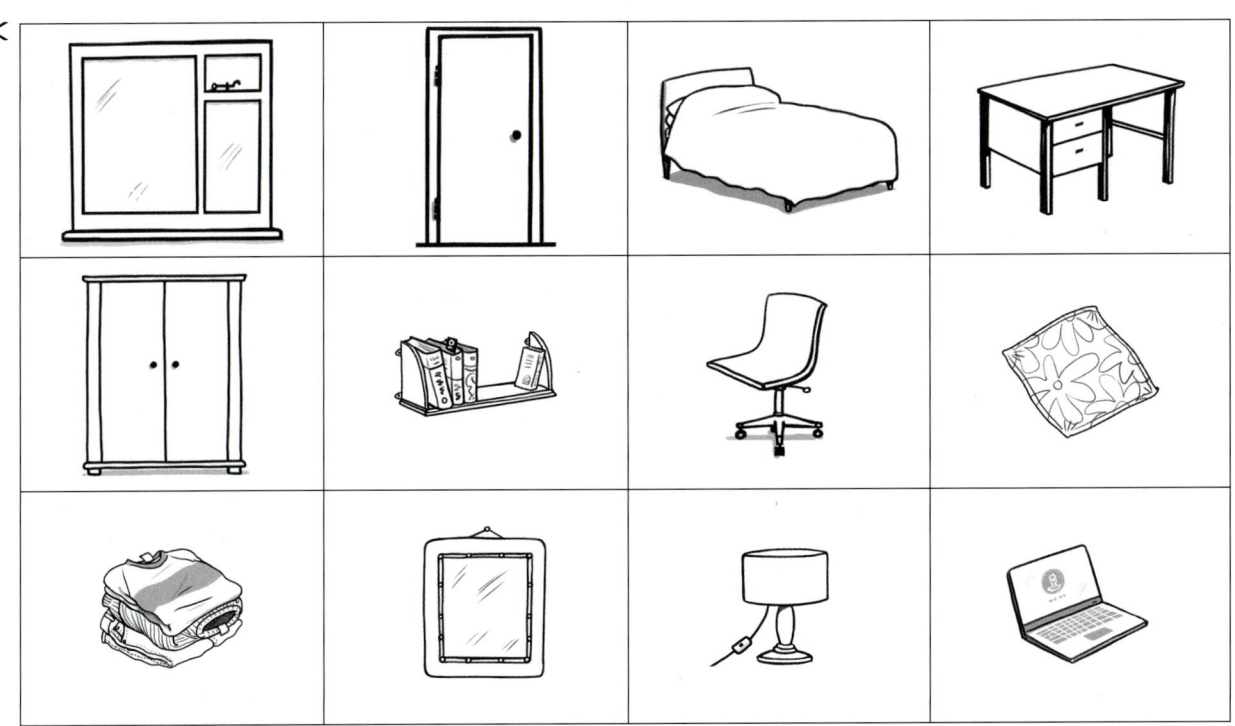

Lighthouse 1 | Lehrkräftefassung Plus
Illustrationen: Cornelsen/Karen Donnelly

My little flat

a) Cut out the lines a–i.

b) Listen to the song and put the lines in the right order.

c) Listen again and check on **p. 74** in your book.

d) Describe the flat in one sentence.

It's _____

e) Do you like the song? Talk to a partner.

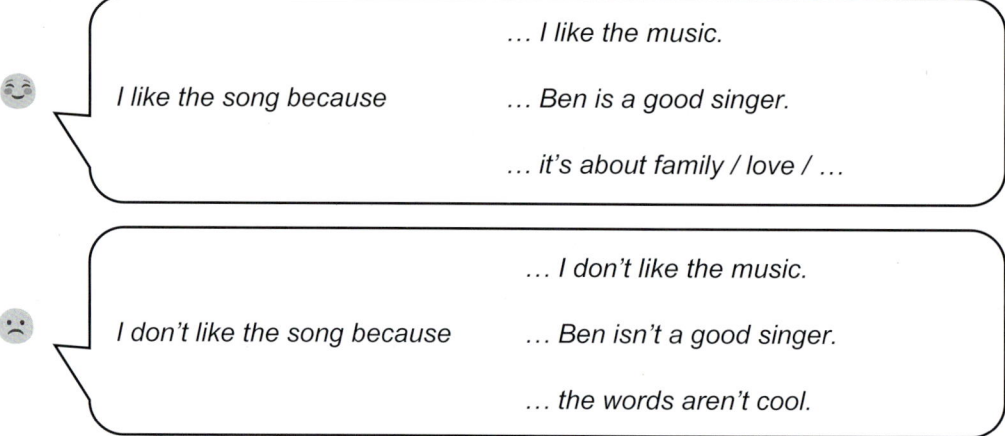

| ☺ | I like the song because | … I like the music.
… Ben is a good singer.
… it's about family / love / … |
| ☹ | I don't like the song because | … I don't like the music.
… Ben isn't a good singer.
… the words aren't cool. |

✂

a	And the living room is always very messy
b	There are two small bedrooms, there aren't three
c	And it isn't new or modern at all
d	There aren't expensive pictures on the wall
e	But my little flat is perfect for me
f	People ask, 'Is your flat big?' No, it's small
g	There's my family, that's enough
h	My little flat is perfect for me
i	Because there's music, there's love

1 WORDS Jay's favourite picture

I can talk about my family.

(9 points)

This is my favourite photo. It's my (1) **family** at my flat. That's my (2) m**um**/m**other**, Priya, and my (3) d**ad**, Rahi, behind the sofa. Next to me is my (4) s**ister**, Anika. She's nice! Then there's my (5) a**unt**, Meera, with her (6) d**aughter**, Sunita. Sunita is my (7) c**ousin**. Behind Sunita is her (8) b**rother**, Nish. My (9) g**randpa**/g**randfather** is on the sofa too. He's my mum's dad.

2 WORDS Priya's pictures

(6 points)

1 A • 2 A • 3 B • 4 B • 5 A • 6 B

15–13	12–10	9–7	6–0

3 On the phone with *FindAPet*

I can talk about pets (questions and short answers).

(6 points)

a) 1 **Are** you good with animals? – Yes, I **am.**
2 **Is** your flat big? – No, it **isn't**.
3 **Is** your home quiet? – Yes, it **is**.
4 **Are** you and your family cat fans? – No, **we aren't / are not**.
5 **Are** your neighbours dog fans? – No, they **aren't / are not**.
6 **Are** you scared of lizards? – No, I**'m not / am not**.

6	5–4	3	2–0

4 WRITING Amira's message to Jay

I can describe my home or dream home.

(5 points)

I live with my parents and my brother. We live in a small house near Bremen. It's a modern house and it's always tidy. There's a kitchen, a living room, two bedrooms and a bathroom. There's a big garden too. Our neighbours are friendly.

(Es sind mehr als 5 Sätze möglich. Für jeden korrekten Satz gibt es einen Punkt.)

5	4	3	2–0

5 LISTENING Noah's room

I can describe my room.

a) C • D • F

(3 points)

b) 1 C • 2 A • 3 B • 4 C

(4 points)

7–6	5	4	3–0

Lighthouse 1 | Lehrkräftefassung Plus
Smileys: Shutterstock.com/Yefym Turkin

6 READING Lily wants a new pet

I can understand a problem and talk about it. ✓

a) D • B • A • E • C

(5 points)

b) B Lily is often alone and wants to play with a pet.

(1 point)

😄	🙂	😏	😫
6	5–4	3	2–0

7 STUDY SKILLS Sunita's message

I can spell words correctly. ✓

(8 points)

1 Ben's music is too **loud** – again!
2 Hi, Lily, the art **homework** is hard – can you help me?
3 Coding isn't easy to **learn**, but it's fun!
4 Nish, thank you for the **chocolate**!
5 Have a **nice** weekend, Anika.
6 Mum, what's for **dinner**? I'm really hungry.
7 Hello, Zane. What's your **address**, please?
8 Hi, Mum. I'm **back** at home now. See you.

8 LISTENING At the vet

(8 points)

1 Pet's name: **Queenie**
   Animal: **hamster**
   Family name: **Fruin**
   Phone number: **4960162**

2 Pet's name: **Hermes**
   Animal: **parrot**
   Family name: **Lui**
   Phone number: **07700900835**

😄	🙂	😏	😫
16–14	13–11	10–8	7–0

9 SPEAKING Zane's dream room

I can present my dream room. ✓

(5 points)

(Lösungsbeispiel) This is Zane's dream room. It's very big and quite messy.
The walls are yellow. There are football posters on the walls.
There's a cat on the bed. There's a guitar on the sofa.
There's a desk with a computer.

(Es sind mehr als 5 Sätze möglich. Für jeden korrekten Satz gibt es einen Punkt.)

😄	🙂	😏	😫
5	4	3	2–0

Talk about Scout's day

a) Match the pictures to the correct verbs.

b) Choose six pictures. Then tell a partner about Scout's day.

> *Scout gets up.*
> *Then she …*

1 get up	
2 eat breakfast	
3 go for a walk	
4 go swimming	
5 go shopping	
6 do her homework	
7 listen to music	

8 take photos
9 meet friends
10 play football
11 sing a song
12 dance
13 watch TV
14 go to bed

Cornelsen

Lighthouse 1 | Lehrkräftefassung Plus
Illustrationen: Cornelsen/Irina Zinner

Play a domino game

PREPARATION Complete the domino cards. Then cut out the cards.

art • computer games • ~~cricket~~ • cycling • dancing • drama • ~~hiking~~ • music •
running • singing • ~~swimming~~ • table tennis • trampolining • windsurfing

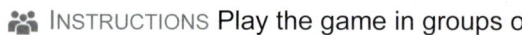 INSTRUCTIONS Play the game in groups of three.

1 Put all the domino cards face down on the table.
2 Each player draws three cards. Put the other cards on a pile[1].
3 The youngest player starts by putting a card face up in the middle.
4 The next player puts down a matching card. Take a card from the pile if you do not have a matching one.

> *I do not have a matching card.*

> *Then take a card from the pile.*

[1] pile *Stapel*

swimming	 🥾	hiking	 🏏
cricket	 🩰		 🎤🎵
	🎨		🎭
	🏓		🎮
	🏄		🎼
	🏃		🤸
	🚴		🏊

Lighthouse 1 | Lehrkräftefassung Plus
Piktogramme: von links oben nach rechts unten: 1: Shutterstock.com/HuHu; 2, 7, 9, 11, 13, 14: Shutterstock.com/
browndogstudios; 3, 4, 5, 6, 10: Shutterstock.com/ArnaPhoto; 8: stock.adobe.com/rashadaliyev;
12: Shutterstock.com/elenabsl

1 Let's meet

a) Write the phrases from the box in the correct place.

> Let's … • No, thanks. • I'd love to. • I'm busy. • Good idea! • Yes, please! •
> Are you free on …? • Sorry, I can't. • What about …?

Ask to meet	Say *yes*	Say *no*

2 Are you free?

BEFORE YOU START WITH THE DOUBLE CIRCLE: Choose four activities and write them in your calendar. You can choose ideas from the box or your own ideas.

> **Ideas:** go to the beach • go to the park • go to the skatepark • go skateboarding • go swimming •
> go cycling • meet at my house/flat • play football • go dancing • play basketball

	Friday	**Saturday**	**Sunday**
9.00	SCHOOL	activity: _____ with: _____	activity: _____ with: _____
1.00	SCHOOL	activity: _____ with: _____	activity: _____ with: _____
5.00	activity: _____ with: _____	activity: _____ with: _____	activity: _____ with: _____

⊠ 3 My plans

Tell your partner about your plans. You can replace *(ersetzen)* the underlined words.

> *Do you have plans for <u>Friday</u> at <u>five</u> o'clock in the <u>afternoon</u>?*

> *Yes, I do. <u>Friday</u> at <u>five</u> o'clock in the <u>afternoon</u> I have plans with <u>Lea</u> to <u>go swimming</u>. What about you?*

> *No, I don't. But I have plans for <u>Sunday</u> at <u>nine</u> o'clock in the <u>morning</u> to <u>go to the beach</u> with <u>Kim</u>. What about you?*

👥 1 Describe the pictures to a partner.

Who can you see in the pictures? How do they feel?
Say at least two sentences for each picture.
Take turns.

> *In picture 1 I can see …*

> *In picture 2 …*

_____

_____

_____

_____

_____

_____

_____

_____

_____

_____

_____

_____

_____

_____

_____

_____

_____

_____

2 Choose headings for parts 1–6.

Choose headings from the box and write them under the pictures.

a Zane says thank you.	**d** Zane tells his friends he's the winner.
b Zane's friends tell him they know.	**e** Zane explains about his mum.
c Zane's friends find out about his mum.	**f** Zane's mum is happy.

Lighthouse 1 | Lehrkräftefassung Plus
Illustrationen: Cornelsen/Harald Ardeias

1 READING Zara's school journey

b) 1 false   (5 points)
   2 true
   3 false
   4 false
   5 true

c) 1 Zara's car journey is **good** because it's **fast**.   (5 points)
   2 Zara's bus journey is **bad / not good** because the bus is **slow / loud**
     and **it's loud / it is loud / it's slow / it is slow**.

10–9	8–7	6–5	4–0

2 WORDS Sunita's morning

1 I **get up / get out of bed** at six fifteen.   (6 points)
2 At six thirty I **have a shower**.
3 And I **brush my teeth**.
4 After that I **get dressed**.
5 Then I **have breakfast / eat breakfast**.
6 I **go to school / leave home / leave for school** at 8 o'clock.

3 LANGUAGE Sunita's evening

I come home from school at 4 p.m. Sometimes Nish (1) **makes** a snack for us – we're   (9 points)
always hungry after school! Then I (2) **do** my homework. That (3) **takes** thirty minutes.
We (4) **eat** dinner at 7 p.m. and then Ben (5) **tidies** the kitchen.
After dinner I (6) **watch** TV and Nish (7) **does** his homework on the computer.
Mum and Ben often (8) **read** the newspaper. On weekdays I
(9) **go** to bed at 9 p.m.

15–13	12–10	9–7	6–0

4 SPEAKING A conversation with Ryan

(Lösungsbeispiel) Yes, I'm in the school art club. I also like parkour.
It's really fun. I sometimes play tennis and I sometimes walk with my dad.

(Es sind mehr als 4 Sätze möglich. Für jeden korrekten Satz gibt es einen Punkt.)

4	3	2	1–0

Lighthouse 1 | Lehrkräftefassung Plus
Smileys: Shutterstock.com/Yefym Turkin

5 WORDS Next weekend

I can make plans to meet friends. ✓

(8 points)

1 h • **2** d • **3** a • **4** g • **5** f • **6** c • **7** e • **8** b

Lily: Are you free on **Saturday**?
Alice: Sorry Lily, I'm **busy**.
Lily: That's a **shame**!
Alice: What about Sunday? Are you **free**?
Lily: Yes, I **am**.
Alice: Great. Let's go **cycling**.
Lily: Good **idea**!
Alice: Let's meet at the park at **11 a.m**.

😄	🙂	😏	😮
8–7	6	5–4	3–0

6 LISTENING Saturday plans

I can understand feelings in a story. ✓

(8 points)

a)

	Saturday morning	Saturday afternoon
1 Zane	see grandpa	swimming
2 Lily	homework	shopping
3 Noah	free	free
4 Sunita	yoga	free

(4 points)

b) 1 Zane is **sorry**.
   2 Lily is **tired**.
   3 Noah is **sad**.
   4 Sunita is **happy**.

😄	🙂	😏	😮
12–11	10–8	7–6	5–0

7 STUDY SKILLS The computer club

I can look up and learn new words. ✓

(5 points)

b) amazing • classmates • memes • stressed • swap

d)

(5 points)

emails	**classmates**	angry	good	give
headphones	friends	sad	interesting	tell
memes	students	scared	important	share
websites	teachers	**stressed**	**amazing**	**swap**

😄	🙂	😏	😮
10–9	8–7	6–5	4–0

8 WRITING Fabian's week

I can share the highlights of my week. ✓

(5 points)

(Lösungsbeispiel) On Monday afternoon I go cycling with my friend. **On Tuesday I have a guitar lesson. On Wednesday I go to my grandpa's house. On Thursday afternoon I go to the school drama club. On Friday evening I play computer games. On Saturday and Sunday I have a big breakfast.**

😄	🙂	😏	😮
5	4	3	2–0

Lighthouse 1 | Lehrkräftefassung Plus
Smileys: Shutterstock.com/Yefym Turkin

1 READING Lily's homework

a) BEFORE YOU READ Make six pairs of opposites to describe a neighbourhood:

big • boring • clean • dirty • friendly • horrible • interesting • loud • nice • quiet • small • unfriendly

big – small, _____

_____

_____

b) Read Lily's homework.
Underline the words (*adjectives*) from **a)** Lily uses in the text and complete the table.

1 the shop: small _____	4 the fields: _____
2 her neighbours: _____	5 some places on the estate: _____
3 activities at the youth centre: _____	6 the cars: _____

My neighbourhood

I live in Brighton on the Whitehawk Estate. There are a lot of flats and houses and a small shop. We don't have a car – we go to the town centre by bike or bus.

I like our neighbours, they're really friendly. I like the youth centre because it has interesting activites. I sometimes go to the homework club after school because my parents work late. My sister doesn't live with us because she's married.

I like the sports centre. It doesn't have parkour, but I like playing table tennis there. And I like the big fields near the estate too. I walk there with my dad. But we don't go very often because he doesn't have a lot of free days.

Some people don't look after our estate. They don't put rubbish in the bins and some places on the estate are really dirty. I don't like all the rubbish. I also don't like all the cars, they're very loud.

My neighbourhood has some problems. But I think it's nice and I like it.

c) Read Lily's homework again. <u>Underline</u> what Lily likes 😊 and what Lily doesn't like ☹.
Use two different colours. Complete Lily's table with notes:

😊	☹
the neighbours	the rubbish

d) Say what Lily likes or doesn't like from Lily's table in **c)**.

Lily likes …

She doesn't like …

e) Say why Lily likes or doesn't like things.

Lily likes … because …

She doesn't like … because …

> 💡 Look at the adjectives in **a)** and **b)**.

2 LOOKING AT LANGUAGE Simple present: negative sentences

a) Find all the sentences with *don't* and *doesn't* in Lily's homework.

don't	doesn't
We <u>don't</u> have a car.	My sister <u>doesn't</u> live with us.

b) Complete the rule.

Wenn wir im *simple present* ausdrücken wollen, dass wir etwas nicht machen, verwenden wir:			
I You We They	+ _____ + have, live, like, go, …	He She It	+ _____ + have, live, like, go, …

1 PREPARATION Match the activities with the pictures and cut the cards.

do homework • eat a big breakfast • listen to music • meet friends • ~~play computer games~~ •
sing a song • tidy the room • walk in the fields • watch a film

play computer games

The Sea

2 PREPARATION Cut out the symbols.

X	X	X
✓	✓	✓

3 GAME Play the game in groups of three.

INSTRUCTIONS Make a pile¹ with activity cards and a pile with symbols.
Take an activity card and a symbol. Then throw the dice and make
a sentence.

She listens to music.

I don't watch a film.

We …

✓ = a positive sentence
X = a negative sentence

1 = I
2 = you
3 = he, she, it
4 = we
5 = you
6 = we

¹pile *Stapel*

Lighthouse 1 | Lehrkräftefassung Plus
Illustration: Cornelsen/Karen Donnelly

1 SONG Kasia's town

a) Listen to Kasia's song again. What places do you hear?
Collect them on the board and write them down here.

_____

_____

_____

_____

b) Listen again. Complete the song with the places.

c) Say what Kasia likes about her town.

> *Kasia likes …*

Kasia's town

I think that my town is boring

And I don't like living here.

My town doesn't have a (1) _____.

It doesn't have a (2) _____

or (3) _____.

There isn't anything for me

No (4) _____,

 no (5) _____.

The only thing here that is good

Are my friends in the neighbourhood.

---

2 Now you

a) Write your own song. What do you like about your town or village?
You can use the structure in the box.

_____

_____

_____

_____

_____

_____

_____

> • I think my town/village is great /
>   And I love living here.
> • My town/village has a … and a … /
> • It has a … and a …
> • There are lots of things for me /
> • A … and a …
> • The only thing(s) that is (are) bad /
>   Is (are) … in my neighbourhood.

b) Record your song and present it to the class.

Step 4: Practise your group presentation. Then give feedback.

Checklist for the slide show	Yes ✓	No ✗
Make the title big.		
Use short notes.		
Use some colour.		
Use big pictures.		

Step 5: Give another group feedback and ask them questions.

Checklist for the presentation	☺	🙂	☹
Speak loudly.			
Speak clearly.			
Look at the group.			

Questions:

1 _____

2 _____

✂ -

Step 4: Practise your group presentation. Then give feedback.

Checklist for the slide show	Yes ✓	No ✗
Make the title big.		
Use short notes.		
Use some colour.		
Use big pictures.		

Step 5: Give another group feedback and ask them questions.

Checklist for the presentation	☺	🙂	☹
Speak loudly.			
Speak clearly.			
Look at the group.			

Questions:

1 _____

2 _____

Lighthouse 1 | Lehrkräftefassung Plus
Smileys: Shutterstock.com/Yefym Turkin

1 MEDIATION Jack's favourite place

I can understand information about Brighton. ✓

a) **C** Jack meint, dass wir den Hove Skatepark in Brighton besuchen sollten.
(1 point)

b) **1** Nein, er ist nicht im Zentrum.
(4 points)
2 Neben dem Skatepark ist der Bahnhof Portslade und die Bushaltestelle Wish Road South.
3 Nein, man muss keinen Eintritt zahlen.
4 Der Skatepark ist immer offen.

5	4	3	2–0

2 LANGUAGE We live in Hove

I can describe my neighbourhood (simple present: negative sentences). ✓

I live with my family in Hove. Our neighbourhood has nice shops and parks, (6 points)
but it (1) **doesn't** have a cinema. There's a great beach in Hove. Nish and I often
go there after school, but we (2) **don't** go there at the weekend because it's really busy.
There's a museum too, but I (3) **don't** go there very often. I (4) **don't** like museums!
I like my neighbourhood, but Nish (5) **doesn't** like it. He wants to live in London, but my
mum (6) **doesn't** want to live there!

3 WRITING Lea's neighbourhood

(5 points)

(Lösungsbeispiel) Hi, Sunita! I live in a **small village. My neighbourhood is
clean. My neighbourhood has fields, three shops and a nice cinema.
It doesn't have a youth centre. I don't like my neighbourhood because
it's boring.**

11–10	9–8	7–5	4–0

4 Tour of Chester

I can talk about my town or village (simple present: questions and short answers). ✓

a) **Zane:** (1) **Do** you like your town?
(6 points)
Sophie: Yes, I (2) **do.** It's a nice place.
Zane: (3) **Does** your town have a good park?
Sophie: Yes, it (4) **does.** I often go cycling there.
Zane: (5) **Does** your town have a beach?
Sophie: No, it (6) **doesn't.** It's a shame!

b) **a** stadium • **b** ice rink • **c** supermarket • **d** hospital • **e** train station • **f** library
(6 points)

c) **1** c • **2** a • **3** e • **4** f • **5** d • **6** b
(5 points)

17–15	14–12	11–8	7–0

Lighthouse 1 | Lehrkräftefassung Plus
Smileys: Shutterstock.com/Yefym Turkin

5 Photos of Brighton

I can talk about sights in Brighton and the weather (simple present: *wh*-questions). ✓

a) 1 What do you see in the picture? (3 points)
   2 What's the weather like?
   3 Why do you like the picture?

b) (Lösungsbeispiele) (4 points)

Picture A: I can see a big park. There are some trees and there are a lot of children. The weather is cold and snowy. I like the picture because I love the snow.

Picture B: I can see the beach and the sea. There is the pier and there are many people. The weather is warm and sunny. I like the picture because I like the beach.

(Es sind mehr als 4 Sätze möglich. Für jeden korrekten Satz gibt es einen Punkt.)

7–6	5	4	3–0

6 READING At the Swap Place

I can understand a story about green activities. ✓

a) C Zane's things. (1 point)

b) 1 true (5 points)
   2 false
   3 false
   4 true
   5 true

c) 1 Saturday (5 points)
   2 toys
   3 messy
   4 home
   5 jigsaw puzzle

11–10	9–8	7–5	4–0

7 STUDY SKILLS Buddy's favourite places

I can plan and practice a presentation. ✓

a) Slide number 2 is the best because it has a big title, short notes and a big picture. (1 point)

b) 1 My **presentation** is about Buddy's favourite places. (6 points)
   2 In this **photo** you can see the Pavilion Gardens.
   3 In the **next** photo we have the beach.
   4 Let's **look** at these pictures of Buddy's toys in the garden.
   5 Thank you for **listening**.
   6 Do you have any **questions**?

7–6	5	4	3–0

8 SPEAKING Ideas for a rainy day

I can give a presentation to a group. ✓

(Lösungsbeispiel) Hello. My presentation is about ideas for a rainy day. (10 points)
When it's rainy, I like to go to the sports centre. It has lots of activities and it's not expensive.
Next, we have the ice rink. It costs ten euros but it's really fun!
The cinema is great too. It has interesting films and a nice cafe.
Thank you for listening. Do you have any questions?

(Es sind mehr als 10 Sätze möglich. Für jeden korrekten Satz gibt es einen Punkt.)

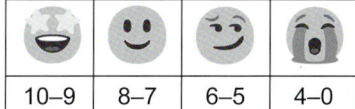

10–9	8–7	6–5	4–0

What are they doing?

a) Cut out the swap cards and fold the grey parts so that they are on the backside of the card.

b) Every student gets one card. Show your picture to another student. They have to make a sentence about the picture. Check the answer and correct them if there is a mistake.

I

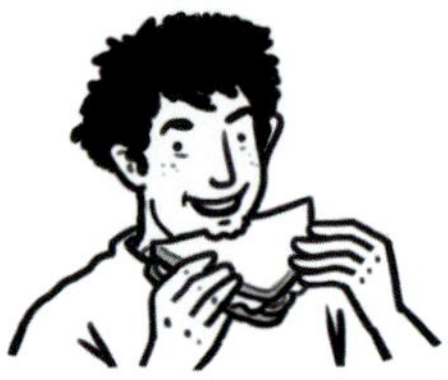

I'm eating a sandwich.

Tanja

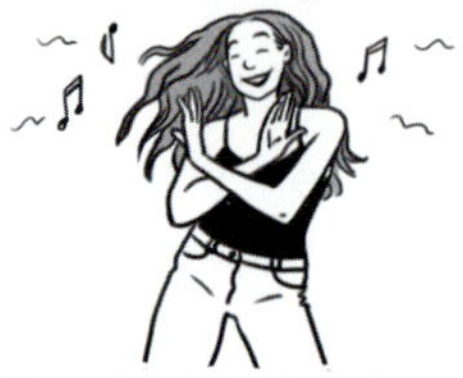

Tanja is dancing.

Cleo and Mara

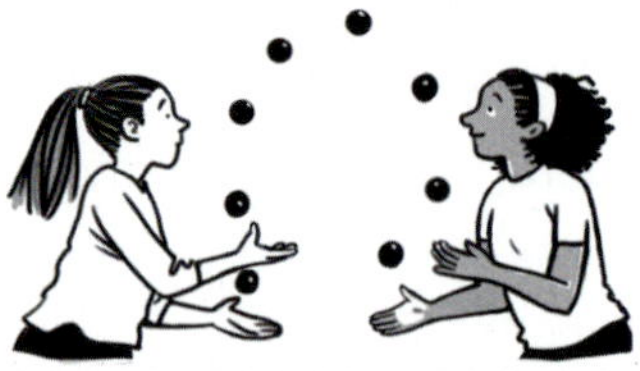

Cleo and Mara are juggling.

Max and Ben

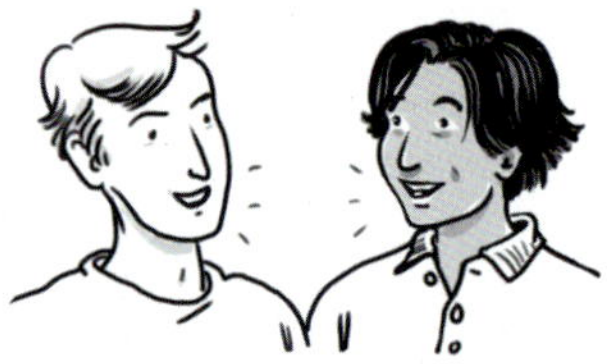

Max and Ben are talking.

Chris

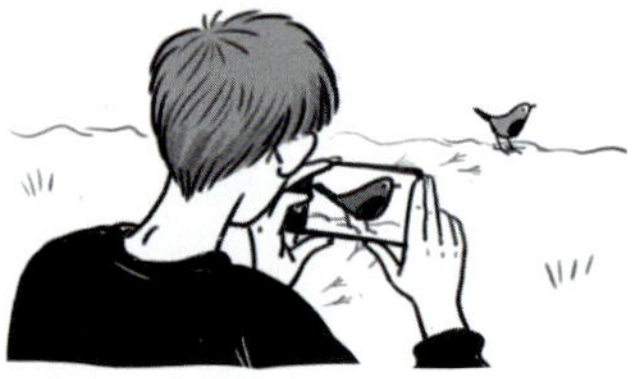

Chris is taking photos.

Sam's father

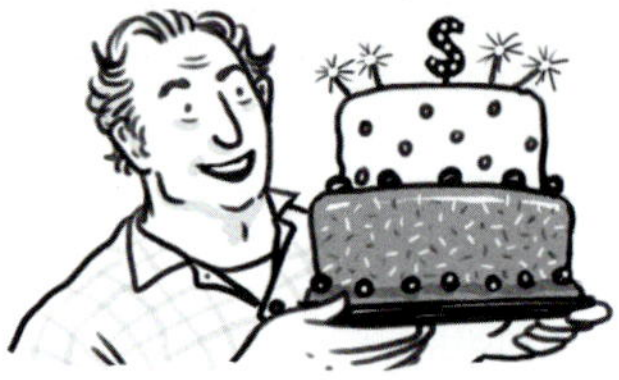

Sam's father is bringing the birthday cake.

Sam

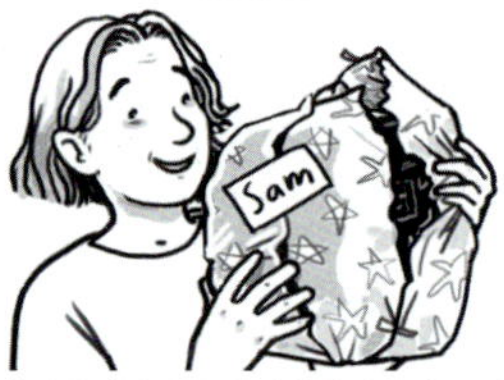

Sam is opening his birthday present.

Clara

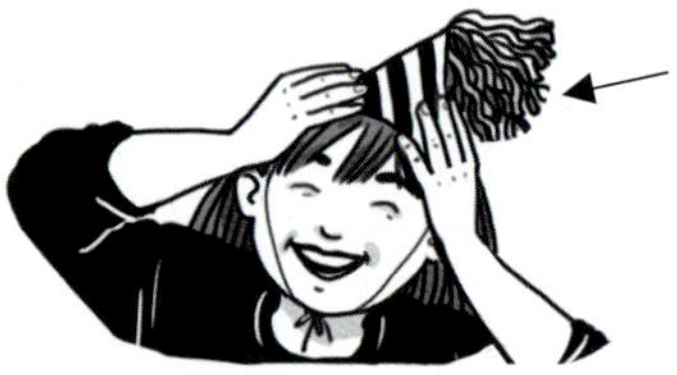

Clara is wearing a party hat.

Mike and Nick

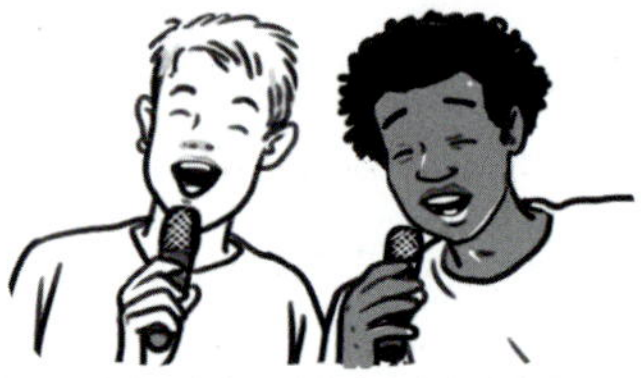

Mike and Nick are singing.

Hissy

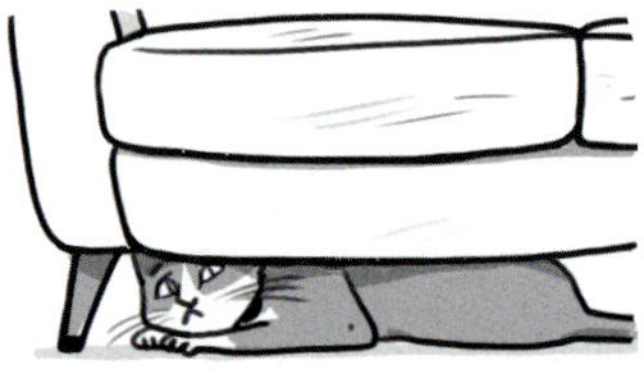

Hissy is lying under the sofa.

Zorro

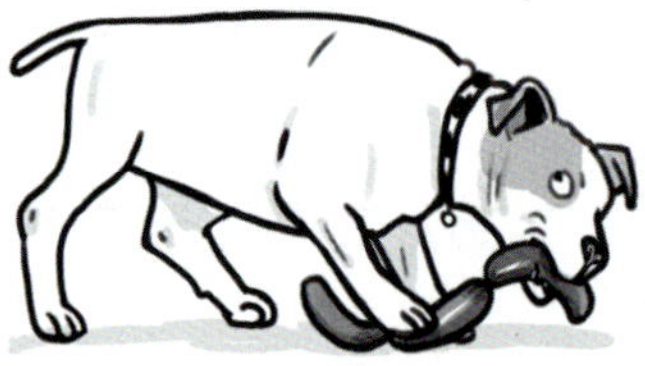

Zorro is eating sausages.

I

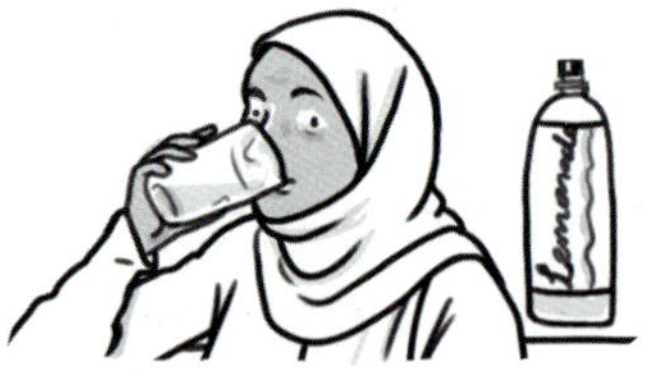

I'm drinking water.

Sam's mum

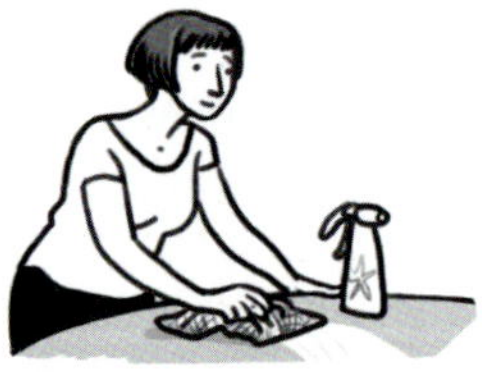

Sam's mum is cleaning the table.

We

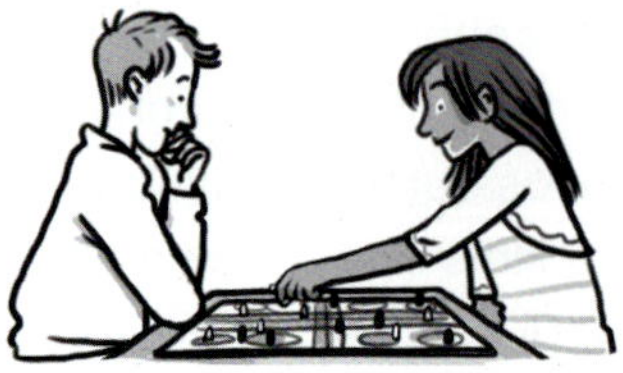

We're playing a game.

We

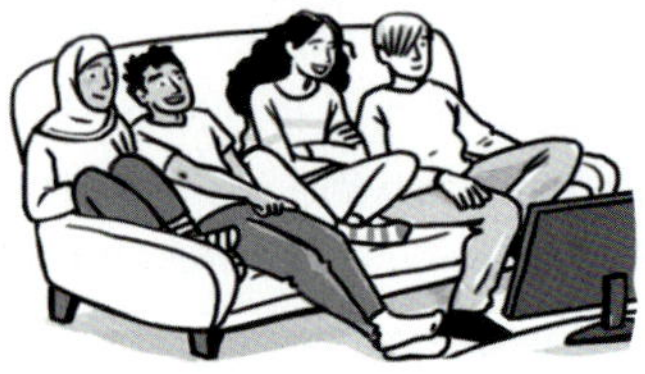

We're watching TV.

Illustrationen: Cornelsen/Karen Donnelly

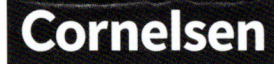

How to make a ham and cheese sandwich

a) Find the words and write them in the boxes with the right pictures.   ⇨ ⬂ ⬇ ⬆

v	s	c	p	a	g	o	p	n
f	c	h	z	l	s	u	z	e
b	r	e	a	d	a	g	r	f
u	q	e	w	m	m	t	x	i
t	d	s	l	a	h	b	e	n
t	l	e	t	t	u	c	e	k
e	c	z	n	w	p	f	o	r
r	b	t	o	m	a	t	o	w

some _____

two slices[1] of _____

a slice of _____

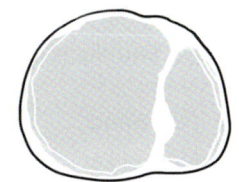
a slice of _____

a _____

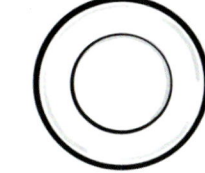
a _____

some _____

one _____

b) Cut the stripes and put them in the right order.

✂ -

Enjoy your sandwich.

Slice[2] the tomato.

Next, put the ham and cheese on one slice of your bread.

Wash the lettuce and tomato.

Put the butter on the bread.

Now, close the sandwich.

First, take two slices of bread and put them on your plate.

Put the lettuce and tomato on the ham or cheese.

c) Make your sandwich.

_____

[1] a slice *eine Scheibe*   [2] (to) slice *(in Scheiben) schneiden*

Lighthouse 1 | Lehrkräftefassung Plus
Illustrationen: Cornelsen/Karen Donnelly

My dish: _____

1 What is special about my dish?
Write about your recipe. Fill in the gaps with the words in brackets or use your own ideas.

_____ is a _____ (starter / main course / a dessert / …).

It comes from _____ and it is _____ (spicy / sweet / cold / …).

You make it with _____.

We usually eat it _____ (every week / for Christmas / for birthdays / …).

2 You need …
Write a list of what you need to make your dish.

🍽 _____   🍽 _____

🍽 _____   🍽 _____

🍽 _____   🍽 _____

🍽 _____   🍽 _____

3 How to make my dish:
a) Draw a picture of the step into the box, or take a picture of how you make the dish and stick it in.
b) Write a short description under each picture. What do you do in this step?

1	2	3

First, _____   Second, _____   Then, _____

_____   _____   _____

_____   _____   _____

_____.   _____.   _____.

4	5	6

Next, _____   After that, _____   In the end, _____

_____   _____   _____

_____   _____   _____

_____.   _____.   _____.

Cornelsen

1 A film night

a) **1** carrots • **2** strawberries • **3** tomatoes • **4** bread • **5** sausages • **6** chocolate • **7** milk • **8** lemonade (8 points)

b) **A:** Let's buy some chocolate. (5 points)
B: Yes, that's a good idea.
A: I love strawberries. Do you like strawberries?
B: I'm allergic to strawberries. Let's buy some bread.
A: Yes, let's buy some bread and some tomatoes.
B: No, I don't want to buy tomatoes. Do you like carrots?
A: Yes, let's buy some carrots.

(Es sind mehr als 5 Sätze möglich. Für jeden korrekten Satz gibt es einen Punkt.)

13–12	11–9	8–6	5–0

2 LANGUAGE A very bad picnic

1 Willow's birthday is in August, so we're **wearing** T-shirts, but it's cold and rainy. (8 points)
2 Mum is **decorating** a tree, but it's very windy.
3 We're **sitting** on the grass because there are no chairs.
4 A dog is **barking** because it wants our food.
5 Nish is on his phone. He's **texting** his friends.
6 A seagull is **eating** my sandwich.
7 Ben is **playing** the guitar.
8 But just one person is **listening** to Ben's music!

8–7	6	5–4	3–0

3 LANGUAGE After the party

a) **1** How **much** lemonade is there?
2 How **many** sandwiches are there?
3 How **much** salad is there?
4 How **many** sausages are there?
5 How **many** carrots are there?

(5 points)

b) **1** There isn't **much** lemonade.
2 There aren't **many sandwiches**.
3 There's a **lot of salad**.
4 There are **a lot of** / **many sausages**.
5 There aren't **many carrots**.

(5 points)

4 READING Zane's dream party

a) Zane's dream party is in the stadium. (1 point)

b) **1** It's special and interesting. (5 points)
2 There's a tour of the stadium, a football lesson and a football match.
3 They are on Sunday mornings.
4 They are two hours long.
5 There are sandwiches, there's fruit and there's cake.

c) (Lösungsbeispiel) (2 points)
I want to have my dream party at the skatepark. I love skateboarding and it's fun.

(Es sind mehr als 2 Sätze möglich. Für jeden korrekten Satz gibt es einen Punkt.)

18–16	15–13	12–9	8–0

5 MEDIATION **My favourite evening meal**

I can describe my favourite dish. ✓

1   Man isst dieses Gericht zu Abend.
2   Man braucht dafür Eier, Milch, Würstchen, Mehl und Öl.
3   Es wird 30 Minuten im Ofen gebacken.

(3 points)

😄	🙂	😏	😮
3	2	1	0

6 LISTENING **Dinner at Sunita's house**

I can understand and talk about differences. ✓

a)   Picture B

(1 point)

b)   1   **Sunita's family** eats dinner in a big dining room.
     2   **Zane's family** has a small dining room.
     3   **Zane's family** eats dinner in the living room.
     4   **Sunita's family** doesn't eat meat.
     5   **Zane's family** has no animals.

(5 points)

😄	🙂	😏	😮
6	5–4	3	2–0

7 STUDY SKILLS **Explaining new words**

I can explain words. ✓

a)   1   carrot: It's a kind of ~~fruit~~.
     2   chicken: It's a kind of ~~cake~~.
     3   dessert: It's the meal ~~before~~ dinner.
     4   milk: It's a kind of ~~food~~.
     5   cornflakes: You eat them with a ~~knife~~.
     6   tea: It's a ~~cold~~ drink.
     7   shopping list: You need it at ~~school~~.
     8   vegetables: They're ~~bad~~ for you.

(8 points)

b)   1   carrot: It's a kind of **vegetable**.
     2   chicken: It's a kind of **meat**.
     3   dessert: It's the meal **after** dinner.
     4   milk: It's a kind of **drink**.
     5   cornflakes: You eat them with a **spoon**.
     6   tea: It's a **hot** drink.
     7   shopping list: You need it at **a supermarket**.
     8   vegetables: They're **good** for you.

(8 points)

😄	🙂	😏	😮
16–14	13–11	10–8	7–0

8 WRITING **A banana and chocolate crepe**

I can research and write a recipe. ✓

(Lösungsbeispiel) Today I want to tell you about my recipe for a chocolate and banana crepe.
You make it with 125 g flour, 2 eggs, 360 ml milk, 1 tablespoon sugar, chocolate sauce
and a banana. You also need a cooking spoon and a frying pan. First mix the flour, eggs,
milk and sugar. Then fry some of the mixture in the frying pan. After two minutes turn the crepe over
and fry the other side. Finally put the crepe on a plate and add the chocolate and banana. Enjoy!

(7 points)

(Es sind mehr als 7 Sätze möglich. Für jeden korrekten Satz gibt es einen Punkt.)

😄	🙂	😏	😮
7–6	5	4	3–0

Lighthouse 1 | Lehrkräftefassung Plus
Smileys: Shutterstock.com/Yefym Turkin